Louis F. Bruchens

Notre Dame, 1946

STALIN

o

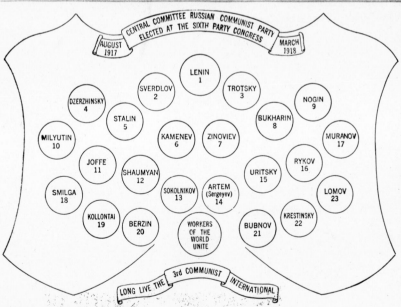

Of the thirty-one members and alternates of the October Central Committee, some of whose portraits appear above, only two were alive in 1946—Stalin and Alexandra Kollontai.

STALIN

AN APPRAISAL OF THE MAN AND HIS INFLUENCE

by

Leon Trotsky

Edited and
Translated from the Russian by
CHARLES MALAMUTH

ILLUSTRATED

HARPER & BROTHERS PUBLISHERS
New York and London

TABLE OF CONTENTS

LIST OF ILLUSTRATIONS

ILLUSTRATIONS

PUBLISHER'S NOTE

THIS BOOK was ready for publication just at the time of the Pearl Harbor disaster. Its appearance was then postponed by the publisher until after the end of the war.

Now that hostilities are over, Harper & Brothers feel that this biography, containing material of historical importance, should be published in accordance with agreements previously made.

March 15, 1946

EDITOR'S NOTE

LEON TROTSKY wrote and revised in the original Russian the first seven chapters and the appendix of this book. He checked in the English translation the first six chapters and the appendix but not the seventh chapter. The first seven chapters were to have been cut and condensed after the writing of the book had been completed. Like most authors, Trotsky was more optimistic than accurate about the expected date of completion, and his case was aggravated not only by the excessive optimism of the revolutionist and the military leader but by continual harassments and attempts on his life. The date of completion was therefore deferred from time to time. Finally, he set August, 1940 as the "deadline," to use his own expression. But his manuscript was not complete on the twentieth of August, when he was struck down by his assassin. Two days later he died. The editor therefore left the first seven chapters and the appendix unrevised, except for a few deletions of repetitious material.

Some of the manuscript of the unfinished portion was in Trotsky's study, strung out in enormously long strips of many sheets pasted end to end, at the time of the murderous attack upon him, and in the struggle with the assassin portions of the manuscript were not only spattered with blood but utterly destroyed. Moreover, no part of this posthumous manuscript had been put in final form by the author. It was made up of notes to be more fully developed, of excerpts from the works of other writers, of various documents, of dictated material not yet corrected by the author, all tentatively grouped for further use. Some of it was roughly blocked out under tentative chapter headings. Most of it was undigested material filed under eighty-one subheadings in more than twice that many folders. Out of this largely raw material the Introduction, the chapters from eight to twelve inclusive, and the two supplements have been edited.

Under the circumstances, extensive interpolations by the editor were unavoidable but were, nevertheless, kept down to a minimum consistent with achieving the maximum of clarity and fluency. In every case, including the editor's introduction of single words, these are set off from the author's text by brackets. Of course, the captions, arrangement and selection of the frontispiece and of all the other illustrations; the lists of Stalin's aliases, of Communist Party Congresses, the glossary and chronological guide are entirely the work of the editor. Portions of the author's notes summarized by the editor are distinguished from the main body of the text by closer printing. Wherever quoted material found in Trotsky's portfolio on the Stalin biography is not a component part of Trotsky's text, such quoted material is marked by a star. In many cases that material bore identifying notations in Trotsky's handwriting.

The editorial policy in regard to the unfinished portion of the manuscript was to publish Trotsky's text entire, except for repetitious and utterly extraneous material which he obviously would have cut had he survived. Many of the documents are published here for the first time, without benefit of censorship either by Trotskyists or by Stalinists.

The editor wishes to thank the author's widow, Natalia Ivanovna Sedoff-Trotsky, for her contribution to this book. He desires also to acknowledge the assistance of Leon Trotsky's principal secretary, M. Jean Van Heijinoort; the Director of the Harvard University Library, Mr. Keyes D. Metcalf; the Registrar of the Harvard Library, Mr. Edward L. Gookin, and his staff; the Curator of Rare Books in the Treasure Room of the Widener Library at Harvard, Mr. William A. Jackson, Mr. W. H. McCarthy, and the Misses Fritzi Oldach and Rita Fitzpatrick. Their generous co-operation and unfailing patience facilitated the editor's access to Trotsky's posthumous manuscript. Although the editor did not always follow their advice, his very special appreciation is reserved for Marguerite Hoyle Munson, Alexandre Barmine and Max Eastman, who read the book before publication and offered extremely valuable critical comments.

C. M.

INTRODUCTION

THE reader will note that I have dwelt with considerably more detail on the development of Stalin during the preparatory period than on his more recent political activities. The facts of the latter period are known to every literate person. Moreover, my criticisms of Stalin's political behavior since 1923 are to be found in various works. The purpose of this political biography is to show how a personality of this sort was formed, and how it came to power by usurpation of the right to such an exceptional role. That is why, in describing the life and development of Stalin during the period when nothing, or almost nothing, was known about him, the author has concerned himself with a thoroughgoing analysis of isolated facts and details and the testimony of witnesses; whereas, in appraising the latter period, he has limited himself to a synthetic exposition, presupposing that the facts—at least, the principal ones—are sufficiently well known to the reader.

Critics in the service of the Kremlin will declare this time, even as they declared with reference to my *History of the Russian Revolution*, that the absence of bibliographical references renders a verification of the author's assertions impossible. As a matter of fact, bibliographical references to hundreds and thousands of Russian newspapers, magazines, memoirs, anthologies and the like would give the foreign critical reader very little and would only burden the text. As for Russian critics, they have at their disposal whatever is available of the Soviet archives and libraries. Had there been factual errors, misquotations, or any other improper use of material in any of my works, that would have been pointed out long ago. As a matter of fact, I do not know of a single instance of any anti-Trotskyist writings that contain a single reference to incorrect use of source material by me. I venture to think that this fact alone is sufficient guarantee of authenticity for the foreign reader.

In writing my *History* [of the Russian Revolution] I avoided personal reminiscences and relied chiefly on data already published and therefore subject to verification, including only such of my own testimony, previously published, as had not been controverted by anyone in the past. In this biography I ventured a departure from this too stringent method. Here, too, the basic warp of the narrative is made up of documents, memoirs and other objective sources. But in those instances where nothing can take the place of the testimony of the author's own memories, I felt that I had the right to interpolate one or another episode from my personal reminiscences, many of them hitherto unpublished, clearly indicating each time that in the given case I appear not only as the

xi

author but also as a witness. Otherwise, I have followed here the same method as in my *History of the Russian Revolution*.

Numerous of my opponents have conceded that the latter book is made up of facts arranged in a scholarly way. True, a reviewer in the *New York Times* rejected that book as prejudiced. But every line of his essay showed that he was indignant with the Russian Revolution and was transferring his indignation to its historian. This is the usual aberration of all sorts of liberal subjectivists who carry on a perpetual quarrel with the course of the class struggle. Embittered by the results of some historical process, they vent their spleen on the scientific analysis that discloses the inevitability of those results. In the final reckoning, the judgment passed on the author's method is far more pertinent than whether all or only a part of the author's conclusions will be acknowledged to be objective. And on that score this author has no fear of criticism. This work is built of facts and is solidly grounded in documents. It stands to reason that here and there partial and minor errors or trivial offenses in emphasis and misinterpretation may be found. But what no one will find in this work is an unconscientious attitude toward facts, the deliberate disregard of documentary evidence or arbitrary conclusions based only on personal prejudices. The author did not overlook a single fact, document, or bit of testimony redounding to the benefit of the hero of this book. If a painstaking, thoroughgoing and conscientious gathering of facts, even of minor episodes, the verification of the testimony of witnesses with the aid of the methods of historical and biographical criticism, and finally the inclusion of facts of personal life in their relation to our hero's role in the historical process—if all of this is not objectivity, then, I ask, What is objectivity?

Again new times have brought a new political morality. And, strangely enough, the [swing of the pendulum of history has] returned us in many respects to the epoch of the Renaissance, even exceeding it in the extent and depth of its cruelties and bestialities. Again we have political condottieri, again the struggle for power has assumed a grandiose character, its task—to achieve the most that is feasible for the time being by securing governmental power for one person, a power denuded to a merciless degree [of all restraints previously formulated and hitherto deemed necessary]. There was a time when the laws of political mechanics painstakingly formulated by Machiavelli were considered the height of cynicism. To Machiavelli the struggle for power was a chess theorem. Questions of morality did not exist for him, as they do not exist for a chess player, as they do not exist for a bookkeeper. His task consisted in determining the most practicable policy to be followed in regard to a given situation and in explaining how to carry that policy through in a nakedly ruthless manner, on the basis of experiences tested in the political crucibles of two continents. This approach is explained not only by the task itself but also by the character of the epoch during which this task was posed. It proceeded essentially from the state of development of feudalism and in accordance with the crucial struggle for power between the masters of two epochs—dying feudalism and the bourgeois society which was being born.

But throughout the nineteenth century, which was the age of parliamentarism, liberalism and social reform (if you close your eyes to a few international wars and civil wars), Machiavelli was considered absurdly old-fashioned. Political ambition was confined within the parliamentary framework, and by the same token its excessively venturesome trends were curbed. It was no longer a matter of outright seizure of power by one person and his henchmen but of capturing mandates in as many electoral districts as possible. In the epoch of the struggle for ministerial portfolios Machiavelli seemed to be the quaint ideologist of a dimly distant past. The advent of new times had brought a new and a higher political morality. But, amazing thing, the twentieth century—that promised dream of a new age for which the nineteenth had so hopefully striven—has returned us in many respects to the ways and methods of the Renaissance!

This throw-back to the most cruel Machiavellism seems incomprehensible to one who until yesterday abided in the comforting confidence that human history moves along a rising line of material and cultural progress. [Nothing of course is further from the truth. That is too clearly apparent today to require verbal proof. But whatever our qualifications or disagreements on this] score, all of us, I think, can say now: No epoch of the past was so cruel, so ruthless, so cynical as our epoch. Politically, morality has not improved at all by comparison with the standards of the Renaissance and with other even more distant epochs. [No social order dies gently and willingly when the day of its usefulness passes. All epochs of transition have been epochs of violent social struggles free of traditional moral restraints, epochs of life and death struggles.] The epoch of the Renaissance was an epoch of struggles between two worlds. Social antagonisms reached extreme intensity. Hence the intensity of the political struggle.

By the second half of the nineteenth century political morality had supplanted materialism (at least, in the imagination of certain politicians) only because social antagonisms had softened for a time and the political struggle had become petty. The basis of this was a general growth in the well-being of the nation and certain improvements in the situation of the upper layers of the working class. But our period, our epoch, resembles the epoch of the Renaissance in the sense that we are living on the verge of two worlds: the bourgeois-capitalistic, which is suffering agony, and that new world which is going to replace it. Social contradictions have again achieved exceptional sharpness.

Political power, like morality, by no means develops uninterruptedly toward a state of perfection, as was thought at the end of the last century and during the first decade of the present century. Politics and morals suffer and have to pass through a highly complex and paradoxical orbit. Politics, like morality, is directly dependent on the class struggle. As a general rule, it may be said that the sharper and more intense the class struggle, the deeper the social crisis, and the more intense the character acquired by politics, the more concentrated and more ruthless becomes the power of the State and the more frankly [does it cast off the garments of morality].

Some of my friends have remarked that too much space in this book is occupied by references to sources and my criticism of these sources. I fully realize the inconveniences of such a method of exposition. But I have no choice. No one is obliged to take on faith the assertions of an author as closely concerned and as directly involved as I have been in the struggle with the person whose biography he has been obliged to write. Our epoch is above all an epoch of lies. I do not therewith mean to imply that other epochs of humanity were distinguished by greater truthfulness. The lie is the fruit of contradictions, of struggle, of the clash of classes, of the suppression of personality, of the social order. In that sense it is an attribute of all human history. There are periods when social contradictions become exceptionally sharp, when the lie rises above the average, when the lie becomes an attribute of the very acuteness of social contradictions. Such is our epoch. I do not think that in all of human history anything could be found even remotely resembling the gigantic factory of lies which was organized by the Kremlin under the leadership of Stalin. And one of the principal purposes of this factory is to manufacture a new biography for Stalin . . . Some of these sources were fabricated by Stalin himself . . . Without subjecting to criticism the details of progressively accumulating falsifications, it would be impossible to prepare the reader for such a phenomenon, for example, as the Moscow trials . . .

Hitler is especially insistent that only the vivid oral word marks the leader. Never, according to him, can any writing influence the masses like a speech. At any rate, it cannot generate the firm and living bond between the leader and his millions of followers. Hitler's judgment is doubtless determined in large measure by the fact that he cannot write. Marx and Engels acquired millions of followers without resorting throughout their life to the art of oratory. True, it took them many years to secure influence. The writer's art ranks higher in the final reckoning, for it makes possible the union of depth with height of form. Political leaders who are nothing but orators are invariably superficial. An orator does not generate writers. On the contrary, a great writer may inspire thousands of orators. Yet it is true that for direct contact with the masses living speech is indispensable. Lenin became the head of a powerful and influential party before he had the opportunity to turn to the masses with the living word. His public appearances in 1905 were few and passed unnoticed. As a mass orator Lenin did not appear on the scene until 1917, and then only for a short period, in the course of April, May and July. He came to power not as an orator, but above all as a writer, as an instructor of the propagandists who had trained his cadres, including also the cadres of orators.

In this respect Stalin represents a phenomenon utterly exceptional. He is neither a thinker, a writer nor an orator. He took possession of power before the masses had learned to distinguish his figure from others during the triumphal processions across Red Square. Stalin took possession of power, not with the aid of personal qualities, but with the aid of an impersonal machine. And it was not he who created the machine, but the machine that created him. That machine, with its force and its authority, was the product of the prolonged and heroic struggle of the Bolshevik Party, which itself grew out of ideas. The machine was the bearer of the idea before it became an end in itself. Stalin headed the machine from the moment he cut off the umbilical cord that bound it to the idea and it became a thing unto itself. Lenin created the machine through constant association with the masses, if not by oral word, then by printed word, if not directly, then through the medium of his disciples. Stalin did not create the machine but took possession of it. For this, exceptional and special qualities were necessary. But they were not the qualities of the historic initiator, thinker, writer, or orator. The machine had grown out of ideas. Stalin's first qualification was a contemptuous attitude toward ideas. The idea had. . . .

[On August 20, 1940, Trotsky was struck a mortal blow on the back of his head with a pickaxe and his brain wrenched out while he was reading a manuscript brought to him by the assassin. That is why this and other portions of this book remain unfinished.]

STALIN

○

Chapter I

FAMILY AND SCHOOL

THE late Leonid Krassin, old revolutionist, eminent engineer, brilliant Soviet diplomat and, above all, intelligent human being, was the first, if I am not mistaken, to call Stalin an "Asiatic." In saying that, he had in mind no problematical racial attributes, but rather that blending of grit, shrewdness, craftiness and cruelty which has been considered characteristic of the statesmen of Asia. Bukharin subsequently simplified the appellation, calling Stalin "Genghis Khan," manifestly in order to draw attention to his cruelty, which has developed into brutality. Stalin himself, in conversation with a Japanese journalist, once called himself an "Asiatic," not in the old but rather in the new sense of the word: with that personal allusion he wished to hint at the existence of common interests between the U.S.S.R. and Japan as against the imperialistic West. Contemplating the term "Asiatic" from a scientific point of view, we must admit that in this instance it is but partially correct. Geographically, the Caucasus, especially Transcaucasia, is undoubtedly a continuation of Asia. The Georgians, however, in contradistinction from the Mongolian Azerbaijanians, belong to the so-called Mediterranean, European race. Thus Stalin was not exact when he called himself an Asiatic. But geography, ethnography and anthropology are not all that matters; history looms larger.

A few spatters of the human flood that has poured for centuries from Asia into Europe have clung to the valleys and mountains of the Caucasus. Disconnected tribes and groups seemed to have frozen there in the process of their development, transforming the Caucasus into a gigantic ethnographic museum. In the course of many centuries the fate of these people remained closely bound up with that of Persia and Turkey, being thus retained in the sphere of the old Asiatic culture, which has contrived to remain static despite continual jolts from war and mutiny.

Anywhere else, on a site more traversed, that small, Georgian branch of humanity—about two and a half millions at the present time—undoubtedly would have dissolved in the crucible of history and left no trace. Protected by the Caucasian mountain range, the Georgians preserved in a comparatively pure form their ethnic physiognomy and their language, for which philology to this day seems to have difficulty in finding a proper place. Written language appeared in Georgia simultaneously with the penetration of Christianity, as early as the fourth century, six hundred years earlier than in Kievian Russia. The tenth, eleventh, twelfth and thirteenth centuries are considered the epoch in which Georgia's military power, and its art and literature flourished. Then followed centuries of stagnation and decay. The frequent bloody raids into the Caucasus of Genghis Khan and Tamerlane left their traces upon the national epos of Georgia. If one can believe the unfortunate Bukharin, they left their traces likewise on the character of Stalin.

At the beginning of the eighteenth century the Georgian Tsar acknowledged the suzerainty of Moscow, seeking protection against his traditional enemies, Turkey and Persia. He attained his immediate goal in that his life became more secure. The Tsarist government laid down the necessary strategic roads, partially renovated the cities, and established a rudimentary network of schools, primarily for the purpose of Russifying these alien subjects. Of course, in two centuries the Petersburg bureaucracy could not replace the old Asiatic barbarism with a European culture of which its own country was still in sad need.

Despite its natural wealth and supernal climate, Georgia continued to be a poor and backward country. Its semifeudal social structure was based on a low level of economic development and was therefore distinguished by the traits of Asiatic patriarchy, not excluding Asiatic cruelty. Industry was almost nonexistent. Agriculture and house-building were carried on virtually as they had been two thousand years before. Wine was pressed out with the feet and stored in large clay pitchers. The cities of the Caucasus, comprising no more than one-sixth of the population, remained, like all Asia's cities, bureaucratic, military, commercial, and only to a small extent industrial. Above the basic peasant mass rose a stratum of gentry, for the most part not rich and not generally cultured, in some instances distinguishable from the upper layers of the peasantry only by their pompous titles and affectations. Not without reason Georgia—with its tiny past "power," its present economic stagnation, its beneficent sun, its vineyards, its irresponsibility, and its abundance of provincial hidalgos with empty pockets—has been called the Spain of the Caucasus.

The young generation of the nobility knocked at the portals of Russian universities and, breaking with the threadbare tradition of their caste, which was not taken any too seriously in Central Russia, joined sundry radical groups of Russian students. The more prosperous peasants and townsmen, ambitious to make of their sons either government officials, army officers, lawyers, or priests, followed the lead of the noble families. Wherefore Georgia acquired an excessive number of intellectuals, who, scattered in various parts of Russia, played a prominent role in all the progressive political movements and in the three revolutions.

The German writer Bodenstedt, who was director of a teachers' institute at Tiflis in 1844, came to the conclusion that the Georgians were not only slovenly and shiftless, but less intelligent than the other Caucasians; at school they could not hold their own against the Armenians and the Tartars in the study of science, the acquisition of foreign languages and aptitude for self expression. Citing this far too cursory opinion, Élisée Reclus expressed the altogether sound surmise that the difference might be due not to nationality but rather to social causes—the fact that the Georgian students came from backward villages while the Armenians were the children of the city bourgeoisie. Indeed, further development soon erased that educational lag. By 1892, when Joseph Djugashvili was a pupil in the second form of the parochial school, the Georgians, who made up approximately one-eighth of the population in the Caucasus, contributed virtually a fifth of all the students (the Russians—more than a half, the Armenians—about fourteen per cent, the Tartars—less than three per cent . . .). It seems, however, that the peculiarities of the Georgian language, one of the most ancient tools of culture, do indeed impede the acquisition of foreign languages, leaving a decided imprint on pronunciation. But it does not follow that the Georgians are not gifted with eloquence. Like the other nations of the empire, under Tsarism they were doomed to silence. But as Russia became "Europeanized," Georgian intellectuals produced numerous—if not first rate, at least outstanding—orators of the judiciary and later of the parliamentary rostrum. The most eloquent of the leaders of the February Revolution was perhaps the Georgian Iraklii Tseretelli. Therefore it would be unjustified to account for the absence of oratorical ability in Stalin by citing his national origin. Even in his physical type he hardly represents a happy example of his people, who are known to be the handsomest in the Caucasus.

The national character of the Georgians is usually represented as trusting, impressionable, quick-tempered, while at the same time devoid of energy and initiative. Above all, Reclus noted their gaiety, sociability and forthrightness. Stalin's character has few of these attributes, which, indeed, are the most immediately noticeable in personal intercourse with Georgians. Georgian émigrés in Paris assured Souvarine, the author of Stalin's French biography, that Joseph Djugashvili's mother was not a Georgian but an Osetin and that there is an admixture of Mongolian blood in his veins. But a certain Iremashvili, whom we shall have occasion to meet again in the future, asserts that Stalin's mother was a pure-blooded Georgian, whereas his father was an Osetin, "a coarse, uncouth person, like all the Osetins, who live in the high Caucasian mountains." It is difficult, if not impossible, to verify these assertions. However, they are scarcely necessary for the purpose of explaining Stalin's moral stature. In the countries of the Mediterranean Sea, in the Balkans, in Italy, in Spain, in addition to the so-called Southern type, which is characterized by a combination of lazy shiftlessness and explosive irascibility, one meets cold natures, in whom phlegm is combined with stubbornness and slyness. The first type prevails; the second augments it as an exception. It would seem as if each national group is doled out its due share of basic character elements, yet these are less happily distributed under the southern than under the northern sun. But we must not venture too far afield into the unprofitable region of national metaphysics.

The county town of Gori is picturesquely situated on the banks of the Kura River, seventy-six kilometers from Tiflis along the Transcaucasian Railway.

One of the oldest of Georgia's cities, Gori has an intensely dramatic history. Tradition has it that it was founded in the twelfth century by Armenians seeking refuge from the Turks. Thereafter the little town was subjected to repeated raids, for by that time the Armenians were already a commercial and urban class notable for such great wealth that they were a tempting prey. Like all Asiatic cities, Gori grew little by little, gradually drawing into its walls settlers from Georgian and Tartar villages. At about the time the shoemaker Vissarion Djugashvili migrated there from his native village of Didi-Lilo, the little town had a mixed population of approximately six thousand, several churches, many stores and more inns for the peasantry of the adjacent regions, a teachers' seminary with a Tartar department, a preparatory classical school for girls and a junior high school.

Serfdom was abolished in the Tiflis Government only fourteen years prior to the birth of Joseph, the future General Secretary [of the Communist Party Central Committee]. Social relations and customs still reflected its effects. It is doubtful that his parents could read and write. True, five Georgian language daily newspapers were published in Transcaucasia, but their total circulation was less than four thousand. The life of the peasantry still lay outside history.

Shapeless streets, widely scattered houses, fruit orchards—these gave Gori the appearance of a rambling village. The houses of the city poor, at any rate, were scarcely distinguishable from peasant dwellings. The Djugashvilis occupied an old adobe hut with brick corners and a sand-covered roof which freely admitted the wind and the rain. D. Gogokhiya, a former classmate of Joseph's, describing the family dwelling, writes: "Their room was no more than eight square yards and was located next to the kitchen. The entrance was directly from the court yard into the room, without a single step. The floor was laid with brick. The small window let in scarcely any light. The furnishings of the room consisted of a small table, a stool, and a wide couch, something like a plank-bed, covered with a *chilopya*—a straw mat." To this was later added his mother's old and noisy sewing machine.

No authentic documents have yet been published about the Djugashvili family and Joseph's childhood. Nor could they be numerous. The cultural level of their milieu was so primitive that life went unrecorded and flowed on almost without leaving any trace. Only after Stalin himself was more than fifty years old did reminiscences of his father's family begin to appear. They were usually second-hand, written either by embittered and not always conscientious enemies, or by forced "friends," at the initiative—one might almost say, by order—of official commissions on Party history, and therefore, for the most part, they are exercises on an assigned theme. It would be, of course, too simple to seek the truth along the diagonal between the two distortions. However, putting the two in juxtaposition, weighing on the one hand the reticences and on the other, the exaggerations, critically evaluating the inherent thread of the narrative itself in the light of future developments, it is possible to approximate the truth. Without seeking to paint artificially complete pictures, as I proceed, I shall endeavor to present to the reader the elements of those source materials on which rest either my surmises or my conclusions.

Most profuse in details are the reminiscences of the aforementioned [Joseph] Iremashvili, published in 1932 in the German language at Berlin, under the title, *"Stalin und die Tragödie Georgiens."* Since their author is a former Menshevik who subsequently became something in the nature of a National Socialist, his political record as such does not inspire great confidence. It is, nevertheless, impossible to ignore his essay. Many of its pages are so patently convincing that they leave no room for doubt. Even incidents which seem doubtful at first glance, find direct or indirect confirmation in official reminiscences published several years later. It might not be amiss for me to add that certain of the guesses I had made on the basis of intentional silences or evasive expressions in Soviet publications found their confirmation in Iremashvili's book, which I had the opportunity to read only at the very last moment. It would be an error to assume that as an exile and a political enemy Iremashvili tries to belittle Stalin's figure or to paint it all black. Quite the contrary: he recounts Stalin's abilities almost triumphantly, and with obvious exaggerations; he recognizes Stalin's readiness to make personal sacrifices for his ideals; he repeatedly emphasizes Stalin's attachment to his mother and sketches Stalin's first marriage in most affecting strokes. A more probing examination of this former Tiflis high school teacher's reminiscences produced the impression of a document composed of various layers. The foundation is undoubtedly made up of the remote recollections of childhood. But that basic layer has been subjected to the inevitable retrospective elaboration by memory and fantasy under the influence of Stalin's latter-day fate and the author's own political views. To that must be added the presence in the reminiscences of dubious, although in their essence, unimportant, details which should be ascribed to a failing rather frequent among a certain kind of memoirist—an endeavor to invest their presentation with "artistic" finish and completeness. Thus forewarned, I deem it quite proper, as I proceed, to lean upon Iremashvili's reminiscences.

The earlier biographical references invariably speak of Stalin as the son of a peasant from the village of Didi-Lilo. Stalin for the first time referred to himself as a workingman's son only in 1926. But this contradiction is more apparent than real: like most of Russia's workers, Djugashvili the father continued to be listed in his passport as a peasant. However, that does not exhaust the difficulties. The father is invariably called: "worker of Alikhanov's shoe factory in Tiflis." Yet the family lived at Gori, not in the capital of the Caucasus. Does it mean, then, that the father lived apart from the family? Such a supposition might be justified, had the family remained in the village. It is most unlikely that the family and its provider would live in different towns. Besides, Gogokhiya, Joseph's comrade at the theological school, who lived in the same yard with him, as well as Iremashvili, who frequently visited him, both say outright that Vissarion worked nearby, on Sobornaya Street, in an adobe with a leaky roof. We therefore surmise that the father's employment at Tiflis was temporary, probably while the family still lived in the village. At Gori, however, Vissarion Djugashvili no longer worked in a shoe factory—there were no factories in the county seat—but as an independent petty tradesman. The intentional lack of clarity on that point is dictated undoubtedly by the desire not to weaken the impression of Stalin's "proletarian" heritage.

Like most Georgian women Ekaterina Djugashvili became a mother when still quite young. The first three children died in infancy. On the twenty-first of December, 1879, when her fourth child was born, she was scarcely twenty years old. Joseph was in his seventh year when he fell ill with smallpox. Its traces remained for the rest of his life as witness of his plebeian origin and environment. To his pockmarks, Stalin's French biographer, Souvarine, adds cachexia of the left arm, which, in addition to the two toes grown together, according to his information, should serve as proof of alcoholic heredity on his father's side. Generally speaking, shoemakers, at least in Central Russia, were so notorious as drunkards that "drunk as a shoemaker" became a by-word. It is hard to tell how near the truth are the speculations on heredity communicated to Souvarine by "various persons," most likely Menshevik émigrés. In the enumeration of Joseph Djugashvili's "distinctive marks" by Tsarist gendarmes, a withered arm was not listed, but the adhering toes were recorded once, in 1903, by Colonel Shabelsky. It is not impossible that, prior to publication, the gendarmerie documents, like all others, had been subjected to an insufficiently thorough purge by the censor. It is impossible not to remark, however, that in later years Stalin was wont to wear a warm glove on his left hand, even at sessions of the Politburo. Rheumatism was the generally accepted reason for that. But after all, these secondary physical characteristics, whether real or imaginary, are in themselves scarcely of passing interest. It is far more important to try to assay the true character of his parents and the atmosphere of his family.

The first thing that strikes the eye is the fact that the officially collected reminiscences hardly mention Vissarion, passing him by in almost total silence, while at the same time dwelling sympathetically on Ekaterina's hard life of drudgery. "Joseph's mother earned very little," relates Gogokhiya, "working as a washerwoman or baking bread in the homes of Gori's well-to-do inhabitants. She had to pay a ruble and a half a month for her room. But she was not always able to save that ruble and a half." We thus learn that the responsibility of paying rent for their home rested with the mother, not the father. Furthermore, "The poverty and the mother's hard life of toil left their imprint on Joseph's character . . ."—as if his father were not a part of the family. Only later, in passing, the author inserts this sentence: "Joseph's father, Vissarion, spent the entire day in work, stitching and repairing footwear." However, the father's work is not mentioned in connection with the family's home life or its problems of making a living. The impression is thus created that the father is mentioned at all only in order to fill a gap.

Glurdzhidze, another classmate at the theological school, ignores the father altogether when he writes that Joseph's mother "earned her living by cutting, sewing or laundering underwear." These reticences, which are not accidental, deserve all the more attention because the customs of the people did not assign the leading role in the family to the woman. On the contrary, according to Old Georgian traditions, exceedingly persistent among the conservative mountaineers, woman was relegated to the position of a household slavey, was scarcely ever admitted into the august presence of her lord and master, had no voice in family affairs, and did not so much as dare to punish her own son. Even at church mothers, wives and sisters were placed behind fathers, husbands and brothers. The fact that the authors of the reminiscences place the mother where normally the father should be cannot be interpreted otherwise than as a desire to avoid characterizing Vissarion Djugashvili altogether. The old Russian encyclopedia, commenting on the extreme abstinence of Georgians in the matter of food, adds: "There is scarcely another people in the world that drink as much wine as the Georgians." True, after moving to Gori, Vissarion could hardly have maintained his own vineyard. But to make up for that, the city had *dukhans* on every corner, and in them vodka successfully competed with wine.

On that score Iremashvili's evidence is especially convincing. Like the other memoirists, but antedating them by five years, he is warmly sympathetic in his characterization of Ekaterina, who evinced great love for her only son and friendliness for his mates in play and in school. A true Georgian woman, Keke, as she was generally called, was profoundly religious. Her life of toil was one uninterrupted service: to God, to husband and to her son. Her eyesight became weak in consequence of constant sewing in a half-dark dwelling, so she began to wear eye-glasses early in life. But then any Georgian matron past thirty was regarded as almost an old woman. Her neighbors treated her with all the greater sympathy because her life had turned out to be so very hard. According to Iremashvili, the head of the family, Bezo (Vissarion) was a person of stern disposition as well as a heartless dipsomaniac. He drank up most of his meager earnings. That was why the responsibility for rent and for the support of the family fell as a double burden on the mother. In helpless grief Keke observed Bezo, by mistreating his son, "drive out of his heart the love of God and people, and fill him with aversion for his own father." "Undeserved, frightful beatings made the boy as grim and heartless as was his father." In bitterness Joseph began to brood over the eternal mysteries of life. He did not grieve over the premature death of his father; he merely felt freer. Iremashvili infers that when still quite young, the boy began to extend his smoldering enmity and thirst for vengeance against his father to all those who had, or could have, any power at all over him. "Since youth the carrying out of vengeful plots became for him the goal that dominated all his efforts." Granting these words are based on retrospective judgments, they still retain the full force of their significance.

In 1930, when she was already seventy-one, Ekaterina, who then lived in the unpretentious rooms of a servant at what was formerly the palace of the Viceroy in Tiflis, replying to the questions of journalists, said through an interpreter: "Soso (Joseph) was always a good boy . . . I never had occasion to punish him. He studied hard, always reading or discussing, trying to understand everything . . . Soso was my only son. Of course, he was precious to me . . . His father Vissarion wanted to make of Soso a good shoemaker. But his father died when Soso was eleven years old . . . I did not want him to be a shoemaker. I wanted only one thing—that he should become a priest." Souvarine, it is true, collected quite different information among Georgians in Paris: "They knew Soso when he was already hard, unfeeling, treating his mother without respect, and in support of their reminiscences they cite 'ticklish facts.'" The biographer himself remarks, however, that his information came from Stalin's political enemies. In that set, too, circulate not a few legends, only in reverse. Iremashvili, on the contrary, speaks with great persistence of Soso's warm attachment for his mother. Indeed, the boy could have had no other feelings for the family's benefactress and his protectress against his father.

The German writer Emil Ludwig, our epoch's court portrait painter, found at the Kremlin another occasion for applying his method of asking leading questions, in which moderate psychological insight is combined with political wariness. Are you fond of nature, Signore Mussolini? What do you think of Schopenhauer, Doctor Masaryk? Do you believe in a better future, Mister Roosevelt? During some such verbal inquisition Stalin, ill at ease in the presence of the celebrated foreigner, assiduously drew little flowers and boats with a colored pencil. So, at any rate, recounts Ludwig. On the withered arm of Wilhelm Hohenzollern this writer had constructed a psychoanalytic biography of the former Kaiser, which old man Freud regarded with ironic perplexity. Ludwig did not notice Stalin's withered arm, nor did he notice, needless to say, the adhering toes. Nonetheless he attempted to deduce the revolutionary career of the master at the Kremlin from the beatings administered to him in childhood by his father. After familiarizing oneself with Iremashvili's memoirs it is not difficult to understand where Ludwig got his idea. "What made you a rebel? Did it perhaps come to pass because your parents treated you badly?" It would be rather imprudent to ascribe to these words any documentary value, and not only because Stalin's affirmations and negations, as we shall have frequent occasions to see, are prone to change with the greatest of ease. In an analogous situation anyone else might have acted similarly. In any event, one cannot blame Stalin for having refused to complain in public of his father who had been dead a long time. One is rather surprised by the deferential writer's lack of delicacy.

Family trials were not however the only factor to mold the boy's harsh, willful and vengeful personality. The far broader influences of social environment furthered the same quality. One of Stalin's biographers relates how from time to time the Most Illustrious Prince Amilakhviri would ride up on a spirited horse to the poor home of the shoemaker to have his boots repaired, which had just been torn at the hunt, and how the shoemaker's son, a great shock of hair over his low forehead, pierced the Prince with eyes of hate, clenching his childish fists. By itself, that picturesque scene belongs, we think, in the realm of fantasy. However, the contrast between the poverty surrounding him and the relative sumptuousness of the last of the Georgian feudal lords could not help but make a sharp and lasting impression on the consciousness of the boy.

The situation of the city population itself was not much better. High above the lower classes rose the county officialdom, which ruled the city in the name of the Tsar and his Caucasian Viceroy, Prince Golitsyn, a sinister satrap who was universally and deservedly hated. The landowners and the Armenian merchants were in league with the county authorities. Despite its general low level, and partly in consequence of it, the basic plebeian mass of the population was itself divided by barriers of caste. Each one who ever so slightly rose above his fellow, guarded his rank vigilantly. The Didi-Lilo peasant's distrust of the city was transformed at Gori into the hostile attitude of the poor artisan toward the more prosperous families for whom Keke was obliged to sew and to wash. No less crudely did the social gradations assert themselves in school, where the children of priests, petty gentry and officials more than once made it quite clear to Joseph that he was their social inferior. As is evident from Gogokhiya's stories, the shoemaker's son first sensed the humiliation of social inequality early in life and poignantly. "He did not like to call on people who lived prosperously. Despite the fact that I visited him several times a day, he very rarely came to see me, because my uncle lived richly, according to the standards of those days." Such were the first sources of a social protest, as yet instinctive, which, in the atmosphere of the country's political ferment, would later transform the seminary student into a revolutionist.

The lowest layer of the petty bourgeoisie knows but two high careers for its gifted or only sons: those of civil servant or priest. Hitler's mother dreamed of a pastor's career for her son. The same fond hope was Ekaterina Djugashvili's some ten years earlier, in an even more modest milieu. The dream itself —to see her son in priestly robes—indicates incidentally how little the family of the shoemaker Bezo was permeated with the "proletarian spirit." A better future was conceived, not in consequence of the class struggle, but as the result of breaking with one's class.

The Orthodox priesthood, despite its low social rank and cultural level, belonged to the hierarchy of the privileged in that it was free of compulsory military service, the head tax, and . . . the whip. Only the abolition of serfdom gave the peasants access to the ranks of the priesthood, that privilege being conditioned, however, by a police limitation: in order to be appointed to a church position, a peasant's son had to have the special dispensation of the governor.

The future priests were educated in scores of seminaries, the preparatory step for which were theological schools. By their rating in the government system of education, the seminaries approximated the middle schools, with this difference, that in them lay studies were supposed to be no more than a slender pillar for theology! In old Russia the well-known *boorsy* were notorious for the horrifying savagery of their customs, medieval pedagogy and the law of the fist, not to mention dirt, cold, and hunger. All the vices censured by Holy Scripture flourished in these hotbeds of piety. The writer Pomyalovsky found a permanent place in Russian literature as the ruthlessly veracious author of "Theological School Sketches" [*Ocherki Boorsy*—1862]. One cannot but quote at this juncture the words Pomyalovsky's biographer used with reference to Pomyalovsky himself: "that period of his school life developed in him mistrust, dissimulation, animosity, and hatred for his environment." True, the reforms of Alexander the Second's reign brought about certain improvements even in the mustiest region of ecclesiastical education. Nonetheless, as late as the last decade of the last century the theological schools, especially in remote Transcaucasia, remained the darkest blots on the "cultural" map of Russia.

The Tsarist government long ago, and not without bloodshed, broke the independence of the Georgian Church, subjecting it to the Petersburg Synod. But hostility toward the Russifiers continued to smolder among the lower ranks of the Georgian clergy. The enslavement of their church shook the traditional religiousness of the Georgians and prepared the ground for the influence of the Social-Democracy, not only in the city but in the village as well. The fustian atmosphere of the theological schools was even more marked, for they were designed not only to Russify their charges but to prepare them for the role of the church's police of the soul. A spirit of sharp hostility permeated the intercourse between teachers and pupils. Instruction was carried on in Russian; Georgian was taught only twice a week, and was not infrequently slighted, as the language of an inferior race.

In 1890, evidently soon after his father's death, the eleven-year old Soso, carrying a calico school-bag under his arm, entered the theological school. According to his schoolmates, the boy evinced a great urge for learning his catechism and his prayers. Gogokhiya remarks that, thanks to "his extraordinary memory," Soso remembered his lessons from the words of his teacher and had no need to review them. As a matter of fact, Stalin's memory—at least, his memory for theories—is quite mediocre. But all the same, in order to remember in the class room it was necessary to excel in attentiveness. At that time the sacerdotal order was no doubt Soso's own crowning ambition. Determination stimulated both aptitude and memory. Another school comrade, Kapanadze, testifies that throughout the thirteen years of tutelage and throughout the later thirty-five years of activity as a teacher he never had occasion once "to meet such a gifted and able pupil" as Joseph Djugashvili. Yet even Iremashvili, who wrote his book not in Tiflis but in Berlin, maintains that Soso was the best pupil in the theological school. In other testimonies there are, however, substantial shadings. "During the first years, in the preparatory grades," relates Glurdzhidze, "Joseph studied superbly, and with time, as he disclosed increasingly brilliant abilities, he became one of the best pupils." In that article, which bears all the earmarks of a panegyric ordered from above, occurrence of the circumspect expression "one of the best" indicates too obviously that Joseph was not the best, was not superior to the entire class, was not an extraordinary pupil. Identical in nature are the recollections of another schoolmate, Elisabedashvili. Joseph, says he, "was one of the most indigent and one of the most gifted." In other words, not the most gifted. We are thus constrained to the surmise that either his scholastic standing varied in the various grades or that certain of the memoirists, belonging themselves to the rear-guard of learning, were poor at picking the best pupils.

Without being definite as to Joseph's exact rating in his class, Gogokhiya states that in development and knowledge he ranked "much higher than his schoolmates." Soso read everything available in the school library, including Georgian and Russian classics, which were, of course, carefully sifted by the authorities. After his graduation examinations Joseph was rewarded with a certificate of merit, "which in those days was an extraordinary achievement, because his father was not a clergyman and plied the shoemaking trade." Truly a remarkable touch!

On the whole the memoirs written in Tiflis about "the Leader's youthful years" are rather insipid. "Soso would pull us into the chorus, and in his ringing, pleasant voice would lead us in the beloved national songs." When playing ball, "Joseph knew how to select the best players, and for that reason our group always won." "Joseph learned to draw splendidly." But not a single one of these attributes developed into a talent: Joseph became neither a singer nor a sportsman nor an artist. Even less convincing sound reports like these: "Joseph Djugashvili was remarkable for his great modesty, and he was a kind, sensitive comrade."—"He never let anyone feel his superiority," and the like. If all of that is true, then one is forced to conclude that with the years Joseph became transformed into his opposite.

Iremashvili's recollections are incomparably more vivid and closer to the truth. He draws his namesake as a lanky, sinewy, freckled boy, extraordinarily persistent, uncommunicative and willful, who could always obtain the goal he had set before him, be it a matter of bossing his playmates, throwing rocks or scaling cliffs. Although Soso was decidedly a passionate lover of nature, he had no sympathy for its living creatures. Compassion for people or for animals was foreign to him. "I never saw him weeping."—"Soso had only a sarcastic sneer for the joys and sorrows of his fellows." All of that may have been slightly polished in memory, like a rock in a torrent; it has not been invented.

Iremashvili commits one indubitable error when he ascribes to Joseph rebellious behavior as far back as the Gori school. Soso was presumably subjected to almost daily punishments as the leader of schoolboy protests; particularly, hooting against "the hated Inspector Butyrski." Yet the authors of official memoirs, this time without any premeditated purpose, portray Joseph as an exemplary pupil even in behavior all through those years. "Usually he was serious, persistent," writes Gogokhiya, "did not like pranks and mischief. After his schoolwork he hurried home, and he was always seen poring over a book."

According to the same Gogokhiya, the school paid Joseph a monthly stipend, which would have been quite impossible had there been any lack of respectfulness toward his superiors and above all toward "the hated Inspector Butyrski." All the other memoirists place the inception of Joseph's rebellious moods at the time of his Tiflis seminary days. But even then no one states anything about his participation in stormy protests. The explanation for Iremashvili's lapses of memory, as well as for those of certain others, with reference to the place and time of individual occurrences, lies evidently in the fact that all the participants regarded the Tiflis seminary as the direct continuation of the theological school. It is more difficult to account for the fact that no one except Iremashvili mentions the hooting under Joseph's leadership. Is that a simple aberration of memory? Or did Joseph play in certain "concerts" a concealed role, of which only a few were informed? That would not be at all at variance with the character of the future conspirator.

The moment of Joseph's break with the faith of his fathers remains uncertain. According to the same Iremashvili, Soso, together with two other schoolboys, gladly sang in the village church during summer vacations, although even then—that is, in the higher grades of the school—religion was already something he had outgrown. Glurdzhidze recalls in his turn that the thirteen-year old Joseph told him once: "You know, they are deceiving us. There is no God . . ." In reply to the amazed cry of his interlocutor, Joseph suggested that he read a book from which it was evident that "the talk of God is empty chatter." What book was that? "Darwin. You must read it." The reference to Darwin ends a shade of the incredible to the episode. A thirteen-year old boy in a backward town could hardly have read Darwin and derived atheistic convictions from him. According to his own words, Stalin took to the road of revolutionary ideas at the age of fifteen; hence, when already in Tiflis. True, he could have broken with religion earlier. But it is equally possible that Glurdzhidze, who likewise left the theological school for the seminary, erred in his dates, anticipating by a few years. To repudiate God, in whose name the cruelties against the schoolboys were perpetrated, was undoubtedly not difficult. At any rate, the inner strength necessary for that was rewarded when the instructors and the authorities as a whole had the moral ground snatched from under their feet. From then on they could not perpetrate violence merely because they were stronger. Soso's expressive formula, "they are deceiving us," sheds a bright light on his inward world, irrespective of where and when the conversation took place, whether at Gori, or a year or two later, at Tiflis.

As to the time of Joseph's matriculation at the seminary, various official publications offer the choice of three dates: 1892, 1893 and 1894. How long was he in the seminary? Six years, answers "The Communist's Calendar." Five, states the biographical sketch written by Stalin's secretary. Four years, asserts his former schoolmate, Gogokhiya. The memorial shingle on the building of the former seminary states, as it is possible to decipher from a photograph, that the "Great Stalin" studied in these walls from the first of September, 1894, to the twenty-first of July, 1899; consequently, five years. Is it possible that the official biography avoids that last date, because it presents the seminary student Djugashvili as too overgrown? At any rate, we prefer to rely on the memorial shingle, because its dates are based in all likelihood upon the documents of the seminary itself.

The certificate of good conduct from the Gori school in his satchel, the fifteen-year old Joseph found himself for the first time in the autumn of 1894 in the big city that could not have failed to astound his imagination, Tiflis, the ancient capital of Georgian kings. It will be no exaggeration to say that the half-Asiatic, half-European city laid an impress on young Joseph that remained for the rest of his life. In the course of its history of almost 1,500 years Tiflis fell many times into the power of its enemies, was demolished fifteen times, on several occasions razed to its very foundations. The Arabs, the Turks and the Persians, who smashed their way in, left a profound impression upon the architecture and the customs of the people, and the traces of that influence have been preserved to this day. European sections developed after the Russian conquest of Georgia, when the former capital became the provincial seat and the administrative center of the Transcaucasian Region. Tiflis numbered more than 150,000 inhabitants the year Joseph entered the seminary. The Russians, who composed one-fourth of that number, were either exiled religious dissenters, rather numerous in Transcaucasia, or the military and civil servants. Trade and industry were concentrated in the hands of the Armenians, since ancient days and the most numerous (38%) and the most prosperous sector of the population. The Georgians, who were connected with the village and who, like the Russians, formed approximately one-fourth of the population, provided the lower layer of artisans, traders, petty civil servants and officers. "Alongside of streets which bear a contemporary European character . . ." states a description of the city published in 1901, ". . . nests a labyrinth of narrow, crooked and dirty, purely Asiatic lanes, squarelets and bazaars, framed by open stalls of the Eastern type, by stands, coffee houses, barber shops, and filled with a clamorous throng of porters, water carriers, errand boys, horsemen, lines of pack mules and donkeys, caravans of camels, and the like." The absence of a sewage disposal system, insufficiency of water, the torrid summers, the caustic and infiltrating dust of the streets, kerosene lighting in the center of the city and the absence of any light at all in the outlying streets—such were features of Transcaucasia's administrative and cultural center at the turn of the century.

"We were admitted into a four-storey house," relates Gogokhiya, who arrived there together with Joseph, "into the huge rooms of our dormitory, which held from twenty to thirty people. This building was the Tiflis Theological Seminary." Thanks to his successful graduation from the theological school at Gori, Joseph Djugashvili was admitted to the seminary, with everything provided, including clothes, shoes and textbooks, a circumstance that would have been utterly impossible, it must be reiterated, had he revealed himself as a rebel. Who knows, perhaps the authorities had high hopes that he might become an ornament of the Georgian Church? As in preparatory school, instruction was in Russian. Most of the instructors were Russians by nationality and Russifiers by duty. Georgians were admitted to teaching only in the event that they exhibited double zeal. The rector was a Russian, the monk Hermogenes; the inspector, a Georgian, the monk Abashidze, the most sinister and detestable person in the seminary. Iremashvili, who has not only given the first but also the most complete information about the seminary, recalls:

> Life in school was sad and monotonous. Locked in day and night within barrack walls, we felt like prisoners who must spend years there, without being guilty of anything. All of us were despondent and sullen. Stifled by the rooms and corridors that cut us off from the outer world, youthful joy almost never asserted itself. When, from time to time, youthful temperament did break through, it was immediately suppressed by the monks and monitors. The Tsarist inspection of schools forbade us the reading of Georgian literature and newspapers. . . . They feared our becoming inspired with ideas of our country's freedom and independence, and the infection of our young souls with the new teachings of socialism. Even the few literary works the lay authorities allowed us to read were forbidden to us by the church authorities because we were future priests. The works of Tolstoy, Dostoyevsky, Turgeniev and other classics remained inaccessible to us.

The days in the seminary passed as in a prison or in a barracks. School life began at seven o'clock in the morning. Prayers, tea drinking, classes. Again prayers. Instruction, with recesses, until two o'clock in the afternoon. Prayers. Dinner. Poor and insufficient food. Permission to leave the walls of the seminary prison was granted only for the interval between the hours of three and five. After that the gates were locked. Roll-call. At eight o'clock, tea. Preparation of lessons. At ten o'clock—after more prayers—all went to their cots. "We felt trapped in a stone gaol," confirms Gogokhiya. During Sunday and holiday services the students stood on their feet for three or four hours at a stretch, always on one and the same stone slab of the church floor, shifting from one numb foot to the other, under the gaze of the monks who watched them incessantly. "Even the most pious should have unlearned to pray under the influence of the interminable service. Behind devout grimaces we hid our thought from the monks on duty."

As a rule the spirit of piety went hand and glove with the spirit of police repression. Inspector Abashidze, hostile and suspicious, observed the boarders, their train of thought, their manner of spending their time. More than once when the pupils returned to their rooms from dinner, they would find fresh evidence of a raid perpetrated during their absence. Not infrequently the monks searched the seminary students themselves. Punishment was meted out in the form of crude upbraiding, the dark cell, which was seldom vacant, low marks for deportment, which threatened the collapse of all hopes, and finally, expulsion from the holy of holies. Those who were physically weak left the seminary for the graveyard. Hard and thorny was the path of salvation!

The methods of seminary pedagogy had everything that the Jesuits had invented to curb the children's souls, but in a more primitive, a cruder and therefore a less effective form. But the main thing was that the situation in the country was hardly conducive to the spirit of humility. In almost all of the sixty seminaries of Russia there were undergraduates who, most frequently under the influence of university students, rejected their priestly robes even before they had time to put them on, who were filled with contempt for theological scholasticism, read didactic novels, radical Russian journalism and popular expositions of Darwin and Marx. In the Tiflis seminary the revolutionary ferment, nurtured by nationalistic and general political sources, already enjoyed a certain tradition. In the past it had broken through in the form of sharp conflicts with teachers, openly expressed indignation, even the killing of a rector. Ten years prior to Stalin's matriculation at the seminary Sylvester Dzhibladze had struck his teacher for a slighting reference to the Georgian language. Dzhibladze subsequently became a founder of the Social-Democratic movement in the Caucasus and one of Joseph Djugashvili's teachers.

In 1885 Tiflis saw the appearance of its first socialist circles, in which the graduates of the seminary at once took the leading place. Alongside of Sylvester Dzhibladze we meet here Noah Jordania, the future leader of the Georgian Mensheviks, Nicholas Chkheidze, the future Deputy of the Duma and Chairman of the Petrograd Soviet during the month of the February Revolution of 1917, and a number of others who were destined to play a notable role in the political movement of the Caucasus and of the entire country. Marxism in Russia was still passing through its intelligentsia stage. In the Caucasus the Theological Seminary became the principal hearth of Marxist infection simply because there was no university at Tiflis. In backward, non-industrial districts, like Georgia, Marxism was accepted in a particularly abstract, not to say scholastic form. The seminarists had at least some training in the use of logical deductions. But at the base of the turn toward Marxism lay, of course, the profound social and national dissatisfaction of the people, which compelled the young Bohemians to seek the way out along the revolutionary road.

Joseph did not have occasion to lay new roads in Tiflis, notwithstanding the attempts of the Soviet Plutarchs to present the matter in this light. The blow Dzhibladze struck was still reverberating within the seminary walls. The former seminarists were already leading the left wing of public opinion, nor did they lose contact with their step-mother, the seminary. Sufficient was any occasion, a personal encounter, a mere push, for the dissatisfied, embittered, proud youth, who needed merely a formula in order to find himself, to drift naturally into the revolutionary track. The first stage along this road had to be a break with religion. If it is possible that from Gori the boy had brought with him remnants of faith, surely they were forthwith dispelled at the seminary. Henceforth Joseph decidedly lost all taste for theology.

"His ambition," writes Iremashvili, "reached such heights that he was away ahead of us in his achievements." If that is true, it applies only to a very brief period. Glurdzhidze remarks that of the studies in the seminary curriculum, "Joseph liked civil history and logic," occupying himself with the other subjects only sufficiently to pass his examinations. Having grown cold toward Holy Scriptures, he became interested in lay literature, natural science and social problems. He was aided by students in the advanced classes. "Having found out about the capable and inquiring Joseph Djugashvili, they began to converse with him and to supply him with magazines and books," relates Gogokhiya. "The book was Joseph's inseparable friend, and he did not part with it even while eating," testifies Glurdzhidze. In general, avidity for reading was the distinguishing characteristic during those years of burgeoning. After the final check-up at night, the monks having put out the lamps, the young conspirators would produce their hidden candles and by their flickering flames would immerse themselves in books. Joseph, who had spent many sleepless nights poring over his books, began to look ill and in need of sleep. "When he began to cough," relates Iremashvili, "I would take his books away from him and put out his candle, more than once." Glurdzhidze recalls how, in stealth, the seminary students would swallow Tolstoy, Dostoyevsky, Shakespeare, Shelley, Lippert's "History of Culture," the Russian radical publicist Pisarev . . . "At times we read in church, during service, hiding in the pews."

At that time the writings of Georgian national literature made the strongest impression upon Soso. Iremashvili describes the first explosions of the revolutionary temperament, in which an idealism still fresh combined with the sudden awakening of ambition. "Soso and I," recalls Iremashvili, "frequently talked about the tragic fate of Georgia. We were enraptured by the works of the poet Shota Rustaveli . . ." Soso's model became Koba, the hero of the romance "Nunu" by the Georgian author of "Kazbek." In their fight against the Tsarist authorities the oppressed mountaineers, because of betrayal, suffer defeat and lose their last remnants of freedom, while the leader of the rebellion sacrifices everything, even his life, for the sake of his country and his wife, Nunu. From then on Koba "became a divinity for Soso . . . He wanted to become another Koba, a fighter and a hero, as renowned as 'Koba' himself . . ." Joseph called himself by the name of the leader of the mountaineers, and did not want to be called by any other name. "His face shone with pride and joy when we called him Koba. Soso preserved that name for many years, and it became likewise his first pseudonym when he began to write and propagandize for the party . . . Even now everybody in Georgia calls him *Koba* or *Koba-Stalin*." Concerning young Joseph's enthusiasm for the national problem of Georgia, official biographers say nothing at all. In their writings Stalin appears at once as a finished Marxist. Nonetheless, it is not hard to understand that in the naive "Marxism" of that first period, nebulous ideas of Socialism lived on in peace with the nationalistic romanticism of "Koba."

In the course of that year, according to Gogokhiya, Joseph developed and matured to such an extent that in his second year he began to lead a group of comrades at the seminary. If Beriya,[1] the most official of the historians, is to be believed, "in 1896-1897 Stalin led two Marxist circles at the Tiflis Theological Seminary." Stalin himself was never led by anyone. Much more probable is Iremashvili's story. Ten seminarists, among them Soso Djugashvili, organized, according to him, a secret socialist circle. "The oldest undergraduate, Devdariyani, elected leader, undertook his task in all seriousness." He worked out, or rather received from his inspirers outside the walls of the seminary, a program according to which the members of the circle had to train themselves within six years into accomplished Social-Democratic leaders. The program began with Cosmogony and finished with a Communist society. At the secret meetings of the circle papers were read, accompanied by a heated exchange of opinions. Matters were not limited, Gogokhiya assures us, to oral propaganda. Joseph "founded and edited" in the Georgian language a manuscript journal which appeared twice a month and circulated from hand to hand. The wideawake Inspector Abashidze once found on Joseph's person "a notebook with an article for our manuscript magazine." Similar publications, irrespective of their contents, were strictly forbidden, not only in theological, but even in lay institutions of education. Since the result of Abashidze's discovery was only a "warning" and a bad mark in behavior, we are bound to conclude that the magazine was rather innocuous. It is noteworthy that the very thoroughgoing Iremashvili says nothing at all about that magazine.

In the seminary Joseph must have sensed his poverty even more sharply than in preparatory school. ". . . He had no money," Gogokhiya mentions by the way, "while we received from our parents packages and pin money. During the two hours allowed for sojourning outside the school walls, Joseph could not afford any of the things accessible to the sons of the more privileged families. All the more unbridled were his dreams and plans of the future and more marked the effect on his instincts in dealing with his schoolmates.

"As boy and youth," testifies Iremashvili, "he was a good friend to those who submitted to his domineering will." But only to those. The more imperative was self-restraint in the presence of his preceptors, the more freely did his despotism assert itself in the circle of his comrades. The secret circle, fenced off from the entire world, became the natural arena on which Joseph tried his strength and the endurance of others. "He deemed it something unnatural," writes Iremashvili, "that any other fellow-student might be a leader and organizer of the group . . . since he read the greater part of the papers." Who-

[1] Lavrentii Pavlovich Beriya (1899-), People's Commissar of Internal Affairs, head of the political police of the Soviet Union, was for many years head of the G.P.U. of Georgia. Hitherto known only as a ruthless Chekist, he acquired sudden fame as an historian after the publication of his lecture, "On the Question of the History of Bolshevik Organizations in Trans-Caucasia," originally delivered to the Communist Party activists of Tiflis at two sessions, July 21 and 22, 1935. In those lectures he created a romantic early revolutionary career for Stalin. Today Beriya is one of Stalin's most trusted lieutenants.—C. M.

ever dared to refute him or even to attempt to explain something to him, immediately evoked his "merciless enmity." Joseph knew how to persecute and how to avenge himself. He knew how to strike at weak spots. Under such circumstances the initial solidarity of the circle could not long endure. In his struggle for mastery, Koba, "with his supercilious and poisonous cynicism, injected personal squabbles into the society of his friends." These complaints about his "poisonous cynicism," his rudeness and his vengefulness, occur many, many times during Koba's life.

In the rather fantastic biography written by Essad-Bey it is told that presumably prior to his seminary days young Joseph led a vagabond life in Tiflis in the company of *"kintos"*—heroes of the street, fast talkers, singers and hooligans—and that from them he acquired his crude ways and his virtuosity at swearing. All of that is quite obvious invention. From the theological school Joseph went directly to the seminary, so that there was no interval left for vagabondage. But the point is that the nickname *"kinto"* does not occupy the last place in the Caucasian dictionary. It signifies a clever schemer, a cynic, a person capable of the lowest sort of conniving. In the autumn of 1923 I first heard that appellation with reference to Stalin from the lips of the old Georgian Bolshevik Philip Makharadze. Is it not possible that this sobriquet had been acquired by Joseph in his more youthful years and gave birth to the legend concerning the street chapter of his life?

The same biographer speaks of the "heavy fist," with the aid of which Joseph Djugashvili presumably assured himself of his triumph on the occasions when peaceful means proved ill-suited. That too is hard to believe. Risky "direct action" was never a part of Stalin's character, in all likelihood not even in those remote years. He preferred and knew how to find others to do the actual fighting, himself remaining in the shadows if not altogether behind the curtains. "What brought him adherents," states Iremashvili, "was fear of his crude anger and his vicious mockery. His partisans surrendered to his leadership, because they felt secure under his power . . . Only such human types as were quite poor spiritually and inclined to fights could become his friends . . ." The inevitable results were not far behind. Some members of the circle left, others took less and less interest in the discussions. "Two groups, *for* and *against* Koba, formed in the course of a few years; the struggle for a cause developed into a disgusting personal squabble . . ." This was the first big "squabble" on Joseph's path of life, but it was not the last. Many of them were ahead.

It is impossible not to tell here, although considerably anticipating, how Stalin, already the General Secretary of the Communist Party, having painted at one of the sessions of the Central Committee a depressing picture of the personal intrigues and squabbles which were developing in the various local committees of the Party, quite unexpectedly added: "but these squabbles have also their positive side, because they lead to the monolithicism of leadership." His hearers looked at each other in surprise; the orator continued his report undisturbed. The essence of that "monolithicism" even in his youthful years was not always identical with the idea. Says Iremashvili: "His concern was not with finding and determining the truth; he would contend against or defend that which he had previously affirmed or condemned. Victory and triumph were much more precious to him."

It is impossible to ascertain the nature of Joseph's views in those days, since they left no traces in writing. According to Soso Iremashvili, his namesake stood for the most forcible actions and for "the dictatorship of the minority." The participation of a purposeful imagination in the work of memory is quite obvious here: at the end of the past century the very question of "dictatorship" did not yet exist. "Koba's extreme views did not take form," continues Iremashvili, "in consequence of 'objective study,' but came as the natural product of his personal will to power and of his merciless ambition, which dominated him physically and spiritually." Behind the undoubted prejudice in the judgments of the former Menshevik one must know how to find the kernel of truth. In Stalin's spiritual life, the personal, practical aim always stood above the theoretical truth, and the will played an immeasurably greater part than the intellect.

Iremashvili makes one more psychological observation, which, although it contains a measure of retrospective evaluation, still remains extremely pertinent: Joseph "saw everywhere and in everything only the negative, the bad side, and had no faith at all in men's idealistic motives or attributes." This point of view, which had already revealed itself during his youth, when the entire world is usually still covered with the film of idealism, was in the future to run through Joseph's entire life as its leit-motif. Precisely because of that, Stalin, despite the other prominent traits of his character, was to remain in the background during periods of historical progress, when the finest qualities of selflessness and heroism awaken among the masses. Inversely, his cynical disbelief in men and his special ability to appeal to the worst in their nature were to find ample scope during the epoch of reaction, which crystallizes egoism and perfidy.

Joseph Djugashvili not only did not become a priest, as his mother had dreamed, but he did not even receive the certificate that could have opened for him the doors to certain provincial universities. As to how that happened and why, there are several versions, which cannot be readily reconciled. In reminiscences written in 1929, with obvious intent to eradicate the unfavorable impression of the reminiscences written by him in 1923, Abel Yenukidze states that at the seminary Joseph began to read secret books of harmful tendency. His offense did not escape the attention of the Inspector and hence the dangerous pupil "flew out of the seminary." The official Caucasian historian Beriya informs us that Stalin was "expelled for unreliability." There is, of course, nothing unlikely in that; similar expulsions were not infrequent. What does seem strange is that so far the seminary documents on that subject have not been published. That they have not been destroyed by fire and have not been lost in the maelstrom of the revolutionary years is apparent at least from the previously mentioned memorial shingle and even more so from the complete silence as to their fate. Are the documents being kept from publication because they contain inauspicious facts or because they refute certain legends of latter-day origin?

Most frequently one finds the assertion that Djugashvili was expelled for leading a Social-Democratic circle. His former classmate at the seminary, Elisabedashvili, not a very reliable witness, informs us that in the Social-Democratic circles, "organized by direction and under the leadership of Stalin," there were "a hundred to one hundred twenty" seminarists. Had this referred to the years 1905-1906, when all the waters had overflowed their banks and all the authorities were in utter bewilderment, this might have been believed. But for the year 1899 that figure is utterly fantastic. Had the organization numbered as many members as that, the affairs could not have been limited to mere expulsion: the intervention of the gendarmes would have been quite unavoidable. Joseph nevertheless not only was not immediately arrested, but remained at liberty for nearly three years after leaving the seminary. Therefore, the version that the Social-Democratic circles were the cause of his expulsion has to be definitely rejected.

That issue is presented much more cautiously by Gogokhiya, who as a rule tries not to stray too far from the groundwork of facts. "Joseph stopped paying attention to his lessons," he writes, "studied for no more than passing marks, so as to pass the examinations. The ferocious monk Abashidze guessed why the talented, well-developed Djugashvili, who possessed an incredibly rich memory, studied only for passing marks . . . and succeeded in obtaining a decision to expel him from the seminary." As to what the monk had "guessed," only more guesses are possible. From Gogokhiya's words the conclusion is inevitable that Joseph was expelled from the seminary for failure in his studies, which was the result of his break with theological super-wisdom. The same conclusion might be drawn from Kapanadze's story about the "break" which occurred at the time he studied in the Tiflis seminary: "he was no longer the assiduous pupil he had been before." It is noteworthy that Kapanadze, Glurdzhidze and Elisabedashvili entirely avoid the question of Joseph's expulsion from the seminary.

But most astounding of all is the circumstance that Stalin's mother in the last period of her life, when official historians and journalists began to take an interest in her, categorically denied the very fact of expulsion. At the time he entered the seminary the fifteen year old boy was remarkable, according to her words, for his glowing health, but close application to his studies exhausted him to such an extent that physicians feared tuberculosis. Ekaterina added that her son did not want to leave the seminary and that she "took" him against his will. That does not sound very likely. Ill health might have called for a temporary interruption of studies, but not for a complete break with the school, not for a mother's complete repudiation of so alluring a career for her son. Also, in the year 1899 Joseph was already twenty years old, he was not distinguished by submissiveness, and it is hardly possible that his mother could have disposed of his fate so easily. Finally, after leaving the seminary, Joseph did not return to Gori and place himself under his mother's wing, which would have been the most natural thing in the event of illness, but remained in Tiflis, without occupation and without means. Old Keke did not tell the whole truth when she talked with the journalists. It might be supposed that at the time his mother had regarded her son's expulsion as a dire disgrace to herself, and since the event took place in Tiflis, she had assured her neighbors at Gori that her son had not been expelled but had voluntarily left the seminary because of the state of his health. To the old woman, moreover, it must have seemed that it was unbecoming for "the leader" of the State to have been expelled from school in his youth. It is hardly necessary to seek other, more recondite, reasons for the persistence with which Keke repeated, "he was not expelled, I took him out myself."

But perhaps Joseph was not actually subjected to expulsion in the precise sense of the word. Such a version, perhaps the most likely, is given by Iremash-vili. According to him, the seminary authorities, having become disappointed in their expectations, began to treat Joseph with ever-increasing disfavor and to find fault constantly. "It so developed that Koba, who was convinced of the fruitlessness of any earnest study, gradually became the worst pupil in the seminary. He would reply to the reproachful remarks of his teachers with his poisonous and contemptuous leer." The certificate which the school authorities gave him for passing from the sixth to the last form was so bad that Koba himself decided to leave the seminary the year before graduation. Taking into consideration that explanation, it at once becomes clear why Yenukidze wrote "flew out of the seminary," avoiding the more precise expressions, "was expelled," or, "left the seminary"; why most of his schoolmates say nothing at all about that significant moment of Joseph's seminary life; why no documents are published; why, finally, his mother felt she had the right to say that her son had not been expelled, although she herself gave the episode a different coloring, transferring responsibility from her son to herself. From the point of view of Stalin's personal characterization or his political biography, the details of his break with the seminary have scarcely any significance. But they are not a bad illustration of the difficulties which totalitarian historiography places in the way of research even on such subsidiary questions.

Joseph entered the preparatory theological school at the age of eleven, in 1890, passed four years later into the seminary, and abandoned it in 1899, thus remaining altogether in the ecclesiastical schools for nine years. Georgians mature early. Joseph left the seminary a grown man, "without diploma," writes Gogokhiya, "but with definite, firm views on life." The nine year period of theological studies could not fail to have left a profound influence on his character, on the manner of his thought, and on his style, which form an essential part of personality.

The language of the family and of their milieu was Georgian. His mother, even in her old age, did not know Russian. The situation could scarcely have been otherwise with his father. The boy studied Russian speech only in school, where again the majority of the pupils were Georgians. The spirit of the Russian language, its free nature, its inherent rhythm, Joseph never acquired. Moreover he was called upon to study the foreign language, which was to take the place of his native tongue, in the stilted atmosphere of a theological school. He imbibed the turns of Russian speech together with the formulae of churchly scholasticism. He learned the speech itself, not as a natural and inseparable spiritual organ for the expression of his own feelings and thoughts, but as an artificial and external instrument for transmitting a foreign and hated mysticism. In later life he was even less able to become intimate with or to assimilate the language, to use it precisely or to ennoble it, because he habitually employed words to camouflage thought and feeling rather than to express them. Consequently, Russian always remained for him not only a language half-foreign and makeshift, but, far worse for his consciousness, conventional and strained.

It is not hard to understand that from the moment Joseph inwardly broke with religion the study of homiletics and liturgy became insufferable to him. What is hard to understand is how he was able to lead a double life for such a long time. If we are to credit the tale that at the early age of thirteen Soso had counterposed Darwin to the Bible, we must conclude that from then on for seven whole years he patiently studied theology, although with diminishing eagerness. Stalin himself placed the inception of his revolutionary *Weltanschauung* at the fifteenth or sixteenth year of his life. It is quite possible that he turned away from religion two or three years before he turned toward socialism. But even if we were to allow that both changes occurred simultaneously, we shall see that the young atheist in the course of five whole years continued to explore the mysteries of Orthodoxy.

True, in Tsarist educational institutions many free-thinking youths were obliged to lead a double life. But that has reference principally to universities, where the régime nevertheless was distinguished by considerable freedom and where official hypocrisy was reduced to a ritualistic minimum. In the middle schools this divergence was more difficult to endure, but it usually lasted only a year or two, when the youth saw ahead of him the doors of the university, with its relative academic freedom. The situation of young Djugashvili was extraordinary. He did not study in a lay educational institution, where the pupils were under surveillance only part of the day and where the so-called "Religion" was actually one of the secondary subjects; but in a closed educational institution, where all of his life was subjected to the demands of the church and where his every step was taken before the eyes of the monks. In order to endure this régime for seven or even five years, extraordinary cautiousness and an exceptional aptitude for dissimulation were needed. During the years of his sojourn in the seminary no one noticed any kind of open protest by him, any bold act of indignation. Joseph laughed at his teachers behind their backs, but he was never impudent to their faces. He did not slap any chauvinistic pedagogue, as Dzhibladze had done; the most he did was to retort "with a contemptuous leer." His hostility was reserved, underhanded, watchful. The seminarist Pomyalovsky during his life as a pupil was, as we heard, inoculated with "suspiciousness, secretiveness, enmity and hatred for the surrounding milieu." Almost the same attitude, but even more pointed, Iremashvili states, was characteristic of Koba: "In 1899 he left the seminary, taking with him a vicious, ferocious enmity against the school administration, against the bourgeoisie, against everything that existed in the country and embodied Tsarism. Hatred against all authority."

Chapter II

"PROFESSIONAL REVOLUTIONIST"

IN 1883, when Soso was going on his fourth year, Baku, the oil capital of the Caucasus, was connected by rail with the Black Sea port of Batum. To the backbone of its mountain ranges, the Caucasus added its backbone of railways. After the oil industry the manganese industry began to grow. In 1896, when Soso had already begun to have dreams about the name of Koba, the first strike in the railway shops of Tiflis broke out.

In the development of ideas, as in industry, the Caucasus was in the tow of Central Russia. During the second half of the 'nineties, beginning in Petersburg, the ruling tendency of the radical intelligentsia was toward Marxism. When Koba was still pining away in the fusty atmosphere of seminarist theology, the Social-Democratic movement had already managed to attain broad dimensions. A tempestuous wave of strikes was rolling over the length and breadth of the land. At first the initial hundreds, and then thousands of intellectuals and workers suffered arrest and banishment. A new chapter opened in the revolutionary movement.

In 1901, when Koba became a member of the Tiflis Committee, there were approximately forty thousand industrial workers in Transcaucasia engaged in nine thousand enterprises, without counting the artisan shops. A negligible number, considering the extent and the riches of this region, washed by two seas; yet, the corner stones of Social-Democratic propaganda were already at hand. Fountains of Baku oil, the first extractions of Chitaurian manganese, the vivifying activities of the railways, these gave an impetus, not only to the strike movement of the workers, but also to the theoretical thought of the Georgian intelligentsia. The liberal newspaper *Kvali* (The Furrow) recorded, in surprise rather than with hostility, the appearance on the political arena of representatives of the new movement: "Since 1893 young men representing a singular trend and advocating a unique program have been contributing to Georgian publications; they are supporters of the theory of economic materialism." To distinguish them from the progressive nobility and the liberal bourgeoisie, which dominated the preceding decade, the Marxists were given the nickname *"Mesame-dasi,"* meaning "the third group." At the head of it was Noah Jordania,[1] the future leader of the Caucasian Mensheviks and the future head of the ephemeral Georgian democracy.

[1] Noi Nikolayevich Zhordaniya (1870-   ), also known as An, Kostrov, etc., was member

The petty bourgeois intellectuals of Russia, who aspired to escape the oppression of the police régime and the backwardness of that impersonal ant-heap which was the old society, were obliged to jump over the intervening stages because of the country's extremely belated development. Protestantism and Democracy, under whose banner the revolutions of the seventeenth and eighteenth centuries had taken place in the West, had long ago become transformed into conservative doctrines. The semi-mendicant Caucasian Bohemians could nowise be tempted by liberal abstractions. Their hostility to the privileged classes had acquired a natural social coloration. For the impending battle ahead these intellectuals needed a fresh theory, one that had not yet been compromised. They found that in Western Socialism, in its highest scientific expression— Marxism. The point at issue was no longer equality before God or equality before the law, but economic equality. Actually, by resorting to the remote Socialist perspective, the intellectuals insured their anti-Tsarist struggle against the skepticism that threatened it prematurely in consequence of the disillusioning experiences of Western Democracy. These conditions and circumstances determined the character of Russian, and even more so of Caucasian, Marxism, which was exceedingly limited and primitive because it was adapted to the political needs of backward, provincial intellectuals. Itself lacking in theoretical realism, that Marxism nevertheless rendered a very real service to the intellectuals in that it inspired them in their struggle against Tsarism.

The critical edge of the Marxism of the 'nineties was directed first of all against jejune Populism,[2] which superstitiously feared capitalistic development, hoping to find for Russia "exceptional," privileged historical paths. The defense of the progressive mission of capitalism became therefore the principal theme of the Marxism of the intellectuals, who not infrequently pushed into the background the program of the proletarian class struggle. In the legal press Noah Jordania preached assiduously the unity of the "nation's" interests: in connection with that he had in mind the necessity of the union of the proletariat and the bourgeoisie against the autocracy. The idea of such a union was subsequently to become the cornerstone of Menshevik policy and in the end was to cause their ruin. Official Soviet historians continue to this very day to take cognizance of Jordania's idea, and to present it in all sorts of ways, although it was long ago lost in the course of battle. At the same time they shut their eyes to the fact that three decades later Stalin was applying that Menshevik policy not only in China but in Spain and even in France, and under circumstances immeasurably less justifiable than those prevailing when feudal Georgia was under the heel of Tsarism.

But even in those days, Jordania's ideas did not meet with universal recognition. In 1895, Sasha Tsulukidze,[3] who subsequently became one of the out-

---

of the Russian Social-Democratic Labor Party's Central Committee after 1907, a defensist during World War I, First President of the First Georgian Republic (1918-1921) until the invasion of his country by the Red Army, when he escaped to France.—C. M.

[2] See glossary.

[3] Aleksandr Grigoryevich Tsulukidze (1876-1905) died June 10, 1905.—C. M.

standing propagandists of the Left Wing, joined *Mesame-dasi*. He died of tuberculosis at twenty-nine, in 1905, leaving behind him a number of journalistic works which testified to his considerable Marxist training and literary talent. In 1897 the ranks of *Mesame-dasi* were joined by Lado Ketskhoveli[4] who, like Koba, was a former pupil of the Gori theological school and of the Tiflis seminary. He was, however, several years older than Koba and had served him as a guide during the first stages of his revolutionary career. Yenukidze recalled in 1923, when memoirists still enjoyed sufficient freedom, that "Stalin many times stressed with amazement the extraordinary talents of the late Comrade Ketskhoveli who even in those days knew how to pose questions correctly in the spirit of revolutionary Marxism." That testimony, especially the reference to "amazement," refutes the more recent tales that even then the leadership was Koba's and that Tsulukidze and Ketskhoveli were merely his "assistants." It might also be added that young Tsulukidze's articles in their content and form rank considerably higher than anything Koba wrote two or three years later.

Having taken his place in the Left Wing of *Mesame-dasi*, Ketskhoveli drew young Djugashvili into it the following year. At that time it was not a revolutionary organization, but a circle of like-minded people centering around the legal newspaper *Kvali*, which in 1898 passed from the hands of the liberals into the hands of the young Marxists, led by Jordania.

"In secret we frequently visited the offices of *Kvali*," relates Iremashvili. "Koba went with us several times, but later made fun of the members of the editorial board." The differences of opinion in the Marxist camp in those days, however elementary they might have been, were nevertheless quite substantial in character. The Moderate Wing did not really believe in revolution, still less that it was near, reckoning on prolonged "progress" and longing for a union with the bourgeois liberals. The Left Wing, on the other hand, sincerely hoped for a revolutionary upheaval of the masses and therefore stood for a more independent policy. In essence the Left Wing consisted of revolutionary democrats who fell into a natural opposition to the "Marxist" semi-liberals. Because of his early environment as well as his personal character, it was natural that Soso should instinctively incline toward the Left Wing. A plebeian democrat of the provincial type, armed with a rather primitive "Marxist" doctrine—it was as such that he entered the revolutionary movement, and such in essence he remained to the very end, despite the fantastic orbit of his personal fate.

The differences of opinion between the two still vaguely differentiated groups temporarily converged on the question of propaganda and agitation. Some stood for circumspect educational work among small groups; others, for leadership of strikes and for agitation by means of leaflets. When those who favored mass work won out, the subject of their differences became the content of the leaflets. The more circumspect stood for agitation on the ground of exclusively

---

[4] Vladimir Zakharyevich Ketskhoveli (1877-1903) died August 17, 1903, shot by his prison guard.—C. M.

economic needs, determined to "refrain from frightening the masses." They received from their opponents the contemptuous appellation of "Economists." The Left Wing, on the other hand, deemed unpostponable the transition to revolutionary agitation against Tsarism. Such was Plekhanov's position among the émigrés abroad. Such in Russia was the position of Vladimir Ulyanov and his friends.

"The first Social-Democratic groups arose in Tiflis," relates one of the pioneers. "As early as 1896-1897 that city had circles in which workers were the preponderant element. These circles were at first of a purely educational character . . . The number of these circles constantly increased. In 1900 they already numbered several score. Each circle consisted of ten to fifteen people." With the growth of the number of circles, their activity became bolder.

In 1898, while still a seminary student, Koba established contact with workers and joined the Social-Democratic organization. "One evening Koba and I," recollects Iremashvili, "secretly made our way from the seminary at Mtatsminda to a small house, which stood leaning against a cliff and which belonged to a worker of the Tiflis Railway. After us, secretly arrived others from the seminary who shared our views. There also met with us a Social-Democratic labor organization of railway workers." Stalin himself told about it in 1926 at a meeting in Tiflis:

> I recall the year 1898, when the first circle of workers from the railway shops was assigned to me. I remember how in the home of Comrade Sturua, in the presence of Sylvester Dzhibladze (he was at that time one of my teachers) . . . and other advanced workers of Tiflis, I received lessons in practical work. . . . Here, in the circle of these comrades, I then received my first revolutionary baptism by fire: here, in the circle of these comrades, I then became a pupil of the revolution . . .

In the years 1898-1900, in the railway shops and in a number of Tiflis factories, strikes broke out with the active, and at times leading, participation of young Social-Democrats. Proclamations, printed by hand with the aid of a bootblack brush in an underground printing shop, were distributed among the workers. The movement was still developing in the spirit of "economism." Part of the illegal work fell to Koba; exactly what part it is not easy to determine. But apparently he had already managed to become an initiate in the world of the revolutionary underground.

In 1900 Lenin, who had just then completed his Siberian exile, went abroad with the express intention of founding a revolutionary newspaper, in order, with its aid, to muster the scattered party and to switch it definitely onto the rails of revolutionary endeavor. Simultaneously an old revolutionist, the engineer Victor Kurnatovsky, who was confidentially initiated into these plans, journeyed from Siberia to Tiflis. It was he, and not Koba, as the Byzantine historians now aver, who brought the Tiflis Social-Democracy out of its "economistic" limitations and invested its activities with a more revolutionary trend.

Kurnatovsky had begun his revolutionary activity with the terroristic *Narod-*

naya Volya ("People's Will") party. At the time of his third exile, toward the end of the century, he, who was already a Marxist, became very friendly with Lenin and his circle. The newspaper *Iskra* (The Spark), founded abroad by Lenin, whose adherents began to be known as Iskrovites, had in the person of Kurnatovsky its principal representative in the Caucasus. Old Tiflis workers recall: "On the occasion of any arguments and discussions all the comrades turned to Kurnatovsky. His conclusions and judgments were always accepted without argument." From that testimony one gathers the significance for the Caucasus of this tireless and inflexible revolutionist, whose personal fate was composed of two elements: the heroic and the tragic.

In 1900, undoubtedly upon Kurnatovsky's initiative, the Tiflis Committee of the Social-Democratic Party was established. It was composed entirely of intellectuals. Koba, who evidently fell soon after, like many others, under Kurnatovsky's spell, was not yet a member of that committee which, incidentally, did not long survive. From May through August, a wave of strikes affected Tiflis business establishments; among the strikers of the railroad shops are listed the locksmith Kalinin, the future President of the Soviet Republic, and another Russian worker, Alliluyev, Stalin's future father-in-law.

In the meantime, in the North, upon the initiative of university students, a cycle of street demonstrations began. A large First of May demonstration at Kharkov in 1900 brought to its feet a majority of the city's workers and aroused an echo of amazement and exultation throughout the country. Other cities followed suit. "The Social-Democracy understood," wrote the Gendarme General Spiridovich, "the tremendous agitational significance of going forth into the street. From then on it took upon itself the initiative for demonstrations, attracting to them an ever greater number of workers. Not infrequently the street demonstrations grew out of strikes." Tiflis did not remain quiet for long. The First of May celebration—let us not forget that the old calendar still reigned in Russia—was marked on April 22, 1901, by a street demonstration in the heart of the city, in which nearly two thousand people took part. At the time of the encounter with the police and the Cossacks, fourteen were wounded and more than fifty of the rioters arrested. *Iskra* did not neglect to notice the important symptomatic significance of the Tiflis demonstration: "From that day on an open revolutionary movement began in the Caucasus."

Kurnatovsky, who was in charge of the preparatory work, had been arrested on the night of March the twenty-second, a month before the demonstration. That same night a search was made in the observatory where Koba was employed; but he was not caught because he was away at the time. The gendarme administration resolved ". . . to locate the aforementioned Joseph Djugashvili and to question the accused." Thus Koba passed to the "status of illegality" and became a "professional revolutionist" for a long time to come. He was then twenty-two years old. There still remained sixteen years before the victory would be won.

Having escaped arrest, Koba spent the next few weeks in hiding at Tiflis, and so managed to take part in the May Day demonstration. Beriya states that categorically, adding, as always, that Stalin "personally" led it. Unfortunately, Beriya is not to be trusted. In this case, however, there is also the testimony of Iremashvili, who, it is true, was at that time not in Tiflis but in Gori where he had become a teacher. "Koba, as one of the leaders who were being sought," he says, "managed to hide by leaving the market square as he was on the verge of arrest . . . He fled to his home town of Gori. He could not live in his mother's lodgings, because that was the first place where he would be sought. He therefore had to hide even in Gori. Secretly, during the hours of the night, he frequently visited me at my lodgings."

The Tiflis demonstration made an exceedingly strong impression on Koba. "Not without alarm" Iremashvili had noticed that it was precisely the bloody outcome of the clash that had inspired his friend. "The movement was to grow strong in a life and death struggle: in the opinion of Koba the bloody struggle was to bring the quickest decision." Iremashvili did not guess that his friend was merely repeating the preachings of *Iskra*.

From Gori Koba evidently again returned illegally to Tiflis, for according to the information of the gendarme administration, "in the Autumn of 1901 Djugashvili was elected to the Tiflis Committee . . . participated in two sessions of that committee, and toward the end of 1901 was assigned to propaganda activity in Batum . . ." Since the gendarmes were not inclined toward any "trend" other than the catching of revolutionists, and were, thanks to the internal agency, usually well informed, we can consider it established that in 1898-1901, Koba did not play the leading role in Tiflis which has been ascribed to him in recent years; until the fall of 1901 he was not even a member of his local committee, but was merely one of the propagandists, that is, a leader of circles.

Toward the end of 1901, Koba moved from Tiflis to Batum on the shores of the Black Sea, close to the Turkish border. This move can be explained on the grounds of double necessity—to hide from the eyes of the Tiflis police and to introduce revolutionary propaganda in the provinces. Menshevik publications, however, give another reason. According to them, from the very first days of his activities in workers' circles Djugashvili attracted attention to himself by his intrigues against Dzhibladze, the principal leader of the Tiflis organization. In spite of warnings, he continued to spread slander "for the purpose of undermining the true and recognized representatives of the movement and in order to obtain a leading position." Placed on trial before a Party court, Koba was found guilty of slander unbecoming a comrade and unanimously expelled from the organization. There is hardly any possibility of verifying that story, which comes, we must not forget, from Stalin's bitterest opponents. The documents of the Tiflis gendarme administration—at any rate, those that have been published to date—say nothing at all about Joseph Djugashvili's expulsion from the Party, and on the contrary, speak of his assignment to Batum "for propaganda." We might therefore set aside the Menshevik version without further ado if other testimony did not indicate that his removal to Batum was the result of some unpleasantness.

One of the first and most conscientious historians of the labor movement in the Caucasus was T. Arkomed, whose book was published in Geneva in 1910. In it, he tells about the bitter conflict that broke out in the Tiflis organization in the autumn of 1901 over the question of inducting into the committee elected representatives of the workers: "Against it spoke a certain young, indiscriminately 'energetic,' and in all matters intelligent comrade, who, pleading conspirative considerations, the lack of preparation and the lack of class consciousness among the workers, came out against admitting workers into the committee. Turning to the workers, he ended his speech with the words: 'Here they flatter the workers; I ask you, are there among you even one or two workers fit for the committee? Tell the truth, placing your hand on your heart!'" The workers, however, did not listen to the orator and voted to include their representatives on the committee. Arkomed did not mention the name of that "indiscriminately energetic" young man, for in those days circumstances did not permit the disclosure of names. In 1923, when this book was republished by the Soviet publishing house, that name remained undisclosed, and, we are prone to think, not through oversight. The book itself, however, contains a valuable indirect clue. "The aforementioned young comrade," Arkomed continues, "transferred his activity from Tiflis to Batum, from where the Tiflis workers received information about his unseemly behavior, his hostile and disorganizing agitation against the Tiflis organization and its workers." According to this author, the hostile behavior was dictated not by motives based on principle, but "by personal caprice and the striving for absolute power." All of this is similar to what we have heard from Iremashvili concerning the squabble in the seminary circle. The "young man" closely resembles Koba. There can be no doubt that the reference was to him, since numerous reminiscences attest that he was the only one of the Tiflis Committee who went to Batum in November, 1901. It is therefore probable that the change in his sphere of activity was made because Tiflis became too hot to hold him. If not actually "expelled," he may have been removed merely to make the atmosphere of Tiflis healthier. From that, in turn, follows Koba's "incorrect attitude" toward the Tiflis organization and the subsequent rumors about his expulsion. Let us note at the same time the cause of the conflict: Koba was protecting "the *apparat*" [political machine] against pressure from below.

Batum, which at the beginning of the century had a population of nearly thirty thousand, was a significant industrial center in the Caucasus, according to the scale of those days. The number of workers in the factories reached almost eleven thousand. The working day, as was quite customary then, exceeded fourteen hours, at wretched pay. It is no wonder then that the proletariat was in the highest degree responsive to revolutionary propaganda. As in Tiflis, Koba did not have to begin from scratch: illegal circles had been in existence at Batum since 1896. Co-operating with the worker Kandelyaki, Koba extended the network of these circles. At a New Year's Eve party they united to form a single organization, which however was not granted the prerogatives of a committee and remained dependent upon Tiflis. This evidently was one of the causes of the new friction to which Arkomed alluded. Koba, as a rule, could not endure anyone in authority over him.

At the beginning of 1902 the Batum organization managed to establish an illegal printshop, a very primitive one, which was located at Koba's lodgings. This direct violation of the rules of conspiracy was undoubtedly due to the dearth of material resources. "A crowded little room dimly lighted with a kerosene lamp. At a small round table Stalin sits and writes. To one side of him is the printing press, at which several typesetters are busy. The type is laid out in match and cigarette boxes and on pieces of paper. Stalin frequently hands over to the typesetters what has just been written." That is how one of the participants of the organization recalls the scene. It must be added that the text of the proclamation was approximately on the same level as the technique of printing. Somewhat later, with the co-operation of the Armenian revolutionist Kamo, something like a printing press, a cash register and type were brought in from Tiflis. The print shop widened and became more efficient. The literary level of the proclamations remained the same. But that did not detract from their influence.

On February the twenty-fifth, 1902, the management of Rotschild's kerosene plant posted a notice which proclaimed the dismissal of 389 workers. In reply a strike broke out on the twenty-seventh. The disturbance affected other factories as well. There were clashes with strike-breakers. The police chief asked the governor to help him with troops. On the seventh of March the police arrested 32 workers. The following morning almost 400 workers of the Rotschild plant gathered at the prison, demanding either the release of those under arrest or the arrest of all the others. The police moved all of them into deportation barracks. At that time the feeling of solidarity was welding the laboring masses of Russia closer together, and this new unity asserted itself in a new way each time in the most desolate corners of the country; the revolution was only three years off . . . The very next day, on the ninth of March, a bigger demonstration took place. The barracks were approached, according to the indictment, by "a huge crowd of workers, with leaders at their head, marching in well-formed ranks, with song, noise and whistling." There were nearly two thousand people in that crowd. The workers Khimiryants and Gogoberidze, as spokesmen, demanded that the military authorities either liberate the imprisoned ones or arrest all. The crowd, as the court later acknowledged, was "in a peaceful mood and unarmed." The authorities managed, however, to bring it out of its peaceful mood. The workers responded to the attempt of the soldiers to clear the square with their rifle butts by throwing stones. The troops began to shoot, killing 14 and wounding 54. The occurrence stirred the entire country: in the beginning of the century human nerves reacted with far greater sensitiveness to mass slaughter than they do now.

What was Koba's role in that demonstration? It is not easy to say. Soviet compilers are torn between contradictory problems: to ascribe to Stalin participation in the greatest possible number of revolutionary events, and at the same time to expand as much as possible the terms of his imprisonment and exile. Court artists have been known, in portraying two concurrent events, to represent Stalin at one and the same moment as a hero of the streets and a prison martyr. On April twenty-seventh, 1937, the official Moscow *Izvestiya* published the photograph of a painting by the artist E. Khutsishvili, portraying Stalin as organizer of the strike of the Tiflis railroad workers in 1902. The next day the editorial board was compelled to apologize for the error. "From the biography of Comrade Stalin," its statement proclaimed, "it is known that he . . . from February, 1902, until the end of 1903 was in the Batum and Kutais prisons. Therefore, Comrade Stalin could not have been the organizer of the strike at Tbilisi (Tiflis) in 1902. Asked about that, Comrade Stalin declared that portraying him as the organizer of the railway strike at Tbilisi in 1902, from the point of view of historical truth, is a complete misunderstanding, since at that time he was in prison in Batum." But if it is true that Stalin was in prison from February, then "from the point of view of historical truth" he could not have led the Batum demonstration, which occurred in March. However, on that occasion not only did the assiduous artist err badly, but likewise the *Izvestiya* editorial board, despite its reference to the primary source. Koba was, as a matter of fact, arrested not in February, but in March. He could not have led the Tiflis strike, not because he was in prison but because he was on the shores of the Black Sea. There is still the possibility that he participated in the Batum events. It remains only to discover the nature of this participation.

Stalin's French biographer, Barbusse, who wrote to the Kremlin's dictation, asserts that Koba took his place at the head of the Batum demonstration "as a target." That flattering phrase contradicts not only the evidence of the police records but the very nature of Stalin, who never and nowhere took his place as a target (which, by the way, is not at all necessary). The publishing house of the Central Committee, which is directly under Stalin's orders, in 1937 devoted an entire volume to the Batum demonstration, or rather, to Stalin's part in it. However, the 240 handsome pages complicated the question even more, because the dictated "reminiscences" are at complete variance with the partial accounts previously published. "Comrade Soso was constantly on the scene of action and guided the central strike committee," Todria writes obligingly. "Comrade Soso was always with us," affirms Gogoberidze. The old Batum worker Darakhvelidze says that Soso was "in the midst of the tempestuous sea of workers, directly leading the movement; he personally led out of the mob the worker G. Kalandadze, who was wounded in the arm during the shooting, and took him home." The leader could scarcely have abandoned his post in order to rescue one wounded man; the duties of a stretcher bearer could have been discharged by any rank and file participant of the demonstration. None of the other authors, and they number twenty-six, mentioned that dubious episode. But in the final reckoning that is a mere detail. The tales concerning Koba as the direct leader of the demonstration are more conclusively refuted by the circumstance that the demonstration, as became only too clear in court, took place without any leadership whatever. Despite the insistence of the prosecutor, the Tsarist court admitted that even the workers Gogoberidze and Khimiryants, who actually marched at the head of the crowd, were only rank and file participants of the procession. The name of Djugashvili, despite the great number of defendants and witnesses, was not so much as mentioned throughout the court trial. The legend thus collapses of itself. Koba's participation in the Batum events was apparently of an obscure character.

After the demonstration Koba, according to Beriya, carried through "tremendous" work, writing proclamations, organizing their printing and distribution, transforming the funeral procession in honor of the victims of the ninth of March into "a grandiose political demonstration," and the like. Unfortunately, these prescribed exaggerations are not supported by anything at all. At that time Koba was being sought by the police and could hardly have displayed "tremendous" activity in a small town where, according to the same writer, he had previously played a prominent role before the eyes of the demonstrating crowd, the police, the troops and observers in the street. On the night of April fifth, during a session of the leading party group, Koba was arrested along with other collaborators and lodged in prison. Wearisome days began. Many of them.

Published documents disclose at this juncture an exceedingly interesting episode. Three days after Koba's arrest, during the regular meeting between the prisoners and their visitors, someone threw two notes out of a window into the prison yard, reckoning that one of the visitors might pick them up and take them to their indicated destination. One of these notes contained a request to look up the school teacher Soso Iremashvili at Gori and to tell him that "Soso Djugashvili has been arrested and asks him immediately to inform his mother about it, so that in case the gendarme should ask her 'When did thy son leave Gori?' she would say, 'All summer and winter until the fifteenth of March he was here.'" The second note addressed to the teacher Elisabedashvili, touched upon the need to continue revolutionary activities. Both scraps of paper were intercepted by the prison guards, and the gendarme cavalry captain Djakeli without much difficulty reached the conclusion that the author was Djugashvili and that he had "played a prominent role in the labor troubles at Batum." Djakeli immediately sent to the chief of the Tiflis gendarme administration a demand to search Iremashvili's lodgings, to question Djugashvili's mother and also to search and arrest Elisabedashvili. About the consequences of these operations the documents say nothing.

It is with relief that we greet on the pages of an official publication a name already familiar to us: Soso Iremashvili. True, Beriya had already mentioned him among the members of the seminary circle, but he said very little about the relationship of the two Sosos. However, the nature of one of the notes intercepted by the police is incontestable proof that the author of the reminiscences to which we have already referred more than once was actually on intimate terms with Koba. It is to him, his childhood friend, that the man under arrest entrusts his instruction to his mother. It likewise confirms the fact that Iremashvili also enjoyed the confidence of Keke, who, as he tells us, called him in childhood her "second Soso." The note dispels the last doubts concerning the credibility of his very valuable reminiscences, which are entirely ignored by Soviet historians. The instructions which Koba as confirmed by his own depositions during the interrogation, attempted to transmit to his mother, were intended to deceive the gendarmes as to the time of his arrival in Baku and thus to keep him out of the impending trial. There is no reason, of course, to see anything prejudicial in that attempt. The deception of gendarmes was a rule in that very serious game which was called revolutionary conspiracy. However one cannot help pausing with amazement at the carelessness with which Koba subjected two of his comrades to danger. The purely political aspect of his act merits no less attention. It would be natural to expect a revolutionist who had helped to prepare a demonstration that had ended so tragically to desire to share the prisoners' dock with the rank and file workers. Not for sentimental considerations, but in order to shed political light on the events and to condemn the behavior of the authorities—that is, in order to utilize the tribune of the courtroom for purposes of revolutionary propaganda. Such opportunities were not any too frequent! The absence of such desire in Koba can be explained only by the narrowness of his outlook. It is quite evident that he did not understand the political significance of the demonstration and that his chief aim was to escape its consequences.

The very plot to deceive the gendarmes would not have been feasible, we might say, if Koba had actually led the street procession and had been marching at the head of the crowd, had offered himself as a "target." In that event scores of witnesses would inevitably have identified him. Koba could have stayed out of the trial only if his participation in the demonstration had remained secret, anonymous. Actually, only one police constable, Chkhiknadze, testified at the preliminary investigation that he had seen Djugashvili "in the crowd" before the prison. But the testimony of a single policeman could not carry any great weight as evidence. At any rate, despite that testimony and the interception of Koba's own notes, he was not indicted in the case of the demonstration. The trial was held a year later and lasted nine days. The political direction of the court arguments was relegated entirely to the tender mercies of liberal lawyers. They did indeed obtain minimum punishments for the twenty-one defendants, but only at the price of lessening the revolutionary significance of the Batum events.

The police constable who made the arrests of the Batum organization's leaders characterized Koba in his report as one "who had been expelled from the theological seminary, living in Batum without written documents or definite occupation and without lodgings of his own, the Gori denizen Joseph Djugashvili." The reference to expulsion from the seminary is not documentary in character, for a simple constable could have no archives at his disposal, and was apparently repeating rumors in his written report; far more significant is the reference to the fact that Koba had no passport, no definite occupation nor place of residence: the three typical characteristics of the revolutionary troglodyte.

In the old and neglected provincial prisons of Batum, Kutais, and again Batum, Koba spent more than a year and a half. In those days that was the customary period of imprisonment while awaiting investigation and banishment. The régime of the prisons, as of the country as a whole, combined barbarism with paternalism. Peaceable and even familiar relations with the prison administration would be suddenly terminated by stormy protests, when the prisoners would bang their boots against the doors of their cells, shout, whistle, break up the dishes and the furniture. After the storm subsided there would again be a lull. Lolua tells briefly about one such explosion in the Kutais prison—of course, "upon the initiative and under the leadership of Stalin." There is no reason for doubting that Koba played a prominent part in prison conflicts and that in contacts with the prison administration he knew how to defend himself and others.

"He established an orderly routine in his prison life," Kalandadze wrote thirty-five years later. "He rose early in the morning, exercised, then set to studying the German language and economic literature . . . He liked to share with his comrades his impressions of the books he had just read . . ." It is not at all difficult to imagine a list of those books: popular compositions on natural science; a bit from Darwin; Lippert's "History of Culture;" perhaps Buckle and Draper in translations of the 'seventies; the "Biographies of Great Men" in Pavlenkov's edition; the economic teachings of Marx, as expounded by the Russian professor Sieber; something or other on the history of Russia; Beltov's famous book on historical materialism (under this pseudonym the émigré Plekhanov appeared in legal literature); finally, the weighty investigation of the development of Russian capitalism, published in 1899, written by the exile V. Ulyanov, the future N. Lenin, under his legal pseudonym of V. Ilyin. All of those were there, more or less. In the theoretical knowledge of the young revolutionist there were, of course, great gaps. Yet he seemed to be not badly armed against the teachings of the Church, the arguments of Liberalism and especially the prejudices of Populism.

In the course of the 'nineties the theories of Marxism won their victory over the theories of Populism, a victory which found support in the successes of capitalism and in the growth of the labor movement. However, the strikes and demonstrations of the workers stimulated the awakening of the village, which, in turn, led to a revival of Populist ideology among the city intelligentsia. Thus, at the beginning of the century there began to develop rather rapidly that hybrid revolutionary tendency which took a bit from Marxism, repudiated the romantic terms ("Land and Freedom") and *"Zemlya: Volya"* ("The Will of the People") and gave itself the more European title, "Party of Socialists-Revolutionists" *Narodnaya Volya* [the S-R (Essar) Party]. The fight against "Economism" was fundamentally finished in the Winter of 1902-1903. The ideas of *Iskra* found too convincing a confirmation in the successes of political agitation and street demonstrations. Beginning with 1902, *Iskra* devoted more and more of its space to attacks against the eclectic program of the Socialists-Revolutionists and against the methods of individual terror, which they preached. The passionate polemic between "the gray-haired" and the "gray"[5] penetrated all corners of the land, including, of course, the prisons as well. On more than one occasion Koba was obliged to cross swords with his new opponents; it is credible that he did so with sufficient success: *Iskra* provided him with excellent arguments.

Since Koba was not indicted and placed on trial in the case of the demonstration, his judicial examination was conducted by the gendarmes. The methods of secret investigation, as well as the prison régime, differed considerably in different parts of the country. At the capital the gendarmes were more cultured and more circumspect; in the provinces they were cruder. In the Caucasus, with its archaic customs and colonial social relations, the gendarmes resorted to the crudest forms of violence, especially when dealing with untutored, inexperienced and weak-willed victims.

> Pressure, threats, terrorization, torments, falsifying the depositions of witnesses, the subornation of false witnesses, the concoction and inflation of cases, ascribing decisive and absolute significance to the hearsay reports of secret agents—such were the special features of the method pursued by the gendarmes in disposing of cases.

Arkomed, who wrote the above lines, states that the gendarme Lavrov was wont to resort to inquisitorial methods in securing "confessions" he knew beforehand to be false. These police proceedings must have left a lasting impression on Stalin, for thirty years later he was to apply Captain Lavrov's methods on a colossal scale. From the prison reminiscences of Lolua we learn, by the way, that "Comrade Soso did not like to address his comrades by using *vy*," saying that the Tsar's servitors used *vy* in addressing revolutionists when sending them to the gallows. As a matter of fact, the use of *ty* was customary in revolutionary circles, especially in the Caucasus. A few decades later Koba was to send to the gallows not a few of his old comrades with whom, unlike the "Tsar's servitors," he had been on terms of *ty*[6] since their early years. But that is still quite far off.

---

[5] In Russian "gray-haired" is *sedoy* and "gray" *sery*. The etymon of each word consists of its consonants, which are initials, the *s d* in *SeDoy* standing for Social-Democrat and the *s r* in *SeRy* for Socialist-Revolutionist.—C. M.

[6] In Russian, as in French and in many other languages, *vy*, the second person plural, literally the equivalent of the English *you*, is used in polite intercourse; whereas, *ty*, the second person singular, literally the equivalent of the English *thou*, is used either affectionately with intimates, or as a mark of superiority when addressing servants, animals and inferiors generally.—C. M.

It is surprising that the records of Koba's police examinations pertaining to that first arrest, as well as all the records pertaining to his subsequent arrests, have not yet been published. As a rule, the *Iskra* organization demanded that its members refuse to testify. Revolutionists usually wrote: "I have been a Social-Democrat by conviction for a long time; I repudiate and deny the accusations against me; I refuse to give testimony or to take part in any secret investigation." Only at a trial in open court, to which the authorities resorted however only in exceptional circumstances, did the Iskrovites come out with their banner unfurled. The refusal to give testimony, which was quite justified from the point of view of the Party's interests as a whole, in certain cases made the situation of the arrested person rather difficult. In April, 1902, Koba, as we have seen, attempted to establish his alibi by a ruse for which others were obliged to suffer. It may be supposed that on other occasions as well he relied more on his own cunning than on the standard behavior obligatory for all. Consequently, the entire series of his police depositions present, we should think, not a very attractive—at any rate, not a "heroic"—record. That is the only possible explanation why the records of Stalin's police examinations are still unpublished.

The preponderant majority of revolutionists were subjected to punishment by the so-called "administrative order." On the basis of the reports of local gendarmes, the "Special Conference" at Petersburg, composed of four high-ranking officials from the Ministries of the Interior and Justice, brought out verdicts without the presence of the accused, and these verdicts were confirmed by the Minister of the Interior. On July 25, 1903, the Tiflis Governor received from the capital a verdict of that sort, ordering him to banish sixteen political prisoners to Eastern Siberia under the direct surveillance of the police. The names were listed as was customary according to the gravity of offense or the offender's culpability, and their specific place of exile in Siberia was correspondingly better or worse. The first two places in that list are occupied by Kurnatovsky and Franchesky, who were sentenced to four years. Fourteen other persons were banished for three years, the first place here being filled by Sylvester Dzhibladze, who is already known to us. Joseph Djugashvili occupies the eleventh place on that list. The gendarme authorities did not yet regard him among the important revolutionists.

In November Koba, with other exiles, was sent from Batum Prison to the Government of Irkutsk. Transported from one halting place for convicts to the next, their journey lasted nearly three months. In the meantime the revolution was seething, and everyone was trying to escape as soon as possible. By the beginning of 1904 the exile system had become a sieve. In most cases it was not very difficult to escape; each province had its own secret "centers," which provided forged passports, money, addresses. Koba remained in the village of Novaya Uda not more than a month, i.e., precisely the time necessary to look around, find the indispensable contacts, and work out a plan of action. Alliluyev, the father of Stalin's second wife, states that during his first attempt to escape, Koba froze his face and ears and was obliged to return to acquire warmer clothing. A strong Siberian troika, driven by a reliable coachman, raced him quickly over the snow-laden highway to the nearest railway station. The return journey through the Urals took not three months, but about a week.

It is pertinent here, and only fair, to complete the story of the engineer Kurnatovsky, who really inspired the revolutionary movement at Tiflis at the beginning of the century. After two years in the military prison, he was banished to the Yakut Region, from which escapes were immeasurably more difficult than from the Irkutsk Government. At Yakutsk, on the road, Kurnatovsky participated in the armed resistance of the exiles against the outrages of the authorities, and was sentenced by the court to twelve years at hard labor. Amnestied in the fall of 1905, he reached Chita, which was then deluged with combatants of the Russo-Japanese War. There he became chairman of the Soviet of Workers', Soldiers' and Cossaks' Deputies—the head of the so-called "Chita Republic." At the beginning of 1906 Kurnatovsky was again arrested and sentenced to death. General Rennenkampt, the pacifier of Siberia, carried the condemned man in his train so that he might witness with his own eyes the executions of workers at every railway station. Because of the new liberal tendency in connection with elections to the First Duma, his death sentence was commuted to life-long banishment to Siberia. Kurnatovsky managed to escape from Nerchinsk to Japan. From there he went to Australia, where he was in great need, worked as a lumberjack and strained himself. Ill, with inflammation in his ears, he somehow managed to make his way to Paris. "An exceptionally difficult lot," relates Krupskaya, "finally undermined him. In the autumn of 1910, after his arrival, Ilyitch and I called on him at the hospital." Two years later, when Lenin and Krupskaya were already living at Cracow, Kurnatovsky died. On the shoulders of the Kurnatovskies and over their corpses the revolution marched forward.

The revolution marched forward. The first generation of the Russian Social-Democracy, headed by Plekhanov, started its critical and propagandistic activity at the beginning of the 'eighties. The pioneers were counted singly; later, by tens. The second generation, which Lenin led—he was fourteen years younger than Plekhanov—entered the political arena at the beginning of the 'nineties. Social-Democrats were counted by hundreds. The third generation, composed of people some ten years younger than Lenin, enlisted in the revolutionary struggle at the end of the past and the beginning of the present century. To that generation, which was already numbered by thousands, belonged Stalin, Rykov, Zinoviev, Kamenev, the author of this book and others.

In March, 1898, at the provincial town of Minsk, the representatives of nine local committees convened and founded the Russian Social-Democratic Labor Party. All the participants were promptly arrested. It is hardly possible that the resolutions of the Congress were received very soon in Tiflis, where the seminary student Djugashvili contemplated joining the Social-Democracy. The Minsk congress, prepared by Lenin's coevals, merely proclaimed the Party, but did not yet create it. One strong blow by the Tsarist police proved sufficient to demolish the weak party contacts for a long time to come. In the course of the next few years the movement, which was preponderantly economic in character, sank its roots locally. The young Social-Democrats usually carried out their activities on the home ground until subjected to arrest and banishment. Such a thing as Party workers traveling from one city to another was an exception. Transition to illegal status, for the purpose of eluding arrest, was almost never practiced; they had neither the experience nor the technical means nor the necessary contacts for that.

Beginning with 1900, "Iskra" began to build a centralized organization. Without question the leader of that period was Lenin, who rightfully pushed into the background "the old people" headed by Plekhanov. Party construction found its support in the incomparably broader sweep of the labor movement, which roused the new revolutionary generation, considerably more numerous than the one from which Lenin himself had emerged. The immediate task of *Iskra* was to select from among the local workers the persons of greatest stamina and to use them in the creation of a central apparatus capable of guiding the revolutionary struggle of the entire country. The number of *Iskra* adherents was considerable, and it was constantly growing. But the number of genuine Iskrovites, of trusted agents of the foreign center, was of necessity limited: it did not exceed twenty to thirty persons. Most characteristic of the Iskrovite was his severance from his own city, his own Government, his own province, for the sake of building the party. In the *Iskra* dictionary "localism" was a synonym for backwardness, narrowness, almost for retrogression. "Welded into a compact conspirative group of professional revolutionists," wrote the Gendarme General Spiridovich, "they traveled from place to place wherever there were party committees, established contacts with their members, delivered illegal literature to them, helped to establish printshops and garnered the information needed by the *Iskra*. They penetrated into local committees, carried on their propaganda against 'Economism,' eliminated their ideological opponents and in this way subjected the committees to their influence." The retired gendarme gives here a sufficiently correct characterization of the Iskrovites. They were members of a wandering order, above the local organizations which they regarded as an arena for the exercise of their influence.

Koba took no part in that responsible work. He was first a Tiflis Social-Democrat, then a Batum Social-Democrat—in other words, a revolutionist in a small, local way. The contact of the Caucasus with "Iskra" and with Central Russia was through Krassin, Kurnatovsky and others. The entire work of unifying the local committees and groups into a centralized party was accomplished without Koba. That circumstance—which is established beyond the shadow of a doubt on the basis of the correspondence of those days, memoirs and other documents—is very important in the estimation of Stalin's political development; he moved forward slowly, uncertainly, groping his way.

In June, 1900, Krassin, in his capacity as a prominent young engineer, arrived to assume a responsible post in Baku. "No less intensive," writes Krassin, "was the activity in a different sphere; namely, underground Social-Democratic work in Baku itself, as well as throughout the Caucasus—in Tiflis, Kutais, Batum, whither I journey from time to time to maintain contact with the local organizations there." Krassin remained in Baku until 1904. Hampered by his official position, he could not participate directly in the work of the masses. The workers were not aware of his actual role and later even attempted to insist that he be removed as manager at the electric station. Krassin dealt only with the tops of the organization; he was the leader of the local leaders. Among the revolutionists with whom he had occasion to come directly in contact he mentions the brothers Yenukidze, Lado Ketskhoveli, Alliluyev, Shelgunov, Halperin and others. It is noteworthy that the one man who carried on the leading work in the Caucasus from 1900 to 1904 does not mention Stalin even once. No less significant is the fact that as late as 1927 this pretermission passed entirely unnoticed, and Krassin's autobiography was printed by *Gosizdat* (the State Publishing House) without any annotations or corrections. Similarly, no place whatever is accorded to Stalin in the reminiscences of other Bolsheviks who were in any way connected with the movement in the Caucasus during those years. This is true, of course, only of reminiscences written prior to the beginning of the official revision of Party history, i.e., not later than 1929.

In February, 1902, there was supposed to take place in Kiev a conclave of the Iskrovites who were agents of the foreign center. "To that conference," writes Pyatnitsky, "came representatives from all parts of Russia." Discovering that they were under surveillance, they began to leave the city hastily in various directions. However, all of them were caught, some in Kiev, some en route. Several months later they made the famous jail break from the Kiev prison. Koba, who at that time worked in Batum, was not invited to the Kiev meeting, and undoubtedly knew nothing about it.

Koba's political provincialism is most instructively exemplified by his relations with the foreign center, or rather, by the absence of any relations at all with it. Beginning with the middle of the past century, the émigrés continued almost invariably to play the dominant role in the Russian revolutionary movement. What with constant arrests, exiles and executions in Tsarist Russia, the haunts of these émigrés, who were the most outstanding theoreticians, publicists and organizers, were the only continuously active sectors of the movement and hence by the nature of things laid their imprint upon it. The editorial board of the *Iskra* became unquestionably at the beginning of the century the center of the Social-Democracy. From there emanated not only the political slogans but also the practical directions. Every revolutionist passionately desired as soon as possible to spend some time abroad, to see and to hear the leaders, to verify the correctness of his own views, to establish permanent contact with *Iskra* and, through it, with the underground workers in Russia itself. V. Kozhevnikova, who at one time was close to Lenin in connection with work abroad, tells how "from exile and on the road to exile there began a general flight abroad to the editorial office of *Iskra* . . . and then again to Russia for active work." The young workingman Nogin—to take one example out of a hundred —in April, 1903, fled from exile to go abroad, "in order to catch up with life," as he wrote to one of his friends, "in order to read and learn." A few months later he returned illegally to Russia as an *Iskra* agent. All of the ten participants of the aforementioned Kiev jail break, among them the future Soviet diplomat Litvinov, soon found themselves abroad. One after another they subsequently returned to Russia, to prepare the congress of the party. Concerning these and other trusted agents, Krupskaya writes in her reminiscences, "*Iskra* carried on active correspondence with all of them. Vladimir Ilyich looked through every letter. We knew in minute detail which *Iskra* agent did what, and discussed with them each phase of their entire activity; we re-established broken contacts, informed them of arrests and the like." Among these agents were coevals of Lenin as well as of Stalin. But as yet, Koba was not included among that upper layer of revolutionists, the disseminators of centralism, the builders of a unified party. He remained a "local worker," a Caucasian, and a congenital provincial.

In July, 1903, the Party congress prepared by *Iskra* finally convened in Brussels. Under pressure from Tsarist diplomats and the Belgian police subservient to them, it was obliged to transfer its deliberations to London. The congress adopted the program worked out by Plekhanov, and passed resolutions on tactics; but when it came to organizational questions, unexpected differences of opinion suddenly arose among the Iskrovites themselves, who dominated the congress. Both sides, including the "hard" ones, headed by Lenin and the "soft" ones, headed by Martov, at first supposed that the differences were not fundamental. All the more amazing therefore was the sharp clash of these differences. The party, which had but recently been unified, suddenly found itself on the verge of a split.

"As far back as 1903, while sitting in prison, and having learned through comrades returning from the Second Congress about the very serious differences of opinions between the Bolsheviks and the Mensheviks, Stalin resolutely joined the Bolsheviks." So runs a biography, written at the dictation of Stalin himself, which is in the nature of an instruction to Party historians. It would be, however, most incautious to regard that instruction with any excess of confidence. At the congress which led to the split were three Caucasian delegates. With which one of these did Koba meet, and how precisely did he meet him, being at that time in solitary confinement? How and in what way did he express his solidarity with the Bolsheviks? The only confirmation of this version of Stalin's comes from Iremashvili. "Koba, who had always been an enthusiastic partisan of Leninist violent methods," he writes, "immediately, of course, took his place on the side of Bolshevism and became its most passionate defender and leader in Georgia." However, that testimony, its categorical character notwithstanding, is flagrantly anachronous. Prior to the congress no one, including Lenin himself, had ever advocated "Leninist violent methods" as opposed to the methods of those members of the editorial board who were the future leaders of Menshevism. At the congress itself the arguments were not concerned with revolutionary methods; tactical differences of opinion had not yet arisen. Iremashvili is obviously in error, and no wonder: throughout 1903 Koba was in prison, so Iremashvili could not have had any direct impressions of him. In general, although his psychological observations and reminiscences of actual incidents are quite convincing and almost always confirmable, his political observations are less reliable. It would seem that he lacked both the instinct and the background requisite for an understanding of the evolution of the warring revolutionary tendencies; in that sphere he presents us with retrospective guesses, dictated by his own latter-day views.

The wrangle at the Second Congress flared up, as a matter of fact, over the question of party membership; whether it should include only those who were members of the illegal organization, or anyone who systematically participated in the revolutionary struggle under the leadership of local committees. At the time of the discussion Lenin said: "I do not deem the difference of opinion among us so substantial that the life or death of our party is dependent on it. We are far from perishing because of a bad clause in our party regulations." Toward the end of the congress there was also argument over the question of the personnel of the editorial board of *Iskra* and of the Central Committee; and never once did the differences of opinion spread beyond those narrow limits. Lenin attempted to obtain sharp and explicit boundaries for the Party, a compact composition of the editorial board and severe discipline. Martov and his friends preferred a looser organization, more on the order of a family circle. However, both sides were still merely feeling their way and, despite the sharpness of the conflict, no one yet thought these differences of opinion "most serious." According to Lenin's pointed observation of a later day, the struggle at the congress was in the nature of an "anticipation."

Lunarcharsky, the first Soviet leader in the field of education, wrote subsequently:

> The greatest difficulty in that struggle consisted in this, that the Second Congress, having split the Party, had not yet plumbed the really profound differences between the Martovists on the one hand and the Leninists on the other. These differences still seemed to turn on the one paragraph of the party statutes and the personnel of the editorial board. Many were embarrassed by the insignificance of the reason that led to the split.

Pyatnitsky, later a prominent official of the Comintern, but at that time a young workman, writes in his reminiscences: "I could not understand why petty differences kept us from working together." The engineer Krzhizhanovsky, who was very close to Lenin in those years, and later the head of the State Planning Commission, recalls, "To me personally, the thought about Comrade Martov's opportunism seemed particularly far-fetched." There is a lot of such testimony.

From Petersburg, from Moscow, from the provinces came protests and wails. No one wanted to acknowledge the split which transpired at the congress among the Iskrovites. The parting of the ways took place in the course of the following period, slowly, with inevitable shifts to one side and the other. Not infrequently the first Bolsheviks and Mensheviks continued to work peaceably together.

In the Caucasus, because of its backward social and political development, what had occurred at the Congress was understood even less than anywhere else. True, all three of the Caucasian delegates, in the heat of passion, joined the majority in London. But it is significant that all three subsequently became Mensheviks: Topuridze deserted the Majority[7] by the end of the Congress itself; Zurabov and Knunyants came over to the Mensheviks in the course of the next few years. The famous Caucasian illegal printshop, in which Bolshevik sympathies predominated, continued in 1904 to reprint the Menshevik *Iskra*, which formally remained the central organ of the Party. "Our differences of opinion," write Yenukidze, "were absolutely not reflected in our work." Only after the Third Congress of the Party, i.e., not earlier than the middle of 1905, did the printshop pass into the hands of the Bolshevik Central Committee. There is therefore no reason whatever to credit the assertion that Koba, sitting in an out-of-the-way prison, had at once estimated the differences as "most serious." Anticipation was never his strong suit. And it would hardly be possible to censure a young revolutionist even less circumspect and suspicious, had he then departed for Siberia without taking a stand on the struggle within the Party.

From Siberia Koba returned directly to Tiflis; that fact cannot help but evoke amazement. Fugitives who were in the least conspicuous seldom returned to their native haunts, where they could too easily be observed by the ever-vigilant police, especially when that place was not Petersburg or Moscow but a small provincial city like Tiflis. But the young Djugashvili had not yet severed his Caucasian umbilical cord; Georgian still remained almost exclusively the language of his propaganda. Moreover, he did not feel himself to be a focus for police attention. He had not yet made up his mind to try his talents in Central Russia. He was unknown abroad, nor did he try to go there. It would seem also that a more personal reason kept him in Tiflis: if Iremashvili is not confused in his chronology, Koba was already married at that time. During his imprisonment and exile he had left his young wife behind him at Tiflis.

The war with Japan, which began in January, 1904, at first weakened the labor movement, but gave it unprecedented momentum by the end of that year. The military defeats of Tsarism quickly dispelled the patriotic moods which had at first affected liberal and partly student circles. Defeatism, although with a varying coefficient, increasingly overcame, not only the revolutionary masses, but even the oppositionist bourgeoisie. Despite all of that, the Social-Democracy, before the great upheaval which was impending, lived through months of stagna-

[7] See Glossary.

tion and internal ailment. The differences between the Bolsheviks and the Mensheviks, overtaxing because as yet indeterminate, little by little began to seep through the cramped confines of the Party headquarters and subsequently encompassed the entire field of revolutionary strategy.

"Stalin's work during the period of 1904-1905 passed under the flag of fierce struggle against Menshevism," states his official biographer. "Literally on his own shoulders he bore the brunt of the entire struggle with the Mensheviks in the Caucasus, beginning in 1904 and ending with 1908," writes Yenukidze in his newly-revised reminiscences. Beriya affirms that after his flight from exile Stalin "organized and directed the struggle against the Mensheviks, who after the Second Congress of the Party, during Comrade Stalin's absence, became particularly active." These authors want to prove too much. If one were to accept on faith the statement that as early as 1901-1903 Stalin was already playing a leading role in the Caucasian Social-Democracy, that he had joined the Bolsheviks as early as 1903, and, beginning with February, 1904, had already begun his struggle against Menshevism, then one must pause with amazement before the fact that all these efforts had yielded such pitiful results: on the eve of the revolution of 1905 Georgian Bolsheviks were literally counted singly. Beriya's reference to the fact that the Mensheviks became particularly active "during Stalin's absence" sounds almost like irony. Petty bourgeois Georgia, including Tiflis, remained the fortress of Menshevism for a score of years quite irrespective of anyone's presence or absence. In the revolution of 1905 the Georgian workers and peasants followed indivisibly behind the Menshevik faction; in all the four Dumas[8] Georgia was invariably represented by Mensheviks; in the February Revolution of 1917 Georgian Menshevism provided all of Russia with leaders of national caliber—Tseretelli, Chkheidze and others. Finally, even after the establishment of the Soviet Government in Georgia, Menshevism continued to exert considerable influence, which was subsequently expressed in the uprising of 1924. "All of Georgia must be plowed under!" that was how Stalin summarized the lessons of the Georgian uprising at the session of the Political Bureau in the autumn of 1924, i.e., twenty years after he had "opened a fierce struggle against Menshevism." It would therefore be more correct and more just to Stalin not to exaggerate Koba's role during the first years of the century.

Koba returned from exile as a member of the Caucasian Committee, to which he had been elected *in absentio*, during his tenure in prison, at a conference of the Transcaucasian organizations. It is possible that at the beginning of 1904 a majority of the Committee members, eight in all, was already sympathetic to

[8] The first two Dumas were elected in accordance with the election law of December 24 (11 o.s.), 1905, the First Duma sitting from May 10 (April 27 o.s.) to July 22 (9 o.s.), 1906, and the Second Duma from March 5 (February 20 o.s.) to June 15 (2 o.s.), 1907. The last two Dumas were elected in accordance with the more restrictive election law of June 16 (3 o.s.), 1907. The Third Duma sat throughout its allotted term, from November 14 (1 o.s.), 1907 to June 22 (9 o.s.), 1912, and the Fourth Duma very nearly so, from November 28 (15 o.s.), 1912 to March 10 (February 25), 1917.—C. M.

the Majority of the London Congress; but that alone is no indication of Koba's own sympathies. The local Caucasian organizations obviously tended in the direction of the Mensheviks. The conciliationist Central Committee of the Party, under the leadership of Krassin, was at the time opposed to Lenin. *Iskra* was entirely in the hands of the Mensheviks. Under these conditions the Caucasian Committee, with its Bolshevik sympathies, seemed suspended in mid-air. Yet Koba preferred to have firm ground under his feet. He prized the apparatus more than the idea.

Official information about Koba's activities in 1904 is exceedingly sketchy and unreliable. It remains unknown whether he carried on any activity in Tiflis, and if he did, the nature of his work. It is hardly possible that a fugitive from Siberia could have shown himself in workers' circles, where many knew him. It is likely that precisely for that reason Koba moved to Baku as early as June. Concerning his activity there we are informed in the stereotyped phrases: "he directed the struggle of the Baku Bolsheviks," "he exposed the Mensheviks." Not a single fact, not a single specific recollection! If Koba wrote anything at all during those months, it is being withheld from publication, and probably not through mere oversight.

On the other hand, the belated attempts to represent Stalin as the founder of the Baku Social-Democracy are based on nothing at all. The first workers' circles in the smoky and gloomy city poisoned by the Tartar-Armenian feud appeared as early as 1896. The basis for a more complete organization was laid three years later by Abel Yenukidze and several workmen expelled from Moscow. At the very beginning of the century, the very same Yenukidze, in collaboration with Lado Ketskhoveli, organized the Baku Committee, which was Iskrovite in sympathies. Due to the efforts of the Yenukidze brothers, who were closely connected with Krassin, a large underground printshop was established at Baku in 1903. It played an important part in laying the groundwork for the First Revolution. In that very printshop Bolsheviks and Mensheviks worked together in the friendliest fashion until the middle of 1905. When the aged Abel Yenukidze, for many years Secretary of the Central Executive Committee of the Soviet Union, lost favor with Stalin, he was compelled in 1935 to revise his recollections of 1923 anew, substituting for well-established facts mere assertions about the inspiring and leading role of Soso in the Caucasus and particularly in Baku. His submission did not save Yenukidze from his doom. Neither did it add a single vivid stroke to Stalin's biography.

When Koba first appeared on the Baku horizon in June, 1904, the local Social-Democratic organization had to its credit a record of eight years of revolutionary activity. The "Black City" had played a particularly important part in the labor movement during the preceding years. The Spring had brought to Baku a general strike that unleashed an avalanche of strikes and demonstrations throughout the South of Russia. Vera Zasulitch was the first to appraise those developments as the beginning of the Revolution. Due to the more proletarian character of Baku, especially by comparison with Tiflis, the

Bolsheviks managed to secure there an earlier and a more stable foothold than elsewhere in the Caucasus. The same Makharadze, who had used the Tiflis term *"kinto"* with reference to Stalin, states that in the autumn of 1904 there was created in Baku, "under the direct leadership of Soso, a special organization for revolutionary work among the backward oil industry workers, Tartars, Azerbaijanians, and Persians." That testimony might evoke less doubt if Makharadze had made it in the first edition of his memoirs and not ten years later, when under the whip of Beriya he again rewrote the entire history of the Caucasian Social-Democracy. The process of his step-by-step approach to the official "truth" was supplemented by his castigation of each preceding edition of his book in its turn as a spawn of the Evil Spirit and its withdrawal from circulation.

Upon return from Siberia, Koba undoubtedly met Kamenev, who was born in Tiflis[9] and who was one of the first of Lenin's young followers there. It is possible that it was Kamenev, recently returned from abroad, who had helped to convert Koba to Bolshevism. But Kamenev's name was expunged from the history of the Party a few years before Kamenev himself was shot on a fantastic charge. In any event, the real history of Caucasian Bolshevism began, not with Koba's return from exile, but in the autumn of 1904. That date is established in various connections even by official authors wherever they are not obliged to refer specifically to Stalin. In November, 1904, a Bolshevik conference convened at Tiflis, composed of fifteen delegates from local Caucasian organizations, for the most part insignificant groups. It passed a resolution in favor of convoking a new Party congress. That act was an outright declaration of war, not only against the Mensheviks but also against the conciliationist Central

[9] Lev Borisovich Kamenev was born in Moscow July 31 (18 o.s.), 1883. However, he was connected with Tiflis off and on for about ten years. In 1896 he moved with his family to Tiflis, where his father found employment with the Transcaucasian Railway, and young L. B. transferred from the Wilno *Gimnasia* (high school) to the Second Tiflis *Gimnasia*, from which he was graduated in 1901. During his last couple of years in the Tiflis *gimnasia* young Kamenev had been so active as a Marxist that upon graduation he was debarred from matriculating at any Russian university or engineering school. After petitioning the then Minister of Public Instruction Bogolepov, he was finally granted permission to matriculate in the Faculty of Jurisprudence of Moscow University, where he continued to "misbehave" and landed first in the Butyrki and then in the Taganka prisons. He was denied the right to return to the university and was sent back to Tiflis under police surveillance. In Tiflis as an active Iskrist he taught a circle of railway workers and another of shoemakers until the autumn of 1902, when he went to Paris. There he met many of the leaders of the Iskra group, and wrote articles on the student movement for *Iskra*. Several months later Lenin came to Paris from London to deliver a lecture. Kamenev met him, fell under his spell, and when Lenin moved from London to Geneva young Kamenev moved from Paris to Geneva. There he studied Marxism under Lenin's guidance and made his debut as an orator in a debate with Martov, who at the time was traveling through Europe on Kamenev's passport. In Paris Kamenev met Trotsky's sister, Olga, who later became his wife. Immediately after the Second Congress of the Party Lenin sent Kamenev back to Tiflis as a Bolshevik organizer. There he also took part in organizing a strike on the Transcaucasian Railway. He had to leave Tiflis again after a police raid on his apartment, January 18-19, 1904. After five months' imprisonment in Moscow, he was sent back to Tiflis on July 28, 1904. There he remained, except for organizational tours, until the spring of 1905; when he went to London as delegate to the Third Congress.—C. M.

Committee. Had Koba participated in that first conference of the Caucasian Bolsheviks, Beriya and the other historians would not have failed to report that thè conference had been held "at the initiative and under the leadership of Comrade Stalin." Utter silence on that score means that Koba, who was at the time in the Caucasus, did not participate in the conference. In other words, not a single Bolshevik organization sent him as a delegate. The conference elected a Bureau. Koba did not become a member of that important body. All of that would have been inconceivable had he enjoyed a position of any prominence at all among Caucasian Bolsheviks.

Victor Taratuta, who was at the conference as a delegate from Batum and who was subsequently a member of the Party's Central Committee, gives us a fairly definite and unquestionable hint as to who was then the leader among the Bolsheviks in the Caucasus. "At the Caucasus regional conference, which took place at the end of 1904 or at the beginning of 1905," he writes, ". . . I first met also Comrade Kamenev, Lev Borisovich, in his capacity as leader of the Caucasian Bolshevik organizations. At that regional conference Comrade Kamenev was elected traveling propagandist and was to canvass the country far and wide in order to agitate for the convocation of a new Party congress. At the same time he was delegated to visit the committees of the entire country and to establish contact with our foreign centers of those days." This authoritative witness does not say a word about Koba's participation in that activity.

Under those circumstances there naturally could not have been any reason at all for including Koba in the general Russian center of the Bolsheviks, the "Bureau of the Committees of the Majority," composed of seventeen members, which was formed for the purpose of convoking the congress. Kamenev became a member of that Bureau as the representative of the Caucasus. Among the others on the list of the Bureau members who subsequently became famous Soviet leaders we find the names of Rykov and Litvinov. It might not be amiss to add that Kamenev and Rykov were two or three years younger than Stalin. On the whole the Bureau was composed of representatives of the "third" generation.

Koba came to Baku for the second time in December, 1904, that is, soon after the Tiflis Bolshevik Conference had taken place. On the eve of his arrival a general strike broke out in the oil fields and factories, catching all of Russia by surprise. The Party's organizations manifestly had not yet learned to understand the nature of the insurrectionary mood of the masses, which was aggravated by the first year of the war. The Baku strike directly preceded the famous Bloody Sunday in Petersburg, the tragic march of the workers under the leadership of the priest Gapon to the Winter Palace on January twenty-second, 1905. One of the "memoirs" fabricated in 1935 vaguely mentions that Stalin led the strike committee in Baku and that everything transpired under his leadership. But according to the same author, Koba arrived in Baku after the strike had begun and remained in the city only ten days in all. As a matter of fact, he came on a special assignment, which probably had something to do with preparations for the congress. By that time he might have made his choice in favor of Bolshevism.

Stalin himself attempted to set back the date of his joining the Bolsheviks. Not satisfied with the statement that he had become a Bolshevik before his release from prison, he declared in 1924, at the memorial evening of the Kremlin cadets, that he had first established contact with Lenin as far back as the time of his first exile:

> I first met Comrade Lenin in 1903. True, it was not a person to person meeting, but by correspondence, in the course of an exchange of letters. Yet it left me with an indelible impression that remained with me throughout the entire tenure of my work in the Party. At that time I was in Siberia, in exile. Familiarity with Comrade Lenin's revolutionary activity at the beginning of the 'nineties, and especially since 1901, after the appearance of "Iskra," led me to the conviction that in Comrade Lenin we had an extraordinary man. I did not regard him then as only a leader of the Party, but as its actual creator, for he alone understood our Party's inner substance and its urgent needs. When I compared him with the other leaders of our Party, it always seemed to me that Comrade Lenin's companions-in-arms—Plekhanov, Martov, Axelrod, and others—ranked a whole head lower than Comrade Lenin, that by comparison with them, Lenin was not only one of the leaders, but a leader of the highest type, a mountain eagle who knew no fear in the fight and who boldly led the Party forward over the unexplored paths of the Russian revolutionary movement. That impression sank so deep into my soul that I felt the necessity to write about it to one of my close friends, who was at the time in emigration, requesting a reply from him. Sometime later, when I was already in exile in Siberia— that was toward the end of 1903—I received an exultant answer from my friend and simple yet profoundly pregnant letter from Comrade Lenin, to whom it would seem my friend had shown my letter. Comrade Lenin's little letter was comparatively brief, but it subjected the practices of our Party to bold and fearless criticism and gave a remarkably clear and cogent exposition of the entire plan of the Party's work for the impending period. Only Lenin could write a letter about the most complicated matters so simply and clearly, so cogently and boldly that each phrase did not so much speak as shout. That simple and audacious letter strengthened my conviction that in Lenin we had the mountain eagle of our Party. I cannot forgive myself that due to the habits of an old underground worker, I burned Comrade Lenin's letter along with many other letters. My acquaintance with Comrade Lenin began at that time.

The chronology of that story, so typical of Stalin because of its psychological and stylistic primitiveness, is not all that is wrong with it. Koba did not reach his place of exile until January, 1904; consequently he could not have received the alleged letter there in 1903. Furthermore, it is not at all clear where and just how he wrote "to one of my closest friends" abroad, since prior to his banishment to Siberia he had been in prison for a year and a half. Exiled persons never knew ahead of time to what place they would be banished; hence, Koba could not have communicated his Siberian address in advance to his friend abroad, and certainly there was no time for a letter from exile and a reply from abroad in the course of the one month Koba spent in exile. According to Stalin's own version, Lenin's letter was not of a personal but of a programmatic character. Copies of that type of letter were invariably sent out by Krupskaya to a number of addresses, while the original was kept in the Party archives abroad. It is most unlikely that in this one instance an exception was made for the sake of an unknown young Caucasian. Yet the archives do not contain the original of that letter, the copy of which Koba burned "due to the habits of an old underground worker" (he was at the time exactly twenty-four years old). But most amazing is the fact that Stalin says nothing at all about his reply to Lenin. Having received a letter from the leader whom he admittedly venerated as a demigod, it stands to reason that Koba would have answered him at once. Yet Stalin is silent about that—and not by accident: the archives of Lenin and Krupskaya do not contain Koba's reply. Of course, it might have been intercepted by the police. But in that event the copy would have been preserved in the files of the police department and would have been reproduced in the Soviet press years ago. But that relationship would not have been limited to one letter. A young Social-Democrat could not have failed to regard permanent contact with the leader of his Party, with its "mountain eagle," as most precious to him. As for Lenin, he regarded every contact with Russia as precious and meticulously replied to every letter. Yet no correspondence between Lenin and Koba has come to light in the course of recent years. Everything in this tale evokes perplexity—everything except its purpose.

The year 1904 was perhaps the most difficult in Lenin's life, barring the last years of his illness. Without desiring it and without foreseeing it, he broke with all the prominent leaders of the Russian Social-Democracy and for a long time thereafter could find no one capable of replacing his former companions-in-arms. Bolshevik literary men were recruited slowly and with great effort. Nor were they up to the par of the *Iskra* editors. Lyadov, one of the most active Bolsheviks in those days, who in 1904 was with Lenin at Geneva, recalled twenty years later: "Olminsky came, Vorovsky came, Bogdanov came . . . we awaited the coming of Lunacharsky, for whom Bogdanov vouched that immediately upon arrival he would join us." These men were returning from exile. Their reputations preceded them. They were expected. But when mobilizing the editorial staff of the factional newspaper no one suggested Koba as a possibility. Yet nowadays he is portrayed as a prominent Bolshevik leader of that period. The first issue of the newspaper *Vperyod* [Forward] was finally published in December twenty-second at Geneva. Koba had nothing whatever to do with that momentous event in the life of his faction. He did not so much as get in touch with the editors. The newspaper contains neither his articles nor his news reports. That would have been unthinkable had he been a leader of the Caucasian Bolsheviks at the time.

Finally, there is direct and documentary testimony in support of the conclusion we made on the basis of circumstantial evidence. In an extensive and exceedingly interesting statement on Joseph Djugashvili written in 1911 by the chief of the Tiflis Secret Police Department, Karpov, we read:

> He has been active in the Social-Democratic organization since 1902, at first as a Menshevik and later as a Bolshevik.

Karpov's report is the only document known to us which states explicitly that during a certain period after the split Stalin was a Menshevik. The Tiflis newspaper *Zarya Vostoka* which was careless enough to have published that document in its issue of December twenty-third, 1925, either did not think of offering, or could not offer, any explanations whatsoever. No doubt the editor was later cruelly punished for that blunder. It is most significant that even Stalin did not find it convenient to refute that statement. Not a single one of the official biographers or historians of the Party ever again referred to that important document, while at the same time scores of insignificant bits of paper were reproduced, requoted and rephotographed without end. Let us suppose for the moment that the Tiflis gendarmerie, which in any event should have been best informed on that score, had given incorrect information. Then immediately the supplementary question arises: how was such an error possible? Had Koba actually been at the head of the Caucasian Bolsheviks, the Secret Police Department could not have failed to know it. It could have committed such a crude error in political characterization only with reference to some green neophyte or some third-rate figure, but never with reference to a "leader." Thus, the one document which fortuitously found its way into print demolishes in one fell swoop the official myth reared with such great effort. And how many more such documents are being preserved in fireproof vaults, or, on the contrary, are solicitously relegated to the flames!

It may seem that we have wasted altogether too much time and effort, in order to establish a very modest conclusion. Is it not really all the same whether Koba joined the Bolsheviks in the middle of 1903 or on the eve of 1905? Yet that modest conclusion, apart from the fact that incidentally it discloses to us the mechanics of Kremlin historiography and iconography, has very significant bearing on the proper understanding of Stalin's political personality. The majority of those who have written about him accept his transition to Bolshevism as something inherent in his character, self-evident, natural. Yet such a view is definitely one-sided. True, firmness and resoluteness predetermine a person to the acceptance of the methods of Bolshevism. Yet these characteristics in themselves are not decisive. There were any number of persons of firm character among Mensheviks and Socialist-Revolutionists. On the other hand, weak people were not so very rare among the Bolsheviks. Psychology and character are not all that there is to the nature of Bolshevism, which, above all, is a philosophy of history and a political conception. Under certain historical conditions workers are pushed onto the path of Bolshevism by the entire pattern of their social circumstances. That happens almost regardless of the hardness or softness of individual characters. An intellectual needed exceptional political intuition and theoretical imagination, unusual faith in the dialectic historical process and in the revolutionary attributes of the working class, in order seriously and firmly to tie his fate to the Bolshevik Party in the days when Bolshevism was no more than a historical anticipation. The preponderant majority of intellectuals who joined Bolshevism in the period of its revolutionary rise abandoned it in subsequent years. It was more difficult for Koba to join, but it was likewise more difficult for him to break with it, because he had neither theoretical imagination nor historical intuition nor the gift of foresight, just as, on the other hand, he was devoid of light-mindedness. His intellect always remained immeasurably inferior to his will. In a complex situation, when confronted with new considerations, Koba prefers to bide his time, to keep his peace, or to retreat. In all those instances when it is necessary for him to choose between the idea and the political machine, he invariably inclines toward the machine. The program must first of all create its bureaucracy before Koba can have any respect for it. Lack of confidence in the masses, as well as in individuals, is the basis of his nature. His empiricism always compels him to choose the path of least resistance. That is why, as a rule, at all the great turning points of history this near-sighted revolutionist assumes an opportunist position, which brings him exceedingly close to the Mensheviks and on occasion places him to the right of them. At the same time he invariably is inclined to favor the most resolute actions in solving the problems he has mastered. Under all conditions well-organized violence seems to him the shortest distance between two points. Here an analogy begs to be drawn. The Russian terrorists were in essence petty bourgeois democrats, yet they were extremely resolute and audacious. Marxists were wont to refer to them as "liberals with a bomb." Stalin has always been what he remains to this day—a politician of the golden mean who does not hesitate to resort to the most extreme measures. Strategically he is an opportunist; tactically he is a "revolutionist." He is a kind of opportunist with a bomb.

Soon after his departure from the seminary Koba became something in the nature of a bookkeeper at the Tiflis Observatory. Despite its "miserly salary," he liked his job, Iremashvili informs us, because it left him a lot of free time for revolutionary activity. "He was least of all concerned with his personal welfare. He made no demands on life, regarding them as incompatible with Socialist principles. He had sufficient integrity to make sacrifices for his ideal." Koba was true to that vow of poverty which was taken unostentatiously and without any ado by all the young people who went into the revolutionary underground. Besides, unlike many others who took that vow, he had not been accustomed to comforts since childhood. "I visited him several times in his small, squalid, poorly furnished room on Mikhailovskaya Street," relates the irreplaceable second Soso. "Every day Koba wore a simple black Russian blouse and the red necktie that was then characteristic of all Social-Democrats. In the winter he wore an old brown cape over it. As headgear he knew only the Russian peak cap. Although when Koba left the seminary he was far from friendly with most of the young seminary Marxists, they would nevertheless make up a collection from time to time in order to help him out of his dire needs." Barbusse informs us that in 1900, that is, a year after his departure from the seminary, Joseph found himself entirely without means: "His comrades made it possible for him to obtain food." Police documents indicate that Koba remained in the service of the observatory until March, 1901, when he was obliged to go into hiding. His job, as we have heard, scarcely gave him a living. ". . . His income did not make it possible for him to dress adequately," continues Iremashvili. "Yet it is also true that he did not make any effort to keep his clothes at least clean and in order. He could never be seen otherwise than in a dirty blouse and in an unpolished pair of shoes. He detested from the bottom of his heart everything that reminded him of the bourgeois." The dirty blouse, the unpolished boots, the tousled hair were likewise generally characteristic of all young revolutionists, especially in the provinces.

Passing in March, 1901, to illegal status, Koba became a professional revolutionist. From then on he had no name because he had many names. At various periods, and upon occasions at one and the same time, he was called, "David," "Koba," "Nizheradze," "Chizhikov," "Ivanovich," "Stalin." Similarly the gendarmes invested him with their nicknames. The most persistent of these was "Ryaboi," which alluded to his pock-marked face. Henceforth Koba would revert to legal status only in prison and in exile, that is, between each two periods of underground.

"He never lacked singleness of purpose," Yenukidze wrote about the young Stalin in his corrected memoirs. "All of his actions, encounters, friendships were directed toward a definite objective . . . Stalin never sought personal popularity," he adds, and there limited his circle of contacts "to the advanced workers and to professional revolutionists." The purpose of that refrain, repeated in many official memoirs, is to explain why until his very accession to power Stalin remained unknown to the nation's masses and even to the general membership of the Party. It is untrue, however, that he presumably did not seek popularity. He sought it greedily, but he could not find it. From the first, the absence of popularity rankled in his heart. It was precisely his inability to win fame by a frontal attack that drove this forceful personality into devious and crooked ways.

Since early youth Koba had sought power over people, who for the most part seemed to him weaker than himself. Yet he was neither wiser nor more educated nor more eloquent than others. He did not possess a single one of those attributes which attract sympathy. But he was richer than others in cold persistence and practical common sense. He did not yield to impulses: rather, he knew how to subject them to his calculations. That characteristic had already shown itself when he was a schoolboy. "Usually Joseph replied to questions unhurriedly," writes Glurdzhidze. "Whenever his answer was in all its aspects well founded, he would reply; if not, he would procrastinate with his answer for a more or less brief period of time." Quite apart from the exaggeration concerning his answer having been "in all its aspects well founded," these words contain mention of the one rather vital trait of the young Stalin that gave him an important advantage among the young revolutionists, who for the most part were big-hearted, precipitate, and naïve.

Even in that early period Koba did not hesitate to set his opponents against each other, to slander them, and to carry on intrigues against every one who in any way seemed superior to him or who seemed a hindrance to his path. The moral unscrupulousness of the young Stalin generated an atmosphere of suspicion and of sinister rumors about him. Much of which he was not guilty was beginning to be ascribed to him. The Socialist-Revolutionist Vereshchak, who came in close contact with Stalin in prison, related in the émigré press in 1928 how, presumably after Joseph Djugashvili had been expelled from the seminary, the director received from him a denunciation of a former comrade in his revolutionary group. When Joseph was obliged to give an account of himself in this affair before the Tiflis organization, he presumably not only admitted that he had been the author of the denunciation, but even deemed it something in his favor: instead of becoming transformed into priests and teachers, those expelled would be forced to become, according to his alleged reckoning, revolutionists. This entire episode, pounced upon by certain gullible biographers, bears the obvious brand of invention. A revolutionary organization can maintain its existence only through ruthless strictness in regard to anything at all which in the slightest way smacks of denunciation, provocation, or betrayal. The smallest indulgence in that sphere spells the beginning of gangrene for it. Had Soso been proven capable of resorting to such means, compounded of one-third Machiavelli to two-thirds Judas, it is altogether inadmissible that the Party would have tolerated him in its ranks after that. Iremashvili, who at the time belonged to the same seminarist circle as Koba, knows nothing at all about that episode. He himself succeeded in graduating from the seminary and became a teacher. Yet it is no mere accident that so vicious an invention is connected with Stalin's name. Nothing of the kind was ever rumored about any of the other old revolutionists.

Souvarine, who wrote the best documented of Stalin's biographies, attempts to deduce his moral personality from his membership in the ominous order of "professional revolutionists." In this instance, as in many others, Souvarine's generalizations are most superficial. A professional revolutionist is a person who completely dedicates himself to the labor movement under conditions of illegality and forced conspiracy. Not everyone is capable of that, and certainly, in any event, not the worst kind of person. The labor movement of the civilized world knows numerous professional officials and professional politicians; the preponderant majority of that caste is noted for its conservatism, egotism and narrow-mindedness, living not for the movement, but at its expense. By comparison with the average labor bureaucrat of Europe or America, the average professional revolutionist of Russia cut an incomparably more attractive figure.

The youth of the revolutionary generation coincided with the youth of the labor movement. It was the epoch of people between the ages of eighteen and thirty. Revolutionists above that age were few in number and seemed old men. The movement was as yet utterly devoid of careerism, lived on its faith in the future and on its spirit of self-sacrifice. There were as yet no routine, no set formulae, no theatrical gestures, no ready-made oratorical tricks. The struggle was by nature full of pathos, shy and awkward. The very words "committee," "party" were as yet new, with an aura of vernal freshness, and rang in young ears as a disquieting and alluring melody. Whoever joined an organization knew that prison followed by exile awaited him within the next few months. The measure of ambition was to last as long as possible on the job prior to arrest; to hold oneself steadfast when facing the gendarmes; to ease, as far as possible, the plight of one's comrades; to read, while in prison, as many books as possible; to escape as soon as possible from exile abroad; to acquire wisdom there; and then return to revolutionary activity in Russia.

The professional revolutionists believed what they taught. They could have had no other incentive for taking to the road to Calvary. Solidarity under persecution was no empty word, and it was augmented by contempt for cowardice and desertion. "Turning over in my mind the mass of comrades with whom I had occasion to meet," writes Eugenia Levitskaya concerning the Odessa underground of 1901-1907, "I cannot recall a single reprehensible, contemptible act, a single deception or lie. There was friction. There were factional differences of opinion. But no more than that. Somehow everyone looked after himself morally, became better and more gentle in that friendly family." Odessa was not, of course, an exception. The young men and young women who devoted themselves entirely to the revolutionary movement, without demanding anything in return, were not the worst representatives of their generation. The order of "professional revolutionists" cannot suffer by comparison with any other social group.

Joseph Djugashvili was a member of that order and shared many of its traits; many, but not all. He saw the purpose of his life in overthrowing the powers that be. Hatred of them was immeasurably more active in his soul than love for the oppressed. Prison, exile, sacrifices, privations did not frighten him. He knew how to look danger straight in the eye. At the same time he was keenly sensitive about such of his traits as his slowness of intellect, lack of talent, the general colorlessness of his physical and moral countenance. His overweening ambition was tinged with envy and ill will. His pertinacity marched hand in hand with vindictiveness. The jaundiced glint of his eyes impelled sensitive people to take notice. As far back as his schooldays he displayed an aptitude for noting the weaknesses of people and for harping upon them pitilessly. The Caucasian environment proved most favorable for nurturing these basic attributes of his nature. Without being swept off his feet while in the midst of enthusiasts, without catching fire while in the midst of those who were easily inflamed yet quick to cool down, he learned early in life to prize the advantages of icy grit, of circumspection and especially of astuteness, which in his case became subtly transformed into wiliness. Special historical circumstances were to invest these essentially secondary attributes with primary significance.

Chapter III

THE FIRST REVOLUTION

ACCORDING to our surmise, Koba did not join the Bolsheviks until some time after the November Conference, which met at Tiflis. That conference resolved to take an active part in preparations, already under way, for a new congress of the Social-Democratic Labor Party. Without any objection, we accepted Beriya's bare assertion that Koba had left Baku in December on a propaganda tour in favor of that congress. That much is not improbable. It was clear to all that the Party was split in two. By that time the Bolshevik faction had already gained such strength that organizationally it was superior to its Menshevik opponent. Forced to choose between the two, it is not unlikely that Koba joined the Bolshevik faction. But we would be hard put to it, if we had to offer positive proof that Koba was already a member of the Bolshevik faction by the end of 1904. Beriya goes so far as to marshal a number of quotations from leaflets published at the time, yet he does not venture to say that Koba wrote any of them. That shy reticence about the authorship of these leaflets speaks louder than words. Beriya's quotations from leaflets written by others than Koba serve, of course, the obvious purpose of filling in the gaping lacunae in Stalin's biography.

Meantime, the differences of opinion between the Mensheviks and the Bolsheviks passed from the domain of party regulations to the domain of revolutionary strategy. The campaign of banquets—launched by zemstvo[1] workers

[1] Zemstvo—semi-official local self-government principally in the provinces of Central Russia (there were no zemstvos in the Western Russian provinces, in Poland, in the Baltic provinces, in the Cossack districts, in the Caucasus, Turkestan, and Siberia), administered under the supervision of the landed gentry ostensibly for public benefit. The institution was introduced by the Tsar-Liberator Alexander II (edict of January 1, 1864) shortly after the liberation of the serfs, liberalizing the police régime of the autocracy and representing a progressive step toward a constitutional régime. From its very inception the zemstvo had no real political authority, being dependent on the good will of the provincial governor and other appointees of the tsarist autocracy. Under Alexander III the self-governing ambit of the zemstvo was further limited by introducing in 1889 the office of zemski nachalnik, or Lands Administrator, a nobleman who functioned as judge over the peasantry, and who tightened his reins over the zemstvo's administrative power in local affairs. Barring these important limitations, the zemstvo outwardly resembled a county council. It took care of the roads, public health, fire-insurance, relief of the indigent, public education and other cultural and economic functions. In an extremely limited and rather timid way, the zemstvo was likewise a sounding board for liberal political sentiments. Always loyal to the Tsar, zemstvo leaders as a class were in favor of a constitutional régime in Russia. The Tsar used the zemstvo as a tool of the autocracy; whereas, from time to time, the revolutionists attempted to utilize individual zemstvo members, at least, as an auxiliary force in their struggle against the autocracy. Zemstvo physicians,

and other liberals, and which grew apace during the autumn of 1904, largely because the distracted Tsarist authorities were too negligent to do anything about it—posed point-blank the question of relations between the Social-Democracy and the oppositionist bourgeoisie. The Menshevik plan called for an attempt to transform the workers into a democratic chorus supporting liberal soloists, a chorus sufficiently considerate and circumspect not only to "refrain from frightening" the liberals, but, more than that, one dedicated to bolstering the liberals' faith in themselves. Lenin immediately launched his offensive. He derided the very idea of this plan—to substitute diplomatic support of a helpless opposition for the revolutionary struggle against Tsarism. The victory of the revolution can be secured only under pressure of the masses! Only a bold social program can rouse the masses to action: yet that is precisely what liberals fear. "We would have been fools had we taken their panic into consideration." A smallish pamphlet by Lenin, which appeared in November, 1904, after a long silence, raised the spirits of his comrades and played an important part in developing Bolshevism's tactical ideas. Was it not perhaps this pamphlet that had won Koba over? We do not venture to answer in the affirmative. In years to come, whenever he had occasion to exercise his own discretion in assuming a position with reference to the liberals, he invariably floundered toward the Menshevist notion of the importance of "refraining from frightening" the liberals. (Witness the revolutions in Russia in 1917, in China, in Spain and elsewhere.) The possibility is not excluded, however, that on the eve of the First Revolution, the plebeian Democrat appeared to be sincerely indignant with the opportunistic plan, which evoked great dissatisfaction even among rank and file Mensheviks. It must be said that, on the whole, among the radical intelligentsia, the tradition of maintaining a contemptuous attitude toward liberalism had not yet had time to fade away. It is also possible, however, that only Bloody Sunday[2] in Petersburg and the wave of strikes that swept the country in its wake had nudged the cautious and suspicious Caucasian to the path of Bolshevism. In any event, the milestone of that turn remained unrecorded in the annals of history.

The two old Bolsheviks, Stopani and Lehman, in their elaborately detailed reminiscences list all the revolutionists with whom they had occasion to deal at Baku and Tiflis toward the end of 1904 and the beginning of 1905: Koba is not on that list. Lehman names the people "who were at the head" of the Caucasian Union: Koba is not one of them. Stopani names the Bolsheviks who,

---

engineers, statisticians, clerks and other employees came to be with increasing frequency revolutionists or sympathizers of the revolutionary parties.—C. M.

[2] January 22, 1905 (commonly known in Russia as The Ninth of January) went down into the annals of Russian history as "Bloody Sunday" after Tsar Nicholas II met a procession of loyal and unarmed Petersburg workingmen, come to petition him for redress of grievances under the leadership of Priest Gapon, with volleys of gunfire that killed hundreds of them. More than any other single factor, that act of monumental brutality undermined the faith of the average Russian in the good intentions of their "Little Father" and swept Russian workingmen in droves toward the revolutionary parties. That day marked the beginning of Russia's first revolutionary year, 1905.—C. M.

jointly with the Mensheviks, led the famous Baku strike in December, 1904: again Koba's name is among the missing. Yet Stopani should know whereof he writes, since he was himself a member of that strike committee. The reminiscences of both authors were published in the official Communist historical journal, and both memoirists, far from being "enemies of the people," were good Stalinists; but they wrote their pieces in 1925, before planned falsification on assignment from above was developed into a system. In an article written as recently as 1926, Taratuta, a former member of the Bolshevik Central Committee, discussing "The Eve of the Revolution of 1905 in the Caucasus," makes no mention whatever of Stalin. In the commentaries to the correspondence of Lenin and Krupskaya with the Caucasian organization Stalin's name does not appear so much as once throughout the entire fifty pages. It is simply impossible to find around the latter part of 1904 and the beginning of 1905 any trace of activity by him who is nowadays portrayed as the founding father of Caucasian Bolshevism.

Nor does this conclusion run counter to the very latest of the interminable asseverations about Stalin's implacable campaigning against the Mensheviks. All that is needed to reconcile these apparent contradictions is to push his campaigning some two years back, which is not hard, since there is no need to cite documents and no occasion to apprehend disproof. On the other hand, there is no reason to doubt that, having once made his choice, Koba waged his fight against the Mensheviks in the harshest, crudest and most unscrupulous manner. That penchant for underhand ways and intrigues, which had been charged against him while he was a participant in the seminarist circles, a propagandist of the Tiflis Committee and a member of the Batum group, now found a far wider and bolder expression in the factional struggle.

Beriya names Tiflis, Batum, Chituary, Kutais and Poti as the places at which Stalin had engaged in debates against Noah Jordania, Irakli Tsereteli, Noah Ramishvili and other Menshevik leaders, as well as against the Anarchists and the Federalists. But Beriya cavalierly ignores all dates—an omission far from unintentional. As a matter of fact, the first of these discussions, which he fixes with some semblance of exactitude, took place in May, 1905. The situation is exactly the same in the case of Koba's published writings. His first Bolshevik composition, a thin little pamphlet, was issued in May, 1905, under the rather odd title, "Slightly About Party Differences."[3] Beriya deems it necessary to remark, without revealing on what grounds, that this pamphlet was written "at the beginning of 1905," thereby disclosing more flagrantly than ever his attempt to shorten the two-year gap. One of the correspondents, evidently the future Litvinov, who did not know any Georgian, reported abroad the appearance in Tiflis of a pamphlet "which created a sensation." This "sensation" can be explained only by the circumstance that the Georgian audience had heretofore heard nothing but the voice of the Mensheviks. In substance, this pamphlet amounts to no more than a sophomoric summary of Lenin's writings. No won-

[3] Officially translated in English as "A Glance at the Disagreements in the Party."—C. M.

der that it has never been reprinted. Beriya cites from it painstakingly culled quotations, which easily explain why the author himself was content to cast over that pamphlet, as over his other literary works of that period, the pall of oblivion.

In August, 1905, Stalin restated that chapter of Lenin's book, "What To Do?", which attempted to explain the correlation of the elemental labor movement and socialistic class-consciousness. According to Lenin's representations, the labor movement, when left to its own devices, was inclined irrevocably toward opportunism; revolutionary class-consciousness was brought to the proletariat from the outside, by Marxist intellectuals. This is not the place for a criticism of that concept, which in its entirety belongs in a biography of Lenin rather than of Stalin. The author of "What To Do?" himself subsequently acknowledged the biased nature, and therewith the erroneousness, of his theory, which he had parenthetically interjected as a battery in the battle against "Economism" and its deference to the elemental nature of the labor movement. After his break with Lenin, Plekhanov came out with a belated, but all the more severe, criticism of "What To Do?". The question of introducing revolutionary class-consciousness into the proletariat "from the outside" became timely again. The central organ of the Bolshevik Party recorded "the splendid posing of the question" concerning the introduction of class-consciousness "from the outside" in an anonymous article in a Georgian newspaper. That praise is cited nowadays as a kind of testimonial of Koba's maturity as a theorist. As a matter of fact, it was nothing more than one of the customary encouraging remarks usually made by the foreign center whenever some provincial publication placed itself on record in defense of the ideas or the leaders of its own faction. As to the quality of the article, a sufficiently clear idea of it may be obtained from the following quotation in Beriya's Russian translation:

> Contemporary life is arranged capitalistically. In it exist two great classes: the bourgeoisie and the proletariat; a life or death struggle is waged between them. The circumstances of life compel the former to uphold the capitalistic order. The same circumstances compel the latter to undermine and to destroy the capitalistic order. Corresponding to these two classes, a two-fold class-consciousness, bourgeois and socialistic, is likewise created. Socialistic class-consciousness corresponds to the situation of the proletariat . . . But what significance can socialistic class-consciousness alone have, when it is not disseminated in the proletariat? It remains merely an empty phrase, and no more! Matters will take quite a different turn when that class-consciousness finds circulation in the proletariat: the proletariat will then realize its situation and will strive at an increasing pace to achieve the socialist way of life . . .

and so forth. Such articles were rescued from duly merited oblivion only by the subsequent fate of their author. Yet, it is quite self-evident that the articles in themselves do not explain that fate; rather, they render it even more enigmatic.

Throughout 1905 Koba did not figure at all among Lenin's and Krupskaya's

Caucasian correspondents, even as he had not figured prior to that. On the eighth of March a certain Tari, writing from Tiflis, summarized the reactions of certain Caucasian Mensheviks in the following words: "Lenin grasped the meaning of our times before anyone else and better than anyone else." The same Tari wrote: "Lenin is referred to as a kind of Bazarov among these Arcady Nikolayeviches." The reference is, of course, to Turgenev's heroes: Bazarov, the practical realist type; and Arcady Nikolayevich, the idealist and phrasemonger. Under the name of Tari the editors of the historical journal indited the footnote, "Author unknown." But the pointed literary reference alone suffices to show that Stalin could not have been the author of that letter. In Lenin's articles and letters for the second half of 1905—at least in those published to date—are mentioned more than thirty Social-Democrats who had worked in Russia; of these, nineteen are closest in age to Lenin and twelve to Stalin. Stalin himself does not figure in that correspondence, either as a direct participant or as a third person. We are therefore obliged to adhere as firmly as ever to the conclusion we have already enunciated—that Stalin's tale of having received a letter from Lenin in 1903 is simply a fabrication.

After his break with the editorial board of *Iskra*, Lenin, who was then about thirty-four years old, lived through months of wavering—a condition doubly difficult for him because so flagrantly at variance with his character—before he became convinced that his followers were comparatively numerous and his young authority sufficiently strong. The successful culmination of the arrangements for the new congress made plain beyond a doubt that the Social-Democratic organizations were preponderantly Bolshevik. The conciliatory Central Committee, led by Krassin, finally capitulated to the "illegal" Bureau of the Committees of the Majority and participated in the congress it could not prevent. Thus, the Third Congress—which convened in April, 1905, in London, and from which the Mensheviks deliberately stayed away, satisfying themselves with a conference in Geneva—became the constituent congress of Bolshevism. The twenty-four voting and fourteen advisory delegates were all, almost without exception, those Bolsheviks who had been faithful to Lenin from the moment of the split at the Second Congress and had aroused the Committees of the Party against the combined authority of Plekhanov, Axelrod, Vera Zasulich, Martov, and Potresov. At this Congress was legitimatized that view on the moving forces of the Russian Revolution which Lenin developed in the course of his forthright fight against his former teachers and closest collaborators on the *Iskra*, and which thenceforth acquired greater practical significance than the Party's official program worked out in common with the Mensheviks.

The ill-starred and inglorious war with Japan was hastening the disintegration of the Tsarist régime. Coming after the first great wave of strikes and demonstrations, the Third Congress reflected the approach of the revolutionary denouement. "The entire history of the past year has shown," Lenin said in his report to the assembled delegates, "that we had underestimated the significance and the inevitability of insurrection." The Congress took a resolute step forward on the agrarian question by acknowledging the necessity of supporting the peasant movement then current even to the extent of confiscating the lands of the landed gentry. More concretely than heretofore, it outlined the general perspective of the revolutionary struggle and the conquest of power, particularly on the question of the provisional revolutionary government as the organizer of civil war. As Lenin put it, "Even if we were to take possession of Petersburg and guillotine Nicholas, we would still be confronted with several Vendées." The Congress undertook, with greater boldness than ever, the technical preparation of the insurrection. "On the question of creating special fighting groups," said Lenin, "I must say that I deem them indispensable."

The greater one's regard for the significance of the Third Congress, the more noteworthy is Koba's absence from it. By that time he had to his credit nearly seven years of revolutionary activity, including prison, exile and escape. Had he been a person of any consequence at all among the Bolsheviks, surely that record would have assured at least his candidacy as a delegate. Koba was moreover at liberty all through the year 1905, and according to Beriya, "took the most active part in the matter of organizing the Third Congress of the Bolsheviks." If that is true, surely he should have been the chief of the Caucasian delegation. Why, then, wasn't he? Had illness or any other exceptional cause prevented his journeying abroad, the official biographers would surely not have failed to tell us about it. Their uncommunicativeness is explicable only on the grounds of their not having at their disposal a single credible explanation for the absence of the "leader of the Caucasian Bolsheviks" from that historically important congress. Beriya's assertions about "the most active" participation of Koba in organizing the Congress is one of those meaningless phrases with which official Soviet historiography is replete. In an article devoted to the thirtieth anniversary of the Third Congress, the well-informed Osip Pyatnitsky says nothing whatsoever about Stalin's participation in the arrangements for the Congress, while the court historian Yaroslavsky limits himself to a vague remark, the substance of which is that Stalin's work in the Caucasus "had undoubtedly tremendous significance" for the Congress, without elucidating the precise nature of that significance. Yet, from all we have so far managed to learn, the situation appears to be quite clear: after hesitating for a considerable period of time, Koba joined the Bolsheviks shortly before the Third Congress; he took no part in the November Conference in the Caucasus; he was never a member of the bureau established by it; and being a newcomer, he could not have even hoped for a delegate's mandate. The delegation consisted of Kamenev, Nevsky, Tskhakaya, and Dzhaparidze; these were the leaders of Caucasian Bolshevism at that time. Their subsequent fate is not irrelevant to our narrative: Dzhaparidze was shot by the English in 1918; Kamenev was shot eighteen years later by Stalin; Nevsky was proclaimed an "enemy of the people" by Stalin's fiat and vanished without a trace; and only the aged Tskhakaya has survived, having managed to outlive himself.

The negative aspect of Bolshevism's centripetal tendencies first became apparent at the Third Congress of the Russian Social-Democracy. The habits peculiar to a political machine were already forming in the underground. The young revolutionary bureaucrat was already emerging as a type. The conditions of conspiracy, true enough, offered rather meager scope for such of the formalities of democracy as electiveness, accountability and control. Yet, undoubtedly the committeemen narrowed these limitations considerably more than necessity demanded and were far more intransigent and severe with the revolutionary workingmen than with themselves, preferring to domineer even on occasions that called imperatively for lending an attentive ear to the voice of the masses. Krupskaya notes that, just as in the Bolshevik committees, so at the Congress itself, there were almost no workingmen. The intellectuals predominated. "The 'committeeman,'" writes Krupskaya, "was usually quite a self-confident person; he was fully aware of the tremendous influence wielded by the Committee's activities on the masses; the 'committeeman,' as a rule, did not recognize any internal party democracy; inherently the 'committeeman' was contemptuous of the 'foreign center,' which raged and ranted and started squabbles: 'they ought to try Russian conditions for a change' . . . At the same time, he did not want any innovations. The 'committeeman' did not desire, and did not know how, to adapt himself to rapidly changing conditions." That restrained yet very pithy characterization is most helpful to an understanding of Koba's political psychology, for he was the "committeeman" *par excellence*. As early as 1901, at the outset of his revolutionary career at Tiflis he opposed drafting workingmen into his Committee. As a "practico"—that is, as a political empiricist—he reacted with indifference, and subsequently with contempt, toward the émigrés, toward the "foreign center." Devoid of personal qualifications for directly influencing the masses, he clung with redoubled tenacity to the political machine. The axis of his universe was his Committee—the Tiflis, the Baku, the Caucasian, before it became the Central Committee. In time to come his blind loyalty to the Party machine was to develop with extraordinary force; the committeeman became the super-machine man, the Party's General Secretary, the very personification of the bureaucracy and its peerless leader.

In this connection it is rather tempting to draw the inference that future Stalinism was already rooted in Bolshevik centralism or, more sweepingly, in the underground hierarchy of professional revolutionists. But upon analysis that inference crumbles to dust, disclosing an astounding paucity of historical content. Of course, there are dangers of one kind or another in the very process of stringently picking and choosing persons of advanced views and welding them into a tightly centralized organization. But the roots of such dangers will never be found in the so-called "principle" of centralism; rather they should be sought in the lack of homogeneity and the backwardness of the toilers—that is, in the general social conditions which make imperative that very centripetal leadership of the class by its vanguard. The key to the dynamic problem of leadership is in the actual interrelationships between the political machine and its party, between the vanguard and its class, between centralism and democracy. Those interrelationships cannot, of their nature, be established *a priori* and remain immutable. They are dependent on concrete historical conditions; their mobile balance is regulated by the vital struggle of tendencies, which, as represented by their extreme wings, oscillate between the despotism of the political machine and the impotence of phrasemongering.

In the pamphlet, "Our Political Problems," written by me in 1904, which contains not a little that is immature and erroneous in my criticism of Lenin, there are, however, pages which present a fairly accurate characterization of the cast of thought of the "committeemen" of those days, who "have foregone the need to rely upon the workers after they had found support in the 'principles' of centralism." The fight Lenin was obliged to wage the following year at the Congress against the high and mighty "committeemen" completely confirmed the justice of my criticism. "The debates assumed a more passionate character," recounts Lyadov, one of the delegates. "There began to emerge definite groupings into theoreticians and practicos, 'literaries' and committeemen . . . In the course of these disputes the rather youngish worker Rykov came most prominently to the forefront. He succeeded in grouping around himself a majority of the committeemen." Lyadov's sympathies were with Rykov. "I could not contain myself," Lenin exclaimed in his concluding remarks, "when I heard it said that there were no workingmen fit for committee membership." Let us recall how insistently Koba had challenged the Tiflis workingmen to acknowledge—"placing your hand on your heart"—that among them there were none fit for taking the holy orders of the priestly caste. "The question is being put off," Lenin persisted. "There is evidently an illness in the Party." That illness was the high-handedness of the political machine, the beginning of bureaucracy.

Lenin understood better than anyone else the need for a centralized organization; but he saw in it, above all, a lever for enhancing the activity of the advanced workingmen. The idea of making a fetish of the political machine was not only alien but repugnant to his nature. At the Congress he spotted the caste tendency of the committeemen at once and opened an impassioned fight against it. "Vladimir Ilyich was very much excited," confirms Krupskaya, "and the committeemen were very much excited." On that occasion the victory was with the committeemen, whose leader was Rykov, Lenin's future successor in the post of Chairman of the Council of People's Commissars. Lenin's resolution, proposing that each Committee should necessarily contain a majority of workingmen, failed to pass. Again against the will of Lenin, the committeemen resolved to place the editorial board abroad under the control of the Central Committee. A year earlier Lenin would have chosen to split rather than consent to have the direction of the Party dependent upon the Russian Center, which was subjected to raids by the police and was, therefore, unstable in its composition. But now he firmly reckoned that the decisive word would be his. Having grown strong in his fight against the old authoritative leaders of the Russian

Social-Democracy, he felt much more self-confident than at the Second Congress and, therefore, calmer. If, as Krupskaya states, he was indeed "excited" during the debates or rather, seemed excited, he was all the more circumspect about the organizational steps he undertook. He not only accepted his defeat on two exceedingly important questions in silence, but even helped to include Rykov in the Central Committee. He did not doubt for a moment that the Revolution, that great teacher of the masses in matters of initiative and enterprise, would be able, simultaneously and without great difficulty, to demolish the youthful and as yet unstable conservatism of the Party's political machine.

In addition to Lenin, to the Central Committee were elected the engineer Leonid Krassin and the naturalist, physician and philosopher A. A. Bogdanov, both coevals of Lenin; Postolovsky, who soon after abandoned the Party, and Rykov. The alternates were the "literary," Rumyantsev and the two practicos Gussev and Bour. Needless to say, no one thought of proposing Koba for the first Bolshevik Central Committee.

In 1934, the Congress of the Communist Party of Georgia, using as a basis Beriya's report, declared that "nothing so far written reflects the real and authentic role of Comrade Stalin, who had actually led the struggle of the Bolsheviks in the Caucasus for a good many years." How that happened, the Congress did not explain. But all the old memoirists and historians were forthwith proscribed, and some of them were eventually shot. Then, to correct all the iniquities of the past, it was decided to establish a special "Stalin Institute." With that was launched a sweeping purge of all the old parchments, which were instanter covered with new characters. Never before under the vault of heaven had there been such large-scale invention of falsehoods. Yet, the situation of the biographer is not utterly hopeless.

[We know that] Koba returned from exile to Tiflis in February, 1904, always invariably and triumphantly "directing the activity of the Bolsheviks." With the exception of brief departures, he spent the major part of the years 1904 and 1905 at Tiflis. According to the latest memoirs, the workers were wont to say, "Koba is skinning the Mensheviks alive." Yet it would seem that the Georgian Mensheviks hardly suffered from that surgical operation. It was only as late as the latter half of 1905 that the Tiflis Bolsheviks entered the "period of lining up together" and "considered" issuing news sheets. What then was the nature of the organization to which Koba belonged during most of 1904 and during the first half of 1905? If he did not stay out of the labor movement altogether, which is unlikely, everything we have heard from Beriya notwithstanding, he must have been a member of the Menshevik organization. By the beginning of 1906 the number of Lenin's followers at Tiflis had increased to three hundred. But the Mensheviks numbered about three thousand. The mere correlation of forces doomed Koba to literary opposition at the very climax of revolutionary development.

"Two years (1905-1907) of revolutionary work among the workers of the oil industry," Stalin testifies, "hardened me." It is decidedly improbable that in a painstakingly edited and re-edited text of his own speech the orator merely happened to be muddled as to where exactly he had been during the year when the nation underwent its revolutionary baptism by fire, as well as the following year, 1906, when the entire country was still in the throes of convulsions and was living in constant apprehension of the dénouement. Such events cannot be forgotten! It is impossible to be rid of the impression that Stalin deliberately avoided mention of the First Revolution because he simply had nothing at all to say about it. Since Baku conjured a more heroic background than Tiflis, he retrospectively moved himself to Baku two and a half years earlier than he had a right to. True, he has no reason to fear objections by Soviet historians. Yet the question, "What did Koba really do in 1905?" remains unanswered.

The first year of the Revolution opened with the shooting of the Petersburg workers who had marched with a petition to the Tsar. The appeal written by Koba on the occasion of the events of January the twenty-second is crowned with this adjuration:

> Let us hold out our hands to each other and rally around our Party's committees. We must not forget even for a minute that only the Party committees can worthily lead us, only they will light our way to the Promised Land . . .

and the like. What self-assurance in the voice of this "committeeman"! During those very days, or perchance hours, in far-off Geneva, Lenin was writing into an article by one of his collaborators the following adjuration to the insurgent masses:

> Make way for the anger and hatred that have accumulated in your hearts throughout the centuries of exploitation, suffering and grief!

All of Lenin is in that phrase. He hates and rebels together with the masses, feels the rebellion in his bones, and does not ask of those in revolt that they act only with the permission of the "committees." The contrast between these two personalities in their attitude toward the one thing that united them polit-ically—toward the Revolution—could not be expressed more concisely or more cogently.

The establishment of the Soviets[4] began five months after the Third Congress, at which no place had been found for Koba. The initiative was that of the Men-sheviks, who, however, had never dreamed whither their handiwork would lead. The Menshevik faction predominated in the Soviets. The rank and file Mensheviks were carried away by the revolutionary developments; the leaders mused in perplexity over the sudden leftward swing of their own faction. The Petersburg Committee of the Bolsheviks was frightened at first by such an innovation as a non-partisan representation of the embattled masses, and could find nothing better to do than to present the Soviet with an ultimatum: imme-diately adopt a Social-Democratic program or disband. The Petersburg Soviet

[4] See Glossary.

as a whole, including the contingent of Bolshevik workingmen as well, ignored this ultimatum without batting an eyelash. Only after Lenin's arrival in November did a radical turn take place in the policy of the "committeemen" toward the Soviet. But the ultimatum had wreaked its havoc by decidedly weakening the Bolshevik position. On that issue, as on the others, the provinces followed the lead of the capital. By that time the profound differences of opinion in the estimation of the historical significance of the Soviets had already begun. The Mensheviks attempted to evaluate the Soviet as no more than a fortuitous form of labor representation—a "proletarian parliament," an "organ of revolutionary self-administration," and the like. All of that was exceedingly vague. Lenin, on the contrary, knew how to eavesdrop thoroughly on the Petersburg masses who called the Soviet "the proletarian government," and at once evaluated that new form of organization as the lever of the struggle for power.

In the writings of Koba for the year 1905, sparse in both form and content, we find nothing at all about the Soviets. This is not only because there were not any in Georgia, but because he simply did not pay any attention to them, passed them by. Is it not astounding? The Soviet as a powerful political machine should have impressed the future General Secretary at first glance. But he regarded it as an *alien* political machine which directly represented the masses. The Soviet did not submit to the discipline of the Committee, requiring more complex and more resilient methods of leadership. In a certain sense, the Soviet was a mighty competitor of the Committee. So, during the Revolution of 1905, Koba stood with his back to the Soviets. Essentially, he stood with his back to the Revolution itself, as though taking umbrage at it.

The reason for his resentment was his inability to see his own way to the Revolution. Muscovite biographers and artists constantly endeavor to represent Koba at the head of one or another demonstration, "as a target," as a fiery orator, as a tribune. All of that is a lie. Even in his later years Stalin did not become an orator; no one ever heard him deliver "fiery" speeches. Throughout 1917, when all the agitators of the Party, beginning with Lenin, went around with cracked voices, Stalin did not address any public meetings at all. It could not have been otherwise in 1905. Koba was not even an orator on the modest scale that other young Caucasian revolutionists were; such as, Knunyants, Zurabov, Kamenev, Tseretelli. At a closed session of the Party he was able to expound fairly well thoughts he had firmly made his own. But there was nothing of the agitator in him. He would force himself to utter sentences with great difficulty, without tonality, without warmth, without emphasis. The organic weakness of his nature, the reverse side of his strength, consisted in his complete inability to catch fire, to rise above the humdrum level of trivialities, to conjure a vital bond between himself and his audience, to arouse in an audience its better self. Unable to catch fire himself, he was incapable of inflaming others. Cold spite is not enough for mastering the soul of the masses.

1905 unsealed the lips of all. The country that had been silent for a thousand years began to speak for the first time. Anyone who was at all capable of expressing his detestation of the bureaucracy and of the Tsar found tireless and grateful listeners. Undoubtedly, Koba, too, tried himself out. But comparison with other extempore orators proved altogether too disadvantageous to him. He could not bear that. Although insensitive to the feelings of others, Koba is extremely easily hurt, exceedingly sensitive about his own feelings, and, although it may seem startling, he is moody to the point of capriciousness. His reactions are primitive. Whenever he feels himself ignored or neglected, he is inclined to turn his back upon developments as well as upon people, creep into a corner, moodily pull on his pipe and dream of revenge. That was why in 1905 he walked into the shadows with hidden resentment and became something in the nature of an editor.

But Koba was far from a born journalist. His thinking is too slow, his associations too single-tracked, his style too plodding and barren. When he desires to produce a forceful effect he resorts to vile expressions. Not a single one of the articles he then wrote would have been accepted by an editorial board in the slightest degree thoughtful or exacting. True enough, underground publications were not, as a rule, notable for their literary excellence, since they were, for the most part, written by people who took to the pen of necessity and not because it was their calling. Koba, at any rate, did not rise above that level. His writing revealed an attempt to attain a systematic exposition of the theme; but that effort usually expressed itself in schematic arrangement of material, the enumeration of arguments, artificial rhetorical questions, and in unwieldy repetitions heavily on the didactic side. The absence of his own thought, of original form, of vivid imagery—these mark every line of his with the brand of banality. Here is an author who never freely expresses his own thoughts, but diffidently restates the thoughts of others. The word "diffidently" may seem startling when applied to Stalin; it nevertheless characterizes his groping manner as a writer most adequately, from his Caucasian period to this very day.

It would, of course, be erroneous to assume that such articles did not lead to action. There was great need for them. They answered a pressing demand. They drew their strength from that need, for they expressed the ideas and slogans of the Revolution. To the mass reader, who could not find anything of the kind in the bourgeois press, they were new and fresh. But their passing influence was limited to the circle for which they were written. Now it is impossible to read these dryly, clumsily, and not always grammatically, formulated phrases, startlingly decorated with the paper flowers of rhetoric, without a sense of constraint, embarrassment, annoyance, and at times laughter over lapses into unconscious humor. And no wonder: even at that time no one looked upon Koba as a journalist. All the Bolshevik writers, prominent and obscure, from the capital and from the provinces, contributed to the first legal Bolshevik daily newspaper *Novaya Zhizn* (New Life), which began publication in October, 1905, at Petersburg under Lenin's guidance. Yet Stalin's name is not among them. It was Kamenev, not Stalin, who was called upon to represent the

Caucasus on that newspaper in an editorial capacity. Koba was no born writer and never became a writer. That he plied the pen with greater than usual diligence in 1905 merely emphasizes the fact that the alternate method of communicating with the masses was even less native to him.

Many of the committeemen proved themselves not big enough for the period of endless meetings, of stormy strikes, of street demonstrations. Revolutionists must harangue crowds in the public square, must write on the spur of the moment, make grave decisions instantaneously. Neither the first nor the second nor the third is a gift of Stalin's: his voice is as weak as his imagination; the gift of improvisation is alien to this plodding thinker, who ever gropes his way. Far brighter luminaries outshone him on the Caucasian firmament. He watched the Revolution with envious alarm, and almost with hostility: it was not his element. "Right along," writes Yenukidze, "in addition to going to meetings and attending to a lot of business in the Party locals, he sat in his little cubbyhole filled with books and newspapers or in the similarly 'roomy' editorial office of the Bolshevik newspaper." One need but visualize for a moment the maelstrom of "the mad year" and recall the grandeur of its pathos, in order fully to appreciate this portrait of a lonely and ambitious young man, who buried himself, pen in hand, in a tiny room—which most likely was not any too neat, either—bound on the fruitless quest of the unyielding phrase that might in some small measure be in tune with the epoch.

Developments followed upon developments. Koba remained on the sidelines, dissatisfied with everybody and with himself. All the prominent Bolsheviks, among them many who in those years were the leaders of the movement in the Caucasus—Krassin, Postolovsky, Stopani, Lehman, Halperin, Kamenev, Taratuta, and others—passed Stalin by, did not mention him in their memoirs, and he himself has nothing to say about them. Some, like Kurnatovsky and Kamenev, undoubtedly came in contact with him in the course of their revolutionary activities. Others might have met him, but did not deem him different from the average run of "committeemen." Not one of them singled him out with so much as a word of appreciation or fellow-feeling, nor did any of them give the future official biographers the slenderest foothold in the way of a sympathetic reference.

In 1926 the official commission on Party history issued a revised edition—that is, one adapted to the new post-Leninist tendency—of source materials about the year 1905. Of the more than a hundred documents nearly thirty were Lenin's articles; there were approximately as many articles by various other authors. Despite the fact that the campaign against Trotskyism was already approaching its paroxysm of rage, the editorial board of true believers could not avoid including in the anthology four of my articles. Yet throughout the four hundred and fifty-five pages there was not a single line by Stalin. In the alphabetical index, which included several hundred names, listing anyone at all who was in the slightest way prominent during the revolutionary years, Stalin's name did not appear even once; only Ivanovich is mentioned as one who had attended the Tammerfors Conference of the Party in December, 1905. Remarkable is the fact that as recently as 1926 the editorial board was still ignorant of the fact that Ivanovich and Stalin were one and the same person. These impartial details are far more convincing than all the retrospective panegyrics.

Stalin seems to stand apart from the revolutionary year, 1905. His "pupilage" had come during the pre-revolutionary years, which he spent at Tiflis, Batum and subsequently in prison and exile. According to his own avowal, he had turned "apprentice" at Baku—that is, in 1907-1908. The period of the First Revolution is thus totally eliminated as a training period in the development of the future "craftsman." Whenever he waxes autobiographic, Stalin does not mention that great year, which brought out into the world and molded the most distinguished revolutionary leaders of the older generation. That should be firmly kept in mind, for it is far from accidental. In his autobiography, the very next revolutionary year, 1917, was to become almost as misty a spot as 1905. Again we shall find Koba, now become Stalin, in an unpretentious editorial office, this time of the Petersburg *Pravda*, unhurriedly writing dull comments on brilliant events. Here is a revolutionist so constituted that a real revolution of the masses upsets him by throwing him out of his rut and kicks him aside. Never a tribune, never the strategist or leader of a rebellion, he has ever been only a bureaucrat of revolution. That was why, in order to find full play for his peculiar talents, he was condemned to bide his time in a semi-comatose condition until the revolution's raging torrents had subsided.

The split into the *Majority* and *Minority* had been ratified at the Third Congress, which declared the Mensheviks "a seceded portion of the Party." The Party was in a state of utter disunion, when the developments transpiring in the autumn of 1905 exerted their beneficent pressure and somewhat softened factional hostility. On the eve of his long-awaited departure from exile in Switzerland to revolutionary Russia in October of that year, Lenin wrote Plekhanov a warm and conciliatory letter, in which he referred to his erstwhile teacher and opponent as "the finest influence among Russian Social-Democrats" and appealed to him for co-operation, declaring, "Our tactical differences of opinion are being swept aside at an astounding rate by the revolution itself . . ." That was true. But not for long, because the revolution itself did not long endure.

There is no doubt that in the beginning the Mensheviks were more resourceful than the Bolsheviks in establishing and utilizing mass organizations. But as a political party they merely floated with the current and almost drowned in it. The Bolsheviks, on the other hand, adjusted themselves more slowly to the sweep of the movement. But they enriched it with their ringing slogans—the product of their realistic estimation of the Revolution's forces. The Mensheviks were preponderant in the Soviet; yet the general direction of the Soviet's policy proceeded in the main along Bolshevik lines. Opportunists to the very marrow of their bones, the Mensheviks were temporarily able to adapt themselves even to the revolutionary upsurge; yet they were incapable either of guiding it or of remaining faithful to its historic tasks during the Revolution's ebb-tide.

After the October General Strike—which snatched the constitutional manifesto from the Tsar, while generating in the workers' districts a mood of optimism and daring—unification tendencies assumed irresistible force in both factions. Unifying or federative committees of Bolsheviks and Mensheviks sprang up in all sorts of places. The leaders succumbed to this tendency. As a step toward complete fusion, each faction convoked its preliminary conference. The Mensheviks convened at Petersburg toward the end of November. In that city the new-fangled "liberties" were still respected. But the Bolsheviks met in December, when the reaction was already in full swing, and they were therefore obliged to hold their conclave on Finnish soil, at Tammerfors.

Initially the Bolshevik conference was conceived as an extraordinary congress of the Party. But the railway strike, the uprising in Moscow and a number of other exceptional developments in the provinces made it imperative for many delegates to remain at home, rendering the representation exceedingly unrepresentative. The forty-one delegates that arrived represented twenty-six organizations with a total voting strength of approximately four thousand. The figure seems insignificant for a revolutionary party contemplating the overthrow of Tsarism and the assumption of its place in the impending revolutionary government. Yet these four thousand had already learned to express the will of hundreds of thousands. Still, because of its numerical inadequacy, the congress transformed itself into a mere conference. Koba, using the pseudonym Ivanovich, and the workingman, Teliya, came as representatives of the Transcaucasian Bolshevik organizations. The stirring events then transpiring in Tiflis did not deter Koba from abandoning his editorial office.

The minutes of the Tammerfors discussions, which proceeded while Moscow was being cannonaded, have not yet been found. The memory of the delegates, overwhelmed by the grandeur of the events then taking place, has retained very little. "What a pity that the minutes of that conference have not been preserved," Krupskaya wrote thirty years later. "It was such an enthusiastic gathering! It took place at the very climax of the Revolution, when every comrade was spoiling for a fight. They practiced shooting between sessions . . . None of the delegates at the conference could have forgotten that. There were Lozovsky, Baransky, Yaroslovsky, and many others. I remember these comrades because their reports of local conditions were exceptionally interesting." Krupskaya did not name Ivanovich: she did not remember him. In the memoirs of Gorev, a member of the conference's praesidium, we read in part: "Among the delegates were Sverdlov, Lozovsky, Stalin, Nevsky and others." Not devoid of interest is the order of these names. It is also known that Ivanovich, who spoke in favor of boycotting the elections to the State Duma, was chosen a member of the committee concerned with that question.

The waves of the surf still beat so high that even the Mensheviks, frightened by their own recent opportunistic mistakes, did not dare to place both their feet on the uncertain board of parliamentarism. In the interests of agitation they proposed to take part only in the preliminary stage of the elections, but not to take their seats in the Duma. The predominant mood among the Bolsheviks was for an "active boycott." In his own peculiar way Stalin described Lenin's position of those days at the unpretentious celebration of Lenin's fiftieth birthday in 1920, as follows:

> I remember how that giant, Lenin, twice admitted the errors of his ways. The first episode was in Finland, in 1905, in December, at the All-Russian Bolshevik Conference. At that time the question was posed concerning the advisability to boycott the Witte Duma[5] . . . The discussion opened, the attack was begun by the provincials, the Siberians, the Caucasians. But what was our surprise, when at the end of our speeches, Lenin stepped forward and declared that he had been in favor of participating in the elections, but that now he saw that he had been mistaken and was ready to support our faction. We were amazed. That produced the impression of an electric shock. We gave him a thunderous ovation.

No one else mentioned that "electric shock" nor the "thunderous ovation" given by fifty pairs of hands. It is nevertheless possible that Stalin's version of the

[5] On October 30, 1905, on the initiative of S. Y. Witte, the Tsarist Government issued a manifesto (popularly known from its old style date as the "Manifesto of the Seventeenth of October"), which, in addition to granting formally a democratic franchise and the fundamental civil liberties, enunciated the principle that no law could henceforth be promulgated in Russia without the consent of the Duma. That virtual capitulation of the autocracy, instigated by Witte, was a maneuver for winning the Liberal groups to the side of the Government and gaining their support against the imminent revolution. Witte was appointed Prime Minister and granted the privilege of choosing his cabinet even from among Oppositionist groupings. It was thus during his administration that the elections to the First Duma took place in March, 1906. At the polls the autocracy sustained a crushing defeat, for, while the Government parties secured but a handful of seats, the majority of the Duma consisted of Opposition deputies, with the Constitutional Democrats (popularly known as the Kadets), led by the prominent Zemstvo leader I. I. Petrunkevich, as the strongest party in the Duma. Whereupon the Tsar dismissed Witte and replaced him with the reactionary and obedient Goremykin. The First Duma was opened by the Tsar on May 10 and was dissolved by his ukase on July 21, with the agrarian problem as the chief bone of contention between the Government and the Opposition. The stormy debates were around a bill, sponsored by the Kadets, which provided for the expropriation of large estates, with compensation to the owners, and distribution of the expropriated lands among the peasants. Having catered to the nobility by dissolving this Duma, Nicholas II made a concession to the Liberals by dismissing Goremykin and appointing Stolypin Prime Minister. The "Witte Duma" was thus the First Duma, which Witte had initiated but which he was denied the opportunity either to guide or to manage.

The Second Duma, elections to which were not boycotted by the Socialist parties, was even more strongly Oppositionist than the First, with a stronger Left Wing (180 Socialists, including the Bolsheviks, as against 85 moderate Laborites in the First Duma), and its conflict with the Government was even sharper than that of the First Duma. Its climax came when the Government charged 55 Socialist deputies with a plot against the Tsar, who forthwith dissolved the Second Duma June 15, 1907, after a three-months session that had begun on March 5.

The Third Duma opened November 14, 1907, after the Government had meantime so altered the electoral law that it secured a majority of reactionary and conservative deputies, with the Liberals and Socialists in a minority. That Duma sat through its legal tenure of office until 1912. It was followed the same year by the Fourth Duma, which continued until 1917.—C. M.

occurrence is substantially correct. In those days Bolshevik "firmness" had not yet become associated with tactical resilience, especially among the "practico," who were devoid of both background and mental outlook. Lenin himself might have wavered; the pressure of the provincials might have seemed to him the pressure of the revolutionary elements themselves. But regardless of whether it was so or not, the conference resolved "to attempt to undermine this police Duma, rejecting all participation in it." The only strange thing about it is that Stalin in 1920 continued to see Lenin's "mistake" in his initial readiness to take part in the elections; by that time Lenin himself had come to acknowledge his yielding in favor of the boycott as his real mistake.

Concerning Ivanovich's participation in the debates on the question of boycotting the Duma elections, there is the colorful tale of a certain Dmitrievsky, which seems to be a pure and simple fabrication. He writes:

> Stalin was at first excited. This was the first time he spoke before a meeting of the Party's leading group. This was the first time he spoke before Lenin. But Lenin regarded him with interested eyes, nodding his head approvingly. Stalin's voice grew stronger. When he finished, everybody approved of him. His point of view was accepted.

Whence this information of the author, who had nothing at all to do with the conference? Dmitrievsky is a former Soviet diplomat, a chauvinist and anti-Semite, who temporarily joined Stalin's faction during its struggle against Trotskyism and later, while abroad, deserted to the camp of the Right Wing of the White emigration. It is significant that even as a functioning outright Fascist Dmitrievsky continues to regard Stalin highly, to detest all of his opponents, and to repeat all the legends of the Kremlin. But let us hear more of his tale. After the session at which the boycott of the Duma was considered, Lenin and Stalin

> together walked out of the People's House, where the conference was being held. It was cold. A sharp wind blew. For a long time they continued to walk through the streets of Tammerfors. Lenin was interested in that man, who he had heard was one of the most resolute and hard-headed revolutionists of Transcaucasia. He wanted to take a good look at him at close range. Attentively, for a long time and in great detail he questioned him about his work, about his life, about the people he had met, about the books he had read. From time to time, Lenin would drop brief comments . . . and their tone was satisfactory, approving. That man was precisely the kind he needed.

Dmitrievsky was not at Tammerfors, he could not have eavesdropped on Lenin's conversation with Stalin in the street at night and, as is evident from his book, he had never talked with Stalin himself, to whose authority he does not refer. Yet in that story of his one senses something vivid and . . . familiar. After some tugs on my memory, I realized that Dmitrievsky had simply adapted to the Finnish climate my own account of my first meeting with Lenin and of our walk in the streets of London in the autumn of 1902. Folklore is rich with the transposition of brilliant episodes from one mythological person to another. The bureaucracy pursues the very same methods in creating its own myths.

Koba was exactly twenty-six years old when he finally pecked his way out of his provincial shell and emerged into the orbit of the Party as a whole. True, that emergence of his was hardly noticed, and seven additional years were to pass before he became a Central Committee member. The Tammerfors conference was nonetheless an important milestone in his life. He visited Petersburg, met the staff of the Party, observed its mechanism, compared himself with other delegates, took part in discussions, was elected to a committee and (as his official biography has it) "definitely connected himself with Lenin." To our regret, very little is known about all of that.

It was possible to convene the unification congress only in April of 1906, at Stockholm. By that time the Petersburg Soviet had been arrested, the Moscow uprising crushed, the Juggernaut of repression had rolled over the entire country. The Mensheviks scattered to the Right. Plekhanov expressed their state of mind in his winged phrase, "We should not have taken up arms!" The Bolsheviks continued to hold true to their course of insurrection. Over the bones of the revolution, the Tsar was convoking the First Duma, in which, from the very beginning of the elections, the victory of the Liberals over the frank monarchical reaction was clearly apparent. The Mensheviks, who a mere few weeks back had stood for a semi-boycott of the Duma, now transferred their hopes from the revolutionary struggle to constitutional conquests. At the time of the Stockholm Congress, the support of the Liberals seemed to them the most important task of the Social-Democracy. The Bolsheviks awaited the further development of the peasant uprisings, which were expected to help the proletarian struggle to resume the offensive, at the same time sweeping aside the Tsarist Duma. Counterposing the Mensheviks, they continued to support the boycott. As always after a defeat, the differences of opinion at once assumed an acute character. It was under such bad auspices that the unifying Congress began its session.

The number of voting delegates at the Congress was 113, consisting of 62 Mensheviks and 42 Bolsheviks. Since theoretically each delegate represented 300 organized Social-Democrats, it might be said that the entire Party had about 34,000 members, of whom 19,000 were Mensheviks and 14,000 Bolsheviks. Considering the vehemence of electioneering, these figures are undoubtedly considerably exaggerated. In any event, at the time the Congress convened the Party was no longer growing, but shrinking. Of the 113 delegates, Tiflis had eleven. Of these eleven, ten were Mensheviks, one was a Bolshevik. That single Bolshevik was Koba, under the pseudonym of Ivanovich. The relationship of forces is herewith expressed in the exact terminology of plain arithmetic. Beriya had the temerity to state that "under the leadership of Stalin" the Caucasian Bolsheviks had isolated the Mensheviks from the masses. These figures hardly bear him out. And besides, the closely-knit Caucasian Mensheviks played a tremendous role in their own fraction[6] at the Congress.

[6] See Glossary.

Ivanovich's rather active participation in the work of the Congress was recorded in the minutes. Yet unless one knew while reading the record that Ivanovich was Stalin, one would not pay the slightest heed to his speeches and remarks. As recently as ten years ago no one quoted those speeches, and even Party historians had not noticed the circumstance that Ivanovich and the General Secretary of the Party were one and the same person. Ivanovich was placed on one of the technical committees set up to find out how the delegates had been elected to the Congress. For all its insignificance, that appointment was symptomatic: Koba was quite in his element when it came to machine technicalities. Incidentally, the Mensheviks twice accused him of lying in the course of his report. It is impossible to vouch for the objectivity of the accusers themselves. Yet it is likewise impossible not to note again that such incidents were always connected with Koba's name.

At the heart of the Congress's business was the agrarian question. The peasant movement had caught the Party virtually napping. The old agrarian program, which had made almost no encroachments on the large land holdings, simply collapsed. Confiscation of the lands of the landed gentry became imminent. The Mensheviks were fighting for the program of "municipalization"—that is, the transference of the land into the hands of the democratic organs of local self-administration. Lenin stood for nationalization, on condition of the passing of all power to the people. Plekhanov, the chief theoretician of Menshevism, recommended not trusting the future central government and not arming it with the land funds of the country. "That republic," said he, "of which Lenin has dreamed, once established would not maintain itself forever. We cannot proceed on the basis that in the near future there will be established in Russia the same sort of democratic order as in Switzerland, in England or in the United States. Considering the possibilities of restoration, nationalization is dangerous . . ." This is how circumspect and modest were the expectations of the founder of Russian Marxism! In his opinion, the transference of land into the hands of the State would have been admissible only in the event that the State itself belonged to the workers. ". . . The seizure of power is compulsory for us," Plekhanov was saying, "when we are making a proletarian revolution. But since the revolution now impending can be only petty bourgeois, we are duty-bound to refuse to seize power." Plekhanov subordinated the question of the struggle for power—and that was the Achilles' heel of his entire doctrinaire strategy—to the *a priori* sociological definition, or rather, nomenclature, of the revolution, and not to the real interrelationship of its inherent forces.

Lenin fought for the seizure of the land of the landed gentry by revolutionary peasant committees and for the sanction of that seizure by the constituent assembly through a law on nationalization. "My agrarian program," he wrote and said, "is entirely a program of peasant insurrection and the complete fulfillment of the bourgeois democratic revolution." On the basic point he remained in agreement with Plekhanov: the Revolution would not only begin, but would also culminate, as a bourgeois revolution. The leader of Bolshevism not only considered Russia unable to establish Socialism independently—it had not even entered anyone's head to pose that question prior to 1924—but he believed that it was impossible to retain even the forthcoming *democratic* conquests in Russia without a Socialist revolution in the West. It was at that very Stockholm Congress that he expressed this view most unequivocally. "The Russian (bourgeois democratic) Revolution can win with its own forces," he said, "but under no circumstances can it retain and strengthen its conquests with its own hand. It cannot attain that unless there is a Socialist upheaval in the West." It would be erroneous to think that, in tune with Stalin's latter-day interpretation, Lenin had in mind the danger of outside military intervention. No, he spoke of the inevitability of an internal restoration, in consequence of the peasant, as a petty proprietor, turning against the revolution after the agrarian upheaval. "Restoration is equally inescapable in the event of municipalization or nationalization or land division, because the petty little proprietor, under any and all forms of possession and ownership, remains the mainstay of the restoration. After the complete victory of the democratic revolution," Lenin insisted, "the petty little proprietor will inevitably turn against the proletariat, and the sooner the common enemy of the proletariat and the petty proprietor will be overthrown, the sooner will he turn . . . Our democratic revolution has no reserve force other than the Socialist proletariat in the West."

But to Lenin, who placed the fate of Russian Democracy in direct dependence on the fate of European Socialism, the so-called "final aim" was not separated from the democratic upheaval by some boundless historical epoch. As early as during the period of the struggle for democracy, he aspired to marshal the points of support for the swiftest advancement toward the Socialist goal. The sense of land nationalization lay in the fact that it opened a window into the future: "In the epoch of the democratic revolution and the peasant uprising," he said, "one cannot limit oneself to mere confiscation of the land of the landed gentry. It is necessary to go beyond that—to strike the fatal blow at the private ownership of land, in order to clear the way for the further struggle for Socialism."

Ivanovich disagreed with Lenin on this crucial question of the Revolution. At this congress he expressed himself resolutely against nationalization and in favor of distributing the confiscated lands among the peasants. To this very day few people in the Soviet Union know of this difference of opinion, which is fully recorded on the pages of the minutes, because no one is permitted either to quote, or to comment upon, Ivanovich's speech during the debate on the agrarian program. Yet, surely it is worthy of notice. "Since we are concluding a temporary revolutionary union with the struggling peasantry," Stalin said, "since we cannot on that account ignore the demands of that peasantry, we must support those demands, if, as a whole and in general, they do not conflict with the tendencies of economic development and with the progress of the revolution. The peasants demand division; division is not inconsistent with the above-mentioned phenomena (?); therefore, we must support complete confiscation and division. From that point of view, both nationalization and municipalization are equally unacceptable." [Years later] Stalin [was to say] that in Tammerfors Lenin had delivered an insuperable speech on the agrarian question which had evoked general enthusiasm [without revealing that] he had not only spoken against Lenin's agrarian program, but had declared it "equally" unacceptable with Plekhanov's. [Moreover, in 1924, he pretended to have been strongly impressed by it in 1906.]

In the first place, the very fact that a young Caucasian who did not know Russia at all dared to come out so uncompromisingly against the leader of his faction on the agrarian question, in which field Lenin's authority was considered particularly formidable, cannot but evoke surprise. The cautious Koba, as a rule, did not relish either stepping on unfamiliar ice or remaining in a minority. He usually engaged in debate only when he felt that the majority was behind him, or, as in later years, when the machine assured his victory, irrespective of the majority. All the more compelling should have been the motives that induced him to speak on that occasion in defense of the not so popular land division. These motives, insofar as it is possible to decipher them some thirty odd years later, were two, and both of them very characteristic of Stalin.

Koba came to revolution as a plebeian democrat, a provincial and an empiricist. Lenin's ideas about the international nature of the revolution were both remote and alien to him. He sought "guarantees" closer at hand. The individualistic approach to land ownership asserted itself more acutely and found a far more spontaneous expression among the Georgian than among the Russian peasants, because the former had no direct experience with communal land holdings. Wherefore the peasant's son from the village of Didi-Lilo decided that investing these small proprietors with additional parcels of land would be the most reliable guarantee against counter-revolution. It is thus clear that in his case "divisionism" was no doctrinaire conviction—he was, indeed, inclined to reject convictions derived from doctrines with the greatest of ease—but rather his organic program, in perfect harmony with the most fundamental inclinations of his nature, his upbringing, his social milieu. Indeed, twenty years later we shall rediscover in him an atavistic reversion to "divisionism."

Almost as unmistakable seems Koba's second motive. In his eyes, Lenin's prestige was decidedly lowered by the December defeat: he always attached greater significance to the fact than to the idea. At this congress Lenin was in a minority. Koba could not win with Lenin. That alone considerably diminished his interest in the nationalization program. Both the Bolsheviks and the Mensheviks looked upon division as the lesser evil by comparison with the program of the opposing faction. Koba had therefore reason to hope that the majority of the congress would in the final reckoning come to terms on the lesser evil. Thus, the organic inclinations of the radical democrat coincided with the tactical calculations of the schemer. But Koba figured wrongly: the Mensheviks had a good majority, so there was no need for them to choose the lesser when they preferred the greater evil.

It is important to note for future reference that during the Stockholm Congress, following in Lenin's footsteps, Stalin regarded the union of the proletariat with the peasantry as "temporary," that is, limited merely to common democratic tasks. It did not even occur to him to maintain that the peasantry as such could ever become an ally of the proletariat in the cause of the Socialist revolution. Twenty years later that "disbelief" in the peasantry was to be proclaimed as the principal heresy of "Trotskyism." Indeed, much was to reappear in an altered aspect twenty years later. Declaring the agrarian program of the Mensheviks and the Bolsheviks "equally unacceptable" in 1906, Stalin deemed land division "not in conflict with the tendencies of economic development." What he really had in mind were the tendencies of capitalistic development. As for the impending socialist revolution, to which he did not devote so much as a single serious thought in those days, he was quite certain that scores of years would elapse before it was likely to come about, and in the interim capitalism's natural laws would perform the task of concentration and proletarianization in the economic structure of the village. Not without reason did Koba refer in his leaflets to the remote Socialist goal with the biblical words, "the Promised Land."

The chief report on behalf of the adherents of division was, of course, not by the virtually unknown Ivanovich, but the more authoritative Bolshevik, Suvorov, who developed the point of view of his group with sufficient amplitude. "It is said that this is a bourgeois measure; but the peasant movement itself is petty bourgeois," Suvorov argued, "and if it is possible for us to support the peasantry, then it must be only in that direction. By comparison with serfdom, the independent economy of the peasants represents a step forward; yet, later it will be outstripped by further developments." The Socialist transformation of society will be able to take its turn only when capitalist development will have "outstripped"—that is, will have ruined and expropriated—the independent farmer created by the bourgeois revolution.

The original author of the land division program was, of course, not Suvorov, but the radical historian Rozhkov, who had joined the Bolsheviks shortly before the revolution. He did not appear as a reporter at the Congress only because he was then in prison. According to Rozhkov's view, which was developed in his polemic against the author of this book, not only Russia, but even the most advanced countries were far from prepared for a socialist revolution. World-wide capitalism still had the prospect of a long epoch of progressive work, the completion of which was lost in the mists of the future. In order to subvert the obstacles in the way of the creative endeavor of Russian capitalism, the most backward of all capitalist systems, the proletariat was bound to pay the price of land division for its union with the peasantry. Capitalism would then make short shrift of such illusions as agrarian leveling by gradually concentrating the land in the hands of the more powerful and progressive landowners. Lenin had named the adherents of this program, which directly preached reliance on the bourgeois farmer, "Rozhkovists," after their leader. It is not superfluous to note that Rozhkov himself, whose attitude was serious in matters of doctrine, passed during the years of reaction to the side of the Mensheviks.

On the first ballot Lenin joined the partisans of division, in order, according to his own explanation "not to break up the votes against municipalization." He regarded the program of division as the lesser evil, adding, however, that although division presented a certain defense against the restoration of the landed gentry and the Tsar, unfortunately it could also create the basis for a Bonapartist dictatorship. He accused the adherents of division of being "one-sided in regarding the peasant movement only from the point of view of the past and the present, without taking into consideration the point of view of the future," of socialism. There was a lot of confusion and not a little of individualism glossed over with mysticism in the peasant view of the land as "God's" or "nobody's;" yet, inherent in that view was a progressive tendency, and it was therefore necessary to discover how to seize upon it and utilize it against the bourgeois social order. The partisans of division did not know how to do that. "The practicos . . . will vulgarize the present program . . . will expand a small error into a large one . . . They will cry to the peasant crowd that the land is nobody's, God's, the government's, will argue for the advantages of division, and in that way they will defame and vulgarize Marxism." On Lenin's lips the word "practicos" signified in this case revolutionists with a narrow outlook, propagandists of the neat little formulae. That blow strikes the nail on the head all the more accurately when we consider that in the course of the next quarter of a century Stalin was to call himself proudly nothing other than a "practico," in distinction from "literaries" and "émigrés." He was to proclaim himself a theoretician only after the political machine secured his practical victory and sheltered him from criticism.

Plekhanov was, of course, right when he placed the agrarian question in unseverable conjunction with the question of power. But Lenin, too, understood the nature of that conjuncture, and rather more deeply than Plekhanov. According to his formulation, in order to make nationalization possible, the revolution must perforce establish "the democratic dictatorship of the proletariat and the peasantry," which he strictly distinguished from the socialistic dictatorship of the proletariat. In distinction from Plekhanov, Lenin thought that the agrarian revolution would be consummated, not by liberal, but by plebeian hands, or it would not be consummated at all. However, the nature of the "democratic dictatorship" he preached remained hazy and paradoxical. According to Lenin, should the representatives of the small property holders obtain a dominant position in a revolutionary government—an unlikely eventuality in a bourgeois revolution occurring in the twentieth century—that very government would threaten to become a tool of reactionary forces. Yet acceptance of the proposition that the proletariat was bound to take possession of the government in the wake of the agrarian revolution removes the fences between the democratic revolution and the socialistic revolution, for the one would naturally pass into the other, the revolution thus becoming "permanent." Lenin had no ready answer for that argument. But needless to say, Koba the "practico" and "divisionist" regarded the perspective of permanent revolution with sovereign contempt.

Arguing against the Mensheviks in defense of the revolutionary peasant committees as instrumentalities for the seizure of the landed gentry's lands, Ivanovich said, "If the liberation of the proletariat can be the act of the proletariat itself, then the liberation of the peasantry can likewise be the act of the peasants themselves." As a matter of fact, that symmetrical formula is a parody on Marxism. The historical mission of the proletariat grows to considerable extent precisely out of the inability of the petty bourgeoisie to liberate itself by means of its own forces. The peasant revolution is impossible, of course, without the active participation of the peasants in the form of armed detachments, local committees, and the like. Yet the fate of the peasant revolution is decided, not in the village, but in the city. A shapeless remnant of medievalism in contemporary society, the peasantry cannot have an independent policy; it needs an outside leader. Two new classes vie for that leadership. Should the peasantry follow the liberal bourgeoisie, the revolution would stop halfway, in order subsequently to roll back. Should the peasantry find its leader in the proletariat, the revolution must inevitably pass beyond bourgeois limits. It was precisely on that peculiar correlation of classes in a historically belated bourgeois society that the perspective of permanent revolution was founded.

No one, however, at the Stockholm Congress defended that perspective, which I again attempted to expound while lodged in a Petersburg prison cell. The uprising had already been repulsed. The revolution was in retreat. The Mensheviks longed for a bloc with the Liberals. The Bolsheviks were in a minority; besides, they were split. The perspective of permanent revolution seemed compromised. It would have to await its return match for eleven years. By a vote of sixty-two against forty-two with seven abstaining, the Congress adopted the Menshevik program of municipalization. That played no role whatsoever in the future course of events. The peasants remained deaf to it, while the Liberals were hostile. In 1917 the peasants accepted land nationalization as they accepted the Soviet Government and the leadership of the Bolsheviks.

Ivanovich's two other speeches at the Congress were no more than a paraphrased digest of Lenin's speeches and articles. On the question of the general political situation, he justly attacked the endeavor of the Mensheviks to abate the movement of the masses by adapting it to the political course of the Liberal bourgeoisie. "Either the hegemony of the proletariat," he reiterated the widespread formula, "or the hegemony of the democratic bourgeoisie—that is how the question stands in the Party, and therein are our differences." But the orator was very far from understanding all the historical implications of that alternative. The "hegemony of the proletariat" means its political supremacy over all the revolutionary forces of the country, and above all, over the peasantry. In the event of the complete victory of the revolution, that "hegemony" must naturally lead to the dictatorship of the proletariat, with all its implied consequences. Yet Ivanovich firmly held on to the view that the Russian Revolution was capable of no more than merely clearing the way for the bourgeois regime. In some incomprehensible way he connected the idea of the proletariat's hegemony with the notion of an independent policy by the peasantry, which would liberate itself by dividing the land into small parcels.

This so-called "unifying" congress did attain the unification of the Party's two main factions as well as of the national organizations—the Social-Democracy of Poland and Lithuania, the Latvian Social-Democracy and the Jewish Bund. The congress thus justified its name. But its real significance, as Lenin put it, was rather in the fact that it "helped to make more distinct the cleavage between the Social-Democracy's Right and Left Wings." If the split at the Second Congress was no more than an "anticipation" and was subsequently overcome, the "unification" at the Stockholm Congress became merely a milestone on the road to the final and definitive split that occurred six years later. Yet during the Congress Lenin was far from thinking that a split was inevitable. The experience of the turbulent months of 1905, when the Mensheviks had made a sharp turn to the left, was altogether too fresh. Despite the fact that thereafter, as Krupskaya writes, they "showed their hand plainly enough," Lenin, according to her testimony, still continued to hope "that the new rise of the revolutionary wave, of which he had no doubt, would overwhelm them and reconcile them to the Bolshevik line." But the new rise of the revolution did not come.

Immediately after the Congress Lenin wrote an appeal to the Party which contained a restrained yet in no way ambiguous criticism of the resolutions adopted. The appeal was signed by delegates from among "the former faction of Bolsheviks," which was considered dissolved on paper. The remarkable thing is that of the forty-two Bolshevik participants of the congress, only twenty-six signed that appeal. Ivanovich's signature is lacking, even as the signature of the leader of his group, Suvorov. Apparently the adherents of division regarded their differences of opinion with Lenin's group so important that they declined to appear jointly with them before the Party, despite the very circumspect formulation of the appeal on the question of land. It would be useless to seek commentaries on that fact in the Party's official publications of today. Yet neither did Lenin refer so much as once to any of Ivanovich's speeches in his extensive printed report about the Stockholm Congress, in which he gave a detailed account of the debates, mentioning all the important speakers, Mensheviks as well as Bolsheviks: evidently Lenin did not deem Ivanovich's speeches as essential to these debates as it has been attempted to represent them thirty years later. Stalin's position inside the Party—outwardly, at any rate—had not altered. No one proposed him for the Central Committee, which was composed of seven Mensheviks and the three Bolsheviks, Krassin, Rykov, and Desnitsky. After the Stockholm Congress, even as prior to it, Koba remained a Party worker of merely "Caucasian caliber."

During the last two months of the revolutionary years the Caucasus was a seething caldron. In December, 1905, the strike committee, having assumed the management of the Transcaucasian railway and telegraph, began to regulate the transport movement and the economic life of Tiflis. The suburbs were in the hands of the armed workers. But not for long. The armed authorities quickly repulsed their enemies. Tiflis Government was declared under martial law. Armed conflicts raged on at Kutais, Chituary and other places. Western Georgia was in the throes of a peasant uprising. On the tenth of December Chief of Police Shirinkin, of the Caucasus, reported to the director of his department at Petersburg: "The Kutais Government is in a state of emergency . . . the gendarmes have been disarmed, the rebels have taken possession of the western sector of the railroad and are themselves selling tickets and looking after public order . . . I have received no reports from Kutais. The gendarmes have been removed from the line and are concentrated in Tiflis. Couriers sent with reports are searched by the revolutionists and their documents confiscated; the situation there is insufferable . . . The Governor-General is ill from nervous exhaustion . . . I shall send details by mail, or, if that is not possible, by courier . . ."

All these developments did not take place of their own free will. The collective initiative of the aroused masses was, of course, chiefly responsible for it; and at every step it had to have individuals as its agents, organizers, leaders. Koba was not among them. Unhurriedly, he commented on the developments after they had transpired. Only that had made it possible for him to go away to Tammerfors during the most stirring of times. No one noticed his absence and no one noticed his return.

Matters were brought to a head by the suppression of the uprising in Moscow. By that time the Petersburg workers, exhausted by preceding battles and lockouts, were already passive. The suppression of rebellions in Transcaucasia, the Transbaltic Region and Siberia came after the pacification of Moscow. Reaction was beginning to come into its own. The Bolsheviks were all the more reluctant to acknowledge this because the surf's belated waves were still running counter to the all-encompassing ebb-tide. All the revolutionary parties were determined to believe that the ninth wave was on the verge of breaking. When some of Lenin's more skeptical followers suggested to him the possibility that the reaction had already set in, he responded, "I'll be the last to admit it!" The pulse beats of the Russian Revolution were still finding their most emphatic expression in labor strikes, ever the basic way of mobilizing the masses. There were two and three quarter million strikers in 1905; nearly a million in 1906: that figure, tremendous in itself, was indicative of acute regression.

According to Koba's explanation, the proletariat had suffered an episodic defeat, "first of all, because it did not have, or had too few, weapons; no matter how class-conscious you might be, you cannot oppose bullets with your bare hands!" Obviously, that explanation oversimplified the problem. Naturally, it is rather hard to "oppose" bullets with bare hands. But there were also more profound causes for the defeat. The peasantry did not rise in its entire mass; it rose less in the center of the country than on the outskirts. The army was only partially won over. The proletariat did not yet really know its own strength or the strength of its opponent. The year 1905 went down into history—and therein is its immeasurable significance—as "the general rehearsal." But Lenin was able to characterize it thus only after the fact. In 1906 he himself awaited a quick showdown. In January, Koba, paraphrasing Lenin, wrote, with oversimplification, as usual: "We must once and for all reject all wavering, cast aside all indefiniteness, and irrevocably assume the point of view of attack . . . A united party, an armed uprising organized by the Party, and the policy of attack— this is what is demanded of us by the victory of the uprising." Even the Mensheviks did not yet dare to say aloud that the Revolution had ended. At the congress in Stockholm Ivanovich had the opportunity to declare without fear of contradiction: "And so, we are on the eve of a new explosion . . . On that all of us are agreed." As a matter of fact, at that time, the "explosion" was already in the past. The "policy of attack" became increasingly the policy of guerrilla clashes and scattered blows. The land was widely inundated with so-called "expropriations"—armed raids on banks, treasuries, and other repositories of money.

The disintegration of the Revolution was relinquishing the initiative of attack, which was passing into the hands of the government, and by that time the government was managing to cope with its own shattered nerves. In the Autumn and Winter the revolutionary parties began to emerge from the underground. The jousts continued, with visors open. The Tsarist police agents came to know the enemy by its face, as a whole and individually. The reign of terror began on the third of December, 1905, with the arrest of the Petersburg Soviet. All those who had compromised themselves and had not managed to hide were in due course arrested. Admiral Dubassov's victory over the Moscow warriors merely added more viciousness to the current acts of repression. Between January, 1905, and the convocation of the First Duma on the Twenty-seventh of April [May 10th], 1906, the Tsarist government, according to approximate calculations, had killed more than fourteen thousand people, had executed more than a thousand, had wounded twenty thousand, had arrested, exiled and imprisoned about seventy thousand. The principal number of victims fell in December, 1905, and during the first months of 1906. Koba did not offer himself "as a target." He was neither wounded nor exiled nor arrested. It was not even necessary for him to go into hiding. He remained, as formerly, in Tiflis. That can in nowise be explained by his personal skill or by a happy accident. It was possible for him to go to the Tammerfors Conference secretly, by stealth. But it was quite impossible to lead the mass movement of 1905 by stealth. No "happy accident" could have possibly shielded an active revolutionist in small Tiflis. As a matter of fact, Koba kept aloof from important developments to such an extent that the police paid no attention to him. In the middle of 1906 he continued to vegetate in the editorial office of a legal Bolshevik newspaper.

In the meantime, Lenin was in hiding in Finland, at Kuokalla, in constant contact with Petersburg and the entire country. The other members of the Bolshevik Center were also there. That was where the torn threads of the illegal organization were picked up and rewoven. "From all the ends of Russia," writes

Krupskaya, "came comrades with whom we discussed our work." Krupskaya mentions a number of names, including that of Sverdlov, who in the Urals "enjoyed tremendous influence," mentions, by the way, Voroshilov, and others. But, despite the ominous reproofs of official criticism, she does not mention Stalin even once during that period. And not because she avoids the mention of his name; on the contrary, wherever she has the slightest foundation in fact, she tries to push him forward. She simply could find no trace of him in her memory.

The First Duma was dissolved on the eighth of July, 1906. The strike of protest, for which the Left Wing parties had appealed, did not materialize: the workers had learned to understand that a strike alone was not enough, and there was no strength left for anything more than that. The attempt by the revolutionists to hamper the mobilization of army recruits failed pitifully. The uprising at the Sveaborg fortress, with the participation of the Bolsheviks, proved to be an isolated flare-up, and was quickly suppressed. The reaction gained strength. The Party went deeper and deeper into the underground. "From Kuokalla, Ilyitch actually guided the entire activity of the Bolsheviks," Krupskaya wrote. Again a number of names and episodes, but no mention of Stalin. Nor is he mentioned in connection with the November session of the Party at Terioki, where the question of elections to the Second Duma was being decided. Koba did not journey to Kuokalla. Not the slightest trace of the alleged correspondence between him and Lenin for the year 1906 has been preserved. No personal contact between them was established, despite the meeting at Tammerfors. Nor did the second meeting, at Stockholm, bring them any closer together. Krupskaya, telling about a walk through the Swedish capital in which Lenin, Rykov, Stroyev, Alexinsky, and others took part, does not name Stalin as being among them. It is also possible that the personal relations, having scarcely arisen, became strained because of the differences of opinion on the agrarian question: Ivanovich did not sign the appeal, so Lenin did not mention Ivanovich in his report.

In accordance with the resolutions adopted at Tammerfors and Stockholm, the Caucasian Bolsheviks united with the Mensheviks. Koba did not become a member of the United Regional Committee. But then, if one is to trust Beriya, he did become a member of the Caucasian Bolshevik Bureau, which existed secretly in 1906 parallel to the Party's official committee. Yet there is no evidence about the activity of that Bureau and about Koba's role in it. One thing is certain: the organizational views of the "committeeman" of the days of the Tiflis-Batum period underwent a change—if not in their essence, at least, in the form of their expression. Koba no longer dared to urge workingmen to confess that they were not yet sufficiently mature to serve on committees. The soviets and the trade unions advanced revolutionary workingmen to the first plane of importance, and they usually proved to be far better prepared to lead the masses than the majority of underground intellectuals. As Lenin had foreseen, the "committeemen" were forced to change their views rather suddenly, or at least, their arguments. Now Koba defended in the press the need for party democracy; more than that, the kind of democracy in which "the mass itself decides the issues and acts by itself." Mere elective democracy was insufficient: "Napoleon III was elected by universal suffrage; yet, who does not know that this elected emperor was the greatest enslaver of the people?" Could Besoshvili (Koba's pseudonym at the time) have foreseen his own future, he would have refrained from referring to a Bonapartistic plebiscite. But there was much that he did not foresee. His gift of foresight was good for short distances only. Therein, as we shall see, was not only his weakness but also his strength—at least, for a certain epoch.

The defeats of the proletariat forced Marxism to retreat to defensive positions. Enemies and opponents silenced during the stormy months again raised their heads. The Left as well as the Right held materialism and dialectics responsible for the rage of the reaction. On the Right, the Liberals, Democrats, Populists; on the Left, the Anarchists. Anarchism played no part at all in the 1905 movement. There were only three factions in the Petersburg Soviet—the Mensheviks, the Bolsheviks, and the Essars. The Anarchists found a more reverberating sounding board in the atmosphere of disillusionment after the downfall of the Soviets. The ebb-tide also left its imprint in backward Caucasus, where in many respects the conditions were more favorable for Anarchism than elsewhere in the country. As part of his defense of Marxist positions then under attack, Koba wrote in his native Georgian a series of newspaper articles on the theme of "Anarchism and Socialism." These articles, which testify to their author's good intentions, do not lend themselves to restatement because they are in themselves no more than a restatement of the works of others. Nor is it easy to cull quotations from them, for they are smoothly stained an even gray that renders the selection of any individualistic expressions even more difficult. It is sufficient to say that this work of his was never republished.

To the right of the Georgian Mensheviks, who continued to regard themselves as Marxist, arose the party of Federalists—a local parody, partly of the Essars and partly of the Kadets. Besoshvili quite justly denounced that Party's penchant for cowardly maneuvers and compromises, but in doing so, he resorted to rather venturesome figures of speech. "As is well known," he wrote, "every animal has its definite coloration. But the nature of the chameleon is not satisfied with that; with a lion, he assumes the coloration of a lion; with a wolf, that of a wolf; with a frog, that of a frog, depending on when which coloration is most advantageous to him . . ." A zoologist would be rather likely to protest against such slander of the chameleon. But since the Bolshevik critic was essentially right, he may be forgiven the style of one who failed to become a village priest.

That is all there is to say about the doings of Koba-Ivanovich-Besoshvili during the First Revolution. It is not much, even in the purely quantitative sense. Yet the author has tried very hard not to omit anything at all worthy of notice. The point is that Koba's intellect, devoid of imagination, was not very productive. The discipline of intellectual labor was alien to him. An overpowering personal motivation was required to stir him to prolonged and systematic application. He did not find that stirring motivation in the Revolution, which brushed him aside. That is why his contributions to the Revolution appear so pitifully meager by comparison with the Revolution's gift to his personal fortunes.

Chapter IV

THE PERIOD OF REACTION

THE personal life of underground revolutionists was always relegated to the background, repressed. Yet it persisted. Like the palms on a Diego Rivera landscape, love struggled toward the sun from under heavy boulders. It was almost always identified with revolution. The same ideas, the same struggle, the same danger, a common isolation from the rest of the world, welded strong bonds. Couples came together in the underground, were parted by prison, and again sought each other out in exile. We know little of young Stalin's personal life, but that little is all the more precious for the light it shed on him as a man.

"He married in 1903," Iremashvili tells us. "His marriage, according to his lights, was a happy one. True, it was impossible to discover in his own home that equality of the sexes which he himself advocated as the basic form for marriage in the new state. But it was not in his character to share equal rights with any other person. His marriage was a happy one because his wife, who could not come up to him in general intelligence, regarded him as a demi-god and because, being a Georgian woman, she was brought up in the sacrosanct tradition which obligates the woman to serve." Although Iremashvili considered himself a Social-Democrat, he himself subscribed almost religiously to the tradition which made the Georgian woman essentially a family slave. He ascribed to Koba's wife the same characteristics that he had ascribed to his mother, Keke. "That truly Georgian woman . . . with all her heart looked after her husband's welfare. Passing countless nights in ardent prayers, she waited for her Soso while he was busy at secret conferences. She prayed that Koba might turn away from his ideas that were displeasing to God and turn to a peaceful home life of toil and contentment."

Not without astonishment do we learn from these lines that Koba, who had repudiated religion at thirteen, was married to a naïvely and profoundly religious wife. That might seem quite an ordinary case in a stable bourgeois environment, in which the husband regards himself as an agnostic or amuses himself with Masonic rites, while his wife, having consummated her latest adultery, duly kneels in the confession box before her priest. But among Russian revolutionists such matters were immeasurably more important. There was no anemic agnosticism at the core of their revolutionary philosophy, but militant atheism. How could they have any personal tolerance toward religion, which was inextricably linked to everything against which they fought at constant risk to themselves?

Among working people, who married early, one might find not a few instances
of the husband turning revolutionist after marriage while his wife continued
to cling stubbornly to the old faith. But even that usually led to dramatic col-
lisions. The husband would keep his new life a secret from his wife and would
grow further and further away from her. In other cases, the husband would
win his wife over to his own views and away from her kinsfolk. Young workers
would frequently complain that it was hard for them to find girls who were free
of the old superstitions. Among the student youth the choice of mates was considerably easier. There were almost no cases of a revolutionary intellectual
marrying a believer. Not that there were any rules to that effect. But such
things were not in keeping with the customs, the views and the feelings of these
people. Koba was undoubtedly a rare exception.

It would seem that the divergence in views led to no dramatic conflict. "This
man, so restless in spirit, who felt himself spied upon, under the constant surveillance of the Tsarist secret police at every step and in everything he did,
could find love only in his impoverished home. Only his wife, his child and his
mother were exempt from the scorn he poured on all others." The idyllic family
picture drawn by Iremashvili allows the inference that Koba was indulgently
tolerant of his intimate companion's beliefs. But since that runs counter to his
tyrannical nature, which appears to be tolerance must really be moral indifference. Koba did not seek in his wife a friend capable of sharing his views or at
least his ambitions. He was satisfied with a submissive and devoted woman.
In his views he was a Marxist; in his feelings and spiritual needs—he was the
son of the Ossetin Beso from Didi-Lilo. He required no more of his wife than
his father had found in the long-suffering Keke.

Iremashvili's chronology, which is not faultless as a rule, is more reliable in
personal matters than in the field of politics. But his marriage date arouses some
doubt. He gives it as 1903. Yet Koba was arrested in April, 1902, and returned
from exile, in February, 1904. It is possible that the wedding took place in prison.
Such cases were not rare. But it is also possible that the marriage took place
only after his flight from exile at the beginning of 1904. In that event a church
wedding did present certain difficulties for one of "illegal" status; yet, in view
of the primitive ways of those times, especially in the Caucasus, police obstacles
were not insurmountable. If Koba's wedding took place after his exile, it can
in part explain his political passivity during 1904.

Koba's wife—we do not even know her name[1]—died in 1907; according to
some accounts, of pneumonia. By that time the two Sosos were no longer on
friendly terms. Iremashvili complains: "The brunt of his struggle was henceforth directed against us, his former friends. He attacked us at every meeting
and discussion in the most savage and unscrupulous manner, trying to sow
poison and hatred against us everywhere. If possible, he would have rooted us
out with fire and sword . . . But the overwhelming majority of Georgian Marx-

---

[1] Ekaterina Svanidze, sister of an obscure comrade, who subsequently became President
of the Soviet Bank for Foreign Trade (*Vnyeshtorgbank*).—C. M.

ists remained with us. That merely enraged and incensed him all the mo
But Georgian customs proved so prepotent that political disagreement did not
deter Iremashvili from visiting Koba on the occasion of his wife's death in order
to bring him words of comfort: "He was very downcast, yet he met me in a
friendly manner, as in the old days. This hard man's pale face reflected the heartfelt anguish caused by the death of his faithful life's companion. His emotional
distress . . . must have been very deepseated and enduring, for he was incapable of hiding it any longer from outsiders."

The deceased was buried in accordance with all the rules of Orthodox ritual.
Her relatives insisted on it. Nor did Koba object. "When the modest procession
reached the entrance to the cemetery," Iremashvili tells us, "Koba firmly pressed
my hand, pointed to the coffin and said: 'Soso, this creature softened my heart
of stone; she died, and with her died—my last warm feelings for all human
beings.' He placed his right hand on his heart: 'It is all so desolate here inside,
so inexpressibly desolate!'" These words may seem theatrically pathetic and
unnatural; yet it is not unlikely that they are true, not only because they refer
to a young man overwhelmed by his first heartfelt sorrow but also because in
time to come we shall rediscover in Stalin the same penchant for strained pathos,
a trait not unusual among persons of harsh character. The awkward style for
expressing his feelings came to him from the seminary training in homiletics.

Koba's wife left him a little boy with fine and delicate features. In 1919-1920
he was a student at the Tiflis secondary school, where Iremashvili was an instructor. Soon after that his father transferred Yasha to Moscow. We shall
meet him again in the Kremlin. That is all we know about this marriage, which
in point of time (1903-1907) fits rather neatly into the framework of the First
Revolution. It is no fortuitous coincidence: the rhythms of the revolutionist's
personal life were too closely intertwined for that with the rhythms of great events.

"Beginning with the day he buried his wife," insists Iremashvili, "he lost
the last vestige of human feelings. His heart filled with the inexpressibly malicious hatred his merciless father had already begun to engender in him when he
was still a child. He crushed with sarcasm his less and less frequently recurring
moral impulses. Ruthless with himself, he became ruthless with all people."
Such was he during the period of reaction which meantime had advanced upon
the country.

The beginning of mass strikes in the second half of the 'nineties signified the
approach of revolution. But the average number of strikers was even less than
fifty thousand a year. In 1905 that number rose at once to two and three-quar-
ter millions; in 1906 it came down to one million; in 1907 to three-quarters
of a million, including repeat strikes. Such were the figures for the three years
of the revolution. Never before had the world witnessed a similar wave of
strikes! The period of reaction opened in 1908. The number of strikers fell at
once to 174,000; in 1909 to 64,000; in 1910 to 50,000. But while the proletariat
was rapidly closing its ranks, the peasants it had aroused not only continued but
even strengthened their offensive. The ravaging of landowners' estates became

particularly widespread during the months of the First Duma's tenure. There came a wave of soldiers' mutinies. After the suppression of the attempted uprisings at Sveaborg and Kronstadt in July, 1906, the monarchy became bolder, introduced courts-martial, and, with the aid of the Senate, vitiated the election law. But it did not attain the requisite results. The Second Duma proved even more radical than the First.

In February, 1907, Lenin characterized the political situation of the country in the following words: "The most unrestrained, the most brazen lawlessness . . . The most reactionary election law in Europe. The most revolutionary body of popular representatives in Europe in the most backward country!" Hence his conclusion: "Ahead is a new, an even more menacing . . . revolutionary crisis." This conclusion proved erroneous. Although the revolution was still strong enough to leave its impress on the arena of Tsarist pseudo-parliamentarism, it was already broken. Its convulsions became increasingly weaker.

The Social-Democratic party was undergoing a similar process. It continued to grow in membership. But its influence on the masses declined. A hundred Social-Democrats were no longer able to lead as many workers into the street as ten Social-Democrats had led the year before. The different aspects of a revolutionary movement, as a homogeneous historical process and generally as a development possessing survival value, are neither uniform nor harmonious in content or movement. Not only workers but even the petty bourgeois attempted to avenge their defeat by Tsarism in open battle by voting on the Left; but they were no longer capable of a new insurrection. Deprived of the apparatus of the Soviets and of direct contact with the masses, who quickly succumbed to gloomy apathy, the more active workers felt the need for a revolutionary party. Thus, this time the leftward swing of the Duma and the growth of the Social-Democracy were symptoms of the revolution's decline, not of its rise.

No doubt, Lenin admitted such a possibility even then. But, pending final verification by experience, he continued to base his policy on a revolutionary prognosis. Such was the fundamental rule of that strategist. "The revolutionary Social-Democracy," he wrote in October, 1906, "must be the first to take its place in the most resolute and the most direct struggle, and the last to resort to the more roundabout methods of struggle." Under direct struggle come demonstrations, strikes, the general strike, clashes with the police, the insurrection. Under roundabout methods—the utilization of legal opportunities, including parliamentarism, for the mobilization of forces. That strategy inevitably implied the danger of resorting to militant methods after the objective conditions for the employment of such methods no longer prevailed. Yet on the scales of the revolutionary party, that tactical risk weighed immeasurably less than the strategic danger of not keeping up with developments and losing sight of a revolutionary situation.

The Fifth Congress of the Party, held in London in May, 1907, was remarkable for the number of people that attended it. In the hall of the "Socialist" Church there were 302 voting delegates (one delegate for each 500 party members), about half a hundred with advisory voices, and not a few guests. Of these, 90 were Bolsheviks and 85 Mensheviks. The national delegations formed the "center" between these two flanks. At the previous congress 13,000 Bolsheviks and 18,000 Mensheviks (one delegate for each 300 party members) were represented. During the twelvemonth between the Stockholm and the London congresses, the Russian section of the Party had increased from 31,000 to 77,000 members, i.e., two and a half times. Inevitably, the keener the factional struggle, the more inflated the figures. Yet, no doubt, the advanced workers did continue to join the Party during that year. At the same time the Left Wing grew stronger at a considerably faster rate than its opponent. In the 1905 Soviet the Mensheviks were preponderant; the Bolsheviks were a modest minority. At the beginning of 1906 the forces of both factions in St. Petersburg were approximately equal. During the interval between the First and the Second Dumas, the Bolsheviks began to get ahead. By the time of the Second Duma, they had already won complete dominance among the advanced workers. Judging by the nature of the resolutions adopted, the Stockholm Congress was Menshevik, the London Congress—Bolshevik.

This shift of the Party leftward was carefully noted by the authorities. Shortly before the Congress the Police Department explained to its local branches that "the Menshevik groups in their present state of mind do not present as serious a danger as the Bolsheviks." In the regular report on the progress of the Congress, presented to the Police Department by one of its foreign agents, the following appraisal was included: "Among the orators who in the course of discussion spoke in defense of the extreme revolutionary point of view were Stanislav (Bolshevik), Trotsky, Pokrovsky (Bolshevik), Tyszko (Polish Social-Democrat); in defense of the opportunist point of view—Martov and Plekhanov," (leaders of the Mensheviks). "There is clear intimation," the Okhrana[2] agent continued, "that the Social-Democrats are turning toward revolutionary methods of struggle . . . Menshevism, which blossomed thanks to the Duma, declined in due time, when the Duma demonstrated its impotence, giving ample scope to Bolshevik, or rather, to extreme revolutionary tendencies." As a matter of fact, as was already pointed out, the shift in sentiment within the proletariat was much more complicated and inconsistent. Thus, while the vanguard, buoyed by its own experiences, moved to the Left, the mass, discour-

[2] The Okhrana (short for Okhránnoye Otdyelyeniye, or Department of Safety) was the political secret service of the Imperial Police Department, the most important branch of the Ministry of the Interior since its founding in 1881. For fifty years prior to that its functions had been performed by the Third Section of the Imperial Court Chancery. Hence, the terms: Okhrana, Okhranka, Third Section, Political Police, Police Department are used interchangeably with reference to the tsarist state's espionage activities directed against revolutionists. The Okhrana was divided into an External and Internal Agency on the basis of methods of espionage, the first consisting of a corps of detectives and the latter of stoolpigeons and agents provocateurs planted inside the revolutionary organizations. The Okhrana was aided in its activities against the revolutionary movement by another branch of the Police Department, the Special Corps of the Gendarmerie. In addition to branches in the important cities of Russia, the Okhrana maintained also a Foreign Agency abroad wherever Russian revolutionary émigrés congregated.—C. M.

aged by defeats, moved to the Right. The breath of the reaction was already
hovering over the congress. "Our revolution is passing through trying times,"
said Lenin at the session of May twelfth. "We need all the strength and will
power, all the self-restraint and perseverance of a united proletarian party, if
we are to endure in the face of the pervasive moods of disbelief, defection, apathy,
submissiveness."

"In London," wrote a French biographer, "Stalin for the first time saw
Trotsky. But the latter hardly noticed him. The leader of the Petersburg Soviet
is not the sort of person who readily strikes up acquaintances or becomes
chummy without genuine spiritual affinity." Whether that is true or not, the
fact remains that I first learned about Koba's presence at the London Congress
from Souvarine's book and subsequently found confirmation of it in the official
records. As in Stockholm, Ivanovich took part not as one of the 302 voting
delegates, but as one of the 42 whose participation was only deliberative. Bolshevism was still so weak in Georgia that Koba could not muster the necessary
500 votes in all of Tiflis! "Even in Koba's and my native town of Gori," writes
Iremashvili, "there was not a single Bolshevik." The complete predominance of
the Mensheviks in the Caucasus was attested to in the course of the Congress
debates by Koba's rival, Sha'umyan, a leading Caucasian Bolshevik and future
member of the Central Committee. "The Caucasian Mensheviks," he complained,
"taking full advantage of their crushing numerical weight and official dominance
in the Caucasus, do everything in their power to prevent Bolsheviks from getting elected." In a declaration signed by the same Sha'umyan and Ivanovich,
we read: "The Caucasian Menshevik organizations are composed almost entirely of the town and village petty bourgeoisie." Of the 18,000 Caucasian members of the Party, no more than 6,000 were workers; but even most of these
followed the Mensheviks.

Koba's appointment as a mere deliberative delegate was accompanied by an
incident not devoid of piquancy. When it was Lenin's turn to preside at the
Congress, he proposed adoption without discussion of a resolution by the mandate commission, which recommended the granting of deliberative participation
to four delegates, including Ivanovich. The indefatigable Martov shouted
from his place: "I should like to know who is being granted an advisory voice.
Who are these people, where do they come from, and so forth?" To which
Lenin responded: *"I really don't know,* but the Congress may rely on the
unanimous opinion of the mandate commission." It is quite likely that Martov
already had some secret information about the specific nature of Ivanovich's
record—we shall touch upon it more fully—and that it was precisely for this
reason that Lenin hastened to dispose of the ominous hint by referring to the
unanimity of the mandate commission. In any event, Martov deemed it proper
to refer to "these people" as nobodies: "Who are they, where do they come
from, and so forth?" while Lenin, for his part, not only did not object to this
characterization but confirmed it. In 1907, Stalin was still utterly unknown, not
only to the Party generally but even to the three hundred delegates of the Con-

THE PERIOD OF REACTION

gress. The mandate commission's resolution was adopted, with a considerable number of delegates not voting.

Most remarkable, however, is the fact that Koba did not even once take advantage of the deliberative voice granted to him. The Congress lasted nearly three weeks, discussions were exceedingly extensive and ample. Yet Ivanovich's name is not listed so much as once among the numerous speakers. His signature appears only on two short statements by Caucasian Bolsheviks about their local conflicts with the Mensheviks, and even then in third place. He left no other traces of his presence at the Congress. To appreciate the full significance of that, it is necessary to know the backstage mechanics of the Congress. Each of the factions and national organizations met separately during recesses between official sessions, worked out its own line of conduct and designated its own speakers. Thus, in the course of three weeks of debates, in which all the more noticeable members of the Party took part, the Bolshevik faction did not deem it fit to entrust a single speech to Ivanovich.

Toward the end of one of the last sessions of the Congress a young Petersburg delegate spoke. All had hastily left their seats and almost no one listened to him. The speaker was obliged to mount a chair in order to attract attention. But notwithstanding these extremely unfavorable circumstances, he managed to draw an ever-growing press of delegates around him and before long the assemblage quieted down. That speech made the novice a member of the Central Committee. Ivanovich, doomed to silence, noted the young newcomer's success —Zinoviev was only twenty-five—probably without sympathy, but hardly without envy. Not a soul paid the slightest heed to the ambitious Caucasian with his unused deliberative voice. The Bolshevik Gandurin, a rank and filer at the Congress, stated in his memoirs: "During the recesses we usually surrounded one or another of the important workers, overwhelming him with questions." Gandurin mentioned among the delegates Litvinov, Voroshilov, Tomsky, and other comparatively obscure Bolsheviks of those days. But he did not mention Stalin even once. Yet he wrote his memoirs in 1931, when it was much harder to forget Stalin than to remember him.

Among the elected members of the new Central Committee, the Bolsheviks were Myeshkovsky, Rozhkov, Teodorovich and Nogin, with Lenin, Bogdanov, Krassin, Zinoviev, Rykov, Shantser, Sammer, Leitheisen, Taratuta and A. Smirnov as alternates. The most prominent leaders of the faction were elected alternates, because persons able to work in Russia were pushed to the forefront. But Ivanovich was neither among the members nor among the alternates. It would be incorrect to seek the reason for that in the tricks of the Mensheviks: as a matter of fact, each faction elected its own candidates. Certain of the Bolsheviks on the Central Committee, like Zinoviev, Rykov, Taratuta and A. Smirnov, were of the same generation as Ivanovich and even younger in actual age.

At the final session of the Bolshevik faction, after the closing of the Congress, a secret Bolshevik Center was elected, the so-called "B. C.," composed of fifteen members. Among them were the theoreticians and "literaries" of the time and of the future, such as Lenin, Bogdanov, Pokrovsky, Rozhkov, Zinoviev, Kámenev, as well as the most prominent organizers, such as Krassin, Rykov, Dubrovinsky, Nogin, and others. Ivanovich was not a member of that collegium either. The significance of that is perfectly obvious. Stalin could not become a member of the Central Committee without being known to the *entire* party. Another obstacle—let us admit for the nonce—was that the Caucasian Mensheviks were particularly hostile to him. But had he any weight and influence inside his own faction, he could not have failed to become a member of the Bolshevik Center, which badly needed an authoritative representative of the Caucasus. Ivanovich himself could not have failed to dream of a place in the "B. C." Yet no such place was found for him.

In view of all this, why did Koba come at all to London? He could not raise his arm as a voting delegate. He proved unnecessary as a speaker. He obviously played no role whatever at the closed sessions of the Bolshevik faction. It is inconceivable that he should have to come out of mere curiosity—to listen and to look around. He must have had other tasks. Just what were they?

The Congress came to an end on May nineteenth. As early as the first of June, Premier Stolypin challenged the Duma with his demand that it immediately expel fifty-five Social-Democratic deputies and sanction the arrest of sixteen of them. Without waiting for the Duma's authorization, the police proceeded to make arrests on the night of June second. On the third of June the Duma was prorogued, and in the course of this governmental shake-up a new election law was promulgated. Mass arrests, carefully prearranged, took place simultaneously throughout the country, with railwaymen among those taken into custody, in an effort to forestall a general strike. The attempted mutinies in the Black Sea Fleet and in a Kiev regiment ended in failure. The monarchy was triumphant. When Stolypin looked into his mirror, he saw there the image of St. George, Bearer of Victory.

The obvious disintegration of the revolution led to several new crises in the Party and in the Bolshevik faction itself, which overwhelmingly assumed the Boycottist position. This was almost an instinctive reaction against the government's violence, but at the same time it was an attempt to cover their own impotence with a radical gesture. While relaxing after the Congress in Finland, Lenin thought the matter over in all its aspects, and came out resolutely against the boycott. His situation in his own faction became rather difficult. It is not any too easy to pass from revolutionary heydays to work-a-day dreariness. "With the exception of Lenin and Rozhkov," wrote Martov, "all the prominent representatives of the Bolshevik faction (Bogdanov, Kamenev, Lunarcharsky, Volsky, and others) came out for the boycott." The quotation is partly interesting in that, while it includes among the "prominent representatives" not only Lunarcharsky but even the long-forgotten Volsky, it does not mention Stalin. In 1924, when the official Moscow historical journal reproduced Martov's testimony, it had not yet occurred to the editorial board to evince interest in how Stalin had voted.

Yet Koba was among the Boycottists. In addition to direct testimonies on that score, which, it is true, come from Mensheviks, there is a bit of indirect testimony which is the most convincing of all: not a single one of the present official historians refers with so much as a single word to Stalin's position on elections to the Third Duma. In a pamphlet entitled "Concerning the Boycott of the Third Duma," which was published shortly after the Revolution, and in which Lenin defended participation in balloting, it was Kamenev who voiced the Boycottists' point of view. It has been all the easier for Koba to preserve his incognito, because it did not occur to anyone in 1907 to ask him to come out with an article. The old Bolshevik Piryeiko recalls that the Boycottists "upbraided Comrade Lenin for his Menshevism." There is no reason to doubt that Koba, too, was not backward in his intimate circle with rather trenchant epithets in Georgian and Russian. As for Lenin, he demanded of his faction readiness and ability to face realities. "The boycott is a declaration of outright war against the old government, a direct attack against it. Barring a widespread revolutionary revival . . . there can be no talk of the boycott's success." Much later, in 1920, Lenin wrote: "It was an error . . . for the Bolsheviks to have boycotted the Duma in 1906." It was an error, because after the December defeat it was impossible to expect a revolutionary attack in the near future; it was therefore senseless to spurn the Duma's tribune for mobilizing the revolutionary ranks.

At the Party Conference which met at Finland in July, all of the nine Bolshevik delegates, with the exception of Lenin, were in favor of the boycott. Ivanovich did not take part in that conference. The Boycottists had Bogdanov as their spokesman. The affirmative resolution on the question of whether to participate in the balloting passed with the united votes of "the Mensheviks, the Bundists, the Poles, one of the Letts, and one Bolshevik," wrote Dan. That "one Bolshevik" was Lenin. "In a small summer house Ilyich ardently defended his position," Krupskaya recalled; "Krassin pedaled up on his bicycle, stopped at a window for a while and listened closely to Ilyich. Then, without coming into the house, he went away, thoughtful . . ." Krassin went away from that window for more than ten years. He returned to the Party only after the October Revolution, and even then not at once. Gradually, under the influence of new lessons, the Bolsheviks came over to Lenin's position, although, as we shall see, not all of them. Quietly, Koba too repudiated Boycottism. His Caucasian articles and speeches in favor of the boycott have been magnanimously relegated to oblivion.

The Third Duma began its inglorious activity on the first of November. The big bourgeoisie and the landed gentry had been previously assured of a majority in it. Then began the gloomiest period in the life of "renovated Russia." Labor organizations were dispersed, the revolutionary press was stifled, courtsmartial came in the wake of the punitive expeditions. But more frightful than the outward blows was the internal reaction. Desertion assumed a mass character. Intellectuals abandoned politics for science, art, religion, and erotic mysticism. The finishing touch on this picture was the epidemic of suicides. The transvaluation of values was first of all directed against the revolutionary parties and their leaders. The sharp change of mood found a bright reflection in the archives of the Police Department, where suspicious letters were censored, thus preserving the most interesting ones for history.

At Geneva Lenin received a letter from Petersburg, which read: "It is quiet both above and below, but the silence below is tainted. Under its cover such anger looms as will make men howl, for howl they must. But so far we, too, suffer the brunt of that anger . . ." A certain Zakharov wrote to his friend in Odessa: "We have absolutely lost faith in those whom we had so highly regarded . . . Think of it, at the end of 1905 Trotsky said in all seriousness that the political revolution had culminated in a grand success, and that it would be followed immediately by the beginning of the social revolution! . . And what about the wonderful tactic of armed insurrection, which the Bolsheviks had bruited about? . . Truly, I have lost all faith in our leaders and in all of the so-called revolutionary intellectuals." Neither did the liberal and radical press spare the vanquished their sarcasm.

News dispatches from local organizations to the Party's central organ, which was again transferred abroad, were no less eloquent in recording the revolution's disintegration. Even in the hard-labor prisons, the heroes and heroines of uprisings and of terrorist acts turned their backs in enmity upon their own yesterdays and used such words as "party," "comrade," "socialism," in no other than the ironic sense.

Desertions took place not only among the intellectuals, not only among those who were here today and gone tomorrow and to whom the movement was but a half-way house, but even among the advanced workers, who had been part and parcel of the Party for years. Religiousness, on the one hand, and drunkenness, card-playing and the like, on the other, waxed stronger than ever in the backward strata of the working class. In the upper stratum the tone was beginning to be set by individualists who strove to raise their personal, cultural, and economic status above that of the mass of their fellow-workers. The Mensheviks found their support in that thin layer of the labor aristocracy which was made up for the most part of metal workers and printers. Workers of the middle stratum, whom the revolution had accustomed to reading newspapers, displayed greater stability. But, having entered political life under the leadership of intellectuals and being suddenly left on their own, they became petrified and marked time.

Not everybody deserted. But the revolutionists who did not wish to surrender ran against insurmountable difficulties. An illegal organization needs sympathetic surroundings and constant renewal of reserves. In an atmosphere of decadence it was not only hard but virtually impossible to abide by the indispensable rules of conspiracy and maintain revolutionary contacts. "Underground work proceeded lackadaisically. During 1909 there were raids on Party printshops at Rostov-on-the-Don, Moscow, Tyumen, Petersburg . . ." and elsewhere; "supplies of proclamations in Petersburg, Byelostok, Moscow; the archives of the Central Committee in Petersburg. In all these arrests the Party was losing good workers." This is recounted almost in a tone of distress by the retired Gendarme General Spiridovich.

"We have no people at all," Krupskaya wrote in invisible ink to Odessa, at the beginning of 1909. "All are scattered in prisons and places of exile." The gendarmes made visible the invisible text of the letter and—increased the population of the prisons. The scantiness of revolutionary ranks led unavoidably to the lowering of the Committee's standards. Insufficiency of choice made it possible for secret agents to mount the steps of the underground hierarchy. With a snap of his finger the provocateur doomed to arrest any revolutionist who blocked his progress. Attempts to purge the organization of dubious elements immediately led to mass arrests. An atmosphere of suspicion and mutual distrust stymied all initiative. After a number of well-calculated arrests, the provocateur Kukushkin, at the beginning of 1910 became head of the Moscow district organization. "The ideal of the Okhrana is being realized," wrote an active participant of the movement. "Secret agents are at the head of all the Moscow organizations." The situation in Petersburg was not much better. "The leadership seemed to have been routed, there was no way of restoring it, provocation gnawed away at our vitals, organizations fell apart . . ." In 1909 Russia still had five or six active organizations; but even they soon sank into desuetude. Membership in the Moscow district organization, which was as high as 500 toward the end of 1908, dropped to 250 in the middle of the following year and half a year later to 150; in 1910 the organization ceased to exist.

The former Duma deputy Samoilov tells how at the beginning of 1910 the Ivanovo-Voznesensk organization, which until recently had been rather influential and active, fell apart. Right after it the trade unions faded away. Their places were taken by gangs of the Black Hundreds. The pre-revolutionary régime was being gradually restored in the textile factories, which meant the lowering of wages, severe penalties, dismissals, and the like. "The workers kept on the job bore it in silence." Yet there could be no return to the old order. Abroad, Lenin pointed to letters from workers, who, telling of the renewed oppression and persecution by the manufacturers, would add, "Wait, 1905 will come again!"

Terror from above was supplemented by terror from below. [The fight of] the routed insurrectionists continued convulsively for a long time in the form of scattered local explosions, guerrilla raids, group and individual terrorist acts. The course of the revolution was characterized with remarkable clarity by statistics of the terror. 233 persons were assassinated in 1905; 768 in 1906; 1,231 in 1907. The number of wounded showed a somewhat different ratio, since the terrorists were learning to be better shots. The terrorist wave reached its crest in 1907. "There were days," wrote a liberal observer, "when several big acts of terror were accompanied by as many as scores of minor attempts and assassinations of lower rank officialdom . . . Bomb laboratories were established in all cities, the bombs destroying some of their careless makers . . ." and the like. Krassin's alchemy became strongly democratized.

On the whole, the three-year period from 1905 through 1907 is particularly notable for both terrorist acts and strikes. But what stands out is the divergence between their statistical records: while the number of strikers fell off rapidly from year to year, the number of terrorist acts mounted with equal rapidity. Clearly, individual terrorism increased as the mass movement declined. Yet terrorism could not grow stronger indefinitely. The impetus unleashed by the revolution was bound to spend itself in terrorism as it had spent itself in other spheres. Indeed, while there were 1,231 assassinations in 1907, they dropped to 400 in 1908 and to about a hundred in 1909. The growing percentage of the merely wounded indicated, moreover, that now the shooting was being done by untrained amateurs, mostly by callow youngsters.

In the Caucasus, with its romantic traditions of highway robbery and gory feuds still very much alive, guerrilla warfare found any number of fearless practitioners. More than a thousand terrorist acts of all kinds were perpetrated in Transcaucasia alone during 1905-1907, the years of the First Revolution. Fighting detachments found also a great spread of activity in the Urals, under the leadership of the Bolsheviks, and in Poland under the banner of the P. P. S. (Polish Socialist Party). On the second of August, 1906, scores of policemen and soldiers were assassinated on the streets of Warsaw and other Polish cities. According to the explanation of the leaders, the purpose of these attacks was "to bolster the revolutionary mood of the proletariat." The leader of these leaders was Joseph Pilsudski, the future "liberator" of Poland, and its oppressor. Commenting on the Warsaw events, Lenin wrote: "We advise the numerous fighting groups of our Party to terminate their inactivity and to initiate some guerrilla operations . . ." "And these appeals of the Bolshevik leaders," commented General Spiridovich, "were not without issue, despite the countermanding action of the [Menshevik] Central Committee."

Of great moment in the sanguine encounters of the terrorists with the police was the question of money, the sinews of any war, including civil war. Prior to the Constitutional Manifesto of 1905 the revolutionary movement was financed principally by the liberal bourgeoisie and by the radical intellectuals. That was true also in the case of the Bolsheviks, whom the liberal opposition then regarded as merely somewhat bolder revolutionary democrats. But when the bourgeoisie shifted its hopes to the future Duma, it began to regard the revolutionists as an obstacle in the way of coming to terms with the monarchy. That change of front struck a powerful blow at the finances of the revolution. Lockouts and unemployment stopped the intake of money from the workers. In the meantime, the revolutionary organizations had developed large political machines with their own printshops, publishing houses, staffs of agitators, and, finally, fighting detachments in constant need of armaments. Under the circumstances, there was no way to continue financing the revolution except by securing the wherewithal by force. The initiative, as almost always, came from below. The first expropriations went off rather peacefully, quite often with a tacit understanding between the "expropriators" and the employees of the expropriated institutions. There was the story of the clerks in the Nadezhda Insurance Company reassuring the faltering expropriators with the words, "Don't worry, comrades!" But this idyllic period did not last long. Following the bourgeoisie, the intellectuals, including the self-same bank clerks, drifted away from the revolution. Police measures became more stringent. Casualties increased on both sides. Deprived of support and sympathy, the "fighting organizations" quickly went up in smoke or just as quickly disintegrated.

A typical picture of how even the most disciplined detachments degenerated is given in his memoirs by the already-cited Samoilov, the former Duma deputy of the Ivanovo-Voznesensk textile workers. The detachment, acting originally "under the directives of the Party Center," began to "misbehave" during the second half of 1906. When it offered the Party only a part of the money it had stolen at a factory (having killed the cashier during the act), the Party Committee refused it flatly and reprimanded the fighters. But it was already too late; they were disintegrating rapidly and soon descended to "bandit attacks of the most ordinary criminal type." Always having large sums of money, the fighters began to preoccupy themselves with carousing, in the course of which they often fell into the hands of the police. Thus, little by little, the entire fighting detachment came to an ignominious end. "We must, however, admit," writes Samoilov, "that in its ranks were not a few . . . genuinely devoted comrades who were loyal to the cause of the revolution and some with hearts as pure as crystal . . ."

The original purpose of the fighting organizations was to assume leadership of the rebellious masses, teaching them how to use arms and how to deliver the most telling blows at the enemy. The main, if not the only, theoretician in that field of endeavor was Lenin. After the December Insurrection was crushed, the new problem was what to do about the fighting organizations. Lenin came to the Stockholm Congress with the draft of a resolution, which, while giving due credit to guerrilla activities as the inevitable continuation of the December Insurrection and as part of the preparation for the impending major offensive against Tsarism, allowed the so-called expropriations of financial means "under the control of the Party." But the Bolsheviks withdrew this resolution of theirs under the pressure of disagreement in their own midst. By a majority of sixty-four votes to four, with twenty not voting, the Menshevik resolution was passed, which categorically forbade "expropriations" of private persons and institutions, while tolerating the seizure of state finances only in the event that organs of revolutionary government were set up in a given locality; that is, only in direct connection with a popular uprising. The twenty-four delegates who either abstained from voting or voted against this resolution made up the Leninist irreconcilable half of the Bolshevik faction.

In the extensive printed report about the Stockholm Congress, Lenin avoided mention of the resolution concerning armed acts altogether, on the grounds that he was not present during the discussion. "Besides, it is, of course, not a question of principle." It is hardly possible that Lenin's absence was accidental: he simply did not want to have his hands tied. Similarly, a year later at the London Congress, Lenin, who as chairman was obliged to be present during the discussion on the question of expropriations, did not vote, in spite of violent protests from the Menshevik benches. The London resolution categorically forbade expropriations and ordered dissolution of the Party's "fighting organizations."

It was not, of course, a matter of abstract morality. All classes and all parties approached the problem of assassination not from the point of view of the Biblical commandment but from the vantage point of the historical interests represented. When the Pope and his cardinals blessed the arms of Franco none of the conservative statesmen suggested that they be imprisoned for inciting murders. Official moralists come out against violence when the violence in question is revolutionary. On the contrary, whoever really fights against class oppression, must perforce acknowledge revolution. Whoever acknowledges revolution, acknowledges civil war. Finally, "guerrilla warfare is an inescapable form of struggle . . . whenever more or less extensive intervals occur between major engagements in a civil war." [Lenin.] From the point of view of the general principles of the class struggle, all of that was quite irrefutable. Disagreements came with the evaluation of concrete historical circumstances. When two major battles of the civil war are separated from each other by two or three months, that interval will inevitably be filled in with guerrilla blows against the enemy. But when the "intermission" is stretched out over years, guerrilla war ceases to be a preparation for a new battle and becomes instead a mere convulsion after defeat. It is, of course, not easy to determine the moment of the break.

Questions of Boycottism and of guerrilla activities were closely interrelated. It is permissible to boycott representative assemblies only in the event that the mass movement is sufficiently strong either to overthrow them or to ignore them. But when the masses are in retreat, the tactic of the boycott loses its revolutionary meaning. Lenin understood that and explained it better than others. As early as 1906 he repudiated the boycott of the Duma. After the coup of June third, 1907, he led a resolute fight against the Boycottists precisely because the high-tide had been succeeded by the ebb-tide. It was self-evident that guerrilla activities had become sheer anarchism when it was necessary to utilize even the arena of Tsarist "parliamentarism" in order to prepare the ground for the mobilization of the masses. At the crest of the civil war guerrilla activities augmented and stimulated the mass movement; in the period of reaction they attempted to replace it, but, as a matter of fact, merely embarrassed the Party and speeded its disintegration. Olminsky, one of the more noticeable of Lenin's companions-in-arms, shed critical light on that period from the perspective of Soviet times. "Not a few of the fine youth," he wrote, "perished on the gibbet; others degenerated; still others were disappointed in the revolution. At the same time people at large began to confound revolutionists with ordinary bandits. Later, when the revival of the revolutionary labor movement began, that revival was slowest in those cities where 'exes' had been most numerous. (As an example, I might name Baku and Saratov.)" Let us keep in mind the reference to Baku.

The sum total of Koba's revolutionary activities during the years of the First Revolution seems to be so inconsiderable that willy-nilly it gives rise to the question: *is it possible that this was all?* In the vortex of events, which passed him by, Koba could not have failed to seek such means of action as would have enabled him to demonstrate his worth. Koba's participation in terrorist acts and in expropriations cannot be doubted. And yet, it is hard to determine the nature of that participation.

"The chief inspirer and general supervisor . . . of fighting activity," writes Spiridovich, "was Lenin himself, aided by trusted people close to him." Who were they? The former Bolshevik Alexinsky, who with the outbreak of the war became a specialist in exposing the Bolsheviks, stated in the foreign press that inside the Central Committee was a "small committee, whose existence was hidden not only from the eyes of the Tsarist police but also from the members of the Party. That small committee, consisting of Lenin, Krassin, and a third person . . . was particularly concerned with the party's finances." By concern with finances Alexinsky means leadership in expropriations. The unnamed "third person" was the naturalist, physician, economist and philosopher Bogdanov, whom we already know. Alexinsky had no reason to be reticent about Stalin's participation in fighting operations. He says nothing about it because he knows nothing about it. Yet during these years Alexinsky was not only very intimate with the Bolshevik Center but was also in touch with Stalin. As a general rule, that muckraker told *more* than he knew.

The notes to Lenin's works state about Krassin: [He] "guided the fighting technical bureau of the Central Committee." Krupskaya in her turn wrote: "The Party members now know about the important work which Krassin carried on at the time of the Revolution of 1905 in arming the fighters, in supervising the manufacture of explosives, and so forth. All of it was done in secrecy without any fanfare, yet a lot of energy was invested in that cause. Vladimir Ilyich knew about that work of Krassin's more than anyone else, and from then on always prized him." Voitinsky, who at the time of the First Revolution was a prominent Bolshevik, wrote: "I have a distinct impression that Nikitich [Krassin] was the only man in the Bolshevik organization whom Lenin regarded with genuine respect and with complete confidence." True, Krassin concentrated his efforts principally in Petersburg. But had Koba guided in the Caucasus operations of a similar type, Krassin, Lenin and Krupskaya could not have failed to know about it. Yet Krupskaya, who, in order to prove her loyalty, tried to mention Stalin as often as possible, did not say anything at all about his role in the Party's fighting activities.

On the third of July, 1938, the Moscow *Pravda* quite unexpectedly declared that "the unprecedented powerful sweep of the revolutionary movement in the Caucasus" in 1905 was connected with the "leadership of the most militant organizations of our Party, created there for the first time directly by Comrade Stalin." But that single official assertion that Stalin had something to do with "the most militant organizations" refers to the beginning of 1905, before the question of expropriation arose; it gives no information about Koba's actual work; finally, it is doubtful from the very nature of things, since there was no Bolshevik organization at Tiflis until the latter half of 1905.

Let us see what Iremashvili has to say about it. Speaking with indignation about terrorist acts, "exes," and the like, he declares: "Koba was the initiator of the crimes perpetrated by the Bolsheviks in Georgia, which played into the hands of the reaction." After his wife's death, when Koba lost "the last remnant of human feelings," he became "a passionate defender and organizer . . . of the vicious systematic murder of princes, priests and bourgeois." We already had occasion to be convinced that Iremashvili's testimony becomes less reliable the further it strays from personal experiences to politics, and from childhood and youth to the more mature years. Political ties between these friends of youthful days terminated at the beginning of the First Revolution. It was only by accident that on the seventeenth of October, on the day the Constitutional Manifesto was published, Iremashvili saw in the streets of Tiflis—only saw, but did not hear—how Koba, hanging onto an iron street lamp (on that day everybody climbed up street lamps), was haranguing a crowd. Being a Menshevik, Iremashvili could find out about Koba's terroristic activity only secondhand or thirdhand. This testimony is therefore obviously unreliable. Iremashvili cites two examples: the famous Tiflis expropriation of 1907, which we shall have occasion to discuss later, and the killing of the popular Georgian writer, Prince Chavchavadze. With reference to the expropriation, which he placed erroneously in 1905, Iremashvili remarks: "Koba was able to deceive the police on that occasion, too; it did not even have sufficient evidence to suspect his initiative in that cruel attempt. But that time the Social-Democratic Party of Georgia expelled Koba officially . . ." Not the slightest proof of Stalin's having anything to do with the assassination of Prince Chavchavadze is adduced by Iremashvili, who limits himself to the meaningless observation: "Indirectly Koba likewise was in favor of murder. He was the instigator of all the crimes, that agitator seething with hatred." Iremashvili's recollections in this part are interesting only insofar as they shed light on Koba's reputation among his political opponents.

The well-informed author of an article in a German newspaper (*Volksstime, Mannheim,* September 2nd, 1932), most likely a Georgian Menshevik, emphasizes that both friends and enemies considerably exaggerated Koba's terroristic adventures. "It is true that Stalin possessed exceptional ability and inclination for organizing attacks of that kind . . . However, in such affairs he usually performed the work of organizer, inspirer, supervisor, but not of direct participant."

Certain biographers are therefore quite incorrect in representing him as "running around with bombs and revolvers and carrying out the wildest sort of adventures." The story of Koba's alleged participation in the assassination of the Tiflis military dictator, General Gryaznov on January 17, 1906, appears to be that sort of invention. "That affair was executed in accordance with the decision of the Social-Democratic Party of Georgia (Mensheviks) through Party terrorists especially designated for that purpose. Stalin, like all other Bolsheviks, had no influence in Georgia and did not take part either directly or indirectly in that affair." This testimony of the anonymous author deserves consideration. Yet in its positive aspect, it is virtually meaningless: acknowledging in Stalin "exceptional aptitude and inclination" for expropriations and assassinations, it does not support that characterization with any data.

The old Georgian Bolshevik terrorist Kotè Tsintsadze, a conscientious and reliable witness, states that Stalin, dissatisfied with the backwardness of the Mensheviks in the matter of the attempt to assassinate General Gryaznov, invited Kotè to help him organize for that purpose a fighting detachment of their own. However, the Mensheviks soon managed to carry out this task themselves. The same Kotè recollects that in 1906 it occurred to him alone to organize a fighting detachment of Bolsheviks for the purpose of robbing state treasuries. "Our prominent comrades, especially Koba-Stalin, approved of my initiative." This testimony is doubly interesting: in the first place, it shows that Tsintsadze regarded Koba as a "prominent comrade"—that is, as a local leader; in the second place, it leaves us free to draw the conclusion that in these matters Koba did not go beyond approving the initiative of others.[3]

Against the direct resistance of the Menshevik Central Committee, but with the active co-operation of Lenin, the fighting groups of the Party managed to convoke a conference of their own at Tammerfors in November, 1906. Among the leading participants of that conference were revolutionists who subsequently played either an important or noticeable role in the Party; such as, Krassin, Yaroslavsky, Zemlyachka, Lalayants, Trilisser, and others. Stalin is not among them, although at the time he was at liberty in Tiflis. It might be supposed that he preferred not to risk putting in an appearance at the conference because of conspiratorial considerations. Yet Krassin, who was then at the head of the Party's fighting activities and who because of his renown was subject to greater risk than anyone else, played a leading role at that conference.

On the eighteenth of March, 1918—that is, a few months after the founding of the Soviet régime—the Menshevik leader, Julius Martov, wrote in his Moscow newspaper: "That the Caucasian Bolsheviks attached themselves to all sorts of daring enterprises of an expropriatory kind should be well known to the same citizen Stalin, who in his time was expelled from his Party organization for having something to do with expropriation." Stalin deemed it necessary to have Martov brought before the judgment of the revolutionary tribunal:

[3] In 1931 Kotè Tsintsadze died in exile, imposed by the "prominent comrade Koba-Stalin."—L. T.

"Never in my life," he told the court and the crowded courtroom, "was I placed on trial before my Party organization or expelled. This is a vicious libel." But Stalin said nothing about expropriations. "With accusations like Martov's, one has a right to come out only with documents in hand. But it is dishonorable to throw mud on the basis of rumors, without having any facts." Wherein is the political source of Stalin's indignation? It was no secret that the Bolsheviks as a whole were involved in expropriations: Lenin openly defended expropriation in the press. On the other hand, expulsion from a Menshevik organization could scarcely be regarded by a Bolshevik as a shameful circumstance, especially ten years later. Stalin, therefore, could not have had any impelling motives for denying Martov's "accusations," had they corresponded to actuality. Besides, to challenge a clever and resourceful opponent to come into court under these conditions meant to risk giving him the chance to try him. Does it mean, then, that Martov's accusations were false? Generally speaking, Martov, carried away by his journalistic temperament and his detestation of the Bolsheviks, had more than once overstepped the pale within which the indubitable nobility of his nature should have confined him. However, in this instance the point at issue was the trial. Martov remained quite categorical in his affirmation. He demanded that certain witnesses be subpoenaed: "First of all, the well-known Georgian Social-Democratic public figure, Isidor Ramishvili, who was the chairman of the revolutionary court which determined Stalin's participation in expropriating the steamship Nicholas I in Baku; Noah Jordania; the Bolshevik Sha'umyan, and other members of the Transcaucasian district committee of 1907-1908. In the second place, a group of witnesses headed by Gukovsky, the present Commissar of Finance, under whose chairmanship was tried the case of the attempted assassination of the worker Zharinov, who, before the Party organization, had exposed the Baku committee and its leader, Stalin, as being connected with an expropriation." In his reply, Stalin said nothing either about the expropriation of the steamship or about the attempt to assassinate Zharinov, at the same time insisting: "I was never tried; if Martov says so, he is a vicious libeller."

In the strictly legal sense of the word, it was impossible to expel "expropriators," since they had themselves prudently resigned from the Party beforehand. But it was possible to pose the question of whether to accept them back in the organization. Direct expulsion could be meted out only to those instigators who remained in the ranks of the Party. But there were apparently no direct incriminations of Koba. It is therefore possible that to a certain extent Martov was right when he affirmed that Koba had been expelled: "in principle" it was so. But Stalin was also right: individually he had never been tried. It was not easy for the tribunal to make head or tail of this, especially in the absence of witnesses. Stalin objected to their being subpoenaed, pleading the difficulty and the unreliability of communications with the Caucasus in those crucial days. The revolutionary tribunal did not delve into the essentials of the case, declaring that libel was not under its jurisdiction, but sentenced Martov to "social censure" for insulting the Soviet government ("the government of Lenin and Trotsky," as the report of the trial in the Menshevik publication proclaimed it ironically). It is impossible not to pause with apprehension at the mention of the attempt on the life of the worker Zharinov for his protest against expropriations. Although we know nothing at all about that episode, it throws off an ominous reflection into the future.

In 1925 the Menshevik Dan wrote that expropriators like Ordzhonikidze and Stalin in the Caucasus provided the Bolshevik faction with the wherewithal; but this is merely a repetition of what Martov had said, and undoubtedly on the basis of the same sources. No one informs us of anything concrete. Yet there was no lack of attempts to raise the curtain over that romantic period in Koba's life. With the ingratiating legerity characteristic of him, Emil Ludwig asked Stalin during their conversation in the Kremlin to tell him "anything" about the adventures of his youth, such as, for example, the robbing of a bank. In reply, Stalin gave his inquiring interlocutor a pamphlet biography in which presumably "everything" was told; but there was not a word in it about robberies.

Stalin himself has never, anywhere, said anything at all, not so much as a word, about his fighting adventures. It is hard to say why. He was never distinguished by autobiographical modesty. What he deems inconvenient to tell, others do by his orders. Beginning with his dizzying rise, he might have been motivated by consideration of governmental "prestige." But in the first years after the October Revolution such considerations were quite foreign to him. The former fighters contributed nothing about it in print during that period when Stalin was not yet the inspirer and the controller of historical reminiscences. His reputation as organizer of fighting activities does not find support in any other documents: neither in police records nor in the depositions of traitors and turncoats. True, Stalin has a firm grip on the police records. But if the gendarme archives contained in them any concrete data about Djugashvili as an expropriator, the punishments to which he had been subjected would have been immeasurably more stringent than they were.

Of all the hypotheses, only one has some verisimilitude. "Stalin does not refer and does not allow others to refer to terroristic acts which in one way or another are connected with his name," writes Souvarine, "otherwise, it would inevitably have been apparent that others took part in these acts while he merely supervised them from afar." At the same time it is quite possible—and this is consonant with Koba's character—that with the aid of understatements and emphases, wherever it was necessary, he circumspectly ascribed to himself those achievements which as a matter of fact he had no right to claim as his own. It was impossible to check up on him under the conditions of underground conspiracy. Hence, the absence of his further interest in disclosures of details. On the other hand, the actual participants in expropriations and persons close to him do not mention Koba in their reminiscences, only because they have nothing to say. Others did the fighting; Stalin supervised them from afar.

Concerning the London Congress Ivanovich wrote the following in his illegal Baku newspaper:

> Of the Menshevik resolutions, only the resolution on guerrilla activities was passed, and that only accidentally: the Bolsheviks did not take up the challenge on that occasion, or rather, they did not wish to carry the fight to the bitter end, simply from the desire to give the Mensheviks at least one chance to be glad about something.

The explanation is astounding, because of its absurdity; "to give the Mensheviks a chance to be glad"—such philanthropic solicitude did not figure among Lenin's political habits. As a matter of fact, the Bolsheviks "did not take up the challenge" only because on that question they had against them not only the Mensheviks, the Bundists and the Lefts, but also their closest allies, the Poles. Moreover, there were very sharp disagreements among the Bolsheviks themselves on the question of expropriations. Yet it would be erroneous to assume that the author of the article had simply talked too much without any ulterior motives. As a matter of fact, he found it necessary to derogate the restrictive decision of the Congress in the eyes of the fighters. That, of course, does not render the explanation itself any the less senseless. Yet such is Stalin's way: whenever he wants to camouflage his purpose, he does not hesitate to resort to the crudest tricks. And not infrequently the very obvious crudity of his arguments does just that, freeing him from the necessity to seek more profound motives. A conscientious Party member would have merely shrugged his shoulders in chagrin after reading how Lenin had failed to take up the challenge in order to "give the Mensheviks something to be glad about," but the simple fighter gladly agreed that the "quite accidental" restriction against expropriations need not be taken seriously. For the next fighting operation that was sufficient.

At ten forty-five in the morning on the twelfth of June [1907], in the Erivan Square of Tiflis, an exceptionally daring armed attack took place on a convoy of Cossacks that accompanied an equipage transporting a bag of money. The course of the operation was calculated with the precision of clockwork. Several bombs of exceptional strength were thrown in a set rotation. There were numerous revolver shots. The bag of money (341,000 rubles) vanished with the revolutionists. Not a single one of the fighters was caught by the police. Three members of the convoy were left dead on the spot; about fifty persons were wounded, most of them slightly. The chief organizer of the enterprise, protected by an officer's uniform, sauntered about the square, observing all the movements of the convoy and of the fighters and at the same time, by means of clever remarks, keeping the public away from the scene of the pending attack, so that there would be no unnecessary victims. At a critical moment, when it might seem that all was lost, the pseudo-officer took hold of the bag of money with amazing self possession and temporarily hid it in a couch belonging to the director of the observatory, the same one in which the youthful Koba had at one time worked as a bookkeeper. This leader was the Armenian fighter Petrosyan, who bore the alias *Kamo*.

Having come to Tiflis at the end of the preceding century, he fell into the hands of propagandists, among them Koba. Knowing almost no Russian, Petrosyan once asked Koba again: "*Kamo* [instead of *komu*, meaning: *to whom*] shall I take this?" Koba began to laugh at him: "Hey, you—*kamo, kamo! . . .*" From that indelicate jest was born a revolutionary alias which became historical. So Kamo's widow, Medvedeva, tells us. She says nothing more about the relations of these two people. But she does tell about the touching attachment of Kamo for Lenin, whom he visited for the first time in 1906 in Finland. "That fearless fighter of limitless audacity and unbreakable will power," writes Krupskaya, "was at the same time an exceedingly sensitive person, somewhat naive, and a tender comrade. He was passionately attached to Ilyich, Krassin and Bogdanov . . . He made friends with my mother, told her about his aunt and about his sisters. Kamo often went from Finland to Petersburg, always taking his weapons with him, and each time, with special care, mother would tie his revolvers on his back." This is all the more remarkable because Krupskaya's mother was the widow of a Tsarist official and did not renounce religion until she was quite old.

Shortly before the Tiflis expropriation, Kamo again visited the staff in Finland. Medvedeva writes: "Disguised as an officer, Kamo went to Finland, called on Lenin, and with arms and explosives returned to Tiflis." The journey took place either on the eve of the London Congress or immediately after it. The bombs came from Krassin's laboratory. A chemist by education, Leonid, when still a student, dreamed of bombs the size of a nut. The year 1905 gave him an opportunity to extend his research in that direction. True, he never succeeded in making one of those ideal dimensions, but the laboratories under his supervision produced bombs of great devastating force. This was not the first time that the fighters tested them on a square in Tiflis.

After the expropriation Kamo appeared in Berlin. There he was arrested upon the denunciation of the provocateur Zhitomirsky, who occupied a prominent place in the foreign organization of the Bolsheviks. During the arrest the Prussian police seized his suitcase, in which presumably bombs and revolvers were discovered. According to the information of the Mensheviks (the investigation was conducted by the future diplomat Chicherin), Kamo's dynamite was intended for an attack on the banking house of Mendelssohn in Berlin. "That is not true," declares the well-informed Bolshevik Pyatnitsky, "the dynamite was prepared for the Caucasus." Let us leave the destination of the dynamite an open question. Kamo remained in a German prison more than a year and a half, continuously simulating violent insanity upon the advice of Krassin. As an incurable madman he was surrendered to Russia, and spent another year and a half in Metekh Castle in Tiflis, subjected to the most trying tests. Declared finally hopelessly insane, Kamo was transferred to a psychiatric hospital, from which he escaped. "After that, illegally, hiding in the hold of a ship, he went to Paris to have a talk with Ilyich." That was in 1911. Kamo suffered frightfully because of the split that occurred between Lenin on the one hand, Bog-

danov and Krassin on the other. "He was ardently attached to all three," Krupskaya repeats. Then follows an idyll: Kamo asked that almonds be brought to
him, sat in the kitchen, which was also the dining room, ate almonds, as in his
native Caucasus, and related the story of the frightful years, told how he simu-
lated madness and how he had tamed a swallow while in prison. "Ilyich listened
to him, and he was poignantly sorry for this recklessly audacious man, who was
childish and naive and warm-hearted and ready for the greatest exploits, and
who after his escape did not know what exactly to do."

Again arrested in Russia, Kamo was condemned to death. The manifesto
issued in 1913, on the occasion of the three hundredth anniversary of the
Romanov dynasty, brought an unexpected commutation to lifelong hard labor
in place of the gibbet. Four years later the February Revolution brought him
unexpected liberation. The October Revolution brought power to the Bolsheviks.
But it threw Kamo out of his rut. He was like a mighty fish flung out on the
shore. During the civil war I tried to interest him in guerrilla warfare in the
enemy's rear, but work on the battlefield was apparently not to his liking. Besides, the frightful years he had endured had not passed without taking their
toll. Kamo was stifling. He had not risked his and other people's lives scores of
times, in order to become a prosperous official. Kotè Tsintsadze, another legend-
ary figure, died of tuberculosis in Stalin's exile. A similar end would undoubtedly
have been Kamo's lot had he not been accidentally run over and killed by an
automobile on one of the streets of Tiflis in the summer of 1922. Most likely
a member of the new bureaucracy sat in that automobile. Kamo was wending his
way through the darkness on a modest bicycle: he had not made a brilliant
career. The very way he perished is symbolic.

Apropos of Kamo, Souvarine writes with unwarranted superciliousness about
"the anachronistic mysticism" which is incompatible with the rationalism of the
advanced countries. As a matter of fact, only a few traits of the revolutionary
type, which is far from being no longer of any use in the countries of "Western
civilization," had found a limited expression in Kamo. Insufficiency of the revolutionary spirit in the labor movement of Europe has already brought about the
triumph of Fascism in a number of countries in which "anachronistic mysticism"
—this is where the word is apt!—finds its most disgusting expression. The
struggle against the iron tyranny of Fascism will undoubtedly bring out among
the revolutionary fighters of the West all those traits which in Kamo so astonish
the skeptical Philistine. In his "Iron Heel" Jack London foretold a whole epoch
of American Kamos in the service of Socialism. The historical process is far
more complex than a superficial rationalist would wish to believe it.

In Party circles, Koba's personal participation in the Tiflis expropriation has
long ago been regarded as indubitable. The former Soviet diplomat Bessedovsky,
who had heard various tales in second and third rate bureaucratic salons, tells
that Stalin, "in accordance with Lenin's instruction" did not take a direct part
in the expropriations but that he himself had presumably "later bragged that

it was he who had worked out the plan of action to its minutest detail and that the first bomb was thrown by him from the roof of the house of Prince Sumbatov." It is hard to tell whether Stalin had actually bragged about his participation or whether Bessedovsky is merely bragging about his information. In any event, during the Soviet epoch Stalin never confirmed or denied these rumors. Evidently he was not at all opposed to having the tragic romanticism of expropriations connected with his name in the consciousness of the youth. In 1932 I still had no doubt about Stalin's leading role in the armed attack on Erivan Square and referred to it incidentally in one of my articles. However, a closer study of the circumstances of those days compels me to revise my view of the traditional version.

In the chronology attached to the twelfth volume of Lenin's Works, under the date of June 12, 1907, we read: "Tiflis expropriation (341,000 rubles), organized by Kamo-Petrosyan." And that is all. In an anthology dedicated to Krassin, in which much is said about the famous illegal printshop in the Caucasus and about the Party's military activities, Stalin is not mentioned even once. An old militant, well informed about the activities of that period writes: "The plans for all the expropriations organized by the latter [Kamo], at the Kvirili and Dushet chancelleries and at Erivan Square, were made and considered by him jointly with Nikitich [Krassin]." Not a word about Stalin. Another former militant states: "Such expropriations as the one in Tiflis and elsewhere were carried out under the direct leadership of Leonid Borissovich [Krassin]." Again nothing about Stalin. Nor is Stalin mentioned even once in Bibineishvili's book, which recites all the minutiae concerning the preparations and performance of the expropriations. It undoubtedly follows from these omissions that Koba was not in direct contact with the members of the detachments, did not instruct them, consequently was not the organizer of the act in the real sense of the word, let alone a direct participant.

The Congress in London came to an end on April twenty-seventh.[4] The expropriation in Tiflis occurred on June twelfth [25th n.s.], a month and a half later. Stalin had too little time left between his return from abroad and the day of the expropriation to supervise the preparation of such a complicated enterprise. It is more likely that the fighters had been selected and had been drawn together in the course of several preceding reckless adventures. Possibly they marked time, pending the Congress's decision. Some of them might have had doubts as to how Lenin would look upon expropriations. The fighters were waiting for the signal. Stalin might have brought them that signal. But did his participation go beyond that?

We know virtually nothing about the relations of Kamo and Koba. Kamo was inclined to attach himself to people. Yet no one speaks of his attachment to Koba. The reticence about their relations leads one to think that there was no

[4] The London Congress was held from May 13 to June 1 (April 30 to May 19, o. s.), 1907. Hence, there was even less than a month and a half from the time it came to an end and the Tiflis expropriation.—C. M.

attachment; that, rather, there were conflicts. The source of that might have been Koba's attempts to boss Kamo or to ascribe to himself what he had no right to claim. Bibineishvili tells in his book on Kamo that "a mysterious stranger" appeared in Georgia after it had become Soviet, and under false pretenses took possession of Kamo's correspondence and of other valuable material. Who needed them and for what purpose? The documents, as well as the man who absconded with them, disappeared without a trace. Would it be too hasty to presume that through one of his agents Stalin had snatched from Kamo certain evidence which for one reason or another he found disturbing? That does not exclude, of course, the possibility of close collaboration between them in June, 1907. Neither is there anything to restrain us from conceding that the relationship between the two might have become worse after the Tiflis "affair," in which Koba might have been Kamo's adviser in working out the final details. Moreover, the adviser might have fostered abroad a highly colored version of his own role. After all, it *is* easier to ascribe to one's self the leadership of an expropriation than the leadership of the October Revolution. Yet Stalin will not hesitate to do even the latter.

Barbusse states that in 1907 Koba went to Berlin and remained there for a certain time "for conversations with Lenin." What sort of conversations the author does not know. The text of Barbusse's book consists mostly of errors. But the reference to the Berlin journey commands our attention all the more, because in the dialogue with Ludwig, Stalin also refers to his having been in Berlin in 1907. If Lenin journeyed especially for that meeting to the capital of Germany, then in any event it was not for the sake of *theoretical* "conversations." The meeting might have taken place either directly before, or more likely, immediately after, the Congress, and almost undoubtedly was devoted to the impending expropriation, the means of forwarding the money, and the like. Why did these negotiations take place in Berlin and not in London? It is quite likely that Lenin might have deemed it careless to meet with Ivanovich in London, where he was in full sight of the other delegates and of numerous tsarist and other spies attracted by the Congress. It is also possible that a third person, who had nothing to do with the Congress, was supposed to participate in these conferences.

From Berlin Koba returned to Tiflis, but a short time after moved to Baku, from where, according to Barbusse, "he again went abroad for a meeting with Lenin." One of the trusted Caucasians (Barbusse was in the Caucasus and while there wrote down a number of stories arranged for him by Beriya) apparently said something about Stalin's two meetings with Lenin abroad, in order to emphasize their close relationship. The chronology of these meetings is very significant: one precedes the expropriation and the other directly follows it. That sufficiently determines their purpose. The second meeting was in all likelihood concerned with the problem: to continue or to stop?

Iremashvili writes: "The friendship of Koba-Stalin with Lenin began with that." The word "friendship" is patently a misnomer. The distance separating these two men precluded personal friendship. But it would seem that just about that time they did begin to know each other. If the assumption is warranted that Lenin had previously made arrangements with Koba about plans for the Tiflis expropriation, then it was quite natural for him to have been filled with admiration for the man he regarded as the organizer of that coup. It is likely that upon reading the telegram about the seizure of the booty without a single loss of life by the revolutionists, Lenin exclaimed to himself, or he might have told Krupskaya, "Splendid Georgian!" These are the words we shall find in one of his letters to Gorky. Enthusiasm for people who showed resoluteness, or were simply successful in carrying out an operation assigned to them, was highly characteristic of Lenin to the very end of his life. Above all, he prized men of action. Basing his judgment of Koba on the latter's vaunted record in the Caucasian expropriations, Lenin apparently came to regard him as a person capable of seeing things through or of leading others unflinchingly. He made up his mind that the "splendid Georgian" would be useful.

The Tiflis booty brought no good. The entire sum consisted of five-hundred ruble notes. It was impossible to circulate currency of such large denomination. After the adverse publicity received by the unfortunate skirmish in Erivan Square, it was senseless to try to exchange these bills at any Russian bank. The operation was transferred abroad. But the provocateur Zhitomirsky, who warned the police about it betimes, participated in the organization of the exchange operations. The future Commissar of Foreign Affairs Litvinov was arrested while attempting to exchange them in Paris. Olga Ravich, who subsequently became Zinoviev's wife, fell into the hands of the police at Stockholm. The future People's Commissar of Public Health Semashko was arrested at Geneva, apparently by accident. "I was one of those Bolsheviks," he wrote, "who at the time was on principle opposed to expropriations." The mishaps connected with the exchange considerably increased the number of such Bolsheviks. "The average Swiss," says Krupskaya, "was scared to death. All they talked about was the Russian expropriators. They talked about it with horror at the boarding house where Ilyich and I took our meals." It is noteworthy that Olga Ravich, as well as Semashko, disappeared during the recent Soviet "purges."

The Tiflis expropriation could in no way be regarded as a guerrilla clash between two battles in a civil war. Lenin could not help but see that the insurrection had been shoved ahead into the hazy future. As far as he was concerned, the problem consisted this time only of a simple attempt to assure financial means to the Party at the expense of the enemy, for the impending period of uncertainty. Lenin could not resist the temptation, took advantage of a favorable opportunity, of a happy "exception." In that sense, one must say outright that the idea of the Tiflis expropriation contained in it a goodly element of adventurism, which, as a rule, was foreign to Lenin's politics. The case with Stalin was different. Broad historical considerations had little value in his eyes. The resolution of the London Congress was only an irksome scrap of paper, to be nullified by means of a crude trick. Success would justify the risk. Souvarine argues that it is not fair to shift responsibility from the leader of the faction to a secondary figure. There is no question here of shifting responsibility. At the time, the majority of the Bolshevik faction was opposed to Lenin on the question of expropriations. The Bolsheviks, in direct contact with the fighting detachments, had extremely convincing observations of their own, which Lenin, again an emigrant, did not have. Without corrections from below, the leader of the greatest genius is bound to make crude errors. The fact remains that Stalin was not among those who understood the inadmissibility of guerrilla actions under conditions of revolutionary retreat. And that was no accident. To him the Party was first of all a machine. The machine required financial means in order to exist. The financial means could be obtained with the aid of another machine, independent of life and of the struggle of the masses. There Stalin was in his own element.

The consequences of this tragic adventure, which rounded out an entire phase of Party life, were rather serious. The fight over the Tiflis expropriation poisoned relations inside the Party and inside the Bolshevik faction itself for a long time to come. From then on, Lenin changed front and came out more resolutely than ever against the tactic of expropriations, which for a time became the heritage of the "Left" Wing among the Bolsheviks. For the last time the Tiflis "affair" was officially reviewed by the Party Central Committee in January, 1910, upon the insistence of the Mensheviks. The resolution sharply condemned expropriation as an inadmissible violation of Party discipline, while conceding that rendering harm to the labor movement was not the intention of the participants, who had been "guided solely by a faulty understanding of Party interests." No one was expelled. No one was mentioned by name. Koba was thus amnestied along with others, as one who had been guided by "a faulty understanding of Party interests."

In the meantime, the disintegration of revolutionary organizations proceeded apace. As early as October, 1907, the Menshevik "literary" Potressov wrote to Axelrod: "We are undergoing complete disintegration and utter demoralization . . . There is not only no organization, but not even the elements for it. And this non-existence is even extolled as a principle . . ." This extoling of disintegration as a principle soon became the task of most leaders of Menshevism, including Potressov himself. They declared the illegal Party liquidated once and for all, and the aim to restore it—a reactionary utopia. Martov insisted that it was precisely "scandalous incidents like the exchange of the Tiflis currency" which forced "the most devoted parties and the most active elements of the working class" to shun all contact with an illegal political machine. The Mensheviks, now known as the Liquidators, saw in the frightful development of provocation another convincing argument in favor of the "necessity" to forsake the mephitic underground. Entrenching themselves in trade unions, educational clubs and insurance societies, they carried on their work as cultural propagandists, not as revolutionists. To safeguard their jobs in the legal organizations, the officials from among the workers began to resort to protective coloration. They avoided the strike struggle, so as not to compromise the scarcely tolerated trade unions. In practice, legality at any price meant outright repudiation of revolutionary methods.

The Liquidators were in the forefront during the most desolate years. "They suffered less from police persecution," writes Olminsky. "They had many of the writers, a good part of the lecturers and on the whole most of the intellectuals. They were the cocks of the walk and they crowed about it." The attempts of the Bolshevik faction, whose ranks were thinning every hour, to preserve its illegal machine were dashed at each turn against hostile circumstances. Bolshevism seemed definitely doomed. "All of present-day development," wrote Martov, "renders the formation of any kind of durable party-sect a pathetic reactionary utopia." In that fundamental prognosis Martov and, with him, Russian Menshevism, made a cruel mistake. The perspectives and the slogans of the Liquidators proved to be the reactionary utopia. There was no place for an open labor party in the Third of June régime. Even the party of the liberals was refused registration. "The Liquidators have shaken off the illegal party," wrote Lenin, "but they have not carried out the obligation to found a legal one either." Precisely because Bolshevism remained loyal to the tasks of the revolution in the period of its decline and degradation, it prepared its unprecedented blossoming in the years of the revolution's new resurgence.

Meantime, at the opposite pole to the Liquidators, in the left wing of the Bolshevik faction, an extremist group formed, which stubbornly refused to recognize the altered situation and continued to defend the tactic of direct action. After the elections, the differences of opinion that arose on the question of boycotting the Duma led to the formation of the Recallist faction, which called for the recall of the Social-Democratic deputies from the Duma. The Recallists were undoubtedly the symmetrical supplement of the Liquidators. While the Mensheviks, always and everywhere, even under the irresistible pressure of revolution, deemed it necessary to participate in any "parliament," even a purely fortuitous one patterned by the Tsar, the Recallists[5] thought that by boycotting the parliament established in consequence of the defeat of the revolution, they would be able to evoke new mass pressure. Since electrical discharges are accompanied by thunderclaps, the "irreconcilables" attempted to evoke electrical discharges by means of artificial thunderclaps.

The period of dynamite laboratories still exerted its powerful influence upon Krassin. That shrewd and sensible man joined for a time the sect of Recallists, in order to abandon the Revolution altogether for years to come. Bogdanov, another of Lenin's closest collaborators in the secret Bolshevik trinity, likewise moved to the Left. With the break-up of this secret triumvirate the old top leadership of Bolshevism fell apart. But Lenin did not budge. In the summer of 1907 the majority of the faction was for the boycott. By the spring of 1908 the Recallists were already a minority in Petersburg and Moscow. Lenin's preponderance was made obvious beyond doubt. Koba speedily took that into ac-

[5] See Glossary.

count. His unfortunate experience with the agrarian program, when he had come out openly against Lenin, made him more circumspect. Noiselessly and unobtrusively, he reneged on his fellow-boycotters. From then on his regular behavior at each turn was to keep out of sight and keep quiet while changing his stand.

The continued splintering of the Party into petty groups, which waged ruthless battles in a vacuum, aroused in sundry factions a longing for reconciliation, for agreement, for unity at any price. It was precisely at that period that another aspect of "Trotskyism" came to the forefront: not the theory of permanent revolution, but "reconciliation" of the Party. That will have to be discussed, however briefly, so as to facilitate understanding of the subsequent conflict between Stalinism and Trotskyism. In 1904—that is, from the moment differences of opinion arose as to the nature of the liberal bourgeoisie—I broke with the Minority of the Second Congress [The Mensheviks] and during the ensuing thirteen years belonged to no faction. My position on the intra-party conflict came down to this: as long as the revolutionary intellectuals were dominant among the Bolsheviks as well as among the Mensheviks and as long as both factions did not venture beyond the bourgeois democratic revolution, there was no justification for a split between them; in the new revolution, under the pressure of the laboring masses, both factions would in any case be compelled to assume an identical revolutionary position, as they did in 1905. Certain critics of Bolshevism to this day regard my old conciliationism as the voice of wisdom. Yet its profound erroneousness had been long ago demonstrated both in theory and practice. A simple conciliation of factions is possible only along some sort of "middle" line. But where is the guaranty that this artificially drawn diagonal line will coincide with the needs of objective development? The task of scientific politics is to deduce a program and a tactic from an analysis of the struggle of classes, not from the [ever-shifting] parallelogram of such secondary and transitory forces as political factions. True, the position of the reaction was such that it cramped the political activity of the entire Party within extremely narrow limits. At the time, it might have seemed that the differences of opinion were unimportant and artificially inflated by the émigré leaders. Yet it was precisely during the period of reaction that the revolutionary party was unable to train its cadres without a major perspective. The preparation for tomorrow was a most important element in the policy of today. The policy of conciliation thrived on the hope that the course of events itself would prompt the necessary tactic. But that fatalistic optimism meant in practice not only repudiation of factional struggle but of the very idea of a party, because, if "the course of events" is capable of directly dictating to the masses the correct policy, what is the use of any special unification of the proletarian vanguard, the working out of a program, the choice of leaders, the training in a spirit of discipline?

Later, in 1911, Lenin observed that conciliationism was indissolubly connected with the very essence of the Party's historical task during the years of counter-revolution. "A number of Social-Democrats," he wrote, "in that period sank into conciliationism, *proceeding from the most varied motives*. Most consistently of all was Conciliationism expressed by Trotsky, about the only one who tried to provide a theoretical foundation for that policy." Just because in those years conciliationism became epidemic, Lenin saw in it the greatest menace to the development of a revolutionary party. He was well aware of the fact that the Conciliators claimed "the most varied motives," opportunistic as well as revolutionary. But in his crusade against that dangerous tendency he felt he had the right not to make any distinction between its subjective sources. On the contrary, he attacked with redoubled ferocity those Conciliators whose basic positions were closest to Bolshevism. Avoiding public conflict with the Conciliationist wing of the Bolshevik faction itself, Lenin chose to direct his polemics against "Trotskyism," especially since I, as has already been said, attempted to provide a "theoretical foundation" for Conciliationism. Quotations from that violent polemic were later to render Stalin a service for which they were certainly not intended.

Lenin's work during the years of reaction—minute and painstaking in its detail, audacious in its sweep of thought—will always offer a great lesson in revolutionary training. "We learned at the time of revolution," wrote Lenin in July, 1909, " 'to talk French,' i.e., . . . to arouse the energy and the sweep of direct mass struggle. We must now, at the time of stagnancy, reaction, disintegration, learn 'to speak German,' i.e., act slowly . . . conquering inch by inch." The leader of the Mensheviks, Martov, wrote in 1911 : "That which two or three years ago the leaders of the open movement [i.e., the Liquidators] acknowledged only in principle—the necessity to build the Party 'in German'—. . . is now everywhere acknowledged as the task to the practical realization of which it is high time to set to work." Although both Lenin and Martov had apparently begun "to speak German," as a matter of fact, they talked different languages. For Martov, "to speak German" meant to adapt himself to the Russian semi-absolutism in the hope of gradually "Europeanizing" it. For Lenin, the same expression meant: to utilize with the aid of the illegal party the meager legal possibilities of preparing a new revolution. As the subsequent opportunistic degeneration of the German Social-Democracy demonstrated, the Mensheviks more truly reflected the spirit of "the German language" in politics. But Lenin understood much more correctly the objective course of development in Germany as well as in Russia: the epoch of peaceful reform was being superseded by the epoch of catastrophes.

As for Koba, he knew neither French nor German. Yet all his inclinations drew him toward Lenin's position. Koba did not seek the open arena, like the orators and journalists of Menshevism, because the open arena exposed his weak rather than his strong attributes. He needed above all a centralized machine. But under the conditions of a counter-revolutionary régime that machine could be only illegal. Although Koba lacked historical perspective, he was more than amply endowed with perseverance. During the years of reaction he was not one of the tens of thousands who deserted the Party, but one of the very few hundreds who, despite everything, remained loyal to it.

Soon after the London Congress both young Zinoviev, who was elected to the Central Committee, and young Kamenev, who became a member of the Bolshevik Center, became émigrés. Koba remained in Russia. Subsequently he credited that to himself as an extraordinary achievement. As a matter of fact, it was nothing of the kind. The selection of place and nature of work depended to a very minor extent on the choice of the individual in question. Had the Central Committee seen in Koba a young theoretician and publicist capable of rising to higher things abroad, he undoubtedly would have been ordered to emigrate and he would have had neither the chance nor the desire to decline. But no one called him abroad. From the time the top leadership of the Party became aware of him, he was looked upon as a "practico," i.e., as a rank and file revolutionist, useful primarily for local organizational activity. And Koba himself, who had tested his own abilities at the congresses in Tammerfors, Stockholm and London, was hardly inclined to join the émigrés, among whom he would have been relegated to third place. Later, after Lenin's death, necessity was transformed into virtue, and the very word "émigré" came to sound on the lips of the new bureaucracy pretty much as it had sounded on the lips of the conservatives of the Tsarist epoch.

Resuming his exile, Lenin felt, according to his own words, as if he were stepping into his grave. "We here are frightfully cut off from everything now . . . ," he wrote from Paris in the autumn of 1909. "These years have actually been hellishly difficult . . ." In the Russian bourgeois press there began to appear disparaging articles about the emigration, which presumably epitomized the defeated revolution repudiated by cultivated circles. In 1912, Lenin replied to these libels in the Petersburg newspaper of the Bolsheviks: "Yes, there is much that is hard to bear in the émigré environment . . . There is more want and poverty here than elsewhere. Especially high among us is the percentage of suicides . . ." However, "only here and nowhere else have been posed and considered the most important fundamental questions of the entire Russian democracy during the years of confusion and interregnum." The leading ideas of the Revolution of 1917 were being prepared in the course of the wearisome and exhausting battles of the émigré groups. In that work Koba took no part at all.

From the autumn of 1907 until March, 1908, Koba carried on revolutionary activity in Baku. It is impossible to establish the date of his removal there. He may have left Tiflis at the very moment that Kamo was loading his last bomb; circumspection was the dominant aspect of Koba's courage. Baku, city of many diverse races, which at the beginning of the century had already a population of more than a hundred thousand, continued to grow rapidly, drawing into the oil industry masses of Azerbaijan Tatars. The Tsarist authorities replied, not without some success, to the revolutionary movement of 1905, by instigating the Tatars against the more advanced Armenians. However, the revolution took hold even of the backward Azerbaijanians. Belatedly, as far as the rest of the country was concerned, they participated *en masse* in the strikes of 1907.

In the "Black City" Koba spent about eight months, from which should be deducted the time he took for his journey to Berlin. "Under the leadership of Comrade Stalin," wrote the not too inventive Beriya, "the Baku Bolshevik organization grew up, gained strength and was tempered during its struggle against the Mensheviks." Koba was sent to regions where the opponents were particularly strong. "Under the leadership of Comrade Stalin, the Bolsheviks broke the influence of the Mensheviks and the Essars," and so forth. We learn little more from Alliluyev. The gathering of Bolshevik forces after the havoc wrought by the police occurred, according to him, "under the direct leadership and with the active participation of Comrade Stalin . . . His organizational talent, genuine revolutionary enthusiasm, inexhaustible energy, firm will and Bolshevik persistence . . ." and the like. Unfortunately, the reminiscences of Stalin's father-in-law were written in 1937. The formula: "under the direct leadership and with the active participation" faultlessly betrays the Beriya trademark. The Essar Vereshchak, who was active in Baku at the same time and observed Koba with the eyes of a political opponent, recognizes in him exceptional organizational talent but completely denies him any personal influence among the workers. "His personality," he writes, "produced a bad first impression. Koba took that into account as well. He never spoke openly at mass meetings . . . Koba's presence in this or that labor district was always a secret matter, and one could guess at it only by the enlivened activity of the Bolsheviks." This is more like the truth. We shall have occasion to meet Vereshchak again.

The reminiscences of Bolsheviks written prior to the totalitarian era give the first place in the Baku organization not to Koba but to Sha'umyan[6] and Dzhaparidze,[7] two exceptional revolutionists killed by the English during their occupation of Transcaucasia, on September 20, 1918. "Of the old comrades in Baku," writes Sha'umyan's biographer Karimyan, "Comrades A. Yenukidze, Koba (Stalin), Timofei (Spandaryan), Alyosha (Dzhaparidze) were then active. The Bolshevik organization . . . had a broad base for activity in the trade union of the oil industry workers. The actual organizer and secretary of all the trade union work was Alyosha (Dzhaparidze)." Yenukidze is mentioned ahead of Koba; the principal role is assigned to Dzhaparidze. Further: "Both of them (Sha'umyan and Dzhaparidze) were the most beloved leaders of the Baku proletariat." It had not yet occurred to Karinyan, who was writing in 1924, to name Koba among "the most beloved leaders."

The Baku Bolshevik Stopani tells how in 1907 he became absorbed in trade union work, "the most burning task for the Baku of those days." The trade union was under the leadership of the Bolsheviks. In the union "a prominent role was played by the irreplaceable Alyosha Dzhaparidze and a lesser role by

[6] Stepan Grigoryevich Sha'umyan (1878-1918).—C. M.
[7] Prokofii Aprasionovich Dzhaparidze (1880-1918).—C. M.

Comrade Koba (Djugashvili), who gave most of his strength primarily to party work, of which he was in charge . . ." Of what this "Party work" consisted, apart from "the most burning task" of leading the trade unions, Stopani does not specify. But he does contribute a very interesting casual remark about disagreements among the Baku Bolsheviks. All of them agreed on the need of organizationally "consolidating" the Party's influence in the trade unions, but "with reference to the degree and form of that consolidation there were also disagreements among ourselves: we had our own 'Left' (Koba-Stalin) and 'Right' (Alyosha Dzhaparidze and others, including myself); the disagreements were not on fundamentals but with reference to the tactics or the methods of establishing that contact." Stopani's deliberately vague words—Stalin was then already very powerful—enable us faultlessly to imagine the actual disposition of figures. Due to the belated wave of the strike movement, the trade union had become of foremost importance. The leaders of the union naturally proved to be those who knew how to talk with the masses and how to lead them: Dzhaparidze and Sha'umyan. Again pushed into second place, Koba entrenched himself in the underground committee. The Party's struggle to win influence in the trade union meant to Koba that the leaders of the masses, Dzhaparidze and Sha'umyan, should submit to his bossing. In the fight for this sort of "consolidation" of his own personal power, Koba, as is evident from Stopani's words, roused against himself all the leading Bolsheviks. The activity of the masses was not favorable to the plans of the underhanded schemer.

Exceptionally bitter became the rivalry between Koba and Sha'umyan. Matters reached such a pass that after Sha'umyan's arrest, according to the testimony of the Georgian Mensheviks, the workers suspected Koba of having renounced his rival to the police, and demanded that he be tried by a party court. Their campaign was terminated only by Koba's own arrest. It is unlikely that the accusers had definite proofs. Their suspicion might have been aroused by any number of circumstantial coincidences. Suffice it, though, that Koba's Party comrades thought him capable of turning informer, when motivated by thwarted ambition. Such things have never been told about anyone else!

Concerning the financing of the Baku Committee at the time of Koba's participation in it, there is circumstantial but far from indubitable evidence concerning armed "expropriation;" financial tributes imposed on industrialists under the threat of death or of firing their oil wells; the fabrication and circulation of counterfeit currency, and the like. It is hard to decide whether these deeds, which actually took place, were imputed to Koba's initiative as far back as those remote years or whether the greater part of them were first connected with his name considerably later. In any event, Koba's participation in such risky enterprises could not have been direct; otherwise, it would have been inevitably revealed. In all likelihood, he guided the militant operations, as he had tried to guide the trade union, from the sidelines. It is noteworthy in this connection that very little is known about the Baku period of Koba's life. The most insignificant episodes are recorded whenever they tend to enhance the "Leader's" fame, yet his revolutionary activity is referred to only in the most general phrases. The amount of suppression is hardly accidental.

The Essar Vereshchak, while still quite young, landed in 1909 in the so-called Ba'ilov Prison of Baku, where he spent three and a half years. Koba, who was arrested on March twenty-fifth, spent a half a year in that prison, left it to go into exile, spent nine months there, returned illegally to Baku, was again arrested in March, 1910, and was again imprisoned there, side by side with Vereshchak, for nearly six months. In 1912 the prison buddies met again at Narym, in Siberia. Finally, after the February Revolution, Vereshchak, then a delegate from the Tiflis garrison, met his old acquaintance at the First Congress of Soviets in Petrograd.

After the rise of Stalin's political star, Vereshchak gave a detailed account of their joint prison life in the émigré press. Perhaps not everything in his story is reliable and not all of his judgments are convincing. Thus, Vereshchak asserts, no doubt on the basis of hearsay, that Koba had himself acknowledged that "for revolutionary reasons" he had betrayed certain of his seminary comrades; the unlikelihood of that tale has already been indicated. The Populist author's discussions of Koba's Marxism are extremely naive. But Vereshchak had the invaluable advantage of observing Koba in an environment where, willy-nilly, the habits and conditions of cultured coexistence atrophy. Intended for four hundred inmates, the Baku prison held at the time more than fifteen hundred. The prisoners slept in the overcrowded cells, in the corridors, on the steps of stairways. There could have been no isolation of any kind under such conditions of overcrowding. All the doors, except those of the punitive cells, were wide open. Criminals and politicals moved freely about from cell to cell, from building to building, and in the yard. "It was impossible to sit or to lie down without stepping on someone's toes." In such circumstances people saw each other, and many saw themselves, in quite unexpected lights. Even cold and reserved persons disclosed traits of character which under ordinary conditions they managed to keep hidden.

"Koba was an extremely one-sided person," writes Vereshchak. "He had no general principles and no adequate educational background. By his very nature he had always been a person of little culture, a crude person. All this in him was combined with a peculiarly studied slyness, which at first obscured from the view of even the most observing person the other traits hidden behind it." By "general principles" the author seems to imply moral principles: as a Populist he was an adherent of the school of "ethical" socialism. Vereshchak was surpised by Koba's stamina. A cruel game was played in that prison, the purpose of which was by hook or crook to drive one's opponent frantic: this was called "chasing into a bubble." "It was never possible to drive Koba off his balance . . ." states Vereshchak, "nothing would get his goat . . ."

That game was quite innocent by comparison with the game the authorities played. Among the imprisoned were persons more or less recently sentenced to death who hourly awaited the culmination of their fate. The condemned ate and slept with the others. Before the eyes of the prisoners, they were led out at night and hanged in the prison yard, so that in the cells "were heard the cries and moans of the hanged." All the prisoners suffered from the nervous strain. "Koba slept soundly," says Vereshchak, "or calmly studied Esperanto (he was convinced that Esperanto was the international language of the future)." It would be silly to think that Koba was indifferent to the executions. But he had strong nerves. He did not feel for others as for himself. Nerves like that were in themselves an important asset.

Despite the chaos, the hangings, the party and personal conflicts, the Baku prison was an important revolutionary school. Koba stood out among the Marxist leaders. He did not participate in person to person discussions, preferring public forums, a sure sign that in education and experience Koba was superior to the majority of his fellow-prisoners. "Koba's outward appearance and his polemical coarseness made his presentation always unpleasant. His speeches were devoid of wit; in form they were a dry and formal exposition." Vereshchak recalls a certain "agrarian discussion," when Koba's comrade Ordzhonikidze, "struck the face of the co-reporter, the Essar Ilya Kartsevadze, for which he was cruelly beaten up by the other Essars." This is no invention: the very ardent Ordzhonikidze preserved his predilection for physical arguments even when he became a prominent Soviet dignitary. Once Lenin even proposed expelling him from the party for that.

Vereshchak was astonished by the "mechanical memory" of Koba, whose little head "with its undeveloped forehead" presumably contained all of Marx's "Capital." "Marxism was his element, in it he was unconquerable . . . He knew how to substantiate anything with the appropriate formulae from Marx. This man made a strong impression on young party people unenlightened in politics." Vereshchak himself was among the "unenlightened." To this young Populist, brought up on homespun Russian belletristic sociology, Koba's Marxist baggage must have seemed exceedingly imposing. As a matter of fact, it was modest enough. Koba had neither theoretical curiosity nor perseverance in study nor discipline of thought. It is hardly correct to speak of his "mechanical memory." It is narrow, empirical, utilitarian, but, despite the seminary training, not in the least mechanical. It is a peasant memory, devoid of sweep and synthesis, but firm and tenacious, especially in rancor. It is not at all true that Koba's head was full of ready quotations for all the occasions of life. Koba was never a bookworm or a scholastic. Through Plekhanov and Lenin he culled from Marxism the most elementary statements on the class struggle and on the subordinate significance of ideas in relation to material factors. Although he over-simplified these propositions, he was nevertheless able to apply them with success against the Populists, even as a person with the crudest sort of revolver is able to fight successfully against a man with a boomerang. But on the whole Koba remained essentially indifferent to the Marxist doctrine.

During his confinement in the prisons of Batum and Kutais, as we remember,

Koba attempted to probe the mysteries of the German language: at the time the influence of the German Social-Democracy on the Russian one was exceedingly great. Yet Koba was even less successful in learning Marx's language than his doctrine. In the Baku prison he began to study Esperanto as "the language of the future." That touch most instructively exposes the quality of Koba's intellectual equipment, which in the sphere of learning always sought the line of least resistance. Although he spent eight years in prison and exile, he never managed to learn a single foreign language, not excluding his ill-starred Esperanto.

As a general rule, political prisoners tried not to associate with criminals. Koba, on the contrary, "could be always seen in the society of ruffians, blackmailers, and among the mauserist robbers." He felt himself on an equal footing with them. "He was always impressed by people of real 'business.' And he looked upon politics as a 'business' which one should know how to 'do' and how to 'outdo.' " This is a very apt observation. But this very observation refutes better than anything else the remarks about his "mechanical memory," filled with ready-made quotations. The company of people with higher intellectual interests than his own was irksome to Koba. In the Palitburo[8] of Lenin's day he almost always sat silent, morose and irritable. Conversely, he became more sociable, more even tempered and more human among people of primitive mentality who were unrestrained by any predilection for brains. During the civil war, when certain sections of the army, usually the cavalry branches, became unruly and went in for violence and roistering, Lenin was wont to say, "Hadn't we better send Stalin there? He knows how to talk with people of that kind."

Koba was not the initiator of prison protests and demonstrations, but he always supported the initiators. "That made him a good comrade in the eyes of the prison public." This observation, too, is apt. Koba was never, in anything or anywhere, an initiator. But he was quite capable of utilizing the initiative of others, of pushing the initiators ahead, and of retaining for himself freedom of choice. That does not mean that Koba was devoid of courage; he merely preferred to spend it economically. The prison régime was a mixture of laxity and cruelty. The inmates enjoyed considerable freedom inside the prison walls. But whenever a certain elusive pale was transgressed, the administration resorted to military force. Vereshchak tells how in 1909 (obviously, he means 1908), on the first day of Easter, a company of the Salyan Regiment beat up all the political prisoners, without exception, forcing them to run the gauntlet. "Koba walked, his head unbowed, under the blows of rifle butts, a book in his hands. And when the free-for-all was let loose, Koba forced the doors of his cell with a slop bucket, ignoring the threat of bayonets." That self-contained man—true, on rare occasions—was capable of blinding rage.

The Moscow "historian" Yaroslavsky restates Vereshchak, as follows: "Stalin ran the gauntlet of soldiers, reading Marx . . ." Marx's name is dragged in here for the same reason that a rose appears in the hands of the Virgin Mary.

[8] See Glossary.

All of Soviet historiography is made up of such roses. Koba holding "Marx" under rifle butts has become the subject of Soviet scholarship, prose and poetry. Yet such behavior was in no way exceptional. Prison beatings, just like prison heroism, were the order of the day. Pyatnitsky tells how after his arrest at Wilno in 1902, the police proposed to send him, then still quite a young worker, to the district police officer, who was notorious for his beatings, in order to force testimony from him. But the elder policeman replied: "He won't say anything there, either. He belongs to the *Iskra* organization." Even in those early days the revolutionists of Lenin's school had the reputation of being unyielding. In order to ascertain that Kamo had actually lost his sensitivity, as alleged, physicians pushed pins under his fingernails, and only because Kamo had adamantly endured such tests for a number of years was he finally declared hopelessly insane. What then is the weight of a few rifle butt blows, by comparison with that? There is no basis for underestimating Koba's courage, but it must be confined within the limits of its time and place.

Because of the prison conditions, Vereshchak had no difficulty in observing a certain trait of Stalin's, which enabled him to remain unknown for such a long time: "That was his ability quietly to incite others while he himself remained on the sidelines." Then follow two examples. On one occasion a young Georgian was being beaten up in the corridor of the "political" building. The evil word "provocateur" resounded through the building. Only the soldiers on guard were able to stop the chastisement. His bloody body was removed on a stretcher to the city hospital. Was he a provocateur? And if so, why was he not killed? "In Bàïlov prison provocateurs, when proved to be such, were usually killed," Vereshchak remarks in passing. "No one knew anything or could make head or tail of it, and only a long time later we learned that the rumor had originated with Koba." It was never found out whether the man who had been beaten up was actually a provocateur. Might he have been simply one of the workers who was opposed to expropriations or who accused Koba of having denounced Sha'umyan?

Another instance. On the steps of the stairway which led into the "political" building a certain prisoner known as "the Greek" stabbed a young worker who had but recently been brought to the prison. The Greek himself regarded the man he had killed as a stoolpigeon, although he had never before met him at any time. This sanguine incident, which naturally aroused the entire prison, remained a mystery for a long time. Finally, the Greek began to intimate that he evidently had been "misled" for no good reason: the misinformation had come from Koba.

Caucasians are easily aroused and easily resort to the knife. The cool and calculating Koba, who knew the language and the customs of these people, found it easy to set one against another. In both instances it was undoubtedly a matter of vengeance. The instigator did not need to have the victims know who was responsible for their mishap. Koba is not inclined to share his feelings, not even the joy of vengeance. He prefers to enjoy it alone, by himself. Both episodes, sordid though they are, do not seem unlikely; subsequent events invest them with inherent verisimilitude . . . In Bàïlov Prison the preparation of future events went on. Koba acquired experience, Koba grew strong, Koba matured. The gray figure of the former seminarist with pock marks on his face cast an ever more sinister shadow.

Vereshchak further mentions, this time obviously on the basis of hearsay, Koba's various risky enterprises during his activities at Baku: the organization of counterfeiters, the robbing of state treasuries, and the like. "He was never tried in court for any of these affairs, although the counterfeiters and the expropriators were in prison together with him." If they had known of his role, someone among them would inevitably have betrayed him. "The ability to achieve his purpose quietly by making use of others, while at the same time remaining unnoticed himself, made Koba a sly schemer who did not spurn any means and who avoided public accounting and responsibility."

We thus learn more about Koba's life in prison than about his activities outside. But in both places he remained true to himself. Between discussions with the Populists and small talk with holdup men, he did not forget about his revolutionary organization. Beriya informs us that from prison Koba managed to establish regular contact with the Baku Committee. That was quite possible: where there was no isolation of politicals from the criminals and of the politicals from each other, it was impossible to remain cut off from the outside. One of the issues of the illegal newspaper was entirely prepared in prison. The pulse of the revolution, although considerably weakened, continued to beat. The prison may not have stimulated Koba's interest in theories, but neither did it break his fighting spirit.

On the twentieth of September Koba was sent to Solvychegodsk, in the northern part of Vologda Province. This was privileged banishment: only for two years; not in Siberia, but in European Russia; not in a village, but in a small town of two thousand inhabitants, with fine opportunities for escape. It is thus obvious that the gendarmes did not have even moderately weighty evidence against Koba. In view of the extremely low cost of living in those remote borderlands, it was not hard for exiles to get along on the few rubles a month the government allotted them; for their extra needs they received aid from friends and from the revolutionary Red Cross. How Koba spent his nine months in Solvychegodsk, what he did, what he studied, we do not know. No documents have been published: neither his essays, nor his diaries, nor his letters. In the local police "case of Joseph Djugashvili," under the heading "behavior," is recorded: "rude, impudent, disrespectful to superiors." "Disrespectfulness" was a trait common to all revolutionists; "rudeness" was his individual trait.

In the spring of 1909 Alliluyev, who was already in Petersburg, received a letter fom Koba, then in exile, asking him for his address. "At the end of that summer of the same year Stalin escaped from exile to Petersburg, where I met him accidentally on one of the streets in the Lityeiny district." It so happened that Stalin did not find Alliluyev at his home nor at his place of work, and was obliged to wander through the streets for a long time without any place of shelter. "When I met him accidentally on the street, he was extremely tired." Alliluyev arranged for Koba to stay at the home of a janitor of one of the guard regiments who was a sympathizer of the revolution. "Here Stalin lived quietly for a while, saw some of the members of the Bolshevik fraction of the Third Duma, and later proceeded southward, to Baku."

Again to Baku! He could hardly have been drawn there by local patriotism. It would be more accurate to suppose that Koba was not known in Petersburg, that the deputies of the Duma did not display any interest in him, that no one asked him to remain or offered the aid which was so indispensable to an illegal resident. "Returning to Baku, he again undertook energetically to strengthen further the Bolshevik organizations . . . In October, 1909, he came to Tiflis, organized and directed the fight of the Tiflis Bolshevik organization against the Menshevik-Liquidators." The reader, no doubt, recognizes Beriya's style.

In the illegal press Koba published several articles, interesting only because they were written by the future Stalin. Owing to the absence of anything more noteworthy, exceptional significance is nowadays accorded to the correspondence written by Koba in December, 1909, for the Party's foreign newspaper. Contrasting the active industrial center of Baku to Tiflis, stagnant with civil servants, storekeepers and artisans, his "Letter From The Caucasus" quite correctly explains the dominance of the Mensheviks at Tiflis in terms of its social structure. Then follows a polemic against the perennial leader of Georgian Social-Democracy, Jordania, who again proclaimed the need "to unite the forces of the bourgeoisie and the proletariat." The workers must renounce their policy of irreconcilability because, Jordania argued, "the weaker the class struggle between the proletariat and the bourgeoisie, the more victorious will be the bourgeoisie . . ." Koba counterposed to that the directly contrary proposition: "The more the revolution will rely on the class struggle of the proletariat, which will lead the village poor against the landlords and the liberal bourgeoisie, the more complete will be the victory of the revolution." All of this was quite right in essence, but did not contain a single new word; beginning with the spring of 1905 such polemics were reiterated a countless number of times. If this correspondence had any value for Lenin, it was not because of the sophomoric reproduction of his own thought, but because it was a living voice from Russia at a time when the majority of such voices had died down. However, in 1937, this "Letter From The Caucasus" was proclaimed "the classic example of Leninist-Stalinist tactics." "In our writings and in all of our teachings," writes one such panegyrist, "not enough light has been shed on this article, extraordinary in its profundity, wealth of implications, and historical significance." The most generous thing to do is to disregard it.

"In March and April, 1910, it was finally possible," the same historian (a certain Rabichev) informs us, "to create a Russian collegium of the Central Committee. Stalin was on the staff of that collegium. However, before that collegium got down to work, it was arrested." If this is true, then Koba, at least formally, joined the staff of the Central Committee in 1910. An important milestone in his biography! But it is not true. Fifteen years prior to Rabichev, the old Bolshevik Germanov (Frumkin) related the following: "At the conference between the writer of these lines and Nogin it was decided to propose that the Central Committee confirm the following list of five as the Russian section of the Central Committee: Nogin, Dubrovinsky, Malinovsky, Stalin, and Milyutin." Thus, under consideration was not a decision of the Central Committee, but merely the project of two Bolsheviks. "Stalin was personally known to both of us," continues Germanov, "as one of the best and most active of Baku workers. Nogin went to Baku to talk things over with him; but for a number of reasons, Stalin could not assume the duties of a Central Committee member." Germanov does not state the exact reason for the difficulty. Nogin himself wrote about his journey to Baku two years later, as follows: ". . . in the deep underground was Stalin (Koba), well known in the Caucasus in those days and forced to hide in the Balakhana oil fields." It follows from Nogin's account that he did not even see Koba.

The reticence about the reasons why Stalin could not enter the Russian collegium of the Central Committee suggests some interesting deductions. 1910 was the period of the most complete degeneration of the movement and of the most widespread flood of conciliatory tendencies. In January, a plenum of the Central Committee was held in Paris, at which the Conciliators gained a very unstable victory. It was decided to restore the Central Committee in Russia with the participation of the Liquidators. Nogin and Germanov were Bolshevik Conciliators. The revival of the "Russian" collegium—that is, of the one acting illegally in Russia—was Nogin's task. Owing to the absence of prominent figures, several attempts were made to draw in the provincials. Among them was Koba, whom Nogin and Germanov knew as "one of the best of the Baku workers." However, nothing came of that idea. The well-informed author of the German article to which we have already referred states that although "the official Bolshevik biographers attempt to present [his] expropriations and expulsion from the Party as never having happened . . . nevertheless, the Bolsheviks themselves hesitated to place Koba in any noticeable post of leadership." It may be safely assumed that the reason for the failure of Nogin's mission was Koba's recent participation in "militant activities." The Paris plenum had branded the expropriators as persons guided by "a faulty understanding of party interests." Fighting for legality, the Mensheviks could in no wise consent to collaboration with an outright leader of expropriations. Nogin came to understand that, it would seem, only in the course of his negotiations with leading Mensheviks in the Caucasus. No collegium with Koba on it was set up. Note that of the two Conciliators whose protegé Stalin was, Germanov is among those missing without a trace; as for Nogin, only his premature death in 1924 saved him from the fate of Rykov, Tomsky, Germanov and other of his closest friends.

Koba's activity in Baku was undoubtedly more successful than in Tiflis, irrespective of whether he played a primary, secondary or tertiary role. But the idea that the Baku organization was the only unconquerable fortress of Bolshevism belongs to the realm of myths. At the end of 1911 Lenin himself accidentally laid the foundation for that myth by listing the Baku organization alongside of the Kiev organization as among "the model and progressive for Russia in 1910 and 1911"—that is, for the years of the Party's complete disintegration and the beginning of its revival. "The Baku organization existed without interruption during the difficult years of reaction and played a most active part in all the manifestations of the labor movement," states one of the footnotes to the fifteenth volume of Lenin's works. Both of these judgments, which are nowadays closely connected with Koba's activities, have proved to be completely erroneous upon investigation. As a matter of fact, after its resurgence, Baku passed through the same stages of decline as the other industrial centers of the country—true, somewhat belatedly, but even more drastically.

Stopani writes in his memoirs: "Beginning with 1910, Party and trade union life in Baku died down completely." Here and there remnants of trade unions still continued to exist for some time, but even they did so with the Mensheviks playing the preponderant role. "Soon Bolshevik activity virtually died down, thanks to constant failures due to arrest, lack of active workers and general chaos." The situation was still worse in 1911. Ordzhonikidze, who visited Baku in March, 1912, when the tide was again beginning to rise noticeably throughout the country, wrote abroad: "Yesterday I managed finally to get together a few workingmen . . . There is no organization, i.e., of the local center; therefore, we had to be content with private conferences . . ." These two testimonials are sufficient. Let us recall in addition the testimony of Olminsky, which has already been cited, that "revival was slowest in those cities where 'exes' had been most numerous (as an example, I might name Baku and Saratov)." Lenin's mistake in estimating the Baku organization is an ordinary instance of the error of an exile who is obliged to judge from afar on the basis of partial or unreliable information, among which might have been the excessively optimistic intelligence supplied by Koba himself.

The general picture thus drawn is clear enough. Koba did not take an active part in the trade union movement, which at that time was the principal arena of struggle (Karinyan, Stopani). He did not speak at workers' meetings (Vereshchak), but sat in "deep underground" (Nogin). He could not "for a number of reasons" enter the Russian collegium of the Central Committee (Germanov). In Baku "exes" had been more numerous than elsewhere (Olminsky) and so were acts of individual terror (Vereshchak). To Koba was ascribed direct leadership of the Baku "militant activities" (Vereshchak, Martov and others). Such activity undoubtedly demanded departure from the masses into the "deep underground." For some time the existence of the illegal organization was artificially sustained by means of monetary plunder. Hence all the stronger was the impact of the reaction and all the more belated the beginning of the revival. That conclusion is not only of biographical but likewise of theoretical significance, for it helps to shed light on certain general laws of the mass movement.

On the twenty-fourth of March, 1910, the gendarme Captain Martynov stated that he had arrested Joseph Djugashvili, known under the alias of "Koba," a member of the Baku Committee, "a most active Party worker who occupied a leading position" (granting that the document had not been corrected by Beriya's hand). In connection with that arrest, another gendarme reported in line of duty: "in view of the persistent participation" of Djugashvili in revolutionary activity and his "two escapes," he, Captain Galimbatovsky, "would suggest that the highest measure of punishment be invoked." But one need not suppose that the reference was to execution: "the highest measure of punishment" by administrative order meant exile to the remote places of Siberia for a term of five years.

Meantime Koba was in the Baku prison, already well known to him. The political situation of the country and the prison regime had undergone profound changes in the course of the intervening year and a half. 1910 was dawning. Reaction was triumphing all along the line. Not only the mass movement, but even the expropriations, the terror, the acts of individual despair struck a new low. The prison became stricter and calmer. There was not even any talk of collective discussion. Koba had sufficient leisure to study Esperanto, if he had not become disillusioned with the language of the future. On the twenty-seventh of August, by order of the Governor-General of the Caucasus, Djugashvili was forbidden to live in Transcaucasia for the duration of the next five years. But the recommendations of Captain Galimbatovsky, who apparently was unable to present any serious charges, fell on deaf ears in Petersburg: Koba was again sent away to Vologda Province to complete his unfinished two-year term of exile. The Petersburg authorities quite obviously did not yet regard Joseph Djugashvili as a serious menace.

Chapter V

THE NEW RESURGENCE

FOR about five years (1906-1911) Stolypin lorded it over the country. He exhausted all of the reaction's resources. The Third of June Regime managed to disclose its worthlessness in all spheres, but above all in the domain of the agrarian problem. Stolypin was obliged to descend from political combinations to the police club. And, as if the better to expose the utter bankruptcy of his system, Stolypin's assassin came from the ranks of his own secret police.

By 1910 the industrial revival became an indisputable fact. The revolutionary parties were confronted with the question: What effect will this break in the situation have on the political condition of the country? The majority of Social-Democrats maintained their schematic position: the crisis revolutionizes the masses, the industrial resurgence pacifies them. Both factions, Bolshevik as well as Menshevik, tended, therefore, to disparage or flatly deny the revival that had actually begun. The exception was the Vienna newspaper *Pravda*, which, notwithstanding its Conciliationist illusions, defended the very correct thought that the political consequences of the revival, as well as of the crisis, far from being automatic in character, are each time determined anew, depending on the preceding course of the struggle and on the entire situation in the country. Thus, following the industrial resurgence, in the course of which a very wide-spread strike struggle had managed to develop, a sudden decline in the situation might call forth a direct revolutionary resurgence, provided the other necessary conditions were present. On the other hand, after a long period of revolutionary struggle which ended in defeat, an industrial crisis, dividing and weakening the proletariat, might destroy its fighting spirit altogether. Or again, an industrial resurgence, coming after a long period of reaction, is capable of reviving the labor movement, largely in the form of an economic struggle, after which the new crisis might switch the energy of the masses onto political rails.

The Russo-Japanese War and the shocks of the revolution prevented Russian capitalism from sharing the world-wide industrial resurgence of 1903-1907. In the meantime, the uninterrupted revolutionary battles, defeats, and repressions, had exhausted the strength of the masses. The world industrial crisis, which broke out in 1907, extended the prolonged depression in Russia for three additional years, and far from inspiring the workers to engage in a new fight, dispersed them and weakened them more than ever. Under the blows of lockouts, unemployment and poverty, the weary masses became definitely discouraged.

Such was the material basis for the "achievements" of Stolypin's reaction. The proletariat needed the resuscitative font of a new industrial resurgence to revive its strength, fill its ranks, again feel itself the indispensable factor in production and plunge into a new fight.

At the end of 1910, street demonstrations—a sight long unseen—took place in connection with the deaths of the liberal Muromtsev, the erstwhile First Duma president, and of Leo Tolstoy. The student movement entered a new phase. Superficially—such is the customary aberration of historical idealism—it might have seemed that the thin layer of the intellectuals was the breeding place of the political revival and that by the force of its own example it was beginning to attract the upper layer of the workers. As a matter of fact, the wave of revival was not proceeding from the top down but from the bottom up. Thanks to the industrial resurgence, the working class was gradually emerging from its torpor. But before the chemical changes that had transformed the masses became apparent, they were transmitted to the students through the intervening social groups. Since the university youth was easier to set in motion, the revival manifested itself first of all in the form of student disturbances. But to the properly prepared observer it was clear beforehand that the demonstrations of the intellectuals were no more than a symptom of much more profound and significant processes within the proletariat itself.

Indeed, the graph of the strike movement soon began to climb. True, the number of strikers in 1911 amounted to a mere hundred thousand (the previous year it had not reached even half of that), but the slowness of the resurgence showed how strong was the torpor that had to be overcome. At any rate, by the end of the year the workers' districts looked quite different than at the beginning of the year. After the plentiful harvests of 1909 and 1910, which gave the impetus to the industrial resurgence, came a disastrous failure of crops in 1911, which, without stopping the resurgence, doomed twenty million peasants to starvation. The unrest, starting in the villages, again placed the agrarian question on the order of the day. The Bolshevik conference of January, 1912, had every right to refer to "the beginning of political revival." But the sudden break did not take place until the spring of 1912, after the famous massacre of the workers on the Lena River. In the deep *taiga*, more than five thousand miles from Petersburg and over fourteen hundred miles from the nearest railway, the pariahs of the gold mines, who each year provided millions of rubles in profit to English and Russian stockholders, demanded an eight-hour day, an increase in wages and abolition of fines. The soldiers, called out from Irkutsk, fired on the unarmed crowd. 150 killed, 250 wounded; deprived of medical aid, scores of the wounded died.

During the debate on the Lena events in the Duma, Minister of the Interior Makarov, a stupid official, no worse and no better than other of his contemporaries, declared, to the applause of the Rightist deputies, "This is what happened and this is what will happen again!" These amazingly brazen words produced an electric shock. At first from the factories of Petersburg, then from all over the country news about declarations and demonstrations of protest began to come in by telephone and telegraph. The repercussion of the Lena events was comparable only to the wave of indignation that had swept the toiling masses seven years before, following Bloody Sunday. "Perhaps never since the days of 1905," wrote a liberal newspaper, "have the streets of the capital been so alive."

In those days Stalin was in Petersburg, at liberty between two exiles. "The Lena shots broke the ice of silence," he wrote in the newspaper *Zvezda* [The Star], to which we shall have occasion to refer again, "and the river of popular resentment was set in motion. It has begun! . . . All that was evil and destructive in the contemporary régime, all that had ailed long-suffering Russia—all of it has merged into the one fact of the events on the Lena. That is why the Lena shots were the signal for strikes and demonstrations."

The strikes affected about three hundred thousand workers. The First of May strike set four hundred thousand marching. According to official data, a total of seven hundred and twenty-five thousand struck in 1912. The total number of workers increased by no less than twenty per cent during the years of industrial resurgence, while, because of the feverish concentration of production, their economic role assumed even greater importance. The revival in the working class affected all the other strata of the population. The hungry village stirred portentously. Flare-ups of dissatisfaction were observed in the army and navy. "In Russia the revolutionary resurgence," Lenin wrote to Gorky in August, 1912, "is not any other kind, but definitely revolutionary."

The new movement was not a repetition of the past, but its continuation. In 1905 the mighty January strike had been accompanied by a naïve petition to the Tsar. In 1912 the workers at once advanced the slogan of a democratic republic. The ideas, traditions and organizational experience of 1905, enriched by the hard lessons learned during the years of reaction, fertilized the new revolutionary period. From the very beginning the leading role belonged to the workers. Inside the proletarian vanguard the leadership belonged to the Bolsheviks. That, in essence, predetermined the character of the future revolution, although the Bolsheviks themselves were not as yet clearly aware of that. By strengthening the proletariat and securing for it a tremendously important role in the economic and political life of the country, the industrial resurgence reinforced the foundation for the perspective of permanent revolution. The cleansing of the stables of the old regime could not be accomplished otherwise than with the broom of the proletarian dictatorship. The democratic revolution could conquer only by transforming itself into the socialist revolution and thus, only by overcoming its own self.

Such continued to be the position of "Trotskyism." But it had its Achilles' heel: Conciliationism, associated with the hope for the revolutionary resurrection of Menshevism. The new resurgence—"not any other kind, but definitely revolutionary"—struck an irreparable blow at Conciliationism. Bolshevism relied on the revolutionary vanguard of the proletariat and taught it to lead the peasant poor behind it. Menshevism relied on the labor aristocracy and inclined toward the liberal bourgeoisie. The moment the masses again entered the arena of open conflict, there could have been no talk of "conciliation" between these two factions. The Conciliators were forced into new positions: the revolutionists among them—with the Bolsheviks, the opportunists—with the Mensheviks.

[Koba's third deportation lasted from September 23, 1910, to July 6, 1911, when he was released upon completing the remainder of his two-year term. About two months of this was spent en route from Baku to Solvychegodsk, with stops in various transfer prisons. Hence,] this time Koba spent more than eight months in [residence as an] exile. Virtually nothing is known about his life at Solvychegodsk, the exiles with whom he maintained contact, the books he read, the problems that interested him. From two of his letters of that period it appears that he received publications from abroad and was able to follow the life of the Party or rather of the emigrants where the conflict between the factions had reached an acute phase. Plekhanov, plus an inconsequential group of his followers, again broke with his closest friends and came to the defense of the illegal Party against the Liquidators. That was the last flare of radicalism in the life of this remarkable man who was rapidly verging toward his decline. Thus arose the startling, paradoxical and short-lived bloc of Lenin with Plekhanov. On the other hand, there was the rapprochement of the Liquidators (Martov and others) the Forwardists (Bogdanov, Lunacharsky) and the Conciliators (Trotsky). This second bloc, utterly devoid of any basis in principles, was formed, in a measure, to the surprise of the participants themselves. The Conciliators still aimed at "conciliating" the Bolsheviks and the Mensheviks; and since Bolshevism, in the person of Lenin, ruthlessly rejected the very idea of any sort of agreement with the Liquidators, the Conciliators naturally shifted to the position of a union or a semi-union with the Mensheviks and the Forwardists. The cement of that episodical bloc, as Lenin wrote to Gorky, was "detestation of the Bolshevik Center for its merciless struggle in defense of its ideas.". The question of the two blocs was subjected to a lively discussion in the thinned Party ranks of those days.

On the thirty-first of December, 1910, Stalin wrote abroad to Paris: "Comrade Simeon! Yesterday I received from comrades your letter. First of all, ardent greetings to Lenin, Kamenev and others." This salutation is no longer reprinted because of Kamenev's name. Then follows his estimate of the situation in the Party. "In my opinion the line of the bloc (Lenin-Plekhanov) is the only normal one . . . Lenin's hand is apparent in the plan of the bloc—he is a smart peasant and knows on which side his bread is buttered. But that does not mean yet that any old bloc is good. The Trotskyist bloc (he would have said—'synthesis')—that's putrid unscrupulousness . . . The Lenin-Plekhanov bloc is vital because it is profoundly principled, is grounded in unity of views on the question of the ways to revive the Party. But precisely because it is a bloc, and not a fusion, precisely for that reason the Bolsheviks need their own faction." All this was quite in line with Lenin's views, was essentially a mere paraphrasing of his articles, and was in the nature of a self-recommendation as to principles. Having further proclaimed, as if *en passant*, that "the main thing" was, after all, not the emigration, but the practical work in Russia, Stalin forthwith hastened to explain that the practical work means "the application of principles." Having thus reinforced his position by repeating the magic word, "principle," Koba came closer to the point. ". . . In my opinion," he writes, "our next task, which must not be postponed, is the organization of a central (Russian) group, which would co-ordinate the illegal, semi-legal and legal work . . . Such a group is as necessary as air, as bread." There was nothing new in the plan itself. Attempts to re-establish the Russian nucleus of the Central Committee had been made by Lenin more than once since the London Congress, but hitherto the dispersion of the Party had doomed them all to failure. Koba proposed the convocation of a conference of Party workers. "It is quite possible that this very conference would bring forth the suitable people for the above-mentioned central group." Having exposed his aim to switch the center of Party gravity from abroad to Russia, Koba again hastened to allay any possible apprehensions of Lenin's: "It will be necessary to act steadfastly and mercilessly, braving the reproaches of the Liquidators, the Trotskyists and the Forwardists . . ." With calculated modesty, he wrote about the central group of his project: "Call it what you like—'the Russian section of the Central Committee' or 'the assistance group of the Central Committee'—that is of no moment." The pretended indifference was supposed to cover Koba's personal ambition. "Now about myself. I have six months left. At the end of the term I am at your service. If the need of organizers is really acute, I can fly the coop at once." The purpose of the letter was clear: Koba advanced his own candidacy. He wanted to become, at last, a member of the Central Committee.

Koba's ambition, in no wise reprehensible, was unexpectedly illuminated by his other letter, addressed to the Moscow Bolsheviks. "The Caucasian Soso is writing to you." (This is the way the letter began.) "You remember in '04 [1904] at Tiflis and Baku. First of all, my ardent greetings to Olga, to you, to Germanov. I. M. Golubev, with whom I am beguiling my days in exile, told me about all of you. Germanov knows me as K . . . b . . . a (he'll understand)." It is curious that as late as 1911 Koba was obliged to remind the old party members about himself by resorting to indirect and purely accidental indications: he was still unknown or in danger of being easily forgotten. "I am ending (exile) in July of this year," he continued. "Ilyich and Co. are calling me to one of two centers, without waiting for the end of the term. However, I should like to finish my term (a legal person has more opportunities) . . . But if the need is great (I am awaiting their answer), then, of course, I'll fly the coop. . . . We here are stifling without anything to do, I am literally choking."

From the point of view of elementary circumspection, that part of the letter seems astounding. An exile, whose letters always run the risk of falling into the hands of the police, for no apparent practical reason sends by mail to members of the Party with whom he is scarcely acquainted, information about his conspiratorial correspondence with Lenin, about the fact that he is being urged to flee from exile and that in case of need he would "of course, fly the coop." As we shall see, the letter actually did fall into the hands of the gendarmes, who without much ado established the identity of the sender and of all the persons mentioned by him. One explanation of this carelessness is inescapable: impatient boastfulness! "The Caucasian Soso," who may not have been sufficiently noticed in 1904, cannot resist the temptation to inform the Moscow Bolsheviks that Lenin himself had included him among the central workers of the Party. However, the motive of boastfulness plays only a subsidiary role. The key to this mysterious letter is in its last part:

> about the "tempest in the teapot" abroad we have heard, of course: the blocs of Lenin-Plekhanov on the one hand and of Trotsky-Martov-Bogdanov on the other. The attitude of the workers to the first bloc, as far as I know, is favorable. But in general the workers are beginning to look disdainfully at the emigration: "let them crawl on the wall as much as their hearts desire; but as for us, whoever values the interests of the movement —work, the rest will take care of itself." That I think is for the best.

Amazing lines! Lenin's struggle against the Liquidators and the Conciliators Stalin regarded as a "tempest in a teapot." "The workers"—and Stalin with them—"are beginning to look disdainfully" at the emigration (including also the general staff of the Bolsheviks). "Whoever values the interests of the movement—work, the rest will take care of itself." The interests of the movement appeared to have no connection with the theoretical struggle which was working out the program of the movement.

A year and a half later, when, under the influence of the beginning of the swing, the struggle among the émigrés became more acute than ever, the sentimental semi-Bolshevik Gorky bemoaned in a letter to Lenin the "squabbles" abroad—the tempest in a teapot. "As to the *squabbles* among Social-Democrats," Lenin answered him reprovingly, "it is a favorite complaint of the bourgeois, the liberals, the Essars, whose attitude toward trying questions is far from serious, who lag behind others, play at diplomacy, sustain themselves with eclecticism . . ." "The business of those who understand the roots these squabbles have in ideas . . . ," he insisted in a subsequent letter, "is to aid the mass in seeking out these roots and not to justify the mass in its attitude toward these debates as the 'personal affair of the generals.' " "In Russia now," Gorky persisted for his part, "among the workers there is a lot of good . . . youth, but it is so fiercely set against the emigration . . ." Lenin replied: "This is actually true. But it is not the 'leaders'' fault . . . That which is torn should be bound together; while it is cheap, popular, but of little use, to scold the leaders . . ." It seems as if in his restrained rebuttals to Gorky, Lenin was indignantly refuting Stalin.

A careful comparison of Stalin's two letters, which their author never intended should be compared, is exceedingly valuable for an insight into his character and his ways. His real attitude toward "principles" is far more truthfully expressed in the second letter: "work, the rest will take care of itself." Such essentially was the attitude of many a not over-sapient Conciliator. Stalin resorted to the crudely contemptuous expressions about the "emigration" not only because rudeness is an integral part of his nature, but chiefly because he counted on the sympathy of the practicos, especially Germanov. He knew all about their moods from Golubev, who had recently been banished from Moscow. Activities in Russia were in a bad way, the underground organization had declined to the lowest point, and the practicos were very apt to take it out on the émigrés for raising much ado about trifles.

To understand the practical aim behind Stalin's double dealing, remember that Germanov, who several months before had proposed Koba's candidacy for the Central Committee, was himself closely connected with other Conciliators influential among the higher-ups of the Party. Koba deemed it useful to show that group his solidarity with it. But he was clearly aware of the strength of Lenin's influence and therefore began with a declaration of his loyalty to "principles." In his letter to Paris he humored Lenin's irreconcilability, for Stalin was afraid of Lenin; in his letter to the Muscovites, he set them against Lenin, who for no good reason "crawls on the wall." The first letter was a crude restatement of Lenin's articles against the Conciliators. The second letter repeated the arguments of the Conciliators against Lenin. All this within twenty-four days.

True, the letter to "Comrade Simeon" contains the cautious phrase: the center abroad "is not everything and not even the main thing. The main thing is to organize activities in Russia." On the other hand, in the letter to the Muscovites there was what appears to be an inadvertently dropped innuendo: the attitude of the workers toward the Lenin-Plekhanov bloc, *"as far as I know,* is favorable." But what in one letter is a subsidiary correction, serves in the other letter as the starting point for developing the contrary line of thought. The task of the vague asides, which are almost mental reservations, is to soften the contradiction between both letters. But, as a matter of fact, they merely betray the author's guilty conscience.

The technique of any intrigue, however primitive, is sufficient unto its goal. Koba purposely did not write directly to Lenin, preferring to address himself to "Simeon." That made it possible for him to refer to Lenin in a tone of admiring intimacy, without making it incumbent upon him to probe into the substance of the question. Doubtless, Koba's actual motivations were no mystery to Lenin. But his was the approach of the politician. A professional revolutionist who in the past had demonstrated will power and resoluteness was now eager to advance himself in the Party machine. Lenin took note of that. On the other hand, Germanov, too, remembered that in Koba's person the Conciliators would have an ally. His goal was thus achieved; at any rate, for the present. Koba had many qualifications for becoming an outstanding member of the Central Committee. His ambition was well-founded. But amazing were the ways by which the young revolutionist approached his goal—the ways of duplicity, deceit, deliberate cynicism!

In conspiratorial life, compromising letters were destroyed; personal contacts with people abroad were rare, so Koba had no fear that his two letters might be compared. The credit for saving these invaluable human documents for the future goes entirely to the censors of the Tsarist post office. On the twenty-third of December, 1925, when the totalitarian regime was still very far from having attained its present automatism, the Tiflis newspaper, *Zarya Vostoka,* was heedless enough to have published a copy of Koba's letter to the Muscovites, taken from the police archives. It is not hard to imagine the drubbing the ill-starred editorial board got for that! The letter was subsequently never reprinted, and not a single one of the official biographers ever refers to it.

Notwithstanding the dire need of organizers, Koba did not "fly the coop at once,"—that is, he did not escape, but this time served his sentence to the end. The newspapers brought information about student meetings and street demonstrations. No less than ten thousand people crowded into Nevsky Prospect.[1] Workers began to join in with the students. "Is this not the beginning of the change?" Lenin asked in an article several weeks before he received Koba's letter from exile. During the first months of 1911 the revival became indisputable, yet Koba, who already had three escapes to his credit, was this time calmly awaiting the end of his term of exile. The awakening of the new spring seemed to have left him cold. Remembering his experiences of 1905, was he fearful of the new resurgence?

All biographers without exception refer to Koba's new escape. As a matter of fact, there was no need of escape; the term of his exile ended in July, 1911. The Moscow *Okhrana,* mentioning in passing Joseph Djugashvili, referred to him this time as one who "completed his term of administrative exile in the city of Solvychegodsk." The conference of the Bolshevik members of the Central Committee, which meantime took place abroad, appointed a special commission to arrange a Party conference, and it appears that Koba, along with four others, was appointed to that commission. After exile, he went to Baku and Tiflis, in order to stir up the local Bolsheviks and to induce them to participate in the conference. There were no formal organizations in the Caucasus, so it was necessary to begin building almost from scratch. The Tiflis Bolsheviks approved the appeal Koba wrote on the need for a revolutionary party:

> Unfortunately, in addition to political adventurers, provocateurs and other riff-raff, the advanced workers in our very own cause of strengthening our own Social-Democratic Party, are obliged to meet a new obstacle in our ranks—namely, people of bourgeois mentality.

The reference was to the Liquidators. The appeal was rounded out with a metaphor characteristic of our author:

> The sombre sanguine clouds of black reaction hanging over the country

[1] The principal street of Petersburg (Leningrad).—C. M.

are beginning to disperse, are beginning to be superseded by the stormy clouds of the people's rage and indignation. The black background of our life is slashed by lightning, while in the distance the dawn is flaring, the storm is approaching . . .

The object of the appeal was to proclaim the emergence of the Tiflis group and thus secure for the few local Bolsheviks participation in the forthcoming conference.

Koba left Vologda Province lawfully. It is doubtful that he went lawfully from the Caucasus to Petersburg: former exiles were usually forbidden for a definite period of time to live in the important cities. But whether with or without permission, the provincial finally set forth to the territory of the capital. The Party was just emerging from its torpor. The best forces were in prison, exile, or had emigrated. It was precisely for that reason that Koba was needed in Petersburg. But his first appearance in the capital was brief. Only two months elapsed between the end of his banishment and his next arrest, and of this from three to four weeks must have been consumed by his journey to the Caucasus. Nothing is known to us about Koba's adjustment to his new environment or how he began to work in the new setting.

The only memento of that period is the very brief news item Koba sent abroad concerning the secret meeting of the forty-six Social-Democrats of the Vyborg district. The main thought of a speech delivered by a prominent Liquidator consisted in this: that "in a party sense no organizations are needed," since for activity in the open it was sufficient to have "initiating groups" that would concern themselves with arranging public speeches and legal meetings on questions of state insurance, municipal politics and the like. According to Koba's news item, this plan of the Liquidators for adaptation to the pseudo-constitutional monarchy was met with the wholehearted resistance of all workers, including the Mensheviks as well. At the end of the meeting, all, with the exception of the principal speaker, voted in favor of an illegal revolutionary party.

Either Lenin or Zinoviev provided this letter from Petersburg with the following editorial note:

> Comrade K's correspondence merits the greatest attention of all to whom the Party is dear . . . One could hardly imagine a better rebuttal to the views and hopes of our peacemakers and Conciliators. Is the incident described by Comrade K exceptional? No, it is typical . . .

Yet it is very rarely that "the Party receives such definite information, for which we are grateful to Comrade K." Referring to this newspaper episode, the Soviet Encyclopaedia writes:

> Stalin's letters and articles testify to the unshakable unity of fighting effort and political line that bound Lenin and the genius who was his companion in arms.

In order to achieve this appreciation it was necessary to issue one after another

several editions of the encyclopedia, liquidating along the way no mean number of editors.

Alliluyev tells how one day early in September, on his way home, he noticed
spies at the gate of his house, and, going upstairs to his flat, he found Stalin and
another Georgian Bolshevik there. When Alliluyev told him about the "tail" he
left downstairs, Stalin retorted, not any too courteously: "What the devil is
the matter with you? . . . Some comrades are turning into scared Philistines
and yokels!" But the spies proved real enough: on the ninth of September Koba
was arrested and by the twenty-second of December he was already in his place
of exile, this time in the provincial capital of Vologda—that is, in more favorable circumstances than heretofore. It is likely that this exile was simply punishment for unlawful residence in Petersburg.

The Bolshevik center abroad continued to send emissaries to Russia, to prepare the conference. The contact between local Social-Democratic groups was
established slowly and was frequently broken. Provocation raged, the arrests
were devastating. However, the sympathy with which the idea of a conference
was met by the advanced workers showed at once, according to Olminsky, that
"the workers merely tolerated liquidationism, and inwardly were far from desiring it." Extremely difficult conditions notwithstanding, the emissaries managed to establish contact with a great many local illegal groups. "It was like
a gust of fresh air," wrote the same Olminsky.

At the conference convoked in Prague on the fifth of January, 1912, were
fifteen delegates from a score of underground organizations—for the most part
very weak ones. The reports of the delegates drew a sufficiently clear picture
of the state of the Party: the few local organizations were composed almost
exclusively of Bolsheviks, with a large percentage of provocateurs, who betrayed
the organization as soon as it began to get on its feet. Particularly sad was the
situation in the Caucasus. "There is no organization of any kind at Chiatury,"
reported Ordzhonikidze about the only industrial spot in Georgia. "Nor is there
any organization in Batum." In Tiflis—"the same picture. During the last few
years there was not a single leaflet and no illegal work of any kind . . ." In
spite of the obvious weakness of local groups, the conference reflected the new
spirit of optimism. The masses were getting into motion, the Party sensed the
trade wind in its sails.

The decisions reached at Prague determined the Party's course for a long
time to come. In the first place, the conference recognized as necessary the
creation of Social-Democratic nuclei surrounded by as extensive a network as
possible of all sorts of legal workers' societies. The poor harvest, which led to
the famine of twenty million peasants, confirmed once more, according to the
conference, "the impossibility of securing any sort of normal bourgeois development in Russia as long as its policy is directed . . . by the class of serfdom-
minded landlords." "The task of the conquest of power by the proletariat, leading
the peasantry, remains as ever the task of the democratic revolution in Russia."
The conference declared the faction of Liquidators outside the Party's ranks

and appealed to all Social-Democrats, "regardless of tendencies and shadings," to wage war on the Liquidators in the name of reconstituting the illegal Party. Having thus gone all the way in breaking with the Mensheviks, the Prague Conference opened the era of the independent existence of the Bolshevik Party, with its own Central Committee.

The newest "History" of the Party, published in 1938 under Stalin's editorial guidance, states:

> The members of that Central Committee were Lenin, Stalin, Ordzhonikidze, Sverdlov, Goloshchekin, and others. Stalin and Sverdlov were elected to the Central Committee in absentio, since at the time they were in exile.

But in the official collection of party documents (1926) we read:

> The conference elected a new Central Committee composed of Lenin, Zinoviev, Ordzhonikidze, Spandaryan, Victor (Ordynsky), Malinovsky and Goloshchekin.

The "History" does not include in the Central Committee either Zinoviev, or the provocateur Malinovsky; but it does include Stalin, who was not on the old list. The explanation of this riddle can throw some light on Stalin's position in the Party of those days as well as on the present methods of Muscovite historiography. As a matter of fact, Stalin was not elected at the conference, but was made a member of the Central Committee soon after the conference by way of what was called co-optation. The above-mentioned official source states that quite definitely:

> Later Comrade Koba (Djugashvili-Stalin) and Vladimir (Belostostky, former worker of the Putilov plant) were co-opted into the Central Committee.

Likewise according to the materials of the Moscow *Okhrana*, Djugashvili was made a member of the Central Committee after the conference on the basis of the right of co-optation reserved for members of the Central Committee. The same information is given by all Soviet reference books, without exception, until the year 1929, when Stalin's instruction, which revolutionized historical scholarship, was published. In the jubilee publication of 1937 devoted to the conference we read:

> Stalin could not participate in the work of the Prague Conference because at the time he was in banishment at Solvychegodsk. At the time Lenin and the Party already knew Stalin as an important leader. . . . Therefore, in accordance with Lenin's proposal, the delegates to the conference elected Stalin to the Central Committee in absentio.

The question whether Stalin was elected at the conference or co-opted later by the Central Committee may seem of minor importance. As a matter of fact, that is not the case. Stalin wanted to become a member of the Central Committee. Lenin deemed it necessary to have him elected to the Central Committee. The choice of available candidates was so limited that second-rate figures became members of the Central Committee. Yet Koba was not elected. Why? Lenin was far from being a dictator in his Party. Besides, a revolutionary party would not brook any dictatorship over itself! After preliminary negotiations with delegates, Lenin apparently deemed it wiser not to advance Koba's candidacy. "When in 1912 Lenin brought Stalin into the Central Committee of the Party," writes Dmitrievsky, "it was met with indignation. Openly no one opposed it. But they gave vent to their indignation among themselves." The information of the former diplomat, which as a rule does not merit confidence, is nevertheless of interest in so far as it reflects bureaucratic recollections and gossip. Lenin undoubtedly met with serious opposition. There was but one thing he could do: wait until the conference came to an end and then appeal to the small leading circle, which either relied on Lenin's recommendation or shared his estimate of the candidate. Thus, Stalin for the first time came into the Central Committee through the back door.

The story about the internal organization of the Central Committee underwent similar metamorphoses.

> The Central Committee . . . upon Lenin's motion, created a Bureau of the Central Committee, headed by Comrade Stalin, for guiding Party activity in Russia. In addition to Stalin, the Russian Bureau of the Central Committee was composed of Sverdlov, Spandaryan, Ordzhonikidze, Kalinin.

So states Beriya, who, while I was at work on this chapter, was appointed chief of Stalin's secret police; his scholarly endeavors did not remain unrewarded. In vain, however, would we look for any documentary support of this version, which is repeated in the latest "History." In the first place, no one was ever placed "at the head" of Party institutions: such a method of election did not exist at all. According to the old official reference books, the Central Committee elected "a bureau composed of: Ordzhonikidze, Spandaryan, Stalin, and Goloshchekin." The same list is given also in the notes to Lenin's works. Among the papers of the Moscow Okhrana the first three—"Timofei, Sergo, and Koba"—are named as members of the Russian Bureau of the Central Committee under their aliases. It is not devoid of interest that in all the old lists Stalin occupies invariably either the last or the next to the last place, which could not have been the case, of course, had he been placed "at the head." Goloshchekin, having been expelled from the Party machine in the course of one of the later purges, was likewise crowded out of the 1912 bureau; his place was taken by the fortunate Kalinin. History is becoming clay in the hands of the potter.

On the twenty-fourth of February, Ordzhonikidze informed Lenin that at Vologda he had visited Ivanovich [Stalin]: "Came to a definite understanding with him. He is satisfied with the way things turned out." The reference is to the decision of the Prague Conference. Koba learned that, at last, he had been co-opted into the recently created "center." On the twenty-eighth of February he escaped from exile, in his new capacity as member of the Central Committee.

After a brief sojourn at Baku, he proceeded to Petersburg. Two months earlier he had turned thirty-two.

Koba's advancement from the provincial arena to the national one coincided with the resurgence of the labor movement and the comparatively widespread development of the labor press. Under the pressure of the underground forces, the Tsarist authorities lost their erstwhile self-assurance. The hand of the censor weakened. Lawful possibilities became more extensive. Bolshevism broke through into the open, at first with a weekly, later with a daily newspaper. At once the possibilities for exerting influence on the workers increased. The Party continued in the underground, but the editorial boards of its newspapers became for the time being the legal staffs of the revolution. The name of the Petersburg *Pravda* colored an entire period of the labor movement, when the Bolsheviks began to be called "Pravdists." During the two and a half years of the newspaper's existence, the government closed it eight times, but each time it reappeared under some similar name. On some of the most crucial questions the *Pravda* was often forced to limit itself to understatements and hints. But its underground agitators and proclamations said for it what it itself could not say openly. Besides, the advanced workers had meantime learned to read between the lines. A circulation of forty thousand may seem all too modest by comparison with Western European or American standards. But under the oversensitive political acoustics of Tsarist Russia, the Bolshevik newspaper, through its direct subscribers and readers, found a responsive echo among hundreds of thousands. Thus, the young revolutionary generation rallied around *Pravda* under the leadership of those veterans who had withstood the years of reaction. "The *Pravda* of 1912 was laying the foundation for the victory of Bolshevism in 1917," Stalin wrote subsequently, hinting at his own participation in that activity.

Lenin, whom the news of Stalin's escape had not yet reached, complained on March fifteenth: "Nothing from Ivanovich—what's the matter with him? Where is he? How is he? . . ." Men were scarce. There were no suitable people even at the capital. In the same letter Lenin wrote that an illegal person was "damnably" needed at Petersburg, "since things are in a bad way there. It's a hard and furious war. We have no information, no leadership, no supervision of the newspaper." Lenin was waging "a hard and furious war" with the editorial board of *Zvezda* [The Star] which balked about waging war with the Liquidators. "Hurry up and fight with *Zhivoye Dyelo* [*The Living Cause,* a journal of the Liquidators]—then victory is assured. Otherwise, it will go badly with us. Don't be afraid of polemics . . ." Lenin insisted again in March, 1912. Such was the leitmotif of all his letters in those days.

"What's the matter with him? Where is he? How is he?" we might well repeat after Lenin. Stalin's actual role—as usual, behind the scenes—is not easy to determine: a thorough appraisal of facts and documents is needed. His duties as a member of the Central Committee in Petersburg—that is, as one of the official leaders of the Party—extended, of course, to the illegal press as well. Yet prior to the instructions to the "historians" that circumstance was relegated to utter oblivion. Collective memory has its own laws, which do not always coincide with Party regulations. *Zvezda* was founded in December, 1910, when the first signs of revival became evident. "Lenin, Zinoviev and Kamenev," states the official notice, "were most closely associated in making arrangements for the publication and in editing it from abroad." The editorial board of Lenin's works names eleven persons among its chief collaborators in Russia, forgetting to mention Stalin among them. Yet there is no doubt that he was a member of this newspaper's staff and by virtue of his position an influential one. The same forgetfulness—nowadays it might be called sabotage of memory—is characteristic of all the old memoirs and reference books. Even in a special issue which in 1927 *Pravda* devoted to its own fifteenth anniversary, not a single article, not even the editorial, mentions the name of Stalin. Studying the old publications, one refuses at times to credit his own eyes!

The only exception is found in the valuable memoirs of Olminsky, one of those most closely associated with *Zvezda* and *Pravda*, who describes Stalin's role in the following words:

> Stalin and Sverdlov appeared in Petersburg at various times after their flight from exile . . . The presence of both at Petersburg (until their new arrest) was brief, but each time managed to produce considerable effect on the work of the newspaper, the faction, and the like.

This bare statement, incorporated, moreover, not in the main text, but as a footnote, probably characterizes the situation most accurately. Stalin would show up in Petersburg for short periods from time to time, bring pressure to bear on the organization, on the Duma faction, on the newspaper, and would again disappear. His appearances were too transitory, his influence too much of the Party machine kind, his ideas and articles too commonplace to have left a lasting impression on anyone's memory. When people write memoirs otherwise than under duress, they do not remember the official functions of bureaucrats but the vital activity of vital people, vivid facts, clear-cut formulae, original proposals. Stalin did not distinguish himself with anything of the kind. No wonder then that the gray copy was not remembered alongside the vivid original. True, Stalin did not merely paraphrase Lenin. Bound by his support of the Conciliators, he continued to ply simultaneously the two lines with which we are already familiar from his Solvychegodsk letters—with Lenin, against the Liquidators; with the Conciliators, against Lenin. The first policy was in the open, the second was masked. Neither did Stalin's fight against the émigré center inspire the memoirists, although for a different reason: all of them, actively or passively, took part in the "conspiracy" of the Conciliators against Lenin and hence preferred to turn away from that page of the Party's past. Only subsequent to 1929 did Stalin's official position as a representative of the Central Committee become the basis for the new interpretation of the historical period preceding the war.

Stalin could not have left the impress of his personality on the newspaper for the simple reason that he is not by nature a newspaperman. From April, 1912, through February, 1913, according to the calculations of one of his intimate associates, he published in the Bolshevik press "no less than a score of articles," which is an average of about two articles a month. And that at the high tide of events when life posed new problems each exciting day! True, in the course of that year Stalin spent nearly six months in exile. But it was much easier to contribute to *Pravda* from Solvychegodsk or Vologda than from Cracow, from where Lenin and Zinoviev sent articles and letters every single day. Sluggishness and inordinate cautiousness, utter lack of literary resourcefulness, and, finally, extreme Oriental laziness combined to make Stalin's pen rather unproductive. His articles, more self-assured in tone than during the years of the First Revolution, continued to bear the indelible imprint of mediocrity.

"Following the economic demonstrations of the workers," he wrote in *Zvezda* of April fifteenth, "came their political demonstrations. Following strikes for increase in pay, came protests, meetings, political strikes occasioned by the Lena shooting . . . There is no doubt that the underground forces of the liberation movement have begun to work. Greetings to you, first swallows!"

The image of "swallows" as a symbol of "the underground forces" is typical of our author's style. But, after all, it *is* clear what he is trying to say. Drawing "conclusions" from the so-called "Lena events," Stalin analyzes—as always, schematically, without regard for living reality—the behavior of the government and of the political parties, accuses the bourgeoisie of shedding "crocodile tears" over the shooting of the workers and concludes with the admonition: "Now that the first wave of the upswing is passing, the dark forces, which had attempted to hide behind a screen of crocodile tears, are again beginning to appear." Notwithstanding the startling effect of his image, "the screen of crocodile tears," which seems particularly whimsical against the otherwise neutral background of the text, the article does state, by and large, what, roughly, should have been said and what scores of others would have said. But it is precisely the "roughness" of his exposition—not only of his style, but of the analysis itself—which makes the reading of Stalin's writings as unendurable as discordant music to a sensitive ear. He wrote in an illegal proclamation:

> It is today, on the day of the First of May, when nature awakens from the slumber of winter, the woods and mountains are covered with greensward, the fields and meadows are decorated with flowers, the sun begins to warm more warmly, the joy of renewal is sensed in the air, while nature indulges in dancing and exultation—it is precisely today that the workers decided to proclaim to the world that they bring to humanity spring and liberation from the gyves of capitalism . . . The ocean of the labor movement spreads ever wider . . . The sea of proletarian anger rises in mounting waves . . . Certain of victory, calm and strong, they march proudly on the road to the promised land, on the road to effulgent socialism.

Here is the Petersburg revolution speaking the language of Tiflis homiletics.

The strike wave swelled, contacts with the workers multiplied. The weekly could no longer fill the needs of the movement. *Zvezda* began to collect money for a daily newspaper. "At the end of the winter of 1912," writes the former deputy Poletayev, "Stalin, who had fled from exile, came to Petersburg. The work of establishing a labor newspaper gained momentum." In his 1922 article on the tenth anniversary of *Pravda* Stalin himself wrote:

> It was in the middle of April, 1912, in the evening, at the apartment of Poletayev, that two Duma deputies (Pokrovsky and Poletayev), two literaries (Olminsky and Baturin) and I, a member of the Central Committee . . . came to agreement on the platform of *Pravda* and made up the newspaper's first issue.

Stalin's responsibility for the *Pravda* platform was thus established by Stalin himself. The essence of that platform may be summarized in the words, "work, the rest will take care of itself." True, Stalin himself was arrested on the twenty-second of April, the very day the first issue of *Pravda* came out. But for almost three months *Pravda* was true to the platform worked out jointly with him. The word "liquidator" was expunged from the newspaper's vocabulary.

"Irreconcilable war with liquidationism was indispensable," writes Krupskaya. "That is why Vladimir Ilyich was so disturbed when from the very start the *Pravda* persistently deleted from his articles all polemics with the Liquidators. He wrote irate letters to *Pravda*." A part of them—evidently, only a small part —has managed to see the light. "At times, although that was rare," she further complains, "Ilyich's articles would be lost without a trace. At other times, his articles were held up, were not published at once. It was then that Ilyich became nervous, wrote irate letters to *Pravda*, but it didn't do much good."

The fight with the editorial board of *Pravda* was a direct continuation of the fight with the editorial board of *Zvezda*. "It is harmful, disastrous, ridiculous to hide differences of opinion from the workers," wrote Lenin on the eleventh of July, 1912. Several days later he demanded that the secretary of the editorial board, Molotov, the present [Vice-] Chairman of the Council of People's Commissars and People's Commissar for Foreign Affairs, explain why the newspaper "persistently and systematically strikes out of my articles and out of the articles of other colleagues any mention of the Liquidators?" Meantime, elections to the Fourth Duma were approaching. Lenin warned: "The elections in the workers' curiae of Petersburg will undoubtedly be accompanied by a fight all along the line with the Liquidators. This will prove the most vital issue for the advanced workers. Yet their newspaper will be silent, will avoid the word, 'liquidator!' . . . To dodge these questions is to commit suicide."

Sitting in Cracow, Lenin discerned sharply enough the tacit yet persistent conspiracy of the conciliatory higher-ups of the Party. But he was thoroughly convinced that he was right. The rapid revitalization of the labor movement was bound to pose sharply the fundamental problems of the revolution, sweeping away the ground not only from under the feet of the Liquidators but of the Conciliators as well. Lenin's strength did not lie so much in his ability to build a machine—he knew how to do that, too—as in his ability at all critical moments to utilize the living energy of the masses for overcoming the limitations and the conservatism characteristic of any political machine. It was so in this instance, too. Under the growing pressure of the workers and under the lash from Cracow, *Pravda,* reluctantly and constantly balking, began to abandon its position of dilatory neutrality.

Stalin spent a little more than two months in the Petersburg prison. On the second of July he left for his new exile of four years, this time across the Urals, in the northern part of Tomsk Province—in Narym Region, famous for its forests, lakes and swamps. Vereshchak, already known to us, again met Koba in the village of Kolpashevo, where the latter spent several days en route to his destination. Here were Sverdlov, I. Smirnov, Lashevich, classic old Bolsheviks. It was not easy to predict then that Lashevich would die in Stalin's exile, that Smirnov would be shot by him and that only premature death would save Sverdlov from a similar fate. "Stalin's arrival at the Narym Region," wrote Vereshchak, "enlivened the activity of the Bolsheviks and was marked by quite a few escapes." After several others, Stalin himself escaped: "He went away almost openly with the first spring steamer . . ." As a matter of fact, Stalin escaped at the end of summer. This was his fourth escape.

Upon his return to Petersburg on September twelfth, he found a considerably altered situation there. Stormy strikes were going on. The workers again poured into the streets with revolutionary slogans. The policy of the Mensheviks was obviously discredited. *Pravda*'s influence grew apace. Besides, Duma elections were near. The tone for the election campaign had already been set by Cracow. The grounds of argument were chosen. The Bolsheviks engaged in the election fight apart from the Liquidators and against them. The workers were to be welded together under the banner of the three main slogans of the democratic revolution: the republic, the eight-hour day, and confiscation of landed estates. Liberate the petty bourgeois democrats from the influence of the liberals, draw the peasants to the side of the workers—such were the leading ideas of Lenin's election platform. Combining painstaking attention to details with audacious sweep of thought, Lenin was practically the only Marxist who had thoroughly studied all the possibilities and pitfalls of Stolypin's election law. Having politically inspired the election campaign, he guided it technically day by day. To help Petersburg, he sent in from abroad articles and instructions and thoroughly prepared emissaries.

Safarov, now among the missing, on his way from Switzerland to Petersburg in the spring of 1912, stopped at Cracow, where he learned that Inessa, a leading Party activist who was close to Lenin, was also going there to help in the election campaign. "For at least a couple of days on end Ilyich pumped us full of instructions." The election of the workers' curiae representatives in Petersburg was set for the sixteenth of September. Inessa and Safarov were arrested on the fourteenth. "But the police did not yet know," wrote Krupskaya, "that on the twelfth Stalin, who had escaped from exile, had arrived. The elections to the workers' curiae were a great success." Krupskaya did not say: "Thanks to Stalin." She merely placed two sentences side by side. That was a measure of passive self-defense. "At extempore meetings in a number of factories," we read in a new edition of the reminiscences of the former Duma deputy Badayev (this was not in the first edition), "Stalin, who had recently escaped from Narym, spoke." According to Alliluyev, who wrote his reminiscences as late as 1937, "Stalin directly managed the entire tremendous Fourth Duma election campaign . . . Living illegally in Petersburg, without a definite permanent haven, and not wishing to disturb any of his close comrades during the late hours of the night, after a workers' meeting that had dragged on and also because of conspiratorial considerations, Stalin would often spend the remainder of the night in some tavern over a glass of tea." Here he also managed occasionally "to take a short nap, sitting in the tavern that reeked of *makhorka* smoke."

Stalin could not have exerted great influence on the issue of the elections in the earlier stages, when it was necessary to come in direct contact with the voters, not only because he was a poor speaker, but because he had no more than four days at his disposal. He made up for that by playing an important part throughout the subsequent stages of the many-storied electoral system, whenever it was necessary to muster the curiae representatives and manage them by pulling wires from behind the scenes, relying on the illegal apparatus. In that activity Stalin undoubtedly proved himself more apt than anyone else.

An important document of the election campaign was, "The Instruction Of The Petersburg Workers To Their Deputy." In the first edition of his memoirs Badayev states that this instruction was composed by the Central Committee, but in the new edition its authorship is ascribed personally to Stalin. In all likelihood the instruction was the product of collective effort, in which the final say might have been Stalin's, as the representative of the Central Committee. ". . . We think," it is stated in the Instruction, "that Russia lives on the eve of impending mass movements probably far more fundamental than in 1905 . . . As in 1905, the initiator of these movements will be the most progressive class of Russian society, the Russian proletariat. Its ally can be only the long-suffering peasantry, which is deeply concerned with the liberation of Russia." Lenin wrote to the *Pravda* editorial board: "Publish without fail . . . this Instruction . . . in large type and in a prominent place." The convention of provincial representatives adopted the Bolshevik Instruction by an overwhelming majority. In those stirring days Stalin also figured more actively as a publicist; I counted four of his articles in *Pravda* within one week.

The election results in Petersburg, as in all the industrial regions generally, were quite favorable. Bolshevik candidates were elected in six of the most important provinces, which altogether comprised about four-fifths of the working class. The seven Liquidators were elected chiefly by the votes of the city petty bourgeoisie. "In contradistinction to the elections of 1907," wrote Stalin in his correspondence to the central organ published abroad, "the elections of 1912 coincided with the revolutionary revival among the workers." Precisely for that reason the workers, who were quite remote from the boycottist tendency, fought actively for their rights of suffrage. The government commission made an attempt to invalidate the elections in some of the largest Petersburg factories. The workers countered that with a unanimous strike of protest, which achieved its purpose. "It is not superfluous to add," the author of this correspondence continues, "that the initiative in this election campaign was that of the Central Committee representative." The reference here is to Stalin himself. His political conclusions on the election campaign were: "The revolutionary Social-Democracy is alive and powerful—such is the first conclusion. The Liquidators are political bankrupts—such is the second conclusion." And that was right.

The seven Mensheviks, largely intellectuals, tried to place the six Bolsheviks, workers with little political experience, under their own control. At the end of November Lenin wrote personally to Vassilyev [Stalin]: "If all of our six are from the workers' curiae, they must not submit in silence to a lot of Siberians.[2] The six must come out with a very clear-cut protest, if they are being lorded over . . ." Stalin's reply to that letter, as to others, remains under lock and key. But Lenin's appeal did not meet with sympathy: the six themselves rated unity with the Liquidators, who had been read "out of the Party," above their own political independence. In a special resolution published in *Pravda*, the united faction acknowledged that "the unity of the Social-Democracy is a pressing need," expressed itself in favor of merging *Pravda* with the Liquidators' newspaper *Lootch'* [The Ray] and, as a step in that direction, recommended that all of its members become contributors to both newspapers. On the eighteenth of December the Menshevik *Lootch'* triumphantly published the names of four of the Bolshevik deputies (two having declined) on its list of contributors; the names of the members of the Menshevik faction appeared simultaneously on the *Pravda* masthead. Conciliationism had won again, which in essence meant a defeat for the spirit and the letter of the Prague Conference.

Soon on the list of the *Lootch'* contributors appeared still another name— Gorky's. That smelled of a plot. "And how did *you* happen to get mixed up with *Lootch'*? ? ?" Lenin wrote to Gorky with three question marks. "Is it possible that you are following in the footsteps of the deputies? But they have simply fallen into a trap!" Stalin was in Petersburg during this ephemeral triumph of the Conciliators, effecting the Central Committee's control over the fraction and over *Pravda*. No one has disclosed anything concerning a protest from him against decisions that struck a cruel blow at Lenin's policy—a sure sign that behind the scenes of the Conciliationist maneuvers stood Stalin himself. Justifying subsequently his sinful behavior, Deputy Badayev wrote: "As on all other occasions, our decision . . . was in agreement with the attitude of those Party circles in which we had then occasion to discuss our activities . . ." This roundabout excuse hints at the Petersburg Bureau of the Central

[2] Referring to political exiles in Siberia, most of whom were intellectuals.—C. M.

Committee and first of all at Stalin. Badayev is circumspectly pleading that the blame should not be shifted from the leaders to the led.

Several years ago it was observed in the Soviet press that not enough light has been shed on the history of Lenin's internal struggle with the Duma fraction and with the editorial board of *Pravda*. In recent years everything has been done to make such enlightenment more difficult than ever. Lenin's correspondence of that critical period has not yet been published in full. At the historians' disposal are only such documents as for one reason or another had been taken out of the archives prior to the institution of totalitarian control. However, even from these scattered fragments a faultless picture emerges. Lenin's intractability was only the other side of his realistic farsightedness. He insisted on division along the line which in the final reckoning was bound to become the battle-line of the civil war. The empiricist Stalin was constitutionally incapable of taking a long-range point of view. He energetically fought the Liquidators during the campaign, in order to have his own deputies: it was a matter of securing an important point of support. But once this organizational task had been performed, he did not deem it necessary to raise a new "tempest in a teapot," especially since even the Mensheviks, under the influence of the revolutionary wave, seemed to be inclined to talk a different language. Truly, there was no reason for "crawling on the wall"! As far as Lenin was concerned, his whole policy came down to the revolutionary education of the masses. The struggle of the election campaign meant nothing to him as long as after the election the Social-Democratic deputies in the Duma remained united. He deemed it necessary to give the workers every opportunity—at each step, with each act—to convince themselves that in all fundamental questions the Bolsheviks were clearly distinguishable from all other political groups. This was the most important point of conflict between Cracow and Petersburg.

The waverings of the Duma fraction were closely connected with *Pravda's* policy. "During that period," wrote Badayev in 1930, "Stalin, whose status was illegal, ran *Pravda*." The well-informed Savelyev wrote likewise: "Remaining in illegal status, Stalin actually ran the newspaper during the autumn of 1912 and the winter of 1912-13. Only for a short while did he leave during that time, going abroad, to Moscow, and other places." These eye-witness accounts, consistent with all the factual circumstances, cannot be questioned. Yet it was not true that Stalin ran the paper in the real sense of the word. The man who really ran the newspaper was Lenin. Every day he sent articles, criticisms of the articles of others, proposals, instructions, corrections. Stalin, a sluggish thinker, could not possibly keep up with this active stream of suggestions and ideas, nine-tenths of which seemed to him superfluous or exaggerated. Essentially the editorial board maintained a defensive position. It had no political ideas of its own, and tried merely to dull the sharp edges of the Cracow policy. Lenin not only knew how to shield these sharp edges, but also how to sharpen them anew. Under these conditions, Stalin naturally became the secret inspirer of the Conciliators' opposition to Lenin's pressure.

"New conflicts," states the editorial board of Lenin's Works (Bukharin, Molotov, Savelyev), "arose in consequence of the weakness of the stand taken against the Liquidators at the end of the election campaign and also in connection with the invitation extended to the Forwardists to contribute to *Pravda*. These relations became still worse in January, 1913, after the departure from Petersburg of J. Stalin . . ." The thoroughly considered expression, "became still worse," testifies that even prior to Stalin's departure Lenin's relations with the editorial board were not marked by friendliness. But Stalin avoided in every way making "a target" of himself.

The members of the editorial staff were figures of little influence in a Party sense and some of them chance figures. It would not have been hard for Lenin to have secured their replacement. But they had support in the attitude of the Party's higher-ups and in the person of the Central Committee's representative. A violent conflict with Stalin, who was closely connected with the editorial board and the fraction, would have meant a shakeup of the Party staff. That is why, for all its persistence, Lenin's policy was circumspect. On November thirteenth he was "deeply grieved" to reproach the editorial board for having failed to have an article on the opening of the International Socialist Congress at Basle: "It would not have been very hard to write such an article, and the *Pravda* editorial board knew that the Congress was opening on Sunday." Stalin, no doubt, was genuinely surprised. An international congress? In Basle? That was utterly remote from him. Yet the chief source of friction were not the incidental, although continually recurring errors, but rather the fundamental divergence in views on the Party's course of development. Lenin's policy made sense only to one with an audacious revolutionary perspective; from the point of view of newspaper circulation or the building of a machine, it could not seem other than highly extravagant. In the depth of his heart Stalin continued to regard the "émigré" Lenin as a sectarian.

We cannot avoid noting a delicate episode that occurred at that time. During those years Lenin was in dire need. When *Pravda* got on its feet, the editorial board designated for its inspirer and chief contributor an honorarium, which, its very modest size notwithstanding, was his financial mainstay. Just when the conflict waxed sharpest, the money stopped coming. Although he was exceptionally sensitive about matters of that sort, Lenin was compelled to remind them rather insistently about himself. "Why don't you send the money due me? The delay causes us considerable embarrassment. Don't be late, please." The holding up of the money can hardly be looked upon as a kind of financial punishment (although subsequently, when he was in power, Stalin did not hesitate to resort to such methods time and again). But even if it was all a matter of simple inattentiveness, it casts a sufficient light on the relations between Petersburg and Cracow. Indeed, they were very far from friendly.

Indignation with *Pravda* breaks through into the open in Lenin's letters immediately after Stalin's departure for Cracow to attend the conference at the Party headquarters. The irresistible impression is created that Lenin was only waiting for that departure in order to break up the Petersburg nest of Conciliators, preserving at the same time the possibility of a peaceful understanding with Stalin. The moment the most influential enemy was neutralized, Lenin launched a devastating attack on the Petersburg editorial board. In his letter of January twelfth, addressed to a trusted person in Petersburg, he refers to "the unpardonable stupidity" committed by *Pravda* in regard to the newspaper of the textile workers, insists on the correction of "your stupidity" and the like. The letter in its entirety was written in Krupskaya's hand. Further, in Lenin's handwriting: "We received a stupid and impudent letter from the editorial board. We will not reply. They must be got rid of . . . We are exceedingly disturbed by the absence of news about the plan for reorganizing the editorial board . . . Reorganization, but better yet, the complete expulsion of all the old timers, is extremely necessary. It's managed absurdly. They praise the Bund[3] and *Zeit* (an opportunist Jewish publication), which is simply despicable. They don't know how to proceed against *Lootch'*, and their attitude toward the articles [that is, the articles of Lenin himself] is monstrous. I've simply lost patience . . ." The tone of the letter shows that Lenin's indignation—and he knew how to contain himself when necessary—had reached the limit. The devastating criticism of the newspaper referred to the entire period when the responsibility for its direct supervision was Stalin's. The identity of the person who wrote the "stupid and impudent letter from the editorial board" has not yet been disclosed, and, of course, not by chance. It could hardly have been written by Stalin: he was too cautious for that; besides, he was most likely already away from Petersburg at the time. It is more likely that the letter was written by Molotov, the official secretary of the editorial board, who is just as inclined to rudeness as Stalin but is devoid of the latter's flexibility.

How resolutely Lenin now tackled the chronic conflict is evident from further lines in his letter: "What has been done about the control of money? Who got the subscription money? In whose possession is it? How much does it amount to?" Lenin apparently did not exclude the possibility of a break and was concerned with keeping the financial resources in his own hands. But it did not come to a break; the disconcerted Conciliators could scarcely have dared to think of it. Passive resistance was their sole weapon. Now even that would be knocked out of their hands.

Replying to Shklovsky's pessimistic letter from Bern and arguing that the affairs of the Bolsheviks were not so bad as they seemed, Krupskaya began with the acknowledgment, "of course, *Pravda* is badly managed." That phrase sounds like common ground, like something beyond dispute. "Every Tom, Dick and Harry[4] is on that editorial staff, and most of them are not literaries . . . The workers' protests against *Lootch'* are not published, in order to avoid polemics." However, Krupskaya promises "substantial reforms" in the near

---

[3] See Glossary.
[4] Literally: *"s boru da s sosenkt"*—"[everyone] from the pine woods and from the small pines."—C. M.

future. This letter was written on January nineteenth. The next day Lenin wrote to Petersburg, through Krupskaya: ". . . we must plant our own editorial staff in *Pravda* and kick the present one out. Things are now in a very bad way. The absence of a campaign for unity from below is stupid and despicable . . . Would you call such people editors? They are not men but pitiful dishrags and they are ruining the cause." This was the style to which Lenin resorted when he wanted to show that he would fight it out to the bitter end.

He opened a parallel fire from carefully placed batteries against the conciliationism of the Duma fraction. As early as the third of January he wrote to Petersburg: "See to it unconditionally that the letter of the Baku workers which we are sending you is published . . ." The letter demands that the Bolshevik deputies break with *Lootch'*. Pointing to the fact that in the course of five years, the Liquidators "have been reiterating in every way that the party has died," the Baku workers asked: "Wherefore now their present urge to unite with a corpse?" The question hits the mark rather neatly. "When will the four [deputies] resign from *Lootch'*?" Lenin persisted for his part. "Must we wait much longer? . . . Even from distant Baku twenty workers are protesting." It would not be amiss to presume that, having failed to obtain through letter-writing the break of the deputies with *Lootch'*, Lenin discreetly began to mobilize the lower ranks while Stalin was still in Petersburg. No doubt it was upon his initiative that the Baku workers protested—not by chance did Lenin choose Baku!—and besides, they sent their protest not to the editorial office of *Pravda*, where the Baku leader Koba was in charge, but to Lenin in Cracow. The complex threads of the conflict become flagrantly apparent. Lenin advances. Stalin maneuvers. With the Conciliators balking, though not without the unwitting aid of the Liquidators, who more and more exposed their opportunism, Lenin managed before long to induce the Bolshevik deputies to resign under protest as contributors to *Lootch'*. But they continued to be bound by the discipline of the liquidationist majority of the Duma fraction.

Preparing for the worst, even for a split, Lenin, as always, did all he could to achieve his political goal with the least disturbance and fewest victims possible. This was exactly why he first asked Stalin to come abroad and then was able to make him understand that it would be best for him to stay away from *Pravda* during the forthcoming "reforms." Meantime another member of the Central Committee was sent to Petersburg—Sverdlov, the future First President of the Soviet Republic. That significant fact has been officially attested. "For the purpose of reorganizing the editorial board," proclaims a footnote in the sixteenth volume of Lenin's Works, "the Central Committee sent Sverdlov to Petersburg." Lenin wrote him: "Today we learned about the beginning of reforms on *Pravda*. A thousand greetings, congratulations and wishes for success . . . You cannot imagine how tired we are of working with an utterly hostile editorial staff." With these words, in which accumulated bitterness mingled with a sigh of relief, Lenin settled scores with the editorial board for the whole period of difficulties during which, as we have been told, "Stalin actually ran the newspaper."

"The author of these lines vividly remembers," wrote Zinoviev in 1934, when the sword of Damocles was already hanging over his head, "what an event was Stalin's arrival in Cracow . . ." Lenin was doubly glad—because during Stalin's absence from Petersburg he would be able to carry out his delicate operation there and because he would probably be able to do it without any shakeup inside the Central Committee. In her sparing and wary account of Stalin's sojourn in Cracow Krupskaya, as if slipping it in, observed: "Ilyich was then very nervous about *Pravda*; Stalin was also nervous. They were parleying as to how to adjust matters." These very significant lines, for all their intentional obscurity, is all that apparently remains from franker text set aside upon the censor's demand. In connection with circumstances already known to us, it is hardly possible to doubt that Lenin and Stalin "were nervous" for different reasons, each trying to defend his policy. However, the struggle was too unequal: Stalin had to retreat.

The conference for which he was called lasted from December twenty-eighth to January first, 1913, and was attended by eleven persons—members of the Central Committee and the Duma fraction and prominent local leaders. In addition to general political problems arising from the revolutionary resurgence, the conference considered the acute questions of internal Party life—the Duma fraction, the Party press, the attitude toward the Liquidators and toward the slogan of "unity." The principal reports were made by Lenin. It must be supposed that the Duma deputies and their leader, Stalin, were obliged to listen to not a few bitter truths, although these were expressed in a friendly tone. It seems that Stalin kept his peace at the conference; only that can explain the fact that in the first edition of his memoirs (1929), the deferential Badayev failed even to list him among the participants. To keep silent under critical conditions is, moreover, Stalin's favorite method. The protocols and other documents of the conference "have not yet been found." Very likely special measures were taken to make sure that they should not be found. In one of Krupskaya's letters of that period to Russia it is stated: "At this conference the reports from locals were very interesting. Everybody was saying that the masses have now grown up . . . During the elections it had become apparent that there were self-made workers' organizations everywhere . . . For the most part they are not connected with the Party, but they are of the Party in spirit." As for Lenin, he noted in a letter to Gorky that the conference "was very successful" and "will play its part." Above all, he had in mind the straightening out of the Party's policy.

Not without a touch of irony, the Police Department informed the man in charge of its agency abroad that, his last report notwithstanding, deputy Poletayev was not present at the conference, while the following persons were: Lenin, Zinoviev, Krupskaya; deputies Malinovsky, Petrovsky, Badayev; Lobov, the worker Medvedev, the Lieutenant of Russian Artillery Troyanovsky,[5] Troyanovsky's wife[6] and Koba. Not devoid of interest is the order of the names: on the Department's list Koba's name is last. In the notes to Lenin's Works (1929) he is named fifth, after Lenin, Zinoviev, Kamenev and Krupskaya, although Zinoviev, Kamenev and Krupskaya had already been long in disfavor at the time. In the listing of the newest era Stalin invariably occupies the second place, directly after Lenin. These shufflings reflect rather aptly the nature of his historical career.

With this letter the Police Department wanted to show that Petersburg was better informed about what was going on in Cracow than its agent abroad. No wonder one of the important roles at the conference was played by Malinovsky, whose real character as a provocateur was known only to the most exalted on the police Olympus. True, certain Social-Democrats who had come in contact with him became suspicious of him as far back as the years of reaction, but they could not substantiate their misgivings with proofs, and their suspicions relaxed. In January, 1912, Malinovsky was delegated by the Moscow Bolsheviks to attend the conference in Prague. Lenin greedily seized upon this capable and energetic worker and helped to advance his candidacy at the Duma elections. The police, for its part, also supported its agent by arresting all his possible rivals. This representative of the Moscow workers at once established his authority in the Duma fraction. Upon receiving from Lenin the ready-made texts of his parliamentary speeches, Malinovsky would transmit the manuscripts for review to the director of the Police Department. The latter attempted at first to introduce emendations; but the régime of the Bolshevik fraction confined the autonomy of the individual deputy within very narrow limits. Consequently, although the Social-Democratic deputy was the best informer of the *Okhrana*, the *Okhrana* agent became the most militant orator of the Social-Democratic fraction.

Suspicions of Malinovsky cropped up again in the summer of 1913 among a number of prominent Bolsheviks; but because of lack of proof, the matter was again dropped. But then the government itself became frightened of possible exposure and of an accompanying political scandal. By order of his superiors, in May of 1914, Malinovsky filed with the President of the Duma a declaration of intention to resign his mandate as a deputy. Rumors of his role spread again and with renewed force, and this time got into the press. Malinovsky went abroad, called on Lenin and demanded an investigation. He had apparently carefully laid out his line of behavior in collaboration with his police superiors. Two weeks later the Party's Petersburg newspaper published a telegram which indirectly declared that the Central Committee, having investigated the Malinovsky affair, was convinced of his personal integrity. After another few days a resolution was published to the effect that by the willful resignation of his

---

[5] Alexander A. Troyanovsky, subsequently Soviet Ambassador to Japan and later to the United States.—C. M.
[6] Not the Mrs. Troyanovsky Washington diplomatic circles knew, but Elena Rozmirovich, an Old Bolshevik.—C. M.

mandate Malinovsky "placed himself outside the ranks of organized Marxists." In the language of the legal newspaper that meant expulsion from the Party.

Lenin's opponents subjected him to a prolonged and cruel barrage for "sheltering" Malinovsky. The participation of a police agent in the Duma fraction, and especially in the Central Committee, was, of course, a great calamity to the Party. As a matter of fact, Stalin had gone to his last exile because of Malinovsky's betrayal. But in those days suspicions, complicated at times by factional hostility, poisoned the atmosphere of the underground. No one presented any direct evidence against Malinovsky. After all, it was impossible to condemn a member of the Party to political—and perhaps even physical—death on the basis of vague suspicion. And since Malinovsky occupied a responsible position and the reputation of the Party depended to a certain extent on his reputation, Lenin deemed it his duty to defend Malinovsky with the energy which always distinguished him. After the overthrow of the monarchy the fact that Malinovsky had served in the Police Department was fully substantiated. After the October Revolution the provocateur, who returned to Moscow from a German war prisoners' camp, was shot by order of the Tribunal.

Notwithstanding the lack of men, Lenin was in no hurry to send Stalin back to Russia. It was necessary to complete "the essential reforms" in Petersburg before he returned. On the other hand, Stalin himself was hardly eager to return to the place of his former labors after the Cracow conference, which, however indirectly, had unmistakably condemned his policy. As usual, Lenin did all he could to obtain an honorable retreat for the vanquished man. Vengeance was altogether alien to his nature. In order to keep Stalin abroad during the crucial period, Lenin got him interested in working on the problem of minor nationalities—an arrangement thoroughly in the spirit of Lenin!

A native of the Caucasus, with its scores of semi-cultured and primitive yet rapidly awakening nationalities, he did not have to have proved to him the importance of the nationalities problem. The tradition of national independence continued to flourish in Georgia. It was from that that Koba himself had received his first revolutionary impulse. His very pseudonym harked back to his own nationality's struggle for national independence. True, according to Iremashvili, during the years of the First Revolution he had grown cool to the Georgian problem. "National liberation . . . no longer meant anything to him. He did not want to set any limitations upon his will to power. Russia and the whole world must henceforth be his prize." Iremashvili obviously anticipates the facts and attitudes of a much later time. The one thing beyond doubt is that, having become a Bolshevik, Koba forsook the nationalistic romanticism that continued to live in peace and harmony with the nerveless socialism of the Georgian Mensheviks. But after repudiating the idea of Georgian independence, Koba could not, like many Great-Russians, remain wholly indifferent to the nationalities problem, because relations between Georgians, Armenians, Tatars, Russians and others constantly complicated revolutionary activities in the Caucasus.

In his views Koba became an internationalist. But did he ever become one in his feelings? The Great-Russian Lenin could not endure any jests or anecdotes that were likely to hurt the sensibilities of an oppressed nationality. Stalin had in him too much of the peasant from the village of Didi-Lilo. During the pre-revolutionary years he did not dare, of course, to trifle with national prejudices, as he did later, when he was already in power. But that disposition disclosed itself in small matters even then. Referring to the preponderance of Jews in the Menshevik faction at the London Congress of 1907, Koba wrote:

> Apropos of that, one of the Bolsheviks jestingly remarked (I think it was Comrade Alexinsky) that the Mensheviks were a Jewish faction while the Bolsheviks were truly Russian, and hence it would not be amiss· for us Bolsheviks to instigate a pogrom in the Party.

It is impossible not to be astonished even now that in an article intended for the workers of the Caucasus, where the air was rife with nationalistic animosities, Stalin ventured to quote a jest of such suspicious odor. It was, moreover, no mere matter of accidental tactlessness but of conscious calculation. In the very same article, the author jauntily "jested" about the congressional resolution on expropriations, for the purpose of dispelling the doubts of the Caucasian fighters. One may confidently assume that the Menshevik faction in Baku was then headed by Jews and that with his "jest" anent a pogrom the author intended to discredit his factional opponents in the eyes of the backward workers. That was easier than to win them through persuasion and education, and Stalin always and in everything sought the line of least resistance. It might be added that neither was Alexinsky's "jest" accidental: that ultra-left Bolshevik subsequently became a downright reactionary and anti-Semite.

Naturally, in his political activities Koba upheld the Party's official position. Yet prior to his journey abroad, his political articles had never been above the level of daily propaganda. Only now, upon Lenin's initiative, did he approach the problem of nationalities from a broader theoretical and political point of view. First-hand knowledge of the intricate national relations in the Caucasus undoubtedly made it easier for him to orient himself in that complicated field, in which abstract theorizing was particularly dangerous.

In two countries of pre-war Europe the national question was of exceptional political significance: in Tsarist Russia and in Hapsburg Austria-Hungary. In each of these the workers' party created its own school. In the sphere of theory, the Austrian Social-Democracy, in the persons of Otto Bauer and Karl Renner, considered nationality independent of territory, economy and class, transforming it into a species of abstraction limited by so-called "national character." In the field of national policy, as for that matter in all other fields, it did not venture beyond a corrective of the status quo. Fearing the very thought of dismembering the monarchy, the Austrian Social-Democracy strove to adapt its national program to the borders of the patchwork state. The program of so-called "national cultural economy" required that the citizens of one and the same nationality, irrespective of their dispersal over the territory of Austria-Hungary and irrespective of the administrative divisions of the state, should be united, on the basis of purely personal attributes, into one community for the solution of their "cultural" tasks (the theater, the church, the school, and the like). That program was artificial and utopian, in so far as it attempted to separate culture from territory and economy in a society torn apart by social contradictions; it was at the same time reactionary, in so far as it led to a forced disunion into various nationalities of the workers of one and the same state, undermining their class strength.

Lenin's position was the direct opposite. Regarding nationality as unseverably connected with territory, economy and class structure, he refused at the same time to regard the historical state, the borders of which cut across the living body of the nations, as a sacrosanct and inviolate category. He demanded recognition of the right to secession and independent existence for each national portion of the state. In so far as the various nationalities, voluntarily or through force of necessity, coexist within the borders of one state, their cultural interests must find the highest possible satisfaction within the framework of the broadest regional (and consequently, territorial) autonomy, including statutory guarantees of the rights of each minority. At the same time, Lenin deemed it the incontrovertible duty of all the workers of a given state, irrespective of nationality, to unite in one and the same class organizations.

The national problem was particularly acute in Poland, aggravated by the historical fate of that country. The so-called P.P.S. (Polish Socialist Party), headed by Josef Pilsudski, came out ardently for Polish independence; the "socialism" of the P.P.S. was no more than a vague appendage of its militant nationalism. On the other hand, the Polish Social-Democracy, whose leader was Rosa Luxembourg, counterposed to the slogan of Polish independence the demand for the autonomy of the Polish region as a constituent part of democratic Russia. Luxembourg proceeded from the consideration that in the epoch of imperialism the separation of Poland from Russia was economically infeasible and in the epoch of socialism—unnecessary. She looked upon "the right of self-determination" as an empty abstraction. The polemic on that question lasted for years. Lenin insisted that imperialism did not reign similarly or equably in all countries, regions and spheres of life; that the heritage of the past represented an accumulation and interpenetration of various historical epochs; that although monopolistic capitalism towers above everything, it does not supersede everything; that, notwithstanding the domination of imperialism, the numerous national problems retained their full force and that, contingent upon the internal and world conjunctures, Poland might become independent even in the epoch of imperialism.

It was Lenin's view that the right of self-determination was merely an application of the principles of bourgeois democracy in the sphere of national relations. A real, full-bodied, all-sided democracy under capitalism was unrealizable; in that sense the national independence of small and weak peoples was likewise "unrealizable." However, even under imperialism, the working class did not refuse to fight for democratic rights, including among them the right of each nation to its independent existence. Moreover, in certain portions of our planet it was imperialism itself that invested the slogan of national self-determination with extraordinary significance. Although Western and Central Europe have somehow managed to solve their national problems in the course of the nineteenth century, in Eastern Europe, Asia, Africa and South America the epoch of national democratic movements had not really begun to unfold until the twentieth century. To deny the right of nations to self-determination is tantamount in effect to offering aid and comfort to the imperialists against their colonies and generally against all oppressed nationalities.

The problem of nationalities was considerably aggravated in Russia during the period of reaction. "The wave of militant nationalism," wrote Stalin, "called attention from above to numerous acts of repressions by those in power, who wreaked their vengeance upon the border states for their love of freedom, calling forth in response a wave of nationalism from below, which at times passed into crude chauvinism." This was the time of the ritual murder trial of the Kiev Jew Bayliss. Retrospectively, in the light of civilization's latest achievements, especially in Germany and in the U.S.S.R., that trial today seems almost a humanitarian experiment. But in 1913 it shocked the whole world. The poison of nationalism began to affect many sections of the working class as well. Alarmed, Gorky wrote to Lenin about the need for counteracting this chauvinistic rabidness. "As for nationalism, I quite agree with you," replied Lenin, "that we must cope with it more earnestly than ever. We have a splendid Georgian staying with us here who is writing a long article for *Prosveshcheniye* [Enlightenment], after garnering all the Austrian and other material. We will bear down on it." The reference was to Stalin. Gorky, long connected with the party, knew all its leading cadres well. But Stalin evidently was utterly unknown to him, since Lenin had to resort to such an impersonal, although flattering, expression as "a splendid Georgian." This is, by the way, the only occasion when Lenin characterized a prominent Russian revolutionist by the token of his nationality. He had in mind, of course, not a Georgian, but a Caucasian: the element of primitiveness undoubtedly attracted Lenin; small wonder that he treated Kamo with such tenderness.

During his two months' sojourn abroad Stalin wrote a brief but very trenchant piece of research entitled "Marxism and the National Problem." Since it was intended for a lawful magazine, the article resorted to a discreet vocabulary. Its revolutionary tendencies were nonetheless distinctly apparent. The author set out by counterposing the historico-materialistic definition of nation to the abstracto-psychological, in the spirit of the Austrian school. "The nation," he wrote, "is a historically-formed enduring community of language, territory, economic life and psychological composition, asserting itself in the community of culture." This combined definition, compounding the psychological attributes of a nation with the geographic and economic conditions of its development, is not only correct theoretically but also practically fruitful, for then the solution to the problem of each nation's fate must perforce be sought along the lines of changing the material conditions of its existence, beginning with territory. Bolshevism was never addicted to the fetishistic worship of a state's borders. Politically the point was to reconstruct the Tsarist empire, that prison of nations, territorially, politically, and administratively, in line with the needs and wishes of the nations themselves.

The party of the proletariat does not enjoin the various nationalities either to remain within the bounds of a given state or to separate from it: that is their own affair. But it does obligate itself to help each of them to realize its actual national will. As for the possibility of separating from a state, that is a matter of concrete historical circumstances and the relation of forces. "No one can say," wrote Stalin, "that the Balkan War is the end and not the beginning of complications. Quite possible is such a combination of internal and external circumstances that one or another nationality in Russia will deem it necessary to postulate and to solve the problem of its own independence. And, of course, it is no business of the Marxists to place barriers in such cases. But for that very reason Russian Marxists cannot get along without the right of nations to self-determination."

The interests of the nations which voluntarily remain within the bounds of democratic Russia would be fenced off by means of "the autonomies of such self-determined units as Poland, Lithuania, the Ukraine, the Caucasus, and the like. Regional autonomy is conducive to a better utilization of the natural wealth of the region; it does not divide citizens along national lines and makes it possible for them to group themselves in class parties." The territorial self-administration of regions in all spheres of social life is counterposed to the extra-territorial—that is, platonic—self-administration of nationalities in matters of "culture" only.

However, most directly and acutely significant, from the point of view of the proletariat's struggle, was the problem of the relations between workers of various nationalities inside the same state. Bolshevism stood for a compact and indivisible unification of workers of all nationalities in the party and in the trade unions on the basis of democratic centralism. "The type of organization does not exert its influence on practical work alone. It places an indelible stamp on the worker's whole spiritual life. The worker lives the life of his organization, within which he develops spiritually and is educated . . . The international type of organization is a school of comradely feelings, of the greatest agitation in favor of internationalism."

One of the aims of the Austrian program of "cultural autonomy" was "the preservation and development of the national idiosyncrasies of peoples." Why and for what purpose? asked Bolshevism in amazement. Segregating the various nationalistic portions of mankind was never our concern. True, Bolshevism insisted that each nation should have the right to secede—the right, but not the duty—as the ultimate, most effective guarantee against oppression. But the thought of artificially preserving national idiosyncrasies was profoundly alien to Bolshevism. The removal of any, even disguised, even the most refined and practically "imponderable" national oppression or indignity, must be used for the revolutionary unification rather than the segregation of the workers of various nationalities. Wherever national privileges and injuries exist, nations must have the possibility to separate from each other, that thus they may facilitate the free unification of the workers, in the name of a close rapprochement of nations, with the distant perspective of the eventual complete fusion of all. Such was the basic tendency of Bolshevism, which revealed the full measure of its force in the October Revolution.

The Austrian program disclosed nothing but its own weaknesses: it saved neither the Empire of the Hapsburgs nor the Austrian Social-Democracy itself. Cultivating the idiosyncrasies of proletarian national groups, while at the same time failing really to satisfy the oppressed nationalities, the Austrian program merely camouflaged the dominance of the Germans and the Magyars, and was, as Stalin justly pointed out, "a refined form of nationalism." However, it should be pointed out in all fairness that while criticizing their concern about "national idiosyncrasies," the author invested his opponents' thoughts with a patently over-simplified interpretation. "Only think," he exclaims, "of preserving such national idiosyncrasies of the Transcaucasian Tatars as self-flagellation during the Shakhsey-Vakhsey festival! To develop such national idiosyncrasies of Georgia as the law of retaliation!" As a matter of fact, the Austro-Marxists did not have in mind, of course, the preservation of any such patently reactionary survivals. As for such "national idiosyncrasies of Georgia as the law of retaliation," it was none other than Stalin who subsequently "developed" it to such an extent as perhaps no one else in human history. But that belongs in another sequence of ideas.

A prominent place in this study was allotted to a polemic against his old opponent Noah Jordania, who during the years of reaction began to lean toward the Austrian program. By example after example, Stalin showed that cultural-national economy, "generally . . . becomes even more senseless and ridiculous from the point of view of Caucasian conditions." No less resolute was his criticism of the policy of the Jewish Bund, which was organized not on the territorial but on the national principle and attempted to impose that system upon the whole party. "One of two things: either the federalism of the Bund, and then the Russian Social-Democracy must be reconstructed on the principle of 'dividing' the workers by nationalities; or an international type of organization, and then the Bund would have to be reconstructed on the principle of territorial economy . . . There is no middle ground: principles conquer, they never become reconciled."

"Marxism And The National Problem" is undoubtedly Stalin's most important—rather, his one and only—theoretical work. On the basis of that single article, which was forty printed pages long, its author is entitled to recognition as an outstanding theoretician. What is rather mystifying is why he did not write anything else of even remotely comparable quality either before or after. The key to the mystery is hidden away in this, that Stalin's work was wholly inspired by Lenin, written under his unremitting supervision and edited by him line by line.

Twice in his life Lenin broke with close collaborators who were high-grade theoreticians. The first time in 1903-1904, when he broke with all of the old authorities of the Russian Social-Democracy—Plekhanov, Axelrod, Zasulich—and with the outstanding young Marxists, Martov and Potressov; the second time—during the years of reaction—when Bogdanov, Lunacharsky, Pokrovsky, Rozhkov, all highly qualified writers, left him. Zinoviev and Kamenev, his closest collaborators, were not theoreticians. In that sense, the new revolutionary resurgence found Lenin stranded. No wonder then that he greedily pounced upon any young comrade who might be useful in working out one or another problem of the party program.

"This time," recalls Krupskaya, "Ilyich talked a lot with Stalin about the national problem, was glad to find a man who was seriously interested in this problem and knew his way about in it. Prior to that Stalin lived approximately two months in Vienna, studying the national problem there, became well acquainted with our Viennese public, with Bukharin, with Troyanovsky." Some things were left unsaid. "Ilyich talked a lot with Stalin"—that means: he gave him the key ideas, shed light on all their aspects, explained misconceptions, suggested the literature, looked over the first drafts and made corrections . . . "I recall," relates the same Krupskaya, "Ilyich's attitude toward authors of little experience. He looked for the substance, for fundamentals, he thought in every way how best to help, how to set them straight. But he did it all somehow with very great care, so that the author in question did not realize that he was being corrected. And Ilyich certainly knew how to help people in their work. If, for example, he wanted to assign the writing of an article to someone but was not certain whether that person would write it properly, he would first start a detailed conversation with him on the theme, develop his own thoughts, get the person interested, sound him out thoroughly, and then he would suggest: 'Won't you write an article on that theme?' And the author did not even notice how the preliminary conversation with Ilyich had helped him, would not realize that he was incorporating in his article even Ilyich's favorite words and expressions." Krupskaya, of course, does not name Stalin. But this characterization of Lenin as coach of young authors is included in that chapter of her memoirs in which she tells about Stalin's work on the problem of nationalities: Krupskaya was not infrequently compelled to resort to roundabout devices, so as to protect at least a portion of Lenin's intellectual rights from usurpation.

Stalin's progress on his article is pictured for us with sufficient clarity. At first, leading conversations with Lenin in Cracow, the outlining of the dominating ideas and of the research material. Later Stalin's journey to Vienna, into the heart of the "Austrian school." Since he did not know German, Stalin could not cope with his source material. But there was Bukharin, who unquestionably had a head for theory, knew languages, knew the literature of the subject, knew how to use documents. Bukharin, like Troyanovsky, was under instructions from Lenin to help the "splendid" but poorly educated Georgian. Evidently, the selection of the most important quotations was their handiwork. The logical construction of the article, not devoid of pedantry, is due most likely to the influence of Bukharin, who inclined toward professorial ways, in distinction from Lenin, for whom the structure of a composition was determined by its political or polemical interest. Bukharin's influence did not go beyond that, since on the problem of nationalities he was much closer to Rosa Luxembourg than to Lenin. Just what was the amount of Troyanovsky's participation, we do not know. But from that time dates the beginning of his contact with Stalin, which several years later, after circumstances had changed, secured for the insignificant and unstable Troyanovsky one of the most responsible of diplomatic posts.

From Vienna Stalin returned with his material to Cracow. Here again came Lenin's turn, the turn of the attentive and tireless editor. The stamp of his thought and the traces of his pen are readily discoverable on every page. Certain phrases, mechanically incorporated by the author, or certain lines, obviously written in by the editor, seem unexpected or incomprehensible without reference to the corresponding works of Lenin. "Not the national but the agrarian problem decides the fate of progress in Russia," writes Stalin without any explanations. "The national problem is subsidiary to it." This correct and profound thought about the relative effect of the agrarian and national problems on the course of the Russian Revolution is entirely Lenin's and was expounded by him innumerable times during the years of reaction. In Italy and in Germany the struggle for national liberation and unification was at one time the crux of the bourgeois revolution. It was otherwise in Russia, where the dominating nationality, the Great-Russians, did not experience national oppression, but, on the contrary, oppressed others; yet it was none other than the vast peasant mass of the Great-Russians themselves that had experienced the profound oppression of serfdom. Such complex and seriously considered thoughts would never have been expressed by their real author as if in passing, as a generality, without proofs and commentaries.

Zinoviev and Kamenev, who long lived side by side with Lenin, acquired not only his ideas but even his turns of phrase, even his handwriting. That cannot be said about Stalin. Of course, he too lived by Lenin's ideas, but at a distance, away from him, and he used them only as he needed them for his own independent purposes. He was too sturdy, too stubborn, too dull and too organic, to acquire the literary methods of his teacher. That is why Lenin's corrections of his text, to quote the poet, look "like bright patches on dilapidated tatters." The exposure of the Austrian school as "a refined form of nationalism" is undoubtedly Lenin's, as are a number of other simple but pertinent formulae. Stalin did not write like that. With reference to Otto Bauer's definition of the nation as "a relative community of character," we read in the article: "Wherein then does Bauer's nation differ from the mystical and self-sufficient 'national spirit' of the spiritualists?" That sentence was written by Lenin. Neither before nor after this did Stalin express himself like that. And further, when, referring to Bauer's own eclectic corrections of his own definition of a nation, the article comments, "thus, the theory sewn with idealistic threads refutes itself," one cannot help but recognize Lenin's pen. The same is true of the characterization of the national type of labor organization as "a school of comradely feelings." Stalin did not write like that. On the other hand, throughout the entire work, notwithstanding its numerous angularities, we find no chameleons assuming the hue of rabbits, no underground swallows, no screens made of tears: Lenin had expunged all these seminarist embellishments. The original manuscript with its corrections can, of course, be hidden. But it is impossible, in any way, to hide the hand of Lenin, as it is impossible to hide the fact that throughout all the years of his imprisonment and exile Stalin produced nothing which even remotely resembles the work he wrote in the course of a few weeks in Vienna and Cracow.

On the eighth of February, when Stalin was still abroad, Lenin congratulated the editorial board of *Pravda* "on the tremendous improvement in all phases of managing the newspaper, which has been noticeable during recent days." The improvement was in the matter of principles, and expressed itself chiefly in intensified fighting against the Liquidators. According to Samoilov, Sverdlov was then carrying out the duties of the actual editor; living in illegal status and never emerging from the apartment of an "immune" deputy, he busied himself all day long with newspaper manuscripts. "He was, besides all that, a very fine comrade in all personal matters as well." This is correct. Samoilov does not say anything of the kind about Stalin, with whom he came in close contact and toward whom he is very respectful. On the tenth of February the police entered the "immune" apartment, arrested Sverdlov, and soon banished him to Siberia, undoubtedly because of Malinovsky's denunciation. Toward the end of February, Stalin, who had returned from abroad, made his home with the same deputies: "He played the leading role in the life of our [Duma] faction[7] and of the newspaper *Pravda*," relates Samoilov, "and he attended not only all the conferences, which we arranged in our apartment, but not infrequently, with great risk to himself, visited also the sessions of the Social-Democratic faction, where, by upholding our position in arguments against the Mensheviks and on various other questions, he rendered us great service."

Stalin found the situation in Petersburg considerably changed. The advanced workers firmly supported Sverdlov's reforms, inspired by Lenin. *Pravda* had a new staff. The Conciliators had been set back. Stalin did not even think of really defending the positions from which he had been torn away two months before. That was not in his spirit. He was now concerned only with saving his

[7] See Glossary.

face. On the twenty-sixth of February he published in *Pravda* an article, in which he called upon the workers "to raise their voice against the separatist efforts inside the fraction, no matter where they come from." In substance, the article was part of the campaign to prepare the split of the Duma fraction, at the same time to place the responsibility on the opponents. No longer bound by his own past record, Stalin attempted to express his new purpose in the old phraseology. Hence, his misleading expression about attempts to split the fraction, "no matter where they come from." In any event, it is evident from the article that, after attending school in Cracow, the author tried to change his line and start off on the new policy as inconspicuously as possible. But he had practically no opportunity to do that, for he was soon arrested.

In March the Bolshevik organization, under the lawful sponsorship of *Pravda*, arranged for a concert and evening of entertainment. Stalin "wanted to go there," relates Samoilov: there one could see many comrades. He asked Malinovsky's advice: was it safe to go, was it not dangerous? The perfidious adviser replied that, in his opinion, there was no danger. However, the danger was prepared by Malinovsky himself. As soon as Stalin came, the hall filled with spies. Comrades attempted to lead him through the stage entrance, having previously dressed him up in a woman's mantle. But he was arrested. This time he was fated to disappear from circulation for exactly four years.

Two months after that arrest Lenin wrote to *Pravda*: "I congratulate you heartily upon your success . . . the improvement is tremendous and important. Let us hope it is permanent and definite and final . . . if only no evil spell is cast on it!" In the interest of completeness, we cannot refrain from quoting also the letter which Lenin sent to Petersburg in October, 1913, when Stalin was already in distant exile and Kamenev was in charge of the editorial board: "Here everybody is satisfied with the newspaper and its editor. In all this time I haven't heard a single word of criticism . . . everybody is satisfied and myself especially, for I have proved to be a prophet. Do you remember?" And at the end of the letter: "Dear Friend, all attention is now devoted to the fight of the six for their rights. I beg you to bear down with all your strength, so as not to let either the newspaper or Marxist public opinion waver even once."

All the cited evidence leads to one inescapable conclusion: in Lenin's opinion, the newspaper was very badly conducted when Stalin was in charge. During that same period the Duma fraction wavered toward conciliationism. The newspaper began to straighten out politically, only after Sverdlov, with Stalin away, brought about "substantial reforms." The newspaper improved and became satisfactory when Kamenev took charge of it. Likewise, under his leadership, the Bolshevik deputies of the Duma won their political independence.

Malinovsky played an active role, even two roles at the same time, in splitting the fraction. The gendarme General Spiridovich wrote apropos of that: "Malinovsky, carrying out the directives of Lenin and of the Police Department, achieved in October, 1913 . . . the final quarrel between the 'seven' and the 'six.'" Then Mensheviks, for their part, gloated repeatedly over the "coincidence" of Lenin's policy with that of the Police Department. Now that the course of events has rendered its own verdict, the old argument has lost its significance. The Police Department hoped that the split of the Social-Democracy would weaken the labor movement. On the contrary, Lenin reckoned that only a split would secure for the workers the needed revolutionary leadership. The police Machiavellis obviously figured wrong. The Mensheviks were doomed to insignificance. The Bolsheviks won all along the line.

Stalin devoted himself to intensive work in Petersburg and abroad for more than six months prior to his last arrest. He helped to conduct the Duma election campaign, managed *Pravda,* participated in an important conference of the Party staff abroad, and wrote his essay on the national problem. That half year was undoubtedly of great importance to his personal development. For the first time he bore responsibility for activities on the soil of the capital, for the first time he came in contact with major politics, for the first time he came in close touch with Lenin. That feeling of supposed superiority which was so much a part of him as a realistic "practico" could not help having been shaken by personal contact with the great émigré. His estimation of himself had to become more critical and sober, his ambition more secretive, guarded. His hurt provincial self-satisfaction must inevitably have been colored with envy, mitigated only by cautiousness.

Chapter VI

WAR AND EXILE

SEEING in the street a man squatting and gesturing strangely, Leo Tolstoy decided that he was looking at a madman; on coming closer he was satisfied that the man was attending to necessary work—sharpening a knife on a stone.

Lenin was fond of citing this example. The interminable discussions, factional squabbles, splits between the Bolsheviks and the Mensheviks, arguments and splits inside the Bolshevik faction itself, seemed to the observer on the sidelines like the activities of maniacs. But the test of events proved that these people were attending to necessary work; the struggle was waged not over scholastic subtleties, as it seemed to the dilettantes, but over the most fundamental questions of the revolutionary movement.

Because of their painstaking and precise definitions of ideas and because they drew clear political boundary lines, only Lenin and his disciples were ready to meet the new revolutionary resurgence. Hence, the uninterrupted series of successes which very quickly secured for the Pravdists dominance over the labor movement. The majority of the older generation had abandoned the struggle during the years of reaction. "Lenin has nothing but boys," the Liquidators were wont to say contemptuously. But in that Lenin saw his Party's great advantage. Revolution, like war, necessarily places the main part of its burden on the shoulders of youth. That socialist party which is unable to draw the "youngsters," is hopeless.

In its secret correspondence, the tsarist police, which came face to face with the revolutionary parties, was far from niggardly with flattering admissions concerning the Bolsheviks. "During the past ten years," wrote the Director of the Police Department in 1913, "the most energetic, courageous element, capable of tireless struggle, resistance and constant organization, have been . . . the organizations and persons concentrating around Lenin . . . The permanent organizational heart and soul of all Party undertakings of any importance is Lenin . . . The faction of Leninists is always better organized than the others, stronger in its singleness of purpose, more resourceful in propagating its ideas among the workers . . . When during the last two years the labor movement began to grow stronger, Lenin and his followers came closer to the workers than others, and he was the first to proclaim purely revolutionary slogans . . . The Bolshevik circles, nuclei and organizations are now scattered through all the cities. Permanent correspondence and contacts have been established with almost all the factory centers. The Central Committee functions almost regularly and is entirely in the hands of Lenin . . . In view of the aforesaid, there is nothing surprising in the fact that at the present time the assembling of the entire underground Party is proceeding around the Bolshevik organizations and that indeed the latter really are the Russian Social-Democratic Labor Party." There is almost nothing to add to this.

The correspondence of the foreign staff acquired a new optimistic tone. Krupskaya wrote to Shklovksy at the beginning of 1913: "All the contacts are somehow different than before. Somehow you feel more as if you were dealing with likeminded people . . . The affairs of Bolshevism are sounder than ever." The Liquidators, who prided themselves on their realism and only yesterday derided Lenin as the head of a degenerate sect, suddenly found themselves relegated to the sidelines and isolated. From Cracow Lenin watched tirelessly for all the manifestations of the labor movement, registering and classifying all the facts that might enable him to take the pulse of the proletariat. From the painstaking calculations in Cracow of money collections for the labor press it was evident that in Petersburg 86% of the reading workers were on the side of *Pravda* and only 14% on the side of the Liquidators; almost the same relation of forces existed in Moscow; in the backward provinces the Liquidators were somewhat better off, but on the whole four-fifths of the advanced workers sided with *Pravda*. Of what value could be abstract appeals to the unity of factions and tendencies, when the correct policy counterposed to these "factions and tendencies" was able, in the course of three years, to rally around Bolshevism the preponderant majority of the advanced workers? During elections to the Fourth Duma, when not Social-Democrats but ordinary voters cast their ballots, 67% of the workers' curiae came out for the Bolsheviks. During the conflict between the two factions of the Duma fraction in Petersburg, five thousand votes were cast for the Bolshevik deputies and only 621 for the Mensheviks. The Liquidators were utterly crushed in the capital. There was the same relation of forces in the trade union movement: of the thirteen Moscow unions, not one belonged to the Liquidators; of the twenty Petersburg unions, only four, the least proletarian and the least important, found themselves partly or entirely in the hands of the Mensheviks. At the beginning of 1914, during the elections of representatives of workers to the Petersburg sick benefit funds, the tickets of *Pravda's* nominees won completely. All the groups hostile to Bolshevism—the Liquidators, the Recallists, all sorts of Conciliators—proved utterly incapable of sinking their roots into the working class. Hence, Lenin drew his conclusions: "Only in the course of fighting against these groups can the real workers' Social-Democratic Party be formed in Russia."

In the spring of 1914 Emile Vandervelde, who was then President of the Second International, visited Petersburg, in order to acquaint himself on the spot with the conflict of the factions inside the working class. The opportunistic skeptic measured the arguments of the Russian barbarians by the rule of Belgian parliamentarism. The Mensheviks, he reported upon his return, wanted to organize legally and demand the right of coalition; the Bolsheviks wanted to demand the immediate proclamation of the republic and the expropriation of the land. This disagreement Vandervelde called "rather childish." There was nothing Lenin could do but smile bitterly. Soon came developments that made possible an incontestable verification of men and ideas. The "childish" differences of opinion between the Marxists and the opportunists gradually spread throughout the world-wide labor movement.

"The war between Austria and Russia," Lenin wrote to Gorky at the beginning of 1913, "would be a very useful thing for the revolution (throughout all of Eastern Europe), but it is hardly possible that Franz-Josef and Nicki would give us this pleasure." Yet they did—although not until a year and a half later.

Meantime the industrial conjuncture had passed its zenith. The first underground tremors of the crisis began to be felt. But they did not stop the strike struggle. On the contrary, they invested it with a more aggressive character. Only a little more than six months prior to the outbreak of the war there were almost a million and a half strikers. The last great explosion occurred on the very eve of mobilization. On the third of July the Petersburg police was shooting into a crowd of workers. In response to an appeal by the Bolshevik Committee, the most important factories struck as a sign of protest. There were as many as two hundred thousand strikers. Meetings and demonstrations were held everywhere. Attempts were made to construct barricades. Into the welter of these events in the capital that became a miliary encampment, came the French President Poincaré for final negotiations with his crowned "friend"; and had the opportunity to peek with one eye into the laboratory of the Russian Revolution. But several days later the government took advantage of the declaration of war to wipe off the face of the earth both the labor organizations and the labor press. The first victim was *Pravda*. The attractive idea of the tsarist government was to stifle the revolution with a war.

The assertion of certain biographers that Stalin was the author of the "defeatist" theory, or the formula for "transforming the imperialist war into a civil war," is pure invention and attests to the complete lack of understanding of Stalin's intellectual and political character. Least of all was he in tune with the spirit of political innovation and theoretical daring. He never anticipated anything; he never ran ahead of anyone. Being an empiricist, he was ever afraid of *a priori* conclusions, preferring to measure ten times before cutting the cloth. Inside this revolutionist always lurked a conservative bureaucrat. The Second International was a powerful political machine. Stalin would never have ventured to break with it on his own initiative. The elaboration of the Bolshevik doctrine on war is in its entirety part and parcel of Lenin's record. Stalin did not contribute to it a single word, even as he contributed nothing to the doctrine of revolution. However, in order to understand Stalin's behavior during the years of exile, and especially during the first critical weeks after the February Revolution, as well as his subsequent break with all the principles of Bolshevism, it is necessary to outline briefly the system of views which Lenin had already elaborated at the beginning of the war and to which he had gradually converted his Party.

The first question posed by the European catastrophe was whether socialists could take upon themselves the "defense of the fatherland." It was not a question of whether the individual socialist should carry out his duties as a soldier. There was nothing else he could do. Desertion was never a revolutionary policy. The question was whether a socialist party should support the war politically —vote from the military budget, terminate its fight against the government, agitate for "defense of the fatherland." Lenin answered: No, it should not, it has no right to do so—not because it was *war*, but because it was a *reactionary* war, a bloody shambles brought about by slave-owners who wanted to divide the world.

The formation of national states on the continent of Europe covered an epoch which began approximately with the Great French Revolution and ended with the Versailles Peace of 1871. During that period, wars for the establishment or defense of national states, as a condition prerequisite to the development of productive forces and culture, had a progressive historical character. Revolutionists not only could, but were duty-bound, to support these national wars politically. From 1871 to 1914 European capitalism, having attained its fruition on the basis of national states, outlived itself, transforming itself into monopolistic or imperialistic capitalism. "Imperialism is that state of capitalism which, having accomplished all that it could accomplish, turns toward decline." The cause of the decline lies in the fact that the productive forces become equally constrained by the framework of private property and by the borders of the national state. Seeking a way out, imperialism strives to divide and to redivide the world. National wars are succeeded by imperialist wars. The latter are thoroughly reactionary in character, epitomizing the historical blind alley, the stagnation, the decay of monopolistic capitalism.

Imperialism can exist only because there are backward nations on our planet, colonial and semi-colonial countries. The struggle of these oppressed peoples for national unity and independence has a twofold progressive character, since, on the one hand, it prepares favorable conditions of development for their own use, and on the other, it strikes blows at imperialism. Hence, in part, the conclusion that in a war between a civilized imperialist democratic republic and the backward barbarian monarchy of a colonial country, the socialists will be entirely on the side of the oppressed country, notwithstanding its monarchy, and against the oppressor country, notwithstanding its "democracy."

Imperialism covers its predatory aims—the seizure of colonies, of markets, of sources of raw materials, of spheres of influence—with the ideas of "protecting peace from the aggressors," "defense of the fatherland," "defense of democracy," and the like. These ideas are false to the core. "The question of whether one or another group struck the first military blow or was the first to declare war," wrote Lenin in March, 1915, "has no significance whatever in determining the tactic of socialists. Phrases about 'defense of the fatherland,' about resisting the invasion of the enemy, about a war of defense, and the like, are an utter deception of the people on both sides . . ." As far as the proletariat is concerned, the objective historical significance of the war is the only thing that has any meaning: which class is waging it and for what aims?—and not the ruses of diplomacy, which knows how to represent the enemy in the role of the aggressor.

Equally spurious are the references of the imperialists to the interests of democracy and culture. Since the war is waged by both camps, not for the sake of defending the fatherland, democracy and culture, but for the sake of partitioning the world and for the sake of colonial enslavement, no socialist has the right to prefer one imperialist camp to another. Utterly useless would be the attempt "to say, from the point of view of the international proletariat, which nation's defeat would be the least evil for socialism." To sacrifice in the name of that supposedly "lesser evil" the political independence of the proletariat, is to betray the future of humanity.

The policy of "national unity" means in time of war, even more than in time of peace, the support of reaction and the eternization of imperialist barbarism. Refusal of that support, which is a socialist's elementary duty, is, however, merely the negative or passive side of internationalism. That alone is not enough. The task of the party of the proletariat is to present "a manifold propaganda of socialist revolution, embracing the army and the theatre of war, propaganda showing the necessity to turn the guns, not against their own brothers, the hired slaves of the other countries, but against the reactionary and bourgeois governments and parties of all countries."

But the revolutionary struggle in time of war may bring defeat to one's own government! Lenin is not frightened by that conclusion. "In every country the struggle with one's own government, which wages the imperialist war, must not stop short before the possibility of the defeat of that country in consequence of revolutionary agitation." Therein is the essence of the so-called theory of "defeatism." Unscrupulous opponents attempted to interpret this as meaning that Lenin admitted the possibility of collaboration between internationalists and foreign imperialists for the sake of victory over one's own national reaction. As a matter of fact, what was under consideration was the general struggle of the world proletariat against world imperialism by way of the simultaneous struggle of the proletariat of each country against its own imperialism as the direct and main enemy. "From the point of view of the interests of the toiling masses and the working class of Russia," wrote Lenin to Shlyapnikov in October, 1914, "we Russians cannot doubt in the slightest way, absolutely cannot doubt at all, that now and at once the least evil would be—the defeat of Tsarism in the present war . . ."

It is impossible to fight against the imperialist war with pious lamentations for peace in the manner of the pacifists. "One of the forms of fooling the working class is pacifism and the abstract preachment of peace. Under capitalism, and especially in its imperialistic stage, wars are inescapable." Peace, concluded by the imperialists, will be a mere breathing spell before a new war. Only a revolutionary mass struggle against war and the imperialism engendered by it is capable of securing a real peace. "Without a series of revolutions the so-called democratic peace is a philistine utopia."

The struggle against the illusions of pacifism is one of the most important elements in Lenin's doctrine. He rejected with particular abhorrence the demand for "disarmament" as flagrantly utopian under capitalism and capable only of deflecting the attention of the workers from the need to arm themselves. "The oppressed class that does not strive to learn how to use guns and to have guns, such an oppressed class deserves to be treated as slaves." And further: "Our slogan must be: the arming of the proletariat in order to win, to expropriate and to disarm the bourgeoisie . . . Only after the proletariat has disarmed the bourgeoisie can it throw all arms on the scrap heap, without playing false to its world-wide historic task . . ." Lenin rejects the bare slogan of "peace," counterposing to it the slogan of "transforming imperialist war into civil war."

Most of the leaders of labor parties found themselves during the war on the side of their own bourgeoisie. Lenin christened their tendency, *"social-chauvinism"*: socialism in words, chauvinism in deeds. The betrayal of internationalism did not, however, fall from the sky but was the inescapable continuation and development of the policy of reformist adjustment to the capitalist state. "The content of political ideas in opportunism and social chauvinism is one and the same: collaboration of classes instead of their struggle, repudiation of the revolutionary need to struggle, aid to 'one's own' government in a difficult situation instead of utilizing those difficulties for the revolution."

The final period of capitalist prosperity before the war (1909-1913) secured the particularly strong attachment of the proletarian upper layer to imperialism. Out of the surplus profit the bourgeoisie secured from the colonies and from the backward countries generally, fat morsels fell into the laps of the labor aristocracy and the labor bureaucracy as well. Their patriotism was thus dictated by direct self-interest in the policy of imperialism. During the war, which exposed all the social relations, "the opportunists and the chauvinists derived their tremendous power from their union with the bourgeoisie, the governments and the general staffs." The opportunists definitely went over to the camp of the class enemy.

The intermediate, and perhaps the broadest tendency in socialism, the so-called Center (Kautsky and others), which in time of peace wavered between reformism and Marxism, became almost wholly the prisoner of the social-chauvinists under the cover of pacifist phrases. As for the masses, they were found unprepared and deceived by their own party machine which they had been building for decades. Having given the sociological and political evaluation of the labor bureaucracy of the Second International, Lenin did not stop half way. "Unity with opportunists is the unity of workers with 'their own' national bourgeoisie and the splitting of the international revolutionary working class."

Hence, his conclusion about the need, once and for all, to sever all contact with the social-chauvinists. "It is impossible to carry out the tasks of Socialism at the present time, it is impossible to achieve the actual international mobilization of the workers, without a resolute break with opportunism," as well as with centrism, "that bourgeois tendency in Socialism." The very name of the party must be changed. "Is it not better to repudiate the sullied and discredited name 'Social-Democrats' and return to the old Marxist name of 'Communists'?" It is high time to break with the Second International and build the Third!

That was where the difference of opinion, which only two or three months before the war had seemed "childish" to Emile Vandervelde. The President of the Second International had meantime himself become a patriotic minister of his king.

The Bolshevik Party was the most revolutionary—indeed, the only revolutionary—section of the Second International. Yet even the Bolshevik Party did not at once find its way in the labyrinth of the war. As a general rule, the confusion was most pervasive and lasted longest among the Party's higher-ups, who came in direct contact with bourgeois public opinion. The Bolshevik Duma fraction at once made a sharp right turn by joining the Mensheviks in an equivocal declaration. True, the document proclaimed in the Duma on July twenty-sixth kept its skirts clear of "false patriotism under the cover of which the ruling classes waged their predatory policy," but at the same time promised that the proletariat "would defend the cultural weal of the people against all encroachments, no matter where they came from, whether from within or from without." Under the subterfuge of "defending culture," the fraction was assuming a patriotic position.

Lenin's theses on the war did not reach Petersburg until the beginning of September. The reception accorded them by the Party was far from one of general approbation. Most of the objections were to Lenin's slogan of "defeatism," which, according to Shlyapnikov, aroused "perplexity." The Duma fraction, which was then led by Kamenev, again tried to smooth down the sharp edges of Lenin's formulations. It was the same story in Moscow and in the provinces. "The war caught the 'Leninists' unprepared," testifies the Moscow *Okhrana*, "and for a long time . . . they could not agree on their attitude toward the war . . ." The Moscow Bolsheviks wrote in code by way of Stockholm for transmission to Lenin that "notwithstanding all respect for him, his advice to sell the house [the slogan of 'defeatism'] has not struck a responsive chord." In Saratov, according to the local leader Antonov, "the workers of the Bolshevik, Menshevik and Essar tendencies did not agree with the defeatist position. More than that . . . they were (with rare exception) decided defensists." Among the advanced workers the situation was more favorable. At Petersburg factories inscriptions appeared, reading: "If Russia wins, we'll not be better off, we'll be oppressed more than ever." And Samoilov wrote: "The Ivanovo-Voznesensk comrades sensed, with the class instinct of proletarians, what was . . . the right road and definitely took to it as early as the very first months of the war."

However, only a very few individuals managed to formulate their opinions. Sweeping arrests blotted out the Social-Democratic organizations. The smashing of the press scattered the workers. All the more important, therefore, became the role of the Duma fraction. Recovering from the first siege of panic, the Bolshevik deputies began to develop important illegal activities. But they were arrested as early as the fourth of November. The chief evidence against them consisted of the documents of the party staff abroad. The authorities charged the arrested deputies with treason. During the preliminary investigation Kamenev and all the deputies, with the single exception of Muranov, repudiated Lenin's theses. At the trial, which took place on the tenth of February, the defendants maintained the same line. Kamenev's declaration that the documents with which he was confronted "decidedly contradict his own views on the current war" was not dictated only by concern for his own safety; essentially, it expressed the negative attitude of the entire Party upper layer toward defeatism. To Lenin's great indignation, the purely defensist tactics of the defendants extremely weakened the agitational effectiveness of the trial. The legal defense could have proceeded hand in hand with a political offensive. But Kamenev, who was a clever and well-educated politician, was not born to meet extraordinary situations. The attorneys, for their part, did whatever they could. Repudiating the charge of treason, one of them, Pereverzev, prophesied at the trial that the loyalty of the labor deputies to their class will be forever preserved in the memory of future generations; whereas their weaknesses—lack of preparation, dependence on their intellectual advisers, and the like—"all of that will fall away, like an empty shell, together with the libelous charge of treason."

By virtue of one of those sadistic jests which history never tires of perpetrating, it fell to none other than Pereverzev in his capacity as Minister of Justice in Kerensky's government, to charge all the Bolshevik leaders with treason to the state and espionage, doing so with the aid of cynical forgeries to which even the Tsarist prosecutor would never have resorted. Only Stalin's prosecutor, Vishinsky, outdid in that respect the democratic Minister of Justice.

Notwithstanding the equivocal behavior of the defendants, the very fact of the trial of the labor deputies delivered a smashing blow to the myth of "civil peace" and aroused the stratum of workers that had gone through the revolutionary school. "About 40,000 workers bought *Pravda*," wrote Lenin in March, 1915, "many more read it. . . . It is impossible to destroy that layer. It lives . . . It alone stands up among the popular masses, and in the very heart of them, as the propagator of the internationalism of the toilers, the exploited, the oppressed." The awakening of the masses began soon, but its influence made its way slowly to the outside. Being subject to military service, the workers were tied hand and foot. Every violation of discipline threatened them with immediate evacuation to the front, accompanied by a special police notation that was tantamount to a death sentence. This was particularly effective in Petersburg, where surveillance was doubly severe.

Meantime, the defeats of the Tsarist army pursued their course. The hypnosis of patriotism and the hypnosis of fear gradually relaxed. During the second half of 1915 sporadic strikes broke out, occasioned by high prices in the Moscow textile region, but they were not developed. The masses were dissatisfied, but they kept their peace. In May, 1916, scattered disturbances among recruits flared up in the provinces. Food riots began in the south, and at once spread to Kronstadt, the fortress that guarded the approaches to the capital. Finally, toward the end of December, came Petrograd's turn. The political strike involved as many as two hundred thousand workers at once, with the unquestionable participation of the Bolshevik organizations. The ice was broken. In February began a series of stormy strikes and disturbances, which developed rapidly into an uprising and culminated when the capital's garrison went over to the side of the workers. "The German course of development," on which the liberals and the Mensheviks relied, did not materialize. As a matter of fact, the Germans themselves soon drifted away from the so-called German way . . . In distant exile Stalin was fated to find out about the triumph of the insurrection and the Tsar's abdication.

Over the approximately thirty thousand square miles of the Turukhansk Region, located in the northern part of Yeniseisk Province, was scattered a population of approximately ten thousand souls, Russians and aliens. The small settlements of two to ten, rarely more, houses were hundreds of miles apart. Since winter endures here for fully eight months, agriculture is non-existent. The inhabitants fish and hunt, for there is an abundance of both fish and game. Stalin reached that inhospitable region in the middle of 1913 and found Sverdlov already there. Soon Alliluyev received a letter, in which Stalin urged him to hurry Deputy Badayev about forwarding the money sent by Lenin from abroad . . . "Stalin explained in detail that he needed the money in a hurry, so as to provide himself with the necessary food supplies, kerosene and other things before the approach of the harsh arctic winter."

On the twenty-fifth of August, the Police Department warned the Yeniseisk gendarmerie about the possibility of an attempt to escape by the exiles Sverdlov and Djugashvili. On the eighteenth of December the Department requested by telegraph that the Governor of Yeniseisk undertake measures to forestall the escape. In January the Department telegraphed the Yeniseisk gendarmerie that Sverdlov and Djugashvili, in addition to the hundred rubles previously received, were to receive another fifty rubles toward the organization of their escape. In March the agents of the *Okhrana* had even heard that Sverdlov had been seen in Moscow. The Governor of Yeniseisk hastened to report that both exiles "are present in person and that measures to forestall their escape have been undertaken." In vain did Stalin write to Alliluyev that the money was sent by Lenin presumably for kerosene and other such necessities: the Department knew first-hand—that is, from Malinovsky himself—that an escape was being prepared.

In February, 1914, Sverdlov wrote to his sister: "Joseph Djugashvili and I are being transferred a hundred versts [nearly seventy miles] north—eighty versts [nearly fifty-five miles] north of the Arctic Circle. The surveillance is stronger. We have been separated from mail delivery, which reaches us once a month through a 'walker' who is frequently late. Actually, we have no more than eight to nine mail deliveries a year . . ." The new place assigned to them was the forsaken settlement of Kureika. But that was not enough. "Because he received money, Djugashvili has been deprived of his allowance for four months. Both he and I need money. But you cannot send it in our names." By sequestering the allowance, the police helped the Tsarist budget and lessened the chances of escape.

In his first letter from Kureika Sverdlov clearly described the manner of his joint life with Stalin. "My arrangements in the new place are considerably worse. For one thing, I no longer live alone in the room. There are two of us. With me is the Georgian Djugashvili, an old acquaintance, for we had already met elsewhere in exile. He is a good chap, but too much of an individualist in everyday life, while I believe in at least a semblance of order. That's why I am nervous at times. But that is not so important. Much worse is the fact that there is no seclusion from our landlord's family. Our room is next to theirs, and has no separate entrance. They have children. Naturally, the youngsters spend many hours with us. Sometimes they are in the way. Besides, grown-ups from the village drop in. They come, sit down, keep quiet for half an hour and suddenly rise: 'Well, I've got to go, good-bye!' No sooner do they leave when someone else comes in, and it's the same thing all over again. They come, as if in spite, at the very best time for study, in the evening. That's understandable: in the daytime they work. We had to part with our former arrangements and plan our day differently. We had to give up the habit of poring over a book until long after midnight. There is absolutely no kerosene. We use candles. Since that provides too little light for my eyes, I do all my studying in the daytime now. As a matter of fact, I don't study very much. We have virtually no books . . ." Thus lived the future President of the Soviet Republic and the future dictator of the Soviet Union.

What interests us most in that letter is the restrained characterization of Stalin as "a good chap, but too much of an individualist." The first part of the testimonial has the obvious aim of softening the second part. "An individualist in everyday life" meant in this case a man who, being obliged to live side by side with another person, did not take into consideration either the latter's habits or interests. "A semblance of order," on which Sverdlov insisted unsuccessfully, called for a certain voluntary self-limitation in the interests of one's roommate. Sverdlov was by nature a considerate person. Samoilov testified that he was "a fine comrade" in personal relations. There was not a shadow of considerateness in Stalin's nature. Moreover, there may have been a goodly measure of vengeance in his behavior: let us not forget that it was Sverdlov who had been commissioned to liquidate the very editorial staff of *Pravda* on which Stalin had relied for support against Lenin. Stalin never forgave such things; he never forgave anything. The publication of Sverdlov's entire Turukhansk correspondence, promised in 1924, never took place; apparently, it contained the history of the subsequent sharpening of relations.

Schweitzer—the wife of Spandaryan, the third member of the Central Committee who journeyed to Kureika on the eve of the war, after Sverdlov had already had himself transferred from there—tells that in Stalin's room "the table was piled with books and large packages of newspapers, while on a rope in the corner hung various tackle, fishing and hunting, of his own making." Evidently, Sverdlov's complaint about the insufficiency of books had led to action: friends added to the Kureika library. The tackle "of his own making" could not, of course, have been a rifle and firearm supplies. It consisted of nets for fish and traps for rabbits and other such game. Subsequently Stalin became neither a marksman nor a hunter, in the sporting sense of the word. Indeed, judging by general appearances, it is easier to imagine him placing traps at night than firing a gun at a bird in flight.

The Socialist-Revolutionary Karganov, who subsequently became an opera singer, places his meeting with Stalin in the Turukhansk exile in 1911 instead of 1913; in such cases chronological errors are usual. Among other things, Karganov tells how Stalin, coming out in defense of a criminal in exile called Tchaika [Sea-gull], who had robbed a peasant, argued that Tchaika could not be condemned, that Tchaika should be brought over to their side, that people of that sort were needed for the forthcoming struggle. We have already heard from Vereshchak about Koba's partiality for criminals. On one occasion, in the course of an argument, Stalin had presumably revealed himself as an anti-Semite, resorting to coarse Georgian expressions against the Jews. Violating the traditions of the political exiles, if one is to believe Karganov, he entered into friendly relations with a police constable, the Osetin Kibirov. Replying to the reproaches of his comrades, Stalin declared that such friendly relations would not deter him, when necessary, from doing away with the constable as a political enemy. According to the same Karganov, Stalin astonished the exiles "by his complete lack of principles, his slyness and exceptional cruelty . . . Even in trifles his extraordinary ambition showed itself." It is hard to decide at what point in this tale truth ends and invention begins. But on the whole, Karganov's story is quite closely reminiscent of Vereshchak's observations in the Baku prison.

For postal and other connections Kureika depended on the village Monastyrskoye, from where the threads led to Yeniseisk and beyond into Krasnoyarsk. The former exile Gaven, now among the missing, tells us that the Yeniseisk commune was in touch with political life, underground as well as lawful. It carried on correspondence with the other regions of exile as well as with Krasnoyarsk, which in its turn had contacts with the Petersburg and Moscow committees of the Bolsheviks and provided the exiles with underground documents. Even in the Arctic Circle people managed to live on party interests, divided into groups, argued until they were hoarse and sometimes to the point of fierce hatred. However, the exiles began to differ on principles only in the middle of 1914, after the arrival in the Turukhansk region of the third member of the Central Committee, the zealous Spandaryan.

As for Stalin, he kept aloof. According to Shumyatsky, "Stalin . . . withdrew inside himself. Preoccupied with hunting and fishing, he lived in almost complete solitude . . . He had practically no need for intercourse with people, and only once in a while would go to visit his friend Suren Spandaryan at the village of Monastyrskoye, returning several days later to his anchorite's cave. He was sparing with his disjointed remarks on this or that question, whenever he happened to be at gatherings arranged by the exiles." These lines, softened and embellished in one of the subsequent versions (even the "cave" for some reason became a "laboratory"), must be understood to mean that Stalin terminated personal relations with the majority of the exiles and avoided them. No wonder that his relations with Sverdlov were likewise severed: under the monotonous condition of exile even more adaptable persons than he were not able to avoid quarrels.

"The moral atmosphere . . ." Sverdlov wrote discreetly in one of his letters that happened to be published, "is not especially favorable . . . A number of encounters (personal conflicts), possible only under the conditions of prison and exile, their pettiness notwithstanding, have had a pretty strong effect on my nerves . . ." Because of such "encounters," Sverdlov secured his transfer to another settlement. Two other Bolsheviks hastened to abandon Kureika: Goloshchekin and Medvedev, who are now likewise among the missing. Choleric, rude, consumed by ambition, Stalin was not easy to get along with.

The biographers obviously exaggerate when they say that this time an escape was physically impossible, although undoubtedly it was bound to involve serious difficulties. Stalin's preceding escapes were not escapes in the true sense of the word, but simply unlawful departures from places of exile. To get away from Solvychegodsk, Vologda, even Narym, involved no great effort, once one decided to dispense with his "legality." The Turukhansk Region was quite different: there one had to effect a rather difficult passage by deer or dogs, or by boat in the summertime, or by carefully hiding under the boards of a ship's hold, provided the captain of the ship was friendly toward political exiles; in a word, the Turukhansk exile intent on escape incurred serious risks. But that these difficulties were not insurmountable was best of all demonstrated by the fact that during those years several persons did manage to escape from the Turukhansk exile. True, after the Police Department learned about their plan of escape, Sverdlov and Stalin were placed under special surveillance. But the Arctic "guards," notoriously lazy and easily tempted by wine, had never deterred others from running away. The Turukhansk exiles enjoyed a sufficient latitude of movement for that. "Stalin often came down to the village of Monastyrskoye," wrote Schweitzer, "where the exiles were wont to foregather. To do that, he employed illegal as well as every legal subterfuge." The surveillance could not have been very active in the limitless Northern wastelands. Throughout the first year Stalin seemed to have been getting his bearings and taking preparatory steps rather unhurriedly: he *was* cautious. But in July of the following year the war broke out. The dangers of illegal existence under the conditions of a war-time régime were added to the physical and political difficulties of an escape. It was precisely that heightened risk that kept Stalin from escaping, as it deterred many others.

"This time," writes Schweitzer, "Stalin decided to remain in exile. There he continued his work on the national question, finished the second part of his book." Shumyatsky, too, mentions Stalin's work on that subject. Stalin actually did write an article on the national question during the first months of exile: with regard to that we have the categorical testimony of Alliluyev. "The same year (1913), at the beginning of winter," he writes, "I received a second letter from Stalin . . . An article on the national question which Stalin asked me to forward abroad to Lenin was enclosed in the envelope." The essay could not have been very extensive if it could have been included in a letter envelope. But what became of that article? Throughout all of 1913 Lenin continued to develop and define the national program. He could not have failed to pounce greedily on Stalin's new effort. Silence about the fate of the article simply testifies that it was considered inadequate for publication. His endeavor to pursue independently the line of the thought suggested to him at Cracow had apparently sidetracked Stalin onto the wrong road, so that Lenin found it impossible to revise the article. Only thus may be explained the astounding fact that during the ensuing three and a half years of exile the offended Stalin made no further effort to appear in the Bolshevik press.

In exile, as in prison, great events seem particularly incredible. According to Shumyatsky, "news of the war stunned our public, some of whom took utterly false notes . . ." "Defensist tendencies were strong among the exiles, everybody was disoriented," writes Gaven. No wonder: even in Petersburg, recently renamed Petrograd, revolutionists were disoriented. "But Stalin's authority among the Bolsheviks was so great," declares Schweitzer, "that his very first letter to the exiles put an end to all doubts and steadied the vacillators." What became of that letter? Such documents were copied as they passed from hand to hand, circulating throughout the colonies of exiles. All of the copies could not have been lost: those that fell into the hands of the police should have been found in its archives. If Stalin's historical "letter" is not available, it is only because it was never written. Despite all its triteness, Schweitzer's testimonial is a tragic human document. She wrote her memoirs in 1937, a quarter of a century after the events, as a compulsory assignment. The political contribution she had been forced to ascribe to Stalin belonged, as a matter of fact, although on a more modest scale, to her husband, the untamable Spandaryan, who died in exile in 1916. Of course, Schweitzer knows well enough what really happened. But the mechanism of falsification works automatically.

Closer to facts are the memoirs of Shumyatsky, published some thirteen years before Schweitzer's article. Shumyatsky ascribed the leading role in the struggle with the patriots to Spandaryan. "He was one of the first to assume an unyielding position of 'defeatism,' and at the rare gatherings of the comrades sarcastically upbraided the social-patriots . . ." Even in the much later edition Shumyatsky, characterizing the general confusion of ideas, preserved the phrase: "The late Spandaryan saw the matter clearly and distinctly . . ." The others, apparently, saw the matter less clearly. True, Shumyatsky, who never visited Kureika, hastens to add that "Stalin, being completely isolated in his cave, without any vacillation at once assumed a defeatist line," and that Stalin's letters "supported Suren in his fight against his opponents." But the credibility of that insertion, which attempts to insure for Stalin second place among the "defeatists," is weakened considerably by Shumyatsky himself. "Only toward the end of 1914 and at the beginning of 1915," he writes further, "after Stalin had managed to visit in Monastyr and support Spandaryan, did the latter cease to be subjected to the attacks of the opposition groups." Had Stalin assumed his internationalist position openly only after meeting with Spandaryan rather than at the beginning of the war? In his attempt to mask Stalin's prolonged silence, but, as a matter of fact, thereby underscoring it more than ever, Shumyatsky eliminated from the new edition all reference to the fact that Stalin's visit to Monastyrskoye occurred "only at the end of 1914 and at the beginning of 1915." As a matter of fact, the journey took place at the end of February, 1915, when, thanks to the experience of seven months of the war, not only the vacillators but even many active "patriots" had managed to recover from the opiate. As a matter of fact, it could not have been otherwise. The leading Bolsheviks of Petersburg, Moscow, and the provinces met Lenin's theses with perplexity and alarm. Not one of them accepted them as they were. There was therefore not the slightest reason for expecting that Stalin's slow and conservative mind would independently reach the conclusions which meant a complete upheaval in the labor movement.

Throughout his term of exile only two documents became known in which Stalin's position on the war found reflection: these were a personal letter of his to Lenin and his signature to a collective declaration of the Bolshevik group. The personal letter, written on the twenty-seventh of February from the village of Monastyrskoye, is Stalin's first and apparently only communication to Lenin throughout the war. We quote it in its entirety:

> My greetings to you, dear Ilyich, warm, warm greetings. Greetings to Zinoviev, greetings to Nadezhda Konstantinovna.[1] How are you, how is your health? I live, as before, chew my bread, completing half of my term. It is rather dull, but it can't be helped. But how are things with you? It must be much livelier where you are . . . I read recently Kropotkin's[2]

[1] Krupskaya, Lenin's wife.—C. M.

[2] Prince Peter Alexeyevich Kropotkin (1842-1921) Russian Anarchist, scientist, historian, critic, social philosopher, who lived in exile in London at the time.—C. M.

articles—the old fool must have completely lost his mind. I also read a short article by Plekhanov in *Ryech*[3]—an incorrigible old gossip. *Ekh-mah!* And the Liquidators with their deputy-agents of the Free Economic Society? There's no one to beat them, the devil take me! Is it possible that they will get away with it and go unpunished? Make us happy and let us know that in the near future a newspaper will appear that will lash them across their mugs, and do it regularly, and without getting tired. If it should occur to you to write, do so to the address: Turukhan Territory, Yeniseisk Province, Village Monastyrskoye, for Suren Spandaryan. Your Koba. Timofeyi [Spandaryan] asks that his sour greetings be conveyed to Guesde,[4] Sembat[5] and Vandervelde[6] on their glorious—ha-ha—post of ministers.

This letter, obviously influenced by conversations with Spandaryan, offers essentially very little for an evaluation of Stalin's political position. The aged Kropotkin, theoretician of pure anarchy, became a rabid chauvinist at the beginning of the war. Plekhanov, whom even the Mensheviks completely repudiated, did not cut any better figure. Vandervelde, Guesde and Sembat were too exposed a target in their role of bourgeois ministers. Stalin's letter does not contain the slightest hint of the new problems which at the time dominated the thoughts of revolutionary Marxists. The attitude toward pacifism, the slogans of "defeatism" and of "transforming the imperialist war into the civil war," the problem of forming a new international—these were then the pivotal points of innumerable debates. Lenin's ideas were far from popular. What would have been more natural than for Stalin to suggest to Lenin his agreement with him, if that agreement were a fact? If one is to believe Schweitzer, it was here, at Monastyrskoye, that Stalin first became acquainted with Lenin's theses. "It is hard to express," she writes in the style of Beriya, "with what feeling of joy, confidence and triumph Stalin read Lenin's theses, which confirmed his own thoughts . . ." Why then did he not drop a single hint about those theses in his letter? Had he worked independently over the problems of the new International, he could not have refrained from sharing at least a few words with his teacher about his own conclusions or from consulting him about some of the most trying questions. But there is no evidence of that. Stalin assimilated from Lenin's ideas those which suited his own outlook. The rest seemed to him the dubious music of the future, if not a foreign "tempest in a teapot." It was with these views that he subsequently came to the February Revolution [of March. 1917].

[3] *Ryech,* daily newspaper of the Kadets (Constitutional Democrats), a bourgeois liberal party.—C. M.

[4] Jules Basile Guesde (1845-1922), ex-Left-Wing leader of French Socialist Party, was Minister Without Portfolio (August, 1914-October, 1915).

[5] Marcel Sembat (1862-1922), French reformist Socialist politician, Minister of Public Works (1914-1916).—C. M.

[6] Emile Vandervelde (1866-1938), Belgian reformist Socialist, chairman of the International Socialist Bureau, Minister of State during World War I, held various cabinet posts. —C. M.

The letter from Monastyrskoye, poor in content, with its artificial tone of jaunty bravado ("the devil take me," "ha-ha" and the like), reveals a lot more than its author intended to reveal. "It is rather dull, but that can't be helped." A man capable of living an intense intellectual life does not write like that. "If it should occur to you to write, do so to the address of . . ." A man who really values an exchange of theoretical thoughts, does not write like that. The letter bears the characteristic threefold stamp: slyness, stupidity and vulgarity. No systematic correspondence with Lenin developed throughout his four years of exile, despite the importance Lenin attached to contacts with likeminded people and his penchant for keeping up a correspondence.

In the autumn of 1915 Lenin asked the émigré Karpinsky: " I have a great favor to ask: find out . . . the surname of 'Koba' (Joseph Dj . . . ? ? we forgot). Very important!!" Karpinsky replied: "Joseph Djugashvili." What was it about: a new money order, or a letter? The need to make inquiry about his surname certainly shows that there was no constant correspondence.

The other document which bears Stalin's signature is an address by a group of exiles to the editorial board of a legal journal devoted to workers' insurance:

> *Voprosy Strakhovaniya*[7] should also devote all its diligence and endeavor to the cause of insuring the working class of our country with ideas against the thoroughly corrupting anti-proletarian preachments of Messrs. Potressovs, Levitskies, and Plekhanovs, which run radically counter to the principles of internationalism.

This was undoubtedly a declaration against social patriotism, but, again, strictly within the limits of ideas common not only among Bolsheviks but even among Left-Wing Mensheviks. The letter, which, judging from the style, must have been written by Kamenev, was dated March 12, 1916—that is, at a time when revolutionary pressure had already gained considerable impetus while patriotic pressure had largely relaxed.

Kamenev and the convicted deputies arrived for their exile at Turukhansk in the summer of 1915. The deputies' behavior at the trial continued to be a source of great controversy among Party members. About eighteen Bolsheviks, including four members of the Central Committee—Spandaryan, Sverdlov, Stalin and Kamenev—came together at Monastryskoye. Petrovsky delivered a report on the trial and Kamenev supplemented it. The participants of the discussion, relates Samoilov, "pointed to the mistakes we had made at the trial: Spandaryan did it particularly sharply, all the others expressing themselves more indulgently." Samoilov does not mention at all Stalin's participation in the discussion. But then Spandaryan's widow was forced to ascribe to Stalin what had actually been done by her husband. "After the discussion," continued Samoilov, "a resolution was passed which, on the whole, approved . . . the

[7] Although ostensibly devoted to workers' insurance, *Voprosy Strakhovaniya* [Insurance Problems], founded October 29, 1913, as an outgrowth of *Pravda's* insurance department, discussed general politics as well, and, after *Pravda's* suppression by the tsarist authoritie. during the war, published articles on the dangerous war question.—C. M.

behaviour of the fraction at the trial." Such indulgence was very far from the irreconcilability of Lenin, who publicly castigated Kamenev's behavior as "unworthy of a revolutionary Social-Democrat." At Lenin's request, Shklovsky, from Berne, wrote to Samoilov, at Monastyrskoye, in roundabout terms: "I am very glad that you have no desire to quarrel with my family, yet how many unpleasantnesses he (Kamenev) caused us (and not he alone) . . . Any man can make a mistake or do something foolish, but he must rectify his mistake at least through a public apology, if he and his friends have any regard for my honor and the honor of my kinsmen." Samoilov explains that the words "my family" and "my kinsmen" must be understood as "the Party Central Committee." The letter was in the nature of an ultimatum. However, neither Kamenev nor the deputies made the declaration Lenin demanded of them. And there is no reason for assuming Stalin's support of that demand, although Shklovsky's letter was received at Monastyrskoye just before the conference.

Stalin's tolerance of the deputies' behavior was essentially a discreet expression of solidarity. In the face of a trial pregnant with dire consequences, Lenin's sharpened formulae must have seemed doubly out of place: what is the sense of making sacrifices for something you regard as a mistake? In the past Stalin himself had not displayed any inclination to use the prisoners' dock as a revolutionary tribune: while the trial of the Baku demonstrators was pending, he had resorted to rather dubious tricks in order to set himself apart from the other defendants. He judged Kamenev's tactic at the trial as a stratagem rather than as an opportunity for political agitation. Anyway, he remained an intimate friend of Kamenev's throughout their term of exile and during the revolution. They stand together on the group photograph taken in Monastyrskoye. Twelve years would pass before Stalin, not as a matter of principle, merely as a weapon in the struggle for personal power, would bring out Kamenev's behavior at the trial as a dire accusation against him. However, the tone of Shklovsky's letter should have intimated to Stalin that the issue was far more crucial than he had supposed and that he could no longer continue marking time. It was precisely because he understood this that he wrote the above-cited letter to Lenin; its free and easy form was intended to cover up his unwillingness to commit himself politically.

In 1915 Lenin tried to publish in Moscow a legal Marxist anthology, in order to express at least in an undertone the Bolshevik Party's views on the war. The anthology was held up by the censor, but the articles were preserved and were published after the revolution. Besides Lenin, we find among the authors the literary Stepanov, Olminsky (whom we already know), the comparatively recent Bolshevik Milutin, the Conciliator Nogin, all émigrés. We also find there an article entitled, "On the Split of the German Social-Democracy," by Sverdlov. But there was no contribution to this anthology by Stalin, who lived under the same conditions of exile as Sverdlov. That might be explained either by Stalin's apprehension that he would not be in tune with the others or by his annoyance at his failure to place his article on nationalities: touchiness and capriciousness were just as much a part of him as cautiousness.

Shumyatsky states that Stalin was called to the colors while in exile, apparently in 1916, when the older ages were being mobilized (Stalin was then going on thirty-seven), but was not inducted into the army because of his unbending left arm. Patiently he bided his time beyond the Arctic Circle, fishing, setting his traps for rabbits, reading and possibly also writing. "It is rather dull, but it can't be helped." A recluse, taciturn, choleric, he was far from the central figure among the exiles. "Clearer than many others," writes Shumyatsky, a Stalin adherent, "in the memory of the Turukhanites is the monumental figure of Suren Spandaryan . . . the intransigent revolutionary Marxist and magnificent organizer." Spandaryan reached Turukhansk on the eve of the war, a year later than Stalin. " 'What peace and quiet here!' " he was wont to remark sarcastically. " 'Everybody agrees with everybody else on everything—the Essars, the Bolsheviks, the Mensheviks, the Anarchists . . . Don't you know that the Petersburg proletariat is listening to the voice of the exiles? . . .' " Suren was the first to assume an anti-patriotic position and made everybody listen to him. But in personal influence on his comrades Sverdlov held first place. "Lively and sociable," an extrovert constitutionally incapable of being self-centered, Sverdlov always rallied the others, gathered important news and circulated through the various colonies of exiles, and organized an exiles' co-operative, besides conducting systematic observations at the meteorological station. The relations between Spandaryan and Sverdlov came to be strained. The exiles grouped themselves around these two figures. Although both groups fought together against the administration, rivalry "for spheres of influence," as Shumyatsky puts it, never stopped. It is not easy to ascertain today that struggle's basis in principles. Antagonistic to Sverdlov, Stalin supported Spandaryan discreetly and at arm's length.

In the first edition of his memoirs Shumyatsky wrote: "The administration of the region realized that Suren Spandaryan was the most active of the revolutionists and regarded him as their leader." In a subsequent edition this sentence was stretched to include two persons: Sverdlov as well as Spandaryan. Constable Kibirov, with whom Stalin had presumably established friendly relations, had established a prying surveillance of Spandaryan and Sverdlov, considering them "the ringleaders of all the exiles." Losing for a time the official thread, Shumyatsky entirely forgot to mention Stalin in that connection. The reason is not hard to understand. The general level of the Turukhansk exiles was considerably above the average. Here were held simultaneously the men who constituted the essential nucleus of the Russian center: Kamenev, Stalin, Spandaryan, Sverdlov, Goloshchekin, and several other prominent Bolsheviks. There was no official Party machine in exile and it was impossible to lead anonymously, pulling the strings behind the scenes. Everyone was in full view of the others. Slyness, firmness and persistence were not enough to win these thoroughly experienced people: one had to be cultured, an independent thinker and a skilled debater. Spandaryan, apparently, was distinguished for the superior daring of his thinking, Kamenev for his broader scholarship and greater catholicity of views, Sverdlov for his greater receptivity, initiative and flexibility. It was for that reason that Stalin "became self-centered," content with mono-syllabic remarks, which Shumyatsky thought of describing as "pointed" only in a later edition of his composition.

Did Stalin study in exile and what did he study? He had long passed the age when one is satisfied with aimless and random reading. He could advance only by studying specific questions, taking notes, trying to formulate his own ideas in writing. Yet apart from the reference to his article on the national question, no one has anything to say about Stalin's intellectual life during those four years. Sverdlov, who was in no sense a theoretician or a literary, wrote five articles during those years, translated from foreign languages, contributed regularly to the Siberian press. "In that way my affairs are not in bad shape," he wrote in an optimistic tone to one of his friends. After the death of Ordzhoni-kidze, who had absolutely no predilection for theory, his wife wrote about her late husband's prison years: "He studied and read without end. Long excerpts from what he had read during that period were preserved in the thick oilcloth-bound copybook issued to Sergo by the prison authorities." Every revolutionist brought out from prison and exile such oilcloth-bound copybooks. True, much was lost during escapes and searches. But from his last exile Stalin could have brought out anything he liked and under the best of conditions, and in the years to come it was not he who was subjected to searches but, on the contrary, he who subjected others to them. Yet it is useless to seek any traces of his intellectual life throughout that entire period of solitude and leisure. For four years—the years of the revolutionary movement's resurgence in Russia, of the World War, of the international Social-Democracy's collapse, of a vehement struggle of ideas in Socialism, of laying the groundwork for the new International—it is impossible that throughout that entire period Stalin did not take pen in hand. Yet in all that he then wrote there does not seem to be even a single line that could have been used to enhance his latter-day reputation. The years of war, the years of paving the way for the October Revolution are a blank space in the history of Stalin's ideas.

Revolutionary internationalism found its finished expression under the pen of the "émigré" Lenin. The arena of a single country, moreover, of backward Russia, was too limited to permit the proper evaluation of a world-wide perspective. Just as the émigré Marx needed London, which was in his day the hub of capitalism, in order to integrate German philosophy and the French Revolution with English economics, so Lenin had to be during the war at the focal point of European and world events, in order to draw the decisive revolutionary inferences from the premises of Marxism. Manuilsky, the official leader of the Communist International after Bukharin and preceding Dimitrov, wrote in 1922: ". . . *Sotsial-Demokrat* [The Social-Democrat], published in Switzerland by Lenin and Zinoviev, and the Paris *Golos* [The Voice] (*Nashe Slovo*

[Our Word]), published by Trotsky, will be to the future historian of the Third International the basic fragments out of which was forged the new revolutionary ideology of the international proletariat." It is cheerfully conceded that Manuilsky overestimated Trotsky's role. However, he did not even have a pretext for naming Stalin. But then, years later he would do his utmost to rectify that omission.

Tranquilized by the monotonous rhythms of the snowy waste, the exiles were far from expecting the events that transpired in February [March], 1917. All of them were caught by surprise, notwithstanding that they always lived by their faith in the inevitability of revolution. "At first," writes Samoilov, "we seemed to have suddenly forgotten our differences of opinion . . . Political disagreements and mutual antipathies seemed suddenly to have vanished . . ." That interesting confession is confirmed by all the publications, speeches and practical steps of that time. The barriers between the Bolsheviks and the Mensheviks, between the Internationalists and the Patriots, fell down. The whole country was flooded with buoyant but nearsighted and verbose conciliationism. People floundered in the welter of heroic phrases, the principal element of the February Revolution, especially during its first weeks. Groups of exiles started from all the ends of Siberia, merged into one stream and flowed westward in an atmosphere of exultant intoxication.

At one of the meetings in Siberia, Kamenev, who sat in the praesidium together with Liberals, Populists and Mensheviks, as it was later told, joined in signing a telegram which greeted the Grand Duke Michael Romanov on the occasion of his presumably magnanimous but, as a matter of fact, cowardly renunciation of the throne, pending the decision of the Constituent Assembly. It is not impossible that Kamenev, sodden with sentimentality, thought it best not to worry his colleagues in the praesidium with a disrespectful refusal. In the great confusion of those days no one paid the slightest heed to that, and Stalin, whom no one even thought of including in the praesidium, did not protest against Kamenev's fall from grace until a pitiless struggle began between them.

The first great point on the way, which contained a considerable number of workers, was Krasnoyarsk. Here a Soviet of deputies was already in existence. The local Bolsheviks, who were members of the general organization together with the Mensheviks, awaited directives from the leaders who were traveling through. Caught entirely by the wave of unification, these leaders did not even require the establishment of an independent Bolshevik organization. What was the use? The Bolsheviks, like the Mensheviks, stood for supporting the provisional government which was headed by the Liberal Prince Lvov. Differences of opinion were also voided on the question of the war: it was necessary to defend Revolutionary Russia! In such a mood Stalin, Kamenev and others were proceeding toward Petrograd. "The path along the railroad," recalls Samoilov, was "extraordinary and tumultuous, a mass of welcoming demonstrations, meetings and the like." At most stations the exiles were met by the exultant populace with military bands playing the *Marseillaise*[8]: the day of the *Internationale* had not yet dawned. At the larger railway stations there were gala banquets. The amnestied had to "talk, talk without end." Many lost their voices, became ill from fatigue, refused to leave their cars; "but even in the cars we were not left in peace."

Stalin did not lose his voice, for he made no speeches. There were many other, more skilled orators, among them the puny Sverdlov with his powerful bass. Stalin remained on the sidelines, sullen, alarmed by the flood of nature at springtide and, as always, malevolent. He was again being elbowed out of the way by persons of far smaller caliber. He had already established a record of well-nigh a score of years of revolutionary activity, intersected by unavoidable arrests and resumed after escapes. Almost ten years had passed since Koba had abandoned "the stagnant morass" of Tiflis for industrial Baku. He had worked in the capital of the oil industry for nearly eight months, he had spent nearly six months in the Baku prison, nearly nine months in the Vologda exile. A month of underground activity was paid for with two months of punishment. After escaping he had again worked in the underground for nearly nine months, spent about six months in prison, stayed nine months in exile—a somewhat more favorable ratio. At the end of exile—less than two months of illegal work, nearly three months of prison, nearly two months in Vologda province: two and a half months of punishment for one month of activity. Again two months of underground, nearly four months of prison and exile. Another escape. More than half a year of revolutionary activity, then—prison and exile, this time until the February Revolution; that is, lasting four years. On the whole, of the nineteen years of his participation in the revolutionary movement, he spent two and three quarters years in prison, five and three quarters years in exile. That was not a bad proportion; most professional revolutionists spent much longer periods in prison.

During those nineteen years Stalin did not emerge as a figure of either primary or even secondary rank. He was unknown. Referring in 1911 to Koba's intercepted letter from Solvychegodsk to Moscow, the chief of the Tiflis *Okhrana* wrote a detailed report on Joseph Djugashvili that contained neither notable facts nor striking features, barring perhaps the mention that "Soso," alias "Koba" had begun his career as a Menshevik. At the same time, referring to Gurgen (Tskhakaya), who was mentioned incidentally in the same letter, the gendarme remarked that the latter "has long been one of the important revolutionists . . ." According to this record, Gurgen was arrested "together with the famous revolutionist Bogdan Knuniants." The latter was not only a fellow-

---

[8] The *Marseillaise* was the battle-hymn common to all opponents of tsarist autocracy, in the patriotic and republican tradition of the Great French Revolution; whereas, the *Internationale* (written by Eugene Pottier in 1871) was confined exclusively to Socialists, champions of a new social order predicated on the self-liberation of all toilers throughout the world, irrespective of race or nationality, from exploitation and oppression.—C. M.

Georgian but the same age as Koba. As for the "fame" of Djugashvili himself, there is not even the remotest suggestion of it.

Two years later, characterizing in detail the structure of the Bolshevik Party and its general staff, the Director of the Police Department remarked in passing that Sverdlov and "a *certain* Joseph Djugashvili" had been inducted by co-optation into the Bureau of the Central Committee. The expression, "a certain" indicates that Djugashvili's name did not yet mean anything to the Chief of Police in 1913, notwithstanding such a source of information as Malinovsky. Until recently, Stalin's revolutionary biography up to March, 1917, was quite unremarkable. Scores of professional revolutionists, if not hundreds, had done the same sort of work as he, some better, others worse. Industrious Moscow researchers have figured out that during the three years, 1906-1909, Koba wrote sixty-seven appeals and newspaper articles, or less than two a month. Not one of these articles, which were no,more than a mere rehash of other people's ideas for his Caucasian readers, was ever translated from the Georgian language or reprinted in the leading organs of the party or the faction. There is no article by Stalin or any reference to him in any list of contributors to the Petersburg, Moscow or foreign publications of that period, legal or illegal, newspapers, magazines, or anthologies. He continued to be regarded not as a Marxist writer, but as a small-time propagandist and organizer.

In 1912, when his articles began to appear more or less regularly in the Bolshevik press of Petersburg, Koba gave himself the pseudonym Stalin, taking it from the word for steel, just as Rosenfeld before him had taken the pseudonym Kamenev from the word for stone: it was fashionable among young Bolsheviks to choose hard pseudonyms. Articles under Stalin's signature do not arrest anyone's attention: they are devoid of personality, barring crudity of exposition. Beyond the narrow circle of leading Bolsheviks, no one knew who the author of the articles was, and hardly anyone wondered about it. In January, 1913, Lenin wrote in a carefully considered note on Bolshevism for the famous Rubakin bibliographic reference book: "The principal Bolshevik writers are: G. Zinoviev, V. Ilyin,[9] Yu. Kamenev,[10] P. Orlovsky, and others." It could not have occurred to Lenin to name Stalin among the "principal writers" of Bolshevism, although at that very time he was abroad and at work on his "nationality"[1] article.

Pyatnitsky, who was uninterruptedly connected with the entire history of the Party, with its foreign staff as well as with its underground agency in Russia, with the literary men as well as with the illegal transporters,[11] in his careful and on the whole conscientious memoirs, embracing the period 1896-1917, discusses all more or less prominent Bolsheviks but never once mentions Stalin; that name is not included even in the index at the end of the book. This fact deserves all the more attention because Pyatnitsky was far from hostile to Stalin; on

[9] Lenin.—C. M.
[10] L. B. Kamenev.—C. M.
[11] See Glossary.

the contrary, he remains to this day in the second rank of his entourage. In a large anthology of materials of the Moscow *Okhrana*, which covers the history of Bolshevism from 1903 to 1917, Stalin is mentioned three times: with reference to his co-optation into the Central Committee, with reference to his appointment to the Bureau of the Central Committee, and with reference to his participation in the Cracow Conference. There is nothing there about his work, not a word of evaluation, no mention of a single distinguishing individual trait.

Stalin emerges for the first time within range of police vision, as within range of party vision, not as a personality but as a member of the Bolshevik Center. In the gendarme reports, as in the revolutionary memoirs, he is never mentioned personally as a leader, as an initiator, as a writer in connection with his own ideas or actions, but always as part of the Party machine—as member of the local Committee, as member of the Central Committee, as one of the contributors to a newspaper, as one of many others in a list of names, and then never in the first place. It was no accident that he found himself on the Central Committee considerably later than others of his age, and not through election but by way of co-optation.

This telegram from Perm was sent to Lenin in Switzerland: "Fraternal greetings. Leaving today for Petrograd. Kamenev, Muranov, Stalin." The thought of sending the telegram was, of course, Kamenev's. Stalin signed last. That trinity felt itself bound by ties of solidarity. The amnesty had liberated the best forces of the Party and Stalin thought with trepidation of the revolutionary capital. He needed Kamenev's relative popularity and Muranov's title of deputy. Thus the three of them together arrived in a Petrograd shaken by revolution. "His name," writes Ch. Windecke, one of his German biographers, "was at that time known only in narrow Party circles. He was not greeted like Lenin was a month later . . . by an inspired crowd of the people with red banners and music. He was not greeted, as two months later Trotsky, hurrying from America, had been, by a deputation which rode out to greet him halfway and which carried him on its shoulders. He arrived without a sound and without any noise, and sat down to work . . . Outside the borders of Russia no one had any idea of his existence."

Chapter VII

THE YEAR 1917

THIS was the most important year in the life of the country and of Joseph Djugashvili's generation of professional revolutionists. As a touchstone, that year tested ideas, parties, men.

At Petersburg, now called Petrograd, Stalin found a state of affairs he had not expected. Bolshevism had dominated the labor movement prior to the war's outbreak, especially in the capital. In March, 1917, the Bolsheviks in the Soviet were an insignificant minority. How had that happened? The impressive mass that had taken part in the movement of 1911-1914 actually amounted to no more than a small fraction of the working class. Revolution had made millions, not mere hundreds of thousands, spring to their feet. Because of mobilization, nearly forty per cent of these workers were new. The old-timers were at the front, playing there the part of the revolutionary yeast; their places at the factories were taken by nondescript newcomers fresh from the country, by peasant lads and peasant women. These novices had to go through the same political experiences, however briefly, as the vanguard of the preceding period. The February Revolution in Petrograd was led by class-conscious workers, Bolsheviks mostly, but not by the Bolshevik Party. Leadership by rank-and-file Bolsheviks could secure victory for the insurrection but not political power for the Party.

Even less auspicious was the state of affairs in the provinces. The wave of exultant illusions and indiscriminate fraternization, coupled with the political naïveté of the recently-awakened masses, swept in the natural conditions for the flourishing of petty bourgeois socialism, Menshevism and Populism. Workers—and following their lead, the soldiers, too—were electing to the soviet those who, at least in words, were opposed not only to the monarchy but to the bourgeoisie as well. The Mensheviks and the Populists, having gathered very nearly all of the intellectuals into their fold, had a countless number of agitators at their disposal, all of them proclaiming the need of unity, fraternity and other equally attractive civic virtues. The spokesmen for the Army were for the most part the Essars, those traditional guardians of the peasantry, which alone sufficed to bolster that party's authority among the proletarians of recent vintage. Hence, the dominance of the compromisers' parties seemed assured—at least, to themselves.

Worst of all, the course of events had caught the Bolshevik Party napping. None of its tried and trusted leaders were in Petrograd. The Central Committee's Bureau there consisted of two workingmen, Shlyapnikov and Zalutsky, and one college boy, Molotov. The "manifesto" they issued in the name of the Central Committee after the victory of February called upon "the workers of plants and factories, and the insurrectionary troops as well, immediately to elect their chosen representatives to the provisional revolutionary government." However, the authors of this "manifesto" themselves attached no practical significance to this call of theirs. Furthest from their intentions was the launching of an independent struggle for power. Instead, they were getting ready to settle down to the more modest role of a Leftist opposition for many years to come.

From the very beginning the masses repudiated the liberal bourgeoisie, deeming it no different from the nobility and the bureaucracy. It was out of the question, for example, that either workers or soldiers should vote for a Kadet. The power was entirely in the hands of the Socialist Compromisers, who had the backing of the people in arms. But, lacking confidence in themselves, the Compromisers yielded their power to the bourgeoisie. The latter was detested by the masses and politically isolated. The régime based itself on *quid pro quo*. The workers, and not only the Bolsheviks, looked upon the Provisional Government as their enemy. Resolutions urging the transfer of governmental power to the Soviets passed almost unanimously at factory meetings. The Bolshevik Dingelstead, subsequently a victim of the purge, has testified: "There was not a single meeting of workers that would have refused to pass such a resolution proposed by us . . ." But, yielding to the pressure of the Compromisers, the Petrograd Committee of the Bolshevik Party stopped this campaign. The advanced workers tried their utmost to throw off the tutelage on top, but they did not know how to parry the learned arguments about the bourgeois nature of the revolution. Several shades of opinion clashed in Bolshevism itself, but the necessary inferences from the various arguments were not drawn. The Party was in a state of abysmal chaos. "No one knew what were the slogans of the Bolsheviks," the prominent Saratov Bolshevik Antonov subsequently recalled, "It was a most distasteful spectacle."

The twenty-two days that elapsed between Stalin's arrival from Siberia [Sunday, March 12/25] and Lenin's from Switzerland [Monday, April 3/16] are exceptionally significant for the light they throw on Stalin's political complexion. He was suddenly thrust into a wide-open field of action. Neither Lenin nor Zinoviev was yet in Petrograd. Kamenev was there, the Kamenev compromised by his recent behavior in court and generally renowned for his opportunistic tendencies. There was also young Sverdlov, scarcely known in the Party, more of an organizer than a politico. The furious Spandaryan was no more: he had died in Siberia. As in 1912, so now again Stalin was for the time being, if not the leading, at least one of the two leading, Bolsheviks in Petrograd. The disoriented party expected clear instructions. It was no longer possible to evade issues by keeping still. Stalin had to give answers to the most urgent questions—about the Soviets, the government, the war, the land. His answers were published; they speak for themselves.

As soon as he reached Petrograd, which was one vast mass meeting in those days, Stalin went directly to Bolshevik headquarters. The three members of the Central Committee Bureau, assisted by several writers, were deciding *Pravda*'s complexion. Although the Party leadership was in their hands, they went about the job helplessly. Letting others crack their voices addressing workers' and soldiers' meetings, Stalin entrenched himself at headquarters. More than four years ago, after the Prague conference, he had been co-opted into the Central Committee. Since then much water had run over the dam. But the exile from Kureika had the knack of keeping his hold on the Party machine: he still regarded his old mandate as valid. Aided by Kamenev and Muranov, he first of all removed from leadership the "Leftist" Central Committee Bureau and the *Pravda* editorial board. He went about it rather rudely, the more so since he had no fear of resistance and was in a hurry to show that he was boss.

"The comrades who arrived," Shlyapnikov wrote later, "were critical and negative in their attitude toward our work." They did not find fault with its colorlessness and indecisiveness, but, on the contrary, with its persistent effort to draw the line between themselves and the Compromisers. Like Kamenev, Stalin stood closer to the Soviet majority. *Pravda*, after passing into the hands of the new editorial board, declared as early as March 15 (28) that the Bolsheviks would resolutely support the Provisional Government "in so far as it fights reaction or counter-revolution." The paradox of this declaration was that the only important agent of counter-revolution was the Provisional Government itself. Stalin's stand on war showed the same mettle: as long as the German Army remained subservient to its Emperor, the Russian soldier should "staunchly stand at his post, answering bullet for bullet and salvo for salvo." As if all there was to the problem of imperialism was the Emperor! The article was Kamenev's, but Stalin raised not the slightest objection to it. If he differed at all from Kamenev in those days, it was in being more evasive than his partner. "All defeatism," *Pravda* explained, "or rather what the venal press stigmatized by that name under the aegis of tsarist censorship, died the moment the first revolutionary regiment appeared on the streets of Petrograd." This was an outright disclaimer of Lenin, who had preached defeatism out of reach of the tsarist censorship, and at the same time a reaffirmation of Kamenev's declaration at the trial of the Duma fraction. But on this occasion it was countersigned by Stalin. As for "the first revolutionary regiment," all its appearance meant was a step from Byzantine barbarism to imperialist civilization.

"The day the transformed *Pravda* appeared . . ." recounts Shlyapnikov, "was a day of triumph for the Defensists. The whole Tauride Palace, from the businessmen of the Duma Committee to the Executive Committee, the very heart of revolutionary democracy, buzzed with but one news item—the triumph of the moderate and sensible Bolsheviks over the extremists. In the Executive Committee itself we were greeted with malicious smiles . . . When that issue of *Pravda* reached the factories, it created confusion and indignation among our Party members and sympathizers, spiteful satisfaction among our opponents . . . The indignation in the outlying districts was stupendous, and, when the proletarians found out that *Pravda* had been taken in tow by three of its former managing editors recently arrived from Siberia, they demanded the expulsion of the latter from the Party."

Shlyapnikov's account was retouched and softened by him in 1925 under the pressure of Stalin, Kamenev and Zinoviev, the "triumvirate" that then ruled the Party. Yet it does record clearly enough Stalin's initial steps in the arena of the Revolution and the reaction to them of class-conscious workers. The sharp protest of the Viborgites, which *Pravda* was soon obliged to publish in its own columns, forced the editorial board henceforth to formulate its opinions more circumspectly but not to change its policy.

Soviet politics was shot through and through with compromise and equivocation. The great need of the masses was above all to find someone who would call a spade a spade; that is, of course, the sum and substance of revolutionary politics. Everybody shied from that, for fear of upsetting the delicate structure of dual power.

The greatest amount of falsehood accumulated around the war issue. On March 14 (27) the Executive Committee proposed to the Soviet its draft of the manifesto "To the Peoples of the World." This document called upon the workers of Germany and Austria-Hungary to refuse "to serve as a tool of conquest and violence in the hands of kings, landowners and bankers." But the Soviet leaders themselves had not the slightest intention of breaking with the kings of Great Britain and Belgium, the Emperor of Japan, or the bankers and landowners, their own and those of all the Entente countries. The newspaper of the Minister of Foreign Affairs Miliukov noted with satisfaction that "the appeal is blossoming into an ideology shared by us and our allies." That was quite right—and quite in the spirit of the French Socialist ministers since the outbreak of war. During practically the very same hours, Lenin was writing to Petrograd by way of Stockholm that the revolution was threatened with the danger of having the old imperialist policy camouflaged behind new revolutionary phrases. "I shall even prefer to split with anyone at all in our Party rather than yield to social-patriotism . . ." But in those days Lenin's ideas did not have a single champion.

Besides marking a victory for the imperialist Miliukov over the petty bourgeois democrats, the unanimous adoption of this manifesto by the Petrograd Soviet meant the triumph of Stalin and Kamenev over the Left Wing Bolsheviks. All bowed their heads before the discipline of patriotic hypocrisy. "We welcome wholeheartedly," Stalin wrote in *Pravda*, "the Soviet's appeal of yesterday . . . This appeal, if it reaches the broad masses, will undoubtedly bring back hundreds and thousands of workers to the forgotten slogan: *Workers of the world, unite!*" There was really no lack of similar appeals in the West, and all they did was to help the ruling classes preserve the mirage of a war for democracy.

Stalin's article on the manifesto is not only highly revealing as to his stand on this particular issue but also of his way of thinking in general. His organic opportunism, forced by time and circumstance to seek temporary cover in abstract revolutionary principles, made short shrift of these principles when it came to an issue. He began his article by repeating almost word for word Lenin's argumentation that even after the overthrow of tsarism, Russia's participation in the war would continue to be imperialistic. Nevertheless, when he came to draw his practical conclusions, he not only welcomed the social-patriotic manifesto with equivocal qualifications but, following Kamenev's lead, rejected out of hand revolutionary mobilization of the masses against war. "First of all," he wrote, "it is undeniable that the bare slogan, 'Down with War!' is utterly inapplicable as a practical solution . . ." And his suggested solution was: "pressure on the Provisional Government with the demand that it immediately express its readiness to start peace negotiations . . ." With the aid of friendly "pressure" on the bourgeoisie, to whom conquest was the whole purpose of the war, Stalin wanted to achieve peace "on the basis of the self-determination of nations." Since the beginning of the war Lenin had been directing his hardest blows against precisely this sort of philistine utopianism. No amount of "pressure" can make the bourgeoisie stop being the bourgeoisie: it must be overthrown. But Stalin stopped short before this conclusion, in sheer fright—just like the compromisers.

No less significant was Stalin's article, "On the Abolition of National Limitations." [in *Pravda*, April 7 (March 25), 1917.] His basic idea, acquired from propagandist pamphlets as far back as Tiflis Seminary days, was that national oppression was a relic of medievalism. Imperialism, viewed as the domination of strong nations over weak ones, was a conception quite beyond his ken. "The social basis of national oppression," he wrote, "the force that inspires it, is the degenerating landed aristocracy . . . In England, where the landed aristocracy shares its power with the bourgeoisie . . . national oppression is softer, less inhuman, provided of course we do not take into consideration the special consideration that during the war, when the power passed into the hands of the landlords, national oppression increased considerably (persecution of the Irish, the Hindus)." The absurd assertions with which his article bristles—that supposedly racial and national equality is secure in the democracies; that in England during the war the power had passed to the landlords; that the overthrow of the feudal aristocracy would mean the abolition of national oppression—are shot through and through with the spirit of vulgar democratism and parochial obtuseness. Not a word to the effect that imperialism was responsible for national oppression on a scale of which feudalism was utterly incapable, if only because of its indolent provincial make-up. In theory he had not moved forward since the beginning of the century; more than that, he seemed to have entirely forgotten his own work on the national question, written early in 1913 under Lenin's fescue.

"To the extent that the Russian Revolution has won," the article concluded, "it has already created actual conditions [for national freedom] by having overthrown the sovereignty of feudalism and serfdom . . ." As far as our author was concerned the Revolution was already completely a thing of the past. In prospect, quite in the spirit of Miliukov and Tseretelli, were "the drafting of laws" and "their statutory ratification." Yet still untouched was not only capitalistic exploitation, the overthrow of which had not even occurred to Stalin, but even the ownership of land by the landed gentry, something he himself had designated as the basis of national oppression. The government was run by Russian landlords like Rodzianko and Prince Lvov. Such was—hard though it is to believe even now!—Stalin's historical and political slant a mere ten days before Lenin was to proclaim the course toward socialist revolution.

The All-Russian Conference of Bolsheviks, convoked by the Central Committee Bureau, opened in Petrograd on March 28, simultaneously with the conference of representatives of Russia's most important Soviets. Although fully a month had elapsed since the Revolution, the Party was still in the throes of utter confusion, which was further enhanced by the leadership of the past two weeks. Differentiation of political trends had not yet crystallized. In exile that had needed the arrival of Spandaryan; now the Party had to wait for the arrival of Lenin. Rabid chauvinists like Voitinsky and Eli'ava, among others, continued to call themselves Bolsheviks and took part in the Party Conference alongside those who considered themselves internationalists. The patriots vented their sentiments far more explicitly and boldly than the semi-patriots, who constantly backed down and apologized. Since a majority of the delegates belonged to the Swamp [middle-of-the-roaders of unstable views], their natural spokesman was Stalin. "We all feel alike about the Provisional Government," said the Saratov delegate Vassilyev. "There are no differences as to practical steps between Stalin and Voitinsky," Krestinsky chimed in with pleasure. The very next day Voitinsky joined the Mensheviks and seven months later he led a detachment of Cossacks against the Bolsheviks.

It seems that Kamenev's behavior at the trial had not been forgotten. It is possible that there was also talk among the delegates about the mysterious telegram to the Grand Duke. Perhaps Stalin took the trouble to remind others of these errors by his friend. Anyway, it was not Kamenev but the far lesser known Stalin who was delegated to present the chief political report, on the policy toward the Provisional Government. The protocol record of that report has been preserved; it is a priceless document to historians and biographers. Its subject was the central problem of the revolution—the relations between the Soviets, directly supported by the armed workers and soldiers, and the bourgeois government, existing only by the grace of the Soviet leaders. "The government," said Stalin in part, "is split into two organs, neither of which has full sovereignty . . . The Soviet has indeed taken the initiative in revolutionary changes; the Soviet is the sole revolutionary leader of the insurgent people— the organ that controls the Provisional Government. The Provisional Government has undertaken the task of actually fortifying the achievements of the revolutionary people. The Soviet mobilizes the forces and exercises control, while the Provisional Government, balking and bungling, takes upon itself the role of defender of those achievements of the people which the latter have already actually made." This excerpt is worth a whole program!

The reporter presented the relationship between the two basic classes of society as a division of labor between two "organs." The Soviets, i.e., the workers and soldiers, make the Revolution; the government, i.e., capitalists and liberal landed gentry, "fortify" it. During 1905-1907 Stalin himself wrote over and over again, reiterating after Lenin: "The Russian bourgeoisie is anti-revolutionary; it cannot be the prime-mover, let alone the leader, of the Revolution; it is the sworn enemy of revolution, and a stubborn struggle must be waged against it." Nor was this guiding political idea of Bolshevism in any sense nullified by the course of the February Revolution. Miliukov, the leader of the liberal bourgeoisie, said at the conference of his party a few days before the uprising: "We are walking on a volcano . . . Whatever the nature of the government—whether good or bad—we need a firm government now more than ever before." When the uprising began, notwithstanding the resistance of the bourgeoisie, there was nothing left for the liberals to do except take their stand on the ground prepared by its victory. It was none other than Miliukov who, having declared only yesterday that a Rasputinite monarchy was better than a volcanic eruption, was now running the Provisional Government which, according to Stalin, was supposed to be "fortifying" the conquests of the revolution but which actually was doing its utmost to strangle it. To the insurgent masses the meaning of the Revolution was in the abolition of the old forms of property, the very forms the Provisional Government was defending. Stalin presented the irreconcilable class-struggle which, defying all the efforts of the Compromisers, was straining day after day to turn into civil war, as a mere division of labor between two political machines. Not even the Left Menshevik Martov would have put the issue in such fashion. This was Tseretelli's theory —and Tseretelli was the oracle of the Compromisers—in its most vulgar expression: "moderate" and more "resolute" forces perform in an arena called "democracy" and divide the act between them, some "conquering" and others "fortifying." Here ready-made for us is the formula of future Stalinist policy in China (1924-1927), in Spain (1934-1939) as well as generally in all his ill-starred "popular fronts."

"It is not to our advantage to force the course of events now," the reporter continued, "accelerating the secession of the bourgeois layers . . . We have to gain time by checking the secession of the middle bourgeois layers, in order to get ready for the struggle against the Provisional Government." The delegates listened to these arguments with vague misgivings. "Don't frighten away the bourgeoisie" had ever been Plekhanov's slogan, and in the Caucasus, Jordania's. Bolshevism attained its maturity in fierce combat with that trend of thought. It is impossible to "check the secession" of the bourgeoisie without checking the proletariat's class struggle; essentially, both are merely the two aspects of the same process. "The talk about not frightening away the bourgeoisie . . ."

Stalin himself had written in 1913, shortly before his arrest, "evoked only smiles, for it was clear that the task of the Social-Democracy was not merely 'to frighten away' the very same bourgeoisie but to dislodge it in the person of its advocates, the Kadets." It is even hard to understand how any old Bolshevik could have so forgotten the fourteen-year-old history of his faction as to resort at the most crucial moment to the most odious of Menshevik formulae. The explanation is to be found in Stalin's way of thinking: he is not receptive to general ideas, and his memory does not retain them. He uses them from time to time, as they are needed, and casts them aside without a twinge, almost as a reflex. In his 1913 article he was referring to Duma elections. "To dislodge" the bourgeoisie meant merely to take mandates away from the liberals. The present reference was to the revolutionary overthrow of the bourgeoisie. That was a job that Stalin relegated to the remote future. For the present, quite like the Mensheviks, he deemed it necessary "not to frighten them away."

After reading the Central Committee's resolution, which he had helped to draw up, Stalin declared rather unexpectedly that he was not in complete accord with it and would rather support the resolution proposed by the Krasnoyarsk Soviet. The secret significance of this maneuver is not clear. On his way from Siberia Stalin might have had a hand in drafting the resolution of the Krasnoyarsk Soviet. It is possible that, having sensed the attitude of the delegates, he thought it best to edge away from Kamenev ever so little. However, the Krasnoyarsk resolution ranked even lower in quality than the Petersburg document: ". . . to make completely clear that the only source of the Provisional Government's power and authority is the will of the people, to whom the Provisional Government must wholly submit, and to support the Provisional Government . . . only in so far as it pursues the course of satisfying the demands of the working class and of the revolutionary peasantry." The nostrum brought out of Siberia proved quite simple: the bourgeoisie "must wholly submit" to the people and "pursue the course" of the workers and peasants. Several weeks later the formula of supporting the bourgeoisie "in so far as" was to become the butt of general ridicule among Bolsheviks. But already several of the delegates protested against supporting the government of Prince Lvov: the very idea ran too drastically counter to the whole tradition of Bolshevism. Next day the Social-Democrat Steklov, himself a supporter of the "in so far as" formula, and at the same time as a member of the "contact commission" close to the ruling spheres, was careless enough at the conference of the Soviets to draw such a dismal picture of the Provisional Government's actual machinations—opposition to social reforms, efforts on behalf of the monarchy and annexations—that the conference of Bolsheviks recoiled in alarm from the formula of support. "It is now clear," was the way the moderate delegate Nogin expressed the feeling of many others, "that it is not support we should be discussing but counter-action." The Left Wing delegate Skrypnik expressed the same thought: "Much has changed since Stalin's report of yesterday . . . The Provisional Government is plotting against the people and the revolution . . .

yet the resolution speaks of support." The crestfallen Stalin, whose appraisal of the situation could not stand the test of time even to the extent of twenty-four hours, moved "to instruct the committee to alter the clause about support." But the conference went one better: "By a majority against four, the clause about support is stricken from the resolution."

One might think that henceforth the reporter's whole schema about the division of labor between the proletariat and the bourgeoisie would be cast into oblivion. Actually, only the phrase was stricken from the resolution, not the thought. The dread of "frightening away the bourgeoisie" remained. In substance the resolution was an appeal exhorting the Provisional Government to wage "the most energetic struggle for the total liquidation of the old régime" at the very time it was busy waging "the most energetic struggle" for the restoration of the monarchy. The conference did not venture beyond friendly pressure on the liberals. No mention was made of an independent struggle for the conquest of power—if only for the sake of democratic objectives. As if intent upon exposing in the most lurid light the true spirit behind the resolutions passed, Kamenev declared at the conference of Soviets, which was going on simultaneously, that on the issue of power he was "happy" to add the vote of the Bolsheviks to the official resolution which had been moved and sponsored by the Right Menshevik leader Dan. In the light of these facts, the split of 1903, made permanent by the Prague conference of 1913, must have seemed a mere misunderstanding.

Hence it was not by chance that at the next day's session the Bolshevik conference was deliberating the proposal of the Right Menshevik leader Tseretelli to merge the two parties. Stalin reacted to this in the most sympathetic manner: "We ought to do it. It is necessary to define our proposals as to the terms of unification. Unification is possible along the line of Zimmerwald-Kienthal." The reference was to the "line" of two socialist conferences in Switzerland at which moderate pacifists had been preponderant. Molotov, who two weeks earlier had been punished for his Leftism, came out with timid objections: "Tseretelli wants to unite divergent elements . . . Unity along that line is wrong . . ." "More resolute was Zalutsky's protest: "Only a philistine can be motivated by the mere desire for unity, not a Social-Democrat . . . It is impossible to unite on the basis of superficial adherence to Zimmerwald-Kienthal . . . It is necessary to advance a definite platform." But Stalin, who had been dubbed a philistine, stuck to his guns: "We ought not to run ahead and anticipate disagreements. Party life is impossible without disagreements. We will live down these trivial disagreements inside the Party." It is hard to believe one's eyes: Stalin declared differences with Tseretelli, the inspirer of the dominant Soviet bloc, to be petty disagreements that could be "lived down" inside the Party. The discussion took place on April first (Apr. 14, o.s.). Three days later Lenin was to declare war unto death against Tseretelli. Two months later Tseretelli was to disarm and arrest Bolsheviks.

The conference of March, 1917, is extraordinarily important for insight into the state of mind of the Bolshevik Party's leading members immediately after the February Revolution—and particularly of Stalin as he was upon his return from Siberia after four years of brooding on his own. He emerges from the scanty chronicle of the protocols as a plebeian democrat and oafish provincial forced by the trend of the times to assume the Marxist tinge. His articles and speeches of those weeks cast a faultlessly clear light on his position during the years of war: had he drawn the least bit toward Lenin's ideas during his Siberian sojourn, as memoirs written twenty years after the fact avow, he could not have gotten as hopelessly stuck in the morass of opportunism as he did in March, 1917. Lenin's absence and Kamenev's influence made it possible for Stalin to show himself at the outbreak of the revolution for what he really was, revealing his most deeply rooted traits—distrust of the masses, utter lack of imagination, short-sightedness, a penchant for the line of least resistance. These characteristics continued to reassert themselves in later years whenever Stalin had occasion to play a leading role in important developments. That is why the March conference, at which Stalin revealed himself so utterly as a politician, is today expunged from Party history and its records are kept under lock and key. In 1923, three copies were secretly prepared for the members of the "triumvirate"—Stalin, Zinoviev, Kamenev. Only in 1926, when Zinoviev and Kamenev joined the opposition against Stalin, did I manage to procure from them this remarkable document, which enabled me to have it published abroad in Russian and English.

But after all, this record does not differ in any essential from his *Pravda* articles and merely supplements them. Not a single declaration, proposal, protest in which Stalin more or less articulately counterposed the Bolshevik point of view to the policy of the petty bourgeois democrats has come down to us from those days. An eye-witness of those times, the Left Wing Menshevik Sukhanov —author of the already-mentioned manifesto, "To the Toilers of the World"— wrote in his invaluable "Notes On The Revolution": "In addition to Kamenev, the Bolsheviks then had Stalin on the Executive Committee . . . During his nondescript tenure . . . [he] made—and not only on me—the impression of a gray spot which was occasionally dimly apparent and left no trace. There is really nothing more that can be said about him." For that description, which was admittedly rather one-sided, Sukhanov later paid with his life.

On the third [16] of April, having traversed belligerent Germany, Lenin, Krupskaya, Zinoviev and others crossed the Finnish border and arrived in Petrograd . . . A group of Bolsheviks headed by Kamenev had gone to meet Lenin in Finland. Stalin was not one of them, and that little fact shows better than anything else that there was nothing even remotely resembling personal intimacy between him and Lenin. "The moment Vladimir Ilyich came in and sat down on the couch," relates Raskolnikov, an officer of the Navy and subsequently a Soviet diplomat, "he opened up on Kamenev: 'What have you people been writing in *Pravda*? We saw several issues and were very angry with you . . .'" During his years of working with Lenin abroad Kamenev had grown quite used to such cold showers. They did not deter him from loving Lenin, even from worshiping him, all of him, his passion, his profundity, his simplicity, his witticisms, at which Kamenev laughed before they were uttered, and his handwriting, which he involuntarily imitated. Many years later somebody remembered that on the way Lenin had asked about Stalin. That natural question (Lenin undoubtedly inquired about all the members of the old Bolshevik staff) later served as the starting point for the plot of a Soviet motion picture.

An observant and conscientious reporter of the revolution wrote the following about Lenin's first public appearance before the foregathered Bolsheviks: "I shall never forget that speech which, like thunder, shook and astonished not only me, a heretic who had accidentally wandered in, but even all the faithful. Decidedly, no one expected anything of the kind."

It was not a question of oratorical thunder, with which Lenin was sparing, but of the whole trend of his thought. "We don't want a parliamentary republic, we don't want a bourgeois democracy, we don't want any government except the Soviet of Workers', Soldiers' and Poor Peasants' Deputies!" In the coalition of socialists with the liberal bourgeoisie—i.e., in the "popular front" of those days—Lenin saw nothing but treason to the people. He jeered fiercely at the fashionable phrase "revolutionary democracy," which lumped into one workers and petty bourgeoisie, Populists, Mensheviks and Bolsheviks. The compromisist parties which ruled in the Soviets were not allies to him but irreconcilable enemies. "That alone," remarks Sukhanov, "sufficed in those days to make the hearers' heads spin!"

The Party was as unprepared for Lenin as it had been for the February Revolution. All the criteria, slogans, turns of speech accumulated during the five weeks of revolution were smashed to smithereens. "He resolutely attacked the tactics of the leading Party groups and individual comrades prior to his arrival," wrote Raskolnikov, referring first and foremost to Stalin and Kamenev. "The most responsible Party workers were on hand. Yet even to them Ilyich's speech was something utterly new." There was no discussion. All were too stunned for that. No one wanted to expose himself to the blows of this desperate leader. In corners, they whispered among themselves that Ilyich had been too long abroad, that he had lost touch with Russia, that he did not understand the situation, and worse than that, that he had gone over to the position of Trotskyism. Stalin, yesterday's reporter at the Party Conference, was silent. He realized that he had made a frightful mistake, far more serious than on that occasion at the Stockholm Congress when he had defended land division, or a year later, when for a while he was one of the boycottists. Decidedly, the best thing to do was to make himself scarce. No one cared to know Stalin's opinion on the question anyway. Subsequently, no one could remember anything, for his memoirs, about what Stalin did during the next few weeks.

Meantime Lenin was far from idle: he surveyed the situation with his sharp eyes, tormented his friends with questions, sounded out the workers. The very next day he presented the Party with a short résumé of his views. These came to be the most important document of the revolution, famous as "The Theses of April Fourth." Lenin was not only unafraid "to frighten away" liberals but even members of the Bolshevik Central Committee. He did not play hide and seek with the pretentious leaders of the Bolshevik Party. He laid bare the logic of class war. Casting aside the cowardly and futile formula, "in so far as," he confronted the Party with the task of seizing the government. But first and foremost it was necessary to determine who was the enemy. The Black Hundred Monarchists cowering in their nooks and corners were of no consequence whatever. The staff of the bourgeois counter-revolution was made up of the central committee of the Kadet Party and the Provisional Government inspired by it. But the latter existed by grace of the Social-Revolutionists and the Mensheviks, who in their turn held power because of the gullibility of the masses. Under these conditions, application of revolutionary violence was out of the question. First of all the masses had to be won. Instead of uniting and fraternizing with the Populists and the Mensheviks, it was necessary to expose them before the workers, soldiers and peasants as agents of the bourgeoisie. "The real government is the Soviet of Workers' Delegates . . . Our Party is a minority in the Soviet . . . That can't be helped! It is up to us to explain—patiently, persistently, systematically—the erroneousness of their tactics. As long as we are a minority, our job is to criticize in order to undeceive the masses." Everything in that program was simple and reliable and every nail was driven in firmly. These theses bore only one single signature: "Lenin." Neither the Party Central Committee nor the editorial board of *Pravda* would countersign this explosive document.

On that very Fourth of April Lenin appeared before the same Party Conference at which Stalin had expounded his theory of peaceful division of labor between the Provisional Government and the Soviets. The contrast was too cruel. To soften it, Lenin, contrary to his custom, did not subject the resolutions that had been passed to analysis but merely turned his back on them. He raised the conference to a much higher plane. He forced it to see new perspectives—perspectives at which the makeshift leaders had not even guessed. "Why didn't you seize power?" the new reporter demanded, and proceeded to recapitulate the current explanations: the revolution was presumably bourgeois; it was only in its initial stage; the war created unforeseen difficulties; and the like. "That's all nonsense. The point is that the proletariat is not sufficiently conscious and not sufficiently organized. That should be admitted. The material force is in the hands of the proletariat, but the bourgeoisie is wide awake and ready." Lenin shifted the issue from the sphere of pseudo-objectivism, where Stalin, Kamenev and others tried to hide from the tasks of the revolution, into the sphere of awareness and action. The proletariat failed to seize power in February, not because seizure of power was forbidden by sociology, but because their failure to seize power enabled the Compromisers to deceive the proletariat in the interests of the bourgeoisie—and that was all! "Even our Bolsheviks," he continued, so far without mentioning any names, "display confidence in the government. That can be explained only by intoxication with the revolution. This is the end of socialism . . . If that's the case, I cannot go along. I would rather remain in a minority." It was not hard for Stalin and Kamenev to recognize the reference to themselves. The entire conference understood to whom the speech referred. The delegates had no doubt that Lenin was not joking when he threatened to break away. This was a far cry from the "in so far as" formula and from the generally homespun policy of the preceding days.

The axis of the war issue was no less resolutely shifted. Nicholas Romanov had been overthrown. The Provisional Government had half promised a republic. But did this change the nature of the war? France had long been a republic, and more than once. Yet its participation in the war remained imperialistic. The nature of war is determined by the nature of the ruling class. "When the masses declare that they do not want any conquests, I believe them. When Guchkov and Lvov say that they do not want any conquests—they are liars." This simple criterion is profoundly scientific and at the same time understandable to every soldier in the trenches. Lenin then delivered a direct blow, calling the *Pravda* by its right name. "To demand from a government of the capitalists that it should repudiate annexation is nonsense, crying mockery . . ." These words struck directly at Stalin. "It is impossible to end this war without a peace of violence unless capitalism is overthrown." Yet the Compromisers were supporting the capitalists, and *Pravda* was supporting the Compromisers. "The appeal of the Soviet—not a single word of it has a semblance of class consciousness. It is all phrasemongering." The reference is to the very manifesto that had been welcomed by Stalin as the voice of internationalism. Pacifist phrases, while preserving the old alliances, the old treaties, the old aims, were meant only to deceive the masses. "What is unique for Russia is the incredibly rapid transition from uncontrollable violence to the most subtle deception." Three days ago Stalin had declared his readiness to unite with Tseretelli's party. "I hear," said Lenin, "that there is a unification tendency afoot in Russia: unity with a Defensist is treason to Socialism. I think that it is better to remain alone, like Liebknecht, one against a hundred and ten!" It was no longer permissible even to bear the same name as the Mensheviks, the name of Social Democracy. "I propose for my part that we change the Party name, that we call ourselves the Communist Party." Not a single one of the participants of the conference, not even Zinoviev, who had just arrived with Lenin, supported this proposal, which seemed a sacrilegious break with their own past.

Pravda, which continued to be edited by Kamenev and Stalin, declared that Lenin's theses were his personal opinion, that the Central Committee Bureau did not share his opinion, and that *Pravda* itself pursued its old policy. That declaration was written by Kamenev. Stalin supported him in silence. He would have to be silent for a long time. Lenin's ideas seemed to him the phantasmagoria of an émigré, yet he bided his time to see how the Party machine would react. "It must be openly acknowledged," wrote subsequently the Bolshevik Angarsky, who had passed through the same evolution as the others, "that a great many of the Old Bolsheviks . . . maintained the Old Bolshevik opinions of 1905 on the question of the character of the Revolution of 1917 and that the repudiation of these views was not easily accomplished." As a matter of fact, it was not a question of "a great many of the Old Bolsheviks" but of all of them without exception. At the March conference, at which the Party cadres of the entire country met, not a single voice was heard in favor of striving to win the power for the Soviets. All of them had to re-educate themselves. Out of the sixteen members of the Petrograd Committee, only two supported the theses, and even they did not do it at once. "Many of the comrades pointed out," Tsikhon recalled, "that Lenin has lost contact with Russia, did not take into consideration present conditions, and so forth." The provincial Bolshevik Lebedev tells how in the beginning the Bolsheviks condemned Lenin's agitation, "which seemed Utopian and which was explained by his prolonged lack of contact with Russian life." One of the inspirers of such judgments was undoubtedly Stalin, who always had looked down at the "émigrés." Several years later Raskolnikov recalled that "the arrival of Vladimir Ilyich laid down a sharp Rubicon in the tactic of our Party. It must be acknowledged that prior to his arrival there was decidedly great chaos in the Party . . . The task of taking possession of the power of the State was conceived of as a remote ideal . . . It was considered sufficient to support the Provisional Government with one or another kind of qualification . . . The party had no leader of authority capable of welding it together into a unit and leading it." In 1922 it could not have occurred to Raskolnikov to see Stalin as the "leader of authority." Wrote the Ural worker Markov, whom the revolution had found at his lathe, "Our leaders were groping until the arrival of Vladimir Ilyich . . . Our Party's position began to clarify with the appearance of his famous theses." "Remember the reception given to Vladimir Ilyich's April Theses," Bukharin was saying soon after Lenin's death, "when part of our own Party looked upon them as a virtual betrayal of accepted Marxist ideology." This "part of our own Party" consisted of its entire leadership without a single exception. "With Lenin's arrival in Russia in 1917," wrote Molotov in 1924, "our Party began to feel firm ground under its feet . . . Until that moment it had merely felt its way weakly and uncertainly. . . . The Party lacked the clarity and resoluteness required by the revolutionary moment . . ." Earlier than the others, more precisely and more clearly, did Ludmilla Stahl define the change that had taken place: "Until Lenin's arrival all the comrades wandered in darkness . . ." she said on April 4 [17], 1917, at the time of the sharpest moment of the Party crisis. "Seeing the independent creativeness of the people, we could not help taking it into consideration . . . Our comrades were content with mere preparations for the Constituent Assembly through parliamentary methods and did not even consider the possibility of proceeding further. By accepting Lenin's slogans we shall be doing that which life itself urges us to do."

The Party's rearmament of April was a hard blow to Stalin's prestige. He had come from Siberia with the authority of an Old Bolshevik, with the rank

of a member of the Central Committee, with the support of Kamenev and Muranov. He too began with his own kind of "rearmament," rejecting the policy of
the local leaders as too radical and committing himself through a number of
articles in *Pravda*, a report at the conference, and the resolution of the Krasnoyarsk Soviet. In the midst of this activity, which by its very nature was the
work of a leader, Lenin appeared. He came into the conference like an
inspector entering a classroom. After having heard several sentences, he turned
his back on the teacher and with a wet sponge wiped off the blackboard all of
his futile scrawls. The feelings of astonishment and protest among the delegates
dissolved in the feeling of admiration. But Stalin had no admiration to offer.
His was a sharp hurt, a sense of helplessness and green envy. He had been
humiliated before the entire party far worse than at the closed Crakow conference after his unfortunate leadership of the *Pravda*. It was useless to fight
against it. He, too, now beheld new horizons at which he had not even guessed
the day before. All he could do was to grit his teeth and keep his peace. The
memory of the revolution brought about by Lenin in April, 1917, was stamped
forever on his consciousness. It rankled. He got hold of the records of the
March Conference and tried to hide them from the Party and from history. But
that in itself did not settle matters. Collections of the *Pravda* for 1917 remained
in the libraries. Moreover, those issues of *Pravda* came out in a reprint edition
—and Stalin's articles spoke for themselves. During the first years of the Soviet
régime innumerable reminiscences about the April crisis filled all the historical
journals and the anniversary issues of newspapers. All this had to be gradually
removed from circulation, counterfeited, and new material substituted. The very
word, "rearmament" of the Party, used by me casually in 1922, became subject
in time to increasingly ferocious attacks by Stalin and his satellite historians.

True, as late as 1924, Stalin still deemed it the better part of wisdom to admit, with all due indulgence for himself, the error of his ways at the outset of
the revolution: "The Party . . . ," he wrote, "accepted the policy of pressure
by the Soviets on the Provisional Government in the question of peace, and
did not at once decide to take a forward step . . . toward the new slogan of
power to the Soviets . . . That was a profoundly erroneous position, for it multiplied pacifist illusions, poured water into the mill of defensism and hampered
the revolutionary education of the masses. I shared that erroneous position at
that time with other comrades in the Party and repudiated it completely only
in the middle of April, after subscribing to Lenin's theses." This public admission, necessary in order to protect his own rear in the struggle against Trotskyism, which was then beginning, proved too circumscribing two years later. In
1926 Stalin categorically denied the opportunist character of his policy in March,
1917—"This is not true, comrades, this is gossip!"—and admitted merely that
he had "certain waverings . . . but who among us did not have momentary
waverings?" Four years later, Yaroslavsky, who in his capacity as historian
mentioned the fact that Stalin at the beginning of the revolution had assumed
"an erroneous position," was subjected to ferocious persecution from all sides.

It was no longer permissible so much as to mention the "passing waverings." The idol of prestige is a voracious monster! Finally, in the "history" of the Party edited by himself Stalin ascribes to himself Lenin's position, reserving his own views as the portion of his enemies. "Kamenev and certain workers of the Moscow organization, as for example, Rykov, Bubnov, Nogin," proclaims this remarkable history, "stood on the semi-Menshevik position of conditional support for the Provisional Government and the policy of the Defensists. Stalin, who had just returned from exile, Molotov and others, together with the majority of the Party, defended the policy of no confidence to the Provisional Government, came out against defensism," and the like. Thus, by way of gradual change from fact to fiction, black was transformed into white. This method, which Kamenev called "doling out the lie," runs through Stalin's entire biography, finding its culminating expression, and at the same time its collapse, in the Moscow trials.

Analyzing the basic ideas of the two factions of the Social Democracy in 1909, I wrote: "The anti-revolutionary aspects of Menshevism are already apparent in all their force; the anti-revolutionary characteristics of Bolshevism are a threat of tremendous danger only in the event of a revolutionary victory." In March, 1917, after the overthrow of Tsarism, the old cadres of the Party carried these anti-revolutionary characteristics of Bolshevism to their extreme expression: the very differentiation between Bolshevism and Menshevism appeared to have been lost. Imperative was a radical rearmament of the Party. Lenin, the only man big enough for the job, accomplished that in the course of April. Apparently, Stalin did not want to come out publicly against Lenin. But neither did he come out for him. Without much ado he shook clear from Kamenev, just as ten years before he had deserted the Boycottists and just as at the Cracow Conference he quietly abandoned the Conciliators to their fate. He was not in the habit of defending any idea that did not promise immediate success. The conference of the Petrograd organization was in session from the fourteenth to the twenty-second of April. Although Lenin's influence already predominated, the debates were pretty sharp now and then. Among those who participated were Zinoviev, Tomsky, Molotov and other well known Bolsheviks. Stalin did not even show up. Obviously, he sought to be forgotten for a while.

The All-Russian Conference convened in Petrograd on April twenty-fourth. It was supposed to clear up any matters left over from the March conference. About 150 delegates represented 79,000 Party members, of whom 15,000 were in the capital. This was not at all a bad record for an anti-patriotic party that had emerged from the underground only yesterday. Lenin's victory became clear from the very start, with the elections to the presidium of five members, for among those elected were neither Kamenev nor Stalin, the two men responsible for the opportunist policy in March. Kamenev had sufficient courage to demand the privilege of a minority report at the conference. "Recognizing that formally and factually the classic remnant of feudalism, the ownership of land by the landed gentry, has not yet been liquidated . . . it is too soon to assert that bourgeois democracy has exhausted all of its possibilities." Such was the basic thought of Kamenev and of Rykov, Nogin, Dzerzhinsky, Angarsky and others. "The impetus for social revolution," Rykov was saying, "should have come from the West." The democratic revolution has not ended, the orators of the opposition insisted, supporting Kamenev. That was true. However, the mission of the Provisional Government was not to complete the revolution but to reverse its course. Hence it followed that the democratic revolution could be completed only under the rule of the working class. The debates were animated yet peaceful, since in all essentials the issue had been decided beforehand and Lenin did everything possible to make his opponents' retreat easy.

During these debates Stalin came out with a brief statement against his ally of yesterday. In his minority report Kamenev had argued that since we were not calling for the immediate overthrow of the Provisional Government, we must demand control over it; otherwise the masses would not understand us. Lenin protested that the proletariat's "control" of a bourgeois government, especially under revolutionary conditions, would either be fictitious or amount to no more than mere collaboration with it. Stalin decided this was a good time to register his disagreement with Kamenev. To provide some semblance of an explanation for the change in his own position, he took advantage of a note issued on the nineteenth of April by Minister of Foreign Affairs Miliukov. The latter's extreme imperialist frankness literally drove the soldiers into the street and caused a government crisis. Lenin's conception of the revolution was based on the interrelationship of classes, not on some isolated diplomatic note, which differed little from other acts of the government. But Stalin was not interested in general ideas. All he needed was some obvious pretext in order that he might make his shift with the least damage to his vanity. He was "doling out" his retreat. At first, as he put it, "it was the Soviet that outlined the program, while now it is the Provisional Government." After Miliukov's note "the government is advancing upon the Soviet, while the Soviet is retreating. After that to speak of control is to speak nonsense." It sounded strained and false. But it turned the trick: Stalin managed thus to separate himself in time from the opposition, which got only seven votes when the ballots were cast.

In his report on the question of national minorities, Stalin did whatever he could to bridge the gap between his March report, which saw the source of national oppression solely in the landed aristocracy, and the new position, which the Party was now assimilating. "National oppression," he said, unavoidedly arguing against himself, "is not only supported by the landed aristocracy but also by another force—the imperialistic groups, which apply the method of enslaving nations learned in the colonies to their own country as well . . ." Moreover, the big bourgeoisie is followed by "the petty bourgeoisie, part of the intellectuals and part of the labor aristocracy, who also enjoy the fruits of this robbery." This was the very theme Lenin had so persistently harped upon during the war years. "Thus," his report continued, "there is a whole chorus of social forces that supports national oppression." In order to put an end to this oppression, it was necessary "to remove this chorus from the political scene." By placing the imperialistic bourgeoisie in power, the February Revolution certainly did not lay the ground for the liberation of national minorities. Thus, for example, the Provisional Government resisted with all its might all efforts to broaden the autonomy of Finland. "Whose side should we take? It is clear that it must be the side of the Finnish people . . ." The Ukrainian Pyatakov and the Pole Dzerzhinsky came out against the program of national self-determination as Utopian and reactionary. "We should not advance the national question," Dzerzhinsky was saying naïvely, "since that retards the moment of social revolution. I would therefore suggest that the question of Poland's independence should be removed from the resolution." "The social democracy," Stalin replied, "in so far as it pursues a course directed toward a socialist revolution, should support the revolutionary movement of the nationalities against imperialism." Here for the first time in his life Stalin said something about "a course directed toward a socialist revolution." The sheet of the Julian calendar that day bore the date: April 29, 1917.

Having assumed the prerogatives of a congress, the Conference elected a new Central Committee, which consisted of Lenin, Zinoviev, Kamenev, Milutin, Nogin, Sverdlov, Smilga, Stalin, Fedorov; and the alternates: Teodorovich, Bubnov, Glebov-Avilov and Pravdin. Of the 133 delegates, for some reason only 109 took part in the secret balloting with full vote; it is possible that part of them had already left town. Lenin got 104 votes (was Stalin perhaps one of the five delegates who refused to support Lenin?), Zinoviev 101, Stalin 97, Kamenev 95. For the first time Stalin was elected to the Central Committee in the normal party way. He was going on 38. Rykov, Zinoviev and Kamenev were about 23 or 24 when first elected by party congresses to the Bolshevik general staff.

At the Conference an attempt was made to leave Sverdlov out of the Central Committee. Lenin told about it after the latter's death, treating it as his own glaring mistake. "Fortunately," he added, "we were corrected from below." Lenin could hardly have had any reason for opposing Sverdlov's candidacy. He knew him only through correspondence as a tireless professional revolutionist. It is not unlikely that the opposition came from Stalin, who had not forgotten how Sverdlov had had to straighten things out after him in Petersburg and reorganize *Pravda*; their joint life in Kureika had merely enhanced his enmity. Stalin never forgave anything. He apparently tried to take his revenge at the conference and in one way or another, we can only guess how, managed to win Lenin's support. But his attempt did not succeed. If in 1912 Lenin met with the resistance of the delegates when he tried to get Stalin onto the Central Committee, he now met with no less resistance when he tried to keep Sverdlov off. Of the members of this Central Committee elected at the April Conference, only Sverdlov managed to die a natural death. All the others—with the exception of

Stalin himself—as well as the four alternates, have either been officially shot or have been done away with unofficially.

Without Lenin, no one had known what to make of the unprecedented situation; all were slaves of old formulae. Yet clinging to the slogan of democratic dictatorship now meant, as Lenin put it, "actually going over to the petty bourgeoisie." It may well be that Stalin's advantage over the others was in his lack of compunction about going over and his readiness for rapprochement with the Compromisers and fusion with the Mensheviks. He was not in the least hampered by reverence for old formulae. Ideological fetishism was alien to him: thus, without the least remorse he repudiated the long-held theory of the counter-revolutionary role of the Russian bourgeoisie. As always, Stalin acted empirically, under the pressure of his natural opportunism, which has always driven him to seek the line of least resistance. But he had not been alone in his stand; in the course of the three weeks before Lenin's arrival, he had been giving expression to the hidden convictions of very many of the "Old Bolsheviks."

It should not be forgotten that the political machine of the Bolshevik Party was predominantly made up of the intelligentsia, which was petty bourgeois in its origin and conditions of life and Marxist in its ideas and in its relations with the proletariat. Workers who turned professional revolutionists joined this set with great eagerness and lost their identity in it. The peculiar social structure of the Party machine and its authority over the proletariat (neither of which is accidental but dictated by strict historical necessity) were more than once the cause of the Party's vacillation and finally became the source of its degeneration. The Party rested on the Marxist doctrine, which expressed the historical interests of the proletariat as a whole; but the human beings of the Party machine assimilated only scattered portions of that doctrine according to their own comparatively limited experience. Quite often, as Lenin complained, they simply learned ready-made formulae by rote and shut their eyes to the change in conditions. In most cases they lacked independent daily contact with the laboring masses as well as a comprehensive understanding of the historical process. They thus left themselves exposed to the influence of alien classes. During the War, the higher-ups of the Party were largely affected by compromisist tendencies, which emanated from bourgeois circles, while the rank and file Bolshevik workingmen displayed far greater stability in resisting the patriotic hysteria that had swept the country.

In opening a broad field of action to democratic processes, the revolution was far more satisfying to "professional revolutionists" of all parties than to soldiers in the trenches, to peasants in villages and to workers in munition factories. The obscure underground men of yesterday suddenly became leading political figures. Instead of parliaments they had Soviets, and there they were free to argue and to rule. As far as they were concerned, the very class contradictions that had caused the revolution seemed to be melting away under the rays of the democratic sun. That was why almost everywhere in Russia Bolsheviks and

Mensheviks joined hands. Even where they remained apart, as in Petrograd, the urge for unity was decidedly compelling in both organizations. At the same time, in the trenches, in the villages and in the factories, the chronic antagonisms assumed an ever more open and more intense character, foreboding civil war instead of unity. As often happens, a sharp cleavage developed between the classes in motion and the interests of the party machines. Even the Bolshevik Party cadres, who enjoyed the benefit of exceptional revolutionary training, were definitely inclined to disregard the masses and to identify their own special interests with the interests of the machine on the very day after the monarchy was overthrown. What, then, could be expected of these cadres when they became an all-powerful state bureaucracy? It is unlikely that Stalin gave this matter any thought. He was flesh of the flesh of the machine and the toughest of its bones.

But by what miracle did Lenin manage in a few short weeks to turn the Party's course into a new channel? The answer should be sought simultaneously in two directions—Lenin's personal attributes and the objective situation. Lenin was strong not only because he understood the laws of the class struggle but also because his ear was faultlessly attuned to the stirrings of the masses in motion. He represented not so much the Party machine as the vanguard of the proletariat. He was definitely convinced that thousands from among those workers who had borne the brunt of supporting the underground Party would now support him. The masses at the moment were more revolutionary than the Party, and the Party more revolutionary than its machine. As early as March the actual attitude of the workers and soldiers had in many cases become stormily apparent, and it was widely at variance with the instructions issued by all the parties, including the Bolshevik. Lenin's authority was not absolute, but it was tremendous, for all of past experience was a confirmation of his prescience. On the other hand, the authority of the Party machine, like its conservatism, was only in the making at that time. Lenin exerted influence not so much as an individual but because he embodied the influence of the class on the Party and of the Party on its machine. Under such circumstances, whoever tried to resist soon lost his footing. Vacillators fell in line with those in front, the cautious joined the majority. Thus, with comparatively small losses, Lenin managed in time to orient the Party and to prepare it for the new revolution.

Every time that the Bolshevik leaders had to act without Lenin they fell into error, usually inclining to the Right. Then Lenin would appear like a *deus ex machina* and indicate the right road. Does it mean then that in the Bolshevik Party Lenin was everything and all the others nothing? Such a conclusion, which is rather widespread in democratic circles, is extremely biased and hence false. The same thing might be said about science. Mechanics without Newton and biology without Darwin seemed to amount to nothing for many years. This is both true and false. It took the work of thousands of rank and file scientists to gather the facts, to group them, to pose the problem and to prepare the ground for the comprehensive solutions of a Newton or a Darwin. That solution in turn affected the work of new thousands of rank and file investigators. Geniuses do not create science out of themselves; they merely accelerate the process of collective thinking. The Bolshevik Party had a leader of genius. That was no accident. A revolutionist of Lenin's makeup and breadth could be the leader only of the most fearless party, capable of carrying its thoughts and actions to their logical conclusion. But genius in itself is the rarest of exceptions. A leader of genius orients himself faster, estimates the situation more thoroughly, sees further than others. It was unavoidable that a great gap should develop between the leader of genius and his closest collaborators. It may even be conceded that to a certain extent the very power of Lenin's vision acted as a brake on the development of self-reliance among his collaborators. Nevertheless, that does not mean that Lenin was "everything" and that the Party without Lenin was nothing. Without the Party Lenin would have been as helpless as Newton and Darwin without collective scientific work. It is consequently not a question of the special sins of Bolshevism, conditioned presumably by centralization, discipline and the like, but a question of the problem of genius within the historical process. Writers who attempt to disparage Bolshevism on the grounds that the Bolshevik Party had the good luck to have a leader of genius merely confess their own mental vulgarity.

The Bolshevik leadership would have found the right line of action without Lenin, but slowly, at the price of friction and internal struggles. The class conflicts would have continued to condemn and reject the meaningless slogans of the Bolshevik Old Guard. Stalin, Kamenev and other second-raters had the alternative of giving consistent expression to the tendencies of the proletarian vanguard or simply deserting to the opposite side of the barricades. We must not forget that Shlyapnikov, Zalutsky, Molotov, tried to take a more Leftist course from the very beginning of the revolution.

However, that does not mean that the right path would have been found anyway. The factor of time plays a decisive role in politics—especially, in a revolution. The class struggle will hardly bide its time indefinitely until the political leaders discover the right thing to do. The leader of genius is important because, in shortening the learning period by means of object lessons, he enables the party to influence the development of events at the proper moment. Had Lenin failed to come at the beginning of April, no doubt the Party would have groped its way eventually to the course propounded in his "Theses." But could anyone else have prepared the Party in time for the October denouement? That question cannot be answered categorically. One thing is certain: in this situation—which called for resolute confrontation of the sluggish Party machine with masses and ideas in motion—Stalin could not have acted with the necessary creative initiative and would have been a brake rather than a propeller. His power began only after it became possible to harness the masses with the aid of the machine.

It is hard to trace Stalin's activities during the next two months. He was suddenly relegated to a third-rate position. Lenin himself was now directly in charge of the *Pravda* editorial board day in and day out—not merely by remote control, as before the War—and *Pravda* piped the tune for the whole Party. Zinoviev was lord and master in the field of agitation. Stalin still did not address any public meetings. Kamenev, half-hearted about the new policy, represented the Party in the Soviet Central Executive Committee and on the floor of the Soviet. Stalin practically disappeared from that scene and was hardly ever seen even at Smolny. Sverdlov assumed paramount leadership of the most outstanding organizational activity, assigning tasks to Party workers, dealing with the provincials, adjusting conflicts. In addition to his routine duties on the *Pravda* and his presence at sessions of the Central Committee, Stalin was given occasional assignments of an administrative, technical or diplomatic nature. They are far from numerous. Naturally lazy, Stalin can work under pressure only when his personal interests are directly involved. Otherwise, he prefers to suck his pipe and bide his time. For a while he felt acutely unwell. Everywhere he was superseded either by more important or more gifted men. His vanity was stung to the quick by the memory of March and April days. Violating his own integrity, he slowly reversed the trend of his thoughts. But in the final reckoning it was a half-hearted turn.

During the stormy "April days," when the soldiers went out into the streets in protest against Miliukov's imperialistic note, the Compromisers were busy as always with exhortations addressed to the government and soothing promises addressed to the masses. On the twenty-first the Central Executive Committee sent one of its Pastoral telegrams, under the signature of Chkheidze, to Kronstadt and to other garrisons, conceding that Miliukov's militant note was undeserving of approval, but adding that "negotiations, not yet concluded, have begun between the Executive Committee and the Provisional Government" (by their very nature these negotiations could never come to an end). [It continued], "recognizing the harm of all scattered and unorganized public appearances, the Executive Committee asks you to restrain yourself," and so forth.

From the official protocols we note, not without surprise, that the text of the telegram was composed by a commission that consisted of two Compromisers and one Bolshevik, and that this Bolshevik was Stalin. It is a minor episode (we find no important episodes pertaining to him throughout that period), but decidedly a typical one. The reassuring telegram was a classic little example of that "control" which was an indispensable element in the mechanics of dual power. The slightest Bolshevik contact with that policy of futility was denounced by Lenin with particular vehemence. If the public appearance of the Kronstadtites was not opportune, the commission should have told them so in the name of the Party, in its own words, and not taken upon itself responsibility for the "negotiations" between Chkheidze and Prince Lvov. The Compromisers placed Stalin on the commission because the Bolsheviks alone enjoyed any authority in Kronstadt. This was all the more reason for declining the appointment. But Stalin did not refuse it. Three days after the telegram of reassurance, he spoke at the Party conference in opposition to Kamenev, selecting none other than the controversy over Miliukov's note as particularly cogent proof that "control" was senseless. Logical contradictions never disconcerted that empiricist.

At the conference of the Bolshevik military organizations in June, after the basic political speeches by Lenin and Zinoviev, Stalin reported on "the nationalist movement in the nationalist regiments." In the active army, influenced by the awakening of the oppressed nationalities, there was a spontaneous regrouping of army units in accordance with nationality. Thus there sprang up Ukrainian, Mussulman, Polish regiments, and the like. The Provisional Government openly combated this "disorganization of the army," while here, too, the Bolsheviks came out in defense of the oppressed nationalities. Stalin's speech was not preserved. But it could hardly have added anything new.

The First All-Russian Congress of Soviets, which opened on the third of June, dragged on for almost three weeks. The score or two of Bolshevik delegates from the provinces, lost in the mass of Compromisers, constituted a group far from homogeneous and still subject to the moods of March. It was not easy to lead them. It was to this Congress that an interesting reference was made by a Populist already known to us, who had at one time observed Koba in a Baku prison. "I tried in every way to understand the role of Stalin and Sverdlov in the Bolshevik Party," wrote Vereshchak in 1928. "While Kamenev, Zinoviev, Nogin and Krylenko sat at the table of the congress praesidium, and Lenin, Zinoviev and Kamenev were the main speakers, Sverdlov and Stalin silently directed the Bolshevik Fraction. They were the tactical force. It was then for the first time that I realized the full significance of the man." Vereshchak was not mistaken. Stalin was very valuable behind the scenes in preparing the Fraction for balloting. He did not always resort to arguments of principle. However he did have the knack of convincing the average run of leaders, especially the provincials. But even on that job the pre-eminent place was Sverdlov's, who was permanent chairman of the Bolshevik Fraction at the Congress.

Meantime, the Army was being treated to "moral" preparation for the offensive, which unnerved the masses at home as well as at the front. The Bolshevik Fraction resolutely protested against this military venture and predicted a catastrophe. The Congress majority supported Kerensky. The Bolsheviks decided to counter with a street demonstration, but while this was being considered differences of opinion arose. Volodarsky, mainstay of the Petrograd Committee, was not sure that the workers would come out into the streets. The representatives of the military organizations insisted that the soldiers would not come out without arms. Stalin thought it "a fact that there is ferment among the soldiers, while there is no such definite mood among the workers," yet he nevertheless supposed that it was necessary to offer resistance to the Government. The demonstration was finally set for Sunday, June tenth. The Compromisers were alarmed and in the name of the Congress forbade the demonstration. The Bolsheviks submitted. But frightened by the bad impression of their own interdict against the masses, the Congress itself appointed a general demonstration for the eighteenth of June. The result was unexpected: all the factories and all the regiments came out with Bolshevik placards. An irreparable blow had been struck at the authority of the Congress. The workers and soldiers of the capital sensed their own power. Two weeks later they attempted to cash in on it. Thus developed the "July Days," the most important borderline between the two revolutions.

On May fourth Stalin wrote in *Pravda*: "The Revolution is growing in breadth and depth . . . The provinces are marching at the head of the move-ment. Just as Petrograd marched in front during the first days of the Revolution, so now it is beginning to lag behind." Exactly two months later the "July Days" proved that the provinces were lagging considerably behind Petrograd. What Stalin had in mind when he made his appraisal were the organizations, not the masses. "The Soviets of the capital," Lenin observed as early as the April con-ference, "are politically more dependent upon the bourgeois central government than the provincial Soviets." While the Central Executive Committee tried with all its might to concentrate the power in the hands of the government, the Soviets in the provinces, Menshevik and Essar in their composition, in many cases took over the local governments against their will and even attempted to regulate economic life. But the "backwardness" of the Soviet institutions in the capital was due to the fact that the Petrograd proletariat had advanced so far that the radicalism of its demands frightened the petty bourgeois democrats. When the July demonstration was under discussion, Stalin argued that the workers were not eager for the fray. That argument was disproved by the July Days themselves, when, defying the proscription of the Compromisers and even the warnings of the Bolshevik Party, the proletariat poured out into the street, shoulder to shoulder with the garrison. Both of Stalin's mistakes are notably characteristic of him: he did not breathe the air of workers' meetings, was not in contact with the masses and did not trust them. The information at his dis-posal came through the machine. Yet the masses were incomparably more revo-lutionary than the Party, which in its turn was more revolutionary than its committeemen. As on other occasions, Stalin expressed the conservative inclina-tions of the Party machine and not the dynamic force of the masses.

By the beginning of July Petrograd was already completely on the side of the Bolsheviks. Acquainting the new French Ambassador with the new situation in the capital, the journalist Claude Anet pointed across the Neva to the Vyborg district, where the largest factories were concentrated. "There Lenin and Trotsky reign as masters." The regiments of the garrison were either Bolshevik or wavering in the direction of the Bolsheviks. "Should Lenin and Trotsky desire to seize Petrograd, who will deter them from it?" The characterization of the situation was correct. But it was not yet possible to seize power because, not-withstanding what Stalin had written in May, the provinces lagged consider-ably behind the capital.

On the second of July, at the All-City Conference of the Bolsheviks, where Stalin represented the Central Committee, two excited machine gunners appeared with the declaration that their regiments had decided to go out into the street immediately, fully armed. The conference went on record against this move. Stalin, in the name of the Central Committee, upheld this decision of the conference. Thirteen years later Pestkovsky, one of Stalin's collaborators and a repentant oppositionist, recalled this conference. "There I first saw Stalin. The room in which the conference was taking place could not hold all those present: part of the public followed the course of the debates from the corridor through the open door. I was among that part of the public, and therefore, I did not hear the report very well . . . Stalin appeared in the name of the Central Committee. Since he spoke quietly, I did not make out much of what he said from the corridor. But there was one thing I noticed: each of Stalin's sentences was sharp and crisp, his statements were distinguished by their clarity of formulation . . ."

The members of the conference parted and went to their regiments and factories in order to restrain the masses from a public demonstration. "About five o'clock," Stalin reported after the event, "at the session of the Central Executive Committee I declared officially in the name of the Central Executive Committee at the conference that we decided not to come out." Nevertheless, the demonstration developed by about six o'clock. "Did the Party have the right to wash its hands . . . and stand apart? . . . As the party of the proletariat we should have intervened in its public demonstration and given it a peaceful and organized character, without aiming at armed seizure of power." Somewhat later Stalin told about the July Days at a Party congress: "The Party did not want the demonstration, the Party wanted to bide its time until the policy of the offensive at the front should be discredited. Nevertheless, the elemental demonstration, evoked by the chaos in the country, by the orders of Kerensky, by the dispatch of detachments to the front, took place." The Central Committee decided to make the demonstration peaceful in character. "To the question posed by the soldiers whether it was permissible to go out armed, the Central Committee answered no. But the soldiers said that it was impossible to go out unarmed . . . that they would take their arms only for self-defense."

At this point, however, we come across the enigmatic testimony of Dyemyan Byedny. In a very exultant tone, the poet laureate told in 1929 how in the quarters of the *Pravda* Stalin was called to the telephone from Kronstadt and how in reply to the question asked of him, whether to go out with arms in hand or without arms, Stalin replied: "Rifles? . . . You comrades know best! . . . As for us scribblers we always take our arms, pencils, everywhere with us . . . As for you and your arms, you know best! . . ." The story was probably stylized. But one senses a grain of truth in it. In general, Stalin was inclined to underestimate the readiness of the workers and soldiers to fight: he was always mistrustful of the masses. But wherever a fight started, whether on a square in Tiflis, in the Baku prison, or on the streets of Petrograd, he always strove to make it as sharp in character as possible. The decision of the Central Committee? That could always be cautiously turned upside down with the parable about the pencils. However, one must not exaggerate the significance of that episode. The question probably came from the Kronstadt Committee of the Party. As for the sailors, they would have gone out with their arms anyway.

Without developing into an insurrection, the July Days broke through the framework of a mere demonstration. There were provocative shots from windows and rooftops. There were armed clashes without plan or clear purpose but with many killed and wounded. There was the accidental half-seizure of the Fortress of Peter and Paul by the Kronstadt sailors, there was the siege of the Tauride Palace. The Bolsheviks proved themselves complete masters in the capital, yet deliberately repudiated the insurrection as an adventure. "We could have seized power on the Third and Fourth of July," Stalin said at the Petrograd Conference. "But against us would have risen the fronts, the provinces, the Soviets. Without support in the provinces, our government would have been without hands and feet." Lacking a direct goal, the movement began to peter out. The workers returned to their factories, the soldiers to their barracks. There remained the problem of the Peter and Paul Fortress, still occupied by the Kronstadtites. "The Central Committee delegated me to the Peter and Paul Fortress," Stalin has told, "where I managed to persuade the sailors present not to accept battle . . . As a representative of the Central Executive Committee I went with the [Menshevik] Bogdanov to [the Commanding Officer] Kozmin. He was ready for battle . . . We persuaded him not to resort to armed force . . . It was apparent to me that the Right Wing wanted blood in order to teach a 'lesson' to the workers, soldiers and sailors. We made it impossible for them to attain their wish." Stalin was able to carry out such a delicate mission successfully only because he was not an odious figure in the eyes of the Compromisers: their hatred was directed against other people. Besides, he was able, like no one else, to assume in these negotiations the tone of a sober and moderate Bolshevik who avoided excesses and was inclined to compromise. He surely did not mention his advice about "the pencils" to the sailors.

In the teeth of the obvious facts, the Compromisers proclaimed the July demonstration an armed uprising and accused the Bolsheviks of conspiracy. When the movement was already over, reactionary troops arrived from the front. In the press appeared news, based on the "documents" of the Minister of Justice Pereverzev, that Lenin and his collaborators were outright agents of the German General Staff. Then began days of calumny, persecution and rioting. The *Pravda* offices were demolished. The authorities issued an order for the arrest of Lenin, Zinoviev and others responsible for the "insurrection." The bourgeois and Compromisist press ominously demanded that the guilty surrender themselves to the hands of justice. There were conferences in the Central Committee of the Bolsheviks: should Lenin appear before the authorities, in order to give open battle to the calumny, or should he hide? Would the matter go as far as a court trial? There was no lack of wavering, inevitable in the midst of such a sharp break in the situation.

The question of who "saved" Lenin in those days and who wanted to "ruin" him occupies no small place in Soviet literature. Dyemyan Byedny told some time ago how he rushed to Lenin by car and argued with him not to imitate Christ who "gave himself up into the hands of his enemies." Bonch-Bruyevich, the former office manager of the Sovnarkom [People's Council of Commissars], completely contradicted his friend by telling in the press how Dymyan Byedny passed the critical hours at his country place in Finland. The implication that the honor of having convinced Lenin "belonged to other comrades" clearly indicates that Bonch was obliged to annoy his close friend in order to give satisfaction to somebody more influential.

In her reminiscences Krupskaya states: "On the 7th I visited Ilyich at his quarters in the apartment of the Alliluyevs together with Maria Ilyinichna [Lenin's sister]. This was just at the moment when Ilyich was wavering. He marshalled arguments in favor of the necessity to appear in court. Maria Ilyinichna argued against him hotly. 'Gregory [Zinoviev] and I have decided to appear. Go and tell Kamenev about it,' Ilyich told me. I made haste. 'Let's say good-bye,' Vladimir Ilyich said to me, 'we may never see each other again.' We embraced. I went to Kamenev and gave him Vladimir Ilyich's message. In the evening Stalin and others persuaded Ilyich not to appear in court and thereby saved his life."

These trying hours were described in greater detail by Ordzhonikidze. "The fierce hounding of our Party leaders began . . . Some of our comrades took the point of view that Lenin must not hide, that he must appear . . . So reasoned many prominent Bolsheviks. I met Stalin in the Tauride Palace. We went together to see Lenin . . ." The first thing that strikes the eye is the fact that during those hours when "a fierce hounding of our Party leaders" was going on, Ordzhonikidze and Stalin calmly meet at the Tauride Palace, headquarters of the enemy, and leave it unpunished. The same old argument was renewed at Alliluyev's apartment: to surrender or to hide? Lenin supposed that there would be no open trial. More categorical than any other against surrender was Stalin: "The Junkers [military students, equivalent of West Pointers] won't take you as far as prison, they'll kill you on the way . . ." At that moment Stassova appeared and informed them of a new rumor—that Lenin was, according to the documents of the Police Department, a provocateur. "These words produced an incredibly strong impression on Lenin. A nervous shudder ran over his face, and he declared with the utmost determination that he must go to jail." Ordzhonikidze and Nogin were sent to the Tauride Palace, to attempt to persuade the parties in power to guarantee "that Ilyich would not be lynched . . . by the Junkers." But the frightened Mensheviks were seeking guarantees for themselves. Stalin in his turn reported at the Petrograd Conference: "I personally posed the question of making a declaration to Lieber and Anissimov [Mensheviks, members of the Soviet Central Executive Committee], and they replied to me that they could not give guarantees of any kind." After this feeler in the camp of the enemy, it was decided that Lenin should leave Petrograd and hide securely underground. "Stalin undertook to organize Lenin's departure."

To what extent the opponents of Lenin's surrender to the authorities were right was proved subsequently by the story of the officer commanding the troops, General Polovtsev. "The officer going to Terioki [Finland] in hopes of catching Lenin asked me if I wanted to receive that gentleman whole or in pieces . . . I replied with a smile that people under arrest very often try to escape." For the organizers of judicial forgery it was not a question of "justice" but of seizing and killing Lenin, as was done two years later in Germany with Karl Liebknecht and Rosa Luxemburg. Stalin was more convinced than the others of the inevitability of a bloody reprisal; such a solution was quite in accord with his own cast of thought. Moreover, he was far from inclined to worry about what "public opinion" might say. Others, including Lenin and Zinoviev, wavered. Nogin and Lunarcharsky became opponents of surrender in the course of the day, after having been in favor of it. Stalin held out more tenaciously than others and was proved right.

Let us see now what the latest Soviet historiography has made of this dramatic episode. "The Mensheviks, the Essars and Trotsky, who subsequently became a Fascist bandit," writes an official publication of 1938, "demanded Lenin's voluntary appearance in court. Also in favor of it were those who have since been exposed as enemies of the people, the Fascist hirelings Kamenev and Rykov. Stalin fought them tooth and nail," and so on. As a matter of fact, I personally took no part in those conferences, since during those hours I was myself obliged to go into hiding. On the tenth of July, I addressed myself in writing to the Government of the Mensheviks and Essars, declaring my complete solidarity with Lenin, Zinoviev and Kamenev, and on the twenty-second of July I was arrested. In a letter to the Petrograd Conference Lenin deemed it necessary to note particularly that "during the difficult July days (Trotsky) proved himself equal to the situation." Stalin was not arrested and was not even formally indicted in this case for the very simple reason that he was politically non-existent as far as the authorities or public opinion were concerned. During the fierce persecution of Lenin, Zinoviev, Kamenev, myself and others, Stalin was hardly ever mentioned in the press, although he was an editor of *Pravda* and signed his articles. No one paid the slightest attention to these articles and no one was interested in their author.

Lenin hid at first in Alliluyev's apartment, then moved to Sestroretsk, where he stayed with the worker Emelyanov, whom he trusted implicitly and to whom he refers respectfully without mentioning him by name in one of his articles. "At the time of Vladimir Ilyich's departure for Sestroretsk—that was in the evening of July eleventh—Comrade Stalin and I," relates Alliluyev, "escorted Ilyich to the Sestroretsk station. During his sojourn in the tent at Razliv, and later in Finland, Vladimir Ilyich sent notes to Stalin through me from time to time. The notes were brought to me at my apartment; and, since it was necessary to answer them immediately, Stalin moved in with me in the month of August and lived with me in the very room in which Vladimir Ilyich hid out during the July days." Here he evidently met his future wife, Alliluyev's daughter Nadezhda, who was a mere adolescent at the time. Another of the veteran Bolshevik workers, Rahia, a Russified Finn, told in print how Lenin instructed him on one occasion "to bring Stalin the next evening. I was supposed to find Stalin in the editorial offices of *Pravda*. They talked very long." Along with Krupskaya, Stalin was during that period an important connecting link between the Central Committee and Lenin, who undoubtedly trusted him completely as a cautious conspirator. Besides, all the circumstances naturally pushed Stalin into that role: Zinoviev was in hiding, Kamenev and I were in jail, Sverdlov was in charge of all the organizational work. Stalin was freer than others and less in the eye of the police.

During the period of reaction after the July movement, Stalin's role grew considerably more important. Pestkovsky wrote in his apologetic reminiscences about Stalin's work during the summer of 1917: "The laboring masses of Petrograd knew Stalin very little then. Nor was he seeking popular acclaim. Having no talent as an orator, he avoided addressing mass meetings. But no Party conference, no serious organizational conclave got along without a political speech by Stalin. Because of that, the Party activists knew him well. When the question arose about Bolshevik candidates from Petrograd to the Constituent Assembly, the candidacy of Stalin was advanced to one of the foremost places upon the initiative of the Party activists." Stalin's name in the Petrograd list was in the sixth place . . . As late as 1930, in order to explain why Stalin did not enjoy popularity, it was still deemed necessary to point out that he lacked "the oratorical talent." Now such an expression would be utterly impossible: Stalin has been proclaimed the idol of the Petrograd workers and a classic orator. But it is true that, although he did not appear before the masses, Stalin, alongside of Sverdlov, carried out in July and August extremely responsible work at headquarters, at conclaves and conferences, in contacts with the Petersburg Committee, and the like.

Concerning the leadership of the Party during that period, Lunarsharsky wrote in 1923: ". . . Until the July days Sverdlov was, so to speak, at the chief headquarters of the Bolsheviks, in charge of all that happened, together with Lenin, Zinoviev and Stalin. During the July days he advanced to the forefront." That was true. In the midst of the cruel devastation which fell upon the Party that little dark man in eye-glasses behaved as if nothing untoward had happened. He continued to assign people to their tasks, encouraged those who needed encouragement, gave advice, and when necessary gave orders. He was the authentic "General Secretary" of the revolutionary year, although he did not bear that title. But he was the secretary of a party whose unchallenged political leader, Lenin, remained underground. From Finland Lenin sent articles, letters, drafts of resolutions, on all the basic questions of policy. Although the fact that he was at a distance led him not infrequently into tactical errors, it enabled him all the more surely to define the Party's strategy. The daily leadership fell to Sverdlov and Stalin, as the most influential members of the Central Committee remaining at liberty. The mass movement had in the meantime weakened considerably. Half of the Party had gone underground. The preponderance of the machine had grown correspondingly. Inside of the machine, the role of Stalin grew automatically. That law operates unalterably through his entire political biography and forms, as it were, its mainspring.

It was the workers and soldiers of Petrograd who suffered the direct defeat in July. In the final reckoning, it was their impetuousness that was smashed to pieces against the relative backwardness of the provinces. The defeatist mood among the masses of the capital was therefore deeper than anywhere else. But it lasted only a few weeks. Open agitation was resumed in the middle of July, when at small meetings in various parts of the city three courageous revolutionists appeared: Slutsky, who was later killed by the White Guards in Crimea; Volodarsky, killed by the Essars in Petrograd; and Yevdokimov, killed by Stalin in 1936. After losing accidental fellow-travelers here and there, by the end of the month the Party again began to grow.

On the twenty-first and twenty-second of July an exceptionally important conference, which remained unnoticed by the authorities and by the press, was held in Petrograd. After the tragic failure of the adventurous offensive, delegates from the front began to arrive at the capital more and more often with protests against the suppression of liberties in the army and against continuation of the war. They were not admitted to the Central Executive Committee, because the Compromisers had nothing to tell them. The soldiers from the front got acquainted with one another in the corridors and reception rooms, and exchanged opinions on the grandees of the Central Executive Committee in vigorous soldierly words. The Bolsheviks, who had the knack of insinuating themselves everywhere, advised the bewildered and irate delegates to confer with the workers, soldiers and sailors of the capital. The conference that thus originated was attended by representatives of 29 front-line regiments, of 90 Petrograd factories, of Kronstadt sailors and of several surrounding garrisons. The front-line soldiers told about the senseless offensive, about the carnage, and about the collaboration between the Compromisist commissars and the reactionary officers, who were again getting cocky. Although most of the front-line soldiers continued to regard themselves as Essars, the sharply-worded Bolshevik resolution was passed unanimously. From Petrograd the delegates went back to the trenches as matchless agitators for a workers' and peasants' revolution. It would seem that the leading roles in the organization of this remarkable conference were played by Sverdlov and Stalin.

The Petrograd Conference, which had tried in vain to keep the masses from demonstrating, dragged on, after considerable interruption, until the night of the twentieth of July. The course of its activities sheds considerable light on Stalin's role and his place in the Party. The organizational leadership on behalf of the Central Committee was borne by Sverdlov, who unpretentiously and without any false airs of modesty, left the sphere of theories and important questions of policy to others. The conference was mainly concerned with appraising the political situation as it developed after the havoc of July. Volodarsky, leading member of the Petrograd Committee, declared in the very beginning: "On the current moment only Zinoviev can be the reporter . . . It would be well to hear Lenin . . ." No one mentioned Stalin. The conference, cut short by the mass movement, was resumed only on the sixteenth of July. By that time Zinoviev and Lenin were in hiding, and the basic political report fell to Stalin, who appeared as a substitute for Zinoviev. "It is clear to me," he said, "that at the given moment the counter-revolution has conquered us. We are isolated and betrayed by the Mensheviks and the Essars, lied about . . ." The reporter's chief point was the victory of the bourgeois counter-revolution. However, it was an unstable victory; as long as the war continued, as long as the economic collapse had not been overcome, as long as the peasants had not received their land, "there are bound to be crises, the masses will repeatedly come out into the streets, and more, there will be bolder battles. The revolution's peaceful period is over . . ." Hence the slogan, "All power to the Soviets," was no longer practical. The Compromisist Soviets had helped the militaristic bourgeois counter-revolution to crush the Bolsheviks and to disarm the workers and soldiers, and in that way they themselves had forfeited actual power. Only yesterday they could have removed the Provisional Government with a mere decree; within the Soviets the Bolsheviks could have secured power in simple by-elections. But now this was no longer possible. Aided by the Compromisers, the counter-revolution had armed itself. The Soviets themselves had become a mere camouflage for the counter-revolution. It would be silly to demand power for these Soviets! "It is not the institution, but what class policy an institution pursues that matters." Peaceful conquest of power was out of the question now. There was nothing left to do but prepare for an armed uprising, which would become possible as soon as the humblest villagers, and with them the soldiers at the fronts, turned toward the workers. But this bold strategic perspective was followed by an extremely cautious tactical directive for the impending period. "Our task is to gather forces, to strengthen the existing organizations and to restrain the masses from premature demonstrations . . . That is the general tactical line of the Central Committee."

Although quite elementary in form, this report contained a thoroughgoing appraisal of the situation that had developed within the last few days. The debates added comparatively little to what the reporter had said. In 1927 the editorial board of the protocols recorded: "The basic propositions of this report had been agreed upon jointly with Lenin and developed in accordance with Lenin's article, 'Three Crises,' which had not yet had time to appear in print." Moreover the delegates knew, most likely through Krupskaya, that Lenin had written special theses for the reporter. "The group of the conferees," declares the protocol, "requested that Lenin's theses be made public. Stalin stated that he did not have the theses with him . . ." The demand of the delegates is all-too understandable: the change in orientation was so radical that they wanted to hear the authentic voice of their leader. But Stalin's reply is incomprehensible: had he simply left the theses at home, they could have been presented at the next session; however, the theses were never delivered. The impression thus created was that they had been hidden from the conference. Even more astonishing is the fact that the "July Theses," quite unlike all the other documents written by Lenin in the underground, have not been published to this day. Since the only copy was in Stalin's possession, we must presume that he lost them. However, he himself said nothing about having lost them. The editorial board of the protocols expresses the supposition that Lenin's theses were composed by him in the spirit of his articles, "Three Crises" and "About Slogans," written before the conference but published after it at Kronstadt, where there was still freedom of the press. As a matter of fact, a juxtaposition of texts shows that Stalin's report was no more than a simple exposition of these two articles, without a single original word added by him. Evidently Stalin had not read the articles themselves and did not suspect their existence; but he used the theses, which were identical with the articles in the tenor of their thought, and that circumstance sufficiently explains why the reporter "forgot" to bring Lenin's theses to the conference and why that document was never preserved. Stalin's character makes that hypothesis not only admissible but unavoidable.

Inside the conference committee, where a fierce struggle was going on, Volodarsky, who refused to admit that the counter-revolution had won a decisive victory in July, gathered a majority. The resolution that had now emerged from the committee was no longer defended before the conference by Stalin but by Volodarsky. Stalin made no demand for a minority report and took no part in the debate. There was confusion among the delegates. Volodarsky's resolution was finally supported by 28 delegates against 3, with 28 not voting. The group of Vyborg delegates excused their abstention from voting by the fact that "Lenin's theses had not been made public and the resolution was not defended by the reporter." The hint at the improper hiding of the theses was plain enough. Stalin said nothing. He had sustained a double defeat, since he had evoked dissatisfaction with his concealment of the theses and could not secure a majority for them.

As for Volodarsky, he continued to defend in substance the Bolshevik schema for the Revolution of 1905: first, the democratic dictatorship; then the inevitable break with the peasantry; and, in the event of the victory of the proletariat in the West, the struggle for the socialist dictatorship. Stalin, supported by Molotov and several others, defended Lenin's new conception: the dictatorship of the proletariat, resting on the poorest peasants, can alone assure a solution of the tasks of the democratic revolution and at the same time open the era of socialist transformations. Stalin was right as against Volodarsky, but he did not know how to prove it. On the other hand, in refusing to recognize that the bourgeois counter-revolution had won a decisive victory, Volodarsky was proved right against both Lenin and Stalin. That debate was to come up again at the Party Congress several days later. The conference ended with passing an appeal written by Stalin, "To All the Toilers," which read in part: ". . . The corrupt hirelings and cowardly calumniators dare openly to accuse the leaders of our Party of 'treason' . . . Never before have the names of our leaders been as dear and as close to the working class as now when the impudent bourgeois rabble is throwing mud at them!" Besides Lenin, the chief victims of persecution and calumny were Zinoviev, Kamenev and myself. These names were especially dear to Stalin "when the bourgeois rabble" threw mud at them.

The Petrograd Conference was in the nature of a rehearsal for the Party Congress that convened on the twenty-sixth of July. By that time nearly all the district Soviets of Petrograd were in the hands of the Bolsheviks. At the headquarters of the trade unions, as well as in factory and shop committees, the influence of the Bolsheviks had become dominant. The organizational preparation for the Congress was concentrated in Sverdlov's hands. The political preparation was guided by Lenin from underground. In letters to the Central Committee and in the Bolshevik press, which began to come out again, he shed light on the political situation from various angles. He it was who wrote the drafts of all the basic resolutions for the Congress, carefully weighing all the arguments at clandestine meetings with the various reporters.

The Congress was called "Unifying," because in it was to take place the fusion into the Party of the Petrograd Inter-district [*Mezhrayonnaya*] organization, to which belonged Joffe, Uritsky, Ryazanov, Lunacharsky, Pokrovsky, Manuilsky, Yurenev, Karakhan and I, as well as other revolutionists who in one way or another entered into the history of the Soviet Revolution, "During the years of the War," states a footnote to Lenin's Works, "the Inter-districters [*Mezhrayontsy*] were close to the Bolshevik Petersburg Committee." At the time of the Congress the organization numbered about 4,000 workers.

News of the Congress, which met semi-legally in two different working class districts, got into the newspapers. In government circles there was talk of breaking it up. But when it came to a showdown, Kerensky decided that it would be more sensible not to butt into the Vyborg District. As far as the general public was concerned, the people in charge of the Congress were unknown. Among the Bolsheviks at the Congress who subsequently became famous were Sverdlov, Bukharin, Stalin, Molotov, Voroshilov, Ordzhinikidze, Yurenev, Manuilsky . . . The praesidium consisted of Sverdlov, Olminsky, Lomov, Yurenev and Stalin. Even here, with the most prominent figures of Bolshevism absent, Stalin's name is listed in the last place. The Congress resolved to send greetings to "Lenin, Trotsky, Zinoviev, Lunacharsky, Kamenev, Kollontai and all the other arrested and persecuted comrades." These were elected to the honorary praesidium. The 1938 edition records only Lenin's election.

Sverdlov reported on the organizational work of the Central Committee. Since the April Conference the Party had grown from 80,000 to 240,000 members, i.e., had tripled in size. The growth, under the blows of July, was a healthy one. Astonishing because of its insignificance was the total circulation of the entire Bolshevik press—a mere three hundred and twenty thousand copies for such a gigantic country! But the revolutionary set-up is electric: Bolshevik ideas made their way into the consciousness of millions.

Stalin repeated two of his reports—on the political activity of the Central Committee and on the state of the country. Referring to the municipal elections, at which the Bolsheviks won about twenty per cent of the vote in the capital, Stalin reported: "The Central Committee . . . did its utmost to fight not only the Kadets, the basic force of the counter-revolution, but likewise the Mensheviks and Essars, who willy-nilly followed the Kadets." Much water had gone under the bridge since the days of the March Conference, when Stalin had considered the Mensheviks and the Essars as part of "the revolutionary democracy" and had relied on the Kadets to "fortify" the conquests of the Revolution.

Contrary to custom, questions of war, social patriotism, the collapse of the Second International and the groupings inside of world socialism, were excerpted from the political report and assigned to Bukharin, since Stalin could not make head or tail of international matters. Bukharin argued that the campaign for peace by way of "pressure" on the Provisional Government and the other governments of the Entente had suffered complete collapse and that only the overthrow of the Provisional Government could bring an early approach to a democratic liquidation of the war. Following Bukharin, Stalin made his report on the tasks of the Party. The debates were carried on jointly on both reports, although it soon became apparent that the two reporters were not in agreement.

"Some comrades have argued," Stalin reported, "that, because capitalism is poorly developed in our country, it is utopian to pose the question of the socialist revolution. They would have been right, had there been no war, no collapse, had not the very foundations of national economy gone to pieces. But today these questions of intervention in the economic sphere are posed in all countries as imperative questions . . ." Moreover, "nowhere did the proletariat have such broad organizations as the Soviets . . . All this precludes the possibility that the laboring masses should refrain from intervening in economic life. Therein is the realistic foundation for posing the question of the socialist revolution in Russia."

Amazing is the obvious incongruity of his main argument: if the weak development of capitalism makes the program of socialist revolution utopian, then the demolition of the productive forces through war should not bring the era of socialism any closer but on the contrary make it more remote than ever. As a matter of fact, the tendency to transform the democratic revolution into the socialist one is not grounded in the demolition of the productive forces through war, but in the social structure of Russian capitalism. That tendency could have been perceived—as indeed it was—before the war and independently of it. True, the war accelerated the revolutionary process in the masses to an immeasurably more rapid tempo, but it did not in the least change the social content of the revolution. However, it should be added that Stalin cribbed his argument from some isolated and undeveloped remarks of Lenin, whose purpose was to get the old cadres used to the need of rearming.

During the debates, Bukharin tried partly to defend the old Bolshevik schema: in the first revolution the Russian proletariat marches shoulder to shoulder with the peasantry, in the name of democracy; in the second revolution—shoulder to shoulder with the European proletariat, in the name of socialism. "What is the sense of Bukharin's perspective?" Stalin retorted. "According to him, we are working for a peasant revolution during the first stage. But that cannot . . . fail to coincide with the workers' revolution. It is impossible that the working class, which is the vanguard of revolution, should at the same time fail to fight for its own demands. Therefore, I consider Bukharin's schema light-minded." This was absolutely right. The peasant revolution could not win otherwise than by placing the proletariat in power. The proletariat could not assume power, without beginning the socialist revolution. Stalin employed against Bukharin the very same reflections which, expounded for the first time in the beginning of 1905, were branded "utopian" until April, 1917. But in a few years Stalin was to forget these arguments which he voiced at the Sixth Congress; instead, jointly with Bukharin he was to revive the "democratic dictatorship" formula, which would have an important place in the program of the Comintern and play a fatal role in the revolutionary movement of China and other countries.

The basic task of the Congress was to change the key-note from peaceful transition of power to the Soviets to preparedness for armed insurrection. To do that, it was first of all necessary to understand the shift in the correlation of forces that had taken place. Its general direction was obvious—from the people to the bourgeoisie. It was far more difficult to determine the extent of the change: only another open clash between the classes could measure the new correlation of forces. This test came toward the end of August with General Kornilov's revolt, which made it immediately clear that the bourgeoisie continued to have no support either among the people or the army. The July shift was consequently superficial and episodic in character; nevertheless it was real enough. Henceforth, it was unthinkable to suggest peaceful transition of power to the Soviets. Formulating the new course, Lenin was above all concerned with making the Party face the changed correlation of forces as resolutely as possible. In a certain sense he resorted to deliberate exaggeration: it is more dangerous to underestimate the enemy's forces than to overestimate them. But an overdrawn appraisal would have made the Congress balk, just as it had done at the Petrograd Conference—especially, because of Stalin's oversimplified expression of Lenin's ideas.

"The situation is clear," Stalin was saying. "No one talks any more about dual authority. The Soviets, which were once a real force, are now merely powerless organs for rallying the masses." Certain of the delegates were absolutely right in protesting that the triumph of the reaction in July was temporary, that the counter-revolution had not won and that dual authority had not yet been abolished to the advantage of the bourgeoisie. Stalin replied to these arguments as he had done at the Conference, with the stock phrase: "Reaction does not occur during revolution." As a matter of fact, the orbit of every revolution is made up of exceptional curves of ascent and descent. Counter-jolts by the enemy, or resulting from the very backwardness of the masses themselves, which render the régime more acceptable to the needs of the counter-revolutionary class, bring forth reaction, without yet displacing those in power. But the victory of the counter-revolution is quite another matter: that is inconceivable without the passing of power into the hands of another class. No such decisive transition took place in July. To this very day, Soviet historians and commentators continue to copy Stalin's formula from book to book, without asking themselves this question: if the power had passed into the hands of the bourgeoisie in July, why did the bourgeoisie have to resort to an uprising in August? Until the July events, under the régime of dual authority the Provisional Government was a mere phantom while real power reposed in the Soviet. After the July events, part of the real power passed from the Soviet to the bourgeoisie, but only a part: dual authority did not disappear. That was the very thing that subsequently determined the character of the October Revolution.

"Should the counter-revolutionaries manage to last a month or two," Stalin said further, "it would be only because the principle of coalition has not been abolished. As the forces of the revolution develop, explosions will occur, and the moment will come when the workers will arouse and rally around themselves the strata of the poor peasantry, raise the banner of the workers' revolution and start the era of socialist revolution in the West." Let us note: the mission of the Russian proletariat is to start "the era of socialist revolution in the West." That was the Party formula for the ensuing years. In all essentials Stalin's report gives the correct appraisal of the situation and the correct prognosis—Lenin's appraisal and prognosis. But, as usual, his report lacks elaboration of thought. The orator asserts and proclaims; he never proves or argues. His appraisals are made by rule of thumb or taken ready-made; they do not pass through the laboratory of analytic thinking and there is no indication of that organic connection between them which in itself generates the necessary arguments, analogies and illustrations. Stalin, as a polemicist, is given to reiterating propositions already expressed, at times in the form of aphorisms, which assume as already proved the very things that need proving. Often the arguments are spiced with churlishness, especially in the peroration, when there is no need to fear an opponent's rebuttals.

In a 1938 publication concerning the Sixth Congress, we read: "Lenin, Stalin, Sverdlov, Dzerzhinsky and others were elected members of the Central Committee." Only three dead men are named side by side with Stalin. Yet the protocols of the Congress inform us that 21 members and 10 alternates were elected to the Central Committee. In view of the Party's semi-legality the names of persons elected by secret ballot were not announced at the Congress, with the exception of the four who had received the largest number of votes. Lenin—

133 out of a possible 134, Zinoviev—132, Kamenev—131, Trotsky—131. Besides them the following were elected: Nogin, Kollontai, Stalin, Sverdlov, Rykov, Bubnov, Artem, Uritsky, Milutin, Berzin, Dzerzhinsky, Krestinsky, Muranov, Smilga, Sokolnikov, Sha'umyan.[1] The names are arranged in the order of the number of votes received. The names of eight alternates have been definitely established: Lomov, Joffe, Stassova, Yakovleva, Dzhaparidze, Kisselev, Preobrazhensky, Skrypnik.

The Congress ended on the third of August. The next day Kamenev was liberated from prison. From then on he not only spoke regularly in Soviet institutions but exerted an unmistakable influence on the Party's general policy and on Stalin personally. Although in varying degrees both of them had adapted themselves to the new line, it was not so easy for them to rid themselves of their own mental habits. Wherever possible, Kamenev rounded out the sharp angles of Lenin's policy. Stalin did not object to that; he merely kept out of harm's way. An open conflict flared up on the issue of the Socialist conference in Stockholm, the initiative for which had come from the German Social-Democrats. The Russian patriots and compromisers, inclined to grasp at any straw, saw in that conference an important means of "fighting for peace." But Lenin, who had been accused of connections with the German General Staff, came out resolutely against participation in this enterprise, which was obviously sponsored by the German Government. At the session of the Central Executive Committee of August sixth Kamenev openly came out for participation in the conference. It did not even occur to Stalin to come to the defense of the Party position in the *Proletarian* (which was then *Pravda's* name). Instead, Stalin held back from publication Lenin's sharp article against Kamenev, which appeared only after a delay of ten days and only because of its author's persistent demands, reinforced by his appeal to other members of the Central Committee. Nevertheless, even then, Stalin did not come out openly in support of Kamenev.

Immediately after Kamenev's liberation a rumor was launched in the press by the democratic Ministry of Justice to the effect that he had had some connections with the Tsarist secret police. Kamenev demanded an investigation. The Central Committee commissioned Stalin "to discuss with Gotz [one of the Essar leaders] a commission in the case of Kamenev." He had been given similar assignments in the past: "to discuss with the Menshevik Bogdanov the case of the Kronstadtites, "to discuss" with the Menshevik Anissimov guarantees for Lenin. Remaining behind the scenes, Stalin was more suitable than others for all sorts of delicate assignments. Besides, the Central Committee was always sure that in discussions with opponents Stalin would not let anyone pull the wool over his eyes.

"The reptilian hissing of the counter-revolution," wrote Stalin on August thirteenth about the calumny against Kamenev, "is again becoming louder. The disgusting serpent of reaction thrusts its poisonous fang from round the corner. It will sting and slink back into its dark lair . . ." and so forth in the

[1] Bukharin's name is missing from this list.—C. M.

typical style of his Tiflis "chameleons." But the article is interesting not only stylistically. "The infamous baiting, the bacchanal of lies and calumnies, the shameless deception, the low-grade forgery and falsification," the author continued, "assume proportions hitherto unknown in history . . . At first they tried to smear the tested revolutionary fighters as German spies, and that having failed, they want to make them out Tsarist spies. Thus they are trying to brand those who have devoted their entire conscious life to the cause of the revolutionary struggle against the Tsarist regime as . . . Tsarist varlets . . . The political meaning of all this is self-evident: the masters of the counter-revolution are intent at all cost to render Kamenev harmless and to extirpate him as one of the recognized leaders of the revolutionary proletariat." It is a pity that this article did not figure in Prosecutor Vyshinsky's material during Kamenev's trial in 1936.

On August 30, Stalin published without a word of reservation an unsigned article by Zinoviev, "What Not To Do," which was obviously directed against preparations for the insurrection. "It is necessary to face the truth: in Petrograd there are now many circumstances favorable to the emergence of an insurrection typified by the Paris Commune of 1871." Without mentioning Zinoviev, Lenin wrote on September third: "The reference to the Commune is very superficial and even foolish . . . The Commune could not at once offer to the people all that the Bolsheviks can offer them when they become the government: namely, land to the peasants, immediate peace proposals." The blow at Zinoviev rebounded at the editor of the newspaper. But Stalin kept silent. Anonymously, he was ready to support any Right Wing polemic against Lenin. But he was careful not to involve himself in it. At the first sign of danger he stepped aside.

There is practically nothing to say about Stalin's newspaper work during that period. He was the editor of the central organ, not because he was a writer by nature, but because he was not an orator and simply did not fit into any public activity. He did not write a single notable article; did not pose a single new question for discussion; did not introduce a single slogan into general circulation. His comments on events were impersonal, and strictly within the framework of current Party views. He was a Party functionary assigned to a newspaper, not a revolutionary publicist.

The revival of the mass movement and the return to activity of the Central Committee members who had been temporarily severed from it, naturally threw Stalin out of the position of prominence he held during the July congress. From then on, his activities were carried on in obscurity, unknown to the masses, unnoted by the enemy. In 1924 the Commission on Party History published a copious chronicle of the revolution in several volumes. The 422 pages of the fourth volume, dealing with August and September, record all the happenings, occurrences, brawls, resolutions, speeches, articles in any way deserving of notice. Sverdlov, then practically unknown, was mentioned three times in that volume; Kamenev, 46 times; I, who spent August and the beginning of September in prison, 31 times; Lenin, who was in the underground, 16 times; Zinoviev, who shared Lenin's fate, 6 times; Stalin was not mentioned even once. Stalin's name is not even in the index of approximately 500 proper names. In other words, throughout those two months the press did not take cognizance of anything he did or of a single speech he spoke and not one of the more or less prominent participants in the events of those days mentioned his name even once.

Fortunately, it is possible to trace Stalin's role in the life of the Party, or rather of its headquarters staff, more or less closely through the protocols of the Central Committee for seven months (August, 1917 to February, 1918), which have been preserved but which, true enough, are incomplete. During the absence of the political leaders, Milutin, Smilga, Glebov, figures of little influence but better fit for public appearances than Stalin, were delegated to the various conferences and congresses. Stalin's name seldom occurs in Party decisions. Uritsky, Sokolnikov and Stalin were delegated to organize a committee for elections to the Constituent Assembly. The same three were delegated to draft the resolution on the Stockholm Conference. Stalin was delegated to negotiate with a printshop about re-establishing the central organ. He was on still another committee for drafting a resolution, and the like. After the July congress Stalin's motion to organize the work of the Central Committee on the principle of "strict allocation of functions" was passed. However, that motion was easier to write than to execute: the course of events was to continue for some time to confound functions and to upset decisions. On the second of September the Central Committee designated editorial boards for the weekly and monthly journals, in both of which Stalin participated. On the sixth of September—after my liberation from prison—Stalin and Ryazanov were replaced on the editorial board of the theoretical journal by Kamenev and me. But that decision, too, remained only in the protocol. As a matter of fact, both journals published only one issue each, and the actual editorial board was quite different from the one designated.

On the fifth of October the Central Committee appointed a committee to prepare a Draft Party Program for the forthcoming convention. That committee was made up of Lenin, Bukharin, myself, Kamenev, Sokolnikov and Kollontai. Stalin was not included in it, not because there was any opposition to his candidature, but simply because his name never occurred to anyone when it was a matter of drafting a theoretical Party document of prime importance. But the program committee never met—not even once. Quite different tasks were on the order of the day. The Party won the insurrection and came to power without having a finished program. Even in purely Party matters, events did not always dispose of people in correspondence with the foresight and plans of the Party hierarchy. The Central Committee designated editorial boards, committees, groups of three, of five, of seven, which, before they could meet, were upset by new events, and everybody forgot yesterday's decision. Besides, for reasons of conspiracy, the protocols were securely hidden away, and no one ever referred to them.

Rather strange was Stalin's comparatively frequent absence. He was absent six times from 24 sessions of the Central Committee for August, September and the first week of October. The list of participants for the other six sessions is not available. This lack of punctuality is all the more inexcusable in Stalin's case, because he took no part in the work of the Soviet and its Central Executive Committee and never spoke at public meetings. He himself evidently did not attach the importance to his own participation in the sessions of the Central Committee which is ascribed to him nowadays. In a number of cases his absence was undoubtedly explained by hurt feelings and irritation: whenever he cannot carry his point he is inclined to sulk in hiding and dream of revenge. Noteworthy is the order in which the presence of Central Committee members at its sessions was recorded in the protocol: September 13th: Trotsky, Kamenev, Stalin, Sverdlov and others; September 15th: Trotsky, Kamenev, Rykov, Nogin, Stalin, Sverdlov, and others; September 20th: Trotsky, Uritsky, Bubnov, Bukharin, and others (Stalin and Kamenev absent); September 21st: Trotsky, Kamenev, Stalin, Sokolnikov, and others; September 23rd: Trotsky, Kamenev, Zinoviev, and so forth (Stalin absent). The order of the names was not of course regulated and was sometimes violated. Yet it was not accidental, especially when we consider that in the preceding period, when Trotsky, Kamenev and Zinoviev were absent, Stalin's name was occasionally listed in first place. These are, of course, trifling matters. But there is nothing bigger to be found with reference to Stalin; besides, these trifles mirror impartially the Party's life from day to day and Stalin's place in it.

The greater the sweep of the movement, the smaller is Stalin's place in it and the harder it is for him to stand out among the ordinary members of the Central Committee. In October, the decisive month of the decisive year, Stalin was less noticeable than ever. The truncated Central Committee, his only substantial base, was itself devoid of innate self-confidence during those months. Its decisions were too often nullified through outside initiative. On the whole, the Party machine never felt itself firmly grounded in the revolutionary turmoil. The broader and deeper the influence of Bolshevism's slogans, the harder it was for the committeemen to grasp the movement. The more the Soviets fell under the influence of the Party, the less of a place did the machine find for itself. Such is one of the paradoxes of revolution.

Transferring to 1917 conditions that crystallized considerably later, when the waters of the floodtide had receded inside the banks, many historians, even quite conscientious ones, tell the story as if the Central Committee had directly guided the policy of the Petrograd Soviet, which became Bolshevik about the beginning of September. As a matter of fact, that was not the case. The protocols undoubtedly show that, with the exception of several plenary sessions in which Lenin, Zinoviev and I participated, the Central Committee did not play a political role. It did not assume the initiative in a single important issue. Many of the Central Committee decisions for that period remained hanging in the air, having clashed with the decisions of the Soviet. The most important resolutions of the Soviet were transformed into action before the Central Committee had the time to consider them. Only after the conquest of power, the end of the civil war, and the establishment of a stable régime, would the Central Committee little by little begin to concentrate the leadership of Soviet activity in its hands. Then would come Stalin's turn.

On the eighth of August the Central Committee launched a vigorous campaign against the Government Conference convoked by Kerensky in Moscow, which was crudely manipulated in the interests of the bourgeoisie. The conference opened on the twelfth of August under the stress of the general strike of protest by the Moscow workers. Not admitted to the conference, the Bolsheviks found a more effective expression for their power. The bourgeoisie was frightened and furious. Having surrendered Riga to the Germans on the twenty-first, Commander-in-Chief Kornilov started his march on Petrograd on the twenty-fifth, intent on a personal dictatorship. Kerensky, who had been deceived in his calculations about Kornilov, declared the Commander-in-Chief "a traitor to the fatherland." Even at that crucial moment, on the twenty-seventh of August, Stalin did not show up at the Soviet Central Executive Committee. Sokolnikov appeared there in the name of the Bolsheviks. He proclaimed the readiness of the Bolsheviks to come to terms about military measures with the organs of the Soviet majority. The Mensheviks and the Essars accepted the offer with thanks and with gritting of teeth, for the soldiers and workers were now following the Bolsheviks. The rapid and bloodless liquidation of the Kornilov mutiny completely restored the power the Soviets had partly lost in July. The Bolsheviks revived the slogan, "All Power to the Soviets!" In the press Lenin proposed a compromise to the Compromisers: let the Soviets take power and guarantee complete freedom of propaganda, and the Bolsheviks would take their stand entirely on the ground of Soviet legality. The Compromisers bellicosely rejected a compromise with the Bolsheviks. They continued to seek their allies on the Right.

The high-handed refusal of the Compromisers only strengthened the Bolsheviks. As in 1905, the preponderance which the first wave of revolution brought to the Mensheviks soon melted in the atmosphere of the sharpening class struggle. But unlike its tendency in the First Revolution, the growth of Bolshevism now corresponded to the rise rather than the decline of the mass movement. The same essential process assumed a different form in the villages: a Left Wing split off from the Essar Party, which was dominant among the peasantry, and tried to march in step with the Bolsheviks. The garrisons of the large cities were almost entirely with the workingmen. "Indeed, the Bolsheviks worked hard and tirelessly," testified Sukhanov, a Left Wing Menshevik. "They were among the masses at the lathe, daily, constantly . . . The mass lived and breathed with the Bolsheviks. It was in the hands of the Party of Lenin and

Trotsky." It was in the hands of the Party, but not in the hands of the Party's machine.

On the thirty-first of August the Petrograd Soviet for the first time passed a political resolution of the Bolsheviks. Trying hard not to yield, the Compromisers decided on a new test of strength. Nine days later the question was put point-blank in the Soviet. The old praesidium and the coalition policy received 414 votes with 519 opposed and 67 not voting. The Mensheviks and the Essars reaped the harvest of their policy of compromise with the bourgeoisie. The Soviets greeted the new coalition government they organized with a resolution which I, as its new president, introduced. "The new government . . . will enter the history of the revolution as the government of civil war . . . The All-Russian Congress of Soviets will organize a genuinely revolutionary government." That was an outright declaration of war against the Compromisers who had rejected our "compromise."

The so-called Democratic Conference, convoked by the Soviet Central Executive Committee, ostensibly to offset the Government Conference but actually to sanction the same old thoroughly rotten coalition, opened in Petrograd on the fourteenth of September. The Compromisers were getting frantic. A few days earlier Krupskaya had gone on a secret trip to Lenin in Finland. In a railroad coach full of soldiers the talk was not about coalition but about insurrection. "When I told Ilyich about this talk of the soldiers, his face became thoughtful; later, no matter what was under discussion, that thoughtfulness did not leave his face. It was clear that he was saying one thing and thinking of something else—the insurrection and how best to prepare for it."

On the day the Democratic Conference opened—(the silliest of all the pseudo-parliaments of democracy)—Lenin wrote to the Party Central Committee his famous letters, "The Bolsheviks Must Take Power" and "Marxism and the Insurrection." This time he demanded immediate action: the rousing of regiments and factories, the arrest of the government and the Democratic Conference, the seizure of power. Obviously the plan could not be carried out that very day; but it did direct the thinking and activity of the Central Committee into new channels. Kamenev insisted on a categorical rejection of Lenin's proposal —as disastrous! Fearing that these letters might circulate through the Party as well as in the Central Committee, Kamenev gathered six votes in favor of destroying all copies except the one intended for the archives. Stalin proposed "to send the letters to the most important organizations and to suggest their discussion." The latest commentary declares that the purpose of Stalin's proposal was "to organize the influence of local Party Committees on the Central Committee and to urge it to carry out Lenin's directives." Had such been the case, Stalin would have come right out in defense of Lenin's proposals and would have countered Kamenev's resolution with—his own! But that was far from his thought. Most of the committeemen in the provinces were more Rightist than the Central Committee. To send them Lenin's letters without the Central Committee's endorsement was tantamount to expressing disapproval of them. Stalin's proposal was made to gain time and in the event of a conflict to secure the possibility of pleading that the local Committees were balking. The Central Committee was paralyzed by vacillation. It was decided to defer the question of Lenin's letters to the next session. Lenin was awaiting the answer in frenzied impatience. But Stalin did not even put in an appearance at the next session, which met no sooner than five days later, and the question of the letters was not even included in the order of the day. The hotter the atmosphere, the colder are Stalin's maneuverings.

The Democratic Conference resolved to organize in agreement with the bourgeoisie some semblance of a representative institution, to which Kerensky promised to grant consultative rights. What should be the Bolshevik attitude toward this Council of the Republic or Pre-Parliament, became at once a crucial issue of tactics among the Bolsheviks: should they participate in it, or should they ignore it on their way to the insurrection? As reporter of the Central Committee at the forthcoming Party Fraction of the Democratic Conference, I proposed the idea of a boycott. The Central Committee, which divided almost in half on this debatable question (nine for the boycott and eight against), referred the question for decision to the Fraction. To expound the contradictory points of view "two reports were proposed: Trotsky's and Rykov's." "As a matter of fact," Stalin insisted in 1925, "there were four reporters: two for the boycott of the Pre-Parliament (Trotsky and Stalin) and two for participation (Kamenev and Nogin)." This is almost right: when the Fraction decided to terminate the debates, it decided to allow one more representative to speak for each side: Stalin on behalf of the boycottists and Kamenev (but not Nogin) for those favoring participation. Rykov and Kamenev received 77 votes; Stalin and I—50. The defeat of the tactic of the boycott was delivered by the provincials, whose separation from the Mensheviks was quite recent in many parts of the country.

Superficially it might seem that the differences were of minor importance. As a matter of fact, the underlying issue was whether the Party was to prepare to play the part of the Opposition in a bourgeois republic or whether it was to set itself the task of taking power by storm. Stalin later recalled his role as a reporter because of the importance this episode had assumed in the official historiography. The obliging editor added of his own accord that I had come out for "a middle of the road position." In subsequent editing my name has been entirely deleted. The new history proclaims: "Stalin came out resolutely against participation in the Pre-Parliament." But in addition to the testimony of the protocols, there is also Lenin's testimony. "We must boycott the Pre-Parliament," he wrote on the twenty-third of September. "We must go . . . to the masses. We must give them a clear and correct slogan: kick out the Bonapartist Kerensky gang and his fake Pre-Parliament." Then a footnote: "Trotsky was for the boycott. Bravo, Comrade Trotsky!" But, of course, the Kremlin has officially prescribed the elimination of all such sins from the new edition of Lenin's Works.

On the seventh of October the Bolshevik Fraction demonstratively walked out of the Pre-Parliament. "We appeal to the people. All Power to the Soviets!"

This was tantamount to calling for insurrection. That very day at the Central Committee session it was decreed to organize an Information Bureau on Fighting the Counter-Revolution. The deliberately foggy name covered a concrete task: reconnaissance and preparation of the insurrection. Sverdlov, Bubnov and I were delegated to organize that Bureau. In view of the laconic nature of the protocol and the absence of other documents, the author is compelled to resort to his own memory at this point. Stalin declined to participate in the Bureau, suggesting Bubnov, a man of little authority, in place of himself. His attitude was one of reserve, if not of skepticism, toward the idea itself. He was in favor of an insurrection. But he did not believe that the workers and soldiers were ready for action. He lived isolated not only from the masses, but even from their Soviet representation, and was content with the refracted impressions of the Party machine. So far as the masses were concerned, the July experiences had not passed without a trace. Actually blind pressure had disappeared; cautiousness had replaced it. On the other hand, confidence in the Bolsheviks was already colored with misgivings: will they be able to do what they promised? The Bolshevik agitators were complaining at times that they were being somewhat cold-shouldered by the masses. As a matter of fact, the masses were getting tired of waiting, of indecisiveness, of mere words. But in the machine this tiredness was frequently described as "absence of fighting mood." Hence the tarnish of skepticism on many committeemen. Besides, even the bravest of men is bound to feel a little chill in the pit of the stomach just before an insurrection. This is not always acknowledged, but it is so. Stalin himself was in an equivocal frame of mind. He never forgot April, when his wisdom of a "practico" was so cruelly disgraced. On the other hand, Stalin trusted the machine far more than the masses. On all the most important occasions he insured himself by voting with Lenin. But he showed no initiative in support of the resolutions passed, refrained from directly tackling any decisive action, protected the bridges of retreat, influenced others as a dampener, and in the end missed the October Revolution because he was off on a tangent.

True, nothing came of the Bureau on Fighting the Counter-Revolution, but it was not the fault of the masses. On the ninth, Smolny got into a new sharp conflict with the Government, which had decreed the transfer of the revolutionary troops from the capital to the front. The garrison rallied more closely than ever around its protector, the Soviet. At once the preparation of the insurrection acquired a concrete basis. Yesterday's initiator of the Bureau transferred all his attention to the creation of a military staff in the Soviet itself. The first step was taken that very day, on the ninth of October. "For counter-action against the attempts of the General Staff to lead the revolutionary troops out of Petrograd," the Executive Committee decided to launch the Military Revolutionary Committee. Thus, by the logic of things, without any discussion in the Central Committee, almost unexpectedly, the insurrection was started in the Soviet arena and began to recruit its Soviet general staff, which was far more effective than the Bureau of the Seventh of October.

The next session of the Central Committee, with the participation of Lenin in a wig, took place on the tenth of October. It achieved historical significance. The crux of the discussion was Lenin's motion, which proposed armed insurrection as the pressing practical task. The difficulty, even for the most convinced supporter of insurrection, was the question of time. As far back as the days of the Democratic Conference the compromisist Central Executive Committee, under the pressure of the Bolsheviks, had set the twentieth of October as the date for the Congress of the Soviets. Now there was complete assurance of a Bolshevik majority at that congress. At least in Petrograd, the insurrection had to take place before the twentieth; otherwise, the Congress would not be in position to seize the reins of government and would risk being dispersed. It was decided at the Central Committee session, without recording it on paper, to begin the insurrection in Petrograd about the fifteenth. There was, therefore, something like five days left for preparations. Everybody felt that this was not enough. But the Party was a prisoner of the date it had itself imposed upon the compromisers on a different occasion. My announcement that the Executive Committee had decided to organize a military staff of its own did not produce a great impression, because it was more a matter of plan than of fact. Everybody's attention was concentrated on polemics with Zinoviev and Kamenev, who resolutely argued against the insurrection. It seems that Stalin either did not speak at all at this session, or limited himself to a brief remark; at any rate, in the protocols there is no trace of anything he might have said. The motion was passed by ten votes against two. But misgivings about the date remained with all who took part.

Toward the very end of that session, which lasted until way past midnight, on the rather fortuitous initiative of Dzerzhinsky, it was decreed "to organize for the political guidance of the insurrection a bureau consisting of Lenin, Zinoviev, Kamenev, Trotsky, Stalin, Sokolnikov and Bubnov." This important decision, however, led nowhere: Lenin and Zinoviev continued in hiding, Zinoviev and Kamenev became irreconcilably opposed to the decision of October tenth. "The Bureau for the Political Guidance of the Insurrection" did not meet even once. Only its name has been preserved in a pen and ink postscript to the desultory protocol written in pencil. Under the abbreviated name of "the seven" this phantom bureau entered into the official science of history.

The job of organizing the Military Revolutionary Committee of the Soviet went on apace. Of course, the lumbering machinery of Soviet democracy precluded any decided spurt. Yet very little time was left before the Congress. Not without reason did Lenin fear delay. At his request another session of the Central Committee was convoked on the sixteenth of October, with the most important Petrograd organizers present. Zinoviev and Kamenev persisted in their opposition. Formally their position had become stronger than ever: six days had passed and the insurrection had not begun. Zinoviev demanded that the decision be postponed until the Congress of the Soviets met, in order "to confer" with the delegates from the provinces: deep in his heart he was hoping for their support. Passions ran high during the debate. For the first time Stalin took part in this discussion. "Expediency must decide the day of the insurrection," he said, "That alone is the sense of the resolution . . . What Kamenev and Zinoviev propose leads objectively to opportunity for the counter-revolution to organize itself; if we continue to retreat without end, we shall lose the revolution. Why not ourselves name the day and the circumstances, so as not to give the counter-revolution an opportunity to organize itself?" He was defending the Party's abstract right to choose its moment for the blow—when the problem was to set a definite date. Had the Bolshevik Congress of Soviets proved incapable of seizing the reins of government there and then, it would have merely compromised the slogan, "All Power to the Soviets!" by turning it into a hollow phrase. Zinoviev insisted: "We must tell ourselves frankly that we will not attempt an insurrection during the next five days." Kamenev was driving at the same point. Stalin did not meet this issue directly; instead, he wound up with the startling words: "The Petrograd Soviet has already taken the road to insurrection by refusing to sanction the removal of the troops." He was simply reiterating the formula, which had nothing to do with his own abstract speech, that had been recently advocated by the leaders of the Military Revolutionary Committee. But what was the meaning of "being already on the road to insurrection"? Was it a matter of *days* or of *weeks*? Stalin cautiously refrained from making that specific. He was not clear in his own mind about the situation.

The resolution of October tenth was indorsed by a majority of twenty votes to two, with three abstaining. However, nobody had answered the crucial question of whether the decision that the insurrection in Petrograd had to take place prior to the twentieth of October was still valid. It was hard to find that answer. Politically the resolve to have the insurrection before the Congress was absolutely right. But too little time was left for carrying it out. The session of October sixteenth never did manage to reconcile that contradiction. But at this point the compromisers came to the rescue: the very next day, for reasons of their own, they decided to postpone the opening of the Congress, which they hadn't wanted anyway, to the twenty-fifth of October. The Bolsheviks received this unexpected postponement with an open protest but with secret gratitude. Five additional days completely solved the difficulties of the Military Revolutionary Committee.

The Central Committee protocol and the issues of *Pravda* for the last few weeks prior to the insurrection trace Stalin's political career against the background of the insurrection fully enough. Just as before the war he had formally sided with Lenin while at the same time seeking the support of the conciliators against the émigré "crawling on the wall," so now too he aligned himself with the official majority of the Central Committee while simultaneously supporting the Right opposition. As always, he acted cautiously; however, the sweep of events and the acuteness of the conflicts compelled him from time to time to venture farther than he would have liked.

On the eleventh of October, Zinoviev and Kamenev published in Maxim Gorky's newspaper a letter against the insurrection. At once the situation among the leaders of the Party became exceedingly acute. Lenin stormed and fumed in the underground. In order to be free to spread his views about the insurrection, Kamenev resigned from the Central Committee. The question was discussed at the session of October twentieth. Sverdlov made public Lenin's letter which castigated Zinoviev and Kamenev as strikebreakers and demanded their expulsion from the Party. The crisis was unexpectedly complicated by the fact that on that very morning *Pravda* published a declaration by the editorial board in defense of Zinoviev and Kamenev: "The sharpness of the tone of Comrade Lenin's article does not alter the fact that in the main we continue to share his opinion." The central organ deemed it proper to find fault with "the sharpness" of Lenin's protest rather than with the public stand of two Central Committee members against the Party decision on the insurrection and moreover expressed its solidarity with Zinoviev and Kamenev "on fundamentals." As if at that moment there was anything more fundamental than the question of the uprising! The Central Committee members rubbed their eyes with amazement.

Stalin's only associate on the editorial board was Sokolnikov, the future Soviet diplomat and subsequently a victim of the "purge." However, Sokolnikov declared that he had nothing whatever to do with writing the editorial rebuke of Lenin and considered it erroneous. Thus Stalin alone—in opposition to the Central Committee and his own editorial colleague—supported Kamenev and Zinoviev as late as four days before the insurrection. The Central Committee restrained its indignation only because it was apprehensive about extending the crisis.

Continuing to maneuver between the protagonists and opponents of insurrection, Stalin went on record against accepting Kamenev's resignation, arguing that "our entire situation is inconsistent." By five votes, against Stalin's and two others, Kamenev's resignation was accepted. By six votes, again against Stalin's, a resolution was passed, forbidding Kamenev and Zinoviev to wage their fight against the Central Committee. The protocol states: "Stalin declared that he was leaving the editorial board." In his case it meant abandoning the only post he was capable of filling in the circumstances of revolution. But the Central Committee refused to accept Stalin's resignation, thus precluding the development of another rift.

Stalin's behavior might seem inexplicable in the light of the legend that has been created around him; but as a matter of fact, it is quite in line with his inner make-up. Distrust of the masses and suspicious cautiousness force him, in moments of historical decisions to retreat into the shadows, bide his time and, if possible, insure himself coming and going. His defense of Zinoviev and Kamenev was certainly not motivated by sentimental considerations. In April Stalin had changed his official position but not his mental make-up. Although he voted with Lenin, he was far closer in his feelings to Kamenev. Moreover, dissatisfaction with his own role naturally inclined him to align himself with others who were dissatisfied, even if politically he was not in complete accord with them.

All of the last week preceding the insurrection Stalin maneuvered between Lenin, Sverdlov and me on the one hand, and Kamenev and Zinoviev, on the other. At the Central Committee session of October twenty-first he restored the recently upset balance by proposing that Lenin be appointed to prepare the theses for the forthcoming Congress of Soviets and that I be appointed to prepare the political report. Both of these motions passed unanimously. Had there been then any disagreements at all between me and the Central Committee—a canard invented several years later—would the Central Committee upon Stalin's initiative have entrusted me with the most important report at the most crucial moment? Having thus insured himself on the Left, Stalin again retreated into the shadows and bided his time.

The biographer, no matter how willing, can have nothing to say about Stalin's participation in the October Revolution. Nowhere does one find mention of his name—neither in documents nor the numerous memoirs. In order somehow to fill in this yawning gap, the official historiographer implies his participation in the insurrection by connecting the insurrection with some mysterious party "center" that had presumably prepared it. However, no one tells us anything about the activity of that "center," the place and the time of its sessions, the means it employed in directing the insurrection. And no wonder: there never was any such "center." But the story of this legend is noteworthy.

At the October sixteenth conference of the Central Committee with some of the leading Petrograd Party organizers it was decided to organize "a military revolutionary center" of five Central Committee members. "This center," states the resolution hastily written by Lenin in a corner of the hall, "will become a part of the Revolutionary Soviet Committee." Thus, in the direct sense of the decision, "the center" was not designed for independent leadership of the insurrection but to complement the Soviet staff. However, like many other improvisations of those feverish days this idea was fated never to be realized. During the very hours when, in my absence, the Central Committee was organizing a new "center" on a piece of paper, the Petrograd Soviet, under my chairmanship, definitely launched the Military Revolutionary Committee, which from the moment of its origin was in complete charge of all the preparations for the insurrection. Sverdlov, whose name appeared first (and not Stalin's name, as is falsely recorded in recent Soviet publications) on the list of the "center" members, worked before and after the resolution of October sixteenth in close contact with the Chairman of the Military Revolutionary Committee. Three other members of the "center," Uritsky, Dzerzhinsky and Bubnov, were drawn into work for the Military Revolutionary Committee, each of them individually, as late as October twenty-fourth, as if the resolution of October sixteenth had never been passed. As for Stalin, in line with his entire policy of behavior at that period, he stubbornly kept from joining either the Executive Committee of the Petrograd Soviet or the Military Revolutionary Committee, and did not appear at any of its sessions. All of these circumstances are easily established on the basis of officially published protocols.

At the Central Committee session of October twentieth the "center" created four days before was supposed to make a report about its work or at least mention that it had begun working: only five days remained before the Congress of Soviets, and the insurrection was supposed to precede the opening of the Congress. Stalin was too busy for that. Defending Zinoviev and Kamenev, he submitted his resignation from the editorial board of *Pravda* at that very session. But not one of the other members of the "center" present at the session—Sverdlov, Dzerzhinsky, Uritsky—bothered to drop even a hint about it. The protocol record of the October sixteenth session had evidently been carefully put away, in order to hide all traces of Lenin's "illegal" participation in it, and during the ensuing four dramatic days the "center" was all the easier forgotten because the very need of any such supplementary institution was absolutely excluded by the intense activity of the Military Revolutionary Committee.

At the very next session, on October twenty-first, with Stalin, Sverdlov and Dzerzhinsky present, there was again no report about the "center" and not even any mention of it. The Central Committee carried on as if there had never been any resolution whatever passed about a "center." Incidentally, it was at this session that it was decided to put ten more prominent Bolsheviks, among them Stalin, onto the Executive Committee of the Petrograd Soviet for the purpose of improving its activity. But that was just another resolution that remained on paper.

Preparations for the insurrection proceeded apace, but along an entirely different channel. The actual master of the capital's garrison, the Military Revolutionary Committee, was seeking an excuse for openly breaking with the Government. That pretext was provided on October twenty-second by the officer commanding the troops of the district when he refused to let the Committee's commissars control his staff. We had to strike while the iron was hot. The Bureau of the Military Revolutionary Committee, Sverdlov and I participating, decided to recognize the break with the garrison staff as an accomplished fact and to take the offensive. Stalin was not at this conference. It never occurred to anyone to call him. Whenever the burning of all bridges was at stake, no one mentioned the existence of the so-called "center."

The Central Committee session that directly launched the insurrection was held at Smolny, now transformed into a fortress, on the morning of October twenty-fourth. At the very outset a motion of Kamenev's[2] was passed: "No member of the Central Committee may absent himself from Smolny today without special dispensation." The report of the Military Revolutionary Committee was on the agenda. At that very moment when the insurrection began there was no mention of the so-called "center." The protocol states: "Trotsky proposed that two members of the Central Committee be placed at the disposal of the Military Revolutionary Committee for maintaining contact with the post and telegraph operators and the railway men; a third member to keep an eye on the Provisional Government." Dzerzhinsky was assigned to the post and telegraph operators,

[2] Kamenev had meantime been reinstated as a member of the Central Committee.—L. T.

Bubnov to the railwaymen. Sverdlov was delegated to keep a watchful eye over the Provisional Government. Further: "Trotsky proposed the establishment of a reserve staff in the Peter and Paul Fortress and the assignment of one member of the Central Committee there for that purpose. Resolved: 'Sverdlov delegated to maintain constant contact with the Fortress.'" Thus three members of the "center" were for the first time placed at the direct disposal of the Military Revolutionary Committee. Naturally, that would not have been necessary had the "center" existed and been occupied with preparing the insurrection. The protocol records that a fourth member of the "center," Uritsky, made some practical suggestions. But where was the fifth member, Stalin?

Most amazing of all is the fact that Stalin was not even present at this decisive session. Central Committee members obligated themselves not to leave Smolny. But Stalin did not even show up in the first place. This is irrefutably attested to by the protocols published in 1929. Stalin never explained his absence, either orally or in writing. No one made any issue of it, probably in order not to provoke unnecessary trouble. All the most important decisions on conducting the insurrection were made without Stalin, without even the slightest indirect participation by him. When the parts were being assigned to the various actors in that drama, no one mentioned Stalin or proposed any sort of appointment for him. He simply dropped out of the game. Did he perhaps run his "center" from some secret hiding place? But all the other members of the "center" stayed continually at Smolny.

During the hours when the open insurrection had already begun Lenin, who was aflame with impatience in his isolation, appealed to the district leaders: "Comrades! I am writing these lines on the evening of the twenty-fourth . . . I assure you with all my strength that now everything hangs by a thread, that we are confronted with issues which cannot be decided by conferences or by congresses (not even by Soviet Congresses), but exclusively by the struggle of the armed masses . . ." It is perfectly clear from this letter that until the very evening of October twenty-fourth Lenin knew nothing about the launching of the offensive by the Military Revolutionary Committee. Contact with Lenin was chiefly maintained through Stalin, because he was one of those in whom the police showed not the slightest interest. Unavoidable is the inference that having failed to come to the Central Committee session in the morning and having stayed away from Smolny throughout the rest of the day, Stalin did not find out that the insurrection had already begun and was in full swing until rather late that evening. Not that he was a coward. There is no basis for accusing Stalin of cowardice. He was simply politically non-committal. The cautious schemer preferred to stay on the fence at the crucial moment. He was waiting to see how the insurrection turned out before committing himself to a position. In the event of failure he could tell Lenin, and me and our adherents: "It's all your fault!" One must clearly recapture the red-hot temper of those days in order to appreciate according to its deserts the man's cool grit or, if you like, his insidiousness.

No, Stalin did not lead the insurrection—either personally or by means of some "center." In the protocols, reminiscences, countless documents, works of reference, history textbooks published while Lenin was alive, and even later, the so-called "center" was never mentioned and Stalin's name either as its leader or as a prominent participant in the insurrection in some other capacity was not mentioned by anyone. The Party's memory passed him by. It was only in 1924 that the Committee on Party History, in the course of collecting all sorts of data, dug up the minutes of the session of October sixteenth with the text of the resolution to organize a practical "center." The fight against the Left Opposition and against me personally which was then raging called for a new version of Party history and the history of the Revolution. I remember that Serebryakov, who had friends and contacts everywhere, told me once that there was great rejoicing in Stalin's secretariat over the discovery of the "center."

"Of what significance could that possibly be?" I asked in astonishment.

"They are going to wind something around that bobbin," the shrewd Serebryakov replied.

Yet even then the matter of the "center" did not go beyond a repeat reprint of the protocol and vague references to it. The events of 1917 were still too fresh in everybody's memory. The participants of the Revolution had not yet been liquidated. Dzerzhinsky and Bubnov, who were listed as members of the "center," were still alive. Out of sheer factional fanaticism Dzerzhinsky was, of course, quite capable of agreeing to ascribe to Stalin achievements which the latter did not have to his credit; but he was not capable of ascribing such achievements to himself: that was beyond his power. Dzerzhinsky died in due time. One of the causes of Bubnov's fall from grace and his liquidation was undoubtedly his refusal to bear false witness. No one else remembered anything about the "center's" existence. The phantom of the protocol continued to lead its protocolish existence—sans bones or flesh, sans ears or eyes.

That did not preclude it from being turned into the nucleus of a new version of the October Revolution. In 1925 Stalin was already arguing, "It is strange that Comrade Trotsky, the 'inspirer,' 'chief figure,' and 'sole leader' of the insurrection was not a member of the practical center which was called upon to lead the insurrection. How is it possible to reconcile that with the current opinion about Comrade Trotsky's special role?" The argument was patently illogical: according to the precise sense of the resolution, the "center" was to have become a part of the very same Military Revolutionary Committee of which I was Chairman. Stalin fully exposed his intention of "winding" a new history of the insurrection around that protocol. What he failed to explain was the source of "the current opinion about Trotsky's special role." Yet that might be worth considering.

The following is contained under my name in the notes to the first edition of Lenin's Works: "After the Petersburg Soviet passed into the hands of the Bolsheviks [Trotsky] was elected its President and as such organized and led the insurrection of the 25th of October." The "legend" thus found a place for itself in Lenin's Works during their author's lifetime. It never occurred to anyone to challenge it until 1925. Moreover, Stalin himself at one time paid his tribute to this "current opinion." In the first anniversary article, in 1918, he wrote: "All the work of practical organization of the insurrection was conducted under the direct leadership of the President of the Petrograd Soviet, Comrade Trotsky. It may be said with certainty that the swift passing of the garrison to the side of the Soviet, and the bold execution of the work of the Military Revolutionary Committee, the Party owes principally and above all to Comrade Trotsky. Comrades Antonov and Podvoisky were Comrade Trotsky's chief assistants." Today these words sound like a panegyric. As a matter of fact, what the author had in the back of his mind was to remind the Party that during the days of the insurrection, in addition to Trotsky, there existed also the Central Committee, of which Stalin was a member. But forced to invest his article with at least a semblance of objectivity, Stalin could not have avoided saying in 1918 what he did say. Anyway, on the first anniversary of the Soviet Government he ascribed "the practical organization of the insurrection" to Trotsky. What then was the mysterious role of the "center"? Stalin did not even mention it; it was then still six years before the discovery of the protocol of October sixteenth.

In 1920, no longer mentioning Trotsky, Stalin advanced Lenin against the Central Committee as the author of the erroneous plan for. insurrection. He repeated this in 1922, but substituted for Lenin, "one part of the comrades," and cautiously intimated that he (Stalin) had something to do with saving the insurrection from the erroneous plan. Another two years passed, and it seems that Trotsky was the one who had maliciously invented the canard about Lenin's erroneous plan; indeed, Trotsky himself proposed the erroneous plan, which was fortunately rejected by the Central Committee. Finally, the "History" of the Party, published in 1938, represented Trotsky as a rabid opponent of the October Revolution, which had really been conducted by Stalin. Parallel to all this occurred the mobilization of all the arts: poetry, painting, the theater, the cinema, suddenly discovered the urge to invest the mythical "center" with the breath of life, although the most assiduous historians were unable to find any trace of it with a magnifying glass. Today Stalin figures as the leader of the October Revolution on the screens of the world, not to mention the publications of the Comintern.

The facts of history were revised in the same way, although perhaps not quite so flagrantly, with regard to all the Old Bolsheviks, time and time again, depending on changing political combinations. In 1917 Stalin defended Zinoviev and Kamenev, in an attempt to use them against Lenin and me and in preparation for his future "triumvirate." In 1924, when the "triumvirate" already controlled the political machine, Stalin argued in the press that the differences of opinion with Zinoviev and Kamenev prior to October were of a fleeting and secondary character. "The differences lasted only a few days because, and only because, in the person of Kamenev and Zinoviev we had Leninists, Bolsheviks." After the "triumvirate" fell apart, Zinoviev's and Kamenev's behavior in 1917 figured for a number of years as the chief reason for denouncing them as "agents of the bour-

1. Leon Trotsky in his study at Coyoacan, Mexico, at work on his biography of Stalin

2. Gori Theological School, where Soso (Stalin) received his elementary education
(*Inset*) Stalin as a schoolboy

3. Class picture, Gori Theological School: Soso, top row center

4. On June 12, 1905, Stalin delivered his first funeral oration at the bier of mentor and comrade Sasha Tsulukidze

5. Victor Kurnatovsky, organizer of the first Social-Democratic Committee in Tiflis

6. Lado Ketskhoveli, organizer of the first Marxist underground printshop in Trans-Caucasia

7. Professional Revolutionist Stalin as Oganess Vartanovich Totomyants (1909)

9. Baïlov Prison, Baku

8. Rogues Gallery record of Stalin made by the Baku Gendarmerie in
April, 1910, on the occasion of Stalin's return to Baïlov Prison

10. Suren Spandaryan and Stalin in 1915 during their exile in
Monastyrskoye, Turukhansk, Siberia

11. Prokofii Aprasionovich
Dzhaparidze (Alyosha)

12. Stepan Grigoryevich
Sha'umyan

13. Gregory Constantinovich
Ordzhonikidze (Sergo)

14. Vyacheslav Molotov in student uniform during the
underground Bolshevik days

16. Stalin in 1912, about the time of his co-optation to the Bolshevik Central Committee

15. Lenin in 1914

17. A Postcard widely circulated on the first anniversary of the Bolshevik coup, entitled "The Leaders of the Proletarian Revolution," showing (1) Lenin, (2) Trotsky, (3) Zinoviev, (4) Lunacharsky, (5) Kamenev, (6) Sverdlov

18. Stalin in Tsaritsyn, 1918

19. Commissar of War Leon Trotsky addressing Red Army soldiers during the War with Poland in 1920

20. *Kinto* on the Road to Power (1920)

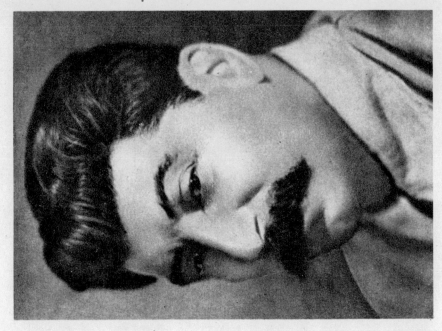

22. Stalin in the spring of 1922, when he became
General Secretary

21. Stalin's Mother—
Ekaterina Georgievna Geladze-Djugashvili

23. Stalin, Lenin, Kalinin—at the Eighth Congress of the Party, in March, 1919

24. Ordzhonikidze   25. Kirov   26. Yenukidze

27. Yagoda   28. Vyshinsky   29. Beriya

30. Stalin and workers, Moscow, March 1, 1927

31. Stalin with his daughter Svetlana in 1935

32. A group of Oppositionists on their way to exile in 1928: from left to right—
seated: Serebryakov, Radek, Trotsky, Boguslavsky, Preobrazhensky;
standing: Rakovsky, Drobnis, Beloborodov, Sosnovsky

33. Stalin and his friends. Reading from left to right:—first row—all unknown;
second row: unknown, Eliava, Stalin, unknown, Voroshilov; third row
(standing): all unknown

34. Red Army Marshals (as of 1936). Reading from left to right: Tukhachevsky, Yegorov, Voroshilov, Budenny. The first two have been liquidated

35. Building up the slogan: "Stalin Is Lenin Today!"

geoisie," until finally it was included in the fatal indictment which brought both of them to the firing squad.

One is forced to pause in sheer amazement before the cold, patient and at the same time cruel persistence directed toward one invariably personal goal. Just as at one time in Batum the youthful Koba had persistently undermined the members of the Tiflis Committee who were his superiors; just as in prison and in exile he had incited simpletons against his rivals, so now in Petrograd he tirelessly schemed with people and circumstances, in order to push aside, derogate, blacken, belittle anyone who in one way or another eclipsed him or interfered with his ambition.

Naturally the October Revolution, as the source of the new régime, has assumed the central position in the ideology of the new ruling circles. How did it all happen? Who led at the center and in the branches? Stalin had to have practically twenty years to impose upon the country a historical panorama, in which he replaced the actual organizers of the insurrecton and ascribed to them roles as the Revolution's betrayers. It would be incorrect to think that he started out with a finished plan of action for personal aggrandizement. Extraordinary historical circumstances invested his ambition with a sweep startling even to himself. In one way he remained invariably consistent: regardless of all other considerations, he used each concrete situation to entrench his own position at the expense of his comrades—step by step, stone by stone, patiently, without passion, but also without mercy! It is in the uninterrupted weaving of intrigues, in the cautious doling out of truth and falsehood, in the organic rhythm of his falsifications that Stalin is best reflected as a human personality and as the leader of the new privileged stratum, which, by and large, has to concoct fresh biographies for itself.

Having made a bad beginning in March, which was not improved in April, Stalin stayed behind the scenes throughout the year of the Revolution. He never knew direct association with the masses and never felt responsible for the fate of the Revolution. At certain moments he was chief of staff, never the commander-in-chief. Preferring to keep his peace, he waited for others to take the initiative, took note of their weaknesses and mistakes, and himself lagged behind developments. He had to have a certain stability of relations and a lot of time at his disposal in order to succeed. The Revolution deprived him of both.

Never forced to analyze the problems of revolution under that mental pressure which is generated only by the feeling of immediate responsibility, Stalin never acquired an intimate understanding of the October Revolution's inherent logic. That is why his recollections of it are so empirical, scattered and inco-ordinate, his latter-day judgments on the strategy of the insurrection so contradictory, his mistakes in a number of latter-day revolutions (Germany, China, Spain) so monstrous. Truly, revolution is not the element of this former "professional revolutionist."

Nevertheless, 1917 was a most important stage in the growth of the future dictator. He himself said later that at Tiflis he was a schoolboy, at Baku he turned an apprentice, in Petrograd he became a craftsman. After four years of political and intellectual hibernation in Siberia, where he descended to the level of the Left Mensheviks, the year of the Revolution, during which he was under the direct leadership of Lenin, in the circle of highly qualified comrades, had immeasurable significance in his political development. For the first time he had the opportunity to learn much that hitherto had been beyond the range of his experience. He listened and observed with malevolence, but sharply and vigilantly. At the core of political life was the problem of power. The Provisional Government, supported by the Mensheviks and the Populists, yesterday's comrades of the underground, prison and exile, enabled him to look more closely into that mysterious laboratory where, as everybody knows, it is not gods that glaze the pots. The unspannable distance, which in the epoch of Tsarism separated the underground revolutionists from the government, shrank into nothing. The government became something close, a familiar concept. Koba threw off much of his provincialism, if not in habits and customs, at least in the measure of his political thinking. He sensed—keenly, resentfully—what he lacked as an individual, but at the same time he tested the power of a closely knit collection of gifted and experienced revolutionists ready to fight to the bitter end. He became a recognized member of the general staff of the party the masses were bearing to power. He stopped being Koba. He definitely became Stalin.

Chapter VIII

PEOPLE'S COMMISSAR

[The Bolsheviks had laid the groundwork of winning over the armed forces of the country so thoroughly that their final victory on November 7th was achieved practically by default. The October coup was "easier than lifting a feather"—to use Lenin's own words. Not a single regiment rose to defend Russian democracy. With the former police force scattered, the Kerensky Government in Petrograd had practically no one other than the military students and the very amateurish women's battalions to oppose the detachments of armed workmen, soldiers and sailors under the command of Bolshevik professional revolutionists. The struggle for supreme power over an empire that comprised one-sixth of the terrestrial globe was decided between amazingly small forces on both sides in the provinces as well as in the two capital cities.

[The civilized democratic West, heading into its fourth year of war, refused to believe the accomplished fact. After the Bolsheviks had been in power for nearly a week, Kerensky sincerely assured the astonished world that Bolshevism "as an organized force . . . no longer exists, even in Petrograd." The Bolshevik victory had been easier and more secure in Petrograd than in Moscow and in the provinces. The Cossacks stationed in Petrograd were "neutral"—even as General Headquarters and all the avowed reactionaries—refraining from extending aid to the Provisional Government and reserving the right to act at their own discretion, while General Krassnov was marching upon the capital with an unknown number of troops. The officials and clerks of the banks, the ministries, and practically all public administration institutions had walked out on strike. The Menshevik-led railway, telephone, telegraph and postal workers' unions threatened to strike and tie up all communication and transportation services unless the victors agreed to a coalition government of all the socialist parties, but without the participation of Lenin and Trotsky. That threat produced a crisis more apparent than real in the leadership of the Bolshevik Party itself.]

Immediately after the insurrection, upon the insistence of the Bolshevik Right Wing—Zinoviev, Kamenev, Rykov, Lunacharsky and others—negotiations were begun with the Mensheviks and the Populists concerning a coalition government. Among the conditions, the parties overthrown by the uprising demanded a majority for themselves, and over and above that, the removal from the government of Lenin and myself as the persons responsible for the October "adventure." The Rightist members of the Central Committee were inclined to accept this demand. The question was considered in the Central Committee during the session of the first (the 14th) of November. This is what the protocol states: "Proposed to expel Lenin and Trotsky. This is a proposal to behead our Party, and we do not accept it." The readiness of the Rightists to go as far as an actual surrender of power was condemned by the Central Committee as "fear of the Soviet Majority to utilize its own majority." The Bolsheviks did not refuse to share their power with other parties, but would share it only on the basis of the proper relation of forces in the Soviets. Lenin declared that the negotiations with the petty bourgeois parties had sense only as a cover for military actions. [As far as Lenin was concerned the negotiations were not in earnest and were meant rather as a political decoy.]

My motion to terminate the negotiations with the Compromisers was passed. Stalin took no part in the debates. But he voted with the majority. In protest, the representatives of the Rightists resigned from the Central Committee and the Government. The majority of the Central Committee addressed the minority with the demand to submit unconditionally to the discipline of the Party. The ultimatum was signed by ten members and candidates of the Central Committee: Lenin, myself, Stalin, Sverdlov and others. Concerning the origin of the document, one of the members of the Central Committee, Bubnov, states: "After writing it he (Lenin) invited into his office individually each of the members of the Central Committee, acquainting them with the text of the declaration and suggesting that they sign it." The story is interesting in so far as it enables us correctly to evaluate the significance of the order of the signatures. Lenin first of all showed the ultimatum to me and, having secured my signature, called out the others, beginning with Stalin. It was always thus, or almost always. Had the document not been directed against Zinoviev and Kamenev, their signatures would probably have stood before Stalin's signature.

Pestkovsky tells how during the October days "it was necessary to select from among the Central Committee the leadership of the insurrection. Selected were Lenin, Stalin and Trotsky." In assigning the leadership to these three, let us note in passing Stalin's collaborator definitely buries the practical "center," of which neither Lenin nor I were members. In Pestkovsky's testimony there is this time a kernel of truth. Not during the days of the uprising but after its victory in the important centers, yet before the establishment of any kind of stable régime, it was necessary to create a compact Party staff, that could enforce locally all the necessary decisions. As the protocol states, on the 29th of November (12th of December) 1917, the Central Committee elected for the solution of pressing questions a bureau composed of four persons: "Stalin, Lenin, Trotsky and Sverdlov." "This foursome was given the right to decide all extraordinary affairs, but with the obligation of drawing into the decision all members of the Central Committee who were present at the time at Smolny." Zinoviev, Kamenev, Rykov, because of their sharp disagreement, had resigned from the Central Committee. This explains the composition of the foursome. Sverdlov, however, was absorbed by the Secretariat of the Party, spoke at meetings, settled conflicts and was seldom at the Smolny. The foursome practically came down to a threesome.

[On the night of February 19th-20th, 1918, the coalition Bolshevik-Left Essar Council of the People's Commissars] elected an executive committee [made up of] Lenin, Trotsky, Stalin, Proshyan and Karelin, which was authorized to carry on all current work in the interim between the sessions of the Council. [This executive committee of the Government was made up of the same three Bolsheviks and the two Left Essars. Nevertheless, there is no ground for imagining that these three made up] a "triumvirate." The Central Committee met frequently and decided all the important and particularly debatable questions. The threesome was necessary for unpostponable practical decisions in connection with the course of the uprising in the provinces, Kerensky's attempts to enter Petrograd, food supply for the capital, and the like. This threesome existed, at least nominally, only until the transfer of the government to Moscow.

Lashing out against the policy of the Bolsheviks after 1917, Iremashvili writes: "The triumvirate, filled with unappeasable vengeance, began to exterminate with inhuman cruelty everything living and dead," and the like. In the triumvirate Iremashvili includes Lenin, myself and Stalin. It may be said with assurance that this idea of the triumvirate arose in the mind of Iremashvili only considerably later, after Stalin had advanced to the first plane of importance. There is, however, a grain of truth—or, at any rate, a semblance of truth—in these words of Iremashvili's. In connection with the negotiations in Brest-Litovsk, Lenin's words, "I'll consult Stalin and give you an answer" are cited time and time again. The point is that such a threesome did actually exist at certain moments, although not always with the participation of Stalin. Dmitrievsky likewise refers to this threesome, although in a somewhat different tone and point of reference:

> Even Lenin at that period felt the need of Stalin to such an extent that when communications came from Trotsky at Brest and an immediate decision had to be made while Stalin was not in Moscow, Lenin would inform Trotsky:
> "I would like first to consult with Stalin before replying to your question."
> And only three days later Lenin would telegraph: "Stalin has just arrived. I will consider it with him and we will at once give you our joint answer."

The most important decisions of that period were not infrequently arrived at by Lenin in agreement with me. But in this case, when such agreement was not reached, a third person was needed. Zinoviev was in Petersburg, Kamenev was not always in Moscow. Besides, he, like other members of the Politburo and the Central Committee, devoted a considerable portion of his time to agitation. Stalin had more free time than all the other members of the Politburo from agitation, leadership of the Soviets, and the rest. That was why prior to his departure from Tsaritsyn he usually carried out the duties of the "third one." Lenin was a stickler for form and therefore naturally did not take it upon himself to reply in his own name alone. Generally, the not infrequent remarks in recent literature to the effect that Lenin directed, ordered and the like, are inspired solely by analogy with the Stalinist régime. As a matter of fact, such a state of affairs didn't exist at all. Directives were actually given, and moreover orders issued, only by the Politburo, and during the absence of the complete staff, by the three-some, which made up the quorum of the five members of the Bureau. When Stalin was away, Lenin would consult with Krestinsky, Secretary of the Central Committee, with the same scrupulousness, and in the archives can be found any number of recorded references to such consultations.

But at the time there was far more talk of a *"duumvirate."* During the Civil War the Soviet "poet laureate" Demyan Byedny wrote verses about "our two-some." No one then spoke of a triumvirate. At any rate any one using that term then would have selected as the third person not Stalin, but Sverdlov, who was the very popular Chairman of the Central Executive Committee of the Soviets, and who signed all the more important decrees. I remember speaking to him several times about the insufficient authority of certain of our directives in the prov-inces. On one such occasion Sverdlov remarked: "Locally, they accept only three signatures: Ilyich's, yours and also to a small extent mine." [Sverdlov was a person of truly remarkable organizational talents and a prodigious capacity for hard work—head and shoulders above Stalin.] "No one could so unite in him-self alone organizational and political work as Sverdlov was able to do," Lenin said at the Party Congress in 1920, "and we had to try to replace his activity with the work of a collegium."

When I arrived in Petrograd at the beginning of May, I hardly remembered Stalin's name. I probably ran across it in the Bolshevik press, signed to articles which hardly held my attention. My first meetings were with Kamenev, Lenin, Zinoviev. With them were carried on negotiations about fusion. Neither at the sessions of the Soviets, nor of its Central Executive Committee, nor at the nu-merous meetings which consumed a considerable part of my time, did I meet Stalin. Upon arrival, I immediately came into close contact with all the leading figures by virtue of my work in the Central Executive Committee, but I did not notice Stalin even among the second-rate members of the Central Committee, such as Bubnov, Milutin, Nogin and others. [After the fusion of the Inter-districters (*Mezhraiontsy*) with the Bolsheviks, Stalin continued to remain an obscure figure.] "In the Praesidium of the Pre-parliament," state the protocols of the Party Central Committee, "Trotsky and Kamenev represented the Bol-sheviks." [When the time came to send leading representatives of the Party to the repeatedly deferred Constituent Assembly, which was supposed to determine in a democratic parliamentary manner the future government of Russia, Stalin was used as the spokesman of the Party Central Committee to nominate them. As the record shows, Stalin's words were:] "Comrades, I propose as candidates to the Constituent Assembly Comrades Lenin, Zinoviev, Kollontai, Trotsky and Lunarcharsky." These were the five persons who were put forth in the name of the entire Party. Let us recall that [according to the official historiography] only two weeks before I, together with the Mensheviks and the Essars, had presumably demanded Lenin's appearance in court.

In the complete list of Bolshevik delegates to the Constituent Assembly headed by Lenin, Stalin's name stands in eighth place. The twenty-five nominees were first official candidates of the Central Committee. The list was worked over by a commission under the leadership of three members of the Central Committee: Uritsky, Sokolnikov and Stalin. Lenin sharply protested against the list: there were too many doubtful intellectuals on it, too few reliable workers.

> ★ Utterly inadmissible also was the disproportionate number of candidates from insufficiently-tested persons who had joined our party quite recently (like U. Larin). Filling the list with such candidates who should have really worked months and months in the Party, the Central Committee opens the door wide for careerism, for the seeking of places in the Constituent Assembly. It is necessary to have an extraordinary review and correction of the list . . . It is self-evident that from among the Inter-districters [Mezhraiontsy] altogether little tested in proletarian work and the direction of our Party no one would contest, for example, such a candidature as that of L. D. Trotsky, for in the first place, Trotsky immediately upon arrival assumed the position of the internationalists; in the second place, he fought among the inter-districters for fusion; in the third place, during the difficult July Days he proved fully equal to the tasks and was loyal champion of the Party of the revolutionary proletariat. It is clear that this cannot be said about many of the members who joined the Party yesterday, whose name appears on the list . . .

Of the twenty-five [Bolshevik representatives], thirteen were subsequently meted out punishments by Stalin or were condemned after death.

After the conquest of power, Stalin began to feel more sure of himself, remaining, however, a figure of the second rank. I soon noticed that Lenin was "advancing" Stalin, valuing in him his firmness, grit, stubbornness, and to a certain extent his slyness, as attributes necessary in the struggle. He did not expect of him any independent ideas, political initiative or creative imagination. Stalin proceeded slowly and cautiously; wherever possible he kept still. But the victory in Petrograd and later in Moscow convinced him. He began to accustom himself to power. "After October," writes Alliluyev, "Stalin moved into the Smolny and settled there in two small rooms on the ground floor." [He was a member of the first Council of People's Commissars as Commissar of Nationalities.] After the Revolution the first session of the Bolshevik Government took place in Smolny, in Lenin's office, where an unpainted wooden partition segregated the cubbyhole of the telephone girl and the typist. Stalin and I were the first to arrive. From behind the partition we heard the thick basso of Dybenko. He was speaking by telephone with Finland, and the conversation had a rather tender character. The twenty-nine-year-old, black-bearded sailor, a jolly and self-confident giant, had recently become intimate with Alexandra Kollontai, a woman of aristocratic antecedents who knew a half dozen foreign languages and was approaching her forty-sixth year. In certain circles of the Party there was undoubtedly a good deal of gossip about this. Stalin, with whom until then I had not carried on a personal conversation, came up to me with a kind of unexpected jauntiness and, pointing with his shoulder toward the partition, said, smirking: "That's he with Kollontai, with Kollontai!" His gestures and his laughter seemed to me out of place and unendurably vulgar, especially on that occasion and in that place. I don't remember whether I simply said nothing, turning my eyes away, or answered drily, "That's their affair." But Stalin sensed that he had made a mistake. His face changed, and in his yellow eyes appeared the same glint of animosity that I had noticed in Vienna.[1] From that time on he never again attempted to engage me in conversation on personal themes.

At the end of January, 1918, as a representative of the Party, Stalin participated in a conference of representatives of several foreign Left Socialist parties. That conference, which decided to convoke the Left Internationalist Conference, came to the conclusion that "an international Socialist conference . . . should be convoked under the following conditions: firstly, that the parties and organizations agree to take the path of revolutionary struggle against 'their own governments' for immediate peace; and secondly, that they support the Russian October Revolution and the Soviet Government."

At the time of the Brest-Litovsk negotiations, the Constituent Assembly was dissolved. The initiative was Lenin's, who also took the lead in working out the corresponding device. During the same days was published "The Declaration of the Rights of Toilers and the Exploited Peoples." On the text of these historical documents are corrections introduced by Bukharin and Stalin. "Most of their corrections," states a footnote to the *Works* of Lenin "do not have a principled character."

The posts that Stalin occupied during the first years after the Revolution and the sundry assignments, predominantly of an organizational and diplomatic character, which he carried out, were exceedingly varied. But such was the portion of the majority of responsible functionaries of those times. Directly or indirectly, everybody was occupied with the Civil War; routine duties were usually placed on the shoulders of the closest assistants. Stalin was listed as a member of the editorial board of the central organ, but as a matter of fact had practically nothing to do with *Pravda*. He carried out more systematic work, interrupted by journeys to the front, in the Commissariat of Nationalities. The Soviet state was just forming itself, and it was not easy to determine in the new fashion this inter-relationship of the various nationalities. The general guidance of this work, not to mention the initiative, was completely Lenin's, who since time immemorial had accorded to the national question a tremendous significance, second in importance only to the agrarian question. It is evident from the diary of his secretariat how often he received all sorts of national delegations and addressed

[1] Trotsky first met Stalin in Vienna early in 1913, when Stalin was engaged in writing his essay, "Marxism and the National Problem." At that time Trotsky was not a member of the Bolshevik faction of the Social-Democratic Party.—C. M.

letters, inquiries and instructions with reference to one or another national group. All the more principal measures had to pass through the Politburo; the less important ones were considered by telephone with Lenin. On the Commissariat of Nationalities was imposed merely the technical performance of decisions already made.

Information concerning the work of this Commissariat can be found in the memoirs of Pestkovsky, published in 1922 and 1930. He was Stalin's closest assistant during the first twenty months of the Soviet régime. An old Polish revolutionist who had been condemned to hard labor in Siberia, and a participant of the October insurrection who held the most varied positions after the victory, including among them the post of Soviet Minister to Mexico in 1924-1926, Pestkovsky was for a long time in one of the oppositional groups, but managed to repent in time. The brand of recent repentance lies on the second edition of these memoirs, but it does not deprive them either of freshness or interest.

The initiative in their collaboration was taken by Pestkovsky, who knocked on various doors, seeking and not finding application for his modest talents.

> ★ "Comrade Stalin," said I, "are you the People's Commissar for the affairs of the nationalities?"
> "Yes."
> "But have you a Commissariat?"
> "No."
> "Well, then, I will make you a Commissariat."
> "All right, but what do you need for that?"
> "For the present, merely a mandate."
> At this point Stalin, who hated to waste words, went to the executive offices of the Council of People's Commissars and several minutes later returned with a mandate.

In one of the rooms of the Smolny already occupied Pestkovsky found a vacant table and placed it against the wall, pinning above it a sheet of paper with the inscription: "People's Commissariat for the Affairs of the Nationalities." To all this two chairs were added.

> ★ "Comrade Stalin," said I, "we haven't a farthing to our name." In those days the new government had not yet taken possession of the State bank.
> "Do you need much?" asked Stalin.
> "To begin with, a thousand roubles will do."
> "Come in an hour."
> When I appeared an hour later Stalin ordered me to borrow three thousand roubles from Trotsky. "He has money. He found it in the former Ministry of Foreign Affairs." I went to Trotsky and gave him the formal receipt for three thousand roubles. As far as I know, the People's Commissariat of Nationalities has not yet returned this money to Comrade Trotsky.

[Stalin was at the side of Lenin] on the 9th (22nd) of November, 1917, from two to half past four in the morning, when Vladimir Ilyich, carrying on negotiations by direct wire with Commander-in-Chief General Dukhonnin, issued orders about the immediate beginning of peace negotiations with all countries at war. After Dukhonnin's refusal, he wrote the order for his removal and the appointment of N. V. Krylenko, as Commander-in-Chief. [Apropos of incidents such as this] Pestkovsky writes that Stalin became "Lenin's deputy in the leadership of fighting revolutionary actions. He was in charge of watching after military operations on the Don, the Ukraine, and in other parts of Russia." The word "deputy" does not fit here; it would be more correct to say "technical assistant." Since observation of the course of the Civil War in the country was carried on principally through the intermediacy of direct telegraphic wire, this function too was carried on by Stalin, because he had more time from his duties than any other member of the Central Committee.

Stalin's conversations by direct wire were essentially semi-technical, semi-political in character. He was carrying out instructions. Extremely interesting is one of his very first conversations by direct wire on the 17th (30th) of November, 1917, with the representative of the Ukrainian Rada, Porsh. The Ukrainian Rada was similar to the government of Kerensky. It was supported by the top layer of the petty bourgeoisie. No doubt it also had the support of the upper bourgeoisie and of the Allies against the Bolsheviks. The Ukrainian Soviets were at the same time falling under the influence of the Bolsheviks and were in direct opposition to the Rada. A clash between the Soviets and the Rada was unavoidable, especially after the October Revolution in Petrograd and Moscow. Porsh, in the name of the Rada, asked what was the attitude of the Petrograd government toward the national question in general and the fate of the Ukraine and its internal régime in particular. Stalin answered with generalities. "The power in the Ukraine, as in other regions," said Stalin, "should belong to the entire totality of Workers', Soldiers' and Peasants' Deputies, including in it also the organization of the Rada. In that sphere there is a broad field for agreement between the Central Rada and the Soviet of People's Commissars." This was precisely the combination that the Mensheviks and the Essars demanded after the October Revolution, and it was on this question that the negotiations conducted by Kamenev had broken down.

At the direct wire in Kiev, alongside the Ukrainian Minister Porsh, was the Bolshevik, Sergei Bakinsky, who likewise demanded answers to questions. They controlled one another. Bakinsky represented the Soviets. He stated that the Central Rada did not deem it possible to transfer the power locally to the Soviets. Replying to Bakinsky, Stalin said that if the Central Rada should refuse to convoke a Congress of Soviets with the Bolsheviks, then "convoke it without the Rada." Further: "The government of the Soviets must be accepted locally. This is the one revolutionary commandment we cannot repudiate, and we do not understand how the Ukrainian Central Rada can argue against an axiom."

A quarter of an hour earlier Stalin had declared that it was possible to combine the Soviets with the democratic organizations of the Rada; now he was declaring for the government of the Soviets without any sort of combination as an axiom. How to explain this contradiction? We have no documents at hand. But the mechanics behind the conversation are quite clear. During the negotiations Stalin was sending the tape from the lower story of the Smolny to the upper story, to Lenin. Having read Stalin's proposal about combining the Soviets with the organizations of the Rada, Lenin could not have done otherwise than to send him a severe note. Perhaps he even ran downstairs into the telegraph room in order to tell Stalin what he thought about it. Stalin did not argue, and in the second part of his conversation gave an instruction directly opposite to the one which he had given in the first part.

As a member of the Politburo, Stalin was included in the delegation from the Russian Communist Party to the Congress of the Finnish Socialist Party. But this inclusion was purely nominal in character. Stalin did not take part in the work of the Congress. "When at the end of December, 1917, the Congress of the Finnish Socialist Party took place," writes Pestkovsky, "there arose the question as to whom the working class of Finland would follow. The Central Committee of the Bolsheviks sent to that Congress as its representative, Stalin." Neither Lenin nor I nor Sverdlov could leave Petrograd; on the other hand, Zinoviev and Kamenev were not suitable at that period for the task of raising an insurrection in Finland. Stalin's candidature appeared the most suitable. It was at that Congress that Stalin evidently met for the first time Tanner, with whom 22 years later he was to carry on negotiations on the eve of the Soviet-Finnish War.

The same Pestkovsky refers to close collaboration between Lenin and Stalin. "Lenin could not get along without Stalin even for a single day. Probably for that reason our office in the Smolny was 'under the wing' of Lenin. In the course of the day, he would call Stalin out an endless number of times, or would appear in our office and lead him away. Most of the day Stalin spent with Lenin. What they did there, I don't know, but on one occasion, upon entering Lenin's office, I discovered an interesting picture. On the wall hung a large map of Russia. Before it stood two chairs. And on them stood Ilyich and Stalin, moving their fingers over the northern part, I think across Finland.

"At night when the commotion in the Smolny subsided a bit, Stalin would go to the direct wire and spend hours there. He carried on the longest negotiations either with our military leaders (Antonov, Pavlunovsky, Muravyov, and others) or with our enemies, with the War Minister of the Ukrainian Rada, Porsh. Occasionally, when he had some pressing business and he was called out, he would send me to the wire." The facts here are given more or less correctly; the interpretation is one-sided. At that period, Lenin had great need of Stalin. There can be no doubt about that. Zinoviev and Kamenev had been waging a struggle against Lenin; I spent my time either at meetings or in Brest-Litovsk, principally in Brest-Litovsk; Sverdlov carried the responsibility for the entire organizational work of the Party. Stalin really had no definite duties. The Commissariat of Nationalities, especially in the beginning, took very little of his time. He, therefore, played the role of chief-of-staff or of a clerk on responsible missions under Lenin. The conversations by direct wire were essentially technical, although very responsible, and Lenin could entrust them only to an experienced man who was fully informed of all the tasks and cares of Smolny.

[Even after the removal from Petrograd to Moscow, Lenin continued to abide by the axiomatic rule of not issuing personal orders. Practically three years later, when] on the 24th of September, 1920, Ordzhonikidze by direct wire from Baku asked for his permission to send a destroyer to Enzeli (Persia), Lenin wrote over the dispatch: "I'll ask Trotsky and Krestinsky." Actually there is a countless number of such inscriptions on telegrams, letters and reports. Lenin never decided himself, always turned to the Politburo. Two or three of its members, and sometimes no more than two, were usually in Moscow. From these hundreds of notations about asking members of the Politburo, only those have been extracted which bore the inscription to "ask Stalin," and these interpreted to mean that Lenin did not take a step without Stalin.

[With reference to the Brest-Litovsk negotiations] Stalin's historiographers have had a veritable holiday. [They had genuine documents to quote in support of their myth-building, documents from the archives of the Commissariat of Foreign Affairs, presided over at the time by Trotsky. Thus, in 1935, a certain Sorin wrote]:

★ In a letter to Lenin from Brest, Trotsky proposed the following essentially profoundly adventuristic plan: not to sign an annexationist peace, but not to continue the war, while demobilizing the army. On the 15th (2nd) of January, in a conversation by direct wire with Trotsky, who asked for an immediate reply, Vladimir Ilyich characterized Trotsky's plan as "disputable" and postponed the final answer until the arrival of Stalin, who at that time was not in Petrograd and whom Vladimir Ilyich wanted to consult. We quote the complete record of these conversations:

15 (2) January—the following conversations by direct wire took place between Trotsky and Lenin: Trotsky asks Lenin whether he received a letter sent to him through a Latvian soldier. Trotsky must have an immediate answer to that letter. The answer should be expressed in words of agreement or disagreement.

"Lenin at the apparatus. I have just now received your special letter. Stalin is not here, and I have not yet been able to show it to him. Your plan seems disputable to me. Is it not possible to postpone taking the final decision until after a special session of the Central Executive Committee here? As soon as Stalin returns I will show the letter to him.

Lenin."

"We shall try to postpone the decision as long as possible, awaiting communication from you. Please try to hurry. The Rada delegation is carrying on a flagrantly treacherous policy. The consideration of the plan in the Central Committee seems to me inconvenient, since it may evoke a reaction before the plan is carried out.

Trotsky."

Reply to Trotsky: "I should like to consult first with Stalin before replying to your question. Today a delegation of the Kharkov Ukrainian Central Executive Committee, which assures me that the Kiev-Rada was breathing its last, has departed to visit you.

Lenin."

When the negotiations of the 18th (5th) January reached a critical moment L. D. Trotsky asked for a directive by direct wire and received one after the other the following two notes:

1. "To Trotsky—Stalin has just arrived. I shall consider with him and we shall give you our joint answer.

Lenin."

2. "Inform Trotsky he is requested to set a recess and come to Petrograd.

Lenin. Stalin."

[The official History of the Bolshevik Party, published in 1939, goes completely overboard. It declares]:

★ On the tenth of February, 1918, the peace negotiations of Brest-Litovsk were interrupted. Notwithstanding the fact that Lenin and Stalin in the name of the Central Committee of the Party insisted on signing peace, Trotsky, who was the Chairman of the Soviet delegation in Brest, treacherously violated the explicit directives of the Bolshevik Party. He declared that the Soviet Republic refused to sign peace on the basis of the conditions proposed by Germany and at the same time informed the Germans that the Soviet Republic would not carry on the war, and would continue to demobilize the Army.

This was monstrous. The German imperialists could ask for no more from this traitor to the interests of the Soviet fatherland.

[Turning from page 207 to 208 of the same book, we find the following elaboration]:

★ Lenin called this decision "strange and monstrous."

At that time it was not yet clear to the Party what was the real reason for this anti-Party behaviour of Trotsky and of the "Left Communists." But as has been recently established by the trial of the Anti-Soviet "Bloc of Rights and Trotskyites" (beginning of 1938), Bukharin and the group of "Left Communists," headed by him, jointly with Trotsky and the "Left" Essars, were already then in a secret conspiracy against the Soviet Government. Bukharin, Trotsky and their fellow-conspirators, it has developed, aimed to annul the Brest Peace Treaty, to arrest V. I. Lenin, J. V. Stalin, Ya. M. Sverdlov, kill them, and form a new government of Bukharinites, Trotskyites and the "Left" Essars.

[Now let us examine the record. Sixty-three Bolsheviks were present at the conference of January 21st (8th), 1918, of whom an absolute plurality (32) voted in favor of waging a revolutionary war. Trotsky's position—neither war nor peace—received 16 votes; Lenin's—peace with Imperial Germany—15 votes. The question was considered again three days later by the Party Central Committee. The protocols recording the session of January 24th (11th), 1918 read as follows]:

★ Comrade Trotsky moves that the following formula be put to the vote:

"We terminate the war, we do not conclude peace, we demobilize the army." This is put to the vote. Ayes 9, Nayes 7.

Lenin's proposition was put to the vote: "we drag out the signing of the peace in every way" (Ayes 12, Nayes 1). L. D. Trotsky's "do we intend to issue a call for a revolutionary war?" (Ayes 2, Nayes 11, not voting 1); and "we stop the war, do not conclude peace, demobilize army" (Ayes 9, Nayes 7).

At that session Stalin based the necessity to sign a separate peace on this argument: "There is no revolutionary movement in the West; there are no facts; there are only potentialities, and we cannot take into account potentialities." "Cannot take into account?" Lenin at once repudiated Stalin's support; it is true that revolution in the West has not yet begun; "however, if we should change our tactics because of that, we would be traitors to international socialism."

The following day, the 25th (the 12th) of January, the question of peace was considered at the joint session of the Central Committees of the Bolsheviks and the Left Social-Revolutionaries [Left Essars]. By a majority of votes, it was resolved to propose for the consideration of the Congress of Soviets the formula: "Not to wage war, not to sign peace."

What was Stalin's attitude toward this formula? This is what Stalin declared a week after that session at which the formula was accepted by nine votes against seven:

> Session of February 1 (January 19) 1918; Comrade Stalin: . . . "The way out of this difficult situation was provided us by the middle point of view—the position of Trotsky."

Stalin's words will become wholly comprehensible if one takes into consideration that throughout that entire critical period the preponderant majority of Party organizations and Soviets stood for revolutionary war and that consequently Lenin's position could only be carried through by way of a party and state revolution (which of course was utterly out of the question). Thus, far from being mistaken, Stalin merely acknowledged an indisputable fact, when he said that my position was at that time the only way out of the situation for the party.

[On the 10th of February] the Soviet delegation at the Peace Conference in Brest-Litovsk made public the official declaration of the refusal of the Soviet Government to sign the annexationist peace and of the termination of the war with the powers of the Quadruple Alliance. [Two days later there was published] the order of Supreme Commander-in-Chief, N. V. Krylenko, for the termination of military activity against the same powers and for the demobilization of the Russian Army.

[Referring to these events a year later, Lenin wrote:]

> ★ How did it happen that not a single tendency, not a single direction, not a single organization of our party was not opposed to that demobilization? What was the matter with us—had we completely lost our minds? Not in the least. Officers, not Bolsheviks, were saying even before October that the Army cannot fight, that it cannot be kept at the front another few

weeks. After October this became self-evident to everyone who wanted to look facts in the face, who wanted to see the unpleasant bitter reality, and not hide himself or pull his hat over his eyes and be satisfied with proud phrases. There was no army. It was impossible to hold on to it. The best that could be done was to demobilize as soon as possible.

This was the sick part of the Russian State organism that could not endure any longer the burden of the war. The sooner we demobilized it, the sooner it was dissolved among parts which were not yet sick, the sooner would the country be able to get ready for its new difficult tasks. This is what we felt when unanimously, without the slightest protest, we passed the resolution, the decision which from the point of view of outward events was absurd—to demobilize the army. It was the right thing to do. We were saying that to keep the army is a frivolous illusion. The sooner we demobilize the army, the sooner will begin the convalescence of the entire social organism as a whole. That is why the revolutionary phrases, "the German cannot advance," from which followed the second, "We cannot declare the state of war terminated; neither war nor the signing of peace," was such a profound error, such an overestimation of events. But suppose the German advances? "No, he will be unable to advance."

Actually the advance of the German troops lasted fourteen days, from the 18th of February to the 3rd of March. The whole of the 18th of February the Central Committee devoted to the question of how to react to the German advance that had begun.

After the breaking off of negotiations in Brest on the 10th of February and the publication by the Russian delegation of the declaration of the termination of the war and the refusal to sign peace with Germany, the "military party"—the party of extreme annexation—had finally won out. At a conference in Hamburg on the 13th of February, which took place under the chairmanship of Emperor Wilhelm, the following statement proposed by him was accepted: "Trotsky's refusal to sign the peace treaty automatically leads to the termination of the Armistice." On the 16th of February the German military Kommando officially informed the Soviet Government of the termination of the Armistice with the Soviet Republic, beginning at twelve noon of the 18th of February, thus violating the stipulated agreement that notice of termination of the Armistice must be given seven days before the beginning of military action.

The question of how to react to the German advance was first broached at the session of the Central Committee of the Party on the evening of the 17th of February. Germany's immediate proposal to enter into new negotiations for the signing of peace was rejected by six votes against five. On the other hand, no one voted "for revolutionary war," while N. I. Bukharin, G. I. Lomov, and A. A. Joffe "declined to vote on such a posing of the question." By a majority of votes a resolution was passed "to postpone the renewal of peace negotiations until the advance shows itself in a sufficient degree and until its influence on the labor movement becomes evident." With three not voting, the following decision was passed unanimously: "When the German advance is as a fact, and yet no revolutionary upsurge begins in Germany and Austria, we shall conclude peace."

On the 18th of February, with the Germans advancing, the Central Committee of the Party was in session throughout the day, with brief interruptions (in one of the Protocols the time indicated is "in the evening," the two others are not dated more precisely). At the first session, after speeches by Lenin and Zinoviev in favor of signing peace, and by me and N. I. Bukharin against, the motion: "to offer immediately a proposal to renew peace negotiations," was voted down by seven to six. At the second, or evening session, after speeches by Lenin, Stalin, Sverdlov and Krestinsky in favor of renewing peace negotiations, Uritsky and Bukharin against, and a speech by me proposing that we do not renew negotiations but ask the Germans for their formulated demands, the following question was put to the vote: "Shall we immediately offer the German Government a proposal to conclude a peace at once?" This proposal was passed by seven votes (Lenin, Smilga, Stalin, Sverdlov, G. Sokolnikov, myself, Zinoviev) against five (Uritsky, Lomov, Bukharin, Joffe, Krestinsky), with one not voting (Stassova). Then it was decided immediately to make out a precise statement of the accepted decision and to work out the text of the communication to the German Government. Lenin's proposal about the points of which the telegram should be composed was put to the vote. All but two abstainers voted for registering and referring to the extortionism of the peace terms; for readiness to sign the old conditions, with the indication that there was no refusal to accept worse conditions: Ayes, seven; nayes, four; not voting, two. The task of working out the text itself was delegated to Lenin and me. The radiogram was then and there written by Lenin, and, with minor corrections which I made, approved at the joint session of the Central Committee of the Bolsheviks and the Left Essars, and sent over the signatures of the Council of People's Commissars to Berlin on the 19th of February.

At the session of the Council of People's Commissars on the 21st of February, the representatives of the Left Essars voted against utilizing the help of the Entente for counteracting the German advance. Negotiations with the Allies about military and technical help had begun soon after the October Revolution. They were carried on by Lenin and me, with Generals Lavergne and Niessel and Captain Jacques Sadoul representing the French, and with Colonel Raymond Robbins representing the Americans. On the 21st of February, in connection with the *continuing advance of the Germans*, the French Ambassador Noulens telegraphed to me: "In your resistance to Germany you may count on the military and financial cooperation of France." Of course, the difference between German militarism and French militarism was not for us a question of principle. It was only a question of securing the necessary neutralization of certain forces antagonistic to us in order to save the Soviet Government. [But the French Government did not keep its word.] Clemenceau proclaimed a holy war against the Bolsheviks. Then we were forced to conclude the peace of Brest-Litovsk.

The reply to the Soviet radiogram which outlined the German conditions of peace was received in Petrograd at 10.30 in the morning [of February 23rd.] By comparison with the conditions of peace presented on the 10th of February, these terms were considerably worse. Livonia and Estonia had to be cleared immediately of the Red Army, and the German police was to occupy them; Russia obligated itself to conclude peace with the bourgeois Ukrainian and Finnish governments; and the like. The question of accepting the German terms of peace was discussed ·[the same day], first at the session of the Central Committee of the Bolshevik Party, then at the joint session of our Central Committee and the Central Committee of the Left Essars, and finally at the Plenary Session of the All-Russian Central Executive Committee itself.

At the session of the Central Committee of the Bolshevik Party Lenin, Zinoviev, Sverdlov and Sokolnikov spoke in favor of accepting these conditions and signing the peace. Bukharin, Dzerzhinsky, Uritsky and Lomov spoke against it. I declared that "if we had unanimity, we could have taken upon ourselves the task of organizing the defense. We could have managed it. . . . But that would require the maximum of unity. Since that is lacking, I will not take upon myself the responsibility of voting for war." The Central Committee resolved by seven votes to four, with four not voting, immediately to accept the German proposal, prepare for a revolutionary war and (unanimously, with three not voting) carry out a poll of the Soviet electors of Petrograd and Moscow, in order to determine the attitude of the masses toward the conclusion of peace.

At that session of the Central Committee on the 23rd of February Stalin declared: "We need not sign, but we must begin peace negotiations." To which Lenin replied: "Stalin is wrong in saying that we need not sign. These conditions must be signed. If you do not sign them, then you will sign the death sentence of the Soviet Government within three weeks." [And the protocol further states]: "Comrade Uritsky argued against Stalin that the conditions had either to be accepted or rejected, but that it was no longer possible to carry on negotiations."

To everyone familiar with the state of affairs at that moment—[even to an ardent and consistent advocate of a revolutionary war against Imperial Germany like Uritsky] it was clear that resistance was hopeless. Stalin's statement was due entirely to the utter lack of any kind of thought-out position. As far back as the 18th of February the German [Army had taken] Dvinsk. Its advance was developing with extraordinary rapidity. The policy of holding back had been exhausted to the very dregs. [Yet] Stalin proposed [five days later], on the 23rd of February, not to sign peace, but . . . to carry on negotiations.

Stalin spoke a second time at the session of the 23rd of February, this time in defense of the necessity to sign the peace treaty. He took advantage of the occasion to correct himself likewise on the question of the international revolution, [in view of] Lenin's [criticism of him. Said Stalin,] "We, too, place our bets on the revolution, but you reckon in weeks, while we reckon in months." This fully corresponded to the moods of those days and to the words of Sergeyev (Artem) [at the session of January 24th (11th), 1918] that all members of the Central Committee were agreed on one thing, that without the victory of the international revolution in the nearest possible time (according to Stalin during the next few months) the Soviet Republic would perish. Thus, "Trotskyism" at that time prevailed unanimously in the Central Committee of the Party.

Essentially, Stalin did not assume any kind of independent position in the period of the Brest negotiations. He hesitated, bided his time, kept his mouth shut—and schemed. "The Old Man is still hoping for peace," he said to me, nodding his head in the direction of Lenin, "but he won't get any peace." Then quite probably he went to Lenin and made the same sort of remarks about me. Stalin never really came into the open. True, no one was particularly interested either in his view or his contradictions. I am sure that my main task, which was to make our attitude toward the question of peace as understandable as possible to the world proletariat, was a secondary consideration with Stalin. He was interested in "peace in one country," just as subsequently he was to become interested merely in "socialism" in one country. During the decisive balloting he joined with Lenin. It was only several years later, in the interests of his struggle with Trotskyism, that he took the trouble to work out for himself a certain semblance of a "point of view" about the Brest events. [Compare his attitude with that of Lenin who, addressing the Seventh Congress of the Party on the 8th of March, immediately after the bitter struggle of factions, said] :

> ★ Further I must touch upon the position of Comrade Trotsky. It is necessary to distinguish two aspects of his activity; when he began negotiations at Brest, splendidly utilizing them for agitation, all of us were in agreement with Comrade Trotsky . . . Trotsky's tactic in so far as it aimed at procrastination, was correct. It became incorrect when the state of war was declared to be terminated while peace had not been signed . . . But since history has swept this aside, it is not worth while to recall it.

There was of course a profound difference between the policy of Lenin throughout the Brest-Litovsk crisis and the policy of Stalin, who stood closer to Zinoviev. It must be said that Zinoviev alone had the courage to demand the immediate signing of the peace, prophesying that putting off the negotiations would increase the severity of the peace conditions more truly, frightening us with it. None of us doubted that from the "patriotic" point of view it would have been more advantageous to sign the conditions immediately, but Lenin thought that the procrastination of the peace negotiations was revolutionary agitation and that the tasks of the international revolution stood above patriotic considerations—above the territorial and all other conditions of the peace treaty. To Lenin it was a question of securing a breathing spell in the struggle for the international revolution. Stalin felt that the international revolution was a "potential" with which we could not reckon. True, later he did amend these words, in order to set himself up against others, but essentially the international revolution in those days, just as considerably later, remained for him a lifeless formula which he did not know how to use in practical politics.

It was precisely at the time of this crisis that it became clear that the factors of world politics were so many unknown quantities to Stalin. He did not know anything about them, and he was not interested in them. In the German working-class passionate debates were raging among the progressive layers as to why the Bolsheviks had entered into negotiations and were preparing to conclude peace. There were not a few who voiced the opinion that the Bolsheviks and the government of Hohenzollern were playing a comedy in which the cues were prearranged. The struggle for the revolution required that we make clear to the workers that we could not act otherwise, that the enemies were walking all over us, that we were forced to sign the peace treaty. Precisely for that reason, the German advance was our best proof of the forced character of the treaty. An ultimatum from Germany would not have been enough; an ultimatum might likewise have been a part of a rehearsed play. Quite a different matter was the actual movement of German troops, the seizure of cities, of military property. We were losing tremendous wealth, but we were winning the political confidence of the working class of the whole world. Such was the sense of the disagreement.

According to the text of the Constitution, a People's Commissariat was made up of the chairman[2] and of the collegium, which in turn consisted of a half dozen and sometimes even a dozen members. It was no easy task to guide a department. According to Pestkovsky, "all members of the Collegium on the National Question were in opposition to Stalin, frequently leaving their People's Commissar in the minority. The repentant author hastens to add: "Stalin decided to re-educate us and worked at it persistently. In this he displayed a lot of gumption and wisdom." Unfortunately Pestkovsky does not go into details on this aspect of the matter. But we do learn from him about the original manner in which Stalin would terminate conflicts with his collegium. "At times he would lose patience," relates Pestkovsky, "but he never made it evident during the sessions. On these occasions, when in consequence of our endless discussions at conferences his patience would be exhausted, he would suddenly disappear, doing it with extraordinary skill; 'just for moment' he would disappear from the room and hide in one of the recesses of the Smolny, and later the Kremlin. It was impossible to find him. In the beginning, we used to wait for him. But finally we would adjourn. I would remain alone in our common office, patiently awaiting his return, but to no avail. Usually at such moments the telephone would ring; it was Vladimir Ilyich calling for Stalin. Whenever I replied that Stalin had disappeared, he would invariably tell me: 'Find him at once.' It was no easy task. I would go out for a long walk through the endless corridors of the Smolny and the Kremlin in search of Stalin. I would find him in the most unexpected places. A couple of times I found him in the apartment of the sailor, Comrade Vorontsov, in the kitchen, where Stalin was lying on a divan smoking a pipe and thinking over his thesis."

Since the best forces of the Party had gone in for military or economic work, the Collegium of the Commissariat of Nationalities consisted of people of minor importance. Nevertheless they indulged in the practice of marshaling arguments

[2] The People's Commissar.—C. M.

to counter Stalin's contentions and of putting questions to him to which he could not find answers. He had power. But that power was utterly insufficient for compulsion; he had to convince or persuade. Stalin could not cope with that situation. The contradictions between his overbearing nature and his insufficient intellectual resources created an insufferable situation for him. He did not enjoy authority in his own department. When his patience would be exhausted he would simply hide "in the most unexpected places." It may be doubted that he was thinking over his thesis in the kitchen of the commandant. It is more likely that he was nursing his hurt inside of himself and brooding on how good it would be if those who disagreed with him would not dare to object. But in those days it did not even enter his head that a time would come when he would merely command and all others would obey in silence.

No less colorful is Pestkovsky's description of the search for the Commissariat's quarters in Moscow, where the government moved the following March from Petrograd. A fierce struggle for the private houses of merchants raged between the departments. The People's Commissariat of Nationalities had absolutely nothing in the beginning. "I brought pressure to bear on Stalin." On whom Stalin brought pressure to bear, I don't know. "After a while, the People's Commissariat of Nationalities was in possession of several private houses. The Central Office and the Byelo-Russians were located on the Povarskya, the Latvians and Estonians on the Nikitskaya, the Poles on the Arbat, the Jews on Prechistenka, while the Tartars were somewhere on the Moscow River Quay. Besides that Stalin and I had offices in the Kremlin. Stalin proved to be quite dissatisfied with this situation. 'Now it is quite impossible to keep an eye on you at all. We ought to find one large house and get everyone together there.' This idea did not desert him for a single minute. Several days later he said to me: 'We have been given the Great Siberian Hotel, but the Supreme Council of National Economy has wilfully taken possession of it. However, we shall not retreat. Tell Alliluyeva to type out the following on several pieces of paper: "These quarters occupied by the People's Commissariat of Nationalities." And take along some thumb tacks.'"

Alliluyeva, Stalin's future wife, was a typist in the Commissariat of Nationalities. Armed with the magic bits of paper and the thumb tacks, Stalin and his assistant went by automobile to the Zlatoustensky Lane. "It was already getting dark. The main entrance to the hotel was closed. The door was decorated by a piece of paper which read—'This dwelling occupied by the Supreme Council.' Stalin tore it off, and we fastened our decoration in its place. 'All we have to do now is get inside,' Stalin said. It was no easy task. With great difficulty we found the back-door entrance. For some inexplicable reason the electricity was not working. We lighted our way with matches. On the second floor we stumbled into a long corridor. We fastened our notices on a number of doors at random. When it was time to go back, we had no more matches. Going down in pitch darkness, we landed in the basement and nearly broke our necks. At long last we did manage to make our way to the automobile."

It takes a certain effort of imagination to visualize the figure of a member of the government under cover of darkness breaking into a building occupied by another ministry, tearing off one set of notices and posting another. It may be said with certainty that it would not have occurred to any of the other People's Commissars or members of the Central Committee to do anything like that. Here we recognize the Koba of the Baku prison days. Stalin could not fail to know that the debatable question of a building would be decided in the final reckoning by the Council of People's Commissars or in the Politburo. It would have been simpler in the very beginning to apply to one of these institutions. Apparently Stalin had reason for supposing that the contest would be decided not in his favor, and tried to confront the Council of People's Commissars with an accomplished fact. The attempt failed; the building was assigned to the Supreme Council of National Economy, which was a more important ministry.[3] Stalin had to hide another grudge against Lenin.

The majority of the Collegium reasoned, according to Pestkovsky's story, in this fashion: every national oppression was merely one of the manifestations of class oppression. The October Revolution had destroyed the basis of class oppression. Therefore, there was no need to organize in Russia national republics and autonomous regions. Territorial division should be exclusively along economic lines. ". . . The opposition to the Leninist policy was, strange though it may seem at first glance, especially strong among the non-Russian Bolsheviks (Letts, Ukrainians, Armenians, Jews and the like). The Bolsheviks in the borderlands that suffered oppression had been brought up in the struggle with local nationalistic parties and were inclined to reject not only the poison of chauvinism but even progressive social demands. The Collegium of the People's Commissariat of Nationalities consisted of these Russified non-Russians, who counterposed their abstract internationalism to the real needs of development of the oppressed nationalities. Actually this policy supported the old tradition of Russification and was in itself a special danger under the conditions of civil war."

The People's Commissariat of Nationalities was created to organize all the formerly oppressed nations of Russia through national commissariats—such as the Armenian, the Byelo-Russian, the Jewish, the Latvian, the Mussulman (which was later renamed the Tataro-Bashkir), the Polish—and the departments of the Mountaineers of the Caucasus, the German, the Kirghiz, the Ukrainian, the Chuvash, the Estonian, the Kalmyk, the Southern Slavs, the Czechoslovaks (for serving the Czech military prisoners), the Votyak and the Komi. The Commissariat tried to organize the education of the nationalities on a Soviet basis. It published a weekly newspaper, *The Life of the Nationalities,* in Russian and a number of publications in various national languages. But it devoted itself

[3] By 1930 Stalin's power was no longer challengeable. But the State Cult of his personality was just then beginning to be established. Thus is to be explained the circumstance that in these memoirs, notwithstanding their general panegyric tone, one still hears a note of familiarity, and even a shade of good-natured irony is permitted. Several years later, when the purges and executions would establish the necessary sense of distance, tales of how Stalin hid in the kitchen of the commandant or took possession of a house at night, would already sound unseemly and render the document taboo. It is likely that this author paid a cruel penalty for violating etiquette.—L. T.

chiefly to organizing national republics and regions, to find the necessary cadres of leaders from among the nationals themselves, to general guidance of the newly-organized territorial entities, as well as to caring for the national minorities living outside of their own segregated territory. In the eyes of the backward nationalities which were for the first time called upon by the Revolution to lead an independent national existence the Commissariat of Nationalities had an undoubted authority. It opened to them the doors leading to an independent existence within the framework of the Soviet régime. In that sphere Stalin was an irreplaceable assistant to Lenin. Stalin knew the life of the aboriginal people of the Caucasus intimately—as only a native could. That aboriginality was in his very blood. He loved the society of primitive people, found a common language with them, was not afraid they would excel him in anything, and therefore with them behaved in a democratic, friendly way. Lenin valued these attributes of Stalin's, which were not shared by others, and in every way tried to bolster Stalin's authority in the eyes of all sorts of national delegations. "Talk it over with Stalin. He knows that question well. He knows the conditions. Discuss the question with him." Such recommendations were repeated by him scores and hundreds of times. On all those occasions when Stalin had serious conflicts with the national delegates, or in his own collegium, the question was referred to the Politburo, where all the decisions were invariably brought out in favor of Stalin. This should have reinforced his authority even more in the eyes of the ruling circles of the backward nationalities; in the Caucasus, on the Volga, and in Asia. The new bureaucracy of the national minorities later became a not unimportant bulwark of Stalin's power.

On the 27th of November, 1919, the Second All-Russian Congress of Mussulman Communist Organizations and Peoples of the East was held in Moscow. The Congress was opened by Stalin in the name of the Central Committee of the Party. Four persons were elected honorary members: Lenin, myself, Zinoviev and Stalin. The president of the Congress, Sultan-Galiyev,[4] one of those who subsequently ended up badly, proposed that the Congress greet Stalin as "one of those fighters who burned with a flame of hatred for international imperialism." Yet it is extremely characteristic of the gradation of leaders at that time that even at this Congress the report of Sultan-Galiyev on the general political revolution concludes with the greeting: "Long Live the Russian Communist Party! Long Live Its Leaders, Comrades Lenin and Trotsky." Even this Congress of the Peoples of the East which was held under Stalin's direct leadership did not deem it necessary to include Stalin among the leaders of the Party.

Stalin was People's Commissar of Nationalities from the moment of the Revolution until the liquidation of the Commissariat in 1923 in connection with the creation of the Soviet Union and the Council of Nationalities of the Central Executive Committee of the U.S.S.R. It may be considered firmly established that at least until May, 1919, Stalin was not very busy with the affairs of the Commissariat. At first Stalin did not write the editorials in *The Life of the Na-*

[4] Cf. Supplement II, p. 417.

tionalities, but later, when the journal began to come out in large format, Stalin's editorials began to appear in one issue after another. But Stalin's literary productivity was not great, and it decreased from year to year. In 1920-21, we find only two or three articles by him. In 1922 not even a single article. By that time Stalin had completely gone over to machine politics.

In 1922 the editorial board of the journal stated: "In the beginning of the publication of *The Life of the Nationalities* Comrade Stalin, the People's Commissar for the Affairs of the Nationalities, took an active part. He wrote during that period not only editorial articles, but often made up the informational review, contributed notes to the department of Party life and the like." Reading these contributions, we recognize the old editor of the Tiflis publications and the editor of the Petersburg *Pravda* of 1913.

Thus, in a number of issues he devoted his attention to the East. This was Lenin's guiding idea. It may be followed in a number of his articles and speeches. No doubt Stalin's interest in the East was in large measure personal in character. He was himself a native of the East. If, before representatives of the West, he, who was familiar neither with the life of the West nor with its languages, felt himself always at a loss, with representatives of the backward nations of the East, he, the Commissar who in large measure decided their fate, felt himself incomparably more confident and on firmer ground. The basic idea was Lenin's. But with Lenin both the Eastern and Western perspectives were closely inter-related. In the foreground in 1918 were the problems of the West, not of the East; the war was coming to an end, there were upheavals in all the countries, revolutions in Germany and Austro-Hungary and elsewhere. Thus, Stalin's article entitled "Don't Forget the East" appeared in the issue of the 24th of November, 1918, i.e., at the very time of the Revolution in Austro-Hungary and Germany. All of us had regarded those revolutions as forerunners of the socialist revolutions of Europe. At that time Stalin wrote that "without the revolutionary movement in the East, it is useless even to think about the final triumph of socialism" —in other words, Stalin considered the final triumph of socialism impossible not only in Russia, but even in Europe without a revolutionary awakening of the East. This was a repetition of Lenin's guiding idea. However, in this repetition of ideas, there was a division not only of labor, but also of interests. Stalin had absolutely nothing to say with reference to the revolutions in the West. He did not know Germany, did not know its life or its language, and others wrote about it with much greater knowledge. Stalin concentrated on the East.

On the 1st of December, 1918, Stalin wrote in *The Life of the Nationalities* an article entitled "The Ukraine is Being Freed." It was the same old seminarist rhetoric. Repetition takes the place of other resources: "We do not doubt that the Ukrainian Soviet Government will be able to offer proper resistance to the new unwelcome guests, the enslavers from England and France. We do not doubt that the Ukrainian Soviet Government will be able to expose their reactionary role," and so on *ad nauseam*. In an article in the same magazine on December 22nd, 1918, Stalin wrote: "With the help of the best Communist forces, the

Soviet state machine (in the Ukraine) is being re-established. The members of the Central Committee of the Soviets in the Ukraine are headed by Comrade Pyatakov . . . The best Communist forces which composed the government of the Ukraine were: Pyatakov, Voroshilov, Sergeyev (Artem) Kviring, Zatonsky, Kotsubinsky." Of these only Voroshilov remained alive and became a Marshal. Sergeyev (Artem) died in an accident; all the others were either executed outright or disappeared without a trace. Such was the fate of "the best Communist forces."

On the 23rd of February, he published an editorial entitled "Two Camps," in which he said in part: "The world has divided itself resolutely and irrevocably into two camps—the camp of imperialism and the camp of socialism . . . The waves of the socialist revolution are growing without restraint, assailing the fortresses of imperialism . . . Their resonance resounds in the lands of the oppressed peoples . . . The ground under the feet of imperialism is catching fire . . ." Notwithstanding the waves, the images are clichés and not in agreement with each other. In all of this there is the unmistakable ring of insincerity under the bathos of bureaucratic fishiness. On the 9th of March, 1919, *The Life of the Nationalities* published an article by Stalin entitled "After Two Years," which expressed his conclusions: "The experience of the two years' struggle of the proletariat has completely confirmed what Bolshevism had foreseen . . . the inevitability of the world proletarian revolution . . ." In those days the perspective of Bolshevism had not yet been reduced to socialism in a separate country. Of the same type were all the other articles, all of them utterly devoid of originality of thought or attractiveness of form. The articles were formally educational in character, dry, flabby and false.

The first Congress of the Chuvash Communists took place in April, 1920, and therefore, more than two years after the establishment of the Soviet Government. The honorary praesidium consisted of the same four persons: Lenin, myself, Zinoviev and Stalin. Describing the opening of the congress, the journal of the People's Commissariat of Nationalities pointed out that the walls were decorated with portraits of the leaders of the world revolution—Karl Marx, Lenin, Trotsky and Zinoviev. At that time there were as yet no portraits of Stalin in existence; they were not hung anywhere and it never occurred to anyone to decorate even the Hall of the Congress with one of them. Yet this occasion was wholly in Stalin's own sphere of activity.

On the 7th of November—that is, on the third anniversary of the October Revolution—we find Stalin in Baku, where he spoke at the solemn session of the Soviets, delivering a report entitled "Three Years of the Proletarian Dictatorship." At the Congress of the People of Daghestan on the 13th of November, Stalin proclaimed the autonomy of Daghestan. "Comrade Stalin's speech," as the journal of the Commissariat of Nationalities informs us, "was in many places interrupted by thunderclaps of applause, the Internationale, and ended in a stormy ovation." On the 17th of November at the Congress of the People of the Terek Territory at Vladikavkaz, Stalin personally "proclaimed the Soviet autonomy of the Gurian people" and appeared with a report about the afore-mentioned autonomous Gurian Soviet Republic. Between the 18th and 21st of December, 1920 there took place the first All-Russian Conference of Represen-tatives of Autonomous republics, territories and regions. Kaminsky transmitted to the Conference greetings in the name of Stalin, who could not be present because of illness. The motion to send greetings to Stalin was adopted unani-mously. But at that Congress of the Peoples of the East the record reads: ". . . Honorary Chairmen of the Congress were elected: Comrades Lenin, Zinoviev and Trotsky . . . storms of applause . . . Honorary members of the Praesidium were elected . . . and Djugashvili-Stalin . . ." Again in the last place!

In Vienna, under the guidance of Lenin, Stalin had written a valuable work on the national problem, but his attempt to continue this work independently in Siberia produced such a result that Lenin deemed it impossible even to publish his article. At the March conference of 1917 Stalin was developing the view that national oppression is the product of feudalism, utterly losing sight of imperialism as the main factor of national oppression in our epoch. In 1923 he was to place on the same plane with Great-Russian nationalism, which had be-hind it age-old traditions and the oppression of weak nations, the defensive nationalism of these latter nations. These crude errors, Stalinist errors, taken together, are explicable, as has already been pointed out, by the fact that not on a single question does he rise to a systematic conception. He utilizes disjointed propositions of Marxism as he needs them at the moment, selecting them just as shoes are selected according to size in a shoe store. That is why at each turn of events he so easily contradicts himself. Thus, even in the field of the national problem, which became his special sphere, Stalin could not rise to an integrated conception.

"Recognition of the right to secede does not mean the recommendation to secede," he wrote in *Pravda* of October 10, 1920. "The secession of the border-lands would have undermined the revolutionary might of Central Russia, which stimulated the liberation movement of the West and the East. The seceded borderlands would have inevitably fallen into slavery to international imperial-ism. It is enough to take a look at Georgia, Armenia, Poland, Finland, etc., which have separated from Russia, and which have preserved merely the ap-pearance of independence, while actually having become transformed into uncon-ditional vassals of the Entente. It is sufficient to recall the recent history of the Ukraine and of Azerbaijan, the former ravished by German capitalism and the latter by the Entente, in order to understand fully the counter-revolutionism of the demand for the secession of a borderland under contemporary international conditions."

"The revolutionary wave from the north," wrote Stalin on the first anniver-sary of the October Revolution, "has spread over all of Russia, pouring over one borderland after another. But at this point it met with a dam in the form of the 'national councils' and territorial 'governments' (Don, Kuban, Siberia) which had been formed even before October. Bourgeois by nature, they did not at all desire to destroy the old bourgeois world. On the contrary, they deemed it their duty to preserve and fortify it with all their strength . . . They naturally became the hearths of reaction, drawing around themselves all that was counter-revolutionary in Russia . . . But the struggle of the 'national' and territorial 'governments' (against the Soviet Center) proved to be an unequal struggle. Attacked from both sides, from the outside by the Soviet Government and on the inside by their own workers and peasants, the 'national governments' had to retreat after the first battle . . . Completely routed, the 'national governments' were obliged to turn for help against their own workers and peasants to the imperialists of the West."

Thus began the wave of foreign intervention and the occupation of the border-lands, populated predominately by non-Russian nationalities, which could not help hating Kolchak, Denikin, Wrangel, or their imperialistic and Russifying policy. In a report Stalin made at Baku on the 8th of November, 1920, under the title, "Three Years of the Proletarian Revolution," we find the following concluding words: "There is no doubt that our road is not one of the easiest, but there is equally no doubt that we are not afraid of difficulties . . ." Paraphrasing certain words of Luther, Russia might have said: "Here I stand on the border between the old capitalistic and the new socialistic world; here on this border I unite the efforts of the proletarians of the West with the efforts of the peasantry of the East, in order to demolish the old world. May the God of History help me in this!"

[According to] Pestkovsky:

★ In the spring of 1918 the Central Committee decreed to create the Tartar-Bashkir Republic. In order to work out this decision more concretely, a special conference was convoked in May at Moscow, composed of representatives of Party and Soviet organizations of the Ural Territory, representatives of the Tartar and Bashkir nationalities, and officials of the People's Commissariat of Nationalities.

The delegates to this conference from the Ural Territory were Comrades Syromolotov and Tintul, and they brought with them a "real" Bashkir Communist, Comrade Shamigulov. All three were resolute opponents of the creation of the Tartar-Bashkir Republic, regarding it as something in the nature of a concession to Pan-Islamistic nationalism. Having received such unexpected support, we "Leftists" in the collegium of the Commissariat of Nationalities perked up in spirit and resolved on firm resistance to Stalin's "opportunism." In this way those who were in favor of creating a republic found themselves in a minority. The only one who resolutely supported Stalin was Nur-Vakhitov, leader of the Tartar Communists, and Ibragimov, a Left Essar and representative of the Ufa Tartars. The one Bashkir Communist, Shamigulov, expressed himself against the Republic, considering it an unnecessary concession to nationalism. Even worse was the action of another Bashkir, Manatov. At the session he voted for the republic, not wishing to "quarrel with his superiors," but in the hall he urged us to fight resolutely against its establishment because according to him the Bashkirs did not want to be in the same republic with the Tartars.

After that Stalin convoked a session of the conference and declared that in view of the fact that the question had already been decided beforehand by the Central Committee, we *must* vote in favor of organizing a republic. But we did not yield, and, making a protest against the decision of the question before the convocation of the conference, we left the fraction meeting and refused to participate in the further deliberations of the council. At the same time we teased Stalin, saying that he "was left with a Left Essar." For that we subsequently received a written reprimand from the Central Committee.

After the proclamation of the Bashkir Autonomous Republic in November, 1917, sympathy for the Soviet Government sprang up among the masses. The leadership of these Bashkir masses passed into the hands of the nationalistic elements headed by Zak-Validov, who represented the interests of the bourgeois-*kulak* portion of the population. Gradually this group degenerated into an outpost of anti-Soviet activity and established contact with Dutov and Kolchak. However, under the pressure of the masses, after the liquidation of Bashkir autonomy by Kolchak, Zak-Validov was compelled to begin negotiations with the Soviet Government. In February, 1919, after the liquidation of Kolchak, the Bashkir government went over to the side of the Soviet Government and toward the end of the same month at Simbirsk, at the staff headquarters of the Eastern Front, the delegation of the Bashkir government signed a preliminary agreement which guaranteed autonomy to the Bashkir people on condition that it establish a government on the basis of the Soviet constitution, open common action of Bashkir detachments with the Red Army against the Whites, and the like.

In the beginning of March, 1919, Stalin commenced negotiations in Moscow with the Bashkir delegation about the formation of the Bashkir Soviet Republic. The result of these negotiations was the agreement of the Central Soviet Government with the Bashkir Government concerning Soviet Autonomous Bashkiria, concluded on the 20th of March, 1919. In the beginning of March, I was obliged to leave Moscow, having declined to participate in the Eighth Congress of the Party in view of military reverses near Ufa. Stalin calmly remained in Moscow at the Congress and until the 20th of March carried on the negotiations with the Bashkir delegation. Nevertheless, Stalin is hardly remembered in connection with that matter by contemporary historians of Bashkiria. [The two quotations below—the first by Antagulov, the second by Samoilov—are typical]:

I.

★ The struggle between the Russian and the Bashkir comrades deepened; complete anarchy began. In one place Russians were arrested in the name of the Bashkir government; in another, Bashkirs were arrested in the name of the local government. Comrade Trotsky's journey to Ufa happened to coincide with this movement (March, 1920). The Bashkir officials again began to carry on negotiations with the Soviet Government in the person of Comrade Trotsky and achieved a degree of agreement.

2.

★ Meantime, as a result of information received from Bashkiria, the Center accorded no little attention to the Bashkir question. In the middle of March Comrade Trotsky, who had arrived in Ufa with special powers, called us there for a conference on Bashkir affairs. To that conference from Sterlitamak, representing the Bashkirs, came Validov, Tukhvatulin, Rakhamatuvin, and Kaspransky; representing the Territorial Committee and the officials of the Center, Dudnik, Samoilov, Sergeyev (Artem), Preobrazhensky, and the Chairman of the Ufa Provisional Executive Committee, Eltsin.

During the initial years of the Soviet régime Bolshevism in the Ukraine was weak. The cause of it is to be sought in the national and social structures of the country. The cities, the population of which consisted of Great-Russians, Jews, Poles, and only to a small extent of Ukrainians, were to a considerable extent colonies in character. Among the industrial workers of the Ukraine, a considerable percentage were Great-Russians. Between the city and the village lay a yawning, almost impassable abyss. Those Ukrainian intellectuals who interested themselves in the village, the Ukrainian language and culture, met with semi-ironical treatment in the city, and that of course pushed them resentfully in the direction of chauvinism. The non-Ukrainian Socialist factions in the cities had no sense of kinship with the life of the masses in the villages. In the Ukrainian cities they represented the culture of the Great-Russians with which most of them, especially the Jewish intellectuals, were not any too well acquainted. Hence, to a considerable extent, the exotic character of Ukrainian Bolshevism, the absence of it during the period when it should have been sending down deep roots, its profound independence, and the multitudinous conflicts, quarrels and constant internal factional struggles.

It was Stalin's duty as People's Commissar of Nationalities to keep the development of the nationalist movement in the Ukraine under constant observation. By virtue of that alone, he was more closely connected than others with the Ukrainian Bolshevik Party. That closer connection began as far back as 1917, soon after the October Revolution, and continued for several years. In the Ukraine, Stalin represented the Russian Central Committee of the Bolsheviks. On the other hand, at certain general Party congresses he represented the Ukrainian organizations. This was customary at that time. He took part in the conferences of the Ukrainian Communist Party as one of its actual leaders, and since the life of the Ukrainian organization was wasted in considerable part on constant squabbles, conflicts, factional groupings, Stalin felt in this atmosphere like a fish in water.

His Ukrainian period was full of failures, and therefore remains completely unrevealed. [Official Stalinist histories, compelled to record failure after failure in the effort to put across the Party line in the Ukraine throughout Stalin's tenure as People's Commissar of Nationalities, carefully avoid mention of his name in connection with this epidemic of failures. They do not state that in the final reckoning "the errors on the peasant and national questions which had been committed in the Ukraine in the beginning of 1919, and which contributed to the fall of the Soviet Government there" were due to Stalin's wholly inadequate defense of the policy laid down by the Central Committee of the Russian Communist Party. In castigating that failure, Lenin said: "Only a very small part of the well-managed farms ought to be turned into Soviet farms, otherwise we will not get a bloc with the peasantry . . . We need a policy similar to the one we needed at the end of 1917 and during many months in 1918 . . . We must therefore now assign a large number of Soviet farms for general land distribution."

[Appearing at the Fourth All-Ukrainian Party Conference on March 16, 1920, as the fully-empowered representative of the Central Committee, armed with the explicit resolution of that body on the Ukrainian question, Stalin was again confronted with a motley opposition, the spearhead of which were the followers of Sapronov's "Democratic Centralism" tendency, which had been routed in debate at the All-Russian Party Conference the previous December. This time all the arguments of that opposition were known beforehand, and the People's Commissar of Nationalities set forth the rebuttals written out for him in advance by Trotsky, that task having been assigned to the latter by the Politburo. Yet he suffered defeat on the floor of the Ukrainian Conference. The Central Committee had to intervene by dissolving the Ukrainian Central Committee elected by the Fourth Conference and by recalling from the Ukraine a number of officials addicted to Great-Russian chauvinism, before it could introduce its policy, which insisted on unswerving enforcement of the principle of "the self-determination of nations." The cardinal point of the Central Committee's resolution adopted at the All-Russian Party Conference in December, 1919, declared]:

> In view of the fact that Ukrainian culture . . . has for centuries been suppressed by Tsarism and the exploiting classes of Russia, the Central Committee of the Russian Communist Party makes it obligatory for all members of the Party to help in every way to get rid of all obstacles to the free development of the Ukrainian language and culture. Owing to the centuries of oppression, nationalist tendencies are to be found among the backward sections of the Ukrainian masses, and in view of this fact, it is the duty of members of the Party to treat them with the utmost forbearance and discretion, putting before them a comradely explanation of the identity of interests of the toiling masses of the Ukraine and of Russia. Members of the Party . . . must actually enforce the right of the toiling masses to study in the Ukrainian language and to use it in all Soviet institutions . . . striving . . . to render the Ukrainian language a weapon for the Communist education of the toiling masses. Steps must immediately be taken to assure a sufficient number of employees in all Soviet institutions who know the Ukrainian language and to see that in the future all employees should be able to speak Ukrainian.

This should have proved an extremely easy thesis to defend. Even though as a rule Stalin was not a successful debater, considering the relation of forces, his defeat still seems surprising. It is quite possible that, having felt previously that the mood of the conference was unfavorable to his thesis, Stalin decided to play at he who loses wins, letting it be understood through intermediaries that he was defending the thesis not from his own conviction, but only from a sense of discipline. He could count in this way on killing two birds with one stone—acquire the sympathy of the Ukrainian delegates and transfer the odium of defeat to me as the author of the thesis. Such an intrigue was quite in the spirit of the man!

The Georgian Social-Democracy not only led the impoverished peasantry of little Georgia, but aspired also, and not without a measure of success, to the leadership of the movement "of the revolutionary democracy of the whole of Russia." During the first months of the Revolution, the leading circles of the Georgian intelligentsia regarded Georgia not as a national fatherland but as a Gironde, a chosen southern province called upon to supply leaders to the whole country. But this continued only as long as there was still hope of harnessing the revolution within the framework of bourgeois democracy. When the danger that Bolshevism would win became definitely clear, the Georgian Social-Democracy immediately broke its ties with the Russian Compromisers and united with the reactionary elements of Georgia itself. When the Soviets won, the Georgian champions of a single indivisible Russia became equally ardent champions of separatism. . . .

[The following documents of the time shed new light on the Sovietization of Georgia] :

I.

★ To the Revolutionary Council of War of the Caucasian Front. For Ordzhonikidze.
Received your complaining letter. You are mistaken in regarding my inquiry, which is my duty, as lack of confidence. I hope that before a personal meeting between us, you will abandon this unbecoming tone of injury.
#96.   Lenin.
April 3, 1920.

2.

★ To Baku via Rostov.
To the Member of the Revolutionary Council of War of the Caucasian Front Ordzhonikidze:
(To be delivered through responsible persons and the delivery reported to Sklyansky of the Revolutionary Council of War of the Republic.)
The Central Committee orders you to remove all units from the territory of Georgia to the border and to refrain from incursion into Georgia. After negotiations with Tiflis, it is clear that peace with Georgia is not excluded.
Immediately report all the most accurate facts about the rebels.
By order of the Politburo:
Lenin. Stalin.
#004/109.
May 5, 1920.

3.

[A letter typed on the stationery of the commander-in-chief of all the armed forces of the Republic dated Moscow, February 17, 1921, #864, superscribed "Secret, Personal," addressed to the Vice-Chairman of the Revolutionary Council of War of the Republic. It bore two inscriptions on the margin—one by Sklyansky, forwarding it to Lenin; the other by Lenin, returning it to Sklyansky. The essence of the text was] :

★ . . . Upon the initiative of the command of the Second Army, we are confronted with the accomplished fact of incursion into Georgia: the borders of Georgia were crossed and the Red Army has already clashed with the Army of Georgia . . .

> Commander-in-Chief, S. Kamenev,
> Military Commissar of the Staff, [S.] Danilov.
> Chief of Staff of the Revolutionary Council
>   of War, [P.] Lebedev.

4.

Ekaterinburg
Secret.

★ To Moscow, To Sklyansky.

Please write me a brief memorandum on the question of military operations against Georgia, when these operations began, by whose order, and the rest. I need the memorandum for the plenum.
#16.   Trotsky.
February 21, 1921.

5.

★(written by Lenin; copy of a secret document)
(typed, signed by Comrade Sklyansky)

Absolutely Secret.

The Central Committee was inclined to permit Army II to support actively the uprising in Georgia and the occupation of Tiflis, while maintaining the international norms, and on condition that all the members of the Revolutionary War Council II, after seriously considering all the evidence, are certain of success. We warn you that we are sitting without bread, because of the transport, and therefore we will not give you a single train or a single car. We are compelled to obtain from the Caucasus only grain and oil. We demand an immediate reply by direct wire under the signature of all the members of the Revolutionary War Council II, as well as Smilga, Sytin, Trifonov, Frumkin. Until our reply to the telegrams of all these persons, do not undertake anything decisive.

By order of the Central Committee:
[undated]   Krestinsky. Sklyansky.

6.

★ Comrade Sklyansky, immediately *in your own presence* have this coded *arch-carefully*, after photographing the original, and send to Smilga, so that he should *personally* stand at the direct wire and personally decode it. (Tell the Commander-in-Chief about it without showing it to him.)

Stalin himself will send Ordzhonikidze.

And so, a threefold and manifold carefulness. Under your responsibility.

February 14, 1921.   Lenin.

(Written in the hand of Comrade Lenin)

Menshevik Georgia could not hold out. That was clear to all of us. However, there was no unanimity as to the movement and methods of sovietization. I stood for a certain preparatory period of work inside Georgia, in order to develop the uprising and later come to its aid. I felt that after the peace with Poland and the defeat of Wrangel there was no direct danger from Georgia and the denouement could be postponed. Ordzhonikidze, supported by Stalin, insisted the Red Army should immediately invade Georgia, where the uprising had presumably ripened. Lenin was inclined to side with the two Georgian members of the Central Committee. The question in the Politburo was decided on the 14th of February, 1921, when I was in the Urals.

The military intervention passed quite successfully and did not provoke any international complications, if one does not take into account the frantic campaign of the bourgeoisie and the Second International. And yet, the method of the sovietization of Georgia had tremendous significance during the next few years. In regions where the toiling masses prior to the Revolution had managed in most cases to go over to Bolshevism, they accepted subsequent difficulties and sufferings as connected with their own cause. This was not so in the more backward regions, where the sovietization was carried out by the Army. There the toiling masses considered further deprivations a result of the régime imposed from the outside. In Georgia, premature sovietization strengthened the Mensheviks for a certain period and led to the broad mass insurrection in 1924, when, according to Stalin's own admission, Georgia had to be "replowed anew."

Chapter IX

THE CIVIL WAR

THERE is a riot at every step as one goes through current historical publications: in Brest-Litovsk Trotsky did not carry out Lenin's instructions; at the Southern Front Trotsky went against Lenin's directives; on the Eastern Front Trotsky acted contrary to Lenin's orders; and so forth and so on. In the first place, it should be pointed out that Lenin could not give me personal directives. Relations in the Party were not like that. We were both members of the Central Committee, which settled all differences of opinion. Whenever there was disagreement between Lenin and me, and such disagreements occurred more than once, the question was automatically referred to the Politburo of the Central Committee, which made the decision. Hence, strictly speaking, it was never in any way a question of my violating Lenin's directives. But this is only one aspect of the matter—the formal one. Getting down to essentials, one cannot help asking: was there any sound reason for carrying out the directives of the Lenin who had placed at the head of the War Department a person who committed nothing but erorrs and crimes; at the head of the national economy—Rykov, a "self confessed" restorer of capitalism and future agent of Fascism; at the head of the Communist International—that future Fascist and traitor, Zinoviev; at the head of the Party's official newspaper and among the leaders of the Communist International—that future Fascist bandit, Bukharin?

All those who headed the Red Army during the Stalinist period—Tukhachevsky, Yegorov, Bluecher, Budenny, Yakir, Uborevich, Gamarnik, Dybenko, Fed'ko, [Kork, Putna, Feldman, Alksnis, Eidemann, Primakov, and many others],—were each in his time advanced to responsible military posts when I was at the head of the War Department, in most cases advanced personally by me during my tours of the fronts and during my direct observation of their war work. However bad, therefore, my own leadership was, it was apparently good enough to have selected the best available military leaders, since for more than ten years Stalin could find no one to replace them. True, almost all the Red Army Leaders of the Civil War, all those who subsequently built our army eventually proved to be "traitors" and "spies." But that does not alter the case. It was they who had defended the revolution and the country. If in 1933 it developed that it was Stalin and not anyone else who had built the Red Army, then it would seem that the responsibility of selecting such a staff of commanders should fall upon him. From this contradiction official historians extricate themselves not without some difficulty, yet with aplomb. The responsibility for the appointment of traitors to commanding positions is placed entirely upon me, while the honor of the victories secured by these very traitors belongs indisputably to Stalin. Today this unique division of historical function is known to every school boy from a *History* edited by Stalin himself.

There were two aspects to military work in the epoch of the Civil War. One was to select the necessary workers, to make proper disposition of them, to establish the necessary supervision over the commanding staff, to extirpate the suspects, to exert pressure, to punish. All of these activities of the administrative machine suited Stalin's talents to perfection. But there was also another side, which had to do with the necessity of improvising an Army out of human raw material, appealing to the hearts of the soldiers and the commanders, arousing their better selves, and inspiring them with confidence in the new leadership. Of this Stalin was utterly incapable. It is impossible, for example, to imagine Stalin appearing under the open sky before a regiment; for that he did not have any qualifications at all. He never addressed himself to the troops with written appeals, evidently not trusting his own seminarist rhetoric. His influence at those sectors of the front where he worked was not significant. It remained impersonal, bureaucratic and policemanlike.

I remember during the Civil War asking a member of the Central Committee, Serebryakov, who at that time was working with Stalin in the Revolutionary Council of War of the Southern Front, whether he could not manage without Stalin for the sake of economizing forces? Serebryakov replied: "No, I cannot exert pressure like Stalin. It is not my specialty." The ability to "exert pressure" was what Lenin prized so highly in Stalin. The more the state machine for "exerting pressure" gained momentum and the further the spirit of the revolution was removed from this machine, the more confident Stalin felt.

If the front attracted Stalin, it also repelled him. The military machine guaranteed the possibility of issuing orders. But Stalin was not at the head of that machine. At first he headed only one of twenty armies; later he was at the head of one of the five or six fronts. He established severe discipline, held his hand firmly on all the levers, did not tolerate disobedience. At the same time, while at the head of an army, he systematically instigated others to violate the orders of the front. In command of the Southern or Southwestern Front, he violated orders of the Chief Command. In the Tsarist Army, in addition to military subordination there existed an unwritten subordination: the Grand Dukes who held one or another commanding or high administrative post often ignored their superior officers and introduced chaos in the administration of the Army and Navy. I remember remarking to Lenin that Stalin, taking undue advantage of his position as member of the Central Committee of the Party, was introducing the régime of the Grand Dukes in our army. [Ten years later] Voroshilov [glibly admitted in his essay on] Stalin and the Red Army, "Stalin was ready to go counter to any regulation, any subordination." Gendarmes are recruited from poachers.

Conflicts between the lower and higher orders are in the nature of things. The army is almost always dissatisfied with the front, the front is always agitating against the General Staff, especially when things do not go very happily. What characterized Stalin is that he systematically exploited these frictions and developed them into bitter feuds. Drawing his collaborators into dangerous conflicts, Stalin thereby welded them together and placed them in dependence upon himself. Twice he was recalled from the front by direct order of the Central Committee. But at each new turn of events he was again sent out. Notwithstanding repeated opportunities, he acquired no prestige in the Army. However, those military collaborators who were under his command, once having been drawn into the struggle against the Center, remained in the future closely connected with him. The Tsaritsyn group became the nucleus of the Stalinist faction.

Stalin's role in the Civil War may perhaps be measured best of all by the fact that at the end of it his personal authority had not grown in the least. It could never enter anyone's head at that time to say or to write that Stalin "saved" the Southern Front or had played an important role on the Eastern Front or even that he had saved Tsaritsyn from falling. In numerous documents, reminiscences and anthologies devoted to the Civil War, Stalin's name either is not mentioned at all or is mentioned among a lot of other names. Moreover, the Polish War placed on his reputation—at least, in the more well-informed circles of the Party—an ineradicable stain. He evaded participation in the campaign against Wrangel, whether actually because of illness or because of other considerations, it is difficult now to decide. In any event, he emerged from the Civil War as unknown and alien to the masses as he had from the October Revolution.

"At that difficult period, 1918-1920," write the latest historians, "Comrade Stalin was transferred from one front to another, to the greatest danger spots of the Revolution." In 1922 the People's Commissariat of Education published an "Anthology for Five Years," made up of fifteen articles, among them one on "Building the Red Army," and another, "Two Years in the Ukraine," both of them dealing with the Civil War. There is not one word about Stalin in either article. The following year a two-volume anthology entitled, "The Civil War" was published. It consisted of documents and other material on the history of the Red Army. At that time no one was yet interested in giving such an anthology a tendentious character. In the whole anthology there is not one word about Stalin. The same year, 1923, the Central Executive Committee of the Soviet published a volume of four hundred pages entitled, "Soviet Culture." In the section devoted to the Army there are numerous portraits under the title, "The Creators of the Red Army." Stalin is not among them. In the section entitled "The Armed Forces of the Revolution During the First Seven Years of October,"[1] Stalin's name is not even mentioned. Yet this section is illustrated not only with my portrait and those of Budenny and Blücher, but

[1] "October" is synonymous with "October Revolution," which is here viewed as having begun in 1917, and still continuing.—C. M.

even with Voroshilov's. And among Civil War leaders named are not only
Antonov-Ovseyenko, Dybenko, Yegorov, Tukhachevsky, Uborevich, Putna,
Sharangovich, but many others, almost all of whom were subsequently proclaimed enemies of the people and shot. Of those [mentioned, only] two—Frunze
and S. Kamenev—died a natural death [only, no doubt, because they managed to die before the great purge.] And a cloud still hangs over the circumstances of Frunze's death. Among those mentioned in this volume, as commander of the Baltic and Caspian Fleets during the Civil War, is Raskolnikov,
[who refused to return to the Soviet Union when recalled from his post as
Soviet Minister to Bulgaria in 1938, at the time that Stalin's purge turned upon
the diplomatic corps. After writing an open letter of accusation against Stalin,
he died suddenly under mysterious circumstances, apparently poisoned.]

Voroshilov contends nonchalantly that "in the period 1918-1920, Stalin was
perhaps the only man in the Central Committee sent from one fighting front
to another." The word "perhaps" is designed, no doubt, as balm for Voroshilov's conscience, for while he wrote that statement he was fully aware of
the fact that any number of members and agents of the Central Committee
played no less a part in the Civil War than Stalin, and others an immeasurably
greater part—among them I. N. Smirnov, Smilga, Sokolnikov, Lashevich,
Muralov, Rosenholtz, Ordzhonikidze, Frunze, Antonov-Ovseyenko, Berzin,
Gussev. All of these, he knew, spent the entire three years at the various fronts
either as members of the Revolutionary Councils of War of the Republic, of
the fronts and of armies, or at the head of armies and fronts, and even (as in
the case of Sokolnikov and Lashevich) as military commanders, while Stalin's
total sojourn at all the fronts was less than one year out of the three years of
the Civil War.

In some of the official publications it is mentioned in passing, seemingly on
the basis of some sort of evidence in the archives, that Stalin was at one time on
the Revolutionary Council of War of the Republic. No specific reference is
made to the precise period of his participation in that highest military organ. In
a special monograph, "The Revolutionary Council of War of the U.S.S.R.
for Ten Years," composed by three authors in 1928, when all power was already
concentrated in Stalin's hands, it is stated:

> On the second of December, 1919, Comrade Gussev was included in the
> Revolutionary Council of War. Subsequently throughout the course of the
> entire period of the Civil War, Comrades Stalin, Podvoisky, Okulov, An-
> tonov-Ovseyenko and Serebryakov were appointed to the Revolutionary
> Council of War at various times.

A history of the Communist Party edited by N. L. Meshcheryakov in 1934,
after glibly repeating the lie that Stalin "spent the period of the Civil War principally at the front," declares that Stalin "was a member of the Revolutionary
Council of War of the Republic from 1920 to 1923." In the twentieth volume
of Lenin's Miscellany (page 9) Stalin is referred to as a "member of the *praesidium* of the Revolutionary Council of War of the Republic . . . since 1920."
In the Red Army Anniversary issue of *Pravda* for 1931 three "unpublished
documents" appeared—all of them telegrams of the year 1920. One of these

telegrams is from Stalin as a member of the Revolutionary Council of War of the Republic to Budenny and Voroshilov, dated June 3rd; the second—a routine report on the situation at the front from Budenny and Voroshilov to Stalin in his above capacity, dated June 25th. The third telegram is from Frunze, in command of the Southern Front, to Lenin, as Chairman of the Council of Defense, announcing termination of military operations against Wrangel—i.e., the end of the Civil War proper—dated November 15th. On the basis of these documents, the only evidence so far published, it would seem that Stalin was actually a member of the Supreme War Council of the Republic at least from June 3rd to June 25th, or for slightly more than three full weeks in 1920. No evidence of his membership is adduced before or after these two dates in June of that year. Why not? True, the five volumes published by the War Department in which my orders, appeals, and speeches were gathered, were not only confiscated and destroyed, but mere reference to them, let alone quotations from them, were tabooed. *The Proletarian Revolution,* the official historical journal of the Party, in its issue of October, 1924, wrote of these five volumes, which contained nothing but documents of the Civil War: "In these . . . volumes the historians of our revolution will find a great quantity of tremendously valuable documentary material."

But in the archives of the War Department remain stenographic transcripts of the sessions of the Council of War. The records of that institution were kept with scrupulous accuracy and preserved in complete security. Why are not these records cited to establish the actual period during which Stalin was a member of the Revolutionary Council of War of the Republic? The answer is simple enough: because Stalin is not mentioned in the minutes of its sessions as among those present, except once or twice as a petitioner on local matters, and never mentioned as an actual member of the Council, let alone its nonexistent "praesidium." Yet Stalin was appointed to membership on that body by order of the Party Central Committee in the spring of 1920.

The explanation of this puzzling circumstance, as far as I can remember it, is rather revealing of Stalin's character. Throughout the years of the Civil War, during every conflict with Stalin, I tried to put him in the position of having to formulate his views on military problems clearly and definitely. I tried to transform his sulking and surreptitious opposition into an open one, or to replace it with his articulate participation in a leading military organ. By agreement with Lenin and Krestinsky, who wholeheartedly supported my military policy, I finally succeeded—I no longer remember under what pretext—in securing Stalin's appointment to the Revolutionary Council of War of the Republic. There was nothing left for Stalin to do but to accept the appointment. But he found a simple way out: under the pretext of being overloaded with work he did not even once appear at any session of [that supreme military body].

Now it may seem strange that no one in the course of the first twelve years of the Soviet régime ever mentioned either the alleged "leadership" of Stalin in military affairs or even his "active" participation in the Civil War. Yet this is easily explained by the simple fact that there were still many thousands of military men about who knew *what* had actually taken place and *how.*

Even in the Red Army Anniversary issue of *Pravda* of 1930 the claim was not yet made that Stalin was the chief organizer of the Red Army as a whole but only of the Red Cavalry. Eight years earlier to the day, on February 23rd, 1922, *Pravda* had published a somewhat different account of the formation of the Red Cavalry in an article on the Civil War:

> ★ Mamontov occupied Kozlov and Tambov for a time, wreaking great havoc. "Proletarians, to horse!" That slogan of Comrade Trotsky's for the formation of the mounted masses was greeted with enthusiasm, and by the 19th of October, Budenny's Army was striking blows at Mamontov under Voronezh.

[As late as] 1926, not only after my removal from the War Department, but after I had already been subjected to cruel persecutions, the War College published a work of historic research, "How The Revolution Was Fought," in which the authors, well-known Stalinists, wrote:

> Comrade Trotsky's slogan, "Proletarians, to horse!" was the stirring slogan for accomplishing the organization of the Red Army in that respect

i.e., in regard to the creation of the Red Cavalry. In 1926 there was as yet no mention of Stalin as organizer of cavalry.

[Voroshilov insists upon] Stalin's great role in organizing the mounted army. "This was," writes Voroshilov, "the first experiment in uniting cavalry divisions into a single unit as large as an army. Stalin foresaw the might of the mounted masses in the Civil War. He thoroughly understood their tremendous significance for a devastating maneuver. But in the past no one had had such a unique experience as action by mounted horse armies. There was nothing written about it in scientific works, and therefore such a measure evoked either amazement or direct opposition. Especially opposed to it was Trotsky." [Arguing thus, Voroshilov merely exposes his ignorance of military affairs, which is exceeded only by his aptitude for prevarication. The point is, that the question of whether to] unite two corps and a sharpshooting brigade into a special mounted army or to leave these three units at the disposal of the command of the front was a problem that had nothing whatever in common with the general appreciation or lack of appreciation of the significance of cavalry. The most important criterion was the question of the command: Will Budenny be able to manage such a mass of horsemen? Will he be able to rise from tactical tasks to strategical ones? Without an exceptional commander of the front, who knew and understood cavalry, and without reliable means of communication, the creation of a special mounted army would have been unwise, since an excessive massing of cavalry always threatens to lessen the unit's basic advantage, [which is its] mobility. The disagreements on this matter had an episodic character, and if history were to repeat itself I would again repeat my doubts. [Nevertheless, the specific circumstances were such that] we did create the mounted army.

[As a matter of fact, the] campaign for the creation of the Red Cavalry made up the major portion of my work during many months in 1919. As I have said [elsewhere], the [Red] Army was built by the worker who was mobilizing the peasant. The worker had an advantage over the peasant not only in his general level of culture, but especially in his knack of using weapons of new technique. This secured a double advantage for the worker in the Army. With the cavalry it was quite a different matter. The homeland of the cavalrymen were the Russian steppes. The best horsemen were the Cossacks. Next to the best were the sons of the rich peasants of the steppes who owned horses and knew horses. The cavalry was the most reactionary part of the old army and it supported the Tsarist régime longer than any other branch of the service. It was, therefore, doubly difficult to form a mounted army. It was necessary to accustom the worker to the horse. It was necessary that the Petrograd and Moscow proletarians actually get on horse back, if only in the role of commissars or rear rank privates. Their task was to create strong and reliable revolutionary cells in the cavalry squadrons and regiments. Such was the sense of my slogan, "Proletarians, to horse!" The whole country, all the industrial cities, were covered with placards bearing that slogan. I toured the country from end to end and assigned tasks concerning the formation of [cavalry] squadrons and [cavalry] regiments by reliable Bolshevik workers. One of my secretaries, Poznansky, was personally occupied—and with great success, I might add—in the formation of the Red Cavalry units. Only this work of proletarians who got up on horseback actually transformed the wobbly guerrilla detachments into well-trained cavalry units [and made possible the formation of a reliable mounted army].

Three years of the Soviet régime were years of civil war. The War Department determined the government work of the entire country. All the other governmental activity was subsidiary to it. After it in importance came the Commissariat of Supplies. Industry worked chiefly for war. All the other departments and institutions were subjected to constant contraction or reduction and some were even completely closed. All who were active and courageous were subjected to mobilization. Members of the Central Committee, People's Commissars, and other [leading Bolsheviks], spent most of their time at the front as members of Revolutionary Councils of War and sometimes as army commanders. The war itself was a hard school of governmental discipline for a revolutionary party which only a few months before had emerged from the underground. War with its pitiless demands, selected the wheat from the chaff within the Party and within the State machines. Very few members of the Central Committee remained in Moscow: Lenin, who was the political center; Sverdlov, who was not only President of the Central [Executive] Committee [of the Soviet], but also General Secretary of the Party, even before [such a] post [had formally been] created; Bukharin, as editor of *Pravda*. Zinoviev, whom everyone including himself regarded as unfit for military affairs, remained in Petrograd as its political leader. Kamenev, the leader of Moscow, was several times sent to the front, although he, too, by nature was decidedly a civilian. Lashevich, Smilga, I. N. Smirnov, Sokolnikov, Serebryakov, [all leading] members of the Central Committee, were almost constantly at the front.

It would carry us too far afield to enumerate even briefly the careers in the revolutionary underground, in October and during the Civil War of these and many another militant. Any number of them were in no way inferior to Stalin and quite a few excelled him in those values that revolutionists prize most—political clarity, moral courage, ability as agitator, propagandist and organizer. It is sufficient to recall that when the Red Army was being organized, other men were considered better fitted than Stalin for the task. The Supreme Council of War, created on March 4th, 1918, consisted of Trotsky as chairman, Podvoisky, Sklyansky and Danishevsky as members; Bonch-Bruyevich as chief clerk and a staff of Tsarist officers as military specialists. When it was reorganized on September 2nd, 1918, into the Revolutionary Council of War of the Republic, it was made up of Trotsky, as Chairman, Vatzetis as Commander-in-Chief of the armed forces, and following as members: Ivan Smirnov, Rosenholtz, Raskolnikov, Sklyansky, Muralov and Yurenev. When on the 8th of July, 1919, it was decided to have a smaller and more compact staff, the Revolutionary Council of War was made up of Trotsky as Chairman, Sklyansky as Vice-Chairman, Rykov, Smilga, Gussev as members and Commander-in-Chief S. Kamenev. Like others, Stalin too found his place in the Army, and the Red Army found due application for his talents. What is contrary to the facts is the latter-day claim of Stalin's pre-eminent role in the organization of the Red Army and in the conduct of the Civil War.

The army was built under fire. The methods of building it, in which improvisation predominated, were subjected to immediate trial in action. In order to solve each new battle problem, it was necessary to organize new regiments and divisions from scratch. The army—growing chaotically by leaps and bounds—was built by the worker, who mobilized the peasant and attracted the former officer to the cause and placed them under his control. This was no easy task. The material conditions were extremely difficult. Industry and transport were completely disorganized, there were no reserve supplies, there was no agricultural economy, and all the processes of industrial disintegration were constantly deepening. Under such conditions, there could be no question of compulsory military service and compulsory mobilization. Temporarily, at least, it was necessary to resort to the volunteer system.

Those who had military training were tired of fighting in the trenches, and to them the Revolution meant deliverance from war. It was no simple matter to mobilize them again for another war. It was easier to mobilize the youngsters who knew nothing of war, but they had to be trained, and the enemy did not allow us sufficient time for that. The number of our own officers, connected in one way or another with our Party and unconditionally trustworthy, was insignificant. They, therefore, played a great political role in the Army. But their military vision was myopic. When their knowledge proved insufficient, they often used their revolutionary and political authority unwisely and thus hampered the task of building the Army. The Party itself, which nine months ago had emerged from the Tsarist underground and several months later had been subjected to the persecution of the Provisional Government, found it difficult, after the brilliant victory of October, to adjust itself to the thought that the Civil War was still ahead. Altogether, insuperable difficulties accumulated in the way of creating the Red Army. At times it seemed that arguments were consuming all the energy spent. *Will we or will we not be able to create an army?* The fate of the Revolution rested on that question.

The transition from the revolutionary struggle against the old state to the creation of a new state, from the demolition of the Tsarist Army to the creation of a Red Army, was accompanied by a Party crisis, or rather by a series of crises. At each step the old methods of thought and the old ways came into conflict with the new tasks. Rearmament of the Party was indispensable. Since the Army is the most necessary of all the organizations of the state and since during the first years of the Soviet régime the center of attention was the defense of the Revolution, it is no wonder that all the discussions, conflicts and groupings inside the Party revolved around the questions of building the Army. An opposition appeared almost from the moment we made our first efforts to pass from disjointed armed detachments to a centralized army. The majority of the Party and of the Central Committee in the end supported the military leadership, since victory after victory spoke in its favor. However, there was no lack of attacks and waverings. The Party enjoyed full freedom of criticism and opposition in the very thick of the Civil War. Even at the front at closed Party meetings the Communists often subjected the policy of the military command to merciless attacks. It never occurred to anyone in those days to persecute the critics. The punishments at the front were very stringent—and they included Communists—but they were imposed only for the non-fulfillment of military duties. Within the Central Committee, the opposition was of a very much weaker character, since I enjoyed the support of Lenin. In general, it must be said that whenever Lenin and I were in agreement, and we were on the majority of occasions, the remaining members of the Central Committee invariably supported us, almost always unanimously; the experience of the October Revolution had entered the life of the Party as a potent lesson.

It must be said, however, that Lenin's support was not unconditional. Lenin wavered more than once, and in several instances was gravely mistaken. My advantage over him was in the fact that I uninterruptedly traveled along the various fronts, came in contact with a tremendous number of people, from local peasants, prisoners of war, and deserters, to the highest Army and Party leaders at the front. This mass of varied impressions was of inestimable value. Lenin never left Moscow, and all the threads were concentrated in his hands. He had to pass judgment on military questions, which were new to all of us, on the basis of information which for the most part came from the higher-ups of the Party. No one was able to understand individual voices coming from below better than Lenin. But these reached him only on exceptional occasions.

In August, 1919, when I was at the front near Svyazhsk, Lenin asked my opinion concerning a proposal introduced by one of the prominent Party members to replace all officers of the General Staff with Communists. I replied sharply in the negative. "True," I replied by direct wire from Svyazhsk to the Kremlin on the 23rd of August, 1918, "of the officers, many are traitors. But there is evidence of sabotage during the movement of troops on the railways as well, yet no one proposes to replace railway engineers with Communists. I consider Larin's proposal thoroughly worthless. We are now creating conditions under which we are carrying on a ruthless selection of officers: on the one hand, concentration camps, and on the other hand, the campaign on the Eastern Front. Catastrophic measures like Larin's are dictated only by panic . . . Victories at the front will enable us to improve our present selections and will give us cadres of reliable General Staff men . . . Those who protest most against the use of officers are either panicky people, or those far removed from the work of the military mechanism, or those Party military workers who themselves are worse than any saboteur; they don't know how to get things done, they behave like satraps, they don't do anything themselves, and when they fail, they place the blame on the General Staff man."

Lenin did not insist. Meantime, victories took their turn with defeats. Victories strengthened confidence in my military policy; reverses, multiplying inevitably the number of betrayals, evoked a new wave of criticism and protest in the Party. In March, 1919, at the evening session of the Council of People's Commissars, in connection with a dispatch concerning the treason of certain Red Army commanders, Lenin wrote me a note: "Hadn't we better kick out all the specialists and appoint Lashevich Commander-in-Chief?" I understood that the opponents of the policy of the War Department, and particularly Stalin, had pressed Lenin with special insistence during the preceding days and had aroused certain doubts in him. I wrote my reply on the reverse side of his query: "Childish!" Apparently the angry retort produced an impression. Lenin appreciated clear-cut formulations. The next day, with the report from the General Staff in my pocket, I walked into Lenin's office in the Kremlin and asked him:

"Do you know how many Tsarist officers we have in the Army?"

"No, I don't know," he answered, interested.

"Approximately?"

"I don't know." He categorically refused to guess.

"No less than thirty thousand!" The figure simply astonished him. "Now count up," I insisted, "the percentage of traitors and deserters among them, and you will see that it is not so great. In the meantime, we have built an army out of nothing. This army is growing and getting stronger."

Several days later at a meeting in Petrograd, Lenin drew the balance sheet of his own doubts on the question of military policy: "When recently Comrade Trotsky told me that . . . the number of officers runs into several tens of thousands, I got a definite idea of how best to make use of our enemy; how to compel those who are the opponents of Communism to build it; how to build

Communism out of the bricks gathered by the capitalists for use against us
. . . We have no other bricks."

Pedantry and set patterns were alien to us. We resorted to all sorts of combinations and experiments in our pursuit of success. One army was commanded by a former non-commissioned officer with a general as chief of staff. Another army was commanded by a former general with a guerrilla fighter as second in command. One division was commanded by a former private, while a neighboring division was commanded by a colonel of the General Staff. This "eclecticism" was forced on us by the circumstances. However, the considerable percentage of educated officers exerted an exceedingly favorable influence on the general level of the command. The amateur commanders learned as they went along, and many of them became first-rate officers. In 1918, 76% of the whole command and administration of the Red Army was composed of former officers of the Tsarist Army and only 12.8% consisted of fledgling Red Commanders, who naturally occupied the lower positions. By the end of the Civil War, the staff of commanders consisted of workers and peasants without any military education except direct battle experience, who had advanced from the ranks in the course of the Civil War; former soldiers and non-commissioned officers of the old army; young commanders who had gone through short term Soviet military schools; and finally, cadre officers and wartime officers of the Tsarist Army. More than 43% of the commanders had no military education, 13% were former non-commissioned officers, 10% had gone through the courses of the Soviet military school, 34% were officers of the Tsarist Army.

From the old officer corps there entered into the Red Army, on the one hand, progressive elements who sensed the meaning of the new epoch (they were a small minority); a broad layer of those who were inert and talentless and who joined the Army only because they did not know how to do anything else; and on the other hand active counter-revolutionists who were awaiting a favorable moment to betray us. The non-commissioned officers of the old army were recruited by means of special mobilization. From among them came a number of exceptional military commanders, the most famous of whom was the former Cavalry Sergeant-Major, Simeon Budenny. But they, too, were not any too reliable as a class, for before the Revolution non-commissioned officers were chiefly the sons of the wealthy peasantry and the city bourgeoisie. From them came no small number of deserters who played an active role in counter-revolutionary uprisings and in the White Army. A commissar, usually a worker Bolshevik with experience in the World War, was attached to each commander. We were looking forward to preparing a reliable officer corps.

"The institution of commissars," I declared when I was at the head of the War Department in December, 1919, "is to serve as a scaffolding . . . Little by little we shall be able to remove this scaffolding." At that time no one foresaw that twenty years later the institution of commissars would again be revived, but this time for opposite purposes. The commissars of the Revolution were representatives of the victorious proletariat watching over commanders who had come mostly from bourgeois classes; the latter-day commissars were representatives of the bureaucratic caste watching over officers who for the most part had come from the rank and file.

[On the 22nd of April, 1918, a decree was published concerning the centralization of village, regional, provincial and territorial commissariats of War.] In July I reported to the Fifth Congress of Soviets—[the Congress which ratified the Brest-Litovsk Treaty and the plan for creating the Red Army]—that many of the lower commissariats had not yet been organized because of lack of competent military men. Our objective was to centralize the military-administrative organs for the purpose of mobilization and the formation of Regular Army units. Each military region was headed by a Revolutionary Council of War, of three members: a representative each from the Party and the government, and one military specialist. Since a considerable number of military specialists were appointed simultaneously to the front as well as to regional, provincial, territorial and township war commissariats, we were of course to a large extent feeling our way in the dark. We organized a military attestant committee. But that did not have at its disposal the necessary information for an adequate appraisal of the old generals and officers from the point of view of their loyalty to the new revolutionary régime. Let us not forget that the job was undertaken in the spring of 1918—that is, a few months after the conquest of power—and that the administrative machine was being built amid the greatest chaos with the aid of the improvisations of chance assistants taken largely upon accidental recommendations. Indeed, there could have been no other way under the circumstances. The verification of the military specialists, their definitive selection and the like took place gradually.

Among the officers there were many, perhaps a great majority, who did not know themselves where they stood. The outright reactionaries had fled in the very beginning, the most active of them to the peripheries, which were then building up the White Fronts. The rest hesitated, bided their time, could not make themselves abandon their families, did not know what would become of them, and by inertia found themselves in the military-administrative or commanding apparatuses of the Red Army. The further behavior of many of them was determined by the treatment they were accorded. Wise, energetic and tactful commissars—and such were in the minority—won over the officers at once, while they, who from force of habit had looked down on the commissars, were amazed by their resoluteness, daring and political definiteness. Such unions of commanders and commissars often lasted for a long time and were distinguished by great stability. When the commissar was ignorant and boorish and baited the military specialist, carelessly compromising him before the Red Army soldiers, friendship was out of the question, and the hesitating officer was finally inclined toward the enemy of the new régime.

The atmosphere of Tsaritsyn, with its administrative anarchy, guerrilla spirit, disrespect for the Center, absence of administrative order and provocative boorishness toward military specialists, was naturally not conducive to winning the good-will of the latter and making them loyal servants of the new régime. It would be, of course, a mistake to think that Tsaritsyn got along without military specialists. Every one of the improvising commanders had to have an officer who knew the routine of military affairs. But the Tsaritsyn sort of specialist was recruited from the dregs of the officers—drunkards or those who had otherwise lost all semblance of human dignity, prideless men who were ready to crawl on their belly before the new boss, flatter him, refrain from contradicting him in anything, and the like. This is the sort of specialist I found in Tsaritsyn. Voroshilov's Chief-of-Staff was precisely that type of specialist. The name of this insignificant officer was never mentioned anywhere else and I don't know anything about his fate. [He was] a docile and submissive former captain of the Tsarist Army irresistibly addicted to alcoholic beverages. Eye to eye with this Chief-of-Staff, the Tenth Army Commander was never obliged to lower his head in embarrassment.

In order to advance the commanders who were closest to the Soviet régime, a special mobilization of former Tsarist non-commissioned officers was made. Most of them had been promoted to non-commissioned ranks during the latter part of the war, so that their knowledge of military affairs was of no great significance. However, the old non-commissioned officers, especially in the artillery and the cavalry, had an excellent comprehension of military matters and were really better informed and far more experienced than the commissioned officers under whose command they served. To that category belonged people like Budenny, Blücher, Dybenko[2] and a number of others. In Tsarist times these men were recruited from among the more literate, the more cultured, those more accustomed to command. Hence it was not surprising to find that these non-commissioned officers were almost exclusively the sons of rich peasants, of the petty gentry, of the city bourgeoisie, of petty officials, teachers, bookkeepers, and the like. Such types of non-commissioned officers gladly assumed command, but were not inclined to submit to and to tolerate the superior authority of commissioned officers.

They were just as little inclined to recognize the authority of the Communist Party, knuckle down to its discipline and sympathize with its aims, especially in the sphere of agrarian affairs. Purchases at fixed prices, not to mention the expropriation of grain from the peasants, was met by them with furious enmity. To that class belonged the cavalry man, Dumenko,[3] the corps commander at Tsaritsyn and Budenny's immediate superior (Budenny at that time commanded

[2] Dybenko was a petty officer in the Navy.—C. M.
[3] The Stalinist historian E. Genkina on p. 109 of her book "The Fight for Tsaritsyn in 1918" (Bor'ba za Tsaritsyn v 1918 godu), published by the political publications section (politizdat) of the All-Union Communist Party in 1940, writes of Dumenko: "Dumenko himself was a kulak by origin, had a windmill, two houses, etc. But during the imperialist war his cattle and horses were confiscated, and the Whites appropriated a few things. That pushed Dumenko temporarily into the camp of the Reds, he began to organize a cavalry detachment, but not at home, in the Cherkass Region of the Don Territory, but in the Sal Region, where he was not known as a kulak."—C. M.

a division). Dumenko was more gifted than Budenny. But he ended up with an insurrection, killed all the Communists of his corps, attempted to join the forces of Denikin, was seized and executed. Budenny and the commanders close to him likewise experienced a period of wavering. One of the Tsaritsyn commanders of a brigade, subordinate to Budenny, revolted; many of the cavalry men joined the Greens.[4] The treason of the former Tsarist officer, Nossovich, who occupied a purely bureaucratic administrative post, produced of course less harm than the treason of Dumenko. But since the military opposition—the breeding ground of the Stalin faction—depended at the front on elements of Dumenko's type, this mutiny is not mentioned at all nowadays.[5]

The reader who is not acquainted with the actual course of events and who at the present time cannot gain access to the archives will find it difficult to imagine the extent to which the proportions of events have been distorted. The whole world has heard by now about the defense of Tsaritsyn, about Stalin's journey to the Perm front, or about the so-called Trade Union Discussion. These episodes loom today as the peaks on the historical range of events. But these alleged peaks have been artificially created. From the tremendous amount of material with which the archives are bulging, certain special episodes have been singled out, and these have been surrounded with imposing historical stage-effects. Subsequent works of official historiography piled up new exaggerations, based on the old exaggerations; to these, outright inventions have been added from time to time. The total effect is the product of stagecraft rather than of historic fact. Practically never does one meet reference to documents. The press abroad, and even learned historians, have come to regard these tall tales as original sources. In various countries one may now find specialists in history who know third-rate details of Tsaritsyn or the Trade Union Discussion but have practically no conception of events which were immeasurably more important and significant. Falsification in this matter has taken on the quality of an avalanche. [Yet it is simply] astonishing how very few documents and other authentic materials have been published concerning Stalin's activity at the front and generally during the Civil War period.

In accounts published during the years of the Civil War, the story of Tsaritsyn was one of the many completely unconnected with the name of Stalin. His role behind the scenes, which was very short-lived at best, was known to only

[4] Although the Civil War was chiefly fought between the Reds and the Whites, smaller groups were also involved in it. The most important of them were the Greens, peasant guerrilla detachments that would sally out of the green forests (hence, their name) to fight either Reds or Whites, but more often the Whites. The Greens regarded themselves as defenders of peasant democracy and were opposed to both Reds and Whites. The Green movement was most active in the Black Sea Basin, the Kuban Territory and the Crimea. As allies of the Reds in the winter of 1919-1920, the Greens played an important part in the disintegration of General Denikin's Army. The Green movement terminated about 1921, when limited freedom of trade was introduced and peasant insurrections generally were liquidated by the Soviet government.—C. M.

[5] The subject is carefully avoided even in the 217-page history of the Tsaritsyn episode cited above with reference to Dumenko—C. M.

a small number of people and offered absolutely no occasion for many words. In the anniversary article on the Tenth Army by Ordzhonikidze, an old pal of Stalin's who proved faithful to him to the point of suicide, Stalin is not even mentioned. It was the same with other such articles. The Bolshevik Minin, Mayor of Tsaritsyn at the time and subsequently a member of the Tenth Army's Revolutionary Council of War, wrote a heroic drama in 1925 entitled "The Encircled City," which had so few references to Stalin in connection with the Tsaritsyn events that Minin ended up eventually as "an enemy of the people." The pendulum of history had to swing very far before Stalin was raised to the heights of a hero of the Tsaritsyn epic.

For years now it has become a tradition to represent matters as if in the spring of 1918 Tsaritsyn was of great strategic importance and Stalin was sent there to save the military situation. It was nothing of the kind. It was entirely a question of provisions. At a session of the Council of People's Commissars on May 28, 1918, Lenin discussed with Tsuryupa, then in charge of supplies, the extraordinary methods then in vogue for supplying the capitals [Moscow and Petrograd] and the industrial centers with provisions. At the close of the meeting Lenin wrote to Tsuryupa: *"This very day get in touch with Trotsky, by telephone, so that by tomorrow he can get everything started."* Further in the same communication, Lenin informed Tsuryupa of the Sovnarkom's[6] decision that People's Commissar of Supplies Shlyapnikov was to leave immediately for the Kuban' to co-ordinate the provisioning activities in the South for the benefit of the industrial regions. Tsuryupa replied in part: "Stalin agrees to go to the Northern Caucasus. Do send him. He knows local conditions there and Shlyapnikov will find it useful to have him around." Lenin agreed: "Send them both off today." During the next few days several additional decisions were made about Stalin and Shlyapnikov. Finally, as recorded in Lenin's Miscellany, "Stalin was sent to the Northern Caucasus and to Tsaritsyn as general manager of provisioning activities in the South of Russia." There was no mention whatever of military tasks.

What happened to Stalin was what happened to many other Soviet officials, to droves of them. They were sent to various provinces to mobilize the collection of grain surpluses. Once there, they ran into White insurrections. Whereupon their provisioning detachments turned into military detachments. Many workers in the commissariats of Education, of Agriculture or other departments were thus sucked into the maelstrom of the Civil War in outlying regions, and, in a manner of speaking, were obliged to change their various professions for the profession of arms. L. Kamenev, who next to Zinoviev was the most unmilitary member of the Central Committee, was sent in April, 1919, to the Ukraine to accelerate the movement of supplies toward Moscow. He found that Lugansk had been surrendered and that danger threatened the entire Don Basin; moreover the situation in the recently-won Ukraine soon became

---

[6] A portmanteau word for the Russian equivalent of Council of People's Commissars— *Soviet Narodnykh Kommissarov.*—C. M.

increasingly less favorable. Just exactly as Stalin had in Tsaritsyn, Kamenev in the Ukraine found himself drawn into military operations. Lenin telegraphed to Kamenev: "Absolutely necessary that you personally . . . should not only inspect and expedite matters, but that you, yourself, should bring the reinforcements to Lugansk and to the entire Don Basin, because otherwise there is no doubt that the catastrophe will be tremendous and scarcely remediable; we will most surely perish, if we do not completely clear the Don Basin in a short time . . ." This was Lenin's customary style in those days. On the basis of such quotations it is possible to prove that Lenin regarded the fate of the Russian Revolution as dependent on the military leadership of Kamenev in the South. At different times the very unmilitary Kamenev[7] played a very prominent rolę at various fronts.

Under totalitarian concentration of all the means of oral and printed propaganda, it is possible to create as false a reputation for a city as for a man. Nowadays many heroic episodes of the Civil War are forgotten. Cities where Stalin played no part are scarcely remembered, while the very name of Tsaritsyn has been invested with mystic significance. It is necessary to bear in mind that our central position and the disposition of the enemy in a large circle made it possible for us to act along internal operational lines and reduced our strategy to one simple idea: the consecutive liquidation of fronts depending on their relative importance. In that profoundly mobile war of maneuvers, various parts of the country acquired exceptional significance at certain important moments, and later lost it. However, the struggle for Tsaritsyn could never have attained the same significance, for example, as the struggle for Kazan', from where the road to Moscow opened, or the struggle for Oryol, from where there was a short road by way of Tula to Moscow, or the struggle for Petrograd, the loss of which would have been a dire blow in itself and would have opened the road to Moscow from the north. Moreover, notwithstanding the assertions of latter-day historians that Tsaritsyn "was the embryo of the War College, where the cadres of the commanders for other numerous fronts were created, commanders who today are at the head of the basic units of the army," the fact is that the most talented organizers and army leaders did not come from

---

[7] The reference is to Lev Borisovich Kamenev, the Bolshevik leader, Trotsky's brother-in-law, deputy chairman under Lenin in the Council of People's Commissars and the Council of Labor and Defense (since 1922), appointed by Lenin himself as Lenin's literary executor and editor of Lenin's *Collected Works*, founder and first president of the Lenin Institute, Lenin's successor as Chairman of the Council of Labor and Defense, etc., etc., who in 1919 was at the front as an extraordinary representative of the Council of Defense. This Kamenev was shot by Stalin's order as a self-confessed traitor in 1936. He is not to be confounded with Sergei Segeyevich Kamenev, scion of a tsarist military family, who was a colonel in command of the 30th Poltava Regiment at the time of the Revolution of 1917, was one of the tsarist officers drawn into the Red Army during Trotsky's tenure as Commissar of War, appointed by Trotsky to the command of the Eastern Front in September, 1918, and made Commander-in-Chief of the Armed Forces of the Soviet Republic in July, 1919, in succession to Joachim Joachimovich Vatzetis. S. S. Kamenev remained Commander-in-Chief until April, 1924, when that office was abolished. He subsequently became a member of the Communist Party and died a natural death.—C. M.

Tsaritsyn. And I do not mean simply central figures, like Sklyansky, the real Carnot of the Red Army; or Frunze, a most talented military leader, who subsequently was placed at the head of the Red Army; or Tukhachevsky, the future reorganizer of the army; or Yegorov, the future Chief-of-Staff; or Yakir or Uborevich, or Kork, but many, many others. Every one of them was tested and trained in other armies and on other fronts. All of them had an extremely negative attitude toward Tsaritsyn, its know-nothing smugness, its constant extortions; on their lips the very word "Tsaritsynite" had a derogatory meaning.

On May 23rd, 1918, Sergo [Ordzhonikidze] telegraphed to Lenin:

> The situation here is bad. We need resolute measures . . . The local comrades are too flabby. Every desire to help is regarded as interference in local affairs. Six trains of grain ready to move for Moscow are standing at the station and not being sent . . . I repeat again that what we need are the most resolute measures . . .

Stalin arrived at Tsaritsyn in June, 1918, with a detachment of Red Guards, with two armored trains and with unlimited powers, in order to arrange for provisioning the hungry political and industrial centers with grain. Soon after his arrival several Cossack regiments surrounded Tsaritsyn. The Cossack villages of the Don and the Kuban had risen against the Soviet Government. The Volunteer Army [of the Whites], which had been wandering and meandering through the steppes of the Kuban, had grown strong. The Soviet Army of the North Caucasus—the only granary of the Soviet Republic at the time—suffered heavily under its blows.

Stalin was not supposed to stay at Tsaritsyn. He was supposed to [organize the dispatch of provisions to Moscow and] proceed to the North Caucasus. But within one week of his arrival in Tsaritsyn, i.e., on June 13th, he wired to Lenin that the situation in Tsaritsyn "has sharply changed, because a detachment of Cossacks have made a sally at a point some forty versts away from Tsaritsyn." From Stalin's telegram of June 13th it is clear that he had been expected by Lenin to go to Novorossiisk, and take charge of the crucial developments in connection with the scuttling of the Black Sea Fleet. For at least the next two weeks he was still supposed to go to Novorossiisk. In his speech of June 28th, 1918, at the Fourth Conference of the Trade-Union and Factory Committees of Moscow [Lenin said]:

> ★ Comrades! I shall now . . . reply to the question about the Black Sea Fleet . . . I am going to tell you that it was Comrade Raskolnikov who acted there . . . Comrade Raskolnikov will be here himself and will tell you how he had urged that we should rather stand for the destruction of the fleet than let the German troops use it against Novorossiisk . . . This was the situation, and the People's Commissars Stalin, Shlyapnikov and Raskolnikov will soon come to Moscow and will tell you how everything happened.

[However, instead of proceeding to the Northern Caucasus or, when the plans were altered by the change in the military situation, to Novorossiisk,] Stalin remained in Tsaritsyn until the latter was surrounded in July by the Whites.

Stalin had expected to find little trouble and great glory in forwarding millions of bushels of grain to Moscow and other centers. But all he managed to send, notwithstanding his ruthlessness, was a shipment of three barges, referred to in his telegram of June 26th. Had he sent more, other telegrams to this effect would have been published and commented on long ago. Instead of that, there are inadvertent admissions of his failure as grain-deliverer in his own reports, culminating on August 4th in his statement that it was useless to expect any further provisions from Tsaritsyn. Unable to make good on his boastful promise to supply food to the Center, Stalin turned from the "food front" to the "military front." He became dictator of Tsaritsyn and of the North Caucasian Front. He acquired extremely broad and practically unlimited powers, as the authorized representative of the Party and the Government. He had the right to carry through local mobilization, requisition property, militarize factories, arrest and try, appoint and dismiss. Stalin exercised authority with a heavy hand. All efforts were concentrated on the task of defense. All of the local Party and workers' organizations were taken in hand, were supplemented with new forces; the freebooting guerrillas were harnessed. The life of the entire city was suddenly squeezed in the vise of a ruthless dictatorship. "On the streets and at crossings were Red Army patrols," writes Tarassov-Rodionov, "and in the middle of the Volga on an anchor, raising its black belly high out of the water, was a large barge, and looking askance at it was a flabby official in a faded uniform cap whispering anxiously to the little old women on shore: 'There . . . is the Cheka!' But that was not the Cheka itself. That was only its floating prison. The Cheka was working in the center of the city, next to the Army headquarters. It was working . . . full blast. Not a day passed without bringing to light all sorts of conspiracies in what seemed the most reliable and respectable places."

[On the 7th of July, approximately one month after his arrival in Tsaritsyn, Stalin wrote to Lenin (on the letter is the notation, "Hurrying to the front— writing only on business.")]:

★ The line south of Tsaritsyn has not yet been re-established. I'm hurrying them, scolding everyone I should. I hope that soon we shall have it re-established. You may be sure that I will not spare anyone, neither myself nor others. But we *will* get you the grain. If our military "specialists" (the shoemakers!) were not asleep, the line would not have been broken, and if the line is restored it will not be thanks to the military, but in spite of them.

[On the 11th of July Stalin again telegraphed Lenin]:

★ Matters are complicated by the fact that the staff of the North Caucasian Military Region proved to be utterly unadapted to the conditions of fighting against counter-revolution. It is not only that our "specialists" are psychologically incapable of resolute struggle with counter-revolution, but also because, being staff men who know only how to sketch blueprints and how to propose plans for reformation, they are utterly indifferent to operative action . . . and generally feel themselves to be outsiders . . . I do not think that I have the right to regard this with indifference, when Kaledin's front has been separated from the provisioning point and the north from the grain region. I will continue to straighten out these and many other deficiencies, wherever I find them; I am undertaking a number of measures and will continue to do so, even if I have to remove all the ranking men and commanders who are inimical, notwithstanding difficulties of formalities, which I will break when necessary. Let it be understood that I assume all responsibility before all the highest institutions.

[On the 4th of August, Stalin wrote from Tsaritsyn "to Lenin, Trotsky and Tsuryupa"] :

★ The situation in the South is not one of the best. The Council of War has received a heritage of utter disorder, due partly to the inertness of the former military leader, partly to the conspiracy of persons brought by the military leader into the various departments of the military region. We had to begin all over again . . . We repealed what I would call the old criminal order, and only after that our advance began . . .

Similar communications were received in those days from all parts of the country, because chaos reigned everywhere. What is surprising are the words about the "heritage of utter disorder." The military regions were established in April and had hardly started working, so that it was rather premature to speak of a "heritage of utter disorder."

The task of provisioning on any sort of wide scale proved to be insoluble because of the military situation: "Contacts with the South and with its loads of provisions are broken," wrote Stalin on the 4th of August, "and the Tsaritsyn region itself, which connects the Center with the Northern Caucasus, is cut off in its turn, or practically cut off from the Center." Stalin explained the cause of the extreme aggravation of the military situation on the one hand by the turn of the strong peasant, "who in October had fought for the Soviet government, against the Soviet government (he hates with all his heart the grain monopoly, stable prices, requisition, the struggle with the baggers) ; on the other hand, by the poor condition of our troops . . . In general it must be said," he concluded, "that until we reestablish contact with the Northern Caucasus we must not rely . . . upon the Tsaritsyn sector for provisions."

Stalin's assumption of the functions of manager of all the military forces at the front had obtained the confirmation of Moscow. The telegram of the Revolutionary Council of War of the Republic, which bore the notation that it was sent by agreement with Lenin, expressly delegated Stalin "to establish order, unite all detachments into regular formations, establish proper command, after expelling all insubordinates." Thus the rights given to Stalin were signed, and as far as one is able to judge from the text, were even formulated by me. Our common task at the time was to subordinate the provinces to the Center, to establish discipline, and to subordinate all sorts of volunteer and guerrilla units to the army and to the front. Unfortunately Stalin's activity at Tsaritsyn took an altogether different direction. At the time I did not know that Stalin had inscribed his resolution, "to be disregarded" on one of my telegrams, since he himself never mustered sufficient courage to report the matter to the Center. My impression was that Stalin did not fight resolutely enough against local self-rule, the local guerrillas and the general insubordination of the local people. I accused him of being too lenient toward the wrong policy of Voroshilov and others, but it never entered my head that he was the actual instigator of that policy. This became evident somewhat later from his own telegrams and from the admissions of Voroshilov and others.

Stalin spent several months at Tsaritsyn. His underhanded work against me, which even then made up an essential part of his activity, went hand in hand with the homespun opposition of Voroshilov who was his closest associate. However, Stalin bore himself so that at any moment he would be able to jump back, his skirts clear. Lenin knew Stalin better than I and apparently suspected that the stubbornness of the Tsaritsynites could be explained by Stalin's activity behind the scenes. I made up my mind to set things right at Tsaritsyn. After a new clash with the command there I decided upon the recall of Stalin. This was accomplished through the good offices of Sverdlov, who went himself in a special train to bring Stalin back. Lenin wanted to reduce the conflict to a minimum, and was of course right in that respect.

At the time, while the Red Army had already managed to win big victories on the Eastern Front, almost completely clearing the Volga, matters continued to go badly in the South, where everything was in chaos because orders were not carried out. On the 5th of October, at Kozlov, I issued an order concerning the unification of all armies and groups of the Southern Front under the command of the Revolutionary Council of War of the Southern Front, consisting of the former General [Sytin and three Bolsheviks—Shlyapnikov, Mekhonoshin and Lazimir] : "All orders and instructions of the Council are subject to unconditional and immediate execution." The order threatened the insubordinates with dire punishments. Then I telegraphed Lenin:

I insist categorically on Stalin's recall. Things are going badly at the Tsaritsyn Front in spite of superabundant forces. Voroshilov is capable of commanding a regiment, not an army of 50,000. However, I shall leave him in command of the Tenth Army at Tsaritsyn, provided he reports to the Commander of the Army of the South, Sytin. Thus far Tsaritsyn has not even sent reports of operations to Kozlov. I have required reports of reconnaissances and operations sent twice daily. If that is not done by tomorrow, I shall remand Voroshilov and Minin to court martial and shall publish the fact in an Army Order. According to the statutes of the Revolutionary Council of War of the Republic, Stalin and Minin, as long as they remain in Tsaritsyn, are nothing more than members of the Revolutionary Council of War of the Tenth Army. We have only a short time left for taking the offensive before the autumn mud sets in, when the local roads will be impassable for either infantry or mounted troops. No serious action will be possible without coordination with Tsaritsyn. There is no time to lose on diplomatic negotiations. Tsaritsyn must either submit or take the consequences. We have a colossal superiority of forces, but there is utter anarchy at the top. I can put a stop to it in twenty-four hours, provided I have your firm and clear-cut support. At all events, this is the only course I can see.

[This was followed the next day by this direct wire to Lenin]:

★ I have received the following telegram: "Stalin's military order #118 must be cancelled. I have issued full instructions to the Commander of the Southern Front, Sytin. Stalin's activities undermine all my plans . . . Vatzetis, Commander-in-Chief; Danishevsky, member of the Revolutionary Council of War."

[Stalin was recalled from Tsaritsyn in the second half of October. This is what he] wrote in *Pravda* (30th of October, 1918) [about the Southern Front]:

★ The point of the greatest attack by the enemy was Tsaritsyn. That was understandable, because the capture of Tsaritsyn and the interruption of communications with the South would have assured the achievement of all the tasks of the enemy. It would have united the Don counter-revolutionists with the upper layer of the Cossacks of the Astrakhan and Ural Armies, creating a united front of the counter-revolution from the Don to the Czecho-Slovaks. It would have secured the South and the Caspian for the counter-revolutionists, internally and externally. It would have left the Soviet troops of the Northern Caucasus in a state of helplessness . . .

[Was Stalin "confessing" that he was guilty of having aggravated the situation by his intrigues and insubordination? Hardly. However, on his way back to Moscow from Tsaritsyn, Sverdlov inquired] cautiously about my intentions and then proposed to me that I have a talk with Stalin, who it developed was on his train.

"Do you really want to dismiss all of them?" Stalin asked me in a tone of exaggerated subservience. "They're fine boys."

"Those fine boys will ruin the Revolution, which can't wait for them to grow up," I answered him. "All I want is to draw Tsaritsyn back into Soviet Russia."

Thereafter, whenever I had occasion to tread on the corns of personal predilections, friendships or vanities, Stalin carefully gathered up all the people whose corns had been stepped on. He had a lot of time for that, since it furthered his personal ends. The leading spirits of Tsaritsyn became from that time on his principal tools. As soon as Lenin fell ill Stalin, through his henchmen, had Tsaritsyn renamed Stalingrad.

[The Tsaritsyn oppositionists were a curious lot. The man who most detested the military specialists was Voroshilov—"the locksmith of Lugansk," as he came to be called by latter-day chroniclers—a hearty and impudent fellow, not overly-intellectual but shrewd and unscrupulous. He never could make head or tail of military theory, but he was a gifted browbeater and had no compunction about utilizing the ideas of brighter subordinates and no false modesty about taking full credit for them. His intellectual naiveté in both military theory and Marxism was to be amply demonstrated in 1921, when,] following uncritically the lead of some obscure ultra-Leftist, he argued that aggressiveness and the tactic of the offensive was a consequence of "the class nature of the Red Army," at the same time offering "proof" of the necessity of the offensive in the form of quotations from the French military regulations of 1921.

His "loyal right hand" was Shchadenko [the political commissar of the Tenth Army, a tailor by trade, whom later chroniclers were to immortalize thus] : "Angrily frowning under his eagle-like eyebrows, his militant eyes squinting, he ran around the front, burning up with the effort to be Klim's loyal right hand."

Equally zealous but quite different from both was Sergei Minin. [He was a curious mixture of poet and demagogue who had given himself heart and soul to the cause and suffered from a blinding phobia of all tsarist officers.] Popular among the workers of Tsaritsyn since his participation as a young student in the Revolution of 1905, Tsaritsyn was proud of him as its leading and most impassioned orator. He was by far the most honest of the lot, but also perhaps the most unreasonable. Sincere in his intransigeance, he contributed his full share of earnest mischief to the aggravation of the military situation in Tsaritsyn. [He was an innocent but all the more effective tool of Stalin's Tsaritsyn intrigue and was cast aside as soon as his usefulness came to an end.]

Then there was the engineer Rukhimovich, former "People's Commissar of War of the Donetz-Krivorog Republic"—[one of the mushroom Red republics of the early days of the Revolution—who had given Voroshilov his first mandate to organize a proletarian army. Placed in charge of supplies, the provincial-minded] Rukhimovitch could conceive of no needs except the needs of the Tenth Army. No other army swallowed as many rifles and bullets, and at the first refusal he yelled about the treason of the specialists in Moscow. [He, like the youngest member of the Council of War, Valerii] Mezhlauk, rose subsequently to second-rank heights in the Stalinist hierarchy, to disappear from view [for reasons unknown. There were] Zhloba, Kharchenko, Gorodovik, Savitsky, Parhomenko and others, whose contributions to the Red Army and the Soviet State did not rank above that of hundreds of thousands of others, but whose names were saved from utter oblivion only because of their early association with Stalin at Tsaritsyn.

"Trotsky," [Tarassov-Rodionov wrote later], "spoke at the Revolutionary Council of War haughtily and irritably. He let loose a hail-storm of stinging rebukes for the tremendous waste of material . . . Trotsky was not interested in explanations . . ." On the first of November I telegraphed to Sverdlov and Lenin from Tsaritsyn:

> The situation with the Tenth Army is as follows: There are many forces here but no operational leadership. The staff of the Southern Front and Vatzetis are inclined to favor changing the commander. I would consider it possible to keep Voroshilov by giving him an experienced operational staff. He objects to that, but I don't doubt that the question could be settled . . . The only serious obstacle is Minin, who carries on an extremely

harmful policy. I insist in every way on his transfer. When will the medals be ready?

After inspecting all the sectors of the Tsaritsyn Army, in a special order of November 5th, 1918, I recognized the services of many of the units and their commanders, at the same time noting that parts of the army consisted of units calling themselves divisions which actually were not such in substance; that "political work in certain units has not even been started yet"; that "the disposition of military reserves does not always proceed with military caution"; that "in certain instances the commander, not wishing to carry out an operational order, would pass it on for the consideration of a meeting . . ." and the like. "As citizens," the order stated, "the soldiers are free during their leisure hours to hold meetings on any question. As soldiers, they must carry out military orders without any objections."

After visiting the Southern Front, including Tsaritsyn, I reported to the Sixth Congress of Soviets on the 9th of November, 1918: "Not all Soviet workers have understood that our administration has been centralized and that all orders issued from above must be final . . . We shall be pitiless with those Soviet workers who have not yet understood; we will remove them, cast them out of our ranks, pull them up with repressions." This was aimed at Stalin to a much greater extent than at Voroshilov, against whom these words were ostensibly directed at the time. Stalin was present at the Congress and kept silent. He was silent at the session of the Politburo. He could not openly defend his behavior. All the more did he store up his anger. It was in those days—recalled from Tsaritsyn, with deep anger and a thirst of vengeance in his heart—that he wrote his piece on the First Anniversary of the Revolution. The purpose of the article was to strike a blow at my prestige, turning against me the authority of the Central Committee headed by Lenin. In that anniversary article, dictated by suppressed anger, Stalin was nevertheless forced to write:

> All the work of practical organization of the insurrection was conducted under the immediate leadership of the President of the Petrograd Soviet, Comrade Trotsky. It is possible to declare with certainty that the swift passing of the garrison to the side of the Soviet, and the bold execution of the work of the Military Revolutionary Committee, the Party owes principally and first of all to Comrade Trotsky.

On the 30th of November, acting on the proposal of the Commissariat of War to organize a Council of Defense, the All-Russian Central Executive Committee, which had already proclaimed the Soviet Republic to be a military camp, passed a resolution calling for the convocation of the Council of Defense, composed of Lenin, myself, Krassin, the Commissar of Ways of Communication, the Commissar of Supplies and the Chairman of the Praesidium of the Central Executive Committee, Sverdlov. By agreement with Lenin I proposed that Stalin be also included. Lenin wanted to give Stalin some satisfaction for removing him from the Army in Tsaritsyn; I wanted to give Stalin the chance to formulate openly his criticisms and proposals, without wetting the powder in the War Department. The first session, which outlined our tasks in a general way, was held in the daytime of the first of December. From Lenin's notes at the session, it appears that Stalin spoke six times, Krassin nine times, Sklyansky nine times, Lenin eight times. Each orator was allowed no more than two minutes. The leadership in the work of the Council of Defense, not only on major questions, but even on details, was concentrated entirely in the hands of Lenin. To Stalin was assigned the task of formulating a thesis on the struggle against regionalism and another on fighting red tape. There is no evidence that either thesis was ever composed. Moreover, in the interest of expediting the work, it was decided that "the decrees of the commission appointed by the Council of Defense, signed by Lenin, Stalin and the representatives of the appropriate department, will have the force of a decree by the Council of Defense." But as far as Stalin was concerned the whole matter boiled down to another title instead of actual work.

[Notwithstanding these concessions, Stalin continued to support the Tsaritsyn opposition secretly, nullifying the efforts of the War Department to enforce order and discipline in that sector. At Tsaritsyn, his principal tool was Voroshilov; in Moscow, Stalin himself exerted all the pressure he could muster upon Lenin. It therefore became necessary to send the following telegram from Kursk on December 14]:

★ To the Chairman of the Council of People's Commissars, Lenin. The question of recalling Okulov cannot be decided by itself. Okulov was appointed as a counterbalance to Voroshilov, as a guarantee that military orders would be carried out. It is impossible to let Voroshilov remain after he has nullified all attempts at compromise. Tsaritsyn must have a new Revolutionary Council of War with a new commander and Voroshilov must go to the Ukraine.

Chairman of the Revolutionary Council of War of the Republic, Trotsky.

[Voroshilov was then transferred to the Ukraine. The fighting capacity of the Tenth Army rose by leaps and bounds. Not only the new commander but Stalin's successor on the Council of War, Shlyapnikov, proved immeasurably more efficient, and the military situation at Tsaritsyn soon improved.

[Several days after Voroshilov's removal, and after the months of enforced abstention from the extremely tempting business of intervening in military affairs following upon his own removal from Tsaritsyn, Stalin got another opportunity to work at the front—this time, for a couple of weeks. He utilized it for sticking a knife into Trotsky's back. The incident began with the following exchange of telegrams between Lenin and Trotsky]:

I.

★ Coded Telegram to Comrade Trotsky at Kursk or any other place where the Chairman of the Revolutionary Council of War of the Republic may be: Moscow, December 13, 1918.

Extremely alarming news from vicinity of Perm. It is in danger. I am afraid we have forgotten about the Urals. Are the reinforcements to Perm and the Urals being sent with sufficient energy? Lashevich told Zinoviev that only units that had been under fire should be sent.

Lenin.

2.

⋆ To Trotsky at Kozlov or wherever the Chairman of the Revolutionary Council of War of the Republic may be:

Moscow, December 31, 1918.

There are several Party reports from around Perm about the catastrophic condition of the Army and about drunkenness. I am forwarding them to you. They ask that you come there. I thought of sending Stalin. I am afraid Smilga will be too soft with Lashevich, who it is said drinks himself and is unable to restore order. Telegraph your opinion.
#66847.

Lenin.

3.

⋆ By direct wire in code to Moscow, Kremlin, for the Chairman of the Council of People's Commissars, Lenin.

Reply to #66847.

Voronezh, January 1, 1919. 19 o'clock [7 P.M.]

From the reports of the operations of the Third Army I concluded that the leadership there is completely at a loss and proposed a change of command. The decision was postponed. Now I deem replacement unpostponable.

I completely share your misgivings concerning the excessive softness of the Comrade who has gone there. I agree to Stalin's journey with powers from both the Party and the Revolutionary Council of War of the Republic for restoring order, purging the staff of Commissars, and severely punishing the guilty. The new commander will be appointed upon agreement with Serpukhov. I propose that Lashevich be appointed a member of the Revolutionary Council of War of the Northern Front, where we do not have a responsible Party man, and the front may soon acquire greater significance.

#9.

Chairman of the Revolutionary Council of
War of the Republic,
Trotsky.

[The matter was then referred to the Central Committee, which decided]:

⋆ to appoint a Party investigating committee of the Central Committee members Stalin and Dzerzhinsky to conduct a detailed investigation into the reasons for the surrender of Perm and the latest defeats on the Ural Front, and also to elucidate all the circumstances surrounding the above facts.

[The Third Army had surrendered Perm to the advancing troops of Admiral Kolchak and took up its position at Vyatka, where it held its ground precariously. Stalin and Dzerzhinsky reached Vyatka while the Third Army was holding it against the attacks of the enemy. On the day of their arrival there, January 5th, 1919, Stalin and Dzerzhinsky telegraphed to Lenin][8]:

[8] The following three excerpts, found in Trotsky's notes for this book, are from the works of S. Dmitrievsky, whom Trotsky quotes also in other places. They tell the story. How accurately, is another question. The possibility that Trotsky might have challenged some of the statements Dmitrievsky ascribes to Stalin and Dzerzhinsky is not excluded.—C. M.

★ The investigation begun. We shall inform you from time to time about the course of the investigation. Meantime we deem it necessary to inform you about such needs of the Third Army as do not bear postponement. The point is, that out of the Third Army of more than 30,000 men, there remain only 11,000 weary, exhausted soldiers, who can hardly withstand the pressure of the enemy. The units sent by the Commander-in-Chief are unreliable, partly even hostile to us, and are in need of serious filtering. In order to save the remnants of the Third Army and to prevent the rapid movement of the enemy upon Vyatka (according to information secured from the commanding staff of the front and of the Third Army, this danger is quite real), it is absolutely necessary at once to transfer from Russia and place at the disposal of the army commander at least three entirely reliable regiments. We insistently urge that you exert the proper pressure in this direction upon the corresponding military institution. We repeat: without this measure the fate of Perm awaits Vyatka.

[On the 15th of January Stalin and Dzerzhinsky informed the Council of Defense]:

★ 1200 reliable bayonets and swords were sent to the front; the next day two squadrons of cavalry. On the 10th the 62nd Regiment of the 3rd Brigade (previously thoroughly filtered) was sent. These units made it possible for us to check the advance of the enemy, to raise the morale of the Third Army and to begin our advance upon Perm, so far successful. A thorough purge of Soviet and Party institutions is going on in the rear of the Army. Revolutionary committees have been organized in Vyatka and at county seats. Strong revolutionary organizations have begun to be set up and continue to be set up in villages. The entire Party and the Soviet work is being reconstructed along new lines. The military control has been cleaned up and reorganized. The provincial Cheka has been purged and staffed with new workers . . .

[After investigating the causes of catastrophe, Stalin and Dzerzhinsky reported to Lenin that these were]:

★ The fatigue and exhaustion of the army at the moment of the enemy's advance, our lack of reserves at that moment, the staff's lack of contact with the army, the mismanagement of the army commander, and inadmissibly criminal methods of administering the front by the Revolutionary Council of War of the Republic, which paralyzed the possibility of offering timely aid to the Third Army, the unreliability of reinforcements sent from the rear due to old methods of recruitment, absolute unsteadiness of the rear due to the complete helplessness and the inability of Local Soviet and Party organizations.

[Almost every statement in this report was a blow at Trotsky. Had Lenin, the Council of Defense, the Central Committee and its Politburo taken these charges against Trotsky seriously, they would have had no alternative but to remove him from office. However, Lenin knew Stalin well enough to consider this report by him and his associate in Vyatka as less factual than recriminative—an act of revenge for the recall from Tsaritsyn, and for Trotsky's refusal to give him another chance at the Southern Front, where he could rejoin Voroshilov and the other Tsaritsynites.

[Meantime in the Ukraine, utilizing his political prerogatives and his rank as Army Commander, Voroshilov continued to antagonize the military specialists, disrupted staff work and interfered with directives from General Headquarters. With the support of Stalin and others, he soon made his presence at the Southern Front so intolerable that on the 10th of January, 1919, it was necessary to telegraph]:

★ To Moscow
To the Chairman of the Central Executive Committee, Sverdlov.
. . . I must state categorically that the Tsaritsyn policy, which has led to the complete disintegration of the Tsaritsyn army, cannot be tolerated in the Ukraine . . . Okulov is leaving for Moscow. I propose that you and Comrade Lenin give the utmost attention to his report on Voroshilov's work. The line of Stalin, Voroshilov and Rukhimovich means the ruin of everything we are doing.

Chairman of the Revolutionary
Council of War of the Republic,
Trotsky.

[While Stalin with the aid of Dzerzhinsky was conniving in Vyatka], Lenin insisted that it was necessary for me to conclude a compromise with Stalin:

★ Stalin would very much like to work on the Southern Front . . . Stalin hopes that on the job he will succeed in convincing us of the correctness of his views . . . In informing you, Lev Davidovich, about all these declarations of Stalin, I beg you to give them your most thoughtful consideration and to answer me: in the first place, whether you agree to let Stalin explain the matter to you in person, for which he is willing to report to you, and in the second place, whether you deem it possible on the basis of certain concrete conditions to adjust the previous conflict and to arrange to work together, which is what Stalin desires so very much. As for me, I think that it is necessary to make every effort for joint work with Stalin.

Lenin.

Lenin's letter was obviously written under the influence of Stalin's insistence. Stalin was seeking agreement, conciliation, further military work, even at the cost of temporary and insincere capitulation. The front attracted him, because here for the first time he could work with the most finished of all the administrative machines, the military machine. As a member of the Revolutionary Council of War who was at the same time a member of the Central Committee of the Party, he was inevitably the dominant figure in every Council of War, in every army, on every front. When others hesitated, he decided. He could command, and each command was followed by a practically automatic execution of his order—not as in the collegium of the Commissariat of Nationalities, where he had to hide from opponents in the commandant's kitchen.

On the 11th of January I replied by direct wire to Lenin:

Compromise is of course necessary, but not a rotten one. The fact of the matter is, that all the Tsaritsynites have now congregated at Kharkov. You can gather what the Tsaritsynites are from Okulov's report, which throughout consists solely of factual material, and the reports of commissars. I consider Stalin's patronage of the Tsaritsyn tendency a most dangerous ulcer, worse than any treason or betrayal by military specialists . . . Rukhimovich is only another name for Voroshilov. Within a month we shall again have to choke on the Tsaritsyn mess, only this time we will not have the Cossacks against us but the English and French. Nor is Rukhimovich the only one. They firmly hang on to each other, raising ignorance to a principle. Voroshilov plus the Ukrainian guerrillas plus the low cultural level of the population plus demagogy—we cannot tolerate that under any conditions. Let them appoint Artem, but not Voroshilov or Rukhimovich . . . Once again I urge a careful reading of Okulov's report on the Tsaritsyn Army and how Voroshilov demoralized it with Stalin's cooperation.

Concerning this first period of Stalin's work at the Southern Front no materials have been published. The point is that this period did not last very long and ended up quite sadly for him. It is a pity that I cannot rely on any material to supplement my memory of this episode, for it left no traces whatever in my personal archives. The official archives have naturally remained in the Commissariat of War. On the Revolutionary Council of War of the Southern Front, with Yegorov commanding, were Stalin and Berzin, who subsequently devoted himself entirely to military work and played a prominent if not a leading role in the military operations of Republican Spain. Once, at night—I regret I cannot state anything with regard to the exact date—Berzin called me to the direct wire and asked me whether he was "obliged to sign an operative order by the Commander of the Front Yegorov." According to the rules, the signature of the commissar or political member of the Council of War on an operative order meant merely that the order did not have any hidden counter-revolutionary significance. As for the operative meaning of the order, that was entirely the responsibility of the commander. In this particular case, the order of the Front Commander was merely a matter of passing on an operative order of the Commander-in-Chief, a transmission and interpretation of that Army order to the army under his command. Stalin declared that Yegorov's order was not valid and that he would not sign it. In view of the refusal of a member of the Central Committee to sign the order, Berzin did not dare to place his own signature on it. At the same time, an operative order signed only by the officer in command had no actual force.

What argument did Stalin advance against an order which, as far as I remember, was of secondary importance and the nature of which I cannot now recall? No argument at all. He simply would not sign it. It would have been quite possible for him to have called me to the direct wire and explained his reasons to me, or, if he preferred, to have called Lenin to the direct wire. The Commander of the Front, if he were in disagreement with Stalin, by the same rule could have expressed his own considerations to the Commander-in-Chief or to me. Stalin's objection would have been immediately discussed in the Politburo, and the Commander-in-Chief would have been requested to submit supplementary explanations. But just as in Tsaritsyn, Stalin preferred a different form of action: "I won't sign it," he declared, in order to show off his importance to his collaborators and to his subordinates. I replied to Berzin: "The order of the Commander-in-Chief certified by a commissar is obligatory for you. Sign it immediately; otherwise, you will be turned over to the Tribunal." Berzin immediately attached his signature to the commander's order.

The question passed to the Politburo. Lenin said, not without embarrassment: "What can we do about it? Stalin again caught in the act!" It was decided to recall Stalin from the Southern Front. This was his second important misfire. I remember, he came back sheepish but apparently not resentful. On the contrary, he even said that he had achieved his purpose, that he had wanted to call attention to improper relations between the chief command and the command at the front, that although the order of the Commander-in-Chief contained nothing inimical, it was issued without previously sounding out the opinion of the Southern Front, which was not right. That, he said, was what he was really protesting against. He felt quite satisfied with himself. My impression was that he had bitten off more than he could chew. Caught in the trap of a chance swaggering remark, he had been unable to extricate himself. At any rate, it was perfectly obvious that he was doing everything possible to cover up his traces and to make believe that nothing had happened. [To save his face, it was then proposed, probably upon Lenin's initiative, to shift him to the Southwestern Front. But Stalin replied] :

> ★ February 4, 1919.
> To the Central Committee of the Party.
> To Comrades Lenin and Trotsky.
>
> . . . My own profound conviction is: no change in the situation can possibly be effected by my going there . . .
>
> Stalin.

[For three or four months after that he held on leash his eagerness to work in the military machine and resumed his contributions to *The Life of the Nationalities*.

[The liquidation of the Tsaritsynites was less real than apparent. Actually, Stalin and his allies had merely changed their field and methods of attack. The new field was the Party, and the methods were adapted accordingly.] As in 1912-1913 with reference to the Conciliators and as during the pre-October days with reference to the opposition of Zinoviev and Kamenev, so at the Eighth Congress [of the Party, Stalin, ostensibly in no way connected with the Military Opposition, worked hard on building it up, and used it as leverage against Trotsky].

The Military Opposition consisted of two groups. There were the numerous underground workers who were utterly worn out by prison and exile, and who now could not find a place for themselves in the building of the Army and the State. They looked with great disfavor on all sorts of upstarts—and there was no lack of them in responsible posts. But in this opposition there were also very many advanced workers, fighting elements with a fresh reserve of energy, who trembled with political apprehension when they saw yesterday's engineers, officers, teachers, professors, once again in commanding positions. This Workers' Opposition reflected, in the final analysis, lack of confidence in its own powers and uncertainty that the new class which had come to power would be able to dominate and control the broad circles of the old intelligentsia.

During the first period, when the Revolution was spreading from the industrial centers toward the periphery, armed fighting detachments were organized of workers, sailors and ex-soldiers, to establish the Soviet régime in various localities. These detachments frequently had to wage minor wars. Enjoying as they did the sympathy of the masses, they easily became victorious. They received a certain tempering, and their leaders a certain authority. There was no proper liaison between these detachments. Their tactics had the character of guerrilla raids, and as far as they went that was sufficient. But the overthrown classes, with the aid of their foreign protectors, began to organize their own armies. Well-armed and well-staffed, they began to take the offensive. Accustomed to easy victories, the guerrilla detachments at once displayed their worthlessness; they did not have adequate intelligence sections; they had no liaison with each other; nor were they ever able to execute a complex maneuver. Hence—at various times, in various parts of the country—guerrillaism met with disaster. It was no easy task to include these separate detachments in a centralized system. The military ability of the commanders was not high, and they were hostile to the old officers, partly because they had no political confidence in them and partly to cover up lack of confidence in themselves. Yet as late as July, 1918, at the Fifth Congress of Soviets the Left Essars still insisted that we could defend ourselves with guerrilla detachments and had no need of a centralized army. "This is tantamount to being told," I replied to them, "that we don't need railways and can get along with horse-carts for transportation."

Our fronts had a tendency to close into a ring of more than eight thousand kilometers in circumference. Our enemies themselves selected the direction, created a base on the periphery, received aid from abroad and delivered the blow in the direction of the center. The advantage of our situation consisted in this, that we occupied a central position and acted along internal operational lines. As soon as the enemy selected his direction for the attack, we were able to select our direction for the counter-attack. We were able to move our forces and mass them for thrusts in the most important directions at any given moment. But this advantage was available to us on the sole condition of complete centralization in management and command. In order to sacrifice temporarily certain of the more remote or less important sectors for the sake of saving the closer and more important ones, we had to be in a position to issue orders and have them obeyed instead of arguing about them. All of this is too elementary to require explanation here. Failure to understand this was due to those centrifugal tendencies which were aroused by the Revolution, the provincialism of the vast land of isolated communities, the elemental spirit of independence that had not yet had the time or the opportunity to mature. Suffice it to say that in the beginning not only provinces but even region after region had its own Council of People's Commissars with its very own Commissar of War. The successes of regular organization induced these scattered detachments to adapt themselves to certain norms and conditions, to consolidate themselves into regiments and divisions. But the spirit and the method often remained as of old. A chief of a division, not sure of himself, was very easy-going with his colonels. Voroshilov, as an army commander, was very indulgent with the chiefs of his divisions. But all the more resentful was their attitude toward the Center, which was not satisfied with the outward transformation of the guerrilla detachments into regiments and divisions, but insisted on the more fundamental requirements of military organization. In an argument with one of Stalin's guerrilla partisans I wrote in January, 1919:

> In one of our armies, it was considered a mark of the highest revolutionism not so very long ago to jeer rather vulgarly and stupidly at "Military specialists," i.e., at all who had studied in military schools; yet in this very same army practically no political work was carried on. The attitude there was no less hostile, perhaps more so, toward Communist commissars than toward the specialists. Who was sowing this hostility? The worst kind of the new commanders—military know-nothings, half-guerrillas, half-Party people who did not want to have anyone around, be they Party workers or serious military workers . . . Hanging on for dear life to their jobs, they fiercely execrated the very mention of military studies . . . Many of them, getting finally into a hopeless mess, ended up by simply rebelling against the Soviet Government.

At a moment of grave danger, the Second Petrograd Regiment, occupying a crucial sector, abandoned the front upon its own initiative and, headed by its commander and commissar, seized a river steamer and sailed down the Volga from the vicinity of Kazan' in the direction of Nizhni-Novgorod. The boat was stopped by my order and the deserters were placed on trial. The commander and commissar of the regiment were shot. This was the first instance of the shooting of a Communist, Commissar Panteleyev, for violation of military duty. In the Party there was a lot of talk and gossip about this incident. In December, 1918, *Pravda* published an article which, without mentioning me by name but obviously hinting at me, referred to the shooting of "the best comrades without a trial." The author of the article, a certain A. Kamensky, was in himself a figure of little importance—obviously, a mere pawn. It seemed incomprehensible that an article containing such dire and weighty accusations could appear in the central organ. Its editor was Bukharin, a Left Communist and therefore opposed to the employment of "generals" in the Army. But, especially at that time, he was utterly incapable of intrigue. The riddle was solved when I discovered upon investigation that the author of the article, or rather the man who signed it, A. Kamensky was on the staff of the Tenth Army and at the time was under the direct influence of Stalin. It is beyond doubt that Stalin surreptitiously assured the publication of the article. The very terminology of the accusation: the brazen reference to the shooting of "the best" comrades, and moreover, "without a trial," was astonishing because of the monstrosity of the fabrication as well as its inherent absurdity. But it was precisely this crude exaggeration of the accusation that revealed Stalin, the organizer of the future Moscow trials. The Central Committee settled the matter. I recall that Kamensky and the editorial board were reprimanded, but Stalin's manipulating hand remained invisible.

[Later, while at the Southern Front, Stalin continued to utilize this discredited story through his tools at the Party Congress. When news of this reached Trotsky, who was away at the front during the sessions of the Eighth Congress, he was obliged to appeal to the Central Committee a second time with the request "to institute an investigation in the case of the shooting of Panteleyev," as the minutes of the Central Committee session for April 18, 1919, state, "in view of the fact that the matter was again brought up at the Party Congress." With Stalin present at the Central Committee session, the request was unanimously referred to the Orgburo, where again with Stalin present (he was a member of both bodies), the Orgburo once more unanimously] appointed a commission composed of Krestinsky, Serebryakov and Smilga, all three members of both the Orgburo and the Central Committee, to look into the entire question. The Commission reached, of course, the conclusion that Panteleyev was shot after a trial and not as a Communist and a [commissar], but as a vicious deserter—"not because his regiment abandoned its position, but because he abandoned the position together with his regiment," [in the words of Army Commander Slavin, commanding officer of the Army to which Panteleyev's regiment belonged]. Ten years later this episode would again play a part in Stalin's campaign against me under the very same title: "The Shooting Of The Best Communists Without A Trial."

The Eighth Congress of the Party was in session from the 18th to the 23rd of March, 1919, in Moscow. On the very eve of the Congress we received a strong blow from the Whites near Ufa. I decided, regardless of the Congress, to go immediately to the Eastern Front. After suggesting the immediate return to the front of all the military delegates, I made ready to go to Ufa. Part of the delegates were dissatisfied; they had come to the capital for the few days' furlough and did not want to leave it. Someone started the rumor that I wanted to avoid debates on military policy. That lie surprised me. I introduced a proposal in the Central Committee on March 16, 1919, to repeal the directive about the immediate return of the military delegates, assigned the defense of the military policy to Sokolnikov and immediately went East. The discussion of the military question at the Eighth Congress, notwithstanding the presence of quite a significant opposition, did not deter me; the situation at the front seemed to me much more important than electioneering at the Congress, especially since I had no doubt that the policy I considered the only correct one was bound to win on its own merits. The Central Committee approved the thesis I had previously introduced and appointed Sokolnikov its official reporter. The opposition's report was to be presented by V. M. Smirnov, an Old Bolshevik and a former artillery officer of the World War. Smirnov was one of the leaders of the Left Communists, who were determined opponents of the Brest-Litovsk Peace and had demanded the launching of a guerrilla war against the German regular army. This continued to be the basis of their platform even as late as 1919, although true enough, they had somewhat cooled off in the interim. The formation of a centralized and regular army was impossible without military specialists and without the substitution of proper and systematic leadership for improvisation. The Left Communists, having managed to cool off to some extent, tried to adapt their views of yesterday to the growth of the State machine and the needs of the regular army. But they retreated step by step, utilizing all they could out of their old baggage, and camouflaging their essentially guerrilla tendencies with new formulas.

A minor but very characteristic episode took place at the beginning of the Congress with regard to the composition of the praesidium. It indicated to a certain extent the nature of the Congress, if only in its preliminary stage. On the order of the day was the trying military question. It was no secret to Lenin that behind the scenes Stalin was in fact at the head of the opposition on that issue. Lenin had come to an agreement with the Petrograd delegation concerning the composition of the praesidium. The oppositionists proposed several supplementary candidatures under various pretexts, naming not only oppositionists but others as well. For example, they proposed the candidature of Sokolnikov, the chief spokesman of the official point of view. However, Bukharin, Stassova, Oborin, Rykov and Sokolnikov declined, honoring as a personal obligation the agreement that had been concluded unofficially concerning the praesidium. But Stalin did not decline. That flagrantly revealed his oppositionist status. He seemed to have been hard at work trying to pack the Congress with his partisans, and electioneering among the delegates. Lenin was aware of this, yet to forestall embarrassment he did his utmost to spare Stalin the test of a vote either for or against him. Through one of the delegates Lenin put the preliminary question: "Are supplementary candidates for members of the praesidium necessary at all?" And without an effort he secured a negative answer to that question. Stalin suffered defeat, which Lenin had made as impersonal and inoffensive as was humanly possible. Today the official version is that Stalin supported Lenin's position on the military question at the Eighth Congress. Why then are not the protocols published now when there is no longer any need to preserve [such] military secrets?

At the Ukrainian conference in March, 1920, Stalin formally defended me, appearing as the reporter representing the Central Committee; at the same time, through trusted people, he exerted no little effort to achieve the failure of his theses. At the Eighth Congress of the Party such a maneuver was difficult, since all the proceedings were directly under the observation of Lenin, several other members of the Central Committee and responsible military workers. But essentially, here too Stalin played quite the same role as at the Ukrainian conference. As a member of the Central Committee he either spoke equivocally in defense of the official military policy or kept quiet; but through his closest friends—Voroshilov and Rukhimovich and other Tsaritsynites, who were the shock troops of the opposition at the Congress—he continued to undermine not so much the military policy, it is true, as its chief spokesman. He incited these delegates to the vilest kind of personal attack against Sokolnikov, who had assumed the defense of the War Commissariat without any reservations. The nucleus of the opposition was the Tsaritsyn group and most prominent among them was Voroshilov. For some time preceding the Congress they were in constant contact with Stalin, who instructed them and held in leash their premature hastiness, at the same time centralizing the intrigue against the War Department. This was the sum and substance of his activity at the Eighth Congress.

"A year ago," Sokolnikov reported to the Eighth Congress of the Party, "at the moment of the complete collapse of the Army, when there was no military organization to defend the proletarian revolution, the Soviet Government resorted to the system of voluntary army formations, and in its day this volunteer army played its part. Now, looking back at this period, as at a stage we have passed, we should take into consideration both the positive and the negative aspects. The essence of the positive side was that the best elements of the working class participated . . . But in addition to these bright aspects of the guerrilla period there were also the dark sides, which in the end outweighed whatever was good in it. The best elements left, died, or were taken prisoner . . . What remained was a conglomeration of the worst elements . . . These evil elements were supplemented by those who chose to enlist in the Volunteer Army because they had been cast out in the street in consequence of the catastrophic collapse of the entire social order . . . These were, finally, supplemented by the demobilized riffraff of the Old Army. That is why during the guerrilla period of our military organization such forces developed as compelled us to liquidate this guerrilla system. In the end it had resulted in a system in which small, independent detachments grouped themselves around separate leaders. These detachments in the final reckoning were devoted not only to the struggle in defense of the Soviet Government, in defense of the victories of the Revolution, but also to banditry and marauding. They turned into guerrilla detachments that were the bulwark of adventurism . . ." On the other hand, "in the present period," Sokolnikov continued, "the building of the State . . . the Army . . . goes forward . . ."

"A great deal of heated discussion," Sokolnikov said, turning to another phase of his report, "arose around the question of military specialists . . . Now this question has been essentially solved both theoretically and practically. Even the opponents of the use of military specialists themselves admit that this question is out of date . . . Military specialists were used in the reorganization of the guerrilla army into the regular army . . . Thus we achieved the stability of the front, thus we achieved military success. Conversely, where the military specialists were not used, we frittered away our forces to the point of utter disintegration . . . In the problem of the military specialists, we are confronted not with a purely military problem but with a general special problem. When the question was brought up of inviting engineers to the factories, of inviting the former capitalist organizers, do you remember how the ultra-Red Left Communists taunted us with their merciless 'super-Communist' criticism . . . that to return the engineers to the factories meant to return the commanding staff of the bourgeoisie? And here we have an analogous criticism, applied now to the building of the Army. We are told that by returning former officers to the Army we will restore the former officer class and the former army. But these comrades forget that side by side with these commanders there are commissars, the representatives of the Soviet Government; that these military specialists are in the ranks of an army which is entirely at the service of the proletarian revolution . . . This Army, which has tens of thousands of old specialists, has shown in practice that it is the army of the proletarian revolution."

By the time of the Eighth Congress, the disagreement on the military question was considerably less pronounced than it had been previously. The opposition no longer put the question as frankly as it had the year before. Then the centralized army was proclaimed to be characteristic of the imperialist State and in its place the opposition advocated the system of guerrilla detachments, rejecting the utilization of contemporary technical means of struggle, such as airplanes and tanks. This time they came out against the "imperialistic" principle of maneuverability: the corps, the division, even the brigade, were declared to be units too heavily weighted. It was proposed to reduce all of the armed forces of the Republic into distinct units of the combined services, each unit about the size of a regiment. This was essentially the ideology of guerrillaism slightly masked. The guerrillaists of the extreme "Left" defended themselves more openly. The use of the old officer corps, especially in commanding positions, was declared incompatible in action with loyalty to the revolutionary military doctrine.

The actual work of organizing the military forces of the workers' government proceeded along entirely different lines. We tried, especially in the beginning, to utilize as much as possible the experience, method, knowledge and means remaining from the old army. We built the revolutionary Army from the human and technical material at hand, striving always and everywhere to secure in it the dominance of the proletarian vanguard. The institution of commissars was under the circumstances an indispensable instrument of proletarian control. We combined the old commanding staff with the new, and only thus were we able to achieve the required results. This had become crystal-clear to a majority of the delegates by the time the Congress convened. No one any longer dared to reject in principle the foundations of the military policy. The opposition turned to criticism of occasional errors and excesses, regaling the Congress with all manner of sad anecdotes.

The reporter of the opposition, Smirnov, replying directly to Sokolnikov's statement that "some presumably stand for a guerrilla army and others for the regular army," pointed out that on the question of using military specialists "there are no disagreements among us over the dominant trend in our military policy." The basic disagreement was over the necessity of broadening the functions of commissars and members of the Revolutionary Council of War so as to ensure their greater participation in the management of the Army and in decisions pertaining to operational matters, and thereby reduce the role of the commanding staff. The Congress met this criticism about half way. It was decided to continue the recruiting of the old military specialists in full force, but on the other hand, it was emphasized that it was necessary to prepare a new commanding staff as an absolutely reliable instrument of the Soviet system. That this and all the other decisions were adopted unanimously with one abstaining vote is explained by the fact that the opposition had in the meantime repudiated most of its principal prejudices. Powerless to counterpose its own line to that of the majority of the Party, it had to join in the general conclusion. Nevertheless, some of the effects of the guerrillaism of the preceding period were evident throughout all of 1919, particularly in the South—in the Ukraine, in the Caucasus and in Transcaucasia, where the elimination of the guerrilla tendency proved no easy task.

In 1920 a prominent military worker wrote: "Notwithstanding all the pain, outcries and noise raised concerning our military policy, concerning the recruitment of military specialists in the Red Army and so forth, the head of the War Department, Comrade Trotsky, proved to be right. With an iron hand he carried through the indicated military policy, disdaining all threats . . . The victories of the Red Army on all the fronts is the best proof of the correctness of the military policy." Yet to this very day in innumerable books and articles the hoary tales of the treason of the "generals" whom I appointed persist without abating. These accusations sound particularly silly when one remembers that twenty years after the October Revolution Stalin accused of treason and exterminated almost the entire commanding staff appointed by himself. It might also be added that Sokolnikov, the official reporter, and V. M. Smirnov, the oppositionist co-reporter, both active participants in the Civil War, subsequently fell victims of the Stalinist purge.

A special military conference was held during the Congress, the minutes of which were kept but never published. The purpose of this conference was to give an opportunity to all participants, especially the dissatisfied members of the opposition, to express themselves fully, freely and frankly. Lenin delivered an energetic speech at this conference in defense of the military policy. What did Stalin say? Did he speak in defense of the Central Committee's position? It is hard to answer this question categorically. There is no doubt that he acted behind the scenes, inciting various oppositionists against the Commissariat of War. There can be no doubt of that because of the circumstances and the recollections of the participants of the Congress. A flagrant piece of evidence is the very fact that the protocols of the military conference of the Eighth Congress have not yet been published—either because Stalin did not speak at it, at all, or because his speech on that occasion would be too embarrassing for him now. [Stalin, along with Zinoviev, was also a member of a] special commission of conciliation for working out the final resolutions. What he did there remains unknown beyond the bare fact that a satellite of his, Yaroslovsky, was advanced as its reporter.

Soon after the Eighth Congress I replied to the declaration of Zinoviev, who, undoubtedly by agreement with Stalin, had taken it upon himself to defend "the insulted" Voroshilov, in a letter to the Central Committee. I said: "The only guilt that I can charge against myself with reference to him [Voroshilov] is that I spent too long, notably two or three months, on the effort to act by means of negotiations, persuasions, personal combinations, when in the interests of the cause, what was necessary was a firm organizational decision. For, in the end, the task in connection with the Tenth Army did not consist of convincing Voroshilov, but of attaining military successes in the shortest possible time." [And that of course depended on the maximum co-ordination of plans throughout the] country, which was divided into eight military districts composed of 46 provincial and 344 regional military commissariats.

[Stalin did his utmost to poison the mind of the Congress on the position taken by the Commissariat of War on the military question.] All documents on hand fully prove that by virtue of his position in the Central Committee and in the Government, Stalin *headed* the opposition. If I had previously suspected it, now I am fully convinced, that Stalin's machinations with the Ukrainians, his wire-pulling in the Central Committee of the Ukrainian Communist Party, and the like, are directly connected with the maneuvers of the military opposition. [Having] reaped no laurels at Tsaritsyn, he tried to reap his revenge [in the dark].

Chapter X

THE CIVIL WAR (*Continued*)

IN THE spring of 1919 the Northwestern Volunteer Army under the command of General Yudenich unexpectedly assumed the offensive and threatened Petrograd. Presently the English Fleet steamed into the Bay of Finland. Colonel Bulak-Balakhovich, at the head of his unit, led the drive against Pskov, and at the same time the Estonian units came to life at the front. On the 14th of May the corps of General Rodzyanko broke through the front of the Seventh Army, which had been considerably weakened by drafts against it for the more active fronts, occupied Yamburg and Pskov, and began a rapid simultaneous advance against Gatchina, Petrograd and Luga. The commander of the Seventh Army, stationed on the outskirts of Petrograd, entered into communication with Yudenich and organized a conspiracy among the garrisons surrounding the capital of the October Revolution—Kronstadt, Oranienbaum, Krasnaya Gor'ka, Syeraya Loshad', Krasnoye Syelo. The conspirators, according to their complot with Yudenich, made ready to occupy the capital simultaneously with the troops of his army. They hoped for the support of the disgruntled sailors and especially the active aid of the fleet. But the sailors of the two Soviet dreadnaughts did not support the insurrection, while the English fleet [restricted itself for the time being to watchful waiting]. The whole enterprise proved abortive. By the twelfth of June, 1919, only Krasnaya Gor'ka [and Syeraya Loshad' remained] in the hands of the conspirators, and for four days no attempt was made to capture them. Finally, after an exchange of shots with Kronstadt, Krasnaya Gor'ka was occupied on the 16th of June by a detachment of red sailors. [Syeraya Loshad' fell just as easily.

[Zinoviev, the head of the Party and the government in the city and region of Petrograd, had become panicky in the face of the advancing enemy and the Politburo had sent Stalin to his rescue.]

With special powers from the Central Committee of the Party and the Soviet Government, Stalin arrived in Petrograd in the latter part of May 1919. [His ruthlessness and resolution made themselves felt immediately. A couple of weeks after his arrival he telegraphed Lenin]:

★ After Krasnaya Gor'ka, Syeraya Loshad' was likewise liquidated. The guns there are in complete order. Lightning mopping up and reinforcement of the forts and fortresses now in full swing. The naval specialists assure me that the capture of Krasnaya Gor'ka from the sea turns upside down all naval science. All I can do about it is to weep over so-called science. The rapid capture of Gor'ka is explained by the rudest intervention by me and by other civilians in operational matters, which reached the point of cancelling orders on land and sea and imposing our own orders. I deem it my duty to declare that in the future I shall continue to proceed similarly notwithstanding all my respect for science.

Lenin was annoyed by this tone of provocative braggadocio. From Petrograd it was possible at any moment to communicate with the Kremlin and its staff, to replace incompetent or unreliable commanders, to strengthen the staff, i.e., to do all that everyone of the responsible military workers of the Party did time and time again at one front after another without violating the elementary rules of good taste, good manners, or the maintenance of correct relations, and without undermining the authority of the Army command and of the General Staff. But Stalin could not act in that way. He could feel his superiority over others only by insulting them. He could not derive any satisfaction from his work without giving violent vent to his contempt for all who were subordinate to him. Having no other resources at his disposal, he converted coarseness into a resource and flaunted his special genius for contumely against institutions and persons that enjoyed the respect of others. His telegram ended with the words:

Quickly send two million rounds of ammunition at my disposal for six divisions.

In this postscript, so typical of Stalin, is a whole system. The Army had of course its own Chief of Supplies. There was always a lack of bullets, and they were distributed upon the direct instructions of the Commander-in-Chief, depending on available reserves and the relative importance of fronts and armies. But Stalin skipped over all the intervening steps and violated every semblance of order. Ignoring the Chief of Supplies, he demanded bullets through Lenin, not even to be placed at the disposal of the Army command, but at his personal disposal, so that he might present them as a gift to a particular division commander whom he wanted to impress with his own importance.

[Ten years later this brief trip of Stalin's to Petrograd in the late spring of 1919 was used by Voroshilov as the germinating element for another falsification of history. By now this seed has grown into a full-blown myth called, "Stalin, the Saviour of Petrograd." It is a cunning myth, implanted, strangely enough, in a deliberate shifting of the seasons. The fact is that] Yudenich tried to capture [Petrograd] *twice* in the course of 1919—in May and again in October.

The first raid by Yudenich with negligible forces was a mere sally, and passed practically unnoticed by the Party, which was absorbed by interest in the Eastern and Southern fronts. The Petrograd situation was brought under control in very short order, and again the entire attention of the Party and the country was transferred to the East and the South. In the meantime Yudenich, under the cover of Estonia and with the highly intensified assistance of England, formed in the course of the next four months a fresh army amply provided

with officers and amply equipped. This second attempt was the real campaign.
It began very successfully for Yudenich. Feeling that we would not be able to
manage all the fronts simultaneously, Lenin proposed to surrender Petrograd.
I opposed it. The majority of the Politburo, including Stalin, decided to support
me. After I had already gone to Petrograd Lenin wrote me on the 17th of
October, 1919:

> Spent last night at the Council of Defense and sent you . . . the decree
> of the Council of Defense. As you see, your plan has been accepted. But
> the removal of the Petrograd workers to the South has not been repealed,
> of course. (It is said that you developed it in conversation with Krassin
> and Rykov) . . . Attached is an appeal which the Council of Defense as-
> signed to me. I was in a hurry. It came out badly. Better put my signature
> under yours. Greetings.
>
> Lenin.

The struggle for Petrograd acquired an extremely dramatic character. The
enemy was in full view of the capital, which was prepared to fight in streets
and squares. When the defense of Petrograd was mentioned in the Soviet press
without any further explanations, it was this second, the autumn campaign of
Yudenich that was understood, not the spring campaign. But in the autumn of
1919 Stalin was at the Southern front and had nothing whatever to do with
the real saving of Petrograd. The official documents pertaining to this basic
operation against Yudenich were published years ago. Yet nowadays both of
Yudenich's campaigns have been merged into one, and the famous defense of
Petrograd is represented as Stalin's handiwork.

[While still in Petrograd, Stalin took advantage of an opportunity to slander
the Revolutionary Council of War of the Republic, and by implication its Chairman, as is evident from the following telegram he sent from Petrograd]:

> ★ June 4, 1919. Secret.
> To Comrade Lenin:
> I am sending you a document taken from the Swiss. It is evident from
> the document that not only the Chief of Staff of the Seventh Army works
> for the Whites (remember the desertion of the 11th Division to the side of
> Krassnov in the autumn of last year near Borisoglebsk or the desertion of
> regiments at the Perm front), but also the entire staff of the Revolutionary
> Council of War of the Republic, headed by Kostyayev. (The reserves are
> allocated and moved by Kostyayev.)
> It is now up to the Central Committee to draw the necessary inferences.
> Will it have the courage to do it?
> The analysis of the evidence continues, and new "possibilities" are open-
> ing up. I would write in greater detail, but I have not a minute to spare.
> Let Peters tell you.
> My profound conviction is:
> 1. Nadezhin is not a commander. He is incapable of commanding. He
> will end up by losing the Western Front.
> 2. Workers like Okulov, who incite the specialists against our commis-
> sars, who are sufficiently discouraged anyway, are harmful, because they
> debilitate the vitality of our army.
>
> Stalin.

[Lenin received this telegram while in conference. Ignoring its obviously wild charges, he wrote the following note to the Vice-Chairman of the Revolutionary Council of War of the Republic, Sklyansky]:

★ Stalin demands the recall of Okulov who *allegedly* is preoccupied with intrigues and disorganizing work.

The ironic "allegedly" speaks for itself. Sklyansky replied on the same piece of paper:

Okulov is the only decent worker there.

[Lenin's reaction to that, recorded immediately, was]:

★ In that case, compose text of telegram (exact exposition of what Okulov accuses the Seventh Army) and I shall send it by code to Stalin and Zinoviev, so that the conflict will not grow and will be adequately settled.

[The matter was then referred to the highest Party Executive, and its decision was immediately communicated to Trotsky at Kharkov by direct wire]:

★ In view of the conflict, which at any rate is growing, between all the Petersburg central-committeemen and Okulov, and recognizing as absolutely necessary the maximum of solidarity in Petersburg military work and the necessity of an immediate victory on that front, the Politburo and the Orgburo of the Central Committee have resolved temporarily to recall Okulov and to place him at the disposal of Comrade Trotsky.
June 4, 1919. #2995.

For the Politburo and the Orgburo of the Central Committee, Lenin, Kamenev, Serebryakov, Stassova.

This was a necessary concession to Stalin and Zinoviev. There was nothing to do but accept it. [As to Kostyayev, that very] able general did not inspire me with confidence either. He gave the impression of an alien among us. However, Vatzetis stood up for him, and Kostyayev complemented the irascible and capricious Commander-in-Chief rather well. It was not easy to replace Kostyayev. [Besides] there were no *facts* against him. There was patently no sense in "taking the document from the Swiss," because it never again figured anywhere. At any rate, obviously crude and forced was the attempt to link Kostyayev with the treason of any of the regiments, which had been organized under the vigilant eye of the Party itself. As for Nadezhin, he had occasion to command the Seventh Army, the army that [actually did save] Petrograd [at its most crucial moment]. As for Okulov's guilt, that consisted solely in his earnest endeavor to abide most faithfully by all orders and regulations and in his outright refusal to take part in any of the intrigues against the Center. [As for] Stalin's provocatively bold and insistent tone, that is explained by the fact that he felt he had at last mustered real support in the Council of War of the Eastern Front, where dissatisfaction with the Commander-in-Chief was turning into dissatisfaction with me.

The disagreement about the strategy on the Eastern Front was between the

Commander-in-Chief Vatzetis and the commanding officer of the Eastern Front, S. S. Kamenev. Both of them had been General Staff colonels of the Tsarist Army. No doubt there was rivalry between them. And the commissars became involved in that conflict. The Communists of our General Staff supported Vatzetis, while the members of the Revolutionary Council of War of the Eastern Front—Smilga, Lashevich, Gussev—sided wholeheartedly with Kamenev. It is hard to say which one of the two colonels was the more gifted. Both undoubtedly were endowed with first-rate talents for strategy, both had wide experience in the World War and both had decidedly an optimistic turn of mind, without which it is impossible to command. Vatzetis was the more stubborn and cranky and undoubtedly prone to yield to the influence of elements hostile to the Revolution. Kamenev was easier to get along with and yielded more readily to the influence of the Communists working with him. But although an able officer and a man of imagination fully capable of taking risks, he was lacking in depth and firmness. Lenin subsequently became disappointed in him and more than once characterized his reports very sharply. [On one occasion Lenin's comment was], "his answer is stupid and in places illiterate."

The Eastern Front was, so to speak, the first-born of the Red Army. It was more amply provided with all that was needed, including Communists, than any other front. [In the autumn of 1918] Kolchak was quite justly regarded as our chief enemy. He had advanced as far as Kazan', threatening Nizhni-Novgorod, from which he had a clear road to Moscow. It was natural then that the revolutionary country had skimmed the cream of everything for the Eastern Front.

On the 7th of September units of the Fifth Army began to attack the approaches to Kazan'. [It was] a stubborn battle. Great losses were sustained. The Czechs did not hold out and retreated. On the 10th of September the Fifth Army took Kazan'. [It was] the first great [Soviet] victory. This was the break which saved the young Republic from a complete rout. It occurred before my eyes at Kazan'. It was a serious and terrifying moment. After the loss of Simbirsk we had surrendered Kazan' practically without battle. Nizhni was next. Had the Whites taken possession of Nizhni-Novgorod, they would have had a clear road to Moscow. That is why the fight for Kazan' acquired decisive significance. The Fifth Army, created in the course of this battle, covered itself with glory. We tore Kazan' out of the grasp of the White Guards and the Czechoslovaks. That day was the turning point in the course of the Revolution. The capture of Kazan' started the liquidation of the counter-revolution in the East. The toilers of the entire country celebrated the capture of Kazan' as a great victory. Even greater was the significance of this victory for the Army.

[But in] March, 1919, with 3000 bayonets and 60,000 swords at his disposal, Kolchak moved quickly toward the Volga. The situation again became precarious. On the eve of the Eighth Party Congress it was Lenin's opinion that I should personally supervise the operations on the Eastern Front. This detail has to be recalled now and substantiated by documentary evidence in rebuttal of the current falsification.

1.

★ April 10, 1919.
To Sklyansky for transmission to Trotsky at Nizhni-Novgorod.

In view of the extremely difficult situation on the Eastern Front, I think it would be best for you to remain there, especially since there will be no serious questions on the 13th. The Orgburo of the Central Committee decided to send you the same telegram yesterday, but I am afraid it did not so do because of Stassova's departure. We are considering hurriedly a series of the most extraordinary measures for aiding the Eastern Front, of which Sklyansky will inform you. Let us have your opinion.

Lenin.

2.

★ By direct wire from Nizhni-Novgorod to Moscow, to Lenin:
Completely agree with the necessity of my remaining on the Eastern Front, *I call the attention of the Central Committee to the Left-Communistic demagogic agitation in the Third Army,* where agitation is carried on against military commanders and against an alleged order introducing saluting and the like. It is necessary to send strong Partymen, centralists. Extremely important that the workers support Simbirsk, where the provincial committee is extremely weak, especially in the counties.
April 10, 1919. #1047   Trotsky.

3.

Secret

★ Excerpt From The Protocol Of The Session Of The Politburo Of The Central Committee, Russian Communist Party (Bolsheviks)
April 18, 1919.
Present: Comrades Lenin, Krestinsky, Stalin, Trotsky.

Considered:

2. Declaration by Comrade Trotsky that the Southern Group of the Eastern Front, consisting of four armies, is under the command of Comrade Frunze, who is insufficiently experienced to manage such a great undertaking and that it is necessary to reinforce the front.

Decided:

To propose to Commander-in-Chief Vatzetis that he go to the Eastern Front, so that the present commander of the front, Comrade Kamenev, may devote himself entirely to the leadership of the armies of the Southern Group.

4.

Secret

★ Excerpt From The Protocol Of The Politburo Of The Central Committee, Russian Communist Party (Bolsheviks) of May 12, 1919.
Present: Comrades Lenin, Stalin, Krestinsky.

Considered:

9. Telegram from Comrade Trotsky to Comrade Lenin about the need to devote special attention to Saratov, which, due to the uprising of the [Ural] Cossacks is becoming an important strategic point.

Decided:

9. a. Immediately recall from Saratov Comrades Antonov, Fedor Ivanov, Ritzberg and Plaksin.

b. Immediately send A. P. Smirnov to work in Saratov as Chairman of the Provincial Executive Committee and member of the fortress council . . .

The advance against Kolchak, after two periods of retreat, was now proceeding with complete success. Vatzetis considered that the chief danger was now in the South and proposed to keep the Army of the Eastern Front in the Urals during the winter, until the danger should subside sufficiently, in order to transfer a number of divisions to the Southern Front. My general position was expounded even earlier in the telegram of January 1st. I was in favor of assuring an uninterrupted offensive against Kolchak. However, the concrete question was determined by the relation of forces and the general strategic situation. If Kolchak had serious reserves beyond the Urals, if our advance with uninterrupted battles had seriously exhausted the Red Army, then to engage in additional battles beyond the Urals would have constituted a danger, for it would have required new replacements of fresh Communists and Commanders, while all of that was at the present necessary for the Southern Front.

It must be added that I had, to a considerable extent, lost contact with the Eastern Front, now that it was quite safe, and that I lived with all my thoughts on the Southern Front. It was hard to judge at a distance to what extent the advancing armies of the Eastern Front had preserved their vitality, i.e. to what extent they were able to pursue a further offensive not only without the aid of the Center, but even with sacrifices to the advantage of the Southern Front, which needed the best divisions. To a certain extent, I permitted Vatzetis freedom of action, considering that if there should be resistance on the part of the Eastern command and if it should develop that a further advance in the East was possible without harm to the Southern Front, there would then be time enough to correct the Commander-in-Chief with a decision of the government.

Under these conditions, a conflict developed between Vatzetis and Kamenev. Objecting to a number of evasive replies by the Eastern Front, which tried to conduct its own policy, Vatzetis demanded the replacement of Kamenev by Samoilov, the former Commander of the Sixth Army. [This was done. But immediately it was protested by the Commissars friendly to Kamenev. Lenin appealed to Trotsky about this and about Stalin's complaint against Kostyayev from Petrograd, and Trotsky replied by direct wire from Kiev]:

★ I agree to the return of Kamenev to the Eastern Front in place of Samoilov, but I don't know where Kamenev is at present. Neither am I opposed to the replacement of Kostyayev; have often raised that question myself, but the difficulty is to find someone to replace him who would not be worse. I don't think that Lashevich is any firmer than Aralov. He simply has a different deviation of softness. *Gussev is more suitable for the field staff*. At any rate, in returning Kamenev, and moreover in replacing Kostyayev, it is necessary to discuss the matter beforehand with the Commander-in-Chief, so as not to disorganize the whole machinery. I suggest that a beginning should be made with the most urgent matters, i.e. the return of Kamenev, and to accomplish that, first of all, to find him and call him immediately to Moscow. At the same time suggest possible substitutes for Kostyayev and Aralov, which is less urgent. Communicate the decision you make.

Trotsky.

P.S. I must say, however, that Kuzmin, Orekhov, Naumov, Vatoshin, have the same opinion of Samoilov as Lashevich, Gussev, Smilga have of Kamenev, as Aralov has of Kostyayev. These loyalties of the front are our common misfortune.
May 21, 1919.

Trotsky.

During the first months of 1919 the Red Army delivered a crushing blow to the Southern counter-revolution, which was composed chiefly of the Don Cossack Army under the command of General Krassnov covered by a curtain of cavalry. But behind Krassnov in the Kuban and the Northern Caucasus, the Volunteer Army of Denikin was being formed. In the middle of May our advancing and in large measure exhausted army clashed with the fresh troops of Denikin and began to roll back. We lost everything we had gained and over and above that all of the Ukraine, which had recently been liberated. Meantime, on the Eastern Front, where the former Colonel Kamenev was in command, with Smilga and Lashevich as members of the Revolutionary Council of War, the situation had improved to such an extent and matters were proceeding so well that I gave up going there altogether and almost forgot what Kamenev looked like. Intoxicated with success, Smilga, Lashevich and Gussev carried their commander on their shoulders, drank *Bruderschaft* with him and wrote the most enthusiastic reports about him to Moscow. When the Commander-in-Chief, i.e. Vatzetis, agreeing with me in principle, had suggested that the Eastern Front remain for the winter in the Urals, in order to transfer several divisions to the South, where the situation was becoming threatening, Kamenev, supported by Smilga and Lashevich, had offered very resolute resistance. [Kamenev contended that he could place several divisions under his command in the East at the disposal of the Southern Front, without stopping his offensive in the Urals. After that, his authority rose at the expense of Vatzetis's, especially since the latter continued to be stubborn after his error had been completely exposed].

Stalin pounced upon the conflict between the Eastern Front and the Commander-in-Chief. He treated Vatzetis, who had officially condemned his intervention in strategic matters, with hostility and lay in wait for an opportunity to wreak vengeance upon him. Now such an opportunity presented itself. Smilga, Lashevich and Gussev proposed, obviously with the co-operation of Stalin, to appoint Kamenev Commander-in-Chief. The success on the Eastern Front bribed Lenin and broke down my resistance.

Kamenev was appointed Commander-in-Chief, and at the morning session of July 3rd, 1919, the Central Committee reconstituted the Revolutionary Council of War of the Republic. It was now to be made up of Trotsky, Sklyansky, Gussev, Smilga, Rykov, and Commander-in-Chief Kamenev.

The first task of the new Commander-in-Chief was to work out a plan for grouping the forces on the Southern Front. Kamenev was distinguished by optimism and a quick strategic imagination. But his outlook was still comparatively narrow. The social factors of the Southern Front—the workers, the Ukrainian peasants, the Cossacks—were not clear to him. He approached the Southern Front from the point of view of the commander of the Eastern Front. The easiest thing to do was to concentrate the divisions removed from the East along the Volga and to strike against the Kuban', the headquarters of Denikin. This had been the basis of his plan when he promised to supply the divisions in time without stopping his advance.

In matters of strategy, I always yielded the first word to the Commander-in-Chief. However, my familiarity with the Southern Front prompted me to believe that this plan was basically erroneous. Denikin had managed to transfer his base from the Kuban' to the Ukraine. To advance against the Cossacks meant to drive them forcibly in the direction of Denikin. It was clear to me that, instead, the main blow should be delivered along the line of division between Denikin and the Cossacks, along the strip where the population was entirely against the Cossacks, against Denikin and for us. But my opposition to Kamenev's plan was interpreted as a continuation of the conflict between the Revolutionary Council of War of the Republic and the Eastern Front. Smilga and Gussev, with the collaboration of Stalin, made it look as if I were against the plan because I did not trust the new Commander-in-Chief on general principles. Lenin apparently had the same misgivings. But these misgivings were fundamentally wrong. I did not overestimate Vatzetis. I greeted Kamenev in a friendly fashion and tried in every way to lighten his burdens. But the error of the plan was so clear beyond any doubt that when it was confirmed by the Politburo, with everybody, including Stalin, voting against me, I submitted my resignation. [On the 5th of July, 1919, the highest Party executive ruled as follows] with reference to my resignation:

> The Organizational and Political Bureaux of the Central Committee, having examined Comrade Trotsky's declaration and having considered it in all its aspects, have come to the unanimous conclusion that they cannot accept Comrade Trotsky's resignation and they are absolutely unable to grant his petition. The Organizational and Political Bureaux of the Central Committee will do everything they can to make Comrade Trotsky's work at the Southern Front—the most difficult, the most dangerous and the most important at the present time, which Comrade Trotsky has himself chosen—as convenient as possible for him and as fruitful as possible for the Republic. As People's Commissar of War and Chairman of the Revolutionary Council of War of the Republic, Comrade Trotsky is fully empowered to act also as a member of the Revolutionary Council of War of the Southern Front in concert with the very same Commander of the Front (Yegoryev),

whom he himself has appointed and the Central Committee has confirmed.

The Organizational and Political Bureaux of the Central Committee offer Comrade Trotsky full opportunity to strive by any means for what he considers an improvement of the policy in the military question, and, if he so desires, will try to expedite the convocation of the Party Congress.

Firmly convinced that the retirement of Comrade Trotsky at the present moment is absolutely impossible and would be most detrimental to the interests of Republic, the Organizational and Political Bureaux of the Central Committee insistently suggest to Comrade Trotsky not to raise that question again, and to carry out his functions in the future to the maximum, curtailing them in the event he so desires, while he concentrates his efforts upon the Southern Front.

In view of the aforesaid, the Organizational and Political Bureaux of the Central Committee likewise reject Comrade Trotsky's resignation from the Politburo as well as from the post of Chairman of the Revolutionary Council of War of the Republic and People's Commissar of War . . :

Lenin, Kamenev, Krestinsky, Kalinin, Serebryakov, Stalin, Stassova. . . .

I withdrew my resignation and immediately went to the Southern Front.

Three days later, while at the front in Kozlov, I received a coded telegram from the Council of People's Commissars, from the Kremlin, to the effect that an officer, accused of treason, confessed and made depositions from which it was possible to infer that Vatzetis had knowledge of a military conspiracy:

Strictly Secret
All in Code

R. S. F. S. R.
Council of People's Commissars
The Kremlin
Moscow

July 8, 1919.

To Trotsky at Kozlov:

Domozhirov, who has confessed and has been completely proved a traitor, has given factual testimony about a conspiracy in which an active part was played by Isayev, who was for a long time attached on duty to the Commander-in-Chief and lived with him in the same apartment. Many other proofs, a whole lot of evidence, convict the Commander-in-Chief of knowing about the conspiracy. The Commander-in-Chief had to be arrested . . .

[This] telegram was signed by Dzerzhinsky [head of the Cheka]; Krestinsky [Secretary of the Central Committee of the Party]; Lenin; and my deputy Sklyansky. It was clear from the names mentioned in the telegram that the reference was to the recently removed Commander-in-Chief. Vatzetis was thus arrested almost immediately after his removal from his post on no less a charge than suspicion of treason. That invested the controversy over strategy with sinister implications. Relations inside the Politburo became more strained, the change of the Chief Command became considerably complicated. To this very day the exact circumstances and implications of this episode are not altogether clear to me. Since Vatzetis was soon set free and even appointed Professor of the War College, it is safe to assume that his knowledge of any military conspiracy was less than infinitesimal. It is not unlikely that, dissatisfied with his removal from the post of Commander-in-Chief, he had engaged in reckless talk with officers close to him. [However, it is decidedly] likely that Stalin played quite a role in his arrest. Stalin had a score of old slights to settle with Vatzetis. Moreover, he derived a sense of impunity and safety from the friendly influence he exerted over the head of the Cheka and from the support of the leaders of the Eastern Front and of the new Commander-in-Chief. He had the added satisfaction of striking an indirect blow at the Commissar of War. One was conscious of the obvious intrigue behind this episode and of the invisible presence of Stalin behind Dzerzhinsky.

[On the 27th of July], I was hastily called out to Kozlov by Sokolnikov "because of extraordinary circumstances." There I discovered that the Commander of the Southern Front, Yegoryev, considered Kamenev's plan of operations [for the South] incorrect and, although he was carrying it out, did not expect success. Such also was the attitude of the Chief of the Operational Department, Peremytov, and such also was the opinion held by Sokolnikov himself. At first I did not discuss the matter with anyone except Sokolnikov and did not ask Yegoryev to elaborate when he referred to the irrationality of the plan, [but immediately telegraphed to Lenin as Chairman of the Council of Defense]:

★ Without going into an analysis of the controversy on its merits, I consider entirely inadmissible a situation under which a plan is carried out by a person who has no faith in its success. The only course is the immediate (before the beginning of operations) replacement of the Commander of the South by a person who recognizes the operative authority of the Commander-in-Chief and agrees with his plan. Perhaps Selivachev will agree with Kamenev. In that case he should be immediately appointed Assistant Commander of the South, so that a week later he may be appointed Commander of the South.
Awaiting instructions.
July 27, 1919. #277/s.   L. D. Trotsky.

[The reply to this telegram was made not by Lenin but in the name of the Politburo. It bore the sole signature of the Central Committee's technical secretary, Helen Stassova—as if to underscore its impersonal nature]:

Secret

★ To Comrade Trotsky in Penza:
The Politburo of the Central Committee has considered your telegram No. 277/s and fully agrees with you concerning the danger of any sort of wavering in the firm execution of an accepted plan. The Politburo fully recognizes the operative authority of the Commander-in-Chief and requests that you make the necessary explanation to all responsible workers. The Politburo appoints as members of the Revolutionary Council of War of the Southern Front, in addition to the present members, Smilga, Serebryakov, Lashevich. By order of the Central Committee,
July 28, 1919.

Stassova.

[The question of strategy on the Southern Front was crucial. Yet the controversy over it, aggravated by the Vatzetis episode, had reached such a pass that it was carried on by innuendo and along exaggeratedly official channels. The immediate acknowledgment of the above instructions was addressed to Trotsky's deputy in Moscow for transmission to the Central Committee. It read]:

Secret

★ To Comrade Sklyansky for transmission to the Central Committee:

Do not understand the sense of your telegram. In view of Yegoryev's doubts, I suggested an assistant for him, who, if necessary, could replace him. This is the least painful solution of the problem. While in Kozlov, I removed the Chief of Operations, Peremytov, who expressed disagreement with the plan of the Commander-in-Chief and replaced him with Berenda, whom I hastily summoned from the Military Inspection. Before I left, by agreement with Sokolnikov and in his presence, I bluntly confronted Yegoryev with the issue of unconditional execution of the Commander-in-Chief's plan. He replied with the utmost categoricalness and as far as I could judge without any mental reservations. Nevertheless, I consider the sending of Selivachev, as assistant, after the preliminary conversation the Commander-in-Chief had with him, extremely desirable. I have received no reply to this single proposal except the recommendation to instill (into whom?) the rule of discipline.

I think it is absurd to add to the Revolutionary Council of War, already overstaffed with six members (Yegoryev, Yegorov, Sokolnikov, Okulov, Vladimirov, Serebryakov) two new ones, and suggest that this decision be revoked, especially since Lashevich has been appointed Commandant of Petrograd, while Smilga is a member of Shorin's group.

Disastrous for the front is the absence of bullets and extreme lack of rifles. The Ninth Army has 20,000 fighters ready, but they are all without rifles, and only half of them expect to receive them. Bullets are issued in frightfully small quantities, which in the event of the slightest complication leads to disastrous consequences. On the basis of observing the situation in the four armies of the Southern Front and conversation with the Commander of the South, I warn you that the whole operation may fail because of lack of bullets.

#284.   Trotsky.
July 29, 1919.

[Preparations for the offensive on the Southern Front according to the plan of the new Commander-in-Chief continued under difficulties. By the end of the first week in August—that is, about a week before the offensive was actually launched—the Politburo was confronted with] several problems of grave importance. [It was perfectly] clear that Denikin was more than likely to direct his main drive against the Ukraine rather than Eastward, in order to establish contact with Rumania and Poland and transfer his base from Ekaterinodar to Odessa and Sebastopol. Irrespective of the measures undertaken by the Commander-in-Chief to obviate this danger, which was the most serious for the moment, it was necessary to decide at once how to proceed with the impending struggle for the Ukraine. First of all it was necessary to unite the 12th Army with the 14th Army, which, owing to the absence of telegraphic connections, was cut off from the Southern Front. Not only were the rears of the two armies already merged by then but both were increasingly obliged to act against one and the same enemy, Denikin. I, therefore, proposed the removal of the 14th Army from the jurisdiction of the Southern Front, fusing the command of the two armies in the person of the commander of the 14th Army, Yegorov, and his staff, calling this new group the Southwestern Front, with headquarters at Konotop, and placing it directly under the jurisdiction of the Comander-in-Chief and the General Staff. To maintain the fighting ability of [this proposed Southwestern Front at the barest minimum, it was necessary] to exert extraordinary effort to put a stop to banditry, the destruction of railway tracks, and the like, with the aid of Communist units temporarily transferred from more secure sectors, regional workers from Moscow and even certain absolutely reliable units of the Czech army. All available Red officers throughout the country were immediately sent to the Ukraine by special trains, irrespective of any prior assignments. All political workers, previously assigned to various other armies, had to be sent to the Ukraine, along with boots, bullets, rifles. The 12th Army was without bullets. For lack of them, it fought against the mutinous colonists in Odessa with hand grenades. The Councils of War of both armies were weak. By agreement between the Ukrainian Council of Defense and the Revolutionary Councils of War of both armies, Voroshilov was appointed to suppress the rebellion in the rears of both armies. All persons and institutions engaged in the suppression of insurrections in the Ukraine were placed under his command.

[Analogous difficulties, as varied as the localities in which they were met yet essentially the same in nature, were confronted everywhere and on every hand. Lenin grew restive. At the very outset of the offensive he wrote to Sklyansky]:

★ I am sick. Had to lie down. Therefore answer by messenger. The delay of the offensive in the direction of Voronezh (from the first of August to the tenth!!) is monstrous. Denikin's success is tremendous.

What's the matter? Sokolnikov said that there our forces were four times as large as theirs.

What then is the matter? How could we have missed the opportunity so badly?

Tell the Commander-in-Chief that things cannot go on like that. He must pay *serious* attention.

Hadn't we better send this sort of telegram to the Revolutionary Council of War of the Southern Front (copy to Smilga) in code:

Utterly inadmissible to delay attack because such delay gives all of Ukraine to Denikin and destroys us. You are responsible for every extra day and even hour of delaying the offensive. Communicate immediately your explanations and when at last you will begin a resolute offensive.

Chairman of the Council of Defense,
Lenin.

[The offensive on the Southern Front, according to the plan of S. S. Kamenev, began in the middle of August. Within six weeks, by the end of September],

I wrote to the Politburo, which had voted against my plan, "The offensive along the line of greatest resistance has proved entirely to the advantage of Denikin, *as was predicted* . . . Right now our situation on the Southern Front is worse than it was when the General Staff began to carry out its *a priori* plan. It would be childish to shut one's eyes to this." By then the fatal error of the plan had become clear to many of its former proponents, including Lashevich, who had been transferred from the Eastern to the Southern Front. Some three weeks earlier, on the 6th of September, I had telegraphed from the front in code to the Commander-in-Chief and to the Central Committee that "the center of difficulty of the struggle on the Southern Front has shifted in the direction of Kursk-Voronezh, where there are no reserves." I called [their] attention also to the following problems:

> The effort to liquidate Mamontov has so far yielded practically no results. The motorized machine-gun units were not formed in consequence of the non-receipt of the machine-guns or even a small number of automobiles. Mamontov is obviously proceeding to unite with his own troops through the Kursk front. Our weak and scattered infantry units hardly disturb him. Lashevich's command is paralyzed by the absence of means of communication. Mamontov's unification may be regarded as assured. The danger of a break through the front at the Kursk-Voronezh sector is becoming apparent. Lashevich's next task is to pursue the enemy in an effort to plug that hole. An attempt will be made to harass Mamontov with guerrilla raids . . . The destruction of railways interferes with transfers from the Tsaritsyn direction to the Kursk. Yet the situation insistently demands the transfer of reserves to the West. It may be possible to transfer the mounted corps of Budenny by forced marches. It is necessary to add that the situation is becoming increasingly worse because of the complete breakdown of the apparatus of the front. The practical tasks appear to us in the following form:
> 1. Immediately appoint Selivachev commander of the Southern Front.
> 2. Selivachev's place should be taken by the assistant commander of the Southern Front, Yegorov.
> 3. Send the reserves, including the 21st Division, after Mamontov in the direction of Kursk.
> 4. Turn the 9th Army from the direction of Novorossiisk to Starobelsk.
> 5. Transfer the corps of Budenny as far as possible to right center.
> 6. Hasten marching reserves and supplies for the 8th and 13th armies.

[In addition], I proposed a number of army regroupings which amounted to a liquidation of the plan that had failed. [That was hardly three weeks after the offensive was launched.] Serebryakov and Lashevich signed the telegram with me. But the new Commander-in-Chief was [as] stubborn [when in error as his predecessor], and the Politburo resolutely supported him. The very same day, on the 6th of September, I received this reply by direct wire at Oryol:

> The Politburo of the Central Committee, having considered the telegram of Trotsky, Serebryakov and Lashevich, has confirmed the reply of the Commander-in-Chief and expresses its surprise with reference to efforts

being made to reconsider the basic strategic plan decided upon September 6, 1919. #96/ sh.

> By order of the Politburo of the Central Committee,
>   Lenin

Within two months the course of military operations had nullified the original plan. Moreover, during these two months of continuous fruitless battles many of the roads were utterly wrecked and the concentration of reserves became incomparably more difficult than in June and July. The radical regrouping of forces was therefore all the more necessary. I suggested that Budenny's mounted corps be sent by forced marches to the Northeast, and that several other units be transferred in that direction. [But the Politburo, including of course Stalin, throughout this period continued to reject these and other suggestions and persistently approved] the directives of the Commander-in-Chief, [who continued to reiterate that] "the basic plan for the advance along the Southern Front remains without alterations; in other words, the main attack is to be delivered by Shorin's special group, its task being to destroy the enemy in the Don and the Kuban'." [Yet] the offensive had utterly bogged down in the meantime. The situation in the Kuban', where the best troops had been sent, became extremely grave, and Denikin was moving to the North.

"In order to evaluate the plan of operation," I wrote at the end of September, "it would not be superfluous to consider its results. The Southern Front has received more forces than any other front has ever had; at the beginning of the offensive the Southern Front had no less than 180,000 bayonets and swords, a corresponding number of guns and machine-guns. After a month and a half of battles, we are pathetically marking time in the Eastern half of the Southern Front, while in the Western half we have a difficult retreat, a loss of units, the destruction of organization . . . The cause of the failure must be sought entirely in the plan of operation . . . Units of average resistance were directed . . . to localities populated entirely by Cossacks, who were not advancing, but were defending their villages and homes. The atmosphere of a national Don War is exerting a disintegrating influence upon our units. Under these conditions Denikin's tanks, skillful maneuvering, and the like, give him a colossal superiority."

[Soon] it was no longer a question of the plan but of its disastrous consequences, material and psychological. The Commander-in-Chief, in consonance with Napoleon's maxim, had apparently hoped, by persisting in his error, to derive from it all possible advantages and in the end to secure victory. The Politburo, losing confidence, persisted in its own decision. On the 21st of September our troops abandoned Kursk. On the 13th of October Denikin took Oryol and opened for himself the road to Tula, where the most important munitions factories were concentrated and beyond which was Moscow. I confronted the Politburo with the alternatives: either to change our strategy or evacuate Tula, destroying the war industries there, and resist the direct threat to Moscow. By that time the stubbornness of the Commander-in-Chief, who was himself already discarding parts of the old plan, and the support of the Politburo were broken. In the middle of October the new grouping of troops for the counterattack was completed. One group was concentrated to the northwest of Oryol for action against the Kursk-Oryol railway. Another group, east of Voronezh, was headed by Budenny's mounted corps. This was tantamount to the plan upon which I had insisted. [In view of these facts it is instructive to consider the latter-day account of the period by Stalinist historiographers] :

★ During September and the beginning of October Denikin achieved considerable success on the Southern Front. He captured Oryol on the 13th of October. In order to remedy the extremely difficult and dangerous situation which arose in consequence of prolonged failures on the Southern Front, the Central Committee of the Party sent Comrade Stalin to the Revolutionary Council of War of the front. Comrade Stalin worked out the new strategic plan of the struggle against Denikin, which was confirmed by Lenin and by the Central Committee of the Party. The realization of this plan brought about the complete defeat and rout of Denikin.

[Stalin's own versions vary from time to time as to who had proposed the right plan which had been rejected and who was to blame for the wrong plan that had proved so very costly. In 1923 Stalin told the story of the Southern Front in order, ostensibly, to demonstrate certain political principles, but actually in order to settle certain political scores of his own] :

★ . . . An analogy might easily be drawn between these principles of political strategy, and the principles of military strategy; for example . . . the struggle with Denikin. Everybody remembers the end of 1919, when Denikin was near Tula. At that time interesting arguments developed among the military on the question of from which direction the decisive blow against Denikin's armies should be struck. Some of the military proposed . . . the line of Tsaritsyn-Novorossiisk . . . Others . . . the line Voronezh-Rostov . . . The first plan was . . . not advantageous because it presupposed our movement along regions . . . hostile to the Soviet Government and thus demanded heavy sacrifices; also, it was dangerous, because it opened to Denikin's armies the road to Moscow by way of Tula and Serpukhov. The second plan . . . was the only correct one, because it presupposed the movement of our basic groups along regions . . . that sympathized with the Soviet Government and therefore did not demand special sacrifices; and also, it disorganized the action of the main body of Denikin's troops marching on Moscow. A majority of the military expressed themselves in favor of the second plan . . . Thus the fate of the entire war with Denikin was settled . . .

Stalin seemed to be using this story as a chance illustration of certain conceptions in the field of political tactics. As a matter of fact, the illustration was not accidental. 1923 was under way; Stalin was [on tenterhooks], expecting a terrible attack by Lenin, and therefore he systematically tried to undermine Lenin's authority. In the leading circles of the Party it was very well known that behind the erroneous and costly plan had been not only certain members of the "military" (like Commander-in-Chief [S. S. Kamenev]) but also the

majority of the Politburo headed by Lenin. However, he preferred to speak
about disagreements among the "military" without touching upon the struggle
within the Politburo. He knew that the leading Party members remembered
altogether too well that it was my plan, the plan I [had been advocating since
early in July], which he came to support only at the end of October or the
beginning of November, after the Commander-in-Chief himself had in actual
practice completely repudiated his own original project. But on November 19,
1924, ten months after Lenin's death, Stalin [went further. He then] made the
first attempt to create a deliberately fictitious version of the struggle on the
Southern Front and to direct it against me:

> It happened in the autumn of 1919. The offensive against Denikin failed
> . . . Denikin takes Kursk. Denikin advances on Oryol. Comrade Trotsky
> is recalled from the Southern Front to a session of the Central Committee.
> The Central Committee recognizes the situation as alarming and decides
> to send new military workers to the Southern Front, recalling Comrade
> Trotsky. The new military workers demand "non-interference" by Com-
> rade Trotsky in the affairs of the Southern Front. Comrade Trotsky retires
> from direct participation in the affairs of the Southern Front. Operations
> on the Southern Front all the way to the capture by us of Rostov-on-the-
> Don and Odessa take place without Comrade Trotsky. Let them try to deny
> these facts!

True, I left the Southern Front about the 10th of October and went to
Petrograd. Our counter-attack on the Southern Front should have begun on
the 10th of October. Everything was prepared; the concentration of units for
the attack was almost completed, and my presence was much more necessary
around Petrograd, which was in mortal danger of capture by Yudenich. Looking
back over three years of Civil War and examining the journals and the correspondence of my trips along the various fronts, I see that I almost never had
occasion to accompany a victorious army, to participate in an attack, directly to
share its victories with others. My journeys did not have a holiday character.
I went only to the sectors in distress after the enemy had broken through the
front. My task was to turn fleeing regiments into an attacking force. I retreated
with the troops, but never advanced with them. As soon as the routed divisions
were restored to order and the command gave the signal to advance, I bade
farewell to the Army and went to another unfavorable sector, or returned for
several days to Moscow, in order to solve the accumulated problems of the
Center. Thus, for three years I literally did not have occasion even once to see
the happy faces of soldiers after the victory or to enter with them into the
captured cities. [That was why, as Stalin could not help knowing], I did not
visit the Southern Front even once throughout the entire period of our victorious
[offensive there after the middle of October. Stalin's falsification thus consists
of investing an undeniable fact with an utterly false implication.

[But there is, as yet, no suggestion that Trotsky was the author of the plan
responsible for the failure of the July-September offensive against Denikin.
At this stage], everything comes down only to the hazy assertion concerning new

military workers who demanded (from whom?) "non-interference" by Comrade Trotsky. As a matter of fact, the thirteen decrees issued by the Central Committee on the 15th of October were proposed by me in written form and unanimously approved by all, including Stalin, Lenin, I, Kamenev and Krestinsky, were on the Commission which, in accordance with my proposal, was charged with the task of sending new workers to the Southern Front to replace the old workers, who had grown altogether too tired in consequence of constant defeats. Stalin was not on it. Which of the new workers demanded my "non-interference," and from whom, in particular, Stalin does not state. [In 1929, Voroshilov declared]:

★ Stalin placed before the Central Committee three main conditions: 1) *Trotsky must not interfere in the affairs of the Southern Front* and must not cross beyond its line of demarcation; 2) a whole series of workers whom Stalin considered incapable of restoring the situation among the troops must be immediately recalled from the Southern Front; and 3) to the Southern Front must immediately be sent new workers selected by Stalin, who would be capable of carrying out this task. These conditions *were accepted fully.*

Where? How? When? By whom? [The answers to these questions concern neither Stalin nor his satellite. Yet even while] crediting Stalin with the revision of the erroneous plan, Voroshilov did not, in 1929, dare to affirm that the erroneous plan was mine. By his very silence on that point he admitted that I was an opponent of this plan. However, this oversight was likewise filled in by the newest historiography. [We have it now on the authority of Zinaida Ordzhonikidze that]:

★ Stalin . . . categorically rejected the old plan to smash Denikin, worked out by the General Staff, headed by Trotsky . . . "This insane proposed march through a roadless, hostile country, threatens us with complete collapse," wrote Stalin in a note to Lenin . . . Instead of the plan already rejected by life itself, Stalin worked out a plan for the advance of the Reds through proletarian Kharkov and the Donetz Basin on Rostov . . . The strategy of the Great Stalin secured victory for the Revolution.

[There is a touch of sardonic humor in this insistence that the plan which finally brought victory on the Southern Front was Stalin's. However, the author of this cynical prevarication is Stalin himself and the documentary evidence on which it is based is Stalin's note to Lenin, in which] Stalin repeats almost word for word those arguments against the July-September plan which I had developed, at first orally and then in writing, and which he had rejected together with the majority of the Politburo. Since all the members of the Politburo were perfectly familiar with the development of the question, it could not, at that time, have even entered Stalin's head to place the responsibility for the old plan on me. On the contrary, he blamed the Commander-in-Chief and the "strategic cockerel" attached to him, the very same Gussev on whom he had relied in July, when the command was changed. [In that note Stalin argued]:

★ . . . What then impels the Commander-in-Chief to defend the old plan?

Evidently, sheer stubbornness, or if you wish factionalism, most stupid and most dangerous to the Republic, fostered in the Commander-in-Chief by the strategic cockerel attached to him . . .

Stalin's telegram [reinforcing the note] came at the very moment that the Commander-in-Chief himself went against his own plan, making a direct frontal attack with a group of shock troops instead of concentrating them in Denikin's Cossack rear. There was nothing the Politburo could do except to sanction after the event the substitution of the new plan for the old. Whether such a decision was brought out, or whether the Politburo simply accepted the accomplished fact, rejoicing inwardly, it is impossible to establish on the basis of published documents, nor is it of much significance. [However, there is the following document, which speaks for itself]:

★ Excerpt   Secret

From the Protocol of the Session of the Political Bureau of the Central Committee of the Russian Communist Party (Bolshevik) of September 14, 1919.

Present: Comrades Lenin, Trotsky, Kamenev, Krestinsky.

Considered:

5. Declaration by Comrades Stalin and Serebryakov concerning reinforcements for the Southern Front and concerning the transfer of certain persons, and Comrade Stalin's telegram in support of this declaration as an ultimatum.

Decided:

5. (a) To commission Comrade Lenin to send Comrade Smilga a coded telegram with inquiry concerning one possible transfer in the opinion of the Politburo.

(b) To commission Comrade Trotsky to transmit to Commander-in-Chief Kamenev in the name of the Government the political-economic directive about the necessity to capture Kursk and to move upon Kharkov and the Donetz Basin, and about the distribution of reinforcements on the basis of this directive between the Southern and Southeastern fronts, these reinforcements to be removed from the Eastern and Kazakhstan fronts (the exact text of the directive is herewith attached). Also, to suggest to Vladimir Ilyich personally to talk matters over with the Commander-in-Chief in accordance with the contents of the above directive.

(c) To inform Comrade Stalin that the Politburo considers absolutely inadmissible the reinforcement of one's business suggestions with ultimatums about resignation.

[On December 4, 1919, Ivan Smirnov reported from the Eastern Front that] "Kolchak has lost his army . . . There will be no more battles . . . I hope to capture the entire mobile staff before Station Taiga . . . The tempo of the pursuit is such that by the 20th of December Barnaul and Novonikolayevsk will be in our hands." [Yudenich had been completely routed in the Northwest. Denikin was on the run in the South. Defeated in his efforts to win peasant support through equivocal "agrarian reforms" and deprived of support among the military and the landed gentry through his disastrous defeat at the front by the Red Army, Denikin lost the confidence of the Whites. On the 26th of March, 1920, he formally relinquished the office of Commander-in-Chief in favor of Baron Wrangel, who had been successful in reforming the scattered ranks of the White Guards in the Crimea.

[The Whites were still trouncing the Red cavalry and infantry units on the Caucasian Front. In the battles of the 1st and 2nd of February, 1920, Mamontov repulsed the offensive of the Red Army and assumed the offensive himself in the vicinity of Novocherkassk. The ranks of the Red Army on the Caucasian Front, which included Budenny's mounted army, had been thinned not only by losses in battles but by the typhus epidemic. The expected reinforcements and provisions had not arrived because of confusion on the railways. Strong-arm methods were needed to move reinforcements and supplies to the Caucasian Front. Lenin and Trotsky turned to Stalin, who was at the time on the Revolutionary Council of War of the Southwestern Front]:

> ★ The Central Committee deems it necessary, in order to save the situation, that you journey immediately to the right wing of the Caucasian Front by way of Debaltsevo, where Shorin is at present. At the same time you will have to undertake extraordinary measures for the transfer of considerable reinforcements and workers from the Southwestern Front. To stabilize the situation, you are inducted into the staff of the Revolutionary Council of War of the Caucasian Front, remaining at the same time on the Revolutionary Council of War of the Southwestern Front.
> #9/sh   Lenin. Trotsky.
> February 3, 1920.

[The text of Stalin's reply is not available, but he apparently raised objections to the new assignment, probably on the grounds of pressing duties in his present position. This drew the following rejoinder]:

> ★ The Central Committee does not insist upon your journey, on condition that in the course of the next few weeks you will concentrate all your attention and all your energy upon servicing the Caucasian Front in preference to the interests of the Southwestern Front. Arzhanov is being sent to Voronezh to expedite the necessary transfers. Please show him the necessary cooperation and inform us accurately about the course of transfers.
> #512.
> February 4, 1920.
>
> Chairman of the Council of Defense, Lenin.
> Chairman of the Revolutionary Council of War of the Republic, Trotsky.

[Two weeks later Lenin telegraphed Stalin]:

★ The Politburo cannot ask you to come in person, since it considers the mopping up of Denikin as the most important and pressing task, which is why you have to expedite reinforcements to the Caucasian Front to the best of your ability.
#34.
February 19, 1920.

Lenin.

[A day later Lenin elaborated further on the same theme]:

★ The situation in the Caucasus is becoming increasingly serious in character. Judging by yesterday's situation, the possibility of our losing Rostov and Novocherkassk is not excluded, as also the enemy's attempt to develop his success further to the North with a threat against the Don Territory. Undertake extraordinary measures for expediting the transfer of the 42nd and the Latvian divisions and for reinforcing their fighting potential. I expect that, realizing the general situation, you will exert your energy to the utmost and will achieve impressive results.
#36/sh   Lenin.

[Stalin's reply follows]:

Absolutely Secret
In Code

★ Lenin, Kremlin, Moscow.
Copy for the Central Committee of the Party.
It is not clear to me why the concern about the Caucasian Front is imposed first of all upon me. In the order of things the responsibility for strengthening the Caucasian Front rests entirely with the Revolutionary Council of War of the Republic, whose members, according to my information, are in excellent health, and not with Stalin, who is overloaded with work anyway.
#970.
February 20, 1920.

Stalin.

[Whereupon Lenin spanked Stalin with the following telegram]:

★ The concern for expediting the shipment of reinforcements from the Southwestern Front to the Caucasian Front has been imposed upon you. Generally one must try to help in every way possible and not quibble about departmental jurisdictions.
#37/sh
February 20, 1920.

Lenin.

Kursk, January 19, 1920.
To the Chairman of the Revolutionary Council of War of the Republic, Comrade Trotsky, Moscow.

I appeal to you with the urgent plea to free me from unemployment. For almost three weeks I have been for no good reason at the headquarters of the Southwestern Front, and have done nothing for two months. I can find out neither the cause of delay nor can I secure a further appointment. If during the almost two years that I have commanded various armies I have demonstrated any merit at all, I beg you to give me the opportunity to apply my talents to actual work, and if none such can be found at the front, then please let me have something to do in transportation or in the Commissariat of War.

\#2.   Army Commander Tukhachevsky.

[Apparently, Stalin had found no application for the talents of Tukhachevsky on the Southwestern Front where he was practically the boss by virtue of his political authority as member of the Central Committee, the Orgburo and the Politburo. Tukhachevsky was still only in his middle twenties. Until the conquest of power by the Bolsheviks, he had been a lieutenant in the Tsarist Army. The October Revolution won him over heart and soul. He not only offered his services to the Red Army but became a Communist. He distinguished himself almost immediately at the front, and within a year had become a general of the Red Army. His brilliance as a strategist was acknowledged by admiring foes who were the victims of that very brilliance. Trotsky inscribed on his telegram: "Inform Comrades Lenin and Stalin." What immediate steps were taken after that is not clear. But one thing is definitely recorded. Tukhachevsky was put in command of the Western Front and was placed in charge of offensive operations against Warsaw.

[The Polish Republic was hostile to the Soviet Government from the moment of its inception. Having seized Wilno in defiance of its award to the Lithuanians by the League of Nations in 1919, the Poles invaded White-Russian territory and by autumn occupied Minsk and considerable portions of Volhynia and Podolia. Then they froze into inactivity in the face of General Denikin's success. They feared that the success of the White Armies, which were pledged to restore the territorial integrity of the Tsarist Empire, would prove inimical to Poland's territorial ambitions not only in the Ukraine and White-Russia but in Poland proper as well. But as soon as the Red Armies began to deliver decisive blows against Denikin, the Polish Army sprang into activity again. Supported by the troops of the recently-formed Latvian Republic, the Polish Armies occupied Dvinsk in January, 1920, forced the Red Army to surrender Latgalia, took Mozyr in March, and under the personal command of Poland's Liberator, Josef Pilsudski, launched a vigorous offensive against the Ukraine in April in alliance with the forces of the defunct Petlura Government. Although the war had thus been imposed on the Red Army, the aim of the Soviet Government was not only to repulse the attack, but to carry the Bolshevik Revolution itself into Poland and thus force open a door for Communism into all Europe].

On the 30th of April, I wrote to the Central Committee of the Party: "Precisely because it is a struggle of life and death, it will have an extremely intensive and severe character." Hence it was necessary "to evaluate the War with Poland not as merely the task of the Western Front but as the central task of all of Worker-Peasant Russia." On the second of May, I issued a general warning through the press against overly-optimistic hopes for a revolution in Poland: "That the war *will end* with the workers' revolution in Poland, there can be no doubt; but at the same time there is no basis for supposing that the war *will begin* with such a revolution . . . It would be extremely frivolous to think that the victory . . . will simply fall into our laps." On the 5th of May, in a report to the Joint Session of All Soviet Institutions, I said: "It would be a grave error to suppose that history will begin by opening for our sakes the Polish workers' revolution and therefore will free us from the necessity to wage an armed struggle." And I concluded: "Comrades, I should like you to carry away from this meeting as your chief conclusion the thought that the struggle still ahead of us will be a hard and intensive struggle." All my military orders and public declarations of that time were permeated with this idea. "At the present time the Western Front is the most important front of the Republic," states an order of the 9th of May, signed by me at Smolensk. "The organs of supply must be prepared for no easy and brief campaign but for a prolonged and stubborn struggle." I was opposed to the march on Warsaw because, considering the weakness of our forces and resources, it could end successfully only on condition of an immediate insurrection in Poland itself, and there was absolutely no assurance of that. I have expounded the essence of the conflict in the most general terms in my autobiography.

The chief initiator of the campaign was Lenin. He was supported against me by Zinoviev, Stalin and even by the cautious Kamenev.[1] Rykov was one of the Central Committee members who sided with me on the issue, but he was not yet a member of the Politburo. Radek was also opposed to the Polish adventure. All the secret documents of that time are at the disposal of the present ruling circles of the Kremlin, and if there were at least one line in those documents affirming the latter-day version of this venture, it would have been published long ago. It is precisely the unsupported character of the version, and moreover the radical contradiction of one assertion by another, which shows that there too we have to deal with the same Thermidorian mythology.

One of the reasons that the catastrophe near Warsaw assumed such extraordinary proportions was the behavior of the command of the Western group of the Southern armies, directed against Lwow (Lemberg). The chief political figure in the Revolutionary Council of War of the group was Stalin. He wanted at any cost to enter Lwow at the same time that Smilga and Tukhachevsky were to enter Warsaw. The rapid advance of our armies toward the Vistula had compelled the Polish command to concentrate all efforts and, with the aid of the French Military Mission, considerable reserves in the regions of Warsaw and Lublin. At this decisive moment, the line of operations on the Southwestern Front diverged at right angles from the line of operations on the main

[1] L. B. Kamenev, the Communist leader, not S. S. Kamenev, the military leader, of course.—C. M.

Western Front: Stalin was waging his own war. When the danger to Tukhachevsky's army became clearly evident and the Commander-in-Chief ordered the Southwestern Front to shift its direction sharply toward Zamostye-Tomashev, in order to strike at the flanks of the Polish troops near Warsaw, the command of the Southwestern Front, encouraged by Stalin, continued to move to the West: Was it not more important to take possession of Lwow itself than to help "others" to take Warsaw? For three or four days our General Staff could not secure the execution of this order. Only after repeated demands reinforced by threats did the Southwestern command change direction, but by then the delay of several days had already played its fatal role. On the 16th of August the Poles took the counter-offensive and forced our troops to roll back.

During the secret debates on the Polish War at a closed session of the Tenth Congress of the Party, Stalin came out with the declaration, equally startling in its viciousness and untruthfulness, that Smilga, the leading member of the Revolutionary Council of War of the Western Front had "deceived the Central Committee" by "promising" to take Warsaw by a definite date and by failing to make good his "promise." The actions of the Southwestern Front, i.e., of Stalin himself, had presumably been determined by the "promise" of Smilga, on whom, therefore, lay the responsibility for the catastrophe. In silent hostility the Congress listened to the sullen orator with that yellow glint in his eyes. With that speech of his Stalin hurt no one but himself. Not a single vote supported him. I protested on the spot against this startling insinuation: Smilga's "promise" meant merely that he had *hoped* to take Warsaw; but that hope did not eliminate the element of the unexpected, which is peculiar to all wars, and under no circumstances did it give anybody the right to act on the basis of an *a priori* calculation instead of the realistic development of operations. Lenin, terribly upset by the dissensions, joined in the discussion and expressed himself to the effect that we did not want to blame anybody personally. Why does not Stalin publish the stenographic record of this debate?

In 1929, A. Yegorov [Commander of the Southwestern Front during the Polish Campaign, made the first public attempt to justify his action in a special monograph entitled] "Lwow-Warsaw," [in which he was constrained to admit]:

★ . . . It is precisely in this respect that all our historians have criticized the campaign on the Southwestern Front. No one acquainted with this campaign on the basis of writings now extant will consider it a secret that the explanation for the failure of the Western operations is directly connected with the actions on the Southwestern Front. Accusations made in this sense against the command of the front come down basically to this, that the Southwestern Front carried on a completely independent operational policy, without taking into consideration either the general situation on the entire Polish Front or the action of the neighboring Western Front; at the decisive moment did not render to the latter the necessary co-operation . . . Such, in general outline, is the version reiterated in all works devoted more or less to the question of the mutual interaction of the front in 1920, without excluding even those published in most recent times . . . We find, for example, in the serious and interesting work of M. Movchin, "The Subsequent Operations according to the Experience of the Marne and the Vistula" (published by the State Publishers in 1928) a direct reference to "the failure by the Southwestern Front to carry out the categorical directives of the Commander-in-Chief concerning the advance of the First Mounted Army upon Zamostye-Tomashev" (page 74). The graduates of our War College have studied the history of the Polish Campaign on the basis of these and analogous statements, and continue to carry away with them into the ranks of our Army corresponding impressions. To put it more briefly, the legend about the disastrous role of the Southwestern Front in 1920 . . . apparently does not evoke at present any doubt and is recognized as a fact which the future generation of tacticians and strategists are supposed to study.

It is not at all surprising that Yegorov, who as Commander-in-Chief of the Southwestern Front, bore serious responsibility for the willful strategy of Stalin, proceeds then to minimize the gravity of his mistake by offering an interpretation of the military events of 1920 less unfavorable to himself. However, suspicion is at once evoked by the fact that Yegorov made his attempt at self-defense only nine years after the event, when "the legend about the disastrous role of the Southwestern Front" had already managed, according to his own words, to find definitive confirmation and even to become a part of military history. This tardiness is explained by the fact that the Army and the country, having suffered a great deal because of the failure of the Polish Campaign, would have indignantly resented any falsification, especially by those responsible for the failure. He had to wait and keep still.

As for me, guided by my concern for the prestige of the Government as a whole and the desire not to inject quarrels into the Army, which was sufficiently disturbed anyway, I did not remind them publicly about the sharp conflict preceding the campaign with so much as a single word. Yegorov had to wait for the establishment of the totalitarian régime before he could come out with a rebuttal. The cautious Yegorov, lacking in independence, was undoubtedly writing by direct assignment from Stalin, although that name, incredible as it may seem, remains entirely unmentioned in the book. Let us remember that 1929 opens the first period of the systematic review of the past.

But if Yegorov tried indirectly to minimize Stalin's guilt along with his own, he did not yet try to place the blame on the other side. Nor was this done by Voroshilov in the thoroughly apologetic article signed by him, "Stalin and the Red Army," published during the same year, 1929. "Only the failure of our troops near Warsaw," Voroshilov states vaguely, "interrupted the advance of the Mounted Army which had made ready to attack Lwow and was at the time ten kilometers from it." However, the matter could not rest with mere self-justification. In such questions Stalin never stops half-way. The moment finally arrived when the responsibility for the failure of the front could be placed on those who had interfered with the march on Lwow. [In

1935 the Red professor] S. Rabinovich [in his] "History of the Civil War" [wrote]:

> ★ The First Army, which became involved in the battle for Lwow, could not directly help the Western Front without taking Lwow. It could not have given greater aid to the Western Front because that would have entailed the transfer of large forces near Lwow. Notwithstanding that, Trotsky categorically demanded the retirement of the First Mounted Army from Lwow and its concentration near Lublin for a blow along the rear of the Polish armies advancing on the flank of the troops of the Western Front . . . In consequence of the profoundly erroneous directive of Trotsky, the First Mounted had to abandon the capture of Lwow without being able at the same time to offer help to the armies of the Western Front.

[Of course], that possibility was lost only because the Budenny-Voroshilov Cavalry, in agreement with the directives of Yegorov-Stalin and contrary to the orders of the Commander-in-Chief, turned toward Lublin several days late. [But the following year, the military journal] *Krasnaya Konnitsa* (Red Cavalry) [went even further in the article], "The Fighting Road of the First Mounted Army." In this the author declared that the Mounted Army . . . "not only could not prevent the Polish Army from retreating behind the River Bug, but did not even break up the counter-attack of the Poles against the flanks of the Red troops marching upon Warsaw." Stalin and Voroshilov, concerned with the new occupation of Galicia, an objective of only secondary importance, simply did not want to help Tukhachevsky in the main task, the advance upon Warsaw. Now Voroshilov argued that only the capture of Lwow would have enabled him "to deliver a crushing blow in the rear of the White Guard Poles and their shock troops."

It is quite impossible to understand how it would have been possible by the capture of Lwow, which was 300 kilometers distant from the main theater of war, to strike at the "rear" of the Polish shock formations, which in the meantime had already pursued the Red Army to within 100 kilometers east of Warsaw. In order to attempt to strike a blow at the Poles in the "rear" it would have been necessary to pursue them in the first place and therefore first of all to abandon Lwow. Why in that case was it necessary to occupy it? The capture of Lwow, which in itself was not devoid of military significance, could have been invested with revolutionary significance only by raising an insurrection of the Galicians against Polish rule. But that required time. The tempos of the military and revolutionary tasks did not coincide in the least. From the moment that the danger of a decisive counter-attack near Warsaw became apparent, the continuation of the advance upon Lwow became not only purposeless but downright criminal. However, at this point the jealousy between the two fronts intervened. Stalin, according to Voroshilov's [own admission], did not hesitate to violate rules and orders.

"Our situation seemed to me utterly hopeless," wrote Pilsudski. "I saw the only bright spot on the dark horizon in Budenny's failure to launch his attack on my rear . . . the weakness which was exhibited by the Twelfth Army," i.e. the army which upon the orders of Commissar Stalin had failed to support Tukhachevsky's army and had broken away from it. [Years later, justifying Stalin's action, the "Red Star" exclaimed indignantly] : "Covering up his disgusting defeatist maneuvers, the traitor Trotsky deliberately and consciously achieved the transfer of the Mounted Army to the north, presumably to aid the Western Front." Unfortunately, I might add, I secured this transfer too late. If Stalin and Voroshilov and the illiterate Budenny had not "had their own war" in Galicia and the Red Cavalry had been at Lublin in time, the Red Army would not have suffered the disaster which forced upon the country the Peace of Riga, which by cutting us off from Germany exerted a tremendous influence on the future development of both countries. After the hopes awakened by the determined drive on Warsaw, the defeat reverberated as an earthquake throughout the Party, upsetting its equilibrium and finding partial expression in the so-called Trade Union Discussion.

[Writing in *Pravda* of February 23, 1930, the Party historian N. Popov, acknowledging that the advance on Warsaw was a mistake of the Politburo, declared that] "Trotsky . . . was opposed to this advance as a petty bourgeois revolutionist who felt that it was inadmissible to carry the revolution into Poland from the outside. For the same reasons, Trotsky was opposed to the Red Army's aiding the rebels in Georgia in February, 1921. Trotsky's anti-Bolshevik, Kautskyist reasoning was emphatically rejected by the Central Committee, both in July, 1920, in the case of Poland, and in February, 1921, in the case of the Menshevik government of Georgia." [Five years later Rabinovich in his "History of the Civil War" ascribed Trotsky's] "errors in the Polish War" [to] "the fundamental political" [position that] "on our part the war was to stimulate and hasten the revolution in Poland, bring the revolution to Europe on the bayonets of the Red Army . . . Otherwise, the victory of Socialism in Russia is impossible. That was why Trotsky in opposition to arguments of Lenin and Stalin, declared that 'the Polish front is the front of life and death for the Soviet Republic.' " The old accusation thus reversed itself. As late as 1930 it was recognized that I was an opponent of the March on Warsaw, and the crime charged against me was my disinclination to introduce Socialism on bayonets. But in 1935, it was proclaimed that I advocated the March on Warsaw, guided by my determination to bring Socialism into Poland on bayonets.

Thus, by degrees, Stalin solved the problem in his own peculiar way. He placed the responsibility for the Warsaw campaign on me. But I, as a matter of fact, was an opponent of the campaign. The responsibility for the disaster to the Red Army, predetermined by the absence of an uprising in the country and made worse by his own independent strategy, he again placed upon me, although I had warned them of the possibility of catastrophe and called for restraint of enthusiasm over ephemeral successes like the capture of Lwow.

To shift the blame bit by bit to his opponent is a fundamental method of political struggle with Stalin and reaches its highest development in the Moscow trials. Let us also note in passing that Stalin contributed no constructive effort to the Polish War that is worthy of any notice. The mail and telegrams of the time show with whom I had occasion to correspond from day to day in determining the daily policy in connection with the Polish War: Lenin, Chicherin, Karakhan, Krestinsky, Kamenev, Radek. Of these six persons, only Lenin managed to die betimes.[2] Chicherin died in disgrace, in complete isolation; Radek is living out the end of his days under arrest; Karakhan, Krestinsky and Kamenev have been executed.

The end of the Polish campaign enabled us to concentrate our forces against Wrangel, who in the spring emerged from the Crimean Peninsula and, by threatening to take the Donetz Basin, placed the coal supply of the Republic in jeopardy. Several overwhelming attacks at Nikopol and Stakhovka dislodged Wrangel's units from their positions, and the Red Army marched ahead, demolishing at the climax of the campaign the fortifications of Perekop and the Sivash Isthmus. The Crimea again became Soviet. [As might be expected, "the basic strategic idea in the impending operation was personally determined by Comrade Stalin." Yegorov wrote in *Pravda*, of November 14, 1935, on the occasion of the fifteenth anniversary of Wrangel's defeat]:

★ Trotsky maintained the most harmful view that the Wrangel front was nothing else than a separate sector of third-rate significance. Against this most dangerous view Comrade Stalin was forced to come out most resolutely. The Central Committee headed by Lenin entirely supported Stalin.

Suffice it to say that S. Gussev, who was a genuine agent of Stalin's in the Red Army, as Mekhlis is now, in his article, "The Rout of Wrangel" [published] in 1925, did not deem it necessary even once to mention the name of Stalin.

Throughout the period of the Civil War, Stalin remained a third-rate figure, not only in the Army but in the field of politics as well. He presided at the congresses of the Collegium of the Commissariat of Nationalities and at the congresses of certain nationalities. He carried on negotiations with Finland, with the Ukraine, with the Bashkirs, i.e., executing essential but nevertheless secondary commissions of the government. He had nothing to do with the matters of major policy presented at the congresses of the Party, of the Soviet or of the Third International. At the Eleventh Conference of the Russian Communist Party, held in December, 1921, Yaroslavsky, in the name of the Organizational Committee, proposed the following list of names for the praesidium: Lenin, Zinoviev, Trotsky, Kamenev, Petrovsky, Ordzhonikidze, Voroshilov, Yaroslavsky, Sulimov, Komarov, Rudzutak, I. N. Smirnov and Rukhimovich. The list is interesting both because of the composition and order of

[2] Cf. the author's statements on the subject elsewhere in this book and particularly on pp. 377, 380, 381.—C. M.

names. The authors of the list, Old Bolsheviks on the order of Yaroslavsky, placed Zinoviev in the second place, so as to remind them that he was an Old Bolshevik. Outside of the first four figures, the remaining members, likewise Old Bolsheviks, were all regional leaders. There was no room for Stalin in this list, yet the calendar indicates the end of the year 1921. The Civil War was completely in the past. It had not made Stalin a leader.

Chapter XI

FROM OBSCURITY TO THE TRIUMVIRATE

[The end of the Civil War found Stalin still in the shadows politically. The Party wheelhorses knew him, of course, but did not regard him as one of the important leaders. To the rank and file of the Party he was one of the least known members of the Central Committee, notwithstanding his membership in the all-powerful Politburo. The country at large had scarcely heard of him. The non-Soviet world did not even suspect his existence. Yet within less than two years his hold on the Party's political machine had become so formidable and his influence was deemed so injurious by Lenin that early in March, 1923, Lenin broke all "comradely relations" with him. Another two years passed, and Trotsky, next in eminence only to Lenin in the leadership of the October Revolution and the Soviet government, had been relegated by Stalin's machine to a precarious political position. Not only did Stalin become a member of the triumvirate that led the Party in place of the sick Lenin, but the most powerful of the triumvirs and subsequently Lenin's sole successor. Moreover, with the years he acquired far greater power than Lenin had ever enjoyed— indeed, more absolute authority than any Tsar in Russia's long history of absolutist rule.

[How did this come about? What were the causes and the steps of Stalin's rise from political obscurity to political pre-eminence?]

Every stage of development, even such catastrophic stages as revolution and counter-revolution, is an outgrowth of the preceding stage, is rooted in it, bears a resemblance to it. After the victory of October, there were writers who argued that the dictatorship of Bolshevism was merely a new version of Tsarism, refusing ostrich-like to take into consideration the abolition of the monarchy and the nobility, the uprooting of capitalism and the introduction of planned economy, the abolition of the State Church and the education of the masses in the principles of atheism, the abolition of landlordism and the distribution of the land to the actual tillers of the soil. Similarly, after Stalin's triumph over Bolshevism many of the same writers—such as the Webbs, the Wellses and the Laskis, who had previously been critical of Bolshevism and had now become fellow-travelers of Stalinism—closed their eyes to the cardinal and stubborn fact that, notwithstanding the measures of repression resorted to under the duress of extraordinary circumstances, the October Revolution brought about an upheaval of social relations in the interests of the toiling masses; whereas, the Stalinist counter-revolution has initiated social upheavals that are steadily transforming the Soviet social order in the interests of a privileged minority of thermidorian bureaucrats. Equally immune to elementary facts are certain renegades of Communism, many

335

of them erstwhile henchmen of Stalin's, who, their heads buried deep in the sands of their bitter disillusion, fail to see that, notwithstanding surface similarities, the counter-revolution headed by Stalin varies in certain definitive fundamental essentials from the counter-revolutions of the Fascist leaders; they fail to see that the difference is rooted in the dissimilarity between the social base of Stalin's counter-revolution and the social base of the reactionary movements headed by Mussolini and Hitler, that it runs parallel to the difference between the dictatorships of the proletariat, however distorted by thermidorian bureaucratism, and the dictatorship of the bourgeoisie, the difference between a workers' state and a capitalist state.

· Moreover, this fundamental dissimilarity is illustrated—and in a certain sense, even epitomized—by the uniqueness of Stalin's career by comparison with the careers of the other two dictators, Mussolini and Hitler, each the initiator of a movement, each an exceptional agitator, a popular tribune. Their political rise, fantastic though it seems, proceeded on its own momentum in full view of all, in unbreakable connection with the growth of the movements they headed from their very inception. Altogether different was the nature of Stalin's rise. It is not comparable with anything in the past. He seems to have no pre-history. The process of his rise took place somewhere behind an impenetrable political curtain. At a certain moment his figure, in the full panoply of power, suddenly stepped away from the Kremlin wall, and for the first time the world became aware of Stalin as a ready-made dictator. All the keener is the interest with which thinking humanity examines the nature of Stalin, personally as well as politically. In the peculiarities of his personality it seeks the key to his political fate.

It is impossible to understand Stalin and his latter-day success without understanding the mainspring of his personality: love of power, ambition, envy—active, never-slumbering envy of all who are more gifted, more powerful, rank higher than he. With that characteristic braggadocio which is the essence of Mussolini, he told one of his friends: "I have never met my equal." Stalin could never have uttered this phrase, even to his most intimate friends, because it would have sounded too crude, too absurd, too ridiculous. There were any number of men on the Bolshevik staff alone who excelled Stalin in all respects but one—his concentrated ambition. Lenin highly valued power as a tool of action. But pure love of power was utterly alien to him. Not so with Stalin. Psychologically, power to him was always something apart from the purposes which it was supposed to serve. The desire to exert his will as the athlete exerts his muscles, to lord it over others—that was the mainspring of his personality. His will thus acquired an ever-increasing concentration of force, swelling in aggressiveness, activity, range of expression, stopping at nothing. The more often Stalin had occasion to convince himself that he was lacking in very many attributes for the acquisition of power, the more intensely did he compensate for each deficiency of character, the more subtly did he transform each lack into an advantage under certain conditions.

The current official comparisons of Stalin to Lenin are simply indecent. If the basis of comparison is sweep of personality, it is impossible to place Stalin even alongside Mussolini or Hitler. However meager the "ideas" of Fascism, both of the victorious leaders of reaction, the Italian and the German, from the · very beginning of their respective movements displayed initiative, roused the masses to action, pioneered new paths through the political jungle. Nothing of the kind can be said about Stalin. The Bolshevik Party was created by Lenin. Stalin grew out of its political machine and remained inseparable from it. He has never had any other approach to the masses or to the events of history than through this machine. In the first period of his rise to power he was himself caught unawares by his own success. He took his steps without certainty, looking to right and left and over his shoulder, always ready to slink back or run to cover. Used as a counterweight against me, he was bolstered and encouraged by Zinoviev and Kamenev, and to a lesser extent by Rykov, Bukharin and Tomsky. No one thought at the time that Stalin would some day loom away above their heads. In the first triumvirate Zinoviev treated Stalin in a circumspectly patronizing manner; Kamenev with a touch of irony. But more of that later.

The Stalinist school of falsification is not the only one that flourishes today in the field of Russian history. Indeed, it derives a measure of its sustenance from certain legends built on ignorance and sentimentalism; such as the lurid tales concerning Kronstadt, Makhno and other episodes of the Revolution. Suffice it to say that what the Soviet government did reluctantly at Kronstadt was a tragic necessity; naturally, the revolutionary government could not have "presented" the fortress that protected Petrograd to the insurgent sailors only because a few dubious Anarchists and Essars were sponsoring a handful of reactionary peasants and soldiers in rebellion. Similar considerations were involved in the case of Makhno and other potentially revolutionary elements that were perhaps well-meaning but definitely ill-acting.

Far from spurning the co-operation of revolutionists of all the currents of Socialism, the Bolsheviks of the heroic era of the revolution eagerly sought it on every occasion and made every possible concession to secure it. For example, Lenin and I seriously considered at one time allotting certain territories to the Anarchists, naturally with the consent of the local population, and letting them carry on their experiment of a stateless social order there. That project died in the discussion stage through no fault of ours. The Anarchist movement itself failed to pass the test of actual events on the proving ground of the Russian Revolution. Many of the ablest and sanest of the Anarchists decided that they could serve their cause best by joining the ranks of *our* Party.

Although we alone seized power in October, we demonstrated our willingness to co-operate with other Soviet parties by engaging in negotiations with them. But their demands were fantastically outrageous; they wanted no less than the decapitation of our Party. We then formed a coalition government with the only other Soviet party with which co-operation seemed possible at the time, the Party of the Left Essars. But the Left Essars resigned from the government in protest against the Peace of Brest-Litovsk in March, 1918, and in July they stabbed the Soviet government in the back by confronting it with the *fait accompli* of the assassination of the German Ambassador Mirbach and an attempted coup d'état. What would the Messieurs Liberals have had us do under the circumstances: let the October Revolution, the country and ourselves be devastated by our treacherous former partners in the coalition government and be trampled under the marching boots of the German Imperial Army? Facts are stubborn things. History records that the Party of the Left Essars crumbled to dust under the impact of impending events and many of its bravest members became stalwart Bolsheviks, among them Blumkin, the assassin of Count von Mirbach. Were the Bolsheviks merely vengeful or were they "liberal" when they perceived the revolutionary motivation behind Blumkin's stupidly disastrous act of provocation and admitted him to full-fledged membership in the Party and to highly responsible work? (And Blumkin was far from the only one.

His case is merely better known than others.) Far from hurting us, the rebellion of the Left Essars, which deprived us of an ally and a fellow-traveler, strengthened us in the final reckoning. It put an end to the defection of the Left Communists. The Party closed its ranks tighter than ever. The influence of Communist cells in the Army and in the Soviet institutions rose tremendously. The policy of the government became considerably firmer.

The Bolsheviks began the heroic period of revolution by erring on the side of tolerance and forbearance in the treatment of all the non-Bolshevik political parties. The bourgeois, Essar and Menshevik newspapers turned from the first days of October into a harmonizing chorus of howling wolves, prowling jackals and baying mad dogs. Only *Novoye Vremya* [The New Times], the shameless organ of darkest Tsarist reaction, attempted super-subtle maneuvering by trying to maintain a "loyal" tone, wagging its tail. Lenin saw through them all and saw the danger of tolerating the whole pack of them. "Are we going to let this rabble get away with it?" Vladimir Ilyich demanded on every occasion. "Good lord! What kind of dictatorship have we!" The newspapers of these hyenas pounced upon the phrase "plunder the plunderers" and made the most of it in editorials, in verse, in special articles. "What aren't they doing to that 'plunder the plunderers,'" Lenin exclaimed once in jocular despair. "Who really said it?" I asked, "Or is it pure fabrication?"—"Not at all!" Lenin retorted. "I did actually use those words. Said them and forgot about them. And here they've made a whole program of them!" He waved his hand humorously.

Yet we did not interfere with public expression of dissident views, although the Mensheviks deliberately sabotaged vital defense activity through their hold on the railway unions, and others elsewhere—until the assassination of Volodarsky and Uritsky and the murderous attempt on the life of Lenin, August 30th, 1918. It was in those tragic days that something snapped in the heart of the revolution. It began to lose its "kindness" and forbearance. The sword of the Party received its final tempering. Resolution increased and, where necessary, ruthlessness, too. At the front the Army's political departments, hand in hand with the shock troops and the revolutionary tribunals, put a backbone into the immature body of the Army. The same process was in time reflected behind the lines. At the front we then recaptured Kazan and Simbirsk. Throughout the country we secured a new lease on life. When Sverdlov and I went to visit Lenin in Gorki, where he was convalescing from his wounds, he showered us with detailed inquiries about the organization of the Army, its morale, the role of the Communists in it, the growth of discipline, interjecting happily, "Now, that's good, that's fine! The strengthening of the Army will be immediately reflected throughout the country in the growth of discipline, the growth of a sense of responsibility . . ." And indeed, by autumn the effects of a great change were evident on every hand. The helplessness we had sensed during the spring months was definitely a thing of the past. Something had happened. It was no longer a respite, a breathing spell, that had saved the Revolution, but the imminence of a new and great danger which had opened in the proletariat hitherto unplumbed subterranean springs of revolutionary energy.

Having deprived the parties of the Mensheviks and the Essars of the Right and Center of Soviet legality in June, 1918, after their direct participation in the Civil War against the Soviet government had been established not only through acts of individual terror, but sabotage, diversion, conspiracy and other overt acts of war, the Bolsheviks were compelled to add the Left Essars to the proscription list after the latter attempted their treacherous coup d'état in July.

But the June 14th decree of the All-Russian Central Executive Committee of the Soviet, which expelled the Mensheviks and the Essars from that body and recommended similar action to other Soviet institutions, was reconsidered five months later, after those parties returned to the class-struggle position axiomatic for professing Socialists. In October, 1918, the Central Committee of the Mensheviks acknowledged in a resolution that the Bolshevik Revolution of October, 1917, was "historically necessary," and repudiating "every kind of political collaboration with classes hostile to the Democracy," refused "to participate in any governmental combinations, even those covered by the democratic flag, that are based on 'general national' coalitions of the democracy with the capitalistic bourgeoisie or which depend on foreign imperialism and militarism." In view of these declarations by the Mensheviks, the All-Russian Central Executive Committee at its session of November 30th, 1918, decreed to regard as void its resolution of the 14th of June "insofar as it refers to the party of the Mensheviks." Several months later the process of "going left" began among a section of the Essars. The conference of the representatives of the various organizations of the Essar parties on the territory of Soviet Russia, which took place on the 8th of February, 1919, in Petrograd, "resolutely repudiated the attempt to overthrow the Soviet Government by way of armed struggle." Whereupon, the All-Russian Central Executive Committee on the 25th of February, 1919, decreed to void its decree of the 14th of June, 1918, "with reference to all groups of the party of the Essars which consider obligatory upon themselves the above-mentioned resolution of the conference of the parties of the Essars."

But in the spring the outbreak of *kulak* uprisings in a number of provinces and the successful advance of Kolchak induced these parties, with the exception of a few of their representatives, to return to their old positions. In view of that the Central Committee of the Russian Communist Party of Bolsheviks in May 1919, issued a directive "concerning the arrest of all prominent Mensheviks and Essars about whom it was not personally known that they were ready actively to support the Soviet Government in its struggle against Kolchak." It thus became obvious that the earlier professions of loyalty to the Soviet "democracy" were mere maneuvers by the Mensheviks and the Essar parties. Their constant agitation for the abolition of the Cheka and the death penalty even for spies and counter-revolutionists played into the hands of the White Guards and spread demoralization in the rear of the Red Army.

[Between arrests by the Soviet government and defections from the ranks by party members sympathetic to the Bolshevik regime, the parties of the Mensheviks and the Essars were reduced to mere skeletons by the end of 1919. Their leaders were either under the constant threat of arrest, imprisoned or in exile. The vaunted democracy of the Soviets—which began as the popular assemblies of the anti-Tsarist and anti-capitalist elements of the country, purporting to represent the vast majority of the common people, and which assumed at first dual and then sole authority over the country—succumbed a year before the end of the Civil War to the absolute rule of the one-party State.

[But meantime the trend toward centralization, that sure precursor of totalitarianism, went on within the Bolshevik Party itself. Although, true enough, it was due in a measure to the anti-Bolshevik activities of the other Socialist parties, which in their effort to become effective were actually anti-Soviet by virtue of the overpowering control of the Soviets by the Bolsheviks, no less important as contributing factors were the disastrous economic, condition of the country, aggravated by the devastation of War Communism and the Civil War, and the "rule or ruin" attitude of the Bolsheviks. The line of development from Soviet democracy and democratic centralism within the Bolshevik Party itself to totalitarianism in both spheres is not always clearly traceable. But it is sufficiently clear that after the seizure of power in October, 1917, in the name of the All-Russian Soviet of Workers' and Soldiers' Deputies, by the Bolshevik Party machine, the Party Central Committee and provincial committees, which had prepared and co-ordinated the coup d'état, yielded priority to the Soviet, in whose name and under whose ostensible auspices the insurrection had been carried out. Within the Soviet itself, the Council of People's Commissars assumed immediate priority of actual power over the Soviet Central Executive Committee, from which it derived its authority. Within the Council itself the Bolshevik majority held the dominant power. When, furthermore, early in March, 1918, the Seventh Party Congress officially approved the Brest-Litovsk Treaty and the Left Essar members of the coalition government withdrew in protest from the Council of People's Commissars, while the Left Communists for the same reason became an organized opposition within the Party and boycotted its Central Committee, the ideal of "democratic centralism" suffered further reverses, for in effect the power within both the government and the Party became concentrated in the hands of Lenin and the immediate retinue of Bolshevik leaders who did not openly disagree with him and carried out his wishes.

[An unfortunate precedent had been set in November, 1917, when Sverdlov, already Secretary of the Central Committee of the Party, and an outstanding organizer, succeeded L. B. Kamenev as Chairman of the Central Executive Committee of the Soviet. Thus, in the person of Sverdlov the Party-State machine found its initial expression in post-October Europe. Unwittingly—and only potentially, of course—the political administration Sverdlov headed was the precursor of the contemporary one-party State.[1]

---

[1] Cf. the resolution adopted in 1904 by the Amsterdam Congress of the Second International, which reads in part: "In order that the working class may put forth all its strength in the struggle against capitalism, it is necessary that in every country there exist vis-à-vis the bourgeois parties only *one* socialist party, as there exists only one proletariat . . ." Experience, particularly the coalition with the Left Essars, convinced the Bolsheviks of the validity of this ideal. Speaking on behalf of the routed Opposition at the Fifteenth Party Congress (Dec. 2-19, 1927), Kamenev declared: "We have to choose between two roads. One of these roads is that of a second party. That road, under the dictatorship of the proletariat, is fatal for the revolution. It is the road of political degeneration and class deviation. This road is closed to us, forbidden by the whole system of our ideas, by all the teachings of Lenin on the dictatorship of the proletariat . . . There remains, consequently, the second road. This road means . . . that we submit completely to the Party. We chose that road, for we are profoundly convinced of the fact that a correct Leninist policy can be realized only inside our Party, not outside the Party and against it . . . But if in addition we are *to renounce our point of view* (which is what this Congress demands), that *would not be . . . Bolshevik. This demand for the renunciation of one's own opinions has never before been posed in our Party.* If we were to declare that we had renounced opinions which we defended only a week or two ago, it would be hypocrisy, and we would not deserve your confidence . . . you would not believe it . . . it would merely introduce

[Lenin's prestige was so overwhelming that he had to resort to an exaggeratedly meticulous observance of the forms of collegialism to avoid becoming a personal dictator. Notwithstanding his unaccommodating disposition and bulldog tenacity in defense of his ideas, and his passion for getting things done as quickly and efficiently as possible, he was strongly inclined to be patient with oppositionists in the Party and in the Soviet. He made an earnest effort to meet his opponents on parliamentary grounds. Had it not been for the withdrawal of the Trotsky faction from the contest, Lenin would have gone down in defeat at the hands of Bukharin in the Central Committee debates on the Treaty of Brest-Litovsk. Nor did he bear a grudge against Bukharin and the other Left Communists for waging a vigorous campaign against him and the Party majority in the press and from the rostrum during the exceedingly critical months of 1918. And on the very day that the Left Essars staged their abortive coup d'état Lenin was answering the arguments of their leader, Maria Spiridonova, on the floor of the Fifth Soviet Congress. But he was no fetishist about parliamentarism. He had written in 1915: "The slogan 'Constituent Assembly' as an independent slogan is incorrect, since the question at present is, who is to call it." Accordingly, in 1918 he made short shrift of it.]

During the very first days, if not hours, after the Insurrection Lenin posed the question of the Constituent Assembly. "We must postpone it," he insisted, "we must postpone the elections. We must broaden electoral rights by giving them to the eighteen-year olds. We must make it possible to revamp the lists of candidates. Our own are no good: too many untried intellectuals, when what we need are workers and peasants. The Kornilovites and the Kadets [Constitutional Democrats] must be deprived of legal status." To those who argued: "It is not politic to postpone it now; it will be construed as liquidation of the Constituent Assembly, especially since we ourselves had accused the Provisional Government of putting it off," Lenin replied: "Nonsense! Facts are important, not words. As against the Provisional Government, the Constituent Assembly was or could have been a step forward, but in relation to the Soviet Government, it can only be a step backward. Why is it not politic to postpone it? And if the Constituent Assembly will prove to be Kadet-Menshevik-Essar, will that be politic?"

"But by that time we shall be stronger," others argued, "while now we are

decay into the very foundation of the reconciliation . . ." and so forth. The key to the difference between the Leninist and Stalinist views on party discipline is in the sentence italicized by me. The Stalinist Congress replied to Kamenev by expelling the Oppositionists and by demanding of them "complete ideological disarmament, the firm condemnation of the views of the Opposition as anti-Leninist and Menshevik." The very next day the same Kamenev with Zinoviev led a procession of twenty-three converts from Leninism to Stalinism up to the praesidium of the Congress with the following words of contrition and moral suicide: ". . . harsh as may be for us the demands of the Congress . . . we . . . bow our will and our ideas to the will and the ideas of the Party . . . the sole supreme judge of what is useful or harmful to the victorious progress of the revolution." They then accepted the ultimatum of the Congress and petitioned for readmission into the Party. This was the beginning of their end.—C. M.

weak. The Soviet Government is practically unknown in the provinces. And should it become known there that we postponed the Constituent Assembly, our position would become even weaker than it is." Sverdlov was particularly energetic in his opposition to postponing it, and he was more closely connected with the provinces than any of us. Lenin proved to be alone in his position. He would shake his head in disapproval and reiterate: "It's a mistake, an obvious mistake, that may cost us dear! I hope this mistake will not cost the revolution its head . . ." Yet once the decision was made against postponement, Lenin concentrated his entire attention on measures for bringing about the convocation of the Constituent Assembly.

Meantime it became clear that we would be in a minority, even with the Left Essars, who ran on the same ticket with the Right Essars and were fooled at every turn. "Of course, we shall have to disperse the Constituent Assembly," Lenin said. "But what about the Left Essars?" However, old man Natanson[2] reassured us on that score. He dropped in to "consult" us, but his very first words were, "I daresay we'll have to disperse the Constituent Assembly forcibly." Lenin exclaimed: "Bravo! What's right is right! But will your people go that far?" Natanson replied: "Some of us are wavering, but I think that in the end they'll all agree to it." The Left Essars were then going through the honeymoon of their extreme radicalism: they actually did consent to it. Lenin devoted himself passionately to the problem of the Constituent Assembly. He was thoroughgoing in all preparations, thinking through all the details and subjecting Uritsky, who to his great distress had been appointed Commissar of the Constituent Assembly, to the rack of pitiless cross-examination. Incidentally, Lenin attended personally to the transfer of one of the Latvian regiments, preponderately proletarian in complexion, to Petrograd. "The muzhik might waver in case of something or other," he observed, "And here we must have proletarian decisiveness."

The Bolshevik delegates to the Constituent Assembly who foregathered from all parts of Russia were—under Lenin's pressure and Sverdlov's management

[2] Mark Andreyevich Natanson, alias Bobrov (1849-1919), one of Russia's great revolutionists and a leading Populist, was one of the organizers of the Chaikovsky Circle, which played a very important revolutionary part in the *"khozhdeniye v narod"* ("going to the people") movement. After exile in Archangel Province, he organized the strongly conspirative *Obshchestvo Severnykh Narodnikov* (Society of Northern Populists) in 1876 and that summer initiated and managed the group which effected the escape of Kropotkin. One of the founders of the *Zemlya i Volya* (Land and Freedom) Party, he became a leader of the *Narodnaya Volya* (People's Will) after the split and a leading protagonist of its terrorist policy. Arrested in 1881, in connection with the assassination of Tsar Alexander II, he was sentenced to 10 years' exile in Siberia. In 1891 he organized with Victor Chernov the *Narodnoye Pravo* (People's Rights) Party. Arrested in 1894, he served his sentence in Peter and Paul Fortress and Eastern Siberia. He was one of the founders of the Essar (Social-Revolutionary) Party, member of its Central Committee, leader of its Left Wing since 1905. During World War I he was a consistent internationalist and one of the leading spirits of the Zimmerwald Conference. He became a leader of the Left Essars after the split in 1917, and in July, 1918, after the abortive Left Essar coup against the Bolsheviks, headed a group of Left Essars opposed to the coup and known as Revolutionary Communists. He was a member of the praesidium of the All-Russian Central Executive Committee of the Soviet. He died abroad in 1919.

—distributed through all the factories, plants and military units. They were an important element in the organizational machine of the "supplementary revolution" of January Fifth. As for the Right Essar delegates, they deemed it incompatible with their high calling to engage in a fight: "The people elected us, let the people defend us." Essentially, these provincial burghers had not the slightest idea what to do with themselves, and most of them had a yellow streak. But to make up for that, they worked out the ritual of the first session most meticulously. They brought along candles, in case the Bolsheviks were to turn out the electric lights, and a large quantity of sandwiches, in the event they were deprived of food. Thus, Democracy came to do battle against Dictatorship—fully armed with sandwiches and candles. It did not even occur to the people to defend those who considered themselves the elect of the people but actually were mere shadows of a period of the revolution gone beyond recall.

I was in Brest-Litovsk during the liquidation of the Constituent Assembly. But as soon as I came for a conference to Petrograd, Lenin told me concerning the dispersal of the Constituent Assembly: "It was of course very risky of us not to have postponed its convocation—very, very incautious of us. But in the final reckoning it was better that it turned out that way. The dispersal of the Constituent Assembly by the Soviet Government is a frank and complete liquidation of formal democracy in the name of the revolutionary dictatorship. Henceforth the lesson will be clear-cut." Thus, theoretical generalization went hand in hand with the utilization of the Latvian Rifle Regiment. It was undoubtedly then that Lenin must have become consciously aware of the ideas he later formulated at the First Congress of the Comintern in his remarkable theses on democracy.

As is generally known, the criticism of formal democracy has its own long history. Both we and our predecessors explained the transitional nature of the Revolution of 1848 by the collapse of *political* democracy. "Social" democracy had come to replace it. But the bourgeois social order was able to force the latter to take the place which pure democracy was no longer able to hold. Political history then passed through a prolonged period during which social democracy, battening upon its criticism of pure democracy, actually carried out the functions of the latter and became thoroughly permeated with the latter's vices. What happened had occurred more than once in history: the opposition was called upon to solve conservatively the very tasks with which the compromised forces of yesterday were no longer able to cope. Beginning as the provisional state of preparation for proletarian dictatorship, democracy became the supreme criterion, the last controlling resort, the inviolable holy of holies, i.e., the ultimate hypocrisy of the bourgeois social order. It was even so with us. After receiving a mortal knock-out in October, the bourgeoisie attempted its own resurrection in January in the phantom sacrosanct form of the Constituent Assembly. The subsequent victorious development of the proletarian revolution after the frank, manifest, blunt dispersal of the Constituent Assembly struck formal democracy the beneficent blow from which it will never again recover.

That is why Lenin was right when he said, "In the final reckoning, it was better that it turned out that way!" In the person of the Essarist Constituent Assembly the February Republic had merely achieved the opportunity to die a second time. [When, during Kamenev's brief tenure as the First President of the Republic —in his capacity as Chairman of the Central Executive Committee of the Soviet —and upon his initiative] the death penalty law against soldiers introduced by Kerensky was repealed, there was no end to Lenin's indignation. "Tommy rot!" he stormed. "How can you expect to conduct a revolution without executions? Do you really think you can deal with all these enemies after disarming yourself? What other measures of repression are there? Imprisonment? Who attaches any significance to it during civil war, when each side hopes to win?" Kamenev tried to argue that it was only a matter of repealing the death penalty which Kerensky had intended especially for deserting soldiers. But Lenin was irreconcilable. It was clear to him that behind this decree was a frivolous attitude toward the unprecedented difficulties we were facing. "A mistake," he reiterated, "unpardonable weakness, pacifist illusions," and the like. He proposed an immediate repeal of the decree. It was objected that this would produce an unfavorable impression. Someone suggested that it would be better to resort to executions when it became clear that there was no other way out. Finally, we let the matter rest there.

"And what," Vladimir Ilyich asked me once quite unexpectedly, "if the White Guards should kill both of us? Will Bukharin and Sverdlov be able to cope with the situation?" [At first, it was Sverdlov rather than Stalin on whom Lenin relied for centralization with a firm hand. Sverdlov it was who first attempted to define the division of functions between the Party and the Soviet political machines. It was Sverdlov who was elected chairman of the first constitutional committee (of which Stalin was a member). It was Sverdlov who incorporated in that first Soviet Constitution not only the theoretical principles of Leninism but the initial practical experience of administration in such matters as the interrelation of central and local organs of the Soviet government, the Committees of the Poor and the Soviets in the villages, the borders and functions of the constituent republics and autonomous regions, and numerous other specific matters that no amount of theorizing could encompass concretely. "Sverdlov," according to an eulogy by Stalin, "was one of the first, if not the first, who skillfully and painlessly solved . . . the complex organizational task . . . of building the new Russia . . . the government of Soviets, the government of workers and peasants," which arose "for the first time in the history of mankind," the task of effecting the transition of "the party, hitherto illegal, to new tracks, creating the organizational forms of interrelation between the Party and the Soviets, securing the leadership of the Party and the normal development of the Soviets. . . ."] Sverdlov was truly irreplaceable: confident, courageous, firm, resourceful, he was the finest type of Bolshevik. Lenin came to know and appreciate Sverdlov fully in those troubled months. How many times was it that Vladimir Ilyich would telephone Sverdlov to suggest one or another urgent measure, and in most cases would receive the reply, "Already!" This meant that the measure had already been undertaken. We often joked about it, saying, "With Sverdlov it is no doubt—already!"

[The process of centralization gained such momentum by the spring of 1919 that the Soviet Central Executive Committee had lost all of its actual power to the Central Committee of the Party, the transfer having been made as it were from Sverdlov's Government office to his Party office, while locally the Soviet committees were entirely subservient to the corresponding Party committees. The latter in turn were under the thumb of the Central Committee in Moscow, which was dominated by Lenin. However, this process had not yet crystallized and was not to achieve completion until years later during Stalin's incumbency.

[At the same Eighth Party Congress this process of increasing centralization at the expense of Party democracy was further stimulated by certain formal proposals of Zinoviev's, who acted ostensibly upon his own initiative but actually as Lenin's instrument. Zinoviev proposed on the one hand that for the sake of efficiency the Central Committee should delegate certain of its functions to three other bodies appointed by it—the Political Bureau, the Organization Bureau and the Secretariat; on the other hand, that a new Commissariat be organized, to be known as the People's Commissariat of Workers' and Peasants' Inspection. The oppositionists at the congress did not take kindly to these proposals. Ossinsky objected most vehemently to the institution of the Political Bureau:

> Permit me to refer to Comrade Zinoviev's theses, according to which . . . the Politburo . . . is to decide all urgent questions. The plenary session of the Central Committee is to meet only twice a month and, as Comrade Zinoviev put it circumspectly, is to discuss questions of general policy . . . In other words, the plenum of the Central Committee merely discusses. What it all comes down to, is that the Political Bureau of five people decides all the important questions, while the plenary session meets for general conversation, for discussion. All of the other fourteen members are thus reduced to the status of second-rate members.

[Ossinsky was right of course. That was precisely what eventually did happen. The Politburo came to pass not only on *urgent* questions but on *all* questions and merely informed the Central Committee of its decisions. In 1919 the Politburo consisted of Lenin, Trotsky, Stalin, Kamenev and Bukharin. The following year at the Ninth Party Congress it was expanded to seven members—the five of 1919 plus Preobrazhensky and Serebryakov. Moreover, after the Tenth Congress in 1921, the relative share of the Central Committee in the function of governing was further limited by statute: that Congress decreed that the Central Committee was to meet no longer semi-monthly but bi-monthly; moreover, the All-Russian Party Conferences, instead of meeting quarterly were to meet semi-annually. This made the Politburo the actual governing body of the Party and ipso facto of the Soviet government and the Communist International.

[At the same Eighth Congress the Organization Bureau, likewise of five members, was created. Its function was personnel work—the appointment and removal of Party members to and from jobs—with the approval of the Politburo. However, at the following Party congress, upon Kamenev's motion, its functions were broadened: the Orgburo was accorded the right "independently without the sanction of the Politburo to decide questions of an organizational character and questions of personnel with reference to workers not above provincial status . . ." Stalin was the only original member of the Politburo who was likewise a member of the Orgburo. Preobrazhensky and Serebryakov, who also became members of both bureaus in 1920, were both too ethical to stoop to the garden variety of machine politics. Thus, after the Ninth Party Congress, i.e., beginning in 1920, Stalin secured practically a free hand in appointing his own candidates to the key posts of provincial Party secretaries without any interference from the other members of the Politburo. Potentially he became the most powerful member of the most powerful governing body in the Party and the country, the Politburo.

[When, moreover, the People's Commissariat of Workers' and Peasants' Inspection was originated, Stalin was appointed its head. In proposing the creation of this new commissariat at the Eighth Party Congress in 1919, Zinoviev described it as "a commissariat of socialist control that will control all the units of our Soviet mechanism, sinking its feelers into all branches of Soviet constructive effort." Lenin made no bones about his support of Stalin in that ministry of the ministries, when, replying to the objections of oppositionists, he said:

> . . . Now about Workers'-Peasants' Inspection. It's a gigantic undertaking . . . It is necessary to have at the head of it a man of authority, otherwise we shall sink in a morass, drown in petty intrigues. I think that even Preobrazhensky could not name any other candidature than that of Comrade Stalin.

[The function of this new commissariat was to root out bureaucracy and red tape in all Soviet institutions. However, under Stalin it soon became a hotbed of political intrigue and one of the chief instruments with which he built his political machine. In a secret memorandum dated April 18, 1922, Trotsky wrote about it:

> It is impossible to shut one's eyes to the fact that the Rabkrin[3] is filled chiefly with persons who had failed in various other spheres. Hence incidentally the extraordinary development of intrigue in the . . . Rabkrin, which has long ago become a by-word throughout the country. There is no reason to assume that this institution (not its small ruling circles only, but the entire organization) can be restored to health and strengthened, because in the future the efficient workers will continue to be assigned to the actual job itself, not to its inspection. Hence, the fantastic nature of

[3] A Russian portmanteau word for the Commissariat of Workers' and Peasants' Inspection. —C. M.

the plan to improve the machinery of the Soviet State through the leverage of the Rabkrin is obvious.

[To this criticism Lenin replied on May 6th:

Comrade Trotsky is radically wrong about the Rabkrin. With our outrageous "departmentalism" even among the best Communists, the low cultural level of our functionaries, the intra-departmental intrigues . . . it is impossible to get along now without the Rabkrin. We can and must work on it systematically and persistently, in order to make of it the machinery for the inspection and improvement of all governmental activities.

[But before long Lenin was to change his opinion on this subject and to grow even more alarmed than Trotsky about the bureaucratization and political corruption of this commissariat especially designed by him to fight bureaucracy.

[The creation of the Secretariat by decision of the Eighth Congress as the third sub-committee of the Central Committee proved far more portentous than anyone at the time had foreseen. It was in that office that Stalin was later to entrench himself. In time the Secretariat was to supersede the Politburo as the seat of power. The Central Committee had a Secretary in Sverdlov but no Secretariat. Between his appointment as President of the Soviet Republic in November, 1917, and the split between the Bukharinists and the Leninists at the Seventh Party Congress in March, 1918, Sverdlov had been more concerned with his governmental duties than his secretaryship of the Party, so that the function of appointing members to jobs was shared indiscriminately by him with other members of the Central Committee and the Central Executive Committee and with the various members of the Council of People's Commissars acting both individually and as a body. As for the technical work, it was actually performed by persons who were not members of the Central Committee. The records of the office were kept largely in Sverdlov's personal notebook and in his head. The man had a phenomenal memory. Although with the emergence of the Party crisis at the Seventh Congress, Sverdlov shifted the emphasis of his attention from the Presidency of the Republic to the Secretaryship of the Party, he continued to conduct his Party office in much the same manner as hitherto, so that he was literally the indispensable hub of the political machine. His death, soon after the opening of the Eighth Congress, placed the Party machine in jeopardy. When the Secretariat was created in March, 1919, Krestinsky was placed at the head of it. He, too, was a man with a phenomenal memory, but he was not allowed to rely on it, and he proceeded to departmentalize his office and to institute the keeping of records. However, the new Secretariat proved ineffectual to the double task of ferreting out oppositionists from important Party and Soviet positions and replacing them with members willing and able to carry through the official policy of centralization. The Ninth Party Congress, held in 1920, therefore carried out a reform of the Secretariat itself. It decreed:

. . . 1.) to reinforce the Secretariat by enlarging it to three members of the Central Committee constantly employed therein; 2.) to transfer to the

> jurisdiction of the Secretariat . . . the current organizational and executive problems, reserving for the Orgburo . . . the general management of the Central Committee's organizational activities . . .

[The object was to increase the authority and prestige of the Secretariat, the better to enable it to cope with oppositionists and forestall the airing of their heretical views at Party congresses, conferences and meetings.

[But the three leading Bolsheviks (Krestinsky, Serebryakov and Preobrazhensky) selected for this high office proved too humane and tolerant for Party police work. Under their administration, oppositionist activities increased instead of subsiding. The three members of the Secretariat became themselves suspected of sympathy for the advocates of democracy. At the Tenth Party Congress, held in March, 1921, they were not only removed from the Secretariat but from the Orgburo, the Politburo and even the Central Committee. Their places were taken by second-raters destined to figure as the rising luminaries of neo-Bolshevik leadership: Molotov, Yaroslavsky, Mikhailov. It is not hard to deduce whose influence figured most potently behind the new "election," when you consider that of the five members of the Orgburo, three were the aforementioned members of the Secretariat discredited in the eyes of Lenin, the fourth was Rykov, until recently in obloquy for his stubborn opposition to Lenin immediately before and after the October Revolution, and the fifth was that master of political wire-pulling and intrigue, Stalin.

[Nor were these three the only rising stars of what was later to become Stalinism. Yaroslavsky was elected alternate member of the Central Committee as early as the Eighth Congress in 1919, Molotov and Petrovsky at the Ninth in 1920. These three plus Mikhailov and Ordzhonikidze were elected full-fledged members of the Central Committee at the Tenth Congress in 1921. Gussev, Andreyev, Kirov, Kuibyshev, Uglanov and Chubar' were other local leaders or minor officials at the Center whom Stalin pushed into political limelight. On the surface relatively a second-rater himself among the Bolshevik leaders, he had already begun convincing a growing group of Bolshevik politicians eager for advancement that he was able to reward the faithful with political plums. At least that attribute of leadership was his].

Stalin found the most loyal of his first collaborators in Ordzhonikidze and Dzerzhinsky, both of whom were at the time in disfavor with Lenin. Ordzhonikidze, who was decidedly gifted with forcefulness, courage and firmness of character, was essentially a man of little culture, irascible and utterly incapable of self-control. As long as he was a revolutionist, his daring and his resolute self-sacrifice predominated. But when he became a high official, his uncouthness and crudity overshadowed his other qualities. Lenin, who had had a warm feeling for him in the past, avoided him more and more. Ordzhonikidze felt it. Their unsatisfactory relationship came to a head when Lenin proposed that Ordzhonikidze be excluded from the Party for a year or two, for misusing his power.

Similarly, Lenin's friendly regard for Dzerzhinsky cooled off. Dzerzhinsky was distinguished by profound inherent honesty, a passionate character and impulsiveness. He remained uncorrupted by power. But he did not always measure up in ability to the tasks imposed upon him. He was invariably re-elected to the Central Committee. But as long as Lenin lived, it was out of the question to include him in the Politburo. In 1921, or it may have been in 1922, Dzerzhinsky, an exceedingly proud man, complained to me, with a note of resignation in his voice, that Lenin did not consider him a political figure. Of course, I tried as best I could to dispel that impression. "He does not consider me an organizer, a statesman," Dzerzhinsky insisted.

"What makes you think so?"

"He stubbornly refuses to accept my report as People's Commissar of Ways of Communication."

Lenin was apparently not enthusiastic about Dzerzhinsky's record in that position. As a matter of fact, Dzerzhinsky was not an organizer in the broad sense of the word. He would call his collaborators together and organize them around his personality, not according to his method. This was obviously no way to bring order into the Commissariat of Ways of Communication. By 1922 Ordzhonikidze and Dzerzhinsky felt thoroughly dissatisfied with their position and in considerable measure hurt. Stalin immediately recruited both of them.

[Another Party institution which played a prominent role in establishing the ascendancy of Stalin was the so-called Control Commissions, first proposed at the All-Russian Party Conference of September, 1920. According to the text of the resolution, the Control Commission was established "in addition to" the Central Committee, not as a part of the latter, like the Politburo, Orgburo and Secretariat. It was invested with the right to consider all complaints and to adjudicate them "by agreement with the Central Committee," arranging "whenever necessary, joint sessions" with the latter or appealing to the Party congress for solution of certain knotty problems. Similar control commissions, independent of the one elected at the All-Russian Party Conference of September, 1920, were elected at provincial Party congresses. Eventually, but not in the beginning, they were to become merely branches subsidiary to the former, which became known as the Central Control Commission.

[At the Tenth Congress, in March 1921, the objectives of the control commissions were defined as follows:

> For the purpose of reinforcing the unity and authority of the Party, Control Commissions are established, within whose competence are the tasks of extirpating the insinuating evils of bureaucratism, careerism, misuse by Party members of their Party and Soviet positions, the violation of comradely relations within the Party, the spread of unfounded and unverified rumors and insinuations and similar information that reflect upon the honor of the Party or any of its members, damaging the unity and authority of the Party.

[This was sufficiently broad to make any member of the Party in disfavor with the ruling group liable to investigation by a control commission. It is no mere coincidence that at the same Party congress the rescript against factions was promulgated. Both were obviously weapons for getting rid of oppositionists. And so was a third resolution—to institute a Party purge.

[At the Eleventh Party Congress in the spring of 1922, the original Control Commission was officially designated as the Central Control Commission and empowered to centralize the activities of the local Control Commissions, which in turn definitely took over punitive functions over recalcitrant Party members from the local and provincial Party committees. Moreover, each constituent republic acquired its own Central Control Commission directly responsible to the one in Moscow. A further proposal to reinforce each Control Commission with a department of investigation and a staff of Party sleuths was also approved. Of the seven members of the top Central Control Commission elected at the Tenth Congress, only Soltz, an Old Bolshevik, was re-elected by the Eleventh Congress. Three other new members of that body elected along with him—Shkiryatov, Korostelev and Muranov—were, like Soltz, political allies of Stalin, who was elected General Secretary for the first time at the same Party Congress. Thus, in the spring of 1922 Stalin secured the support of four out of seven members of the collegium of the supreme Central Control Commission.

[Meantime a subtle but deep-running change had taken place in the Party itself. The struggle for inner-party democracy had been open on the floor of the Tenth Congress. It had revolved principally around the subject of proper relations between the State, the Party and the Trade Unions. The so-called Workers' Opposition, led by Shlyapnikov and Kollontai, proposed a program which the ruling circles had denounced as "an anarcho-syndicalist deviation." According to official historians, this program called for the trade unions as the organizers of production to take over not only the functions of the State but of the Party as well. Trotsky, on the other hand, contended that while it was essential to pursue a policy of equalitarianism in the field of consumption, it was still necessary for some time to come to insist on "shock methods" in the field of production, which according to Trotsky meant "harnessing the trade union machinery to the administrative system of economic management" and according to his opponents, the conversion of the trade unions into State institutions. Lenin maintained that the trade unions should remain under Party control and should become more than ever a vast "school for Communism." In this controversy Stalin supported Lenin's position. There were also other opinions of the subject expressed on the floor of the Congress, but the matter was reduced principally to a three-cornered controversy between the groups whose chief spokesmen were Lenin, Trotsky and Kollontai. The discussion was moreover not confined to the floor of the Party congress. It was carried on publicly and invaded all sorts of Soviet institutions.

[This atmosphere of free discussion had changed radically by the time the Party met for its Eleventh Congress, held between March 27th and April 2nd, 1922.

During the intervening year, factions having been officially proscribed at the Tenth Party Congress, the oppositionists had gone "underground" and had organized clandestinely so well that a number of the resolutions sponsored by the ruling group at the Eleventh Congress were voted down overwhelmingly enough to preclude any fraudulent "revisions" of the ballot.

[Not only did the oppositionists show their mettle secretly, but there were turbulent expressions of approval when the oppositionist Ryazanov upbraided the ruling group openly in one of his speeches and when the delegates stubbornly refused to expel from the Party the leaders of the Workers' Opposition, Shlyapnikov, Medvedev and Kollontai, in open defiance of Lenin's demand for their expulsion. This open opposition was, moreover, symptomatic of a far more widespread secret opposition. The ruling group regarded the secret dissenters as the more dangerous of the two because their machinations were pregnant with painful surprises. It was clear that the system of divided responsibility between three equal members of the Secretariat, each disclaiming full responsibility, was inadequate to cope with the Secretariat's function of appointing "loyal" comrades to key positions and of selecting "loyal" delegates to Party congresses. Lenin and his entourage therefore decided to reinforce the Secretariat in two ways—by establishing the office of General Secretary, with the other two members acting as his assistants rather than equal colleagues, and by selecting for the position of General Secretary the man most capable of strong-arm work, Joseph Stalin. Two of his most loyal henchmen, Molotov and Kuibyshev, were elected as his assistants.

[Stalin was elected General Secretary on the second of April, 1922. Two months later Lenin fell seriously ill. By that time, through a lucky combination of circumstances as much as his own conniving, Stalin was already in a potentially strategic position. Had Lenin recovered rapidly, the chances are that Stalin would have slunk back into obscurity—the chances, not absolute certainty. But Lenin's illness went from bad to worse.]

Lenin's relations with Stalin are officially characterized as a close friendship. As a matter of fact, these two political figures were widely separated not only by the ten years' difference in their ages, but by the very size of their respective personalities. There could be no such thing as friendship between the two. No doubt, Lenin came to appreciate Stalin's ability as a practical organizer during the parlous times of the reaction of 1907-1913. But during the years of the Soviet régime Stalin's coarseness repelled him again and again, and increasingly militated against smooth collaboration between them. Owing largely to that, Stalin continued his clandestine opposition to Lenin. Envious and ambitious, Stalin could not help growing restive as he sensed at every step Lenin's crushing intellectual and moral superiority. [In constantly varying degree, this unstable] relationship persisted [satisfactorily enough for all practical purposes] until Lenin fell so seriously ill [that he retired from active participation in affairs of

State], when it became transformed into an outright struggle that culminated in the final break.

[As early as the spring of 1920] at the celebration in honor of Lenin's fiftieth birthday Stalin went to the length of delivering a speech about Lenin's errors. It is hard to say what impelled him to do it. In any event, the speech seemed so incongruous to all that on the following day, the 24th of April, [in their report of the celebration] both *Pravda* and *Izvestiya* stated merely that "Comrade Stalin spoke of several episodes of their work together before the revolution," and that was all. But at about the same time Stalin also put himself on record in print as to what he had learned and wanted to learn from Lenin, in his general article written for the same occasion under the title, "Lenin as Organizer and Leader of the Russian Communist Party." It would be hardly worth the effort to examine this piece because of its theoretical or literary value. Suffice it to say that the article opens with the assertion:

> While in the West—in France, in Germany—the labor party grew out of the trade-unions under conditions permitting the existence of unions and parties . . . in Russia on the contrary the formation of a proletarian party took place under the cruelest absolutism . . .

His assertion is, of course, true of Great Britain, which he fails to mention as an example, but it is not true of France and monstrously untrue of Germany, where the party had built the trade-unions practically from scratch. To this day, as in 1920, the history of the European labor movement is a closed book to Stalin, and hence it is still useless to expect theoretical guidance from him in that sphere.

The article is interesting because not only in the title but in his whole conception of him, Stalin acclaims Lenin primarily as an organizer, and only secondarily as a political leader. "The greatest credit to Comrade Lenin," which Stalin puts first, was "his furious assault upon the organizational formlessless of the Mensheviks." Lenin is accorded credit for his organizational plan because he "generalized like a master the organizational experience of the best practical workers." Furthermore:

> Only in consequence of such organizational policy could the Party have achieved that internal unity and amazing solidarity which enabled it to emerge effortlessly from the July Crisis and Kerensky, bear on its shoulders the October Revolution, live through the crisis of the Brest period without cracking, and organize the victory over the Entente . . .

Only after that did Stalin add: "But the organizational value of the Russian Communist Party represents only one side of the matter," and turn to the political content of Party work, its program and tactics. It is no exaggeration to say that no other Marxist, certainly no other *Russian* Marxist, would have so constructed an appraisal of Lenin. Surely, organizational questions are not the basis of policy but rather the inferences that follow from the crystallization of theory, program and practice. Yet it is no accident that Stalin looked upon the organizational lever as basic; whatever deals with programs and policies was for him always essentially an ornament of the organizational foundation.

In the same article Stalin formulated for the last time, more or less correctly, the Bolshevik view, rather new at the time, of the role of the proletarian party under the conditions of the bourgeois-democratic revolutions of our epoch. Ridiculing the Mensheviks, Stalin wrote that to those who had poorly digested the history of the old revolutions it seemed that

> the proletariat cannot have the hegemony of the Russian Revolution; the leadership must be offered to the Russian bourgeoisie, the very same bourgeoisie that was opposed to the revolution. The peasantry must likewise be placed under the patronage of the bourgeoisie, while the proletariat should be relegated to the position of an extreme Left opposition. These disgusting echoes of bad liberalism were offered by the Mensheviks as the latest word of genuine Marxism . . .

It is remarkable that a mere three years later Stalin applied this very conception of the Mensheviks, word for word, letter for letter, to the Chinese bourgeois-democratic revolution, and subsequently, with incomparably greater cynicism, to the Spanish Revolution of 1931-1939. Such a monstrous reversal would have been utterly impossible if at the time Stalin had really assimilated and thoroughly understood the Leninist conception of revolution. But what Stalin had assimilated was merely the Leninist conception of a centralized Party machine. The moment he got hold of that, he lost sight of its roots in theoretical considerations, its programmatic base became essentially unimportant, and in consonance with his own past, his own social origin, training and education, he was naturally inclined toward a petty-bourgeois conception, toward opportunism, toward compromise. In 1917 he had failed to realize fusion with the Mensheviks only because Lenin would not let him; in the Chinese revolution he fully achieved the Menshevik conception under the banner of Bolshevism, implementing the Menshevik program with Bolshevik methods, i.e., with the centralized political machine which to him was the essence of Bolshevism. Far more expertly, with a perfected efficiency truly deadly, he carried out the same policy in the Spanish Revolution.

Thus, if Stalin's article on Lenin, which has been republished since then innumerable times in innumerable quantities and in innumerable languages, was a rather simple-minded characterization of its subject, it does give us the key to the political nature of its author. It even contains lines which in a certain sense are auto-biographic:

> Not infrequently our own comrades (not only the Mensheviks) accused Comrade Lenin of being unduly inclined toward polemics and toward splits in his irreconcilable struggle against the compromisers . . . There is no doubt that both took place in their time . . .

In 1920 Stalin still considered Lenin unduly inclined to polemics and splits, as he had deemed him in 1913. Furthermore, he justified this tendency in Lenin without removing the stigma of the accusations that Lenin was given to exaggerations and to extremism.

[Lenin guarded every useful official as the apple of his eye. He was tender with all of them. We find him chatting "for 10-15 minutes" at the bedside of Sverdlov dying from Spanish influenza, notwithstanding the danger of infection; we find him chiding Tsuryupa, "Dear A. D.! You are becoming utterly insufferable in your treatment of government property. Your orders: three weeks' cure! And you must obey the medical authorities who will send you to the sanatorium. So help me, it's unproductive to be careless with poor health. You must get well!" Similarly, when Stalin was laid up with an operation at the Soldatenkovsky Hospital in Moscow in December of 1920, Lenin, according to the testimony of Stalin's attending physician, Dr. Rosanov],

★ called me by telephone every day, twice a day, morning and evening, and not merely inquired about his health but insisted upon the most thoroughgoing and extensive report. Comrade Stalin's operation was a very difficult one. A wide incision had to be made around the appendix at the time of the appendectomy, and we found it hard to guarantee results. It was obvious that Vladimir Ilyich was worried. "If anything should happen," he said to me, "telephone at once—any time, night or day." When on the fourth or fifth day after the operation it became clear that there was no longer any danger and I told him about it, he exclaimed straight from his heart, "Thank you ever so much! . . . But I am going to pester you with my daily phone calls anyway."

Once while calling at Comrade Stalin's apartment, I happened to run into Vladimir Ilyich there. He greeted me cordially, took me aside and again plied me with innumerable questions about Comrade Stalin's illness and cure. I said that it was necessary to send him away for a rest, so that he might properly recuperate from the difficult operation. He chimed in: "That's just what I told him! But he won't listen to me! However, I'll take care of that. But not in one of the sanatoriums. I am told they are good now, but I haven't seen anything good about them yet." I suggested: "Why doesn't he go straight into his native hills?" To which Vladimir Ilyich replied: "You're right! There he'll be further away from everything and no one will bother him. We'll have to see to that."

[But Stalin deferred his visit to his native Georgia until the following July. In the midst of that re-entry of Georgia, where he was confronted with militant opposition, Stalin fell ill again. On July 25, 1921, Lenin telegraphed Ordzhonikidze, Stalin's lieutenant and chief executor of the policy and program of "pacification" in Georgia:

Received your 2064. Send name and address of doctor attending Stalin, also how many days Stalin kept from work. Awaiting your reply to coded telegram. Will you attend plenum August 7? #835. Lenin.

[And on December 28, 1921, Lenin jotted down the following note to one of his secretaries:

Remind me tomorrow, I must see Stalin and *before that* (exec. 29/)
connect me by telephone with OBUKH (Dr.) about Stalin.

[Less than three months later Lenin himself was too ill to attend a Ce
Committee plenum, but rallied for the Eleventh Party Congress. Two months
later, Lenin's speech was impaired as well as the functioning of his right arm
and leg, in consequence of his first acute attack of arteriosclerosis on May 26,
1922, news of which was not made public until June 4th. After recurrent improvements and relapses throughout the summer, Lenin returned to his duties
in October, and the following month even addressed the Fourth Congress of
the Communist International on the fifth anniversary of the October Revolution. He was, however, too ill to attend the Tenth Soviet Congress of the
Russian Republic and the First Soviet Congress of the newly-constituted Soviet
Union at the end of December, for he suffered his second stroke, which paralyzed his entire right side, on December 16. His active participation in the
affairs of the U.S.S.R. was over. Like Moses on Mt. Nebo, he viewed the
promised land of the world proletariat from afar, and during intervals of improvement between recurrent attacks dictated his last commandments—his
Testament, which he completed on January 4th, 1923; his essays *On Cooperation; Our Revolution; How the Workers'-Peasants' Inspection Should Be
Reorganized; Better Less, But Better;* and *Pages From A Diary.* These months
encompassed the last of Lenin's creative effort. It culminated on the night of
March 5th-6th, when he dictated his last letter to Stalin, breaking off all comradely relations with him. On March 9th he suffered his third and most devastating stroke, which flung him into an agony of frightful suffering, aggravated by
insomnia and nervous excitement. His power of speech was gone, one half of his
body in the vise of complete paralysis. But his will to live and function was
indomitable.

[Toward the end of the following summer his health improved slightly, the
continual nightmare of insomnia came to an end, he began to walk, learning all
over again, like a child, and in the autumn he began to learn to speak again.
In October, able already to walk by himself with the aid of a cane, he had himself driven to Moscow, where he revisited his Kremlin office, and on the return
trip to Gorki stopped at the agricultural exhibition then under way. Daily he
chose the books and articles he wanted read to him. His speech was gradually
returning. The day of his recovery seemed not too far off. And then, awaking
out of sorts on January 20th, 1924, he complained of a headache, loss of appetite
and of feeling generally unwell. The following day he was again out of sorts and
ate a little breakfast and dinner under the persuasion of his entourage. After
dinner he lay down to sleep. At six in the afternoon a severe attack set in, his
breathing became increasingly more labored, his face blanched, his temperature
mounted by leaps and bounds, he lay unconscious, dead within fifty minutes.
Hemorrhage of the brain paralyzed his respiratory organs and life burned out
of him. Fifteen years and seven months later to the hour, the life of his partner
in what the world knew as the Lenin-Trotsky Government was to be also

snuffed out by hemorrhage of the brain, induced less subtly this time by the blow of an assassin's pickaxe. Lenin was three months short of fifty-four when he died; Trotsky, seven years older. Stalin, whom his most devoted of apologists among American journalists, after seventeen years of patient service, was to describe as, "an animal of prey which first paws its victim to feel out its strength, then strikes to cripple and steps back to watch the effect and finally kills," has survived both of them. He had planted the means of that survival during Lenin's illness.

[When Lenin suffered his first stroke, the public the world over, including Soviet Russia, was led to believe that his illness was not serious and he would soon return to his duties. He was a man of bulldog tenacity in body and spirit, and only in his early 'fifties. At first the members of the Politburo sincerely shared that conviction. They merely did not bother to disabuse the public—not even the workers and peasants of the Soviet Union or the rank-and-file comrades in the Party—when later it became clear to them that the contrary was true. With Lenin temporarily ill, it was taken for granted that the Politburo would carry on. Although to the public at large Trotsky seemed the most likely successor to Lenin, and although the younger Party members shared that view, the political wheelhorses of the Party machine did not see a fitting successor to their Ilyich either in Trotsky, who not so many years ago had been a factional opponent, or in any other member of the Politburo, all of whom seemed mere armor-bearers by comparison. The only conceivable succession to Lenin, temporarily ill or definitely removed, was a Directory of the top Party leaders, members and alternates of the Politburo and the Central Committee. This was assumed to have happened as soon as Lenin fell ill.

[But actually a variant of this took place. The succession passed to a triumvirate, of which Zinoviev was the leader, Kamenev his alternate and Stalin the junior partner. Zinoviev thus became, for better or for worse, Lenin's successor by virtue of his plurality inside the Politburo, and he secured that plurality not because his fellow-members deemed him the ablest and most deserving, but on the contrary, because they considered him the least capable of leadership and politically the most vulnerable. Of the seven members of the Politburo, Lenin was ill; Trotsky was alone in his opinion that he was the natural successor to Lenin, a widespread opinion outside the Party machine that made him the most feared and hated fellow-member inside the Politburo and among the Party wheelhorses; Zinoviev had the solid support of Kamenev and Bukharin, who felt freest in expression and action and in the opportunity to extend their sphere of influence under his nominal leadership, the grudging support of Stalin, who was not yet ready to assert himself, and the passive support of Tomsky. It was tacitly understood by all but Zinoviev, not only in the Politburo, but on the Central Committee as well, where he likewise enjoyed a plurality, that he was merely a dummy in place of a leader, and that only for as long as he behaved himself in accordance with the secret expectation of each of the others, which was to let him enjoy the glory until the real leader felt ready to reach out for it.

[Whom did Lenin favor as his successor? Until his second stroke, which felled him on December 16, 1922, he had not given the matter serious consideration, fully expecting to recover and resume the leadership. His Testament, written several days later, was patently an effort to offer his own frank opinion of the various candidates rather than to dictate his decision. Precisely because of the power at his command due to his overwhelming prestige, he was reluctant to impose his will. He stated his preferences and his objections, he made recommendations, particularly about the removal of Stalin from the post of General Secretary because of "rudeness" and "disloyalty," but he did not venture beyond advice on how his successors could work best together and beyond the warning that a serious contest between Trotsky and Stalin would be calamitous for the Party and for the Bolshevik cause. However, within two months he found it necessary to take the very definite and irrevocable step of formally severing comradely relations—which meant breaking off all political as well as personal ties—with only one of his lieutenants, Stalin. This "excommunication" took place during preparations for the Twelfth Party Congress, which Lenin, prostrated by his third serious stroke, was unable to attend. It was the first congress without Lenin and the first one packed with delegates hand-picked by the General Secretary. It marked the beginning of the end of the Leninist régime and the dawn of Stalinism as a new political orientation.

[The break between Lenin and Stalin came to a head after patient efforts by Lenin to avert it. When] at the Eleventh Congress, toward the end of March, 1922, Zinoviev and his closest allies were backing Stalin for the post of General Secretary, in the hope of utilizing the latter's hostility toward me for their own ends, Lenin demurred to the candidacy [in an off-the-record discussion among his intimates] with the observation, "That cook will concoct nothing but peppery dishes." Lenin was apprehensive about the recurrence of his illness and was anxious to utilize the period until his next attack, which might prove fatal, to establish a harmonious collective leadership by common agreement and particularly his own agreement with Stalin. [Hence the earnest effort he made to coordinate his own work with that of the Secretariat. He was most meticulous about upholding Stalin's authority. As late as October 21, 1922, Lenin rebuffed the highly indignant protest of the Georgian opposition against Stalin and Ordzhonikidze with a scathing telegram. Similarly, he continued to uphold him or to tone down criticism of him to mild reproof on other issues. Matters came to a head only when Lenin became convinced that Stalin was incorrigible. The Georgian question was only one of the issues which led to the final break.]

The only piece of serious Marxist writing Stalin had ever contributed to the arsenal of Bolshevik theory had been on the national question. That was back in 1913. It contained presumably the *summa summarum* of his own observations in the Caucasus, the results of conclusions from practical revolutionary work, and a number of broad historical generalizations, which, as we had earlier indicated, he had cribbed from Lenin. Stalin had made them his own in a literary sense, i.e., by tying them up with his own conclusions, but without completely digesting them and certainly without assimilating them. This was fully exposed during the Soviet period, when the problems resolved in black and white reappeared as administrative tasks of paramount importance, and as such determined all the other aspects of policy. It was then that the vaunted agreement of Stalin with Lenin in all things and especially their solidarity of principles on the national question, the guarantee of which was Stalin's essay of 1913, proved in large measure to be fictitious.

At the Tenth Congress in March, 1921, Stalin had again read his inevitable report on the national question. As often happens with him because of his empiricism, he proceeded to draw his generalizations not from the living material, not from the experience of the Soviet Government, but from unrelated and un-co-ordinated abstractions. In 1921, as in 1917, he still repeated the general argument that the bourgeois countries could not solve their national questions while the land of the Soviets had every possibility of doing so. The report aroused dissatisfaction, even perplexity. In the course of the ensuing debate the delegates most interested in the question, chiefly representatives of the national minority parties, expressed their dissatisfaction with it. Even Mikoyan, already one of Stalin's close political allies and subsequently one of his most devoted armor-bearers, complained that the Party was in need of instructions as to "what changes should be made in the system, what type of Soviet system should be established in the borderlands . . . Comrade Stalin failed to point that out."

Principles never exerted any influence over Stalin—and on the national question perhaps less than on any other. The immediate administrative task always loomed before him as greater than all the laws of history. In 1905 he came to notice the swelling mass movement only with the permission of his Party Committee. In the years of reaction he defended the underground movement because his nature craved a centralized political machine. After the February Revolution, when that machine was smashed along with illegality, Stalin lost sight of the difference between Menshevism and Bolshevism and was getting ready to unite with Tseretelli's party. Finally, after the conquest of power in October, 1917, all tasks, all problems, all perspectives were subordinated to the needs of that apparatus of apparatuses, the State. As Commissar of Nationalities, Stalin no longer approached the national question from the point of view of the laws of history, to which he had paid his full tribute in 1913, but from the point of view of the convenience of the administrative office. Thus he necessarily found himself at loggerheads with the needs of the most backward and most oppressed nationalities and secured undue advantages for Great-Russian bureaucratic imperialism.

The Georgian people, almost entirely peasant or petty bourgeois in composition, resisted vigorously the sovietization of their country. But the great difficulties thus engendered were considerably aggravated by the manner and method of militaristic arbitrariness wherewith Georgia was subjected to sovietization. Under these conditions a double cautiousness toward the Georgian masses was required of the ruling party. It was on precisely this that the sharp disagreement developed between Lenin, who insisted on an especially resilient, circumspect, patient policy toward Georgia and in Transcaucasia generally, and Stalin, who felt that, since the machinery of the State was in our hands, our position was secure. Stalin's agent in the Caucasus was Ordzhonikidze, the hot-headed, impatient conqueror of Georgia, who regarded every manifestation of resistance as a personal affront. [Stalin seemed to have forgotten that not so long ago] we had recognized the independence of Georgia and had concluded a treaty with her. [That was on May 7th, 1920. But on February 11th, 1921,] detachments of the Red Army had invaded Georgia upon Stalin's orders and had confronted us with a *fait accompli*. Stalin's boyhood friend, Iremashvili writes:

> Stalin was opposed to the treaty. He did not want to let his native land remain outside the Russian State and live under the free rule of the Mensheviks he detested. His ambition pushed him toward rulership over Georgia, where the peaceable, sensible population resisted his destructive propaganda with icy stubbornness . . . Revenge against the Menshevik leaders, who had persistently refused to countenance his utopian plans and expelled him from their ranks, would not let him rest. Against Lenin's will, upon his own egotistical initiative, Stalin achieved the Bolshevization or Stalinization of his native land. . . . Stalin organized the expedition to Georgia from Moscow and led it from there. In the middle of July, 1921, he himself entered Tiflis as a conqueror.

In 1921 Stalin visited Georgia in quite a different capacity from the one in which they had been accustomed to see him in his native land when he was still Soso and later Koba. Now he was the representative of the government, of the omnipotent Politburo, of the Central Committee. Yet no one in Georgia saw in him a leader, especially in the upper tiers of the Party, where he was accorded recognition not as Stalin but as a member of the highest leadership of the Party, i.e., not on the basis of his personality, but on the basis of his office. His former comrades in illegal work regarded themselves at least as competent in the affairs of Georgia as he, freely disagreed with him, and when they were compelled to submit, did it reluctantly, offering sharp criticism and threatening to demand a review of the entire question in the Politburo of the Central Committee. Stalin was not yet a leader even in his own [native haunts. That touched him to the quick. He would never forgive such an affront to his authority] as a representative of the Central Committee of the Party and of the Soviet Government, as People's Commissar of Nationalities. He considered himself with full justification more competent than all other members of the Party Central Committee on all matters pertaining to Georgia. If in Moscow he rested his authority on the fact that he was a Georgian familiar with local conditions, in Georgia, where he appeared as the representative of Moscow independent of local national sympathies and preconceptions, he tried to behave as if he were not a Georgian but a Bolshevik delegated by Moscow, the Commissar of Nationalities, and as if to him the Georgians were just one of many nationalities. He assumed a know-nothing attitude about the national conditions of Georgia—an obvious bit of overcompensation for the strong national feelings of his own youth. [He behaved like a Great-Russian Russifier, riding roughshod over the rights of his own people as a nation]. That was what Lenin meant by Russifying foreigners. This referred as much to Stalin as to Dzerzhinsky, [a Pole turned Russifier. According to Iremashvili, who obviously overstates the case] :

> ★ The Georgian Bolsheviks, who in the beginning were included in the Russian Stalinist invasion, pursued as their aim the independence of the Georgian Soviet Republic, which should have had nothing in common with Russia except the Bolshevik point of view and political friendship. They were still Georgians to whom the independence of their country was more important than anything else . . . But then came the declaration of war by Stalin, who found loyal assistance among the Russian Red Guardsmen and the Cheka he sent there.

Iremashvili tells us that Stalin met with general hostility in Tiflis. At a meeting in a theater convoked by Tiflis Socialists Stalin became the object of a hostile demonstration. Presumably, the old Menshevik Iremashvili himself seized control of the meeting and flung accusations in Stalin's face. Other orators denounced Stalin similarly, we are told. Unfortunately, no stenographic record of these proceedings has been preserved and no one is obliged to accept this part of Iremashvili's recollections too literally:

> For hours Stalin was forced to listen in silence to his opponents and to admit the accusations. Never before and never after did Stalin have to endure such open courageous indignation.

[Following developments can be told briefly.] Stalin again betrayed Lenin's confidence. In order to build solid political support for himself in Georgia he instigated there behind the back of Lenin and the entire Central Committee, with the aid of Ordzhonikidze and not without the support of Dzerzhinsky, a veritable "revolution" against the finest members of the Party, while perfidiously covering himself with the authority of the Central Committee. Taking advantage of the fact that meetings with the Georgian comrades were not accessible to Lenin, Stalin attempted to surround him with false information. Lenin smelled a rat and instructed his private secretariat to collect complete data on the Georgian Question; after studying it, he decided to come out into the open. It is hard to say what shocked Lenin most: Stalin's personal disloyalty or his chronic inability to grasp the gist of Bolshevik policy on the national question; most likely a combination of both.

[Groping for the truth, the bedridden Lenin undertook to dictate a programmatic letter that would outline his fundamental position on the national question, so that there would be no misunderstanding among his comrades as to where he stood on the issues currently under dispute. On December 30th he dictated the following note:

> I think that here the hastiness and administrative impulsiveness of Stalin played a fatal role, and also his spitefulness against the notorious "social nationalism." As a rule, spitefulness plays the worst possible role in politics.

[And the following day he dictated in the programmatic letter itself] :

★ It is of course necessary to hold Stalin and Dzerzhinsky responsible for all this out-and-out Great-Russian nationalistic campaign.

[Lenin was on the right track. If he realized the full seriousness of the situation, his understatement of it was monstrous, for what had actually taken place behind his back, as Trotsky characterized it eight years later, was that] Stalin's faction routed Lenin's faction in the Caucasus. This was the first victory of the reactionaries in the Party. It opened the second chapter of the Revolution [—the Stalinist counter-revolution.

[Lenin was finally constrained to write to the Georgian oppositionists on March 6, 1923] :

★ To Comrades Mdivani, Makharadze and others: (Copies to Comrades Trotsky and Kamenev).
Esteemed Comrades:
I am with you in this matter with all my heart. I am outraged by the arrogance of Ordzhonikidze and the connivance of Stalin and Dzerzhinsky. On your behalf I am now preparing notes and a speech.
With esteem,

Lenin.

The day before he had dictated the following note to me:

Strictly Confidential. Personal★

Esteemed Comrade Trotsky:
I earnestly ask you to undertake the defense of the Georgian matter in the Party Central Committee. It is now being "persecuted" by Stalin and Dzerzhinsky, so that I cannot rely on their impartiality. Indeed, quite the contrary! Should you agree to undertake its defense, I would rest easy. If for some reason you do not agree, please return all the papers. I shall consider that a sign of your disagreement.
With the very best comradely greetings,

Lenin.

[He also sent word by two of his personal secretaries that he wanted Trotsky to see it through at the forthcoming Twelfth Congress as well. Lenin's request was sent by telephone, and the papers—the letter on the national question and the notes—were brought to Trotsky by the Misses Glyasser and Fotieva along with a note from Miss Volodicheva, who had taken the dictation, informing him that Kamenev, who substituted for Lenin as Chairman of the Politburo as well as in the Soviet cabinet, was "going to Georgia on Wednesday, and Vladimir Ilyich asked me to find out whether you have any message of your own for him." Lenin's secretaries had called on Trotsky on Wednesday, March 7, 1923].

"Having read our correspondence with you," Glyasser told me, "Vladimir Ilyich brightened up. That makes things different. He instructed me to transmit to you the manuscript material which was supposed to have made up his bombshell for the Twelfth Congress." Kamenev had informed me that Lenin had just written a letter breaking off all comradely relations with Stalin, so I suggested that since Kamenev was leaving that day for Georgia to attend a Party congress, it might be advisable to show him the letter on the national question so that he might do whatever was necessary. Fotieva replied: "I don't know. Vladimir Ilyich did not instruct me to transmit the letter to Comrade Kamenev, but I can ask him." A few minutes later she returned with the following message: "Absolutely not. Vladimir Ilyich says that Kamenev would show the letter to Stalin, who would make a rotten compromise, in order later to double-cross us."

"In other words, the matter has gone so far that Ilyich does not deem it possible to conclude a compromise with Stalin even along correct lines?" I inquired.

"Yes," she confirmed, "Ilyich does not trust Stalin. He wants to come out openly against him before the whole Party. He is preparing a bombshell."

Lenin's intention now became utterly clear. Using Stalin's policy as an example, he wanted to expose before the Party (and to do so ruthlessly) the danger of the bureaucratic transformation of the dictatorship. But almost immediately after that, possibly within half an hour, Fotieva returned with another message from Vladimir Ilyich, who, she said, had decided to act immediately and had written the [previously-quoted] note to Mdivani and Makharadze, with instructions to transmit copies to Kamenev as well as to me.

"How do you explain the change?" I asked Fotieva.

"Evidently," she replied, "Vladimir Ilyich is feeling worse and is in a hurry to do everything he can."

[Two days later Lenin had his third stroke.

[On the eve of the Congress, at the April 16th session of the Central Committee, Stalin apparently tried to protect himself with an undercover attack on Trotsky in connection with Lenin's notes and letter on the national question and particularly the Georgian issue. The following two documents by Trotsky shed some light on the situation]:

I.

★

Secret # 200T
To the Members of the Central Committee
Re: Comrade Stalin's Declaration of April 16th

1. Comrade Lenin's article was sent to me secretly and personally by Comrade Lenin through Comrade Fotieva and, notwithstanding my expressed intention to acquaint the members of the Politburo with the article, Comrade Lenin categorically expressed himself against this through Comrade Fotieva.

2. Since two days after I had received the article Comrade Lenin's condition became worse, further communication with him on this question naturally terminated.

3. After some time Comrade Glyasser asked me for the article and I returned it.

4. I made a copy of it for my own use (for formulating corrections to Comrade Stalin's thesis, for writing an article, and the like).

5. I know nothing about the instructions Comrade Lenin gave with regard to his article and other documents on the Georgian matter ("I am preparing speeches and articles"); I suppose that the proper instructions are in the possession of Nadezhda Konstantinovna [Krupskaya, Lenin's wife], Maria Ilyinishna [Ulyanova, Lenin's sister], or Comrade Lenin's secretaries. I did not deem it proper to question anyone about it for reasons that do not require clarification.

6. Only from Comrade Fotieva's communication to me yesterday by telephone and from her note to Comrade Kamenev did I learn that Comrade Lenin had made no arrangements about the article. Since Comrade Lenin had not formally expressed his wishes on this matter, it had to be decided on the principle of political feasibility. It stands to reason that I could not personally assume responsibility for such a decision and therefore I referred the matter to the Central Committee. I did it without wasting a minute after I learned that Comrade Lenin had not given any direct and formal instructions as to the future fate of his article, the original of which is kept by his secretaries.

7. If anyone thinks that I acted improperly in this matter I for my part propose that this matter be investigated either by the conflict commission of the congress or by some special commission. I see no other way.
17/IV/23

2.

Personal, written without a copy

★ Comrade Stalin:

Yesterday in personal conversation with me you said it was perfectly clear to you that in the matter of Comrade Lenin's article I did not act improperly and that you will formulate a written declaration in that sense.

Until this morning (11 o'clock) I have not received such a declaration. It is possible that you were delayed by your report of yesterday.

In any event, your first declaration remains until the present moment unrepudiated by you and gives certain comrades a justification for spreading a corresponding version among certain of the delegates.

Since I cannot permit even the shadow of vagueness in this matter—for reasons which, of course, you have no difficulty in understanding—I deem it necessary to expedite its termination. If in reply to this note I do not receive from you a communication to the effect that in the course of today you will send to all members of the Central Committee a declaration that would exclude the possibility of any sort of equivocalness in this matter, then I shall conclude that you have changed your intention of yesterday and will appeal to the conflict commission, requesting an investigation from beginning to end.

You can understand and appreciate better than anyone else that if I have not done this so far, it was not because it could have hurt my interests in any way.

April 18, 1923. Number 201.

Addressing the Congress on the 23rd of April, Stalin said in his concluding remarks on the national question:

Here very many have referred to the notes and articles of Vladimir Ilyich. I shouldn't like to quote my master, Comrade Lenin, since he is not here, for I fear that I may be referring to him incorrectly and not to the point . . .

These words undoubtedly are a model of the most extraordinary Jesuitism on record. Stalin well knew how indignantly Lenin was opposed to his national policy, how his "master" was prevented from blowing this "disciple" sky-high on this very issue only because of grave illness.

Chapter XII

THE ROAD TO POWER

[Early in 1923 it had become clear to the top leaders cognizant of the political situation that Stalin was literally packing the forthcoming Twelfth Congress, the highest authority in the Party, with delegates unswervingly loyal to him personally. Lenin became so alarmed by this trend of affairs that he] summoned me to his room in the Kremlin, spoke of the frightful growth of bureaucratism in our Soviet *apparat*[1] and of the need to find a solution for the problem. He suggested a special commission of the Central Committee and asked me to take an active part in it. I replied:

"Vladimir Ilyich, I am convinced that in the present fight against bureaucratism in the Soviet *apparat* we must not lose sight of what is going on: a very special selection of officials and specialists, Party members and non-partisans, in the Center and in the provinces, even for district and local Party offices, is taking place on the basis of loyalty to certain dominant Party personalities and ruling groups inside the Central Committee itself. Every time you attack a minor official, you run up against an important Party leader . . . I could not undertake the work under present circumstances."

Lenin was thoughtful for a moment and—I am quoting him literally—said: "In other words, I am proposing a campaign against bureaucratism in the Soviet *apparat* and you are proposing to extend the fight to include the bureaucratism of the Party's Orgburo?"

I laughed at the very unexpectedness of this, because no such finished formulation of the idea was in my mind at the time. I replied: "I suppose that's it."

"Very well, then," Lenin retorted, "I propose a *bloc.*"

"It is a pleasure to form a *bloc* with a good man," I said.

It was agreed that Lenin would initiate the proposal for this commission of the Central Committee to fight bureaucratism "in general" and in the Orgburo in particular. He promised to think over "further" organizational details of the matter. On that we parted. Two weeks passed. Lenin's health became worse. Then his secretaries brought me his notes and letter on the national question. For months he was prostrate with arteriosclerosis and nothing could be done about our *bloc* against the bureaucratism of the Orgburo. Obviously, Lenin's plan was directed against Stalin, although his name was not mentioned; it was in line with the train of thought Lenin expressed explicitly in his Testament.

[1] The Communist word for political machine.—C. M.

[If by that time Stalin had the Central Control Commission, the Orgburo and the Secretariat in his grip, Zinoviev still held the plurality in the Politburo and in the Central Committee, by virtue of which he was the leading member of the triumvirate. The contest between him and Stalin, tacit and hidden but nonetheless vehement, was for the majority at the forthcoming Congress. Zinoviev had complete control of the Leningrad organization and his partner Kamenev of the Moscow organization. These two most important Party centers needed only the support of a few other large Party centers to secure a majority of the Congress. This majority was necessary for the election of a Central Committee and the ratification of resolutions favorable to Zinoviev. But Zinoviev failed to secure that majority; most of the Party organizations outside of Leningrad and Moscow proved to be under the firm control of the General Secretary.

[Nevertheless Zinoviev was foolhardy enough to insist on taking Lenin's place at the Twelfth Congress and assumed the role of Lenin's successor by delivering the Political Report at its opening session. During the preparations for the Congress, with Lenin ill and unable to attend,] the most ticklish question was who should deliver this keynote address, which since the founding of the Party had always been Lenin's prerogative. When the subject was broached in the Politburo, Stalin was the first to say, "The Political Report will of course be made by Comrade Trotsky."

I did not want that, since it seemed to me equivalent to announcing my candidacy for the role of Lenin's successor at a time when Lenin was fighting a grave illness. I replied approximately as follows: "This is an interim. Let us hope that Lenin will soon get well. In the meantime the report should be made, in keeping with his office, by the General Secretary. That will eliminate all grounds for idle speculations. Besides, you and I have serious differences on economic questions, and I am in the minority."

"But suppose there were to be no differences?" Stalin asked, letting me understand that he was ready to go far in making concessions, i.e., to conclude a rotten compromise.

Kalinin intervened in this dialogue. "What differences?" he asked. "Your proposals always pass through the Politburo."

I continued to insist on Stalin making the report.

"Under no circumstances," he replied with demonstrative modesty. "The Party will not understand it. The report must be made by the most popular member of the Central Committee."

[The matter was finally decided by Zinoviev's majority in the Central Committee. That made it clear to every Party member that Zinoviev was Lenin's successor as head of the Party. With the delegates he controlled and the majority controlled by his junior partner in the triumvirate, he had every reason to expect an ovation the moment he appeared on the rostrum in the role of Number One Bolshevik to deliver the Political Report. But the General Secretary doublecrossed his fellow-triumvir: Zinoviev was not greeted by the customary applause.

He delivered his keynote address in virtually oppressive silence. The verdict of the delegates was clear: in this new role Zinoviev was an usurper.

[The Twelfth Congress, which lasted for the week between April 17 and 25, 1923, raised Stalin from junior to senior partnership in the triumvirate. Zinoviev's plurality in the Central Committee and the Politburo was destroyed. Stalin gained control of both. But his most important achievement at the Twelfth Congress was in the Central Control Commission and the network of provincial control commissions. At the Eleventh Congress Stalin had become the secret boss of the Central Control Commission; the majority of its members were his men. But the provincial, county and local control commissions, many of them elected before he became General Secretary, were beyond his control. Stalin tackled the problem in characteristic fashion. On one pretext or another, cases subject to the jurisdiction of hostile control commissions and involving the interests of Stalin's political machine were transferred for hearing wherever possible to the Central Control Commission; moreover, whenever it could be done without attracting too much notice, on one or another pretext, a number of hostile control commissions were simply abolished by the Central Control Commission. This, supplemented by organized conniving at provincial and regional conferences of the control commissions, produced fruitful results.

[The Party Collegium, made up of Central Control Commission members and especially created at this Congress to "try" and "liquidate" oppositionists, was made up entirely of Stalinists. The membership of the Central Control Commission itself was raised from 7 to 50, with 10 alternates—more high-placed offices with which to reward the faithful. Moreover, the new definitions of its functions and its actual activities transformed the Central Control Commission into a special OGPU for Communist Party members.

[Having suffered defeat at the Twelfth Congress, Zinoviev tried to recoup his political fortunes by a deal with the top leaders. He wavered between two plans: (1) to reduce the Secretariat to its former status of a subsidiary of the Politburo, by depriving it of its self-aggrandized appointive powers; and (2) to "politicalize" it, which meant establishing a special collegium of three members of the Politburo within it as its highest authority, these three to be Stalin, Trotsky and either Kamenev, Bukharin or Zinoviev. Some such combination, he felt, was indispensable to offset Stalin's undue influence.

[He initiated his conferences on the matter in a cave near Kislovodsk, a famous Caucasian watering place, in September, 1923. Voroshilov, who was in Rostov at the time, received a telegraphic invitation from Zinoviev to attend. So did Stalin's friend Ordzhonikidze. The others present were Zinoviev, Bukharin, Lashevich and Evdokimov. Zinoviev, who wrote down a summary of the views expressed at that conference in a letter addressed to Stalin and personally given by him to his best friend Ordzhonikidze for delivery to the addressee, revealed that:

Comrade Stalin . . . replied with a telegram in a coarse but friendly tone . . . Some time later he arrived and . . . we had several conversations. Finally it was decided that we would not touch the Secretariat, but, in order to coordinate organizational work with political activities, we would place three members of the Politburo. in the Orgburo. This not very practical suggestion was made by Comrade Stalin, and we agreed to it . . . The three members of the Politburo were Comrades Trotsky, Bukharin and I. I attended the sessions of the Orgburo, I think, once or twice, Comrades Bukharin and Trotsky did not come even once. Nothing came of it all . . .

[Actually, all the hopeful Zinoviev had to do was to attend one or two meetings of the Orgburo, to realize the hopelessness of anyone not a member of the Stalin machine trying to "crash the gate" there; Trotsky and Bukharin had at least the foresight and imagination to stay away.

[Meantime, the revolutionary situation in Germany had come to a head. But the triumvirs and their allies in the Politburo were still too busy undermining the prestige of the over-popular Comrade Trotsky and knifing each other, to give more than an occasional perfunctory glance to the paramount problem of world revolution. The German comrades had standing orders to work the lever of the United Front tactic to the limit. Then Zinoviev convoked the enlarged Executive of the Comintern in Moscow, and from June 12th to the 24th the leaders of World Communism talked revolution.

[The desperate German masses—fifteen million of them in the towns, seven million of them in the country—backed the German Section of the Comintern. But with Lenin paralyzed and speechless, with Trotsky hamstrung by Party discipline and rendered politically impotent by his isolation in the Politburo, the Comintern leaders in Moscow had nothing to say to the Communist leaders of Germany. No orders came through and nothing happened. During that fateful August of 1923, Stalin wrote the following lines to Zinoviev (the head of the Communist International) and Bukharin (the officially-acknowledged "chief theoretician of Communism after Lenin")]:

Should the Communists at the present stage try to seize power without the Social-Democrats? Are they sufficiently ripe for that? That, in my opinion, is the question. When we seized power, we had in Russia such resources in reserve as (a) the promise of peace; (b) the slogan: the land to the peasants; (c) the support of the great majority of the working class; and (d) the sympathy of the peasantry. At the moment the German Communists have nothing of the kind. They have of course a Soviet country as neighbor, which we did not have; but what can we offer them? . . . Should the government in Germany topple over now, in a manner of speaking, and the Communists were to seize hold of it, they would end up in a crash. That, in the "best" case. While at worst, they will be smashed to smithereens and thrown away back. The whole point is not that Brandler wants to "educate the masses" but that the bourgeoisie plus the Right Wing Social-Democrats is bound to turn such lessons—the demonstration—

into a general battle (at present all the odds are on their side) and exterminate them [the German Communists]. Of course the Fascists are not asleep; but it is to our advantage to let them attack first: that will rally the entire working class around the Communists (Germany is not Bulgaria). Besides, all our information indicates that in Germany Fascism is weak. In my opinion the Germans should be restrained and not spurred on.

[This opinion of the senior member of the triumvirate and secret boss of the Communist Party of the Soviet Union was virtually an order to the head of the Communist International, who formulated his instructions to the German Communist Party leadership accordingly. Like all such pronouncements, it was "secret" and "confidential" and not generally known at the time. Trotsky, unaware of Stalin's secret "opinion" but very much aware of the seriousness of the German situation, urged that a flexible provisional date eight to ten weeks ahead be set at once for the German Insurrection and corresponding preparations be launched at once. But the majority of the Central Committee was in Stalin's pocket.

[Brandler, who came to Moscow early in September for guidance and help, could not even get an interview with the leaders of the world revolution. After being shunted from office to office day after day and week after week, he finally secured an opportunity to air his knowledge and his views of the German situation in the presence of Stalin as well as Zinoviev. Their advice to Brandler was the same as the decision of the Comintern Executive of the previous June—form a workers' government by entering the Social-Democratic government in Saxony. When Brandler balked he was told the purpose of the maneuver was the better to prepare for the insurrection. Stalin countered further arguments with a peremptory order for immediate entry, and Zinoviev as head of the Comintern sent telegraphic orders to the Communist Party of Saxony to enter the Social-Democratic government at once. Moreover, Brandler himself was instructed to enter that government. He was thus confronted with the alternative of relinquishing the leadership of the German Communist Party, if he did not obey. He bowed his head.

[The hasty preparations begun at the end of September were woefully inadequate and badly mismanaged. The German Communist Party had organized fighting detachments, the so-called Red Hundreds, in each Communist center, and held them in readiness for the signal to be given as a result of a conference to be held in Chemnitz on October 21st. The insurrection was to begin in Saxony. If it developed according to plan the Communist Party would lead it; if it did not, the Communist Party would disclaim all responsibility and hide behind the protective coloration of coalition with the Social Democrats, with whose aid it would attempt to stave off the inevitable reaction.

[It was a typical Stalinist maneuver. He had behaved thus in October, 1917, in Russia, during the debates in the Bolshevik Central Committee, clandestinely supporting Zinoviev and Kamenev who were openly opposed to Lenin's insistence on the insurrection, while keeping a sharp lookout to see which side was actually winning. In Russia it was of no importance where he stood on the issue of insurrection because he was not entrusted with preparing it. But in the German situation of 1923 he was the supreme boss.

[When at the Chemnitz Conference on October 21st the Saxon Social-Democrats turned down Brandler's proposal for a general strike and an armed insurrection, Brandler gave the only signal he could give in keeping with his instructions from Stalin and Zinoviev; he called the revolution off. But this was not the first time that a revolution in Germany had been scheduled, called off and scheduled again. A revolutionary party straining at the leash for action cannot be expected to respond indefinitely with the regularity of a water faucet. Two days after the off signal from Chemnitz, the insurrection was on in Hamburg. All to no purpose. The fighters were leaderless and without an objective. The uprising petered out. What might have been a revolution became a senseless and criminal adventure. It was the first of a progressive series under Stalin's leadership in the international arena, his first great rehearsal for his first capitulation to Hitler in 1933.

[The German failure found immediate repercussion in the Communist Party of the Soviet Union. The sincere Bolsheviks were perturbed; many of them insisted on more than the perfunctory accounting of performance by the Party leaders. They wanted to thrash the problems out in open debate. Their first demand therefore was the restoration of the right to form groupings within the Party, abolished by the Tenth Congress in 1921 during the crucial days of the Kronstadt Rebellion. The dissatisfaction with the rule of the triumvirate had been brewing ever since the Twelfth Congress, nor was it confined to the triumvirs; it was directed against the Central Committee as a whole. Forty-six prominent Bolsheviks, among them Pyatakov, Sapronov, Serebryakov, Preobrazhensky, Ossinsky, Drobnis, Alsky, V. M. Smirnov, issued a statement in which they declared in part:

> The régime which has been set up in the Party is utterly intolerable. It is destructive of initiative within the Party. It is replacing the Party with a political machine . . . which functions well enough when all goes well but which inevitably misfires at moments of crisis and which threatens to prove its absolute bankruptcy in the face of the grave developments now impending. The present situation is due to the fact that the régime of factional dictatorship which developed objectively after the Tenth Congress has outlived its usefulness.

[The Forty-Six were not satisfied with the empty gestures of the September Plenum on "extending democracy" in the Party. Meetings of protest were organized and public agitation against the bureaucratic régime was carried on not only in Soviet institutions but even in Party organizations.

[In an effort to catalyze this growing movement of protest, which threatened to develop into a united opposition from the Left, Zinoviev on behalf of the triumvirate published an article in the November 7th issue of *Pravda*, on the sixth anniversary of the Bolshevik Revolution, which legalized the discussion by announcing the existence of "workers' democracy" within the Party. At the same time, negotiations among the top leaders led finally to a resolution drafted in the Politburo and adopted by the Central Committee on December 5th, 1923, in which all such evils as bureaucracy, special privileges, and the like were condemned and the restoration of the rights to criticize and investigate and to have all offices filled through honest elections was solemnly promised. Trotsky, who had been ill since the beginning of November and therefore unable to participate in the general discussion, attached his signature to it along with all the other members of the Politburo and the Central Committee.

[The struggle at the top had been going on for well-nigh two years in such tight-lipped secrecy that the Party as a whole knew nothing about it and all but a handful of trusted initiates regarded Trotsky by and large as a loyal supporter of the reigning régime. He decided therefore to supplement his signature to the Central Committee Resolution of December 5th with a statement of his own position in which he frankly explained his misgivings about the dangers of bureaucracy, the possibilities of the political degeneration of the Bolshevik movement, called upon the youth to spurn passive obedience, careerism and servility, and drew the explicit inference that the new course outlined in the Central Committee Resolution of December ·5th should lead first of all to clear understanding by everyone "that henceforth no one should terrorize the Party."

[The letter aroused a storm of indignation among the top leaders. Most bitter of all was Zinoviev, who, as Bukharin revealed in the course of a factional fight four years later, insisted on Trotsky's arrest for the "treason" implicit in his "New Course" letter. Moreover, although the discussion had been sanctioned officially, the Central Control Commission worked full blast. So did the entire political machine of the General Secretary and senior triumvir. The Thirteenth Party Conference, which met January 16th to 18th, 1924, to lay the groundwork for the forthcoming Thirteenth Party Congress, to be held in May, adopted a resolution on the basis of Stalin's report which condemned the pro-democracy discussion and Trotsky's role in the following words:

> The opposition headed by Trotsky put forward the slogan of breaking up the Party *apparat* and attempted to transfer the center of gravity from the struggle against bureaucracy in the State *apparat* to the struggle against "bureaucracy" in the Party *apparat*. Such utterly baseless criticism and the downright attempt to discredit the Party *apparat* cannot, objectively speaking, lead to anything but the emancipation of the State *apparat* from Party influence. . . .

and that was of course a "petty-bourgeois deviation." Finally, the Politburo ordered the ailing Trotsky to take a cure in the Caucasus. It was a polite way— (in view of his popularity they were constrained to go easy with him)—of exiling him from the political center for the time being. The sick Trotsky hardly reached the Caucasus, when he received a telegram from Stalin that Lenin, whose health had been improving lately, had suddenly died.]

Politically, Stalin and I have long been in opposite and irreconcilable camps. But in certain circles it has become the rule to speak of my "hatred" of Stalin

STALIN

...ne *a priori* that everything I write, not only about the Moscow ...but about the U.S.S.R. as well, is inspired by that feeling. During the ...re than ten years of my present exile the Kremlin's literary agents have systematically relieved themselves of the need to answer pertinently anything I write about the U.S.S.R. by conveniently alluding to my "hatred" of Stalin. The late Freud regarded this cheap sort of psychoanalysis most disapprovingly. Hatred is, after all, a kind of personal bond. Yet Stalin and I have been separated by such fiery events as have consumed in flames and reduced to ashes everything personal, without leaving any residue whatever. In hatred there is an element of envy. Yet to me, in mind and feeling, Stalin's unprecedented elevation represents the very deepest fall. Stalin is my enemy. But Hitler, too, is my enemy, and so is Mussolini, and so are many others. Today I bear as little "hatred" toward Stalin as toward Hitler, Franco, or the Mikado. Above all, I try to understand them, so that I may be better equipped to fight them. Generally speaking, in matters of historic import, personal hatred is a petty and contemptible feeling. It is not only degrading but blinding. Yet in the light of recent events on the world arena, as well as in the U.S.S.R., even many of my opponents have now become convinced that I was not so very blind: those very predictions of mine which seemed least likely have proved to be true.

These introductory lines *pro domo sua* are all the more necessary, since I am about to broach a particularly trying theme. I have endeavored to give a general characterization of Stalin on the basis of close observation of him and a painstaking study of his biography. I do not deny that the portrait which emerges from that is somber and even sinister. But I challenge anyone else to try to substitute another, more human figure back of these facts that have shocked the imagination of mankind during the last few years—the mass "purges," the unprecedented accusations, the fantastic trials, the extermination of a whole revolutionary generation, and finally, the latest maneuvers on the international arena. Now I am about to adduce a few rather unusual facts, supplemented by certain thoughts and suspicions, from the story of how a provincial revolutionist became the dictator of a great country. These thoughts and suspicions have not come to me full-blown. They matured slowly, and whenever they occurred to me in the past, I brushed them aside as the product of an excessive mistrustfulness. But the Moscow trials—which revealed an infernal hive of intrigues, forgeries, falsifications, surreptitious poisonings and murders back of the Kremlin dictator—have cast a sinister light on the preceding years. I began to ask myself with growing insistency: What was Stalin's actual role at the time of Lenin's illness? Did not the disciple do something to expedite his master's death?

I realize more than anyone else the monstrosity of such suspicion. But that cannot be helped, when it follows from the circumstances, the facts and Stalin's very character. In 1922, the apprehensive Lenin had warned: "That cook will prepare nothing but peppery dishes." They proved to be not only peppery but poisoned, and not only figuratively but literally so. Two years ago[2] I wrote down for the first time the facts which in their day (1923-1924) were known to no more than seven or eight persons, and then only in part. Of that number, besides myself, only Stalin and Molotov are still among the living. But these two—even allowing that Molotov was among the initiated, of which I am not certain—have no motives for confessing that which I am now about to tell. I should add that every fact I mention, every reference and quotation, can be substantiated either by official Soviet publications or by documents preserved in my archives. I had occasion to give oral and written explanations before Dr. John Dewey's commission investigating the Moscow trials, and not a single one of the hundreds of documents that I presented was ever impugned.

The iconography, rich in quantity (we say nothing about its quality), produced in the last few years, invariably portrays Lenin in Stalin's company. They sit side by side, take counsel together, gaze upon each other in friendly fashion. The obtrusiveness of this motif, reiterated in paintings, in sculpture, on the screen, is dictated by the desire to make people forget the fact that the last period of Lenin's life was filled with intense conflict between him and Stalin, which culminated in a complete break between them. As always, there was nothing in any way personal about Lenin's hostility toward Stalin. Undoubtedly he valued certain of Stalin's traits very highly, his firmness of character, his persistence, even his ruthlessness and conniving, attributes indispensable in struggle and consequently at Party Headquarters. But as time went on, Stalin took increasing advantage of the opportunities his post presented for recruiting people personally devoted to him and for revenging himself upon his opponents. Having become in 1919 the head of the People's Commissariat of Inspection,[3] Stalin gradually transformed it into an instrument of favoritism and intrigues. He turned the Party's General Secretariat into an inexhaustible fountainhead of favors and dispensations. He had likewise misused for personal ends his position as member of the Orgburo and the Politburo. A personal motive could be discerned in all of his actions. Little by little Lenin became convinced that certain of Stalin's traits, multiplied by the political machine, were directly harmful to the Party. From that matured his decision to remove Stalin from the machine and thereby transform him into a rank and file member of the Central Committee. In present-day U.S.S.R. Lenin's letters of that time constitute the most tabu of all writings. Fortunately, copies and photostats of a number of them are in my archives, and some of them I have already published.

Lenin's health took a sudden turn for the worse toward the end of 1921. The first stroke came in May of the following year. For two months he was unable either to move, to speak or to write. Beginning with July, he began to convalesce slowly. In October he returned from the country to the Kremlin and took up his work again. He was literally shaken by the spread of bureaucracy, arbi-

---

[2] Probably 1937, for this portion was written by Trotsky in or about October, 1939, in the form of a magazine article.—C. M.

[3] Another name for the Commissariat of Workers' and Peasants' Inspection, for which *Rabkrin* is the Russian portmanteau word.—C. M.

trariness and intrigues in the institutions of the Party and the Government. In December he opened fire against Stalin's persecutions along the line of the nationalities policy, especially as enforced by him in Georgia, where the authority of the General Secretary was openly defied. He came out against Stalin on the question of foreign trade monopoly and was preparing for the forthcoming Party Congress an address which Lenin's secretaries, quoting his own words, called "a bombshell against Stalin." On January twenty-third, to the great trepidation of the General Secretary, he proposed the project for organizing a control commission of workers[4] that would check the power of the bureaucracy. "Let us speak frankly," wrote Lenin on the second of March, "the Commissariat of Inspection does not today enjoy the slightest authority . . . There is no worse institution among us than our People's Commissariat of Inspection . . ." and the like. At the head of the Inspection was Stalin. He well understood the implications of such language.

In the middle of December, 1922, Lenin's health again took a turn for the worse. He was obliged to absent himself from conferences, keeping in touch with the Central Committee by means of notes and telephonograms. Stalin at once tried to capitalize on this situation, hiding from Lenin much of the information which was concentrating in the Party Secretariat. Measures of blockade were instituted against persons closest to Lenin. Krupskaya did whatever she could to shield the sick man from hostile jolts by the Secretariat. But Lenin knew how to piece together a complete picture of the situation from stray and scarcely perceptible indications. "Shield him from worries!" the doctors insisted. It was easier said than done. Chained to his bed, isolated from the outside world, Lenin was aflame with alarm and indignation. His chief source of worry was Stalin. The behavior of the General Secretary became bolder as the reports of physicians about Lenin's health became less favorable. In those days Stalin was morose, his pipe firmly clenched between his teeth, a sinister gleam in his jaundiced eyes, snarling back instead of answering. His fate was at stake. He had made up his mind to overcome all obstacles. That was when the final break between him and Lenin took place.

The former Soviet diplomat Dimitrievsky, who is very friendly toward Stalin, tells about this dramatic episode as it was bandied about in the General Secretary's entourage:

> When Krupskaya, of whom he was thoroughly sick because of her constant annoyances, telephoned him in the country once more for some information, Stalin . . . upbraided her in the most outrageous language. Krupskaya, all in tears, immediately ran to complain to Lenin. Lenin's nerves, already strained to the breaking point by the intrigues, could not hold out any longer. Krupskaya hastened to send Lenin's letter to Stalin . . . "But you know Vladimir Ilyich," Krupskaya said triumphantly to Kamenev. "He would never have ventured to break off personal relations, if he had not thought it necessary to crush Stalin politically."

[4] Not to be confused with the Central Control Commission, already functioning then.—C. M.

Krupskaya did really say that, but far from "triumphantly"; on the contrary, that thoroughly sincere and sensitive woman was frightfully apprehensive and worried by what had taken place. It is not true that she "complained" about Stalin; on the contrary, as far as she was able, she played the part of a shock-absorber. But in reply to Lenin's persistent questioning, she could not tell him more than she had been told by the Secretariat, and Stalin concealed the most important matters. The letter about the break, or rather the note of several lines dictated on the 6th of March to a trusted stenographer, announced dryly the severance of "all personal and comradely relations with Stalin." That note, the last surviving Lenin document, is at the same time the final summation of his relations with Stalin. Then came the hardest stroke of all and loss of speech.

A year later, when Lenin was already embalmed in his mausoleum, the responsibility for the break, as is clearly apparent from Dimitrievsky's story, was openly placed on Krupskaya. Stalin accused her of "intrigues" against himself. The notorious Yaroslavsky, who usually carried out Stalin's dubious errands, said in July, 1926, at a session of the Central Committee: "They sank so low that they dared to come to the sick Lenin with their complaints of having been hurt by Stalin. How disgraceful—to complicate policy on such major issues with personal matters!" Now "they" was Krupskaya. She was being vengefully punished for Lenin's affronts against Stalin. Krupskaya, for her part, told me about Lenin's deep distrust of Stalin during the last period of his life. "Volodya was saying: 'He'" (Krupskaya did not call him by name, but nodded her head in the direction of Stalin's apartment) "'is devoid of the most elementary honesty, the most simple human honesty . . .'"

The so-called Lenin "Testament"—that is, his last advice on how to organize the Party leadership—was written in two installments during his second illness; on December twenty-fifth, 1922, and on January fourth, 1923. "Stalin, having become General Secretary," declares the Testament, "has concentrated enormous power in his hands, and I am not sure that he always knows how to use that power with sufficient caution." Ten days later this restrained formula seemed insufficient to Lenin, and he added a postscript: "I propose to the comrades to find a way to remove Stalin from that position and appoint to it another man," who would be, "more loyal, more courteous and more considerate to comrades, less capricious, etc." Lenin tried to express his estimate of Stalin in as inoffensive language as possible. Yet he did broach the subject of removing Stalin from the one post that could give him power.

After all that had taken place during the preceding months, the Testament could not have been a surprise to Stalin. Nevertheless he took it as a cruel blow. When he first read the text—which Krupskaya had transmitted to him for the forthcoming Party Congress—in the presence of his secretary, Mekhlia, later the political chief of the Red Army, and of the prominent Soviet politician Syrtsov, who has since disappeared from the scene, he broke out into billingsgate against Lenin that gave vent to his true feelings about his "master" in those days. Bazhanov, another former secretary of Stalin's, has described the session of the Central Committee at which Kamenev first made the Testament known. "Terrible embarrassment paralyzed all those present. Stalin, sitting on the steps of the praesidium's rostrum, felt small and miserable. I studied him closely: notwithstanding his self-possession and show of calm, it was clearly evident that his fate was at stake . . . " Radek, who sat beside me at that memorable session, leaned over with the words: "Now they won't dare to go against you." He had in mind two places in the letter: one, which characterized me as "the most gifted man in the present Central Committee," and the other, which demanded Stalin's removal in view of his rudeness, disloyalty and tendency to misuse power. I told Radek: "On the contrary, now they will have to see it through to the bitter end, and moreover as quickly as possible." Actually, the Testament not only failed to terminate the internal struggle, which was what Lenin wanted, but, on the contrary, intensified it to a feverish pitch. Stalin could no longer doubt that Lenin's return to activity would mean the political death of the General Secretary. And conversely: only Lenin's death could clear the way for Stalin.

During Lenin's second illness, toward the end of February, 1923, at a meeting of the Politburo members Zinoviev, Kamenev and the author of these lines, Stalin informed us, after the departure of the secretary, that Lenin had suddenly called him in and had asked him for poison. Lenin was again losing the faculty of speech, considered his situation hopeless, foresaw the approach of a new stroke, did not trust his physicians, whom he had no difficulty catching in contradictions. His mind was perfectly clear and he suffered unendurably. I was able to follow the course of Lenin's illness day by day through the physician we had in common, Doctor Guétier, who was also a family friend of ours.

"Is it possible, Fedor Alexandrovich, that this is the end?" my wife and I would ask him time and again.

"That cannot be said at all. Vladimir Ilyich can get on his feet again. He has a powerful constitution."

"And his mental faculties?"

"Basically, they will remain untouched. Not every note, perhaps, will keep its former purity, but the virtuoso will remain a virtuoso."

We continued to hope. Yet here I was unexpectedly confronted with the disclosure that Lenin, who seemed the very incarnation of the will to live, was seeking poison for himself. What must have been his inward state!

I recall how extraordinary, enigmatic and out of tune with the circumstances Stalin's face seemed to me. The request he was transmitting to us was tragic; yet a sickly smile was transfixed on his face, as on a mask. We were not unfamiliar with discrepancy between his facial expression and his speech. But this time it was utterly insufferable. The horror of it was enhanced by Stalin's failure to express any opinion about Lenin's request, as if he were waiting to see what others would say: did he want to catch the overtones of our reaction to it, without committing himself? or did he have some hidden thoughts of his own? . . . I see before me the pale and silent Kamenev, who sincerely loved Lenin, and Zinoviev, bewildered, as always at difficult moments. Had they known about Lenin's request even before the session? Or had Stalin sprung this as a surprise on his allies in the triumvirate as well as on me?

"Naturally, we cannot even consider carrying out this request!" I exclaimed. "Guétier has not lost hope. Lenin can still recover."

"I told him all that," Stalin replied, not without a touch of annoyance. "But he wouldn't listen to reason. The Old Man is suffering. He says he wants to have the poison at hand . . . he'll use it only when he is convinced that his condition is hopeless."

"Anyway, it's out of the question," I insisted—this time, I think, with Zinoviev's support. "He might succumb to a passing mood and take the irrevocable step."

"The Old Man is suffering," Stalin repeated, staring vaguely past us and, as before, saying nothing one way or the other. A line of thought parallel to the conversation but not quite in consonance with it must have been running through his mind.

It is possible, of course, that subsequent events have influenced certain details of my recollection, though, as a general rule, I have learned to trust my memory. However, this episode is one of those that leave an indelible imprint on one's consciousness for all time. Moreover, upon my return home, I told it in detail to my wife. And ever since, each time I mentally review this scene, I cannot help repeating to myself: Stalin's behaviour, his whole manner, was baffling and sinister. What does the man want? And why doesn't he take that insidious smile off his mask? . . . No vote was taken, since this was not a formal conference, but we parted with the implicit understanding that we could not even consider sending poison to Lenin.

Here naturally arises the question: how and why did Lenin, who at the time was extremely suspicious of Stalin, turn to him with such a request, which on the face of it, presupposed the highest degree of personal confidence? A mere month before he made this request of Stalin, Lenin had written his pitiless postscript to the Testament. Several days after making this request, he broke off all personal relations with him. Stalin himself could not have failed to ask himself the question: why did Lenin turn to him of all people? The answer is simple: Lenin saw in Stalin the only man who would grant his tragic request, since he was directly interested in doing so. With his faultless instinct, the sick man guessed what was going on in the Kremlin and outside its walls and how Stalin really felt about him. Lenin did not even have to review the list of his closest comrades in order to say to himself that no one except Stalin would do him this "favor." At the same time, it is possible that he wanted to test Stalin: just how eager would the chef of the peppery dishes be to take advantage of this opportunity? In those days Lenin thought not only of death but of the fate of the Party. Lenin's revolutionary nerve was undoubtedly the last of his nerves to surrender to death.

When still a very young man in prison, Koba would surreptitiously incite hotheaded Caucasians against his opponents, which usually ended in a beating and on one occasion even in a murder. As the years passed by, he perfected his technique. The monopolistic political machine of the Party, combined with the totalitarian machine of the State, opened to him possibilities which even such of his predecessors as Caesar Borgia could not have imagined. The office in which the investigators of the OGPU carry on their super-inquisitorial questionings is connected by a microphone with Stalin's office. The unseen Joseph Djugashvili, a pipe in his teeth, listens greedily to the dialogue outlined by himself, rubs his hands and laughs soundlessly. More than ten years before the notorious Moscow trials he had confessed to Kamenev and Dzerzhinsky over a bottle of wine one summer night on the balcony of a summer resort that his highest delight in life was to keep a keen eye on an enemy, prepare everything painstakingly, mercilessly revenge himself, and then go to sleep. Later he avenged himself on a whole generation of Bolsheviks! There is no reason here to return to the Moscow judicial frame-ups. The judgment they were accorded in their day was both authoritative and exhaustive.[5] But in order to understand the real Stalin and the manner of his behaviour during the days of Lenin's illness and death, it is necessary to shed light on certain episodes of the last big trial staged in March, 1938.

A special place in the prisoner's dock was occupied by Henry Yagoda, who had worked in the Cheka and the OGPU for sixteen years, at first as an assistant chief, later as the head, and all the time in close contact with the General Secretary as his most trusted aid in the fight against the Opposition. The system of confessions to crimes that had never been committed is Yagoda's handiwork, if not his brainchild. In 1933 Stalin rewarded Yagoda with the Order of Lenin, in 1935 elevated him to the rank of General Commissar of State Defense, that is, Marshal of the Political Police, only two days after the talented Tukhachevsky was elevated to the rank of Marshal of the Red Army. In Yagoda's person a nonentity was elevated, known as such to all and held in contempt by all. The old revolutionists must have exchanged looks of indignation. Even in the submissive Politburo an attempt was made to oppose this. But some secret bound Stalin to Yagoda—apparently, forever. Yet the mysterious bond was mysteriously broken. During the great "purge" Stalin decided to liquidate at the same time his fellow-culprit who knew too much. In April, 1937, Yagoda was arrested. As always, Stalin thus achieved several supplementary advantages:

[5] The Case of Leon Trotsky: Report of Hearings on The Charges Made Against Him In The Moscow Trials: By The Preliminary Commission of Inquiry, John Dewey, Chairman, and others: Harper & Brothers: New York & London: 1937: 617 pp.

Not Guilty: Report of the Commission of Inquiry Into The Charges Made Against Leon Trotsky In The Moscow Trials: By John Dewey, Chairman, and others: Harper & Brothers: New York & London: 1938: 422 pp.

for the promise of a pardon, Yagoda assumed at the trial personal guilt for crimes rumor had ascribed to Stalin. Of course, the promise was not kept: Yagoda was executed, in order the better to prove Stalin's irreconcilability in matters of law and morals.

But exceedingly illuminating circumstances were made public at that trial. According to the testimony of his secretary and confidant, Bulanov, Yagoda had a special poison chest, from which, as the need arose, he would obtain precious vials and entrust them to his agents with appropriate instructions. The chief of the OGPU, a former pharmacist, displayed exceptional interest in poisons. He had at his disposal several toxicologists for whom he organized a special laboratory, providing it with means without stint and without control. It is, of course, out of the question that Yagoda might have established such an enterprise for his own personal needs. Far from it. In this case, as in others, he was discharging his official functions. As a poisoner, he was merely *instrumentum regni*, even as old Locusta at Nero's court—with this difference, that he had far outstripped his ignorant predecessor in matters of technique!

At Yagoda's side in the prisoners' dock sat four Kremlin physicians, charged with the murder of Maxim Gorky and of two Soviet cabinet ministers. "I confess that . . . I prescribed medicines unsuited to the given illness . . ." Thus, "I was responsible for the untimely death of Maxim Gorky and Kuibyshev." During the days of the trial, the basic background of which consisted of falsehood, the accusations, like the confessions of poisoning the aged and ailing writer, seemed fantasmagoric to me. Subsequent information and a more attentive analysis of the circumstances forced me to alter that judgment. Not everything in the trials was a lie. There were the poisoned and the poisoners. Not all the poisoners were sitting in the prisoners' dock. The principal poisoner was conducting the trial by telephone.

Gorky was neither a conspirator nor a politician. He was a softhearted old man, a defender of the injured, a sentimental protester. Such had been his role during the early days of the October Revolution. During the first and second five-year plans famine, discontent and repressions reached the utmost limit. The courtiers protested. Even Stalin's wife, Alliluyeva, protested. In that atmosphere Gorky constituted a serious menace. He corresponded with European writers, he was visited by foreigners, the injured complained to him, he moulded public opinion. But, most important, it would have been impossible for him to acquiesce in the extermination, then being prepared, of the Old Bolsheviks, whom he had known intimately for many years. Gorky's public protest against the frame-ups would have immediately broken the hypnotic spell of Stalin's justice before the eyes of the whole world.

In no way was it possible to make him keep still. To arrest him, to exile him, not to say to shoot him, was even less possible. The thought of hastening the liquidation of the sick Gorky through Yagoda "without bloodshed" must have seemed to the boss of the Kremlin as the only way out under the circumstances. Stalin's mind is so constituted that such decisions occur to him with the impact of reflexes. Having accepted the assignment, Yagoda turned to his "own" physicians. He did not risk anything. Refusal, according to Dr. Levin's own words, "would spell ruin for me and my family." Moreover, "you will not escape Yagoda anyhow. Yagoda is a man who does not stop at anything. He would get you even if you were underground."

But why did not the authoritative and respected Kremlin physicians complain to members of the government, whom they knew well as their own patients? On Dr. Levin's list of patients alone were twenty-four high-ranking officials, including members of the Politburo and of the Council of People's Commissars. The answer is, that Dr. Levin, like everyone else in and around the Kremlin, knew perfectly well whose agent Yagoda was. Dr. Levin submitted to Yagoda because he was powerless to oppose Stalin.

As for Gorky's discontent, his efforts to go abroad, Stalin's refusal to grant him a foreign passport—that was common knowledge in Moscow and was discussed in whispers. Suspicions that Stalin had somewhat aided the destructive force of nature sprang up directly after the great writer's death. A concomitant task of Yagoda's trial was to clear Stalin of that suspicion. Hence, the repeated declarations by Yagoda, the physicians and the other accused that Gorky was "a close friend of Stalin's," "a trusted person," "a Stalinist," fully approved of the "Leader's" policy, spoke "with exceptional enthusiasm" of Stalin's role. If only half of this were true, Yagoda would not have taken it upon himself to kill Gorky, and still less would he have dared to entrust such a plot to a Kremlin physician, who could have destroyed him by simply telephoning Stalin.

Here is a single "detail" taken from a single trial. There were many trials, and no end of "details." All of them bear Stalin's ineradicable imprint. The work is basically his. Pacing up and down his office, he painstakingly considers sundry schemes wherewith he might reduce anyone who displeases him to the utmost degree of humiliation, to lying denunciations of his dearest intimates, to the most horrible betrayal of his own self. For him who fights back, in spite of everything, there is always a little vial. It is only Yagoda who has disappeared; his poison chest remains.

At the 1938 trial Stalin charged Bukharin, as if incidentally, with having prepared in 1918 an attempt on Lenin's life. The naive and ardent Bukharin venerated Lenin, loved him with the love of a child for its mother and, when he pertly opposed him in polemics, it was not otherwise than on his knees. Bukharin, "soft as wax," to use Lenin's expression, did not have and could not have had personal ambitious designs. If in the old days anyone had predicted that the time would come when Bukharin would be accused of an attempt on Lenin's life, each of us, and above all Lenin, would have laughed and advised putting such a prophet in an insane asylum. Why then did Stalin resort to such a patently absurd accusation? Most likely this was his answer to Bukharin's suspicions, carelessly expressed, with reference to Stalin himself. Generally, all the accusations are cut to this pattern. The basic elements of Stalin's frame-ups are not the products of pure fantasy; they are derived from reality—for the most part, from either the deeds or designs of the chef of the peppery dishes himself. The same defensive-offensive "Stalin reflex," which was so clearly revealed in the instance of Gorky's death, disclosed its full force in the matter of Lenin's death as well. In the first case, Yagoda paid with his life; in the second—Bukharin.

I imagine the course of affairs somewhat like this. Lenin asked for poison at the end of February, 1923. In the beginning of March he was again paralyzed. The medical prognosis at the time was cautiously unfavorable. Feeling more sure of himself, Stalin began to act as if Lenin were already dead. But the sick man fooled him. His powerful organism, supported by his inflexible will, re-asserted itself. Toward winter Lenin began to improve slowly, to move around more freely; listened to reading and read himself; his faculty of speech began to come back to him. The findings of the physicians became increasingly more hopeful. Lenin's recovery could not, of course, have prevented the supersedure of the Revolution by the bureaucratic reaction. Krupskaya had sound reasons for observing in 1926, "if Volodya were alive, he would now be in prison."

For Stalin himself it was not a question of the general course of development, but rather of his own fate: either he could manage at once, this very day, to become the boss of the political machine and hence of the Party and of the country, or he would be relegated to a third-rate role for the rest of his life. Stalin was after power, all of it, come what may. He already had a firm grip on it. His goal was near, but the danger emanating from Lenin was even nearer. At this time Stalin must have made up his mind that it was imperative to act without delay. Everywhere he had accomplices whose fate was completely bound to his. At his side was the pharmacist Yagoda. Whether Stalin sent the poison to Lenin with the hint that the physicians had left no hope for his recovery or whether he resorted to more direct means I do not know. But I am firmly convinced that Stalin could not have waited passively when his fate hung by a thread and the decision depended on a small, very small motion of his hand.

Some time after the middle of January, 1924, I left for Sukhum, in the Caucasus, to try to get rid of a dogged, mysterious infection, the nature of which still remains a mystery to my physicians. The news of Lenin's death reached me en route. According to a widely disseminated version, I lost power because I was not present at Lenin's funeral. This explanation can hardly be taken seriously. But the fact of my absence at the mourning ceremonies caused many of my friends serious misgivings. In the letter from my oldest son, who was then nearing eighteen, there was a note of youthful despair: I should have come at any price! Such were my own intentions, too. The coded telegram about Lenin's death found my wife and me at the railway station in Tiflis. I immediately sent a coded note by direct wire to the Kremlin: "I deem it neces-sary to return to Moscow. When is the funeral?" The reply came from Moscow in about an hour: "The funeral will take place on Saturday. You will not be able to return on time. The Politburo thinks that because of the state of your health you must proceed to Sukhum. Stalin." I did not feel that I should request postponement of the funeral for my sake alone. Only in Sukhum, lying under blankets on the verandah of a sanatorium, did I learn that the funeral had been changed to Sunday. The circumstances connected with the previous setting and ultimate changing of the date of the funeral are so involved that they cannot be clarified in a few lines. Stalin maneuvered, deceiving not only me but, so it appears, also his allies of the triumvirate. In distinction from Zinoviev, who approached every question from the standpoint of its immediate effectiveness as agitation, Stalin was guided in his risky maneuvers by more tangible considerations. He might have feared that I would connect Lenin's death with last year's conversation about poison, would ask the doctors whether poisoning was involved, and demand a special autopsy. It was, therefore, safer in all respects to keep me away until after the body had been embalmed, the viscera cremated and a post mortem examination inspired by such suspicions no longer feasible.

When I asked the physicians in Moscow about the immediate cause of Lenin's death, which they had not expected, they were at a loss to account for it. I did not bother Krupskaya, who had written a very warm letter to me at Sukhum, with questions on that theme. I did not renew personal relations with Zinoviev and Kamenev until two years later, after they had broken with Stalin. They obviously avoided all discussion concerning the circumstances of Lenin's death, answering in monosyllables and avoiding my eyes. Did they know anything or were they merely suspicious? Anyway, they had been so closely involved with Stalin during the preceding three years that they could not help being apprehensive lest the shadow of suspicion should fall on them as well.

Over Lenin's bier Stalin read from a scrap of paper his oath of fealty to his master's legacy, couched in the style of the homilectics he had studied at the Tiflis theological seminary. In those days that oath was scarcely noticed. Today it is in all the textbooks, having superseded the Ten Commandments:[6]

> In leaving us, Comrade Lenin commanded us to hold high and pure the great calling of Party Member. We swear to Thee, Comrade Lenin, to honor Thy command.
> In leaving us, Comrade Lenin commanded us to keep the unity of our Party as the apple of our eye. We swear to Thee, Comrade Lenin, to honor Thy command.
> In leaving us, Comrade Lenin ordered us to maintain and strengthen the dictatorship of the proletariat. We swear to Thee, Comrade Lenin, to exert our full strength in honoring Thy command.
> In leaving us, Comrade Lenin ordered us to strengthen with all our might the union of workers and peasants. We swear to Thee, Comrade Lenin, to honor Thy command.
> In leaving us, Comrade Lenin ordered us to strengthen and expand the

[6] The text of Stalin's oath was inserted by the editor.—C. M.

Union of the Republics. We swear to Thee, Comrade Lenin, to honor Thy command.

In leaving us, Comrade Lenin enjoined us to be faithful to the Communist International. We swear to Thee, Comrade Lenin, that we shall dedicate our lives to the enlargement and reinforcement of the union of the workers of the whole world, the Communist International.

The names of Nero and Caesar Borgia have been mentioned more than once with reference to the Moscow trials and the latest developments on the international scene. Since these old ghosts are being invoked, it is fitting, it seems to me, to speak of a super-Nero and a super-Borgia, so modest, almost naive, seem the crimes of that era in comparison with the exploits of our times. It is possible however to discern a more profound historical significance in purely personal analogies. The customs of the declining Roman Empire were formed during the transition from slavery to feudalism, from paganism to Christianity. The epoch of the Renaissance marked the transition from feudal to bourgeois society, from Catholicism to Protestantism and Liberalism. In both instances the old morality had managed to spend itself before the new one was formed.

Now again we are living during the transition from one system to another, in an epoch of the greatest social crisis, which, as always, is accompanied by the crisis in morals. The old has been shaken to its foundations. The new has scarcely begun to emerge. When the roof has collapsed, the doors and windows have fallen off their hinges, the house is bleak and hard to live in. Today gusty draughts are blowing across our entire planet. *All* the traditional principles of morality are increasingly worse off, not only those emanating from Stalin.

But a historical explanation is not a justification. Nero, too, was a product of his epoch. Yet after he perished his statues were smashed and his name was scraped off everything. The vengeance of history is more terrible than the vengeance of the most powerful General Secretary. I venture to think that this is consoling.

Supplement I

THE THERMIDORIAN REACTION

A POLITICAL reaction set in after the prodigious strain of the Revolution and the Civil War. [It differed fundamentally from a parallel social manifestation in the non-Soviet countries.] The reaction was against the [imperialist] war and against those who had led [that utterly useless and wanton carnage which was definitely] unpopular [even in the "victorious" countries]. In England it was primarily directed against Lloyd George and isolated him politically to the end of his life. Clemenceau in France [and Wilson in the United States] suffered in a similar manner.

The tremendous difference in the feeling of the masses after an imperialist war and a civil war was natural. In Russia the workers and peasants were filled through and through with the awareness that their own interests were actually at stake and that the war was in a very direct sense their own. Satisfaction with the victory was very great, and correspondingly great was the popularity of those who had helped to achieve it. [At the same time, there was need to have done with it, to go back at last to civilian pursuits, to re-establish the normal and peaceful processes for the satisfaction of human needs. Heroism itself had become commonplace and people had become fed up with the horrors incidental to it.

[Although it was not directed against the leaders of the Civil War, this over-powering urge for peace turned many eyes in the direction of those who were in charge of such humdrum matters as food rationing, living quarters and employment in good jobs at the best possible wages. Stalin and others like him, whose role in the Civil War had been secondary, came now to the fore and headed the tacit but nonetheless powerful transition movement from war to peace, from self-sacrifice to self-betterment. This mood did not have so strong an effect on the youth and the masses in general—those in the most exposed positions during the Civil War—as it did on the middle-aged with growing family responsibilities and on the job-holders who had acquired a stake in civilian activities. But that does not mean that it was not both strong and widespread.]

The three years of Civil War laid an indelible impress on the Soviet Government itself by virtue of the fact that very many of the administrators, a considerable layer of them, had become accustomed to command and demand unconditional submission to their orders. Those theoreticians who attempt to prove that the present totalitarian régime of the U.S.S.R. is due not to such historical conditions, but to the very nature of Bolshevism itself, forget that the Civil War did not proceed from the nature of Bolshevism but rather from the efforts of the Russian and the international bourgeoisie to overthrow the Soviet régime. There is no doubt that Stalin, like many others, was molded by the environment and circumstances of the Civil War, along with the entire group that later helped him to establish his personal dictatorship—Ordzhoni-kidze, Voroshilov, Kaganovich—and a whole layer of workers and peasants [raised to the status of commanders and administrators.

[Moreover, within five years after the October Revolution more than 97 per cent of the Party consisted of members who had joined it after the victory of the Revolution. Another five years, and] the overwhelming majority of the Party's one million members had only a dim conception of what the Party had been in the first period of the Revolution, not to mention the pre-Revolution under-ground. Suffice it to say that by then fully three-fourths of the Party consisted of members who had joined only after 1923. The number of Party members with a pre-Revolution record—that is, revolutionists of the underground—became less than one per cent. By 1923 the Party had been pretty well diluted by the green and callow mass which was [rapidly being molded and shaped] to play the role of [snappy yes-men] at a prod from the professionals of the machine. This thinning out of the revolutionary nucleus of the Party was a necessary prerequisite to the machine's victories over "Trotskyism" [i.e., over the Bolshevism of Lenin's days.]

In 1923 the situation began to stabilize. The Civil War, like the War with Poland, was definitely in the past. The most horrible consequences of the famine had been overcome, the NEP had given impetus to a vitalizing revival of national economy. The constant shifting of Communists from post to post, from one sphere of activity to another soon became the exception rather than the rule. Communists began to acquire permanent positions, [berths that were their own and led to higher positions, and they] began to rule in a planned fashion the regions or districts of economic and political life entrusted to their adminis-trative discretion. [They were rapidly turning into officials, into bureaucrats, as] the placement of Party members and officials acquired a more systematic and planned character. No longer were assignments to duty regarded as temporary and almost fortuitous. The question of appointments came to have more and more to do with the question of personal life, living conditions of the [ap-pointee's] family, his career.

It was then that Stalin began to emerge with increasing prominence as the organizer, the assigner of tasks, the dispenser of jobs, the trainer and master of the bureaucracy. He chose his men by their hostility or indifference toward his various opponents and particularly toward him whom he regarded as his chief opponent, the chief obstacle in the path of his progress upward. Stalin generalized and classified his own administrative experience, chiefly the experi-ence of systematic conniving behind the scenes, and made it available to those most closely associated with him. He taught them to organize their local political machines on the pattern of his own machine: how to recruit collaborators, how to utilize their weaknesses, how to set comrades at odds with each other, how to run the machine.

As the life of the bureaucracy grew in stability, it generated an increasing need of comfort. Stalin rode in on the crest of this spontaneous movement for creature comfort, guiding it, harnessing it to his own designs. He rewarded the most loyal with the most attractive and advantageous positions. He set the limits on the benefits to be derived from these positions. He hand-picked the membership of the Control Commission, instilling in many of them the need of ruthlessly persecuting the deviators. At the same time he instructed them to look through their fingers at the exceptionally extravagant mode of life led by the officials loyal to the General Secretary. For Stalin measured every situation, every political circumstance, every combination of people [by one criterion —usefulness] to himself, to his struggle for power, to his relentless itch for domination over others.

Everything else was intellectually beyond his depth. He was pushing two of his strongest competitors into a fight. He raised his talent for utilizing personal and group antagonisms to a fine art, an inimitable art in the sense that he had developed an almost faultless instinct for it. In each new situation his first and foremost consideration was how he personally could benefit. Whenever the interests of the whole came into conflict with his personal interests, he always without exception sacrificed the interests of the whole. On all occasions, under any pretext and whatever the result, he did everything possible to make difficulties for his stronger competitors. With the same persistence he tried to reward every act of personal loyalty. Secretly at first and then more openly, equality was proclaimed a petty-bourgeois prejudice. He came out in defense of inequality, in defense of special privileges for the higher-ups of the bureaucracy.

In this deliberate demoralization Stalin was never interested in distant perspectives. Nor did he think through to the social significance of this process in which he was playing the leading role. He acted then, as now, like the empiricist he is. He selects those loyal to him and rewards them; he helps them to secure privileged positions; he requires of them the repudiation of personal political purposes. He teaches them how to create for themselves the necessary machinery for influencing the masses and for holding the masses in submission. Never does he consider that his policy runs directly counter to the struggle that engaged Lenin's interest more and more during the last year of his life— the struggle against bureaucracy. He himself speaks occasionally of bureaucracy, but always in the most abstract and lifeless terms. He has in mind lack of attention, red tape, the untidiness of offices and the like, but he is deaf and blind to the formation of a whole privileged caste welded together by the bond of honor among thieves, by their common interest [as privileged exploiters of the whole body politic] and by their ever-growing remoteness from the people. Without suspecting it, Stalin is organizing not only a new political machine but a new caste.

He approaches matters only from the point of view of selecting cadres, improving the machine, securing his personal control over it, his personal power. No doubt it seems to him, in so far as he is at all concerned with general questions, that his machine will invest the government with greater strength and stability, and thus assure the further development of socialism in a separate country. Beyond that he does not venture to generalize. That the crystallization of a new ruling stratum of professional officials, placed in a privileged situation and camouflaged from the masses by the idea of socialism—that the formation of this new arch-privileged and arch-powerful ruling stratum changes the social structure of the state and to a considerable and ever-growing extent the social composition of the new society—is a consideration that he refuses to contemplate; and whenever it is suggested, he waves it away with his arms or with his revolver. Thus, Stalin, the empiricist, without formally breaking with the revolutionary tradition, without repudiating Bolshevism, became [the most effective betrayer and destroyer of both.]

At the time of the Party discussion in the autumn of 1923, the Moscow organization was divided approximately in half, with a certain preponderance in favor of the Opposition in the beginning. However, the two halves were not of equal strength in their social [potential.] On the side of the Opposition was the youth and a considerable portion of the rank and file; but on the side of Stalin and the Central Committee were first of all the specially-trained and disciplined politicians who were most closely connected with the political machine of the General Secretary. My illness and my consequent non-participation in the struggle was, I grant, a factor of some consequence; however, its importance should not be exaggerated. In the final reckoning, it was a mere episode. [All-important was the fact that] the workers were tired. Those who supported the Opposition were not spurred on by a hope for great and serious changes. On the other hand, the bureaucracy fought with extraordinary ferocity: [it was fighting instinctively for its future prosperity.] True, there was at least one moment of complete confusion in that camp, but we did not know it then. This was subsequently disclosed to us by Zinoviev. Once, upon arriving in Moscow from Petrograd, he found the Central Committee and the Moscow leaders in utter panic. Stalin was evidently thinking up a maneuver with the aim of making peace with the Opposition at the expense of his allies, Zinoviev and Kamenev. This was exactly like him. At the time, the sessions of the Politburo were held in my home because of my illness. He made obvious overtures to me, displaying an utterly unexpected interest in my health. Zinoviev, according to his story, put a stop to this equivocal situation in Moscow by turning to Petrograd for support. He launched the organization of an illegal staff of agitators and shock troops who were sent by automobile from one establishment to another to spread distortions and calumnies. Without breaking with his allies, of course, Stalin carefully protected for himself the road of retreat to the Opposition. Zinoviev was bolder because he was more adventurous and irresponsible. Stalin was cautious. He did not yet appreciate the full extent of the changes that had taken place among the higher-ups of the Party and especially in the Soviet machine, [changes he himself had fostered]. He did not rely on his own individual strength. He was groping, feeling out each resistance, taking each support into account. He let Zinoviev and Kamenev commit themselves, while he himself remained noncommittal.

It was during this very same autumn discussion that the technique of the machine in its struggle with the Opposition was definitely worked out and tested in operation. Under no circumstances was it possible to permit the breaking up of the machine under pressure from below. The machine had to stay put. The Party itself could always be reshuffled, recast or regrouped. Some members might be expelled or compromised and others scared off. Finally, it was possible to juggle facts and figures. The machine men were sent from one factory to another in automobiles. The control commissions, which had been established for the purpose of fighting this very usurpation of power by the machine, became mere cogs in its wheels. At Party meetings specially trusted officials of the control commissions wrote down the name of every speaker suspected of Oppositionist leanings, and were afterwards busy with research into his past. Always, or almost always, it was not too hard to find something more or less tangible— some mistake in the past or simply bad social origin—to justify a charge of, or provoke, a violation of Party discipline. It was then possible to expel, to transfer, to intimidate into silence, or to strike a bargain with the Oppositionist opponent.

This part of the work Stalin took under his direct management. Inside of the Central Control Commission itself he had his own special agency, headed by [Soltz,] Yaroslavsky and Shkiryatov. Their task was to make up black-lists of the non-conformists and later conduct investigations of their genealogy in tsarist police archives. Stalin has a special archive full of all sorts of documents, accusations, libelous rumors against all the prominent Soviet leaders without exception. In 1929, at the time of the open break with the Right members of the Politburo, Bukharin, Rykov and Tomsky, Stalin managed to keep Kalinin and Voroshilov loyal to himself only by the threat of exposing them.

In 1925 in one of the Soviet humorous magazines appeared a caricature which portrayed the head of the government in a very compromising situation. The resemblance was striking. Moreover, in the text, written in highly suggestive style, Kalinin was referred to by his initials, "M. K." I could not believe my eyes. "What does this mean?" I asked several persons close to me, among them Serebryakov, who had known Stalin intimately in prison and exile.

"This is Stalin's last warning to Kalinin," he explained.

"But why?"

"Certainly not because he is concerned about his morals," Serebryakov laughed. "Evidently Kalinin is being stubborn about something."

Kalinin, who knew the recent past only too well, refused at first to acknowledge Stalin as a leader. For a long time he was afraid to tie his own fate to Stalin's. "That horse," he was wont to say to his intimates, "will some day drag our wagon into a ditch." But gradually, groaning and resisting, he turned first against me, then against Zinoviev and finally, with even greater reluctance, against Rykov, Bukharin and Tomsky, with whom he was more closely connected because of his moderate views. Yenukidze passed through the same evolution, following in the footsteps of Kalinin, only more in the shadows and undoubtedly with much keener inward suffering. Because of the very nature of the man, whose principal trait was adaptability, Yenukidze could not help finding himself in the camp of the thermidor. But he was no careerist and certainly not a scoundrel. It was hard for him to break away from old traditions and still harder to turn against those people whom he had been accustomed to respect. At critical moments, Yenukidze not only did not exhibit aggressive enthusiasm but, on the contrary, complained, grumbled and resisted. Stalin knew about it very well and gave Yenukidze more than one warning. I knew about it practically at first hand. Although even in those days the system of denunciation had already poisoned not only political life, but even personal relations, there still remained here and there an oasis of mutual trust. Yenukidze was very friendly with Serebryakov, notwithstanding the latter's prominence as a leader of the Left Opposition, and not infrequently poured out his heart to him. "What more does he [Stalin] want?" Yenukidze complained. "I am doing everything he has asked me to do, but it is not enough for him. He wants me to admit that he is a genius."

Stalin took Zinoviev and Kamenev under his wing when I criticized their behavior in 1917. "It is quite possible that some of the Bolsheviks," he wrote, "actually did shiver in connection with the July defeats. I know, for example, that some of the Bolsheviks then arrested·were even ready to desert our ranks. But to draw this conclusion against certain . . . members of the Central Committee from that, is to distort history unmercifully."

The interesting part of this quotation is not so much the resolute defense of Zinoviev and Kamenev as the gratuitously dragged-in reference to "some of the Bolsheviks then arrested." That was aimed at Lunacharsky. Among the documents seized after the Revolution was found Lunacharsky's testimony at the police investigation. It did not exactly cast honor on his political courage. That by itself would have mattered little to Stalin; less courageous Bolsheviks were in his immediate entourage. What really bothered him was that in 1923 Lunacharsky had published his "Silhouettes of the Leaders of the Revolution," in which he failed to include a silhouette of Stalin. The omission was not deliberate. Lunacharsky was not opposed to Stalin. It simply did not occur to him any more than to anyone else at the time to count Stalin among the leaders of the Revolution. But by 1925 the situation had changed. That was Stalin's way of dropping a hint to Lunacharsky to change his policy accordingly or fall victim to an exposé. It was precisely for this reason that Lunacharsky was not mentioned by name. He was given a certain amount of time to straighten out his "front." Lunacharsky in any event understood to whom reference was made and radically changed his position. His sins of July [1917] were immediately forgotten.

Not all the young revolutionists of the Tsarist era [were story-book heroes.] There were also among them some who did not bear themselves with sufficient courage during investigation [by the secret police.] If they made up for that by their subsequent behavior, the Party did not expel them irrevocably and took them back into its ranks. In 1923 Stalin, as General Secretary, began to concentrate all such evidence in his own hands and to use it to blackmail hundreds of old revolutionists who had more than redeemed this early weakness. By threatening to expose their past record, he browbeat these people into slavish obedience and reduced them step by step to a state of complete demoralization. [And he tied them to himself forever by forcing them to do the dirtiest sort of work in his machinations against the Opposition. Those who refused to be blackmailed were either crushed politically by the machine or destroyed themselves by suicide. So perished one of] my closest collaborators, my personal secretary Glazman, a man of exceptional modesty and [of exemplary] devotion to the Party, [high strung and sensitive, a revolutionist of impeccable honor. He was] a suicide as early as 1924. His desperate act produced such an adverse impression that the Central Control Commission was compelled to exonerate him after his death and to bring out a (very cautious and soft) rebuke to its own executive organ.

[Two years later a direct attempt at bloodshed was made.[1] Although Trotsky and Muralov were already in disgrace, their situation had not yet crystallized. It was the year 1926. In July, Zinoviev, who had in the meantime broken with Stalin and formed an Oppositionist bloc with Trotsky and Kamenev, was expelled from the Politburo. The expulsion of the two other leaders of the Opposition from the same body was to occur three months later, at the very next Plenum of the Central Committee and the Central Control Commission. Meantime Trotsky with Mrs. Trotsky,] accompanied by Muralov and other comrades of Civil War days personally devoted to him, set out for a furlough in the Caucasus. Yenukidze placed [at their disposal] the same villa in Kislovodsk that they had had before. Trotsky was accorded the same deference as ever. The local authorities showed sincere respect and at times even enthusiasm, which they could not hide. At accidental as well as at non-accidental meetings they greeted Lev Davidovich [Trotsky] with genuine warmth. Every sanatorium in Kislovodsk, one after another invited Lev Davidovich to speak. Each met him and saw him off demonstratively. Nevertheless, the pressure from the Center could already be felt. Officially the provinces had not yet received orders about a change of "front." *Stalin did not yet dare to give such orders openly.* But surreptitiously he had made his desires clear to his satraps. Consequently now

---

[1] This account is based on a note by Leon Trotsky. The text proper is by Natalia Ivanovna Sedoff, Trotsky's widow, written at the editor's request. It consists of the unbracketed material on this page and continues to the point indicated on page 391.—C. M.

and then we would run into manifestations of demonstrative coolness by one or another group that had recently come from Moscow. We were told that certain sanatoria debated the question of inviting L. D. But those opposed to extending the invitation were as yet so inconsiderable in number and influence that he was invited by unanimous decision upon the insistence of an enthusiastic majority. Such frank expression of approval of L. D. was no longer possible in Moscow.

Muralov was well informed about everything that took place. He was very sensitive and understanding about such matters. We were apprehensive and constantly on guard. As usual the hunting trips were organized by the local G.P.U., because it knew local conditions best. We continued to be under its guard and protection as formerly. But under the altered circumstances, this G.P.U. guard acquired a double meaning, and one not devoid of danger. We placed our trust not so much in the G.P.U. as in L. D.'s personal guard, who had come with us from Moscow and were tied to L. D. by the close and firm ties of the civil war front.

Once we were returning from a hunt somewhat later than usual. The late return was due to no fault of ours; indeed, we suspected that it had been premeditated. At midnight, just as we were approaching Kislovodsk, the trolley on which we were riding was suddenly derailed, careened in a roundabout circle and stopped with a jolt. We all fell down without realizing at first just what had taken place. The officials who tried to explain to us the cause of this mishap were highly embarrassed. Their explanations did not make sense. It looked very much like a premeditated "accident" that had failed—no doubt, revenge for L. D.'s success at Kislovodsk. The "backward" Caucasus and all of the provinces along with it had to be taught a lesson in one fell blow.[2]

Not very long after this the pressure brought to bear on members and sympathizers of the Left Opposition was increased little by little. The treatment accorded to the hundreds who added their signatures to the Declaration of the 83 of May 26, 1927, was only exceeded in brutality and cynicism by the treatment of the thousands who supported them orally. They were dragged before Party courts, only because at Party meetings they expressed views not in accord with those of the Stalinist Central Committee, which was thus flagrantly depriving them as Party members of their most elementary Party rights. Public opinion in the Party was being prepared for the outright expulsion of the Opposition. This was reinforced by certain extraneous measures taken against members and sympathizers of the Opposition. "You'll be laughing at the labor exchange," a member of the Politburo and of the Central Committee of the Ukrainian Communist Party threatened the Opposition at one of the Party meetings in Kharkov. "We'll throw you out of your jobs," the Secretary of the Moscow Party Committee threatened in Moscow. [These were no idle boasts. When] the threat of hunger failed to silence the Opposition, the Central Committee openly resorted to the G.P.U. One had to be blind not to see that the struggle against the Opposition by such methods was a struggle against the Party.

[2] End of Mrs. Trotsky's text.—C. M.

What was the sense of talking about unity, while wielding such weapons? What did the Stalinists mean by unity? Was it the unity of the wolf with the lamb it was gobbling up? . . .

Menzhinsky, [Dzerzhinsky's successor as] head of the G.P.U., had been in all the opposition movements in Lenin's day. He was with the Boycottists, was carried away by anarcho-syndicalism, and what not. That was in his younger days. But toward the end of his career he was carried away by the machine of police repression. He was not interested in anything except the G.P.U. He devoted all his intellectual faculties to the task of keeping his machine going without interruption. For that, it was first of all necessary to support the government firmly. Once during the Civil War Menzhinsky had warned me unexpectedly about Stalin's intrigues against me. I told about it in my autobiography. When the triumvirate came to power he was faithful to the triumvirate. He transferred his loyalty to Stalin when the triumvirate fell apart. In the autumn of 1927, when the G.P.U. began to intervene in the internal disagreements of the Party, a whole group of us—Zinoviev, Kamenev, Smilga and I, and I think someone else—called on Menzhinsky. We asked him to show us the testimonies of witnesses which he made public at the last session of the Central Committee [with so much damage] to us. He did not deny that essentially those documents were forgeries, but flatly refused to show them to us.

"Do you remember, Menzhinsky," I asked him, "how once you told me on my train at the Southern Front that Stalin was conducting an intrigue against me?" Menzhinsky became embarrassed.

At this point Yagoda, who at the time was Stalin's inspector over the head of the G.P.U., intervened. "But Comrade Menzhinsky," he said, thrusting forward his foxy head, "never even went to the Southern Front."

Yagoda was a pharmacist in his youth. In a peaceful age he might have died the owner of a small town drug store.

I interrupted Yagoda. I told him I was not speaking to him but to Menzhinsky and repeated my question. Then Menzhinsky replied:

"Yes, I was on your train at the Southern Front and warned you about something or other, but I don't think I mentioned any names." The perplexed smile of a somnambulist crept over his face.

It was no use. Stalin dropped in to speak with him after we left empty-handed. Then Kamenev went to see him alone; after all, it was not so long ago that he had been at the disposal of the entire triumvirate against the Opposition.

"Do you really think," Kamenev finally asked him, "that Stalin alone will be able to cope with the tasks of [the October Revolution]?"

Menzhinsky dodged the issue. "Why then did you let him grow into such a formidable force?" he answered question for question. "Now it is too late."

In the spring of 1924, after one of the Plenums of the Central Committee at which I was not present because of illness, I said to [I. N.] Smirnov: "Stalin will become the dictator of the U.S.S.R." Smirnov knew Stalin well. They had shared revolutionary work and exile together for years, and under such conditions people get to know each other best of all.

"Stalin?" he asked me with amazement. "But he is a mediocrity, a colorless nonentity."

"Mediocrity, yes; nonentity, no," I answered him. "The dialectics of history have already hooked him and will raise him up. He is needed by all of them— by the tired radicals, by the bureaucrats, by the *nepmen*, the *kulaks*, the upstarts, the sneaks, by all the worms that are crawling out of the upturned soil of the manured revolution. He knows how to meet them on their own ground, he speaks their language and he knows how to lead them. He has the deserved reputation of an old revolutionist, which makes him invaluable to them as a blinder on the eyes of the country. He has will and daring. He will not hesitate to utilize them and to move them against the Party. He has already started doing this. Right now he is organizing around himself the sneaks of the Party, the artful dodgers. Of course, great developments in Europe, in Asia and in our country may intervene and upset all the speculations. But if everything continues to go automatically as it is going now, then Stalin will just as automatically become dictator."

In 1926 I had an argument with Kamenev, who insisted that Stalin was "just a small town politician." There was of course a particle of truth in that sarcastic characterization, but only a particle. Such attributes of character as slyness, faithlessness, the ability to exploit the lowest instincts of human nature are developed to an extraordinary degree in Stalin and, considering his strong character, represent mighty weapons in a struggle. Not, of course, any struggle. The struggle to liberate the masses requires other attributes. But in selecting men for privileged positions, in welding them together in the spirit of the caste, in weakening and disciplining the masses, Stalin's attributes were truly invaluable and rightfully make him the leader of the bureaucratic reaction. [Nevertheless,] Stalin remains a mediocrity. His mind is not only devoid of range but is even incapable of logical thinking. Every phrase of his speech has some immediate practical aim. But his speech as a whole never rises to a logical structure.

If Stalin could have foreseen at the very beginning where his fight against Trotskyism would lead, he undoubtedly would have stopped short, in spite of the prospect of victory over all his opponents. But he did not foresee anything. The prophecies of his opponents that he would become the leader of the Thermidor, the grave digger of the Party of the Revolution, seemed to him empty imaginings [and phrase-mongering]. He believed in the self-sufficiency of the Party machine, in its ability to perform all tasks. He did not have the slightest understanding of the historical function he was fulfilling. The absence of a creative imagination, the inability to generalize and to foresee killed the revolutionist in Stalin when he took the helm alone. But the very same traits backed by his authority as a former revolutionist enabled him to camouflage the rise of the Thermidorian bureaucracy.

His ambition acquired an untutored Asiatic cast intensified by European technique. He had to have the press extol him extravagantly every day, publish his portraits, refer to him on the slightest pretext, print his name in large type. Today even telegraph clerks know that they must not accept a telegram addressed to Stalin in which he is not called the father of the people, or the great teacher, or genius. The novel, the opera, the cinema, paintings, sculpture, even agricultural exhibitions, everything has to revolve around Stalin as around its axis. Literature and art of the Stalinist epoch will go down in history as examples of the most absurd and abject Byzantinism. [In 1925 Stalin was resentful of Lunacharsky because of his failure to mention him in a book as one of many leading figures. But a dozen or so years later Russia's] great writer, Alexis Tolstoy, who bears the name of one of the mightiest and most independent of the country's writers, wrote about Stalin:

> Thou, bright sun of the nations,
> The unsinking sun of our times,
> And more than the sun, for the sun has no wisdom . . .

[and Stalin takes it in his stride. He is pleased. He is even more pleased, no doubt, when a lesser writer comes closer to his own literary level with the following "Song About the Returned Sun," which chants in part]:

> We receive our sun from Stalin,
> We receive our prosperous life from Stalin . . .
> Even the good life in the tundras filled with snow-storms
> We made together with him,
> With the Son of Lenin,
> With Stalin the Wise.

[Stalin does not realize that such literary effusions sound] more like the grunting of a pig [than like poetry]. The article on the "felicitously reigning" Tsar-Emperor Alexander, the Third, written for an old Russian Encyclopedia by an obsequious courtier is a model of truthfulness, moderation and good taste by comparison with the article on Stalin in the latest Soviet Encyclopedia.

The bloc with Zinoviev and Kamenev restrained Stalin. Having undergone long periods of schooling under Lenin, they appreciated the value of ideas and programs. Although from time to time they indulged in monstrous deviations from the platform of Bolshevism and in violations of its ideological integrity, all under the guise of military subterfuge, they never transgressed certain limits. But when the triumvirate split, Stalin found himself released from all ideological restraints. The members of the Politburo were no longer embarrassed by their lack of background or by their downright ignorance. Discussions and arguments lost all influence, especially with reference to questions of the Comintern. By that time no member of the Politburo would recognize that any of the foreign sections had any independent significance. Everything was reduced to the question of whether they were "for" or "against" the Opposition. In the course of the preceding years one of my tasks in the Comintern had been to observe the

French labor movement. After the upheaval in the Comintern, which began at the end of 1923 and continued throughout 1924, the new leaders of the various sections tended to stray further and further from the old doctrines. I remember I once brought to a session of the Politburo the latest issue of the central organ of the French Communist Party and translated several excerpts of the programmatic article. These excerpts were so expressive of their [authors'] ignorance and opportunism that for a minute there was confusion in the Politburo. But of course they could not let their "boys" down. The only member of that Stalinist Politburo who thought he knew a little French, a wistful echo of adolescent school days, was Rudzutak. He asked me for the newspaper clipping and began to translate it at sight, omitting unfamiliar words and phrases, distorting the meaning of others and supplementing them with his own fantastic comments. At once everybody supported him in chorus. It is hard to convey the feeling of pain, of indignation . . .

Today it would seem hardly worthwhile to subject to a theoretical evaluation the output of literature against Trotskyism which, notwithstanding the shortage of paper, literally flooded the Soviet Union. Stalin himself could not have re-read all that he alone wrote and said approximately from 1923 to 1929, for it is in flagrant contradiction to all that he wrote and said and did in the course of the decade following. So completely is it repudiated by his later testimony that to reproduce this political trash, even in the briefest excerpts, would be sheer Sisyphian labor to me and as dull as dish water for the patient reader. It is sufficient for our purposes merely to indicate the few salient new ideas which gradually crystallized in the course of the polemics between the Stalinist machine and the Opposition and acquired decisive significance in so far as they provided ideological leverage for the initiators of the struggle against Trotskyism. It was around these ideas that the political forces rallied. They were three in number. In time they partly supplemented and partly replaced each other.

The first had to do with industrialization. The triumvirate began by coming out against the program of industrialization proposed by me, and in the interest of polemics branded it super-industrialization. This position was even deepened after the triumvirate fell apart and Stalin established his bloc with Bukharin and the Right Wing. The general trend of the official argument against so-called super-industrialization was that rapid industrialization is possible only at the expense of the peasantry. Consequently, we must move ahead at snail's pace. The question of the tempo of industrialization is really of no significance, and the like. As a matter of fact, the bureaucracy did not want to disturb those strata of the population which had begun to grow rich, i.e., the tops of the nepist petty-bourgeoisie. This was its first serious error in its struggle against Trotskyism. But it never acknowledged its own error. It merely turned a complete somersault on the subject and blithely proceeded to break all previous records of super-industrialization—largely on paper and in speeches, alas!

At the second stage, in the course of 1924, the struggle was launched against the theory of permanent revolution. The political content of this struggle was reduced to the thesis that we are not interested in international revolution but in our own safety, in order to develop our economy. The bureaucracy feared more and more that it was jeopardizing its position by the risk of involvement implicit in an international revolutionary policy. The campaign against the theory of permanent revolution, devoid in itself of any theoretical value whatsoever, served as an expression of a conservative nationalistic deviation from Bolshevism. Out of this struggle emerged the theory of socialism in a separate country. Only then did Zinoviev and Kamenev come to understand the implications of the struggle they themselves had initiated.

The third idea of the bureaucracy in its campaign against Trotskyism had to do with the struggle against leveling, against equality. The theoretical side of this struggle was in the nature of a curiosity. In Marx's letter concerning the Gotha program of the German Social Democracy, Stalin found a phrase to the effect that during the first period of socialism inequality will still be preserved, or, as he expressed it, the bourgeois prerogative in the sphere of distribution. Marx did not mean by this the creation of a new inequality but merely a gradual rather than a sudden elimination of the old inequality in the sphere of wages. This quotation was incorrectly interpreted as a declaration of the rights and privileges of the bureaucrats and their satellites. The future of the Soviet Union was thus divorced from the future of the international proletariat, and the bureaucracy was provided with a theoretical justification for special privileges and powers over the masses of the toilers inside the Soviet Union.

It thus looked as if the Revolution had been fought and won expressly for the bureaucracy, which waged a furious and rabid struggle against leveling, which jeopardized its privileges, and against permanent revolution, which jeopardized its very existence. It is not surprising that in this struggle Stalin found droves of supporters. Among them were former Liberals, Essars, and Mensheviks. They flocked into the State and even the Party machine, singing hosannas to Stalin's practical common sense.

The struggle against super-industrialization was carried on very cautiously in 1922, openly and stormily in 1923. The struggle against the permanent revolution began openly in 1924, and continued after that in different form and with varying interpretations in the course of all the subsequent years. The struggle against Trotsky's charges of inequality began toward the end of 1925 and became in essence the axis of the social program of the bureaucracy. The struggle against super-industrialization was conducted outrightly and directly in the interests of the *kulak*. The snail's pace in the development of industry was needed in order to give the *kulak* a painless antidote against socialism. This philosophy was at the same time the philosophy of the Right wing as well as of the Stalinist center. The theory of socialism in a separate country was championed in that period by a bloc of the bureaucracy with the agrarian and urban petty-bourgeoisie. The struggle against equality welded the bureaucracy more strongly than ever, not only to the agrarian and urban petty-bourgeoisie but to the labor aristocracy as well. Inequality became the common social basis, the source and the *raison d'être* of these allies. Thus economic and political bonds united the bureaucracy and the petty-bourgeoisie from 1923 to 1928.

It was then that the Russian Thermidor displayed its most obvious similarity to its French prototype. During that period the *kulak* was allowed to rent his land from the poor peasant and to hire the poor peasant as his laborer. Stalin was getting ready to lease the land to private owners for a period of forty years. Shortly after Lenin's death he made a clandestine attempt to transfer the nationalized land as private property to the peasants of his native Georgia under the guise of "possession" of "personal parcels" for "many years." Here again he showed how strong were his old agrarian roots and his dominant and deep-seated Georgian nationalism. Upon Stalin's secret instruction, the Georgian People's Commissar of Agriculture prepared a project to transfer the land to the possession of the peasants. Only the protest of Zinoviev, who got wind of the conspiracy, and the alarm raised by the project in Party circles, compelled Stalin, who did not yet feel sure enough of himself, to repudiate his own project. Naturally, the scapegoat in this case proved to be the unfortunate Georgian People's Commissar.

But Stalin and his machine became bolder as time went on, especially after they rid themselves of the restraining influence of Zinoviev and Kamenev. Indeed, the bureaucracy ventured so very far toward meeting the interests and claims of its allies that by 1927 it became as clearly evident to all as it had been right along to every literate economist that the claims of their bourgeois ally were by their very nature unlimited. The *kulak* wanted the land, its outright ownership. The *kulak* wanted to have the right of free disposition of his entire crop. The *kulak* did his utmost to create his very own counter-agents in the city in the form of the free trader and the free industrialist. The *kulak* did not want to put up with forced deliveries at fixed prices. The *kulak*, jointly with the petty industrialist, worked for the complete restoration of capitalism. Thus opened the irreconcilable struggle over the surplus product of national labor. Who will dispose of it in the nearest future—the new bourgeoisie or the Soviet bureaucracy?—that became the next issue. He who disposes of the surplus product has the power of the state at his disposal. It was this that opened the struggle between the petty-bourgeoisie, which had helped the bureaucracy to crush the resistance of the laboring masses and of their spokesman the Left Opposition, and the thermidorian bureaucracy itself, which had helped the petty-bourgeoisie to lord it over the agrarian masses. It was a direct struggle for power and for income.

Obviously the bureaucracy did not rout the proletarian vanguard, pull free from the complications of the international revolution, and legitimize the philosophy of inequality in order to capitulate before the bourgeoisie, become the latter's servant, and be eventually itself pulled away from the state feed-bag. The bureaucracy became mortally frightened by the consequences of its six-year policy. It therefore turned sharply against the *kulak* and the *nepman*. Concurrently, it launched the so-called Third Period[3] and the struggle against the Rightists. In the eyes of simpletons the theory and politics of the Third Period seemed to be a return to the basic tenets of Bolshevism. But it was nothing of the kind. It was merely a means to an end, the end of wiping out the Right Opposition and its satellites. The stupid antics of the notorious Third Period at home and abroad are too recent to warrant description now. They would be laughable if their effects on the masses had not been so tragic. It is no secret to anyone that in the struggle against the Right Wingers Stalin accepted the alms of the Left Opposition. He did not contribute a single new idea. His intellectual work consisted of nothing more than threats and the repetition of the slogans and arguments of the Opposition, naturally with demagogic distortion. Not only did he pick up the old rags of the Opposition, but to avoid recognition, he tore pieces out of them and without taking the trouble to sew them together into some new unit (such niceties never distressed him) he covered his nakedness with them as the need arose. However, it cannot be said that these tatters made up of a left sleeve, a right pocket, a trouser leg—all cut to somebody else's measurement—could be regarded as very satisfactory covering for the Leader's nudity. And his followers could not help him, because they had to keep perfect time with every motion of the Father of Nations.

The literature of the Left Opposition of 1926-27, on the other hand, is distinguished by its exceptional wealth. The Opposition reacted to each fact of life at home and abroad, to each act of the government, to each decision of the Politburo, with individual or collective documents addressed to the various institutions of the Party, mostly the Politburo. These were the years of the Chinese Revolution, of the Anglo-Russian Committee, and of great confusion in internal matters. The bureaucracy was still only feeling its way, casting about from Right to Left and then again from Left to Right. Much of what the Opposition wrote was not intended for the general press but only for the information of the leading institutions of the Party. But even that which was especially written for *Pravda*, or for the theoretical monthly, *The Bolshevik*, was never published in the Soviet press.

The majority of the Politburo had firmly resolved to strangle the Opposition —at least, to choke it off, crowd it out, expel it, arrest it. This was Stalin's way of meeting arguments. Not all the members of the Politburo agreed to this course. But little by little, Stalin drew them into the struggle. He whittled away their mental reservations, wore down their prejudice, made each succeeding step the inevitable consequence of each preceding step. Here he was in his element. In this his mastery was beyond dispute. The time came when the dissenting members of the Politburo gave up protesting even mildly against the outrages of Stalin's crasser "activists." And little by little, they were pushed out of noncommittal silence into public approval of outrage after outrage . . .

That part of the Oppositionist writings that I managed to bring out with me

[3] See Glossary.

at the time of my expulsion to Turkey is now in the Harvard Library and at the disposal of all those who may be interested in studying the record of that remarkable struggle by going to the original sources. Reading over those documents while engaged in the writing of this book—that is, nearly fifteen years later—I had to admit the rightness of the Opposition in two respects: it prophesied correctly and spoke up boldly at the same time; it exhibited remarkable stamina and persistence in carrying out its political line. The arguments of the Opposition were never refuted. It is not hard to imagine the fury they evoked in Stalin and among his closest collaborators. The intellectual and political superiority of the representatives of the Opposition over the majority of the Politburo is clearly apparent in each line of the Oppositionist documents. Stalin had nothing to say in reply, and he did not even attempt to do so. He resorted to the same method that had been a part of him since his early youth, which was not to argue with an opponent by offering his own views in rebuttal, before an audience, but to compromise his opponent personally, and if possible, exterminate him physically. Intellectual impotence before argument, before criticism, gave birth to fury, and fury in its turn drove him to hurry measures for the liquidation of the Opposition. Thus passed 1926-1927. It proved to be merely a rehearsal for the perfidy and degeneration that startled the world ten years later.

On one side of this grand polemic was the Left Opposition, intellectually aflame, tireless in its probings and explorations, earnestly striving to find the right solution for the problems of changing international and internal situations, without violating however the traditions of the Party. On the other side, the cold effort of the bureaucratic clique to make short shrift of its critics, of all opponents, of the disturbers who would not give them rest, who would not give them the chance to enjoy the victory they had won. While members of the Opposition were busy analyzing the basic errors of the official policy in China or subjecting to criticism the bloc with the General Council of the British Trade Unions, Stalin put into circulation the rumor that the Opposition was supporting Austen Chamberlain against the Soviet Union, that it did not want to defend the Soviet Union, that such and such an Oppositionist was improperly using state-owned automobiles, that Kamenev signed a telegram to Michael Romanov, that Trotsky wrote a frantic letter against Lenin. And always the dates, the circumstances, all such details, remained in a fog.

Nor were these the only methods of Stalinist rebuttal. He and his henchmen even stooped to fish in the muddied waters of anti-Semitism. I recall particularly a cartoon in the *Rabochaya Gazeta* [Workers' Gazette] entitled "Comrades Trotsky and Zinoviev." There were any number of such caricatures and doggerels of anti-Semitic character in the Party press. They were received with sly snickers. Stalin's attitude toward this growing anti-Semitism was one of friendly neutrality. But matters went so far that he was forced to come out with a published statement which declared, "We are fighting Trotsky, Zinoviev and

Kamenev not because they are Jews, but because they are Oppositionists," and the like. It was absolutely clear to everyone who thought politically that his deliberately equivocal declaration was aimed merely at the "excesses" of anti-Semitism, while at the same time broadcasting throughout the entire Soviet press the very pregnant reminder, "Don't forget that the leaders of the Opposition are Jews." Such a statement gave carte blanche to the anti-Semites.

Most of the Party members voted for the defeat of the Opposition against their will, against their sympathies, against their very memories. They had been inveigled into voting as they did, little by little, under the pressure of the machine, even as the machine itself was drawn into the fight against the Opposition from the top down. Stalin left the leading roles to Zinoviev, Kamenev, Bukharin, Rykov, because they were much better equipped than he to carry on an open polemic against the Opposition, but also because he did not wish to burn all his bridges behind him. The hard blows struck at the Opposition, blows which seemed decisive at that time, evoked secret but nonetheless deep sympathy for the vanquished and outright hostility toward the victors, especially toward the two leading figures, Zinoviev and Kamenev. Stalin made capital of that, too. He publicly dissociated himself from Kamenev and Zinoviev as the chief culprits in the unpopular campaign against Trotsky. He assumed the role of conciliator, the impartial and moderate mediator in the factional struggle.

In 1925 Zinoviev, trying to impress Rakovsky with his factional victories, said about me: "A poor politician. He could not find the right tactic. That's why he was licked." A year later this unfortunate critic of my tactic was knocking for admission at the door of the Left Opposition. Neither he nor Kamenev had guessed as late as 1925 that they had become tools of bureaucratic reaction— even as they had guessed wrong in 1917. By 1926 they realized there was no other "tactic" possible for a revolutionist, for after all they were of the Old Guard that could not honestly conceive of Bolshevism without its internationalist perspective and its revolutionary dynamism. That was the tradition of which the Old Bolsheviks were the bearers. That was why the entire Party of Lenin's day regarded them as irreplaceable capital. Lenin's special and exceptional concern about the old generation of revolutionists was dictated by this political consideration as much as by comradely solidarity. When Zinoviev boasted to Rakovsky of his own successful "tactic" against me, he was boasting of how he had misused and squandered that capital. From 1923 to 1926, upon the initiative and at first under the leadership of Zinoviev, the struggle against Marxist internationalism under the name of "Trotskyism" was carried on under the slogan of saving the Old Guard. The Opposition was accused of undermining the Old Guard of Bolshevism. A special commission to look after the state of health of the Old Bolshevik veterans was created. The shift in the direction toward the open Thermidor did not express itself so flagrantly in anything else as in the political compromises of the same Old Guard. [That was] followed by its physical extermination. The commission to guard the health of the Old Bolsheviks was finally replaced by a small detachment of [OGPU] executioners, whom Stalin rewarded with the Order of the Red Banner.

Lefebvre [in his book,] "Les Thermidoriens" [makes the point that] the task of the Thermidorians was to represent the 9th of Thermidor as a minor episode —a mere purge of inimical elements for the sake of preserving the basic nucleus of the Jacobins and continuing their traditional policy. In the first period of the Thermidor the attack was not against the Jacobins as a whole but only against the Terrorists. [A parallel process was repeated in the Soviet Thermidor.] The campaign against Trotskyism began in defense of the Old Guard and the Bolshevik line of policy, continued in the name of Party unity, and culminated with the physical extermination of the Bolsheviks as a whole. During both Thermidors this destruction of the revolutionists was carried out in the name of the Revolution and presumably in its best interests. The Jacobins were not destroyed as Jacobins but as Terrorists, as Robespierrists, and the like; similarly, the Bolsheviks were destroyed as Trotskyists, Zinovievists, Bukharinists. There is a remarkable similarity between the Russian term, *"Trotskistskoye okhvostiye,"* which acquired full civic rights in Soviet publications, and the title of a pamphlet "Méhée de la Touche" published on the 9th of Fructidor, *"La queue de Robespierre."* But the similarity of basic Thermidorian methods is even more remarkable. Lefebvre writes that, the very next day after the 9th of Thermidor, speaking in the name of the members of the Committee of Public Safety, Barere reassured the Convention that nothing momentous had happened.

> ★ Speaking in their name on the 10th of Thermidor, Barere declared that the occurrences that had taken place the previous day were no more than a "minor disturbance which left the government unchanged . . ."

[And three weeks later] :

> ★ On the second of Fructidor (the 19th of August) . . . Louchet, the very same man who had brought out the indictment against Robespierre, described the progress of the reaction, called again for the arrest of all suspects, and declared that it was necessary "to keep the Terror on the order of the day."

[This blow against the Left of course unbridled the Right, and passions ran high] :

> ★ The Thermidorians, enforcing the new state of affairs, were above all apprehensive of . . . an uprising. The Rightist elements exploited this fear of the Thermidorians. There began a purge of the clubs, arrests, the murder of Jacobins. The Rightists, upheld by the Thermidorians, did their utmost from then on to represent every manifestation of dissatisfaction, criticism or indignation, whether in Paris or in the provinces, as evidence of conspiracy on the part of the Terrorists.

The prestige of the leaders as a whole, not only the personal prestige of Lenin, made up in its totality the authority of the Central Committee. The principle of individual leadership was utterly alien to the Party. The Party singled out the more popular figures for leadership, gave them its confidence and admiration, while always adhering to the view that the actual leadership came from the Central Committee as a whole. This tradition was used to tremendous advantage by the triumvirate, which insisted upon the paramountcy of the Central Committee over any individual authority. Stalin, schemer, centrist and eclectic par excellence, master of small doses gradually administered, cynically misused that trust [in the Central Committee] for his own advantage.

At the end of 1925 Stalin still spoke of the leaders in the third person and instigated the Party against them. He received the plaudits of the middle layer of the bureaucracy, which refused to bend its neck to any leader. Yet in reality, Stalin himself was already dictator. He was a dictator, but he did not feel yet that he was leader, and no one recognized him as such. He was a dictator not through the force of his personality, but through the power of the political machine that had broken with the old leaders. As late as the Sixteenth Congress, in 1930, Stalin said: "You ask why we expelled Trotsky and Zinoviev? Because we did not want to have aristocrats in the Party, because we have only one law in the Party, and all the Party members are equal in their rights." He reiterated this at the Seventeenth Congress in 1934.

He used the Right as a battering ram against the Left Opposition, for only the Right had a definite platform, interests, and principles, that were jeopardized by a triumph of Left policies. But when he saw that the expulsion of the Left Opposition provoked grave misgivings and dissatisfaction in the Party, and irritation with the triumphant Right, Stalin knew how to utilize this dissatisfaction for a blow against the Rightists. The conflict of class forces in this struggle between Right and Left was of less concern to him than his deceptive role as a conciliator or as the pacifying element which presumably would reduce the inevitable number of victims to a minimum and save the Party from a schism. In his role of super-arbiter, he was able to place the responsibility for the severe measures against certain popular Party members now on one, and now on the other wing of the Party. But classes cannot be fooled. As a maneuver, the pro-*kulak* policy of 1924-1928 was worse than criminal; it was absurd. The *kulak* is nobody's fool. He judges by taxes, prices, profits, not by phrasemongering and declamations: he judges by deeds, not by words. Maneuvering can never replace the action and reaction of class forces; its usefulness is limited at best; and there is nothing so calculated to disintegrate the revolutionary morale of a mass party as clandestine unprincipled maneuvering. Nor is anything deadlier for the morale and the character of the individual revolutionists. Military trickery can never replace major strategy.

Smilga pointed out in conversation with me some ten years after the October Insurrection, that during the first five years there was an underlying tendency to patch up differences—old cracks were plugged, old wounds healed, opponents became reconciled, and the like, while, during the following five years, beginning with 1923, the process was reversed; every crack was broadened, every difference was magnified and sharpened, every wound festered. The Bolshevik Party, in its old form, with its old traditions and its old membership, became more and more opposed to the new ruling stratum.

In this contradiction is the essence of the Thermidor. Sterile and absurd are the Sisyphean labors of those who try to reduce all subsequent developments to a few allegedly basic original attributes of the Bolshevik Party, as if a political party were a homogeneous entity and an omnipotent factor of history. A political party is only a temporary historical instrument, one of very many instruments and schools of history. The Bolshevik Party set for itself the goal of the conquest of power by the working class. In so far as that party accomplished this task for the first time in history and enriched human experience with this conquest, it fulfilled a tremendous historical role. Only the bewildered with a liking for abstruse discussion can demand of a political party that it should subjugate and eliminate the far weightier factors of mass and class hostile to it. The limitation of the party as a historical instrument is expressed in the fact that at a certain point, at a given moment, it begins to disintegrate. Under the tension of external and internal pressures, cracks appear, fissures develop, organs begin to atrophy. This process of decomposition set in, slowly at first, in 1923, and rapidly increased in tempo. The old Bolshevik Party and its old heroic cadres went the way of all flesh; shaken by fevers and spasms and excruciatingly painful attacks, it finally died. In order to establish the régime that is justly called Stalinist, what was necessary was not a Bolshevik Party, but the extermination of the Bolshevik Party.

Numerous critics, publicists, correspondents, historians, biographers, and sundry amateur sociologists, have lectured the Left Opposition from time to time on the error of its ways, saying that the strategy of the Left Opposition was not feasible from the point of view of the struggle for power. However, the very approach to the question was incorrect. The Left Opposition could not achieve power, and did not hope even to do so—certainly not its most thoughtful leaders. A struggle for power by the Left Opposition, by a revolutionary Marxist organization, was conceivable only under the conditions of a revolutionary upsurge. Under such conditions the strategy is based on aggression, on direct appeal to the masses, on frontal attack against the government. Quite a few members of the Left Opposition had played no minor part in such a struggle and had first-hand knowledge of how to wage it. But during the early twenties and later, there was no revolutionary upsurge in Russia, quite the contrary. Under such circumstances it was out of the question to launch a struggle for power.

Bear in mind that in the years of reaction, in 1908-1911 and later, the Bolshevik Party refused to launch a direct attack upon the monarchy and limited itself to the task of preparing for the eventual offensive by fighting for the survival of the revolutionary traditions and for the preservation of certain cadres, subjecting the developing events to untiring analysis, and utilizing all legal and semi-legal possibilities for training the advanced stratum of workers. The Left

Opposition could not proceed otherwise under similar conditions. Indeed, the conditions of Soviet reaction were immeasurably more difficult for the Opposition than the conditions of the Tsarist reaction had been for the Bolsheviks. But, basically, the task remained the same—the preservation of revolutionary traditions, the maintenance of contact among the advanced elements within the Party, the analysis of the developing events of the Thermidor, the preparation for the future revolutionary upsurge on the world arena as well as in the U.S.S.R. One danger was that the Opposition might underestimate its forces and prematurely abandon the prosecution of this task after a few tentative sallies, in which the advance guard necessarily crashed not only against the resistance of the bureaucracy but against the indifference of the masses as well. The other danger was that, having become convinced of the impossibility of open association with the masses, even with their vanguard, the Opposition would give up the struggle and lie low until better times. This threatened with complete loss . . .

Revolution crushes and demolishes the machinery of the old state. Therein is its essence. Crowds fill the arena. They decide, they act, they legislate in their own unprecedented way; they judge, they issue orders. The essence of the revolution is that the mass itself becomes its own executive organ. But when the masses leave the social arena, retire to their various boroughs, retreat into their sundry dwellings, perplexed, disillusioned, tired, the place becomes desolate. And its bleakness merely deepens as it is filled with the new bureaucratic machinery. Naturally, the men in charge, unsure of themselves and of the crowds, are apprehensive. That is why, in the epoch of the victorious reaction, the military-police machine plays a far greater role than under the old régime. In this swing from revolution to thermidor, the specific nature of the Russian Thermidor was determined by the role the party played in it. The French Revolution had nothing of the kind at its disposal. The dictatorship of the Jacobins, as personified by the Committee of Public Safety, lasted only one year. This dictatorship had real support in the Convention, which was much stronger than the revolutionary clubs and sections. Here is the classic contradiction between the dynamics of revolution and its parliamentary reflection. The most active elements of the classes participate in the revolutionary struggle of forces. The remainder—the neutral ones, those who lay low, the backward ones—seem to vote themselves off the books. At election time participation broadens; it is extended to include also a considerable portion of the semi-passive and the semi-indifferent. In times of revolution, parliamentary representatives are immeasurably more moderate and temperate than the revolutionary groups they represent. In order to dominate the Convention, the Montagnards let the Convention rule the people rather than the revolutionary elements of the people outside of the Convention.

Notwithstanding the incomparably deeper character of the October Revolution, the army of the Soviet Thermidor was recruited essentially from the remnants of the former ruling parties and their ideological representatives. The

former landed gentry, capitalists, lawyers, their sons—that is, those of them that had not run abroad—were taken into the State machine, and quite a few even into the Party. A far greater number of those admitted into the State and Party machinery were formerly members of the petty bourgeois parties—Mensheviks and Essars. To these must be added a tremendous number of pure and simple Philistines who had cowered on the sidelines during the stormy epoch of the Revolution and the Civil War, and who, convinced at last of the stability of the Soviet Government, dedicated themselves with singular passion to the noble task of securing soft and permanent berths, if not in the Center, then at least in the provinces. This enormous and varicolored mob was the natural support of the Thermidor.

Its sentiments ran from pale pink to snowy white. The Essars were, of course, ready at all times and in every way to support the interests of the peasants against the threats of the scoundrelly industrializers, while the Mensheviks, by and large, considered that more freedom and territory should be given to the peasant bourgeoisie of which they had also become the political spokesmen. The surviving representatives of the upper bourgeoisie and the landed gentry, who had wedged their way into government jobs, naturally seized upon the peasants as their life-belt. They could not hope for any sort of success as champions of their own class interests for the time being, and clearly understood that they had to pass through a period of defending the peasantry. None of these groups could openly raise its head. All of them needed the protective coloration of the ruling party and of traditional Bolshevism. The struggle against the permanent revolution meant to them the struggle against the permanent establishment of the deprivations they had suffered. It is natural that they gladly accepted as their leaders those of the Bolsheviks who turned against the permanent revolution.

Economy revived. A small surplus appeared. Naturally it was concentrated in the cities and at the disposal of the ruling strata. With it came a revival of theaters, restaurants and entertainment establishments. Hundreds of thousands of people of the various professions who spent the vigorous years of the Civil War in a kind of coma, now revived, stretched out their limbs and began to take part in the re-establishment of normal life. All of them were on the side of the opponents of permanent revolution. All of them wanted peace, growth and the strengthening of the peasantry, and also the continued prosperity of the entertainment establishments in the cities. And they sought permanence for this trend rather than for the revolution. Professor Ustryalov wondered whether the New Economic Policy of 1921 was a "tactic" or an "evolution." This question disturbed Lenin very much. The further course of events showed that the "tactic," thanks to a special configuration of historical conditions, became the source of "evolution." The subsequent strategic retreat of the revolutionary party served as the beginning of its degeneration.

The counter-revolution sets in when the spool of progressive social conquests begins to unwind. There seems no end to this unwinding. Yet some portion of the conquests of the revolution is always preserved. Thus, in spite of monstrous bureaucratic distortions, the class basis of the U.S.S.R. remains proletarian. But let us bear in mind that the unwinding process has not yet been completed, and the future of Europe and the world during the next few decades has not yet been decided. The Russian Thermidor would have undoubtedly opened a new era of bourgeois rule, if that rule had not proved obsolete throughout the world. At any rate, the struggle against equality and the establishment of very deep social differentiations has so far been unable to eliminate the socialist consciousness of the masses or the nationalization of the means of production and the land, which were the basic socialist conquests of the revolution. Although it derogates these achievements, the bureaucracy has not yet ventured to resort to the restoration of the private ownership of the means of production. At the end of the eighteenth century, private ownership of the means of production was a factor of powerful progressive significance. It still had Europe and the whole world to conquer. But in our times private ownership is the greatest single deterrent to the adequate development of productive forces. Although by the nature of its new mode of life, its conservatism, its political sympathies, the overwhelming majority of the bureaucracy was drawn toward the new petty-bourgeoisie, its economic roots were largely in the new conditions of ownership. The growth of bourgeois relations threatened not only the socialist basis of property, but the social foundation of the bureaucracy itself. It may have been willing to repudiate the socialist perspective of development in favor of the petty-bourgeoisie. But under no circumstances was it ready to repudiate its own rights and privileges in favor of the petty-bourgeoisie. It was this contradiction that led to the very sharp conflict between the bureaucracy and the *kulak*.

It is in this respect that the Soviet Thermidor differs radically from its French prototype. The Jacobin dictatorship had been necessary in order to uproot feudal society and defend the survival of the new order from the attacks of the external enemy. That done, the task of the Thermidorian régime was to create the necessary conditions for the development of this new society, which was bourgeois, i.e., based on private ownership of property and unrestricted (or largely unrestricted) trade. The restoration of limited free trading by the NEP in 1921 was a retreat to bourgeois exactions. But actually the freedom of trade was so limited that it did not undermine the foundations of the régime (the nationalization of the means of production), and the reins of government remained in the hands of the Russian Jacobins who had led the October Revolution. Even the further extension of this freedom of trade in 1925 did not alter the basis of the régime, although the threat became greater then. The struggle against Trotskyism was waged in the name of the peasant, behind whose back was the *nepman* with his tongue hanging out, and the greedy bureaucrat. As soon as Trotskyism was defeated, the leasing of land was legalized, and all along the line the general shift of power from Left to Right was unmistakable, notwithstanding occasional shifts to the Left, for these were followed again by shifts even further to the Right. In so far as the bureaucracy used its retreats to the Left for gaining greater momentum for each subsequent jump to the Right, the zigzag course being made consistently at the expense of the toiling masses and in the interests of a privileged minority, its Thermidorian nature is unmistakable.

Rousseau had taught that political democracy was incompatible with excessive inequality. The Jacobins, representatives of the petty-bourgeois rank and file were permeated with this teaching. The legislation of the Jacobin dictatorship, especially the role of the maximum, was along those lines. So was Soviet legislation, which banished inequality even from the Army. Under Stalin all this has been changed, and today there is not only social but economic inequality. It has been fostered by the bureaucracy with cynicism and brazenness in the name of the revolutionary doctrine of Bolshevism. In its campaign against the Trotskyist charges of inequality, in its agitation for the differential table of wages, the bureaucracy invoked the shades of Marx and Lenin and sought justification for its privileges behind the back of the hard-working "middle" peasant and the skilled worker. It charged that the Left Opposition was trying to deprive qualified labor of the higher wage to which it was rightfully entitled. It was the same sort of demagogic camouflage as that employed by the capitalist and the landlord who shed crocodile tears on behalf of the skilled mechanic, the enterprising petty trader and the ever-martyred farmer. It was a masterful maneuver on the part of Stalin, and it naturally found instant support among the privileged officials, who for the first time saw in him their chosen leader. With unbridled cynicism, equality was denounced as a petty bourgeois prejudice; the Opposition was denounced as the chief enemy of Marxism and the principal sinner against the Gospels of Lenin. Lolling in automobiles technically owned by the proletariat, on their way to proletarian-owned summer resorts to which only the chosen few were admitted, the bureaucrats guffawed, "What have we been fighting for?" That ironic phrase was very popular at the time. The bureaucracy had respected Lenin, but it had always found his puritanical hand rather irksome. A witticism current in 1926-1927 characterized its attitude toward the leaders of the United Opposition: "They tolerate Kamenev but do not respect him. They respect Trotsky but do not tolerate him. They neither tolerate nor respect Zinoviev." The bureaucracy sought a leader who would be the first among equals. Stalin's firmness of character and narrowness of outlook inspired confidence. "We are not afraid of Stalin," said Yenukidze to Serebryakov. "As soon as he begins to give himself airs, we'll remove him." But in the end it was Stalin who got rid of them.

The French Thermidor, started by Left Wing Jacobins, turned in the end into reaction against all Jacobins. "Terrorist," "Montagnard," "Jacobin" became terms of abuse. In the provinces the trees of liberty were chopped down and the tricolor cockade was trampled underfoot. This was unthinkable in the Soviet Republic. The totalitarian party contained within itself all the indispensable elements of reaction, which it mobilized under the official banner of the October Revolution. The Party did not tolerate any competition, not even in the struggle against its enemies. The struggle against the Trotskyists did not turn into the struggle against the Bolsheviks because the Party had swallowed this struggle in its entirety, set certain limits to it and waged it in the name of Bolshevism.

In the eyes of simpletons, the theory and practice of the "Third Period" seemed to refute the theory of the Thermidorian period of the Russian Revolution. As a matter of fact, they merely confirmed it. The substance of the Thermidor was, is and could not fail to be social in character. It stood for the crystallization of a new privileged stratum, the creation of a new substratum for the economically dominant class. There were two pretenders to this role: the petty bourgeoisie and the bureaucracy itself. They fought shoulder to shoulder [in the battle to break] the resistance of the proletarian vanguard. When that task was accomplished a savage struggle broke out between them. The bureaucracy became frightened of its isolation, its divorcement from the proletariat. Alone it could not crush the *kulak* nor the petty bourgeoisie that had grown and continued to grow on the basis of the NEP; it had to have the aid of the proletariat. Hence its concerted effort to present its struggle against the petty bourgeoisie for the surplus products and for power as the struggle of the proletariat against attempts at capitalistic restoration.

Here the analogy with the French Thermidor ceases. The new social basis of the Soviet Union became paramount. To guard the nationalization of the means of production and of the land, is the bureaucracy's law of life and death, for these are the social sources of its dominant position. That was the reason for its struggle against the *kulak*. The bureaucracy could wage this struggle, and wage it to the end, only with the support of the proletariat. The best proof of the fact that it had mustered this support was the avalanche of capitulations by representatives of the new Opposition. The fight against the *kulak*, the fight against the Right Wing, the fight against opportunism—the official slogans of that period—seemed to the workers and to many representatives of the Left Opposition like a renaissance of the Dictatorship of the Proletariat and the Socialist Revolution. We warned them at the time: it is not only a question of *what* is being done, but also of *who* does it. Under conditions of Soviet democracy, i.e., self-rule of the toilers, the struggle against the *kulaks* might not have assumed such a convulsive, panicky and bestial form and might have led to a general rise of the economic and cultural level of the masses on the basis of industrialization. But the bureaucracy's fight against the *kulak* was single combat [fought] on the backs of the toilers; and since neither of the embattled gladiators trusted the masses, since both feared the masses, the struggle assumed an extremely convulsive and sanguinary character. Thanks to the support of the proletariat, it ended with victory for the bureaucracy. But it did not lead to a gain in the specific weight of the proletariat in the country's political life.

To understand the Russian Thermidor, it is extremely important to understand the role of the party as a political factor. There was nothing remotely resembling the Bolshevik Party in the French Revolution. During the Thermidor there were in France various social groups [under various] political labels which came out against each other in the name of definite social interests. The Thermidorians attacked the Jacobins under the name of Terrorists. The gilded youth supported the Thermidorians on the Right, threatening them as well.

In Russia, all these processes, conflicts and unions were covered by the name of the single party.

Externally one and the same party was commemorating stages of its existence at the inception of the Soviet Government and twenty years later, resorting to the same methods in the name of the very same aims: the preservation of its political purity and its unity. As a matter of fact, the role of the party and the role of the purges had altered radically. In the early period of the Soviet power the old revolutionary party was purging itself of careerists; in line with that, the committees were composed of revolutionary workers. Adventurers or careerists or simply scoundrels trying to attach themselves to the government in quite considerable numbers were cast overboard. But the purges of recent years were, on the contrary, fully and completely directed against the old revolutionary party. The organizers of the purges were the most bureaucratic and the most low-calibred elements of the Party. The victims of the purges were the most loyal elements, devoted to revolutionary traditions, and above all, its oldest revolutionary generation, the genuine revolutionary proletarian elements. The social significance of the purges has altered fundamentally, yet this change is concealed by the fact that the purges were carried out by the same party. In France, we saw in corresponding circumstances the belated movement of the petty bourgeois and workers' districts against the higher-ups of the petty bourgeoisie and the middle bourgeoisie, represented by the Thermidorians, aided by bands of the gilded youth.

Even these bands of the gilded youth are nowadays included in the Party and in the League of Communist Youth. These were the field detachments, recruited from the sons of the bourgeoisie, privileged young men resolutely ready to defend their own privileged position or the position of their parents. It is sufficient to point to the fact that at the head of the League of Communist Youth for a number of years stood Kossarev, generally known to be a moral degenerate who misused his high position to advance his personal objectives. His entire machine was made up of men of the same type. Such was the gilded youth of the Russian Thermidor. Its direct inclusion in the Party masked its social function as a field detachment of the privileged against the toilers and the oppressed. The Soviet gilded youth cried: "Down with Trotskyism! Long Live the Leninist Central Committee!" just as the gilded youth of the French Thermidor cried, "Down with the Jacobins! Long Live the Convention!"

The Jacobins held on chiefly through the pressure of the street upon the Convention. The Thermidorians, i.e., the deserting Jacobins, strived for the same method, but from the opposite ends. They began to organize well-dressed sons of the bourgeoisie, from among the sans-culottes. These gilded youths, or simply "young men," as they were indulgently called by the conservative press, became such an important factor in national politics that as the Jacobins were expelled from all administrative posts the "young men" took their places. An identical process is still going on in the Soviet Union. Indeed it is considerably more far-reaching under Stalin.

The Thermidorian bourgeoisie was characterized by profound hatred towards the Montagnards, for its own leaders had come from those who had stood at the head of the sans-culottes. The bourgeoisie and with it the Thermidorians, were above all afraid of a new outbreak of the popular movement. It was precisely during that period that the class consciousness of the French bourgeoisie fully formed itself. It detested the Jacobins and the semi-Jacobins with a mad hatred—as betrayers of its most sacred interests, as deserters to the enemy, as renegades. The source of the hatred of the Soviet bureaucracy for the Trotsky-ists has the same social character. Here are people of the same stratum, of the same ruling group, of the same privileged bureaucracy who abandon the ranks only to tie their fate to the fate of the sans-culottes, the disinherited, the proletarians, the village poor. However, the difference is that the French bourgeoisie was already formed before the Great Revolution. It first broke out of its political shell in the Constituent Assembly, but it had to pass through the period of the Convention and the Jacobin Dictatorship in order to settle with its enemies, while during the period of the Thermidor it restored its historical tradition. The Soviet ruling caste consisted entirely of Thermidorian bureaucrats, recruited not only from Bolshevik ranks but from the petty bourgeois and bourgeois parties as well. And the latter had old scores to settle with the "fanatics" of Bolshevism.

The Thermidor rested on a social foundation. It was a matter of bread, meat, living quarters, surplus, if possible, luxury. Bourgeois Jacobin equality, which assumed the form of the reglamentation of the maximum, restricted the development of bourgeois economy and the growth of bourgeois well-being (prosperity). On this point, the Thermidorians were perfectly well aware and clearly understood what they wanted. In the declaration of rights they worked out, they excluded the essential paragraph, "People are born and remain free and equal in their rights." To those who proposed the restoration of this important Jacobin paragraph, the Thermidorians replied that it was equivocal and therefore dangerous; people were of course, equal in their rights, but not in their capabilities and not in their possessions. The Thermidor was a direct protest against the Spartan temper and against the striving for equality.

The same social motivation is to be found in the Soviet Thermidor. It was first of all a matter of throwing off the Spartan limitations of the first period of the Revolution. But it was also a question of achieving increasing privileges for the bureaucracy. It was not a question of introducing a liberal economic régime. Concessions in that direction were temporary in character and lasted a considerably shorter time than had been originally intended. A liberal régime on the basis of private property means concentration of wealth in the hands of the bourgeoisie, especially its higher-ups. The privileges of the bureaucracy have a different source of origin. The bureaucracy took for itself that part of the national income which it could secure either by the exercise of force or of its authority or by direct intervention in economic relations. In the matter of the national surplus product the bureaucracy and the petty bourgeoisie quickly changed from alliance to enmity. The control of the surplus product opened the bureaucracy's road to power.

Supplement II

KINTO IN POWER

BEFORE becoming King in Israel, David herded sheep and played a flute. His extraordinary career becomes comprehensible when we consider that almost all the sons of the semi-nomadic Israelites herded sheep, and that in those days the art of governing people was not much more complicated than the art of herding flocks. Since then, however, society as well as the art of government has greatly increased in complexity. When [a modern] monarch [has] to vacate the throne, [it is no longer necessary] to seek his successor among the shepherds. The delicate question is settled on the basis of dynastic automatism.

Human history has known not a few meteoric careers. Julius Caesar was a natural candidate for power, a member of a not numerous oligarchy by right of birth. Not so Napoleon I. Yet even he [was not so much of an upstart] as the principal dictators of our time. He was, say what you will, [a brilliant soldier.] At least [in that respect] he was true to the same ancient [tradition as Julius] Caesar—[namely, that] a warrior, having demonstrated his ability to command armed men in battle, is all the more entitled to lord it over an unarmed and defenseless populace. This hoary tradition was not strictly observed [in the case of that imitation Napoleon, generally referred to as the Little or] the Third, who was utterly devoid of military gifts. But [even] he was no mere upstart. He was, or was considered to be, the nephew of his [great] uncle. [Besides, he was marked for greatness by] the tame eagle that flew over his head [on a momentous occasion. It would be unkind to conclude that] without this symbolic bird the head of Prince Louis Napoleon [would have had as little on the outside as there was on the inside.]

On the eve of the [First] World War even the career of Napoleon the Third seemed already a fantastic echo of the past. Democracy was firmly established —at least, in Europe, North America and Australia. [Its progress in the] Latin American countries was more instructive [than serious]; it made conquests in Asia; it awakened the people of Africa. The mechanics of constitutionalism seemed to be the only acceptable method for civilized humanity, the only system of government. And since civilization continued to grow and to broaden, the future of democracy seemed unconquerable.

The events in Russia [at the end of that war] delivered the first blow to this historical conception. After eight months of inertia and of democratic chaos, came the dictatorship of the Bolsheviks. But that was after all a mere "episode" of the Revolution, which in itself seemed merely a product of the backwardness of

411

Russia, a reproduction in the twentieth century of those convulsions which England had suffered through in the middle of the seventeenth century and France at
the end of the eighteenth century. Lenin appeared to be a Muscovite Cromwell or
Robespierre. The new phenomena could at least be classified—and there was
consolation in that.

[Then came that] "neurosis of common sense," [as] Schmalhausen [defines]
Fascism, which [was a challenge to the historians.] It was not so easy to find
a historical analogy for Mussolini and eleven years later for Hitler. There
were indistinct mutterings of Caesar and Siegfried—and Al Capone. [But
admittedly they made no sense.] In civilized, democratic countries which had
gone through a prolonged schooling in the representative system, there suddenly rose to power mysterious strangers who in their youth were occupied
with work almost as modest as the work of a David or a Joshua. They had
no feats of military heroism to their credit. They did not proclaim any new
ideas to the world. Behind them did not stand the shadow of a great forebear
in a three-cornered hat. The Roman She-Wolf was not the grandmother
of Mussolini. The swastika is not the family coat-of-arms of Hitler but only
a symbol stolen from the Egyptians and the Indians. Liberal democratic
thought [continued] to stand helpless before the mystery of Fascism. [After
all], neither Mussolini nor Hitler look like geniuses. What then explains their
dizzying success?

[Both leaders of Fascism are representatives of] the petty bourgeoisie,
[which] in this epoch is incapable of contributing either original ideas or creative leadership of its own. Both Hitler and Mussolini have plagiarized and
imitated practically everything and everyone. Mussolini stole from the Bolsheviks and from Gabriele D'Annunzio, and found inspiration in the camp of
big business. Hitler imitated the Bolsheviks and Mussolini. Thus the leaders of
the petty-bourgeoisie, dependent on [the magnates] of capitalism, are typical
second-raters—even as the petty-bourgeoisie itself, whether you view it from
above or from below, invariably assumes a subsidiary role in the class struggle.

The dictatorship of the petty-bourgeoisie was still possible at the end of
the eighteenth century. But it could not maintain itself [for long] even then.
Robespierre was pushed into the abyss from the Right. [The pathetic flounderings
of Kerensky were not entirely due to his personal impotence; even such a
very able and enterprising man as Palchinsky proved utterly helpless. Kerensky
was merely the more fitting representative of this social impotence. Had the
Bolsheviks not seized power, the world would have had a Russian name for
Fascism five years before the March on Rome. Why Russia could not isolate
itself from the profound reaction that swept over post-war Europe in the
early twenties is a subject the author has discussed elsewhere. Suffice it to say
that the coincidence of such dates as the organization of] the first Fascist
ministry under Mussolini on October 30, 1922 in Italy, the coup in Spain of
September 13, 1923, [which placed Primo de Rivera in power, the condemnation of] the Declaration of the 46 Bolsheviks by the joint plenum of the

Central Committee and the Central Control Commission of October 15, 1923 [are not fortuitous. Such signs of the times will bear serious consideration.]

However, within the framework of the historical possibilities [available to him], Mussolini has exhibited great initiative, ability to dodge, tenacity and comprehension. [He is in] the tradition of the long line of Italian improvisers. The gift of improvization is in the very temperament of the nation. Agile and inordinately ambitious, he smashed his socialist career in his greedy quest for success. His anger at the party became a moving force. He created and destroyed theory along his way. He is the very personification of cynical egotism [and of cowardice hiding behind the camouflage of] his braggadocio. Hitler exhibits traits of monomania and messianism. Personal hurt played a tremendous role in his development. He was a declassed petty bourgeois who refused to be a workingman. Normal workers accept their position as normal. But Hitler was a pretentious misfit with a sick psyche. He achieved a vicarious social elevation by execrating Jews and Social-Democrats. He was desperately determined to rise higher. Along his way he created for himself a "theory" full of countless contradictions and mental reservations—a hodge podge of German imperial ambitions and the resentful day dreams of a declassed petty-bourgeois. In attempting to find a historical parallel for Stalin, we have to reject not only Cromwell, Robespierre, Napoleon and Lenin, but even Mussolini and Hitler. [We come] closer to an understanding of Stalin [when we think in terms of] Mustapha Kemal Pasha or perhaps Porfirio Diaz.

At sessions of the Central Committee at which I rose to read a declaration of the Left Opposition, I was constantly interrupted by whistling, shouts, threats, swear words, very much the way I was received ten years earlier, when I rose to read the declaration of the Bolsheviks on the opening day of the Kerensky Pre-Parliament. I remember Voroshilov shouting, "He is bearing himself as he did in the Pre-Parliament!" This was far more apt than the author of the exclamation then realized.

By 1927 the official sessions of the Central Committee became truly disgusting spectacles. No question was discussed on its merits. Everything was decided behind the scenes at a private session with Stalin, who would then strike a political bargain with the Right group—Rykov, Bukharin and Tomsky. There were really at least two official sessions of the Central Committee each time. The line of attack against the Opposition was prearranged and the roles and speeches previously assigned. When the comedy was staged, each time it more closely resembled an obscene and rowdy bar-room burlesque. The tone of that baiting became more unbridled. The more impudent members, the climbers most recently admitted to the Central Committee, exclusively in recognition of their capacity for impudence toward the Opposition, continuously interrupted the speeches of veteran revolutionists with senseless repetitions of baseless accusations, with shouts of unheard of vulgarity and abusiveness. The stage director of all this was Stalin. He walked up and down at the back of the praesidium, looking now and then at those to whom certain speeches were assigned, and made no attempt to hide his approval when the swearing addressed to some Oppositionist assumed an utterly shameless character. It was hard to imagine that we were at a session of the Central Committee of the Bolshevik Party, so low was the tone, so vulgar the participants, and so disgusting the real demoralizer of these foolish people. The habits of the Tiflis streets were transferred to the Central Committee of the Bolshevik Party. Some of us recalled the characterization of Stalin made by one of his old collaborators, Philip Makharadze: "He is simply a—*kinto*!"

At about the same time another old comrade of Stalin's from the Caucasus, Budu Mdivani, told me about a conversation he had with Stalin in the Kremlin. Mdivani was trying to persuade Stalin that it was necessary to reach some sort of agreement with the Opposition: otherwise, the Party would pass from one convulsion to another. Stalin listened in silence with obvious disapproval, walking up and down the room. Then after impressively stalking away to a far corner, he turned, walked in silence toward Mdivani. His muscles tense, rising on tip toes and raising one arm, he stopped short. "They must be crushed," he cried in a dreadful voice. Mdivani said he was simply frightful . . .

According to Besedovsky,

> the murder of the Tsar was Stalin's work. Lenin and Trotsky were in favor of keeping the royal family in Yekaterinburg, while Stalin was afraid that as long as Nicholas II was alive, he would attract the White Guards and the like. On the 12th of July, 1918, Stalin had come to an agreement with Sverdlov. On the 14th of July he initiated Goloshchekin into his plan, and on the 15th of July the latter sent a coded telegram . . . about the intentions of Stalin and Sverdlov to Commissar Beloborodov, who was in charge of guarding the Tsar's family. On the 16th of July Beloborodov telegraphed to Moscow that Yekaterinburg would fall in three days. Goloshchekin saw Sverdlov; Sverdlov saw Stalin. Putting Beloborodov's report in his pocket, Stalin said, "Under no circumstances must the Tsar be surrendered to the White Guards." These words were tantamount to a sentence of death.

My plan: trial—radio—documents.

Undoubtedly characteristic of Stalin is personal, physical cruelty, what is usually called sadism. During confinement in the Baku prison Stalin's cell neighbor was once dreaming of revolution. "Have you a craving for blood?" Stalin, who at that time was still called Koba, asked him unexpectedly. He took out a knife that he had hidden in the leg of his boot, raised high one of the trouser's leg and inflicted a deep gash on himself. "There's blood for you!"—After he had become a Soviet dignitary, he would amuse himself in his country home, by cutting the throats of sheep or pouring kerosene on ant heaps and setting fire to them. Such stories about him, coming from independent observers, are many. But there are few people of such tendencies in the world. Special historical conditions were necessary before these dark instincts of nature found such monstrous developments.

All of his hurts, resentments, bitterness, envy, and attachments he transferred from the small scale of the province to the grand scale of the entire country. He did not forget anything. His memory is above all spiteful. He created his own five-year plan and even ten-year plan of revenge.

(the trials)

The Khevsurs—the custom of the blood feud. If the Khevsur wanted to revenge himself on someone he would throw a dead cat on the grave of his enemy.

"On the grave of the dead," he would say, "lay a dead cat," according to Zinaida Ordzhonikidze.

Stalin's union with Hitler satisfied his sense of revenge. Above all, he wanted to insult the governments of England and France, to avenge the insults to which the Kremlin had been subjected before Chamberlain gave up courting Hitler. He took great personal delight in negotiating secretly with the Nazis while appearing to negotiate openly with the friendly missions of England and France, in deceiving London and Paris, in springing his pact with Hitler as a sudden surprise. He is tragically petty.

If it were possible to cast out the all-powerful and faithless mysticism, the shrill detestation of socialism and of revolution—if, in a manner of speaking, the poem could be secularized—the poem of the Great Inquisitor—the poem of the tragedy of epigonism . . . The idea of degeneration—on another scale; the fifteenth century . . . Dostoyevsky's poem ends with Christ silently kissing the Inquisitor on his lips. The farewell of one of Christianity's bureaucratic epigons. Notwithstanding all his reserve, Lenin would have spit in his eye.

Yaroslavskyism
Old man Soltz—the narrowness of philistinism
Moroz—the Party conscience, only without conscience
Shkiryatov—a crushed, submissive, slightly drunken workingman. Little Shkiryatov would tell Lenin: "Go away, don't bother us, or we'll burn you!"

Alexander and Vladimir—the flower of the Russian intelligentsia. In the person of Alexander the intelligentsia put an end to its tragic past; in the person of Vladimir it laid a bridge to the future.

There are no born leaders, just as there are no born criminals. Madame de

Stael thought that slow but uninterrupted perfectability may be observed in the course of historical development.

It may be said that all of the historical men of genius, all the creators, all the initiators said the essence of what they had to say during the first twenty-five or thirty years of their life. Later came only the development, the deepening and the application. During the first period of Stalin's life we hear nothing but vulgarized reiteration of ready-made formulae.

Stalin was raised to the status of the genius only after the bureaucracy led by its very own General Secretary had utterly wrecked Lenin's entire staff. It is hardly necessary to prove that a man who uttered not a single word on any subject at any time and was automatically raised to the top by his bureaucracy after he had long passed the age of forty cannot be regarded as a genius.

According to Nikolayevsky, Bukharin described Stalin as "apportioner of genius." Apt expression, but only without "genius." I heard it for the first time from Kamenev. He had in mind Stalin's ability to carry out his schemes in driblets, on the installment plan. This possibility presupposes in its turn the presence of a powerful centralized political machine. The task of apportioning consists of gradually insinuating one's way into the machine and then into the public opinion of the country. Accelerate the process and present the change all at once and to its full extent, and it would evoke fright, indignation, resistance.

Of Christ's twelve apostles, Judas alone proved to be a traitor. But if he had acquired power, he would have represented the other eleven apostles as traitors, and also all the lesser apostles, whom Luke numbers as seventy.

On November 19, 1924, in his speech at the Plenum of the Bolshevik Fraction of the Trade Unions, Stalin said:

> After hearing Comrade Trotsky one might think that the Party of the Bolsheviks did nothing else throughout the entire period of preparation from March to October except mark time, corroded by internal contradictions, and hamper Lenin in every way. And if it were not for Comrade Trotsky, the October Revolution might have taken quite another course. It is rather amusing to hear such peculiar speeches about the Party from Comrade Trotsky, who declared in the same foreword to the third volume that: "The basic instrument of the proletarian revolution is the party."

Of course, I had said nothing about the unfitness or worthlessness of the Party and particularly of its Central Committee. I had merely characterized the internal friction. But what really remains mysterious is how a party two-thirds of whose Central Committee was made up of enemies of the people and agents of imperialism could have won. We have not yet heard the explanation of this mystery. Beginning with 1918 the traitors had the preponderant majority in the Politburo and in the Central Committee. In other words, the policy of the Bolshevik Party in the critical years of the Revolution was determined fully and entirely by traitors. Needless to say, Stalin could not have foreseen in 1924 that the logic of his method would lead him to such a tragically monstrous absurdity within [a decade and a half]. What is typical of Stalin is his capacity for blotting out all memory of the past—all except personal grudges, and the insatiable lust for revenge.

Is it possible to draw conclusions about 1924 on the basis of the years 1936-1938, when Stalin had already managed to develop in himself all the attributes of a tyrant? In 1924 he was still only struggling for power. Was Stalin then already capable of such a plot? All the data of his biography compel us to answer that question in the affirmative. From the time of the Tiflis seminary he left a trail of the most malicious suspicions and accusations. Ink and newsprint seemed to him means too insignificant in a political struggle. Only the dead do not awaken. After Zinoviev and Kamenev broke with Stalin in 1925, both of them placed letters in a reliable place:

"If we should perish suddenly, know that this is the work of Stalin's hands."

They advised me to do the very same thing. "You imagine," Kamenev said to me, "that Stalin is preoccupied with how to reply to your arguments. Nothing of the kind. He is figuring how to liquidate you without being punished."

"Do you remember the arrest of Sultan-Galiyev, the former chairman of the Tartar Council of People's Commissars, in 1923?" Kamenev continued. "This was the first arrest of a prominent Party member made upon the initiative of Stalin. Unfortunately Zinoviev and I gave our consent to it. That was Stalin's first taste of blood. As soon as we broke with him, we made up something in the nature of a testament, in which we warned that in the event of our 'accidental' death Stalin was to be held responsible for it. This document is kept in a reliable place. I advise you to do the same thing. You can expect anything from that Asiatic."

Zinoviev added: "He could have put an end to you as far back as 1924, if he had not been afraid of retaliation—of terrorist acts on the part of the youth. That is why Stalin decided to begin by demolishing the Opposition cadres and postponed killing you until he is certain that he could do it with impunity. His hatred of us, especially of Kamenev, is motivated chiefly by the fact that we know too much about him. But he is not yet ready to kill us either." These were not guesses; during the honeymoon months of the triumvirate its members talked quite frankly with each other.

Stalin's uninterrupted success began in 1923, when little by little the conviction grew upon him that the historical process can be flouted. The Moscow trials represent the climax of this policy of deceit and violence. At the same time Stalin began to sense apprehensively that the ground was crumbling and slipping away from under his feet. Every new deception called for a double deception to bolster it; every act of violence broadened the radius of necessary supporting violence. There began a definite period of decline, in the course of which the world was amazed not so much by his force, his will and his implacability as by the low grade of his intellectual resources and political methods.

Stalin's slyness is essentially very crude and designed for primitive minds. If for example we examine the Moscow trials as a whole we shall see that they are amazing for their crudity of conception and execution.

In April, 1925, I was removed from the Post of Commissar of War. My successor, Frunze, was an old revolutionist who had spent many years at hard labor in Siberia. He was not fated to remain long in that post—a mere [seven] months. In November, 1925, he died under the surgeon's knife. During the intervening few months Frunze displayed too much independence in protecting the Army from the supervision of the G.P.U.; that was the very crime for which twelve years later Marshal Tukhachevsky lost his life. Bazhanov has suggested that Frunze was the center of a military conspiracy; that is fantastic nonsense. In Zinoviev's and Kamenev's conflict with Stalin, Frunze was opposed to Stalin. The opposition of the new Commissar of War was full of tremendous risks for the dictator. The mentally limited and submissive Voroshilov seemed to him a much more reliable tool. Rumors spread throughout the Party that Frunze's death took place because it was necessary to Stalin.

On the basis of available data the course of events is reconstructed thus: Frunze suffered from ulcers of the stomach; his personal physicians felt that his heart could not withstand the effects of chloroform; Frunze therefore resolutely rebelled against an operation; Stalin commissioned a physician of the Central Committee, i.e., his trusted agent, to convoke a handpicked concilium, which recommended surgical intervention; the Politburo confirmed the decision; Frunze had to submit, i.e., go and meet his end from narcosis. The circumstances of Frunze's death found distorted reflection in literature [Boris Pilnyak's, "Story of the Unextinguished Moon"]. Stalin immediately confiscated the book and subjected the author to official disfavor. [Pilnyak] later had to repent his "error" in public—and very humbly. Stalin deemed it necessary to follow this up with the publication of documents which indirectly were supposed to establish his innocence. It is hard to say just what the facts are, but the very nature of the suspicion is significant. It shows that by the end of 1925 Stalin's power was already so great that he could rely on a submissive concilium of physicians armed with chloroform and a surgeon's knife. Yet at that time his name was hardly known to one percent of the population.

Bazhanov wrote with reference to my exile to Turkey in February, 1929:

This is only a half measure. I do not recognize my Stalin . . . We have made a certain amount of progress since the days of Caesar Borgia. Then they deftly dropped an active powder into a cup of Falernian wine, or the enemy would die after biting into an apple. Present-day methods of action are inspired by the very latest achievements of science. The culture of Koch bacilli mixed into food and systematically administered will gradually lead to galloping consumption and sudden death . . . It is not clear . . . why Stalin did not follow this method, which is so much a part of his habits and character.

In 1930 when Bazhanov's book appeared this seemed to me merely a literary exercise. After the Moscow trials I took it more seriously. Who had inspired the young man with such speculations? What was the source of it all? Bazhanov had received his training in Stalin's ante-room—there the question of Koch bacilli and Borgia methods of poisoning were evidently under discussion as early as prior to 1926, the year Bazhanov left Stalin's secretariat. Two years later he fled abroad and subsequently became a reactionary émigré.

When Yezhov became chief of the OGPU he changed the toxicological method, of which in all justice Yagoda must be recognized as the originator. But he achieved similar results. At the trial of February,[1] 1938, Yagoda's secretary, Bulanov, was charged among other things with being a poisoner, and he was shot for that. That Bulanov enjoyed Stalin's confidence is evidenced by the fact that he was the man commissioned to escort my wife and me out of our exile in Central Asia to our exile in Turkey. In an effort to save my two former secretaries, Sermuks and Poznansky, I demanded that they be sent out with me. Bulanov, fearing unpleasant publicity at the Turkish border and wishing to arrange everything peacefully, communicated by direct wire with Moscow. A half hour later he brought me the tape of the direct wire on which the Kremlin promised to send Poznansky and Sermuks directly after me. I did not believe it. "You will fool me anyway," I said to Bulanov.
"Then you can call me a scoundrel."
"That is small comfort," I retorted.

Gorky's secretary, Kryuchkov, testified that Yagoda said to him, "It is necessary to lessen Gorky's activity, because he is in the way of the 'big chiefs.' This formula about 'big chiefs' is repeated several times. The reference in court was interpreted as being to Rykov, Bukharin, Kamenev and Zinoviev. But that is a patent absurdity, for at the time these men were Pariahs and victims of OGPU persecution. "Big chiefs" was the pseudonym for the masters of the Kremlin, and above all, Stalin. Let us recall that Gorky died practically on the eve of the Zinoviev trial.

Stalin did not foresee the consequences of the first trial. He hoped that the matter would be limited to the extermination of several of his most hateful enemies—above all, Zinoviev and Kamenev, whose extinction he had been plot-

[1] March 2-13, 1938; see Chronological Guide—C. M.

ting for ten years. But he miscalculated: the bureaucracy became frightened and horrified. For the first time it saw Stalin not as the first among equals but as an Asiatic despot, a tyrant, Genghis-Khan, as Bukharin called him once. Stalin began to fear that he would lose his status as the authority beyond appeal for the old timers of the Soviet bureaucracy. He could not blot out their memories of him, could not subject them to the hypnosis of his self-appointed status as their super-arbiter. Fear and horror grew apace with the number of lives touched, the number of interests threatened. No one of the old timers believed in the accusation. The effect was not what he had expected. He had to go beyond his original intentions.

It was during the preparation of the mass purges of 1936 that Stalin proposed the drafting of a new constitution, "the most democratic in the world." All the Walter Duranties and Louis Fischers sang loud praises to the new era of democracy. The purpose of all this shameless noise-making around the Stalinist constitution was to win the favor of democratic public opinion throughout the world, and then against that auspicious background crush all opposition to Stalin as an agent of Fascism. It is typical of Stalin's intellectual myopia that he was more concerned with personal vengeance than with warding off the menace of Fascism to the Soviet Union and to the workers of the world. While preparing "the most democratic constitution" the bureaucracy was busy with a series of banquets at which a lot was said about "the new and happy life." At each such banquet Stalin was photographed—surrounded by working men and working women, with a laughing child on his lap, and the like. His sick ego had to have this balm. "It's clear," I observed, "that something frightful is being hatched." Other people initiated into the mechanics of the Kremlin were just as apprehensive about Stalin's access of kindness and decency.

A certain type of Moscow correspondent repeats that the Soviet Union emerged from the purges more monolithic than ever. These gentlemen had sung the praises of Stalinist monolithism even before the purges. Yet it is hard to understand how any sound-thinking person can believe that the most important representatives of the government and the party, of the diplomatic corps and the army can be proved to be foreign agents without at the same time being the weather-vanes of profound internal dissatisfaction with a régime. The purges were a manifestation of a serious illness. The removal of the symptoms is hardly a cure. We have a precedent in the autocratic régime of the Tsarist Government, which arrested Minister of War Sukhomilnov during the war on the charge of treason. The allied diplomats observed to Sazonov, "Yours is a strong government, if it dares to arrest its own Minister of War in time of war." As a matter of fact that strong government was then on the verge of collapse. The Soviet Government not only arrested and executed its actual Minister of War, Tukahachevsky, but over and above that it exterminated the entire senior commanding staff of the Army, Navy and the Air Corps. Aided by accommodating foreign correspondents in Moscow, the Stalin propaganda machine has been systematically deceiving public opinion the world over about the actual state of affairs in the Soviet Union. The monolithic Stalinist government is a myth.

With his monstrous trials Stalin proved much more than he wanted; rather, he failed to prove what he set out to prove. He merely disclosed his secret laboratory, he forced 150 people to confess to crimes they never committed. But the totality of these confessions turned into Stalin's own confession.

Within a couple of years Stalin executed all of Voroshilov's deputies and associates, his closest collaborators, his most trusted people. How is this to be understood? Is it possible that Voroshilov began to display signs of independence in his attitude toward Stalin? It is more likely that Voroshilov was pushed by people who were very close to him. The military machine is very exacting and voracious and does not easily endure the limitations imposed upon it by politicians, by civilians. Foreseeing the possibility of conflicts with that powerful machine in the future, Stalin decided to put Voroshilov in his place before he began to get out of hand. Through the OGPU, i.e., through Yezhov, Stalin prepared the extermination of Voroshilov's closest collaborators behind his back and without his knowledge, and at the last moment confronted him with the necessity to choose. Thus trapped by Stalin's apprehensiveness and disloyalty, Voroshilov collaborated tacitly in the extermination of the flower of the commanding staff and ever after was doomed to cut a sorry and impotent figure incapable of ever opposing Stalin. Stalin is a past master of the art of tying a man to him not by winning his admiration but by forcing him into complicity in heinous and unforgivable crimes. Such are the bricks of the pyramid of which Stalin is the peak.

"L'État, c'est moi" [I am the State] is almost a liberal formula by comparison with the actualities of Stalin's totalitarian régime. Louis XIV identified himself only with the State. The Popes of Rome identified themselves with both the State and the Church—but only during the epoch of temporal power. The totalitarian state goes far beyond Caesaro-Papism, for it has encompassed the entire economy of the country as well. Stalin can justly say, unlike the Sun King, "La Société, c'est moi." [I am Society].

APPENDIX: THREE CONCEPTS OF THE
RUSSIAN REVOLUTION

THE Revolution of 1905 came to be not only the "general rehearsal" of 1917 but also the laboratory in which all the fundamental groupings of Russian political life were worked out and all the tendencies and shadings inside Russian Marxism were projected. At the core of the arguments and divergences was, needless to say, the question concerning the historical nature of the Russian Revolution and its future course of development. That conflict of concepts and prognoses has no direct bearing on the biography of Stalin, who did not participate in it in his own right. The few propagandist articles he wrote on that subject are utterly devoid of theoretical interest. Scores of Bolsheviks who plied the pen popularized the same thoughts, and did it considerably better. Any critical exposition of Bolshevism's revolutionary concepts naturally belongs in a biography of Lenin. But theories have their own fate. Although during the period of the First Revolution and subsequently, as late as 1923, at the time when the revolutionary doctrines were elaborated and applied, Stalin had no independent position whatever, a sudden change occurred in 1924, which opened an epoch of bureaucratic reaction and radical transvaluation of the past. The film of the revolution was unwound in reverse order. Old doctrines were subjected either to a new evaluation or a new interpretation. Thus, rather unexpectedly at first glance, attention was focused on the concept of "permanent revolution" as the prime source of all the fallacies of "Trotskyism." For many years to come criticism of that concept formed the main content of all the theoretical—*sit venio verbo*—writings of Stalin and his collaborators. Since on the theoretical plane every bit of "Stalinism" has issued from the criticism of the theory of permanent revolution as it was formulated in 1905, an exposition of that theory, as distinct from the theories of the Mensheviks and the Bolsheviks, clearly belongs in this book, if only as an appendix.

Russia's development is first of all notable for its backwardness. But historical backwardness does not mean a mere retracing of the course of the advanced countries a hundred or two hundred years late. Rather, it gives rise to an utterly different "combined" social formation, in which the most highly developed achievements of capitalist technique and structure are integrated into the social relations of feudal and pre-feudal barbarism, transforming and dominating them, fashioning a unique relationship of classes. The same is true of ideas. Precisely because of its historical tardiness, Russia proved to be the only European country in which Marxism, as a doctrine, and the Social-Democracy, as a party, enjoyed a powerful development even prior to the bourgeois revolution—and naturally so, because the problem of the relation between the struggle for democracy and the struggle for socialism were subjected to the most profound theoretical examination in Russia.

The idealistic democrats—for the most part, the Populists—superstitiously refused to recognize the advancing revolution as a bourgeois revolution. They called it "democratic," attempting to hide under that neutral political label—not only from others, but from themselves as well—its social content. But Plekhanov, the founder of Russian Marxism, in his fight against Populism, showed as far back as the 'eighties of the past century that Russia had no reason whatsoever to rely on preferential ways of development; that, like the "profane" nations, it would have to go through the purgatory of capitalism; and that on this very path it would wrest political freedom, which was indispensable to the proletariat in its continuing fight for socialism. Plekhanov not only segregated the bourgeois revolution, as the immediate task, from the socialist revolution, which he in turn relegated to the vague future, but he foresaw distinct combinations of forces for each of them. The proletariat would secure political freedom jointly with the liberal bourgeoisie; then, after many decades, on a high level of capitalist development, the proletariat would proceed with the socialist revolution in direct conflict against the bourgeoisie.

"To the Russian intellectual . . . ," Lenin wrote toward the end of 1904, "it always seems that to recognize our revolution as bourgeois means to make it colorless, to humiliate it, to vulgarize it. . . . The struggle for political freedom and the democratic republic in bourgeois society is to the proletarian merely one of the necessary stages in the struggle for the social revolution." "The Marxists are thoroughly convinced," he wrote in 1905, "of the bourgeois character of the Russian Revolution. What does that mean? It means that those democratic transformations . . . which became indispensable for Russia, not only do not signify in themselves the undermining of capitalism, the undermining of the domination of the bourgeoisie, but, on the contrary, they will be the first to really clear the ground for a widespread and rapid, a European rather than an Asiatic, development of capitalism; they will be the first to make possible the rule of the bourgeoisie as a class. . . ." "We cannot jump out of the bourgeois-democratic framework of the Russian Revolution," he insisted, "but we can considerably broaden that framework"—that is, create within the bourgeois society more favorable conditions for the further struggle of the proletariat. To that extent Lenin followed in the footsteps of Plekhanov. The bourgeois character of the revolution was the meeting of the crossroads for the two factions of the Russian Social-Democracy.

Under these circumstances it was quite natural that in his propaganda Koba should not have ventured beyond those popular formulae which formed the common heritage of Bolsheviks and Mensheviks. "The Constituent Assembly, elected on the basis of universal, equal, direct and secret suffrage," wrote he in January, 1905, "is what we should now fight for! Only such an assembly will give us a democratic republic, extremely necessary to us in our struggle for socialism." The bourgeois republic as the arena of a prolonged class struggle for the socialist objective—such was the perspective. In 1907, that is, after countless discussions in the foreign and the Petersburg press, and after the earnest verification of theoretical prognoses by the experience of the First Revolution, Stalin wrote: "That our Revolution is bourgeois, that it must end with the demolition of serfdom and not of the capitalist order, that it can be crowned only by a democratic republic—on that, it seems, everybody in our Party is agreed." Stalin was not speaking of what the Revolution was to begin with, but of what it would end with, limiting it beforehand, and rather categorically, to "only a democratic republic." In vain would we seek in his writings of those days for as much as a hint about the perspective of the socialist revolution in connection with the democratic insurrection. Such was to remain his position as late as the beginning of the February Revolution of 1917, until Lenin's very arrival in Petrograd.

For Plekhanov, Axelrod, and the leaders of Menshevism generally, the characterization of the revolution as bourgeois had, above all, the political value of avoiding the premature taunting of the bourgeoisie with the red specter of socialism and thus "frightening it away" into the camp of reaction. "The social relations of Russia have ripened only for a bourgeois revolution," said Axelrod, the chief tactician of Menshevism, at the Unification Congress. "While this general political lawlessness persists, we must not even so much as mention the direct fight of the proletariat against other classes for political power. . . . It is fighting for the conditions of bourgeois development. Objective historical conditions doom our proletariat to an inevitable collaboration with the bourgeoisie in the struggle against our common enemy." The content of the Russian Revolution was thus confined beforehand to changes that were compatible with the interests and the views of the liberal bourgeoisie.

This was the starting point for the fundamental divergence between the two factions. Bolshevism resolutely refused to acknowledge that the Russian bourgeoisie was capable of consummating its own revolution. With immeasurably greater force and consistency than Plekhanov, Lenin advanced the agrarian question as the central problem of the democratic revolution in Russia: "The crux of the Russian Revolution is the agrarian (the land) question. We must make up our minds about the defeat or victory of the revolution . . . on the basis of accounting for the condition of the masses in their struggle for land." At one with Plekhanov, Lenin regarded the peasantry as a petty-bourgeois class and the peasant land program as the program of bourgeois progressivism. "Nationalization is a bourgeois measure," he insisted at the Unification Congress. "It will give impetus to the development of capitalism by intensifying the class struggle, by strengthening the mobilization of land and the investment of capital in agriculture, by lowering the prices on grain." Notwithstanding the admitted bourgeois character of the agrarian revolution, the Russian bourgeoisie was nevertheless hostile to the expropriation of the land owned by the landed gentry, and precisely for that reason strove for a compromise with the monarchy on the basis of a constitution after the Prussian model. To the Plekhanovite idea of union between the proletariat and the liberal bourgeoisie Lenin counterposed the idea of union between the proletariat and the peasantry. He proclaimed the task of the revolutionary collaboration of these two classes to be the establishment of a "democratic dictatorship," as the only means for radically purging Russia of its feudal refuse, creating a free class of farmers and opening the way for the development of capitalism after the American rather than the Prussian model.

The victory of the revolution, he wrote, can be attained "only through dictatorship, because the realization of the transformations immediately and unconditionally necessary for the proletariat and the peasantry will call forth the desperate resistance of the landlords, of the big bourgeoisie and of Tsarism. Without dictatorship it would be impossible to break that resistance, it would be impossible to defeat counter-revolutionary efforts. That would be, needless to say, not a socialist, but a democratic dictatorship. It would not be able to dispose of (without a whole series of intermediary stages in revolutionary development) the foundations of capitalism. At best, it would be able to introduce a radical re-distribution of land ownership for the benefit of the peasantry, carry out a consistent and complete democratization, including a republic; uproot all the oppressive Asiatic characteristics in the life of the factory as well as the village; lay down the beginnings of important improvements in the condition of the workers; raise their standard of living; and finally, last but not least, carry the revolutionary conflagration into Europe."

Lenin's conception represented a tremendous step forward, proceeding, as it did, from the agrarian revolution rather than from constitutional reforms as the central task of the revolution, and indicating the only realistic combination of social forces that could fulfill that task. The weak point of Lenin's concept was its inherently contradictory notion, "the democratic dictatorship of the proletariat and the peasantry." Lenin himself emphasized the basic limitations of that "dictatorship" when he openly called it *bourgeois*. He was thus implying that, for the sake of maintaining unity with the peasantry, the proletariat would be obliged to forego posing the socialist task directly during the impending revolution. But that would have meant the repudiation by the proletariat of its *own* dictatorship. The dictatorship was consequently, in essence, of the peasantry, although with the workers participating. On certain occasions that was precisely how Lenin spoke; for example, at the Stockholm Congress, when he replied to Plekhanov, who had rebelled against the "utopia" of seizing power: "What program are we talking about? About an agrarian program. Who in that program is supposed to seize the government? The revolutionary peasantry. Is Lenin confounding the government of the proletariat with that of the peasantry?" No, he said with reference to himself: Lenin sharply differentiated between the socialist government of the proletariat and the bourgeois-democratic government of the peasantry. "And how is a victorious peasant revolution possible," he exclaimed again, "without seizure of power by the revolutionary peasantry?" In that polemical formulation Lenin very clearly exposed the vulnerability of his position.

The peasantry was dispersed over the surface of an immense country, with cities as points of contact. By itself the peasantry was incapable even of formulating its own interests, for in each region they were differently conceived. Economic contact between provinces was established by the market and by the railroads; but both the market and the railroads were in the city's hands. In trying to break through the confines of the village and pool their interests, the peasantry necessarily succumbed to political dependence on the city. Neither was the peasantry homogeneous in its social relations: its *kulak* stratum naturally strove to entice it to unite with the city bourgeoisie, while the lower strata of the village pulled in the direction of the city workers. Under these circumstances, the peasantry as a whole was utterly incapable of assuming the reins of government.

True, in ancient China revolutions brought the peasantry to power, or rather, the military leaders of peasant insurrections. That led each time to a redivision of the land and the establishment of a new "peasant" dynasty, after which history began all over again: new concentration of lands, a new aristocracy, new usury, new uprisings. So long as the revolution maintained its purely peasant character, society did not emerge from these hopeless rotations. Such was the basis of ancient Asiatic, including ancient Russian, history. In Europe, beginning with the emergence of the Middle Ages, each victorious peasant uprising did not place a peasant government in power but a Leftist burgher party. More precisely, a peasant uprising proved victorious only to the extent that it managed to establish the position of the city population's revolutionary sector. Seizure of power by a revolutionary peasantry was out of the question in twentieth-century bourgeois Russia.

The attitude toward the liberal bourgeoisie thus became the touchstone in the divergence between revolutionists and opportunists among Social-Democrats. How far the Russian Revolution could venture, what character would be assumed by the future provisional revolutionary government, what tasks would confront it, and in what order it would dispose of them—these questions could be correctly posed in all their importance only in reference to the basic character of the proletariat's politics, and that character was determined, above all, by its relation to the liberal bourgeoisie. Plekhanov demonstratively and stubbornly shut his eyes to the fundamental object-lesson of nineteenth-century political history: wherever the proletariat appeared as an independent force, the bourgeoisie shifted to the camp of the counter-revolution. The bolder the struggle of the masses, the quicker the reactionary transformation of liberalism. No one has yet invented a way to paralyze the workings of the law of the class struggle.

"We must prize the support of the non-proletarian parties," Plekhanov was wont to repeat during the years of the First Revolution, "and not drive them away from us by tactless behavior." With such monotonous moralizings the sage of Marxism demonstrated that he was unable to grasp the living dynamics of society. "Tactlessness" might drive away an occasional oversensitive intellectual. But classes and parties are drawn or repelled by their social interests. "It may be safely said," Lenin retorted to Plekhanov, "that the liberals among the landed gentry will forgive you millions of 'tactless' acts, but they will never forgive incitements to take away their land." And not only the landed gentry: the upper crust of the bourgeoisie, bound to the landowners by identity of property interests and even more closely by the banking system, as well as the upper crust of the petty-bourgeoisie and of the intellectuals, materially and morally dependent on the large and middling property owners, dreaded the independent movement of the masses. Yet in order to overthrow Tsarism, it was necessary to arouse scores upon scores of millions of the oppressed for a heroic, self-sacrificing, reckless, supreme revolutionary onslaught. The masses could be aroused to this uprising only under the banner of their own interests; hence, in the spirit of unreconcilable hostility toward the exploiting classes, and first of all, the landlords. The "frightening away" of the oppositional bourgeoisie from the revolutionary peasants and workers was therefore the immanent law of the revolution itself and could not be forestalled by "tactfulness" or diplomacy.

Each new month confirmed Lenin's estimate of liberalism. Notwithstanding the fondest hopes of the Mensheviks, the Kadets not only made no move to lead the "bourgeois" revolution but, on the contrary, more and more found their historic mission in fighting it. After the crushing defeat of the December Insurrection, the liberals, who, thanks to the ephemeral Duma, stepped out before the political footlights, strove with all their might to explain to the monarchy their insufficiently active counter-revolutionary behavior in the autumn of 1905, when the holiest pillars of "culture" were in danger. The leader of the liberals, Miliukov, who carried on *sub rosa* negotiations with the Winter Palace, argued quite properly in the press that by the end of 1905 the Kadets were unable even to appear before the masses. "Those who now blame the [Kadet] party," he wrote, "for not protesting then, by convoking meetings, against the revolutionary illusions of Trotskyism . . . simply do not understand or do not remember the moods then prevalent among the democratic public that attended these meetings." By the "illusions of Trotskyism" the liberal leader meant the independent policy of the proletariat, which attracted to the Soviets the sympathies of the cities' lower classes, soldiers, peasants and of all the oppressed, thus alienating "cultivated" society. The evolution of the Mensheviks developed along parallel lines. Time and again they had to alibi themselves to the liberals for having found themselves in a bloc with Trotsky after October, 1905. The explanations of that talented publicist of the Mensheviks, Martov, came to this—that it was necessary to make concessions to the "revolutionary illusions" of the masses.

In Tiflis political groupings were formed on the same basis of principles as in Petersburg. "The smashing of reaction," wrote the leader of the Caucasian Mensheviks, Jordania, "the winning and attainment of the constitution—will come from the conscious unification and single-minded direction of all the forces of the proletariat and the bourgeoisie . . . True, the peasantry will be drawn into this movement and will invest it with the character of a natural force; nevertheless, it is these two classes that will play the decisive role, while the peasant movement will pour water on their mill." Lenin made sport of Jordania's misgivings that an irreconcilable policy toward the bourgeoisie might doom the workers to helplessness. Jordania "discusses the question of a possible isolation of the proletariat in the democratic insurrection and forgets . . . the peasantry! Of the possible allies of the proletariat, he recognizes and takes delight in the landed gentry of the county councils, but he does not recognize the peasants. And that in the Caucasus!" Lenin's retort, essentially correct, oversimplified the question on one point. Jordania did not "forget" the peasantry, and, as is evident from Lenin's own hint, could not have possibly forgotten it in the Caucasus, where it was then stormily rising under the banner of the Mensheviks. But Jordania saw the peasantry not so much as a political ally as a political battering ram which the bourgeoisie could and should utilize in union with the proletariat. He did not believe that the peasantry could become a leading or even an independent force of the revolution, and in that he was not wrong; but neither did he believe that the proletariat could secure the victory of the peasant uprising in the role of leader—and in that was his fatal error. The Menshevik idea of union between the proletariat and the bourgeoisie actually meant submission of the workers as well as the peasants to the liberals. The reactionary utopianism of that program proceeded from the fact that the far-gone dismemberment of the classes paralyzed the bourgeoisie from the start as a revolutionary factor. In that fundamental question Bolshevism was right: the quest of union with the liberal bourgeoisie was perforce driving the Social-Democracy into the camp opposed to the revolutionary movement of the workers and peasants. In 1905 the Mensheviks merely lacked the courage to draw all the necessary inferences from their theory of "bourgeois" revolution. In 1917, pursuing their ideas to the bitter end, they broke their neck.

On the question of attitude toward the liberals Stalin sided with Lenin during the years of the First Revolution. It must be said that in that period, when it was a question of the oppositionist bourgeoisie, even a majority of the rank and file Mensheviks found themselves closer to Lenin than to Plekhanov. A disdainful attitude toward liberals was a literary tradition of intellectual radicalism. But it would be utterly useless to look for an independent contribution of Koba's on that question, be it an analysis of social relations in the Caucasus or new arguments, or even so much as a new formulation of old arguments. Jordania, leader of the Caucasian Mensheviks, was incomparably more independent of Plekhanov than Stalin was of Lenin. "In vain do the Messieurs Liberals try," wrote Koba after Bloody Sunday, "to save the tottering throne of the Tsar. In vain do they proffer the hand of succor to the Tsar! . . . The agitated masses of people are getting ready for revolution, not for conciliation with the Tsar . . . Yes, gentlemen, vain are your efforts! The Russian Revolution is unavoidable, as unavoidable as the sunrise! Can you stop the rising sun?—that is the question!" and so forth. Koba could not fly higher than that. Two and a half years later, repeating Lenin's words almost literally, he wrote: "The Russian liberal bourgeoisie is anti-revolutionary; it cannot be the propeller, much less the leader, of the revolution; it is the sworn enemy of the revolution; and against it a persistent struggle must be waged." It was on that fundamental issue that Stalin passed through a complete metamorphosis during the ensuing ten years, so that he greeted the February

Revolution of 1917 as a supporter of the bloc with the liberal bourgeoisie, and, in consonance with that, as the herald of fusion with the Mensheviks into one party. Only Lenin, upon arrival from abroad, sharply terminated Stalin's independent policy, which he called a mockery of Marxism.[1]

Populists regarded all workers and peasants as simply "toilers" and "exploited ones," who were equally interested in socialism, while to Marxists a peasant was a petty-bourgeois, capable of becoming a socialist only to the extent that he either materially or spiritually ceased being a peasant. With a sentimentality characteristic of them, Populists saw in that sociological characterization a dire insult to the peasantry. Along that line was fought for two generations the principal battle between the revolutionary tendencies of Russia. In order to understand the subsequent conflict between Stalinism and Trotskyism, it is necessary to emphasize that, in consonance with all Marxist tradition, Lenin never regarded the peasant as a socialist ally of the proletariat; on the contrary, it was the overwhelming preponderance of the peasantry which had led Lenin to conclude that a socialist revolution was impossible in Russia. That idea recurs time and again in all his articles that directly or indirectly touch upon the agrarian question.

"We support the peasant movement," wrote Lenin in September, 1905, "in so far as it is revolutionary and democratic. We are preparing (at once, immediately preparing) to fight against it in so far as it asserts itself as a reactionary anti-proletarian movement. The whole essence of Marxism is in that twofold task . . ." Lenin saw the Western proletariat and to some extent the semi-proletarians of the Russian village as socialist allies, but never the whole of the peasantry. "At first, we support to the very end, with all means, including confiscation," he repeated with persistence typical of him, "the peasant in general against the landed proprietor, but later (and not even later, but at the very same time) we support the proletariat against the peasant in general."

"The peasantry will win in a bourgeois democratic revolution," he wrote in March, 1906, "and thereby will completely exhaust its revolutionism as a peasantry. The proletariat will win in a bourgeois democratic revolution, and thereby will only begin really to unfold its true socialist revolutionism." "The movement of the peasantry," he repeated in May of the same year, "is the movement of another class; it is a struggle not against the foundations of capitalism but for their purging of all the remnants of serfdom." That view may be traced in Lenin from article to article, from year to year, from volume to volume. Expressions and illustrations vary, but the basic thought is unalterable. Nor could it have been otherwise. Had Lenin seen a *socialist* ally in the peasantry, he would not have had the slightest basis for insisting upon the *bourgeois* character of the revolution and limiting it to "the dictatorship of the proletariat and the peasantry," to purely democratic tasks. On the occasions when Lenin accused me of "underestimating" the peasantry, he did not have in mind my failure to recognize the socialist tendencies of the peasantry but rather my failure to realize sufficiently, from Lenin's point of view, the bourgeois-democratic independence of the peasantry, its capacity to create its *own* power and through it impede the establishment of the socialist dictatorship of the proletariat.

The revaluation of that question commenced only during the years of the thermidorian reaction, the beginning of which coincided by and large with Lenin's illness and death. From then on the union of Russian workers and peasants was declared to be in itself sufficient guaranty against the dangers

---

[1] A full account of all this is presented elsewhere in the book.

of restoration and a firm pledge that socialism would be achieved within the borders of the Soviet Union. Having substituted the theory of socialism in a separate country for the theory of international revolution, Stalin began to call the Marxist evaluation of the peasantry "Trotskyism," and moreover not only with reference to the present but retroactively to the entire past.

It is, of course, possible to ask whether the classical Marxist view of the peasantry had not proved erroneous. That theme would lead us far beyond the limits of this appendix. Suffice it to say for the nonce that Marxism never ascribed an absolute and immutable character to its estimation of the peasantry as a non-socialist class. Marx said long ago that the peasant is capable of judgment as well as prejudgment. The very nature of the peasantry is altered under altered conditions. The régime of the dictatorship of the proletariat discovered very great possibilities for influencing the peasantry and for re-educating it. History has not yet plumbed to the bottom the limits of these possibilities. But it is already clear that the growing role of state compulsion in the U.S.S.R., far from refuting, has basically confirmed the very view of the peasantry that distinguished Russian Marxists from Populists. Yet, whatever the situation on that score today, after twenty-odd years of the new régime, the fact remains that prior to the October Revolution, or rather prior to the year 1924, no one in the Marxist camp, and least of all Lenin, had regarded the peasantry as a factor of socialist development. Without the aid of a proletarian revolution in the West, he reiterated time and again, restoration is unavoidable in Russia. He was not mistaken: the Stalinist bureaucracy is nothing else than the first stage of bourgeois restoration.

Such were the divergent positions of the two main factions of the Russian Social-Democracy. But alongside them, as early as the dawn of the First Revolution, a third position was formulated, which met with practically no recognition in those days, but which we must explain—not only because it was confirmed by the events of 1917, but particularly because seven years after the Revolution, after being turned upside down, it began to play an utterly unforeseen role in the political evolution of Stalin and of the entire Soviet bureaucracy.

Early in 1905 I published in Geneva a pamphlet which analyzed the political situation as it existed around the winter of 1904. I came to the conclusion that the independent campaign of liberal petitions and banquets had exhausted its possibilities; that the radical intellectuals, who had shifted their hopes to the liberals, had found themselves in a blind alley together with the latter; that the peasant movement was creating conditions favorable for victory yet incapable of assuring it; that the showdown could be brought about only through an armed insurrection of the proletariat; that the very next stage along that way must be the general strike. This pamphlet called, "Until the Ninth of January," had been written prior to the Bloody Sunday in Petersburg. The powerful wave of strikes which began that day, together with the first armed clashes that supplemented it, was an unequivocal confirmation of the pamphlet's strategic prognosis.

The preface to my work was written by Parvus, a Russian émigré, who had already become by then a prominent German writer. Parvus's was an extraordinarily creative personality, capable of becoming infected with the ideas of others as well as enriching others with his ideas. He lacked the inward balance and application necessary to contribute anything worthy of his talents as a thinker and writer to the labor movement. There is no doubt that he exerted considerable influence on my personal development, especially with respect to the social-revolutionary understanding of our epoch. A few years before our first meeting Parvus passionately defended the idea of a general strike in Germany; but the country was passing through prolonged industrial prosperity, the Social-Democracy was adjusting itself to the Hohenzollern régime, and foreigner's revolutionary propaganda met nothing but ironical indifference. Having read my pamphlet in manuscript, the very next day after the bloody events in Petersburg, Parvus was overwhelmed with the thought of the exceptional role which the proletariat of backward Russia was called upon to play. Several days spent jointly in Munich were filled with conversations that clarified much to both of us and brought us personally close together. The preface Parvus then wrote to the pamphlet entered permanently into the history of the Russian Revolution. In a few pages he shed light on those social peculiarities of backward Russia which, true enough, were already well known, but from which no one before him had drawn all the necessary inferences.

"Political radicalism throughout Western Europe," wrote Parvus, "as everybody knows, depended primarily on the petty bourgeoisie. These were artisans and generally all of that part of the bourgeoisie which was caught up by the industrial development but which at the same time was superseded by the class of capitalists . . . In Russia of the pre-capitalist period cities developed on the Chinese rather than on the European model. These were administrative centers, purely official and bureaucratic in character, devoid of any political significance, while in the economic sense they were trade bazaars for the landlord and peasant milieu of its environs. Their development was still rather inconsiderable, when it was terminated by the capitalist process, which began to establish large cities in its own image, that is, factory towns and centers of world trade . . . That which had hindered the development of petty bourgeois democracy came to benefit the class consciousness of the proletariat in Russia—the weak development of the artisan form of production. The proletariat was immediately concentrated in the factories . . .

"Greater and greater masses of peasants will be drawn into the movement. But all they can do is to aggravate the political anarchy already rampant in the country and thus weaken the government; they cannot become a compact revolutionary army. Hence, as the revolution develops, an ever greater portion of political work will fall to the lot of the proletariat. At the same time its political awareness will be enhanced and its political energy will grow apace . . .

"The Social-Democracy will be confronted with this dilemma: to assume responsibility for the provisional government or to stand aloof from the labor movement. The workers will regard that government as their own, no matter what the attitude of the Social-Democracy . . . In Russia only workers can accomplish a revolutionary insurrection. In Russia the revolutionary provisional government will be a government of the *workers' democracy*. That government will be Social-Democratic, should the Social-Democracy be at the head of the revolutionary movement of the Russian proletariat . . .

"The Social-Democratic provisional government cannot accomplish a socialist insurrection in Russia, but the very process of liquidating the autocracy and establishing a democratic republic will provide it with fertile ground for political activity."

In the heyday of revolutionary events, in the autumn of 1905, I met Parvus again, this time in Petersburg. Remaining organizationally independent of both factions, we jointly edited *Russkoye Slovo*, (The Russian Word), a newspaper for the working class masses, and, in coalition with the Mensheviks, the important political newspaper, *Nachalo* (The Beginning). The theory of permanent revolution was usually associated with the names of "Parvus and Trotsky."

That was only partially correct. Parvus attained revolutionary maturity at the end of the preceding century, when he marched at the head of the forces that fought so-called "Revisionism," i.e., the opportunistic distortions of Marx's theory. But his optimism was undermined by the failure of all his efforts to push the German Social-Democracy in the direction of a more resolute policy. Parvus grew increasingly more reserved about the perspectives of a socialist revolution in the West. At the same time he felt that "the Social-Democratic provisional government cannot accomplish a socialist insurrection in Russia." Hence, his prognosis indicated, instead of the transformation of the democratic into the socialist revolution, merely the establishment in Russia of a régime of workers' democracy, more or less as in Australia, where the first labor government, resting on a farmerist foundation, did not venture beyond the limits of the bourgeois régime.

I did not share that conclusion. Australian democracy, maturing organically on the virgin soil of a new continent, immediately assumed a conservative character and dominated the youthful yet rather privileged proletariat. Russian democracy, on the contrary, could come about only in consequence of a large-scale revolutionary insurrection, the dynamics of which would never permit the labor government to maintain itself within the framework of bourgeois democracy. Our differences of opinion, which began soon after the Revolution of 1905, led to a complete break at the beginning of the war, when Parvus, in whom the skeptic had completely killed the revolutionist, proved to be on the side of German imperialism and subsequently became the counselor and inspirer of the First President of the German Republic, Ebert.

After writing my pamphlet, "Until the Ninth of January," I repeatedly returned to the development and the grounding of the theory of permanent revolution. In view of the significance it subsequently acquired in the intellectual evolution of the hero of this biography, it is necessary to present it here in the form of exact quotations from my works of the years 1905 and 1906.

"The nucleus of population in a contemporary city—at least, in a city of economic and political significance—is the sharply differentiated class of hired labor. It is this class, essentially unknown to the Great French Revolution, which is fated to play the decisive role in our revolution . . . In an economically more backward country the proletariat may come to power sooner than in a country more advanced capitalistically. The conception of a kind of automatic dependence of the proletarian dictatorship on a country's technical forces and means is a prejudice of extremely simplified 'economic' materialism. Such a view has nothing in common with Marxism . . . Notwithstanding the fact that the productive forces of United States industry are ten times greater than ours, the political role of the Russian proletariat, its influence on the politics of its own country and the possibility that it may soon influence world politics are incomparably greater than the role and significance of the American proletariat . . .

"It seems to me that the Russian Revolution will create such conditions that the power may (in the event of victory, *must*) pass into the hands of the proletariat before the politicians of bourgeois liberalism will find it possible fully to unfold their genius for statecraft . . . The Russian bourgeoisie will surrender all the revolutionary positions to the proletariat. It will also have to surrender revolutionary hegemony over the peasantry. The proletariat in power will come to the peasantry as the class liberator . . . The proletariat, leaning on the peasantry, will bring into motion all the forces for raising the cultural level of the village and for developing political consciousness in the peasantry . . .

"But will not perhaps the peasantry itself drive the proletariat away and supersede it? That is impossible. All historic experience repudiates that supposition. It shows that the peasantry is utterly incapable of an *independent* political role . . . From the aforesaid it is clear how I look upon the idea of the 'dictatorship of the proletariat and the peasantry.' The point is not whether I deem it admissible in principle, whether I 'want' or 'do not want' such a form of political co-operation. I deem it unrealizable—at least, in the direct and immediate sense . . ."

The foregoing already shows how incorrect is the assertion that the conception here expounded "jumped over the bourgeois revolution," as has been subsequently reiterated without end. "The struggle for the democratic renovation of Russia . . ." I wrote at the same time, "is in its entirety derived from capitalism, is being conducted by forces formed on the basis of capitalism, and *immediately, in the first place,* is directed against the feudal and vassal obstacles that stand in the way of developing a capitalist society." But the substance of the question was with what forces and by which methods could these obstacles be overcome. "The framework of all the questions of the revolution may be limited by the assertion that our revolution is *bourgeois* in its objective goals and consequently, in all its inevitable results, and it is possible at the same time to close one's eyes to the fact that the principal active force of that bourgeois revolution is the proletariat, which is pushing itself toward power with all the impact of the revolution . . . One may comfort himself with the thought that Russia's social conditions have not yet ripened for a socialist economy—and at the same time overlook the thought that, upon coming to power, the proletariat would inevitably, with all the logic of its situation, push itself toward the management of the economy at the expense of the state . . . Coming into the government not as helpless hostages but as the leading force, the representatives of the proletariat will by virtue of that alone smash the demarcation between the minimal and maximal program i.e., *place collectivism on the order of the day.* At what point in that tendency the proletariat would be stopped will depend on the inter-relation of forces, but certainly not on the initial intentions of the proletariat's party . . .

"But we may already ask ourselves: must the dictatorship of the proletariat inevitably smash itself against the framework of the bourgeois revolution or can it, on the basis of the existing historical situation of the *world* look forward to the perspective of victory, after smashing this limiting framework? . . . One thing may be said with certainty: without the direct governmental support of the European proletariat, the working class of Russia will not be able to maintain itself in power and transform its temporary reign into an enduring socialist dictatorship . . ." But this does not necessarily lead to a pessimistic prognosis: "the political liberation, led by the working class of Russia, will raise the leader to a height unprecedented in history, transmit to him colossal forces and means, and make him the initiator of the world-wide liquidation of capitalism, for which history has created all the objective prerequisites . . ."

As to the extent to which international Social-Democracy will prove capable of fulfilling its revolutionary task, I wrote in 1906: "The European Socialist parties—and in the first place, the mightiest of them, the German party—have developed their conservatism, which grows stronger in proportion to the size of the masses embraced by socialism and the effectiveness of the organization and the discipline of these masses. Because of that, the Social-Democracy, as the organization that embodies the political experience of the proletariat, may at a given moment become the immediate obstacle on the path of an open clash between the workers and the bourgeois reaction . . ." Yet I concluded my analysis by expressing the assurance that "the Eastern revolution will infect the Western proletariat with revolutionary idealism and arouse in it the desire to start talking 'Russian' with its enemy . . ."

To sum up. Populism, like Slavophilism, proceeded from illusions that Russia's course of development would be utterly unique, escaping capitalism and the bourgeois republic. Plekhanov's Marxism concentrated on proving the identity in principle of Russia's historical course with that of the West. The program that grew out of that ignored the very real and far from mystical peculiarities of Russia's social structure and revolutionary development. The Menshevik view of the revolution, purged of its episodic stratifications and individual deviations, was tantamount to the following: the victory of the Russian bourgeois revolution was possible only under the leadership of the liberal bourgeoisie and must put the latter in power. Later the democratic régime would let the Russian proletariat, with incomparably greater success than heretofore, catch up with its elder Western brothers on the road of the struggle for Socialism.

Lenin's perspective may be briefly expressed in the following words: the backward Russian bourgeoisie is incapable of completing its own revolution! The complete victory of the revolution, through the intermediacy of the "democratic dictatorship of the proletariat and the peasantry," would purge the land of medievalism, invest the development of Russian capitalism with American tempo, strengthen the proletariat in city and village and make really possible the struggle for socialism. On the other hand, the victory of the Russian revolution would give tremendous impetus to the socialist revolution in the West, while the latter would not only protect Russia from the dangers of restoration but would also enable the Russian proletariat to come to the conquest of power in a comparatively brief historical period.

The perspective of permanent revolution may be summarized in the following way: the complete victory of the democratic revolution in Russia is conceivable only in the form of the dictatorship of the proletariat, leaning on the peasantry. The dictatorship of the proletariat, which would inevitably place on the order of the day not only democratic but socialistic tasks as well, would at the same time give a powerful impetus to the international socialist revolution. Only the victory of the proletariat in the West could protect Russia from bourgeois restoration and assure it the possibility of rounding out the establishment of socialism.

That compact formula discloses with equal distinctness the similarity of the latter two concepts in their irreconcilable differentiation from the liberal Menshevik perspective as well as their extremely essential distinction from each other on the question of the social character and the tasks of the "dictatorship" which must grow out of the revolution. The not infrequent complaint in the writings of the present Moscow theoreticians that the program of the dictatorship of the proletariat was "premature" in 1905, is beside the point. In an empirical sense the program of the democratic dictatorship of the proletariat and the peasantry proved equally "premature." The unfavorable combination of forces at the time of the First Revolution did not so much preclude the dictatorship of the proletariat as the victory of the revolution in general. Yet all the revolutionary groups were based on the hope of complete victory; the supreme revolutionary struggle would have been impossible without such a hope. The differences of opinion dealt with the 'general perspective of the revolution and the strategy arising from that. The perspective of Menshevism was false to the core: it pointed out the wrong road to the proletariat. The perspective of Bolshevism was not complete: it correctly pointed out the general direction of the struggle, but characterized its stages incorrectly. The insufficiency in the perspective of Bolshevism did not become apparent in 1905 only because the revolution itself did not undergo further development. But then at the beginning of 1917 Lenin was obliged to alter his perspective, in direct conflict with the old cadres of his party.

No political prognosis can pretend to be mathematically exact; suffice it, if it correctly indicates the general line of development and helps to orient the actual course of events, which inevitably bends the main line right and left. In that sense it is impossible not to see that the concept of permanent revolution has completely passed the test of history. During the initial years of the Soviet régime no one denied that; on the contrary, that fact found acknowledgment in a number of official publications. But when the bureaucratic reaction against October opened up in the calmed and cooled upper crust of Soviet society, it was at once directed against the theory which reflected the first proletarian revolution more completely than anything else while at the same time openly exposing its unfinished, limited, and partial character. Thus, by way of repulsion, originated the theory of socialism in a separate country, the basic dogma of Stalinism.

CHRONOLOGICAL GUIDE*

1773-1774

The Pugachov Rebellion in Russia—against serfdom, colonial exploitation, general oppression

1789-1794

The French Revolution

1794

JULY 27—The 9th of Thermidor: reaction against the Revolution in France

1825

DECEMBER 26—The Dekabrist Revolt against tsarism, led by army officers and young noblemen

1847

JUNE 1—The League of the Just reorganized as the Communist League under the influence of Dr. Karl Marx, and its motto "All men are brothers" changed to "Proletarians of all countries, unite!" Utopian socialism becomes "scientific"

1848

JANUARY—The Communist Manifesto, program of the Communist Party, and to this day the basic program of the Marxist movement, written jointly by Karl Marx and Friedrich Engels, completed on the eve of the European revolution of 1848

1852

NOVEMBER 17—The Communist League dissolved at Marx's proposal after being smashed by police persecution

1864

SEPTEMBER 28—The International Working Men's Association, known as the First International, founded in London by Marx and others

1870

MARCH 24—Marx writes, in a proclamation to the Russian Section of the First International: "Your country is also beginning to participate in the general movement of our age."

APRIL 22—Birth of Vladimir Ilyich Ulyanov (Lenin)

SEPTEMBER 1—In letter to Friedrich Sorge, Marx forecasts Russian Revolution of 1917: "What the Prussian donkeys don't see is that the present (Franco-Prussian) war leads just as necessarily to war between Germany and

---

* All dates new style.

435

Russia as the war of 1866 led to war between Prussia and France . . . And this War #2 will act as the wet-nurse of the inevitable revolution in Russia."

1871

MARCH 18-MAY 28—The Paris Commune—the first proletarian government

1872

Actual end of the First International, effected by removal of headquarters to New York City. Last "Congress" held in 1876.

Publication of Russian translation of first volume of Marx's "Capital" (published in German, 1867)

1873

JANUARY 20—Sergei Nechayev (born 1847) condemned by Moscow court to twenty years' hard labor in Siberia but incarcerated in Peter and Paul Fortress where he died of scurvy Nov. 21, 1882. Nechayevism was the *reductio ad absurdum* in deeds of the theories advocated orally and in writing by Michael Bakunin, particularly in his *Catechism of the Revolutionist*—such as "the end justifies the means," "the worse, the better"—which led Marx to dissolve the First International rather than let the movement succumb to "revolutionary" Machiavellism. Nechayev, who resorted to murder, blackmail, betrayal of comrades to the police in his fanatical devotion to revolutionary objectives, was subsequently repudiated even by his teacher, Bakunin

1874

SPRING—The *Khozhdenoye v Narod* (going to the people) movement, chiefly of upper and middle-class intellectuals, finds no response among the peasants and workers for whose benefit it was launched and is savagely suppressed by the tsarist government

AUTUMN—Karl Marx's application for British citizenship refused because he "was not loyal to his king"

1875

Peter Tkachov, in his journal *Nabat* (*The Tocsin*) advocates seizure of the government by revolutionary action, which puts political teeth into *Narodnichestvo* (the Populist movement)

1876

Populists organize as the *Zemlya i Volya* (Land and Freedom) party, adding the fillip of individual terrorism against tsarist bureaucrats to political agitation

1877

FEBRUARY-MARCH—Trial of the Fifty, all Populists, at which the workman Peter Alexeyev delivers the first political speech by a Russian proletarian

1878

JANUARY 24—General Trepov, Governor of Petersburg, shot by the Populist Vera Zasulich, subsequently one of the founders of the Russian Social-Democracy, in protest against his order to whip political prisoners

MARCH 3—Under pressure of public opinion, jury finds Vera Zasulich not guilty; she goes abroad

AUGUST 16—General Mezentsov, Chief of Gendarmes, stabbed by Prince Sergei Mikhailovich Kravchinsky, a Populist, and dies the same day. Kravchinsky immediately writes his pamphlet *Death For Death* in explanation of his act, and refuses to leave Russia until lured abroad by his friends three months later

1879

The Lipetsk and Voronezh Congresses of the *Zemlya i Volya* (Land and Freedom) party. Party splits into a terrorist group—the Executive Committee of the *Narodnaya Volya* (People's Will) party—and a group of agitators led by George Plekhanov, the "father of Russian Marxism"

APRIL 14—The Populist Solovyov tries and fails to kill Tsar Alexander II

NOVEMBER 7—Birth of Lev Davidovich Bronstein (Trotsky)

DECEMBER 21—Birth of Joseph Vissarionovich Djugashvili (Stalin) in Gori, Georgia, the Caucasus; the fourth child of his 21-year-old mother, Ekaterina Georgievna Geladze, wife of Vissarion Ivanovich Djugashvili, shoemaker

1880

FEBRUARY 16—The Populist Stepan Khalturin succeeds in organizing an explosion in the Tsar's Winter Palace

1881

MARCH 13—Tsar Alexander II assassinated by order of the Executive Committee of the People's Will Party. Its leader, Zhelyabov, having been arrested two days before, the order for the assassination is carried out under the leadership of Sophia Perovskaya, the daughter of a general

1882

The Fate of Capitalism in Russia published by the Populist author, V.V. Its thesis is that capitalism was impossible in Russia and therefore a Marxist movement in that country nonsensical

1883

Plekhanov, Zasulich, Paul Axelrod, Leo Deutsch and V. Ignatov organize the Liberation of Labor group and begin publication of the "Library of Contemporary Socialism" in Switzerland for distribution in Russia. Plekhanov criticized the Populists and outlined the principles for the organization of a Social-Democratic Labor Party in Russia in his book *Socialism and the Political Struggle*

1884

The Bulgarian Blagoyev organizes in Petersburg a Social-Democratic circle of college students and a few workingmen

1886

Lenin's older brother, Alexander Ulyanov, helps to organize the Terrorist Group of the People's Will Party, a revival of the organization smashed by the government after the assassination of Tsar Alexander II

1887

MARCH 13—Failure of the attempt of Alexander Ulyanov's Terrorist Group to assassinate Tsar Alexander III on the sixth anniversary of the assassination of Tsar Alexander II

MAY 20—Lenin's brother and hero, Alexander, and his accomplices executed in the Schluesselburg Fortress

DECEMBER 5—Lenin expelled from Kazan University as a student rebel

1889

Founding congress of the Second International in Paris, at which Plekhanov represents the Russian Social-Democracy

1890

Young Stalin matriculates at the Gori Theological School (variant date: 1888); his father dies

1891-1892

Famine in Russia; end of the political passivity of the eighties; revival of the Populist movement; industrial crisis; strikes in Uzovka and Lodz, with mass butchery of strikers

1893

People's Rights Party founded by the veteran Populist Bobrov (Mark Natanson) and the young Populist Victor Chernov (subsequently leading theoretician of the Essar movement, Minister of Agriculture in the Provisional Government under Kerensky, and President of the dispersed Constituent Assembly in 1918)

Lenin argues against the Populists; helps to organize a Social-Democratic circle in Samara; joins the Central Group for Guiding the Labor Movement, in Petersburg

1894

Peter Struve publishes "Critical Notes on the Question of Russia's Economic Development," thus founding the school of Legal Marxism (social-reform capitalism)

Emergence of the Mesame-dasi, a Marxist group, among the intellectuals of the Caucasus, led by Noah Jordania

Stalin is graduated from the Gori school and matriculates at the Tiflis Theological Seminary (variant dates: 1892, 1893)

Lenin publishes his first pamphlet *Who Are the Friends of the People and How They Fight Against the Social-Democrats*, an attack on the Populists; delivers his first "public" lecture, "The Reflection of Marxism in Bourgeois Publications," a criticism of Struve; is active as propagandist in the Petersburg harbor, and business manager of the Central Labor Circle

NOVEMBER 2—Death of Tsar Alexander III

1895

JANUARY 29—Tsar Nicholas II reiterates his predecessor's policy of relentless autocratic rule

APRIL—Butchery of strikers in Yaroslavl and public approval of it by Nicholas II

MAY—Lenin goes abroad to establish contact with Plekhanov's group

SEPTEMBER—Lenin returns to Russia after establishing an organization for efficient smuggling of proscribed publications from abroad; organizes, with several other intellectuals and workingmen, the Petersburg Union of Struggle for the Liberation of the Working Class; lays the organizational groundwork for a new magazine, *Rabocheye Dyelo* (*The Cause of Labor*)

DECEMBER 21—Lenin, and practically entire membership of Union, arrested by police in simultaneous night raids

Stalin's sixteenth birthday

1896

Young Trotsky and another middle-class schoolboy in the Ukraine set out to "find workers" and organize them

Under preliminary arrest in Petersburg, Lenin writes numerous leaflets and pamphlets, including the well-known *On Strikes*, which are smuggled out of prison, a draft program for Russian Social-Democrats, and begins his book *The Development of Capitalism in Russia*

MAY-JUNE—Strike of 30,000 Petersburg textile workers, involving 19 factories; their principal demand is a 10½-hour working day

1897

Lenin, sentenced to three years' exile, travels to his place of banishment, the village Shushinskoye, Yenissei Province, Siberia; there resumes his writing and translates into Russian the Webbs' book, *The Theory and Practice of Trade Unionism*. (Some forty years later the Webbs try to return the compliment by writing two huge volumes, *Soviet Communism, A New Civilization*)

MARCH 29-30—Conference in Kiev of the Kiev, Petersburg and Moscow Social-Democratic organizations, which try, and fail, to organize a nation-wide party

SUMMER—Trotsky helps to organize the South Russian Workers' Union at Nikolayev. Jewish Social-Democrats federate into the Bund

Conference in Zurich, Switzerland, of delegates from Petersburg, Kiev and Wilno organizations with representatives of the Union of Russian Social-Democrats (émigré organization founded in 1895 upon Plekhanov's initiative) discusses plans for a united party

1898

The Marxists in Tiflis, led by Noah Jordania, take over *Kvali* (*The Furrow*), the periodical of the Georgian intellectuals, and recruit a new member, the theology student Joseph Djugashvili (Stalin)

Trotsky arrested after two years' activity as a revolutionary Social-Democrat; shunted from prison to prison, exiled to Siberia

MARCH 13-15—Organization of the Russian Social-Democratic Labor Party at its First Congress in Minsk; Lenin elected in absentio to editorial board of its official organ, *Rabochaya Gazeta* (*The Workers' Gazette*). Congress raided by police who, arresting nearly everyone even remotely conected with it, are satisfied they have nipped the new party in the bud

1899

APRIL—Lenin publishes his first book, *The Development of Capitalism in Russia;* with other orthodox Marxists, under the leadership of Plekhanov, fights Economism (pure and simple Trade-unionism) and Populism; in exile, drafts the Protest of seventeen Social-Democrats against the Economist *Credo* of Eugenia Kuskova

JULY 21—Young Stalin expelled from Tiflis Theological Seminary shortly before graduation (variant date: May 27)

DECEMBER 28—Stalin finds peaceful employment and a home in the Tiflis Geophysical Observatory

1900

FEBRUARY 16—Lenin's Siberian exile ends. He is allowed to return to European Russia but not allowed to reside in Petersburg and several other of the larger cities

FEBRUARY-MARCH—Victor Kurnatovsky, a friend of Lenin, proceeds to Tiflis at the end of his Siberian exile; organizes the first Tiflis Social-Democratic Committee which is soon broken up by the police

FEBRUARY-MAY—His residence officially Pskov, Lenin travels illegally to Petersburg, Moscow, and other important centers, collecting money and mobilizing support for a revival of the *Workers' Gazette* with himself, Martov and Potresov as editors. At a conference in Pskov, Lenin and Potresov are delegated by the Petersburg Social-Democrats to go abroad to re-establish the newspaper in co-operation with Plekhanov's group

MAY DAY—Stalin delivers his first public speech and continues, unmolested by the police, at his job in the Observatory

MAY—Lenin arrested by the police during one of his illegal trips to Petersburg; released after three weeks

JULY-NOVEMBER—Lenin and Potresov go abroad; negotiate with the Plekhanov group, and by autumn reach an agreement for joint publication of a newspaper, each group maintaining its organizational independence. Editorial board to consist of the "oldsters" Plekhanov, Axelrod, Zasulich, and the "youngsters" Lenin, Potresov, Martov, with Lenin's wife, Nadezhda Krupskaya, as secretary of the board. Its name: *Iskra* (*The Spark*); its epigraph: "From the spark the flame will flare," borrowed from a poem on the Dekabrists by Alexander Pushkin; its place of publication, Munich, Bavaria, where twenty-odd years later Nazism would be born. This was to prove the actual beginning of Russian Marxism as an organized political force of national and international significance

DECEMBER—The first issue of *Iskra* appears, with Lenin, assisted by his wife, as the actual manager; a network of Iskrist agents is established throughout Russia; batches of the paper are smuggled into the tsarist empire

1901

MARCH 22—Victor Kurnatovsky and other leading Iskrists of Tiflis arrested during simultaneous raids; Stalin's room at the Observatory searched by the police; Stalin loses his job as a consequence and is forced to "go underground," hiding out in Tiflis

MAY 5—Stalin takes part in a Tiflis street demonstration of 2000, which he helped to organize; demonstration suppressed with bloodshed and many arrests; Stalin flees to Gori

JUNE—Social-Democratic conference in Geneva, Switzerland, works out tentative basis for reunification into a single party and decides to call a congress

OCTOBER 17-19—The congress of Social-Democrats, meeting in Zurich, Switzerland, breaks up with intensified hostilities between the Iskrists and Economists; the Iskrists, outvoted, establish the rival League of the Russian Revolutionary Social-Democracy Abroad, continuing simultaneously their polemics with the Essars and Economists, who had captured *The Cause of Labor*

NOVEMBER 24—Stalin one of 25 delegates to Tiflis conference of Social-Democratic groups, held at Avlabar; conference organizes a new Tiflis Social-Democratic Committee, headed by Dzhibladze, to which Stalin is elected

DECEMBER—Stalin leaves for Batum

1902

JANUARY 12—Stalin and Kandelyaki, at a (Russian) New Year's Eve party, organize the Batum Social-Democratic Committee as a branch of the Tiflis organization; an illegal printshop is established in Stalin's lodgings

APRIL—Underground conference in Bialystok elects an Organizational Committee to prepare the convocation of the Party's Second Congress; police break up both conference and committee

APRIL 18—Stalin arrested for the first time; kept alternately in Batum and Kutais prisons until end of 1903

MAY—Lenin, and the *Iskra* editorial office, move to London

JUNE 14—The editors of *Iskra* and *Zarya* (theoretical journal of the Iskrists, first published in 1901) publish their draft program for the Russian Social-Democratic Labor Party; program officially adopted at the Second Congress the following year

OCTOBER—The Second Bialystok Conference elects a new Organizational Committee, composed entirely of Iskrists

Trotsky arrives in London after his first escape from Siberian exile (having previously joined the Iskra organization at Samara, en route to London); calls on Lenin who examines him on his views and experiences; begins to write for *Iskra*; debates in Whitechapel against the veteran Populist Chaikovsky and the veteran Anarchist Cherkezov in his maiden speech abroad

1903

JANUARY—Rostov the center of a wave of strikes in South Russia

FEBRUARY—Stalin elected member of the Caucasian Federal Committee, in absentio, at First Congress of Caucasian Social-Democrats

MARCH—Strikes in Baku and Batum

SPRING—*Iskra* offices moved to Geneva. Intense activity in Russia and abroad in preparation for the coming congress

JULY—Strikes in Kiev, Odessa, Elizavetgrad

JULY 25—Stalin sentenced to three years' exile in Siberia

JULY 30-AUGUST 23—Second Congress of the Russian Social-Democratic Labor Party (in Brussels and London) ends in split along new lines into Bolshevik and Menshevik factions; elects Central Committee of three Bolsheviks, an editorial board of three instead of six, and establishes a Party Council. Trotsky, beginning as "Lenin's Big Stick," becomes a leading Menshevik.

AUTUMN-WINTER—Strife between Bolsheviks and Mensheviks continues. Lenin resigns from *Iskra* with issue #51. The new *Iskra* (issue #52 on), the émigré League and the Party Council all Menshevik; Central Committee alone remains under Bolshevik control. Trotsky becomes a leading contributor to the Menshevik *Iskra*

NOVEMBER—Stalin begins his journey to Siberia

1904

Mensheviks in full control of Party institutions. Lenin resigns from Central Committee (to which he had been co-opted); wages up-hill fight for a new congress and a new Party régime. Bureau of the Committees of the Majority formed to prepare Third Congress. First issue of Lenin's new periodical *Vperyod* (*Forward*) published; Lenin, Lunacharsky, Vorovsky, editors; Kamenev, Zinoviev among contributors. Leading Bolshevik organizers in Russia at this time include Bogdanov, Litvinov, Gussev, Lyadov, Rykov, Zemlyachka, Kamenev

JANUARY—Stalin arrives at Novaya Uda, Irkutsk Province, to begin three-year term of exile

FEBRUARY 9—Beginning of Russo-Japanese War

FEBRUARY—Stalin makes his first escape, from Siberia to the Caucasus (Batum, Tiflis). Probable time of his marriage to Ekaterina Svanidze, his first wife

SPRING—Stalin in Batum, allegedly "arguing with Mensheviks"

JUNE—Stalin in Baku, his first appearance there

JULY 28—Tsarist Minister Plehve assassinated by the Essar Sazonov

SEPTEMBER—United Front conference in Paris of all Russian anti-Tsarist political parties (with exception of Social-Democrats who refuse to participate) works out common platform

NOVEMBER—Conference of Caucasian Committee in Tiflis favors convocation of Third Congress; joins the All-Russia Bolshevik organization; sends Kamenev on agitational tour. Probable date Stalin joined Bolsheviks in Tiflis

NOVEMBER 2—Second Congress of Union of Liberation (liberals) works out plans to force a Constitution, and a campaign of banquets as a cover for political conferences

NOVEMBER-DECEMBER—Mensheviks urge support of the liberals and their banquets; Trotsky breaks with the Mensheviks and until 1917 belongs to neither faction

DECEMBER—Baku oil strikers supported by Social-Democratic workers' organizations of Balakhna and Bibi-Eibat. Stalin spends ten days in Baku, his second appearance there

1905

The year of the First Russian Revolution

JANUARY 2—The fall of Port Arthur; Japanese winning the war

Conflict between the members of Gapon's workers' organization and the management of the Putilov plant in Petersburg

JANUARY 4—First issue of *Vperyod* (*Forward*) appears in Geneva with Lenin's article, *Concerning Good Demonstrations by the Proletariat and Bad Arguments by Certain Intellectuals*

JANUARY 16—Strike of Putilov workers

JANUARY 19—Gapon writes a petition to the Tsar on behalf of Putilov strikers

JANUARY 22—Bloody Sunday. Gapon leads thousands of Petersburg workers to the gates of Tsar's Winter Palace to petition the Little Father in person; they are met with rifle-fire by the Tsar's guards

FEBRUARY—United Front conference of all anti-Tsarist parties with exception of Social-Democrats

Social-Democratic Central Committee arrested at home of the writer Leonid Andreyev.

Bolshevik Bureau of the Committees of the Majority issue call for Third Party Congress; Menshevik Party Council protests; the new Central Committee (now pro-Bolshevik) endorses the Bolshevik call for Third Congress
Strike movement spreads throughout Russia

FEBRUARY 11—Shidlovsky Commission appointed by the government to investigate the causes for the dissatisfaction of Petersburg workers

FEBRUARY 17—Grand Duke Sergei, Governor-General of Moscow and a leader of reactionaries at the Court, assassinated by the Essar Kalyayev

FEBRUARY 19-22—Pogrom of Armenians in Baku

MARCH—Peasant disturbances spread throughout Russia in spite of ruthless suppression

Bolshevik activities intensified; Bolshevik faction now supported by most of the Social-Democratic Committee

APRIL 25-MAY 10—Third Congress of the Social-Democratic Labor Party—the first constituent congress of the Bolsheviks. Congress abolishes *Iskra* as the central organ; directs establishment of new central organ, *Proletarii (The Proletarian)*, published from May 27 to November 25; abolishes Party Council; vests of all executive authority in Central Committee; changes Paragraph 1 of Party statutes (chief cause of split at Second Congress) to suit Lenin; outlines policy on preparation for insurrection, on provisional government and conditions of Social-Democratic participation, and on dictatorship of the proletariat and peasantry

Mensheviks denounce Third Congress as illegitimate and convoke a Party Conference; Conference elects Organizational Committee to negotiate party unity with Bolsheviks

MAY—Stalin's first pamphlet, *Slightly About Party Differences*, appears

MAY 27—Destruction of Russian Fleet at Tsushima

JUNE —The first Soviet is organized at Ivanovo-Voznesensk in the course of a wide-spread strike. Workers' demonstrations in Lodz, which began immediately after Bloody Sunday, culminate in armed uprising; barricades raised (June 22-24); 2,000 killed

JUNE 12—Stalin makes his first funeral oration at the grave of his friend and mentor, Tsulukidze, who died of tuberculosis

JUNE 26—Barricades raised in Warsaw; general strike in Odessa

JUNE 27—Mutiny on the cruiser *Potemkin*; barricades raised in Odessa

JULY—Soviet organized in Kostroma.

Potemkin mutineers surrender to Rumanians at Constanza.

Lenin's article, *The Paris Commune and the Tasks of the Democratic Dictatorship* is published in *Proletarii* #8; *Two Tactics of the Social-Democracy in the Democratic Revolution*, a pamphlet criticizing Menshevik tactics and insisting on the hegemony of the proletariat in the present revolution, also published; *The Proletariat Fight, The Bourgeois Is Sneaking Its Way to Power,* in *Proletarii* #10, etc. etc.

JULY 19-21—Congress of zemstvo and urban liberal leaders in Moscow

AUGUST 13-14—First (constituent) congress of the All-Russian Peasant Union

AUGUST 19—Tsar's edict in regard to establishment of a purely consultative Duma—the Bulygin Duma—promulgated; no representation for workers and inadequate representation for peasants; edict arouses a storm of protest

SEPTEMBER 5—Peace concluded between Russia and Japan at Portsmouth, New Hampshire, through intervention of President Theodore Roosevelt. Cost of war: 400,000 Russians killed and wounded; one and a half billion gold roubles; destruction of practically entire Russian Navy; loss of best part of Sakhalin, etc.

AUGUST-SEPTEMBER—Lenin, from exile in Switzerland, advocates boycott of Bulygin Duma, arming of workers, insurrection. Protests against too conciliatory policy of Krassin and Bogdanov, members of the Central Committee elected at the Third Congress, in their negotiations for Party unity with

Menshevik Organization Committee, and insists on full recognition by Mensheviks of legitimacy of Third Congress, fusion without preliminary factional congresses, etc.

OCTOBER 3-10—Lenin agrees to fusion with Mensheviks either on basis outlined by Third Congress or on basis to be worked out by a Unifying Fourth Congress, to be convoked jointly. As a result, United Central Committee established by co-opting several Mensheviks; Committee takes charge of preparations for the Fourth Congress

OCTOBER 19-20—On the initiative of the Menshevik-led All-Russian Railways Union, All-Russian Political Strike begun

OCTOBER 20—Moscow-Kazan Railway strike

OCTOBER 21—Strike of all Moscow railways; general strike in Moscow initiated by Bolshevik-led Printers' Union (on strike since Oct. 1)

OCTOBER 25—All railways throughout empire (except Finland) on strike; general strikes in Petersburg, Poltava, Kursk, Saratov, Moscow, and many other places

OCTOBER 25-31—First and constituent congress of the Constitutional Democratic Party (the Kadets) which, although composed of conservative landowners, business and professional men, is regarded as subversive by Tsarist reactionaries. Right Wing favors a constitutional monarchy; Left Wing, a republic

OCTOBER 26—Morning: elections to the Petersburg Soviet of Workers' Deputies held throughout the city's factories, shops, etc. Evening: first meeting of the Petersburg Soviet, which takes charge of the General Strike throughout Russia; the Menshevik S. Zborovsky its first president

OCTOBER 30—Tsar publishes his *Manifesto of the Seventeenth of October*; appoints Count Sergei Witte Prime Minister

The *Izvestiya* (*News*) of the Soviet of Workers' Deputies, under management of Executive Committee member A. A. Simanovsky, assisted by members of the Printers' Union, begins publication

President Zborovsky arrested. The non-partisan but Menshevik sympathizer Khrustalyov (alias of George Nosar, a Petersburg lawyer) elected to succeed him. Trotsky, alias Yanovsky, a leading member of Executive Committee

The Petersburg Soviet assumes functions of the national government; its decrees obeyed, the Tsar's often ignored

NOVEMBER—Legal Social-Democratic newspapers: *Novaya Zhizn'* (*New Life*), managed by Krassin and Litvinov, with Lenin as actual editor-in-chief, in Petersburg; *Nachalo* (*The Beginning*), Trotsky and Parvus principal editors, in Petersburg; *Bor'ba* (*The Struggle*), Bolshevik, in Moscow; *The Moscow Gazette*, Menshevik; and others in various cities

Stalin still a member of the Tiflis Social-Democratic Committee, which is preponderantly Menshevik although he is a Bolshevik; editor, until end of Dec., of *The Caucasian Workers' Newssheet*

Trotsky regarded as the actual leader of the Soviet; his contributions welcomed by the Bolshevik *Novaya Zhizn'* as well as by the largely Menshevik *Nachalo*

Wave of pogroms—anti-Semitic, anti-Socialist, anti-labor, anti-intellectual—sweeps over Russia, instigated by the Black Hundreds, a professedly super-patriotic organization actually managed by Tsarist Minister General Trepov

The Bolshevik Nicholas Muralov, zemstvo agronomist and statistician, caught in anti-Semitic pogrom at Podolsk, blazes his way through a Black Hundreds mob, gun in hand, flees to Moscow where he helps prepare December Insurrection

The Soviet decrees the 8-hr. day

Lenin, returning from abroad in middle of Nov., takes charge of the Bolshevik Fighting Committee (for preparation of armed insurrection), changes Bolshevik opposition to Soviet into support of Soviet, campaigns against "party neutrality" of labor organizations, appeals for boycott of Witte Duma, writes daily articles for Moscow as well as Petersburg Bolshevik newspapers

Coalition Council of Fighting Detachments, uniting Bolshevik, Menshevik, Essar, students' and other armed units, organized in Moscow to repel Black Hundreds assaults; by Dec. becomes nucleus of insurrectionary forces

NOVEMBER 2—The Soviet proclaims freedom of the press

NOVEMBER 15-17—The Petersburg Soviet conducts strike of protest against trial of Kronstadt mutineers and rule of martial law in Poland

DECEMBER 9—Arrest of Khrustalyov-Nosar; Trotsky elected President of the Petersburg Soviet

Tsarist government assumes frankly counter-revolutionary policy; liberal bourgeoisie, shocked by developments, conducts negotiations with Prime Minister Witte

DECEMBER 14—Petersburg Soviet issues its Financial Manifesto urging all Russians to refrain from paying taxes, demanding all payments by government institutions be made in gold, warning foreign governments that revolutionists, when in power, will not repay any loans made to tsarist government

DECEMBER 16—Tsarist government arrests entire Petersburg Soviet

Trotsky awaits trial on charges of treason, sedition, incitement to insurrection, etc. in Petersburg Prison of Preliminary Detention (Dec. 16, 1905-Jan. 17, 1907)

DECEMBER 19—The Moscow Soviet, jointly with Social-Democratic and Essar Moscow Committees, announces beginning of General Political Strike as prelude to insurrection. Strike endorsed by conference of railway union delegates then in session in Moscow, and by congress of postal and telegraph workers' unions

DECEMBER 20—100,000 out on strike in Moscow. Krasnoyarsk Soviet begins insurrection with aid of troops of Railway Battalion; proclaims the Krasnoyarsk Republic which lasts twenty-three days. Insurrection also in Chita, Kansk, Rostov, Nikolayev, etc.

DECEMBER 20-21—General strike of 90,000 workers in Petersburg, unsupported by railway unions, led by new Executive Committee of Soviet which is now headed by Parvus. Insurrection quickly crushed

DECEMBER 21—150,000 out on strike in Moscow

DECEMBER 22—Armed insurrection in Moscow; insurgents resort to guer-rilla tactics

DECEMBER 24—Publication of Law on elections to the First Duma

DECEMBER 24-30—Stalin attends Bolshevik Conference in Tammerfors, Fin-land, as delegate from the Caucasus; meets Lenin for the first time

DECEMBER 28—Government troops begin to gain upper hand in Moscow insurrection

DECEMBER 30—Moscow insurrection ends

1906

JANUARY—Publication of new call for the Fourth Congress by the United Central Committee of Bolsheviks and Mensheviks

Publication of Stalin's pamphlet, *Two Skirmishes*

JANUARY 10-17—First Congress of Essar Party adopts program, splits into Right (National Socialist) and Left (Maximalist) Wings, decides to boycott Duma elections

JANUARY 24-29—Second Congress of Kadet Party defines its attitude toward monarchy, adopts agrarian program

MARCH—Kadets emerge from Duma elections as strongest party

APRIL 15—Stalin arrested and released in raid on Avlabar printing plant

APRIL 23-MAY 10—Fourth Congress of Social-Democratic Party in Stock-holm, Sweden, withdraws boycott of Duma elections. Stalin a delegate to Stockholm Congress, his first trip abroad

MAY 10—Opening session of First Duma

MAY-JUNE—Lenin returns to Petersburg after Stockholm Congress, writes for newly established legal Bolshevik papers *Forward, The Wave, Echo;* re-sumes polemics with Mensheviks

Stalin, in his pamphlet, *The Current Moment and the Unifying Congress,* and in articles for the Georgian newspaper, *Elva,* writing under the pseudonym J. Besoshvili, restates in Georgian what Lenin writes currently in Russian

Conflict between Government and Duma, particularly over Kadet bill to break up large estates in favor of landless peasants with compensation to landowners

JUNE 29—Social-Democratic Fraction in the Duma (Menshevik) proposes support of Kadet demand for a cabinet responsible to the Duma. Lenin op-poses this policy and agitates against support of Duma and Kadet ministry

JULY—Mutinies in Sveaborg and Kronstadt. Lenin, in contact with organ-izers of both mutinies, attempts to exend movement to Petersburg garrison

JULY 21—Tsar dissolves the First Duma, whereupon Duma deputies, under leadership of Kadets, meet in Vyborg and issue appeal to population of Russia to refuse to pay taxes and serve in army. Central Committee of Essar Party issues a Manifesto to All Russian Peasants, calling for insurrection. Prime Minister Stolypin begins his dictatorship

SEPTEMBER 2—Prime Minister Stolypin introduces summary court-martial to cope with revolutionists

SEPTEMBER 3—First issue of Bolshevik underground newspaper *Proletarii* (*The Proletarian*) appears, with article by Lenin, *About the Boycott*

NOVEMBER—Bolsheviks convoke conference of defense and military organizations of various parties in Helsingfors

NOVEMBER 16-20—First All-Russian Party Conference in Tammerfors decides to convoke Fifth Congress "not later than March 15, 1907;" decides to participate in elections to Second Duma, etc.

NOVEMBER 22—Stolypin introduces his agrarian law, designed to develop a small but influential stratum of prosperous peasants as bulwark of the autocracy

1907

Death of Stalin's wife; Stalin left with two-year old son, Yasha

JANUARY-FEBRUARY—Second Duma election campaign

JANUARY 17-23—Trotsky and fourteen other leaders of the Petersburg Soviet in Petersburg Transfer Prison, on way to life-long exile in Siberia

FEBRUARY 23—Trotsky arrives at Berezov, Siberia, on way to his place of exile at Obdorsk; escapes eight days later

MARCH 5—Opening session of Second Duma

MAY 13-JUNE 1—The Fifth Congress of the Social-Democratic Labor Party (the London Congress)—the last until the Revolution of 1917. Stalin, attending but not active, sees and hears Trotsky for the first time

JUNE—Probable time of possible conference between Lenin and Stalin in Berlin with reference to expropriations

Lenin settles in Kuokalla, Finland; Stalin returns to Tiflis

JUNE 14-16—Prime Minister Stolypin requests Duma to surrender for arrest and trial by the government fifty-five of its members—all the Social-Democratic deputies; Duma refuses; deputies arrested by Stolypin, who also dissolves Duma and promulgates new election law for the Third Duma, in violation of the Constitution. This coup begins the so-called Third of June Régime

JUNE 25—The Tiflis expropriation at Erivan Square, led by Kamo

JULY—Stalin settles in Baku

AUGUST 3-5—The July Party Conference, in Helsingfors, Finland

NOVEMBER 14—Third Duma opens

DECEMBER—Lenin goes abroad; does not return to Russia until 1917

1908

JANUARY-FEBRUARY—Wide-spread strikes in Baku

APRIL 7—Stalin arrested, lodged in Bailov Prison at Baku

AUGUST—Central Committee Plenum: Mensheviks propose reorganization of Central Committee into Information Bureau; Bolsheviks object; Foreign Bureau of the Central Committee established. Period of party splits and polemics

AUTUMN-WINTER—Bolsheviks publish the *Proletarii*, with Lenin, Kamenev, Zinoviev, Dubrovinsky as editors; Mensheviks publish *Golos* (*Voice*) *Sotsial-Demokrata*, with Plekhanov, Axelrod, Martov, Dan, Martynov as editors

SEPTEMBER—Stalin exiled to Solvychegodsk, Vologda, Siberia

Lenin argues against the empiriocriticism of Bogdanov, Bazarov, Lunacharsky; writes *Marxism and Revisionism*

OCTOBER 16—*Pravda: A Workers' Gazette,* founded in Lwow by Ukrainian Socialists; moves to Vienna in Nov. and Trotsky becomes chief editor; henceforth known as Vienna *Pravda*

AUTUMN-WINTER—Crisis in the Essar Party: Evno Azev, head of the Fighting Organization, exposed as police spy

Crisis in the Bolshevik faction: Recallists, led by Volsky, demand recall of Social-Democratic deputies from Duma for not carrying out Party directions; Ultimatists, led by Alexinsky, advocate ultimatum to deputies demanding either that they carry out Party directives or resign from Duma

Rise of Liquidationism, policy advocated by Mensheviks (Martov, Dan, Cherevanin, Martynov, Axelrod) of shifting from underground and conspirative to legal activities—trade union, educational, social, etc.—without regard for party framework

1909

JANUARY 3-9—December Conference of the Social-Democratic Party in Paris rebukes Liquidators, Recallists, Ultimatists

SPRING-SUMMER—Bolsheviks split into two main camps: the Lenin-Zinoviev-Kamenev Group, and the *Vperyod* (Forward) Group (a coalition of the Recallists and Ultimatists) led by Bogdanov, Lunacharsky, Alexinsky, Maxim Gorky. Mensheviks split into two main camps: Partyites, led by Plekhanov, and the Liquidators. Trotsky leads principal non-faction group. Plekhanov and Lenin groups co-operate in fighting Liquidators; consider fusion

JUNE-JULY—Stalin escapes from Siberian exile; returns to Baku as Oganess Vartanovich Totomyants

OCTOBER—Stalin journeys to Tiflis-Petersburg-Tiflis-Baku

1910

JANUARY 15-FEBRUARY 5—The January Plenum of the Central Committee, called to re-establish unity in the Social-Democratic Party. Attended by Lenin, Bogdanov, Martov, Trotsky, Kamenev and fourteen other prominent comrades. Stalin not present

APRIL 5—Stalin arrested in Baku; lodged once more in Bailov Prison

OCTOBER 6—Stalin exiled for third time, again to Solvychegodsk

1911

FEBRUARY 6—Stalin writes letter to Lenin, referring to the factional disputes as "a tempest in a teapot." (Russian date: Jan. 24)

SPRING-SUMMER—Liquidationism among Essars: they renounce the terror, turn to work in trade unions, co-operatives, the Duma

JUNE—Lenin proposes abolishing Foreign Bureau of Central Committee by withdrawing Bolshevik members. During consultation of Central Committee members in Paris, it is decided to reorganize Foreign Bureau and convoke general Party conference to elect a new Central Committee. The Party torn by strife, scattered, leaderless

Stalin elected in absentio to the Organization Committee in Russia of the All-Russian Conference of the Social-Democratic Party

JULY 19—Stalin, his term ended, appropriates passport of fellow-exile in Vologda and returns from Solvychegodsk to Petersburg under alias of Chizhikov

SEPTEMBER 19—Prime Minister Stolypin assassinated by Dmitri Bogrov, *Okhrana* agent

SEPTEMBER 22—Stalin arrested in Petersburg

DECEMBER—Stalin exiled to Vologda, capital of the province

1912

JANUARY 9—Conference of Bolshevik groups abroad

JANUARY 19-30—Prague Conference of Party Activists (All-Bolshevik) proclaims itself legitimate All-Russian Conference of the entire Party, expels Liquidators, decides to take part in Fourth Duma election campaign, elects a Central Committee headed by Lenin, elects Lenin Party Representative at the International Socialist Bureau, elects Lenin, Zinoviev, Kamenev editors of official Party newspaper

FEBRUARY—Stalin co-opted into Central Committee after his candidacy, proposed by Lenin, was rejected at the Prague Conference

MARCH—Conference of Social-Democratic Oppositionists in Paris (Plekhanov Partyites, Vperedovists, Trotskyists, Bundists, delegates of the *Sotsial-Demokrat* group) repudiates the Prague Conference as illegitimate, its decisions as not valid, its Central Committee members as usurpers; elects Organization Committee to convoke all-inclusive conference

MARCH 6—Ordzhonikidze, elected to Central Committee at Prague Conference, informs Stalin at Vologda of his co-optation. Stalin decides to escape

MARCH 12—Stalin escapes from Vologda, proceeds first to Baku, then to Petersburg where he reports to Russian Bureau of the Central Committee

MARCH-APRIL—Stalin helps Poletayev and others in Petersburg to organize new legal newspaper, *Pravda*

APRIL 18—Workers of Lena Gold Mines shot by soldiers in cold blood; action initiates wave of political strikes in protest

MAY 5—Stalin arrested day first issue of *Pravda* appears (Russian date: Apr. 22), betrayed by stoolpigeon in Bolshevik Petersburg organization

JUNE 22—Third Duma ends

JULY—Lenin moves Bolshevik Headquarters from Paris to Cracow

JULY 14—Stalin begins his fifth exile, in Narym Territory

JULY-OCTOBER—Fourth Duma election campaign

AUGUST—Conference of what was subsequently termed the August Bloc, in Vienna (Trotskyists, Vperedovists, various Menshevik factions) attempts to unite Party. Bolsheviks repudiate its efforts

SEPTEMBER 14—Stalin escapes from Siberian exile (his fourth escape) and arrives in Petersburg under the pseudonym Vassilyev

NOVEMBER-DECEMBER—Stalin goes to Cracow for special instructions in regard to policy of Bolshevik deputies elected to the Duma, conduct of *Pravda*, etc., and returns to Petersburg

NOVEMBER 28—Opening of Fourth Duma. Social-Democratic deputation consists of seven Mensheviks, led by Chkheidze and Skobelev, and six Bolsheviks, led by Malinovsky, a secret police agent

DECEMBER—Trotsky's Vienna *Pravda* ceases publication

1913

JANUARY 10-14—Stalin attends February Conference in Cracow at Lenin's request. Other conferees: Lenin, Zinoviev, Kamenev, Krupskaya, Malinovsky, Badayev, Lobov, Troyanovsky, Rozmirovich, Medvedev, Petrovsky

JANUARY-FEBRUARY—Stalin, in Cracow and Vienna, writes his dissertation on the problem of minor nationalities under Lenin's supervision, aided in his research by Bukharin and Troyanovsky. Meets Trotsky briefly

MARCH 7—Stalin arrested (for the last time) shortly after his return to Petersburg

JULY—Stalin exiled for the sixth time, to the Arctic Circle: Turukhan Territory—Kostino, Kureika, with occasional visits to Monastyrskoye

AUGUST 8-9—Poronino Conference in Galicia, attended by Lenin, Zinoviev, Kamenev, Malinovsky, Krupskaya

SEPTEMBER—Bolshevik Duma deputies (Malinovsky, Muranov, Badayev, Shagov, Samoilov, Petrovsky) report to Lenin at Poronino for instructions

SEPTEMBER 7—First issue of Bolshevik Moscow newspaper, *Nash Put'* (*Our Road*) appears; last issue, Sept. 25

SEPTEMBER-OCTOBER—The "Ritual Murder" trial of Meyer Beyliss in Kiev, most famous anti-Semitic case since Dreyfuss Affair, stirs liberals and socialists

OCTOBER 8-14—The August Conference, also known as the Summer Conference, held in Bialy Dunajec, a village near Poronino, to discuss Duma policy, self-determination of nations, growth of current strike movement, underground organizations, tasks of current agitation, policy toward Essars, coming International congress. Conferees: Lenin, Zinoviev, Kamenev, Krupskaya, Troyanovsky, the six Duma deputies, representatives of the Polish Social-Democrats

1914

JANUARY—Increasing discontent throughout Russia evidenced by political strikes, demonstrations, clashes with police, etc.

International Socialist Bureau weighs problem of reuniting Bolsheviks and Mensheviks

FEBRUARY—Kamenev sent to Russia to manage Bolshevik deputies in the Duma and supervise *Pravda*

SUMMER—Strikes in Moscow, Ivanovo-Voznesensk, Baku, Petersburg, elsewhere

JULY 1—Unification Conference of Bolsheviks and Mensheviks held in Brussels under aegis of International Socialist Bureau

JULY 21—*Pravda* suppressed by the government

AUGUST—Advent of the World War wipes out all previous factional differences and divides Russian Social-Democrats into two new groups: Defensists, led by Plekhanov, Alexinsky, Chkheidze; and Defeatists, led by Lenin, Zinoviev, Trotsky, Martov. Menshevik deputies in the Duma, led by Chkheidze, become "social-patriots," but Martov and other leading Mensheviks become internationalists. Alexinsky, Bolshevik deputy in the Second Duma and leader of Ultimatists, becomes a rabid chauvinist, and after 1917 a monarchist

SEPTEMBER 14—First appearance of *Golos* (*The Voice*), internationalist newspaper published in Paris

OCTOBER 13-14—First Finnish Conference of Bolshevik Duma Deputies and Party workers: Kamenev and five Duma deputies (Malinovsky having resigned)

NOVEMBER 16-17—Second Conference of Bolshevik Defeatists in Finland

NOVEMBER 18—Conferees arrested, the government ignoring parliamentary immunity of Bolshevik deputies and arresting them along with Kamenev

DECEMBER—Vera Schweitzer (wife of Suren Spandaryan) in exile in Turukhan Territory, receives at Krasnoyarsk copy of Lenin's *Theses on War* which she takes to her husband in Monastyrskoye. Finds Stalin there, visiting Spandaryan. Lenin's main theses: (1) war on war; (2) turning imperialist war into civil war; (3) defeat of tsarist government as least evil under any conditions. Same theses transmitted by Lenin to Conference of Italian and Swiss Socialists at Lugano, Oct. 10

1915

FEBRUARY 4—*Nashe Slovo* (*Our Word*), internationalist newspaper edited in Paris by Trotsky and others, replaces *Golos*, suppressed by French government

FEBRUARY 26—Trial of Kamenev and Bolshevik deputies; sentence: exile to eastern Siberia

FEBRUARY 27—London Conference of Socialists of Allied Countries; Litvinov, in the name of the Central Committee of the Russian Social-Democratic Party and on instructions from Lenin, urges break with own bourgeois imperialist governments and fraternal co-operation with Social-Democrats of Germany and Austria-Hungary

MARCH—*Zhizn'* (*Life*), periodical of Essar Internationalists, begins publication in Geneva

MARCH 2-15—Berne Conference of Bolshevik Sections Abroad, attended by Lenin, Zinoviev, Krupskaya, Troyanovsky, Rozmirovich, Bukharin, and seven representatives of Swiss sections, discusses anti-war agitation

APRIL 2-4—Second Berne Conference discusses anti-war agitation, necessity of creating Third International (Second International having turned chauvinist and failed), etc.

SUMMER—Kamenev and Duma deputies arrive in Turukhansk. Discussion of their behavior at trial, sharply condemned by Spandaryan, leads to resolution of qualified approval by fellow-exiles, including Stalin. Lenin, like Spandaryan, considered Kamenev's behavior unworthy of a Bolshevik and Internationalist

JULY 24—Berne Preliminary Conference of representatives of various European Socialist parties

SEPTEMBER 18-21—Zimmerwald Conference of various European Socialist parties; Angelica Balabanoff, Robert Grimm and others elected to Internationalist Socialist Committee; anti-war Zimmerwald Manifesto issued, signed by Lenin (Bolshevik), Axelrod (Menshevik), Bobrov (Essar) for the Russians

1916

Fight between Defensists and Defeatists

FEBRUARY 18-21—Berne Conference; reports by Socialists of various countries on their efforts to stop the war

MAY 6-12—Kienthal Conference; International Left Opposition, headed by Lenin, Luxemburg, Radek, propose extreme measures to stop the war: general strike, sabotage, insurrection. Bureau of the Zimmerwald Left (Lenin & Co.) advocates turning imperialist war into civil war in all countries

DECEMBER—Stalin called to Krasnoyarsk to report for military service; rejected as physically unfit; settles in Achinsk

DECEMBER 15—Assassination of Rasputin. Country in turmoil; its economy disorganized; strikes; repressive measures

1917

Year of the February and October Revolutions

JANUARY-FEBRUARY—Complete disorganization of governmental machinery; negotiations between Bloc of Progressives in the Duma and Allied diplomats in regard to removal of Nicholas II and institution of a constitutional monarchy; schemes for a Court revolution at the Imperial Court. Strikes and riots in workers' districts of Petrograd. Government's arrest of labor representatives on Central War Industries Board adds fuel to the fire

MARCH 8—The February Revolution begins; housewives riot in the food queues; Bolshevik workers, veterans of 1905, take charge, organize the mobs into demonstrations; International Women's Day celebrated; Petrograd workers, led by Bolshevik rank-and-filers and other Socialist militants, go out on mass strikes

MARCH 10—General strike in Petrograd; mass arrests; street battles

MARCH 11—Fourth Duma dissolved by the Tsar; deputies remain in Petrograd to organize a provisional government

MARCH 12—Petrograd Soviet of Workers' Deputies organized; Provisional Committee of the Duma organized

MARCH 13—*Izvestiya (News)* of the Petrograd Soviet revived; Tsar's ministers arrested; Schluesselburg Fortress stormed and captured

MARCH 14—Moscow Soviet organized. Petrograd Soviet expands into Soviet of Workers' and Soldiers' Deputies, swelled by deputations from mutinous regiments (mutinies begun two days before when soldiers refused to fire on workers and other demonstrators); the Petrograd Soviet issues Order #1 to the Army

MARCH 15—Provisional Committee of the Duma announces formation of Provisional Government: Prince Lvov, Prime Minister; Professor Paul Miliukov (leader of Kadet Party), Minister of Foreign Affairs; Alexander Kerensky (lawyer, obtsreperous Laborite deputy in the Duma), Minister of Justice

Nicholas II abdicates in favor of his brother Michael

MARCH 16—Grand Duke Michael abdicates, pending final determination of the nature of the Russian Government by the Constituent Assembly, to be convoked in the indefinite future

MARCH 18—Publication of *Pravda* resumed in Petrograd under management of Bolshevik Center members Zalutsky, Shlyapnikov, Molotov

Authority in Russia now divided between the Provisional Government, whose authority is largely nominal, and the Petrograd Soviet. Actually, only the qualified support of the Soviet, run by Mensheviks and Essars, enables the government to function at all

The Bolshevik Center (also known as the Russian Bureau of the Central Committee of the Social-Democratic Party) adopts resolution characterizing the Provisional Government as counter-revolutionary and advocating policy of steering toward a democratic dictatorship of the proletariat and the peasantry

MARCH 19—The Provisional Government declares amnesty for all political prisoners, thus recognizing an accomplished fact, for criminals as well as politicals are already streaming out of the prisons

MARCH 25—Stalin arrives in Petrograd with Kamenev and Duma deputy Muranov. The three take over conduct of *Pravda* and introduce a more conciliatory tone toward the Provisional Government

MARCH 27—Stalin's first article since his return from exile appears in *Pravda* (#8), *About the Soviet of Workers' and Soldiers' Deputies*

The Soviet Executive Committee issues a *Manifesto to the Peoples of the World*

MARCH 28—Stalin publishes article in *Pravda* in support of the *Manifesto*; Kamenev publishes article in *Pravda* in support of the Provisional Government

MARCH 29—Stalin's article, *On the War,* appears in *Pravda* (#10)

MARCH 31—Stalin's article, *Conditions for the Victory of the Russian Revolution,* appears in *Pravda* (#12)

APRIL 5—Funeral of the "Martyrs of the Revolution"

APRIL 10—At the All-Russian Conference of Bolsheviks, Stalin reads the key political report, on the official Bolshevik policy in regard to the Provisional Government; a policy of conditional support

APRIL 11—All-Russian Conference of Soviets

APRIL 16—Lenin, Zinoviev, Sokolnikov, Krupskaya and others arrive at Byelo-Ostrov after crossing Germany in a "sealed" train; Lenin immediately chides Kamenev, leader of the welcoming delegation, for the wrong policy of *Pravda*; at Bolshevik headquarters in Petrograd Lenin releases his "thunderbolts" against the non-Bolshevism of the Bolshevik leaders, including Stalin and Kamenev

APRIL 17—Lenin delivers his April Theses; at the same conference, Stalin delivers report advocating friendly division of functions between the Provisional Government and the Soviets, a policy directly opposed in spirit to Lenin's

MAY 1—The first free May Day in Russia

Miliukov's Note to the Allies promises prosecution of war to a victorious end on the old terms

MAY 3—Beginning of the April Days, with armed demonstration of protest against Miliukov's Note

MAY 7-12—All-Russian Conference of the Bolsheviks (the April Conference) elects a Central Committee, declares for peace without annexations or indemnities, supports fraternization at the front, advocates organized seizure of land by peasants, etc. Stalin elected a member of Central Committee for the first time (had previously been co-opted)

MAY 14—Petrograd Soviet votes for a coalition government

MAY 15—Miliukov resigns from Provisional Government

MAY 17—Trotsky arrives in Petrograd from a Canadian concentration camp; is met by cheering crowds at railway station; delivers sensational speech before Soviet in line with Lenin's policies

Lenin, in Open Letter to First All-Russian Congress of Peasant Deputies, advocates ruthless war with the "imperialist bourgeoisie" and the "Social-compromisers" (Mensheviks, Essars)

MAY 18—Coalition government organized with Kerensky as Minister of War

JUNE 7—All-Russian Congress of Essar Party, the most popular party among all classes of Russians between April and September

JUNE 16—First All-Russian Congress of Soviets, Essar-Menshevik majority; Sverdlov and Stalin direct caucus of Bolshevik Faction.

JUNE 29—Kerensky orders offensive at the front; Russia torn between patriotic fervor and determined opposition to war

JULY 1—Essar-Menshevik organized demonstration turns into Bolshevik demonstration; beginning of Bolshevik preponderance in Petrograd

JULY 2—Portraits of Kerensky displayed in patriotic demonstration

JULY 17-19—The "July Days;" abortive mass insurrection in Petrograd. Stalin delegated by Bolshevik Central Committee to prevent sailors in Peter and Paul Fortress from participating in insurrection. Lenin, Trotsky, other leading Bolsheviks, accused of being "German agents" by Provisional Government; Stalin, not so charged, most insistent Lenin and Zinoviev, the principal accused, should not face charge in open court and undertakes to hide them from authorities. Prince Lvov's government collapses

JULY 19—Offensive ordered by Kerensky collapses; German Army smashes through Russian lines at Tarnopol, Kalushch (Galicia)

JULY 20—Salvation of Revolution Government formed with Kerensky as Prime Minister

JULY 24—Stalin and Alliluyev transfer Lenin and Zinoviev to more secure hiding place, Sestroretsk; Stalin becomes important link between Lenin and Central Committee

JULY 29—Stalin succeeds Zinoviev as reporter at conference of Petrograd Bolsheviks

Kornilov replaces Brussilov as Commander-in-Chief of Russian Army

AUGUST 5—Trotsky, Kamenev, Lunacharsky, other leading Bolsheviks arrested; order for Lenin's arrest issued; *Pravda* offices raided, wrecked

AUGUST 8-16—Sixth Congress of the Russian Social-Democratic Labor Party (first since the London Congress of 1907), all-Bolshevik in complexion, the Inter-Districters *(Mezhraiontsy)* and other groups relinquishing their factional status and merging unconditionally; Stalin, Bukharin, Sverdlov and other Bolsheviks not yet wanted by police the leading figures. Congress elects what is later known as "October Central Committee"—many members necessarily in absentio—and endorses policy of the April Conference. Bolsheviks steering toward new revolution

AUGUST 17—Kamenev liberated from prison

AUGUST 25-27—State Conference in Moscow hails Kornilov, provokes general strike in Moscow

AUGUST 31—Germans break through northern front; Riga falls

SEPTEMBER 1—Stalin moves into home of the Alliluyevs at Rozhdestven-skaya #17, Petrograd, "post office" for Lenin's communications with Bolshevik leaders; occupies "best room" where Lenin and Zinoviev hid during July Days, and becomes acquainted with Nadya Alliluyeva, aged sixteen, his future wife

SEPTEMBER 9—Kerensky attempts to remove Kornilov after secretly plotting with him through intermediacy of Savinkov; Kornilov defies Kerensky; marches on Petrograd. United Front of all parties, including Bolsheviks, against Kornilov

SEPTEMBER 14—Kornilov arrested at General Headquarters in Moghilev Bolshevik influence increases, especially in Petrograd; Bolshevik resolution passed for first time by Petrograd Soviet; Bolsheviks generally credited with crushing Kornilov coup

SEPTEMBER 17—Trotsky and other arrested Bolshevik leaders set free on bail

SEPTEMBER 18—Bolshevik resolution carries Moscow Soviet

SEPTEMBER 22—Compromise (Essar-Menshevik) praesidium of Petrograd Soviet resigns; Bolshevik majority dominant

SEPTEMBER 24—Trotsky elected President of Petrograd Soviet, as in 1905, succeeding the Menshevik Chkheidze

SEPTEMBER 27-OCTOBER 4—Democratic Conference in Petrograd; compromise-bourgeois coalition defied by Trotsky as spokesman of Bolsheviks; Conference elects Council of Republic (Pre-Parliament)

OCTOBER 4—Petrograd Soviet issues call for Second All-Russian Congress of Soviets, to meet Nov. 2

OCTOBER 15—Temporary Council of the Russian Republic begins to function

OCTOBER 20—Trotsky leads Bolshevik Fraction out of Council of the Republic; Bolsheviks form bloc with Left Essars

OCTOBER 22—Petrograd Soviet votes to form Military Revolutionary Committee with Trotsky as chairman

OCTOBER 23—Session of Bolshevik Central Committee elects Bureau (which never meets) to lead insurrection; Stalin a member; Central Committee (except Kamenev, Zinoviev) adopts Lenin's resolution citing armed insurrection as immediate task

OCTOBER 26—Soldiers' Section of the Petrograd Soviet votes to transfer all military authority from Headquarters to Military Revolutionary Committee

OCTOBER 29—Session of Bolshevik Central Committee repudiates anti-insurrection stand of Kamenev and Zinoviev; reindorses Lenin's policy

OCTOBER 30—Rumored Bolshevik insurrection; Zinoviev and Kamenev attack Bolshevik policy of insurrection in public press

All-Russian Central Executive Committee (still under Menshevik-Essar influence) postpones meeting of All-Russian Congress of Soviets from Nov. 2 to Nov. 7

NOVEMBER 2—Military Revolutionary Committee begins actual preparations for insurrection

NOVEMBER 4—Review of Soviet forces in Petrograd under guise of huge meetings

NOVEMBER 5—Peter and Paul Fortress, last important obstacle to success of insurrection, declares for Petrograd Soviet

NOVEMBER 6—Provisional Government issues orders for arrest of Military Revolutionary Committee, suppression of Bolshevik papers, replacement of Bolshevik-propagandized troops in Petrograd with loyal troops; Kerensky delivers last speech to Council of the Republic; Lenin comes to Smolny, Bolshevik Headquarters, at night

NOVEMBER 7—October Revolution begins (2 a. m.). Troops of the Military Revolutionary Committee close Council of the Republic (12 noon). Lenin comes out of hiding; appears at session of Petrograd Soviet (3 p. m.); is introduced by Trotsky. Operations against Winter Palace (seat of Provisional Government) begin (9 p. m.). Second All-Russian Congress of Soviets opens (11 p. m.)

NOVEMBER 7-9—Second All-Russian Congress of Soviets, under presidency of Kamenev, adopts Lenin's motions for immediate peace negotiations (Peace Decree), immediate distribution of all lands to tillers of the soil (Land Decree); sets up new government (Council of People's Commissars) "provisionally;" elects Central Executive Committee which holds first session after close of Congress (5 a. m.) with Kamenev, first President of Soviet Republic, presiding

NOVEMBER 8—Winter Palace falls; Provisional Government arrested by Antonov-Ovseyenko of the Military Revolutionary Committee (2 a. m.)

NOVEMBER 9—The first Council of People's Commissars organized: Lenin, Chairman of the Council (prime minister); Trotsky, Foreign Affairs; "J. V. Djugashvili (Stalin) . . . Affairs of the Nationalities," etc.

NOVEMBER 14—Central Committee session considers Essar-Menshevik suggestion for coalition excluding Lenin and Trotsky from the government; rejects Essar-Menshevik condition; forms coalition with Left Essars

NOVEMBER 15—Declaration of the Rights of the Toiling and Exploited People, signed by Lenin and Stalin

NOVEMBER 21—Sverdlov succeeds Kamenev as Chairman of Soviet Central Executive Committee, thus becoming second President of the Soviet Republic; carries on simultaneously as Secretary of Bolshevik Central Committee

NOVEMBER 22-23—Lenin, Stalin at his side, negotiates by direct wire with General Dukhonin, dismisses him, appoints Krylenko Commander-in-Chief in his place

NOVEMBER 23—Decree abolishing ranks, civil service and social gradations

NOVEMBER 27—Decree on Workers' Control

NOVEMBER 30—Trotsky invites Allied missions in Petrograd to participate in forthcoming peace negotiations with Central Powers; receives no reply Stalin begins direct wire negotiations with Ukrainian Rada

DECEMBER 2—Brest-Litovsk negotiations begin. The Joffe delegation

DECEMBER 7—Proclamation of the Council of People's Commissars to the Toiling Moslems of Russia and the East, signed by Lenin and Stalin

DECEMBER 12—Central Committee elects Lenin, Trotsky, Stalin, Sverdlov to bureau of four for problems requiring immediate solution: foreshadow of Politburo

DECEMBER 20—Decree for organization of the Cheka

DECEMBER 21—First meeting of the Cheka collegium—Dzerzhinsky, Peters, Sergo (Ordzhonikidze), Averin, Ksenofontov, Peterson, Yevseyev, Trifonov—limits its duties to "preliminary investigation"

DECEMBER 22-28—Brest-Litovsk Peace Conference. Joffe Delegation

1918

JANUARY 10—Second Brest-Litovsk Peace Conference parleys open. The Trotsky delegation

JANUARY 18-19—The Constituent Assembly meets

JANUARY 21-22—Extraordinary sessions of the Central Committee concerning the Brest-Litovsk parleys; both Lenin's proposal (sign annexationist peace) and Trotsky's (no peace, no war) outvoted in favor of Bukharin's proposal (wage a revolutionary war against the Germans)

JANUARY 23-31—Third Congress of Soviets meets in Petrograd; approves dispersal of Constituent Assembly and constitutes itself the government of Russia by instituting the Congress of Soviets as the highest authority, the Central Executive Committee as its "parliament," and the Council of People's Commissars as its executive organ; acknowledges itself at war with the Ukrainian Rada and the counter-revolutionary forces of Generals Alexeyev, Kaledin, Kornilov (South-east, Don, Kuban)

JANUARY 25—Joint session of Bolshevik and Left Essar Central Committees decides to submit "no war, no peace" policy to Congress of Soviets

FEBRUARY 1—Central Committee approves Trotsky's "no war, no peace" formula

*FEBRUARY 8—New style (Gregorian) calendar adopted

FEBRUARY 9—Central Powers sign separate peace with the Ukrainian Rada

FEBRUARY 10—Trotsky brings Brest-Litovsk Peace Conference to a close: "We are out of the war but we refuse to sign the peace treaty."

FEBRUARY 13—The Homburg Conference—Kaiser Wilhelm II and war lords

FEBRUARY 15—Berlin announces termination of armistice on Feb. 18 but German Army begins to advance at once, and occupies territory relinquished by fleeing Russian Army

* Trotsky follows old style calendar to this date.

FEBRUARY 17—German aeroplanes over Dvinsk, close to Petrograd

FEBRUARY 18—Extraordinary session of Central Committee; at morning session Lenin outvoted by Trotsky and Bukharin supporters; at evening session Lenin's motion for immediate peace adopted after Trotsky swings his support to Lenin

FEBRUARY 19—Petrograd radio broadcast to Berlin announces Soviet readiness to sign a dictated peace under constraint, protests against suspension of armistice; receipt of broadcast acknowledged by General Hoffman but German Army continues its advance

Council of People's Commissars elects executive committee consisting of Lenin, Trotsky, Stalin (Bolsheviks); Proshyan, Karelin (Left Essars)

FEBRUARY 21—Bolshevik government issues orders for holy revolutionary war against "the bourgeoisie and imperialists of Germany," devastating destruction in case of retreat, etc.

FEBRUARY 22—At session of Central Committee, Trotsky proposes asking Allies for aid against Germans and tenders his resignation as Commissar of Foreign Affairs; Lenin, absent, sends note approving "receipt of support and arms from Anglo-French imperialist brigands;" Trotsky's recommendation adopted by a 6 to 5 vote

FEBRUARY 23—New German peace terms, sent by courier from Berlin Feb. 21, received in Petrograd; discussed at session of Central Committee. For immediate acceptance of German terms: Lenin, Zinoviev, Sverdlov, Sokolnikov, Stasova, Smilga, Stalin; against: Bukharin, Uritsky, Bubnov, Lomov; not voting: Trotsky, Dzerzhinsky, Krestinsky, Joffe. Bukharin, Bubnov, Lomov, Yakovleva, Pyatakov, V. M. Smirnov resign in protest from Central Committee; beginning of faction of Left Communists, led by Bukharin

FEBRUARY 28—Arrival of Sokolnikov delegation at Brest-Litovsk

MARCH 3—Signing of Brest-Litovsk Treaty

MARCH 6-8—Seventh Congress of Russian Social-Democratic Labor Party (Bolsheviks) approves Brest-Litovsk Treaty notwithstanding vigorous opposition of Left Communists; renames party Russian Communist Party

MARCH 13-14—Soviet Government and Communist Party Headquarters move to Moscow

MARCH 15-17—Fourth Congress of Soviets in Moscow debates Brest-Litovsk Treaty; vigorous opposition by Left Essars as well as Left Communists. Left Essars resign from coalition with Bolsheviks in Council of People's Commissars; Trotsky becomes Commissar of War; Chicherin, Commissar of Foreign Affairs

APRIL 5—Japanese Army detachments land in Vladivostok, Siberia

APRIL 15—Turks take Batum

APRIL 27—Stalin appointed plenipotentiary for negotiations with Ukrainian Rada

APRIL-MAY—Germans occupy Kharkov, Taganrog, Rostov-on-Don, all of Ukraine, Crimea; dissolve Ukrainian Rada, set up Skoropadsky (Apr. 29)

MAY 10—Stalin begins preparations for Constituent Conference of Tataro-Bashkir Republic

MAY 12—Whites under Mannerheim overthrow Reds in Finland

MAY 25—Czechoslovaks revolt, occupy Central Volga; revolt backed by the French, spreads, cuts off the Trans-Volga, the Urals, Siberia, the Far East, as they capture Novo-Nikolayevsk (May 26), Chelyabink (May 27), Penza (May 29), Omsk (June 7), Samara (June 8), Ufa (July 5), Simbirsk (July 22), Ekaterinburg (July 25), Kazan (August 7), in concert with Whites

Government of the Constituent Assembly establishes its rule in the Urals and Western Siberia

Germans occupy Poti, Georgia, with permission of the Menshevik Government of Georgia

MAY 29—Stalin put in charge of provisioning South Russia, his job to supply Moscow and Petrograd with food

JUNE—Committees of the Poor organized in the villages, campaign to secure peasant support of Soviet government, food supplies, peasant resistance to Whites

JUNE 3—Stalin leaves Moscow for Tsaritsyn with armed guard

JUNE 6—Stalin arrives at Tsaritsyn with detachment of 450 riflemen

JUNE 13—Whites cut off railroad communications from Tsaritsyn to Moscow

JUNE 16—Stalin sends first shipment of provisions to Moscow by water

JUNE 29—Stalin begins active interference in military matters

JULY 1—British and French forces land in Murmansk

JULY 4-10—Fifth Congress of Soviets formally ratifies Brest-Litovsk Treaty, sanctions plan for organizing Red Army (actual organization began Feb. 23). Bitter debates between Left Essars and Bolsheviks over Brest-Litovsk, army, peasantry, etc., lead to complete break

JULY 5—Fifth Congress adopts Constitution of R.S.F.S.R.

JULY 6—German Ambassador Count von Mirbach assassinated by Left Essar Jacob Blumkin in attempt to provoke revolutionary war against imperialist Germany

JULY 6-7—Left Essar insurrection breaks out in Moscow

JULY 6-21—Savinkovist insurrection in Yaroslavl; other insurrections in Murom, Rybinsk, Arzamas

JULY 17—Royal Family executed at Ekaterinburg

JULY 19—Stalin made member of the Council of War of the Tsaritsyn Front, his first official appointment to a military post

JULY 25—Baku Soviet votes (259 ayes to 226 Bolshevik nays) to ask for British troops

AUGUST 1—Allied troops occupy Archangel

AUGUST 13—British, under General Dunsterville, cross from Persia to Baku

AUGUST 14—General Krassnov's Cossacks within 15 kilometers of Tsaritsyn

AUGUST 15—American troops land in Siberia

AUGUST 20—Red troops in Tsaritsyn, under command of Voroshilov, launch counter-offensive against Krassnov's Whites

AUGUST 30—Uritsky assassinated in Petrograd; Lenin wounded during attempted assassination by Fanny Kaplan

AUGUST 31—Beginning of Red Terror: system of hostages, mass executions of individually innocent "class enemies" in reprisal, etc.

SEPTEMBER 2—Soviet Republic proclaimed a single military camp; effort to stamp out local self-rule and centralize military command

SEPTEMBER 10—Kazan retaken by Red Army; Red troops begin to clear Czechoslovaks from Volga territory

SEPTEMBER 11—Southern Front organized by order of Revolutionary Council of War of the Republic with General Sytin in command

SEPTEMBER 12—Stalin leaves Tsaritsyn for trip to Moscow

SEPTEMBER 13—General Dunsterville retires from Baku to Persia, after shooting twenty-six commissars, including Shaumyan, President of the Baku Soviet

SEPTEMBER 17—Stalin reports to Revolutionary Council of War of the Republic in Moscow on situation around Tsaritsyn

SEPTEMBER 22—Stalin arrives in Tsaritsyn

OCTOBER—The Volga cleared by Red troops; Czechs retreat to Urals

OCTOBER 3—Trotsky orders Tsaritsyn commanders to obey orders of their superior, Sytin

OCTOBER 5—Trotsky orders unification of all armies and groups of the Southern Front under command of Sytin, appoints new Council of War for Southern Front, confirms Voroshilov as commander of Tenth Army defending Tsaritsyn with 50,000 troops

Stalin, removed from Council of War of Southern Front, leaves Tsaritsyn for Moscow to talk with Lenin and Sverdlov

OCTOBER 11—Stalin returns to Tsaritsyn

OCTOBER 15—Tsaritsyn again surrounded by Whites; Steel Division reaches Tsaritsyn from North Caucasian Front; saves Tsaritsyn within next couple of days

OCTOBER 18—Stalin recalled from Tsaritsyn by Lenin upon Trotsky's insistence; Stalin stalls and claims credit for victory

OCTOBER 20—Stalin leaves Tsaritsyn in Sverdlov's train

OCTOBER 21—Stalin reports to Trotsky, en route to Tsaritsyn, and asks leniency for Tsaritsyn "boys"

OCTOBER 22—Stalin arrives in Moscow; Trotsky arrives in Tsaritsyn

OCTOBER 29—Stalin speaks before Moscow Soviet on situation at Southern Front; article on same subject in *Pravda,* Oct. 30

OCTOBER 29-NOVEMBER 4—Founding of the Komsomol at its first congress, the Russian Communist Youth Congress

NOVEMBER 5—Trotsky issues special order on Tsaritsyn army

NOVEMBER 6—Stalin publishes anniversary article in *Pravda,* stating Trotsky was directly in charge of October Insurrection and chiefly responsible for its success

NOVEMBER 6-9—Sixth Congress of the Soviets

NOVEMBER 11—Armistice ends hostilities in World War I; end of Hohenzollern rule in Germany

NOVEMBER 13—Soviet Government annuls Brest-Litovsk Treaty

NOVEMBER 22—Allied squadrons enter Black Sea; Winston Churchill promotes intervention and becomes man most hated by Soviet Russia

NOVEMBER 24—The Whites, having secured British support through Winston Churchill, hold Anti-Bolshevik Conference in Jassy, Rumania; proclaim General Denikin dictator of Russia

NOVEMBER 30—Council of Defense organized; includes Lenin, Trotsky, Krassin, Sverdlov, Stalin and others

DECEMBER—German Army begins evacuation of Ukraine; Hetman Skoropadsky's government falls

Coup d'état in Omsk; Kolchak seizes reins of government from Government of the Constituent Assembly (Essar-Menshevik-Liberal) established by Czechoslovaks; Kolchak moves west, threatens Perm

DECEMBER 1—First meeting of Council of Defense

DECEMBER 13—Clemenceau calls for "le cordon sanitaire" around Soviets

DECEMBER 17—French troops land in Odessa

DECEMBER 24—Litvinov appeals to Woodrow Wilson to restore real peace

DECEMBER 26—General Denikin proclaims himself commander-in-chief of all White land and sea forces in South Russia

DECEMBER 31—Lenin considers sending Stalin to Perm

1919

JANUARY 1—Trotsky agrees to sending Stalin to Perm

White Russia becomes a Soviet Republic

JANUARY 2—Soviet troops on Ural Front surrender Perm, retreat to Vyatka

JANUARY 3—Central Committee delegates Stalin and Dzerzhinsky to investigate situation on Ural Front

JANUARY 5—Stalin and Dzerzhinsky arrive in Vyatka; begin purge

JANUARY 10—Lenin conveys to Trotsky Stalin's desire to be transferred to Southern Front and pleads for compromise

JANUARY 11—Trotsky concedes necessity for compromise but points to disruptive tactics of Tsaritsyn "boys" still persisting on Southern Front

JANUARY 15—Stalin and Dzerzhinsky report to Central Committee on situation on Ural Front

JANUARY 20—Probable date of Stalin's appointment to Council of War of Southern Front; he is summarily removed after interfering anew with orders of Commander-in-Chief

FEBRUARY 4—Stalin declines offer of appointment to Council of War of Southwestern Front; remains in Moscow

FEBRUARY 18—Winston Churchill supports Foch's plan for intervention and support of Whites

FEBRUARY-MARCH—Organization of Soviet Ukrainian Government; Stalin in Ukraine at this time

MARCH—Bullitt Mission to Russia

MARCH 2-6—First and founding Congress of Third International, organized and presided over by Lenin; Russian delegates: Lenin, Trotsky, Zinoviev, Bukharin, Stalin; alternates: Osinisky, Vorovsky

MARCH 6—Kolchak advances across the Urals

MARCH 15—Kolchak at gates of Ufa

MARCH 16—Death of Sverdlov. Trotsky leaves for Ufa

MARCH 18-23—Eighth Congress of Communist Party; Sokolnikov reports on military situation; Stalin secret leader of military opposition; Politburo, Orgburo, Secretariat created

MARCH 21—French troops advance on Kherson

MARCH 22—French troops driven back to Odessa

APRIL 2—French ordered to evacuate Odessa in forty-eight hours

APRIL 16—Lloyd George agrees in House of Commons that Kolchak should be supported in operations against Red Army

APRIL 28—Red Army checks Kolchak's advance and begins counter-offensive

MAY—Denikin's Volunteer Army begins offensive in South

MAY 13—Yudenich makes first attempt to capture Petrograd

MAY 15(?)—Stalin sent to Petrograd to aid Zinoviev

MAY 25—Yudenich captures Pskov, Northwest Front

MAY 26—Joint note from Supreme Council of Allies in Paris to Kolchak outlines conditions of support and recognition

MAY 27—Red Army drives Kolchak eastward; captures Sterlitamak

JUNE 4—Kolchak accepts terms of Supreme Council

Stalin in telegram to Lenin makes charges of treason against staff of Revolutionary Council of War of the Republic; charges ignored

JUNE 12—Yudenich driven back from Petrograd

JUNE 13—Winston Churchill undertakes to persuade Finns to join Yudenich, Estonian and British aid having proved fruitless

JUNE 15—Denikin captures Kupyansk, Southern Front

JUNE 16—Red saïlors occupy Krasnaya Gor'ka in Petrograd

JUNE 25—Denikin takes Kharkov

JULY 3—Revolutionary Council of War of the Republic reconstituted; S. S. Kamenev succeeds Vatzetis as Commander-in-Chief

JULY 4—Trotsky disagrees with Kamenev's strategy against Denikin; tenders his resignation as Commissar of War and Navy and as Chairman of Revolutionary Council of War of the Republic

JULY 5—Central Committee resolution (signed by Stalin and others) declines to accept Trotsky's resignation

JULY 8—Trotsky at Southern Front headquarters in Kozlov receives telegram implicating former Commander-in-Chief Vatzetis in anti-Soviet conspiracy; later investigation proves charges false

JULY 27—Trotsky recommends change of commanders at Southern Front since present commander disagrees with Kamenev's strategy; Stalin, a member of Council of War of the Southern Front, approves of Kamenev's plan

AUGUST 10-20—Kamenev's plan, put into operation, begins to show its weaknesses; Mamontov's cavalry breaks through Red lines

SEPTEMBER 4—Denikin enters Kiev, further evidence of failure of Kamenev's plan

SEPTEMBER 6—Trotsky proposes modification of Kamenev's plan; Politburo, including Stalin, disagrees with Trotsky and re-endorses the plan

SEPTEMBER 22—Denikin, marching steadily northward, takes Kursk

SEPTEMBER 25—Moscow Party Headquarters blown up by diversionists in preparation for expected capture of Moscow by Denikin

OCTOBER 1-20—Kamenev's plan modified; strategy on Southern Front altered by Trotsky; Denikin on outskirts of Oryol; Yudenich advancing simultaneously on Petrograd with formidable force. Most critical period of Civil War. Having reorganized Red Army forces on the Southern Front and set new Soviet offensive for Oct. 10, Trotsky leaves for Petrograd and reorganizes defense against Yudenich

OCTOBER 13—Denikin takes Oryol and opens road to Moscow

OCTOBER 15—Central Committee issues thirteen decrees regarding Southern Front, proposed and written by Trotsky

OCTOBER 16—Yudenich takes Gatchina

OCTOBER 20-21—Battle of Pulkovo Heights on outskirts of Petrograd; Red Army under Trotsky's personal command drives Yudenich back

OCTOBER 21—Red Army beats back Denikin in battle on outskirts of Oryol, Southern Front

NOVEMBER 14—Red Army captures Yamburg and Omsk on the Eastern Front; Politburo delegates both Lenin and Trotsky to impress Commander-in-Chief Kamenev with political and economic importance of recapturing Kursk

NOVEMBER 17—Red Army recaptures Kursk

NOVEMBER 27—Order of the Red Banner awarded to Stalin, after similar award was made to Trotsky (variant date: Nov. 20)

NOVEMBER-DECEMBER—Growing disintegration of White Armies of Yudenich, Kolchak, and Denikin under pressure of Red Army offensives

DECEMBER—Final mopping-up operations against Yudenich

DECEMBER 2-4—All-Russian Party Conference

DECEMBER 4—Ivan Smirnov reports from Eastern Front: "Kolchak has lost his army."

DECEMBER 5-9—Seventh Congress of Soviets in Moscow elects new Central Executive Committee; amends constitution

1920

JANUARY—Mopping-up operations against Kolchak in Siberia

JANUARY-FEBRUARY—Trade negotiations with England and France

JANUARY-MARCH—Polish Army, supported by Latvian Army, seizes Dvinsk, Latgalia, Mozyr

FEBRUARY—Mopping-up operations against remnants of Denikin's forces on Southwestern Front

FEBRUARY 2—Peace treaty signed with Estonia

FEBRUARY 3—Lenin and Trotsky ask Stalin, already member of Council of War of Southwestern Front, also to become member of Council of War of Caucasian Front; Stalin declines

FEBRUARY 7—French surrender Kolchak to Red Army; Kolchak summarily executed

FEBRUARY 20—Stalin resents request for dispatch of reinforcements from Southwestern Front to Caucasian Front and is reproved by Lenin

FEBRUARY-MARCH—Denikin reforms White Armies in North Caucasus

MARCH-APRIL—Defeat and final mopping-up of Denikin's forces in Caucasia; Red Army captures Rostov

MARCH 27—Red Army captures Novorossissk, last stronghold of Denikin

MARCH 29-APRIL 4—Ninth Congress of the Communist Party

APRIL 26—Polish Army invades Russia, supported by troops of the defunct Petlura Government

APRIL 28—Azerbaijan proclaimed a Soviet Republic

APRIL-MAY—Baron Wrangel advances from Crimea at head of new White Army

MAY 5—Central Committee orders Ordzhonikidze and entire Council of War of the Caucasian Front to "refrain from aggression into Georgia" in view of pending peace negotiations with Georgian Republic

MAY 7—Soviet Russia signs treaty of friendship with Soviet Georgia

MAY 8—Polish Army captures Kiev

JUNE 13—Polish Army retreats from Kiev; Stalin, on Council of War of Southwestern Front under the command of Yegorov, takes part in offensive operations in southern sector of the front

JUNE-JULY—Main forces of Red Army, under Tukhachevsky, wage rapid offensive on northern sector of Polish Front

JULY 4—Poles retreat to the Bug River

JULY 11—Polish Field Headquarters abandon Minsk

JULY 14—Red Army captures Wilno

JULY 21-AUGUST 6—Second Congress of the Comintern

AUGUST 1—Tukhachevsky's forces take the Brest-Litovsk fortress

AUGUST 11—Tukhachevsky reaches the approaches to Warsaw

AUGUST 12—Commander-in-Chief Kamenev orders Southwestern Front to advance in direction of Zamostye-Tomashev and attack flank of Polish forces defending Warsaw; order is ignored and Southwestern forces continue westward instead of northward, advancing upon Lwow

AUGUST 15—Under threats from Moscow, Southwestern forces change direction of advance as ordered, but are unable to execute the necessary maneuver in time

AUGUST 16—Polish Army, under General Haller, advised by General Weygand, repulses Tukhachevsky's forces near Warsaw; launches a counter-offensive

AUGUST 17—Red Army begins retreat from Poland

AUGUST-SEPTEMBER—Wrangel carries out offensive operations against Red Army in direction of the Don Basin

SEPTEMBER 2—Bokhara proclaimed a Soviet Republic

SEPTEMBER 21—Beginning of peace talks with Poland

SEPTEMBER 22-25—All-Russian Party Conference; Control Commission established

OCTOBER 12—Armistice signed with Poland

OCTOBER 15—Beginning of Red Army offensive against Wrangel

NOVEMBER 9—Red Army inflicts decisive defeat on Wrangel at Perekop

NOVEMBER 10—Red Army recaptures all of Crimea; Wrangel flees

NOVEMBER 13—Stalin proclaims autonomy of Daghestan

NOVEMBER 14—End of mopping-up operations against Wrangel forces

NOVEMBER 17—Congress of the Peoples of Terek Territory at Vladikavkaz during which Stalin proclaims autonomy of the Gurian Republic

DECEMBER—Stalin in hospital for operation

DECEMBER 2—Armenia proclaimed a Soviet Republic

DECEMBER 18-21—First All-Russian conference of representatives of the autonomous republics, territories and regions; Lenin, Zinoviev, Trotsky, elected honorary chairmen; Stalin elected honorary member of praesidium

DECEMBER 22-29—Eighth Congress of Soviets adopts electrification program: beginning of planned industrialization

1921

FEBRUARY 11—Red Army invades Georgia on Stalin's orders and confronts Politburo with accomplished fact

FEBRUARY 14—While Trotsky is in Urals, Politburo sanctions invasion of Georgia, advocated by Ordzhonikidze and Stalin; decision revealed only to Council of War of Second Army; even Commander-in-Chief not told of it

FEBRUARY 17—Commander-in-Chief of Red Army reports the invasion of Georgia to Vice-Chairman Sklyansky of the Revolutionary Council of War

FEBRUARY 21—Trotsky, from Ekaterinburg (Sverdlovsk, in Urals) asks Sklyansky for memorandum on invasion of Georgia: "When these operations began, by whose order," etc.

MARCH 8-16—Tenth Party Congress; culmination of Trade Union discussion (begun in fall of 1920); Workers' Opposition and Democratic Centralists wage strong fight for internal democracy in Party; Stalin delivers his regular report on minor nationalities; New Economic Policy (NEP) adopted; all factions inside the Party proscribed; Molotov, Mikhailov, Yaroslavsky (Stalin's friends) succeed Krestinsky, Serebryakov, Preobrazhensky in Secretariat. Kronstadt Rebellion

MARCH 18—Kronstadt mutiny suppressed on fiftieth anniversary of Paris Commune

MAY 26-JUNE 1—All-Russian Party Conference

JUNE 22-JULY 12—Third Congress of the Comintern

JULY 6—Stalin speaks in Tiflis on Communist tasks in Georgia

JULY 25—Stalin falls ill in Tiflis

AUGUST 11—Decree concerning introduction of New Economic Policy (NEP)

AUTUMN—Stalin enlists Lenin's support in his effort to secure a better apartment in the Kremlin

OCTOBER 19—Crimean Republic established

DECEMBER—Stalin, in ill-health, is treated by Dr. Obukh

1922

FEBRUARY 6—Cheka reorganized as G.P.U.

MARCH—Lenin in failing health

MARCH 12—Trans-Caucasian S.F.S.R. poclaimed

MARCH 27-APRIL 2—Eleventh Party Congress; concerted opposition, both open and secret, against the Lenin ruling group; Leninist Central Committee elects Stalin to office of General Secretary, with Molotov and Kuibyshev as his assistants

APRIL 10—Opening of Genoa Conference (Treaty of Rapallo)

MAY 26—Lenin's first attack of arteriosclerosis impairs his speech, paralyzes right arm and leg

JUNE 4—News of Lenin's grave illness published for first time

JUNE 8—Trial of Essar Party leaders opens

AUGUST 4-7—Twelfth Party Conference adopts new Party constitution

OCTOBER—Lenin's health improves

OCTOBER 25—Vladivostok evacuated by last of Japanese and White Armies

OCTOBER 30—First Fascist ministry under Mussolini

NOVEMBER 4-DECEMBER 5—Fourth Congress of the Comintern; address by Lenin

NOVEMBER 14—Buffer Far-Eastern Republic becomes part of Soviet Russia

DECEMBER 16—Lenin's second stroke; end of his public career. His place taken by the triumvirate, Zinoviev, Kamenev, Stalin

DECEMBER 23-27—Tenth Congress of Soviets (the first without Lenin)

DECEMBER 25—Lenin dictates his Testament

DECEMBER 30—The First and founding Congress of the Union of Soviet Socialist Republics

1923

JANUARY 4—Lenin writes postscript to his Testament

FEBRUARY—Stalin tells Trotsky, Zinoviev, Kamenev, that Lenin has asked him for poison

MARCH 5-6—Lenin dictates letter breaking off all comradely relations with Stalin

MARCH 6-7—Lenin appeals to Trotsky for help against Stalin

MARCH 9—Lenin has third and most devastating stroke

SPRING-SUMMER—Revolutionary situation in Germany ripens

APRIL 17-25—Twelfth Party Congress (the first without Lenin); Stalin becomes senior triumvir and Lenin's successor in all but name; Party machine drastically overhauled; Central Control Commission transformed into a secret police for use against oppositionist Party members

AUGUST-DECEMBER—Organized oppositionist groups agitate against Party leadership; fight for restoration of Party democracy

SEPTEMBER 13—Fascist coup in Spain under Primo de Rivera

SEPTEMBER-OCTOBER—Zinoviev attempts to make a new deal with Stalin; Kislovodsk Cave Conference

OCTOBER 15—Declaration of the 46 Communist leaders against the Party régime condemned by Central Committee

OCTOBER 21-23—Collapse of Communist insurrection in Germany

OCTOBER 23—Trotsky's letter to Central Committee on Party democracy

AUTUMN—Stalin orders the first shooting of a Communist—Sultan Galiyev

NOVEMBER 7—Zinoviev legalizes Party discussion by announcing existence of Party democracy in *Pravda* article, Trotsky, ill, does not take part

DECEMBER 5—Central Committee adopts resolution drafted in Politburo condemning bureaucracy, special privileges; affirming right of Party members to criticize, etc.

DECEMBER 8—Trotsky's New Course letter; Zinoviev charges Trotsky with "treason"; calls for his arrest

1924

JANUARY 16-18—Thirteenth Party Conference condemns the pro-democracy discussion in general and Trotsky in particular

JANUARY 18—Trotsky leaves Moscow for Sukhum

JANUARY 21—Death of Lenin, whose health had been improving since October; Trotsky receives telegram from Stalin at Tiflis, informing him of Lenin's death; continues on to Sukhum

JANUARY 26—Second Congress of Soviets, U.S.S.R.; Stalin reads his oath of fealty to Lenin; Petrograd renamed Leningrad

JANUARY 27—Lenin's funeral, postponed from the 26th

JANUARY 28—Stalin delivers speech to the military kadets of the Kremlin

OCTOBER—Trotsky's book *Lessons of October* condemns behavior of Zinoviev and Kamenev in October, 1917

1925

JANUARY 17—Plenum of Central Committee and Central Control Commission reproves Trotsky

APRIL—Trotsky removed from Commissariat of War; succeeded by Frunze

APRIL 27-29—Fourteenth Party Conference; break between Stalin and Zinoviev-Kamenev faction; Stalin unites with Bukharin-Rykov-Tomsky faction

MAY 13-20—Third Congress of Soviets, U.S.S.R.

NOVEMBER—Death of Frunze; Voroshilov becomes Commissar of War

DECEMBER 18-31—Fourteenth Party Congress; Zinoviev's Leningrad Opposition completely routed; new opposition emerges—Trotsky-Zinoviev-Kamenev

1926

JANUARY—Sergei Mironovich Kirov takes charge of Stalinist forces in Leningrad, seat of Zinoviev's power

FEBRUARY 12—Extraordinary Leningrad Party Conference; Zinoviev removed from leadership of Leningrad; his factional organization smashed

JULY 14-23—Plenary sessions of Central Committee and Central Control Commission; Zinoviev expelled from Politburo and removed from leadership of Communist International

JULY 20—Dzerzhinsky dies suddenly, several hours after speech at one of plenary sessions

OCTOBER 23—Plenary sessions of Central Committee and Central Control Commission; Trotsky and Kamenev expelled from Politburo; Executive Committee of Communist International ordered officially to remove its chairman, Zinoviev

OCTOBER 26—Fifteenth Party Conference

1927

MAY 26—Declaration of the 83 Opposition leaders

JULY 29-AUGUST 9—Joint Plenum of Central Committee and Central Control Commission; Trotsky-Zinoviev-Kamenev oppositionists reproved and warned

OCTOBER 21-23—Joint Plenum of Central Committee and Central Control Commission; Zinoviev and Trotsky expelled from Central Committee

NOVEMBER 7—Oppositionists march with slogans during tenth anniversary of October Revolution in Moscow and Leningrad; repression of Trotsky-Zinoviev faction intensified

NOVEMBER 12—Extraordinary Plenum of Central Committee and Central Control Commission; Trotsky and Zinoviev expelled from Communist Party; Kamenev, Rakovsky, Smilga, Evdokimov expelled from Central Committee; Muralov, Bakayev, others expelled from Central Control Commission, etc.

NOVEMBER 16—Adolf Joffe commits suicide; leaves letter for Trotsky

DECEMBER 2-19—Fifteenth Party Congress; Opposition completely routed; Zinoviev and Kamenev capitulate, petition for readmission into Party as rank-and-file members

1928

JANUARY 16—Trotsky exiled to Alma-Ata

JULY 11—Bukharin calls on Kamenev secretly; pours out his grievances against Stalin whom he regards as dangerous to Communist cause and revolutionary movement

SEPTEMBER 30—Bukharin attempts to criticize Stalin's policies by innuendo in *Pravda* article, *Notes of an Economist*

OCTOBER 19—Publication of Central Committee statement directed against the "Right deviation" (Bukharin-Rykov-Tomsky)

NOVEMBER 26—Plenum of Central Committee; anti-Right Opposition

NOVEMBER 27—Plenum of Moscow Party Committee; expulsion of Rightists

1929

JANUARY 18—Decision taken to expel Trotsky from U.S.S.R.

JANUARY 21—Bukharin criticizes Stalin's peasant policy on fifth anniversary of Lenin's death in article, *Lenin's Political Testament*

FEBRUARY 12—Trotsky arrives in Turkey as exile from U.S.S.R.

MAY 18—Syrtsov succeeds Rykov as Chairman of Council of People's Commissars of R.S.F.S.R.

JUNE 2—Tomsky removed as head of the Trade Unions' Federation

JULY 3—Bukharin removed as head of Communist International

OCTOBER 17—Bubnov succeeds Lunacharsky as Commissar of Education

NOVEMBER 10-17—Plenum of Central Committee; Bukharin expelled from Politburo; Rykov and Tomsky warned; Gamarnik elected to Orgburo

NOVEMBER 25—Bukharin, Rykov, Tomsky capitulate in letter to Central Committee

DECEMBER 21—Celebration of Stalin's fiftieth birthday a national event

DECEMBER 27—Stalin delivers speech to First Conference of Marxist Agronomists

1930

JUNE 26-JULY 13—Sixteenth Party Congress; taunting of Right Opposition leaders, whose repentance is deemed unsatisfactory

DECEMBER 2—Syrtsov and Lominadze expelled from Central Committee

DECEMBER 17-21—Plenum of Central Committee and Central Control Commission; Rykov expelled, Ordzhonikidze elected to succeed him in Politburo

DECEMBER 20—Molotov succeeds Rykov as Chairman of Council of People's Commissars of U.S.S.R.

1931

FEBRUARY 4—Stalin, in speech on difficulties of industrialization, says: "There are no fortresses Bolsheviks cannot take."

1932-33

The Stalin Famine, deliberately brought about as an act of agrarian policy; number of victims estimated variously at from four to ten million dead; many more millions in chronic ill-health

1933

JULY—Suicide of Nikolai Alexeyevich Skrypnik, aged 61, Old Bolshevik, member of the October Central Committee and of the Military Revolutionary Committee in 1917, one of the founders of the Ukrainian Soviet Republic and one of its leaders at time of the Stalin Famine

1934

JANUARY-FEBRUARY—Seventeenth Party Congress, "the congress of victors," marked by complete unanimity on all matters, devotion to Stalin, enthusiasm for his genius

DECEMBER 1—Stalin's friend Kirov, his viceroy in Leningrad, assassinated by Nikolayev

DECEMBER 5-18—"White Guard Terrorists" executed for assassination of Kirov

DECEMBER 28-29—Trial of the Fourteen—Nikolayev-Rumyantsev case; all fourteen condemned to be executed

1935

JANUARY 15-16—Trial of the Nineteen (Zinoviev, Kamenev, et al.) on charges of seeking to "restore capitalism," general "counter-revolutionary activity," "political and moral responsibility" for assassination of Kirov; sentences: imprisonment

JANUARY 23—Trial of the Twelve Leningrad OGPU officials (F. D. Medved and others) for failure to prevent Kirov's assassination; sentences very light

SPRING—Second Kamenev trial (secret) with about thirty defendants; Kamenev's sentence increased by five years

MAY 4—Stalin, in speech to graduating classes of Red Army military academies assembled in the Kremlin, says in part: "We chose our plan of advance and moved forward along the Leninist road, pushing aside . . . those who could not see . . . what was under their noses . . . (those who) threatened to raise a rebellion in the Party against the Central Committee. More: they threatened some of us with bullets."

NOVEMBER 17—First All-Union Conference of Stakhanovists

1936

MARCH 19—Fifteenth anniversary of founding of Georgian Republic celebrated elaborately throughout Soviet Union

JUNE 18—Death of Maxim Gorky in Moscow; Yagoda subsequently held responsible for it and confesses

AUGUST 19-24—Trial of the Sixteen (Zinoviev, Kamenev and others)—the case of the anti-Soviet Trotskyite Center; all defendants executed

SEPTEMBER 27—Nikolai Yezhov succeeds Henry Yagoda as head of OGPU

1937

JANUARY 23-30—Trial of the Seventeen—the case of the anti-Soviet Trotskyite Center; thirteen executed; Sokolnikov, Radek, two others imprisoned

FEBRUARY 18—Sudden and mysterious death of Sergo Ordzhonikidze

JUNE 12—Announcement of execution of Tukhachevsky and seven other of the most famous generals of the Red Army, allegedly after secret trial

DECEMBER—The Yenukidze-Karakhan executions; exact number and exact nature of trial, if any, unknown

1938

MARCH 2-13—Trial of the Twenty-one—the case of the anti-Soviet Bloc of Rights and Trotskyites; eighteen executed, including Bukharin, Rykov, Krestinsky; three imprisoned, including Rakovsky

1939

MARCH 10-21—Eighteenth Congress of the Communist Party

MAY 4—Molotov, Chairman of Council of People's Commissars, takes over portfolio of Foreign Affairs from Litvinov

AUGUST 23—Stalin-Hitler Pact signed in Moscow

AUGUST 29—The Supreme Soviet ratifies Stalin-Hitler Pact

SEPTEMBER 1—World War II begins with German invasion of Poland

NOVEMBER 29—Outbreak of Soviet-Finnish War

DECEMBER 21—Stalin's sixtieth birthday

1940

MARCH 22—End of Soviet-Finnish War

MAY 24—OGPU attempt to assassinate Trotsky fails

AUGUST 20—Trotsky assassinated by OGPU agent

1941

MAY 6—Stalin succeeds Molotov as Chairman of the Council of People's Commissars

JUNE 22—Hitler breaks pact with Stalin and German Army begins invasion of Soviet Union by way of countries recently invaded by Red Army, from Bessarabia to Finland

JULY 3—After eleven-day silence, Stalin makes his first public statement since outbreak of hostilities with Nazi Germany

SEPTEMBER 20—German Army captures Kiev

STALIN'S ALIASES AND PSEUDONYMS

NAME: Joseph Vissarionovich Djugashvili
ALSO KNOWN AS:

J. Besoshvili
Chizhikov
David
Ivanov
Ivanovich
K. Kato
Ko.
Koba (after a hero of Georgian legend)
K. St.
Nizheradze
Ryaboi (police nickname meaning *pockmarked*)
Soselo (affectionate diminutive of Joseph)
Soso (diminutive of Joseph in Georgian)
Stalin (meaning *steel man*)
Oganess Vartanovich Totomyants
Vassily
Vassilyev

COMMUNIST PARTY CONGRESSES

I.	March 13-15, 1898	Minsk
II.	July 30-August 23, 1903	Brussels and London
III.	April 25-May 10, 1905	London
IV.	April 23-May 8, 1906	Stockholm
V.	May 13-June 1, 1907	London
VI.	August 8-16, 1917	Petrograd
VII.	March 6-8, 1918	Moscow
VIII.	March 18-23, 1919	Moscow
IX.	March 29-April 4, 1920	Moscow
X.	March 8-16, 1921	Moscow
XI.	March 27-April 2, 1922	Moscow
XII.	April 17-25, 1923	Moscow
XIII.	May 23-31, 1924	Moscow
XIV.	December 18-31, 1925	Moscow
XV.	December 2-19, 1927	Moscow
XVI.	June 26-July 13, 1930	Moscow
XVII.	January 26-February 10, 1934	Moscow
XVIII.	March 10-21, 1939	Moscow

(Eighteenth All-Union Conference—February 15-20, 1941)

BOOKS AND PAMPHLETS BY LEON TROTSKY
AVAILABLE IN ENGLISH

BETWEEN RED AND WHITE: A Study of Some Fundamental Questions of Revolution, with Particular Reference to Georgia. *Communist Party of Great Britain, London. 1922. 104 pp.*

BOLSHEVIKI AND WORLD PEACE, THE (The War and the International). With an Introduction by Lincoln Steffens. *Boni and Liveright, New York, 1918. 238 pp.*

COMMUNISM AND SYNDICALISM: On the Trade Union Question. *Communist League of America, New York. 63 pp.*

DEFENSE OF TERRORISM, THE (Terrorism and Communism), A Reply to Karl Kautsky. *Geo. Allen and Unwin, London, 1935. 176 pp.*

FROM OCTOBER TO BREST-LITOVSK. *Socialist Pub. Society, New York, 1919. 100 pp.*

GERMANY: The Key to the International Situation. *Pioneer Publishers, New York, 1932. 45 pp.*

HISTORY OF THE RUSSIAN REVOLUTION, THE. *Simon and Schuster, New York, 1932.*

IN DEFENSE OF THE RUSSIAN REVOLUTION. *Pioneer Publishers, New York, 1932.*

IN DEFENSE OF THE SOVIET UNION. *Pioneer Publishers, New York, 1937. 40 pp.*

I STAKE MY LIFE! *Pioneer Publishers, New York, 1937, 23 pp.*

KIROV ASSASSINATION, THE. *Pioneer Publishers, New York, 1935. 32 pp.*

LENIN. *Minton Balch, New York. 1925.*

LEON SEDOV—Son, Friend and Fighter. *Young People's Socialist League (Fourth International), New York, 1938. 31 pp.*

LESSONS OF OCTOBER. *Pioneer Publishers, New York, 1937. 125 pp.*

LESSON OF SPAIN, THE: The Last Warning. *London, 1938.*

LITERATURE AND REVOLUTION. *International Publishers, New York, 1925.*

LIVING THOUGHTS OF MARX. Edited with an Introduction by Leon Trotsky. *Longmans, Green, New York, 1939. 184 pp.*

MY FLIGHT FROM SIBERIA. *American Library Service, 1925. New York. 60 pp.*

MY LIFE. *Charles Scribner's Sons, New York, 1931. 598 pp.*

ONLY ROAD, THE. *Pioneer Publishers, New York, 1933. 93 pp.*

OUR REVOLUTION. Edited with an Introduction by M. J. Olgin. *Henry Holt, New York, 1918. 220 pp.*

PERMANENT REVOLUTION, THE. *Pioneer Publishers, New York, 1931. 157 pp.*

PROBLEMS OF THE CHINESE REVOLUTION. With an Introduction by Max Shachtman. *Pioneer Publishers, New York, 1932. 432 pp.*

PROBLEMS OF LIFE. *Doran, New York, 1924. 114 pp.*

PROLETARIAN REVOLUTION, THE (by Trotsky and Lenin, edited with an introduction by Louis C. Fraina). *Communist Press, New York, 1918. 453 pp.*

REAL SITUATION IN RUSSIA, THE. Edited with an Introduction by Max Eastman. *Harcourt, Brace, New York, 1928. 360 pp.*

REVOLUTION BETRAYED, THE. What is the Soviet Union and Where is it Going? *Doubleday, Doran, New York, 1937. 308 pp.*

REVOLUTION IN SPAIN, THE. *Communist League of America, New York, 1931. 31 pp.*

RUSSIA: PROBLEMS OF DEVELOPMENT OF THE U.S.S.R. *Communist League of America, New York, 1931. 48 pp.*

SOVIET ECONOMY IN DANGER. *Pioneer Publishers, New York, 1933. 67 pp.*

SOVIET UNION AND THE FOURTH INTERNATIONAL, THE. *Pioneer Publishers, New York, 1934. 31 pp.*

SPANISH REVOLUTION IN DANGER, THE. *Pioneer Publishers, New York, 1931. 62 pp.*

STALINISM AND BOLSHEVISM: Concerning the Historical and Theoretical Roots of the Fourth International. *Pioneer Publishers, New York, 1937. 29 pp.*

STALIN SCHOOL OF FALSIFICATION, THE. Edited with an Introduction by Max Shachtman. *Pioneer Publishers, New York, 1937. 326 pp.*

SUPPRESSED TESTAMENT OF LENIN, THE. *Pioneer Publishers, New York, 1935. 47 pp.*

THIRD INTERNATIONAL AFTER LENIN, THE. With an Introduction by Max Shachtman. *Pioneer Publishers, New York, 1936. 357 pp.*

TURN IN THE COMMUNIST INTERNATIONAL AND THE GERMAN SITUATION, THE. *Communist League of America, New York, 1930. 32 pp.*

WAR AND THE FOURTH INTERNATIONAL. *Pioneer Publishers, New York, 1934. 35 pp.*

WHAT HITLER WANTS. *John Day, New York, 1933. 31 pp.*

WHAT NEXT?—Vital Questions for the German Proletariat. *Pioneer Publishers, New York, 1932. 192 pp.*

WHITHER ENGLAND? *International Publishers, New York, 1925. 192 pp.*

WHITHER FRANCE? *Pioneer Publishers, New York, 1936. 160 pp.*

WHITHER RUSSIA—Towards Capitalism or Socialism? *International Publishers, New York, 1926. 128 pp.*

WORLD UNEMPLOYMENT AND THE FIVE YEAR PLAN. *Communist League of America, New York, 1931. 22 pp.*

MANIFESTO OF THE FOURTH INTERNATIONAL ON THE IMPERIALIST WAR. *Pioneer Publishers, New York, 1940. 48 pp.*

GLOSSARY

August Bloc—a united front of various Russian Social-Democratic factions opposed to the Bolsheviks in 1912 and in favor of reuniting into a single party; composed of Trotsky's Non-Factional Social-Democrats, Bundists, Lettish Social-Democrats, the *Vperyod* (Forward) group, the Mensheviks (except the Plekhanovists), and the Caucasian Regional Committee. It originated in protest against Lenin's convocation of the Prague Conference, was followed by a preliminary conference in Paris in March, 1912, which in turn prepared the conference in Vienna in August, 1912—hence, its name. It was short-lived: the *Vperyod* group, Trotsky and others soon withdrew from it and the August Bloc disintegrated.

baggers—illicit traders during the Civil War and later, who bought and sold food and clothing and other necessities, which they usually carried in bags or sacks—*myeshochniki*, from *myeshok*, a bag or sack.

Bezo—Georgian diminutive of Vissarion.

Black Hundreds—members of the Union of Russian People, an organization of reactionary super-patriots sponsored by the tsarist régime, specializing in violence against Jews, Socialists and intellectuals—Russian precursors of the Fascists and the Nazis.

Bloody Sunday—see: footnote p. 56 and Chronological Guide under 1905.

Boorsy—theological schools in Tsarist Russia.

Boycottists—the majority of Bolshevik delegates at the July (August, 1907) Conference of the Russian Social-Democratic Labor Party who, unlike the Menshevik delegates and Lenin, favored a boycott of the Duma. Among its leaders were Bogdanov and Kamenev. They disintegrated as a faction within a couple of years.

Bund—popular name for the All-Jewish Workers' League of Poland, Lithuania and Russia, which played an important part in the Social-Democratic movement of all three countries during the tsarist régime. It was led by generally pro-Menshevik Social-Democrats, but after the advent of the Bolsheviks to power a considerable portion of the Bund split away and formed the nucleus of the Jewish Section (*Yevsektsia*) of the Russian Communist Party. The Bund proper continued to exist in Poland, Lithuania (at least until the advent of the Nazi régime), the United States and parts of Europe in small groups.

bureau—in Socialist and Communist parlance, a small executive committee.

center—the seat of the government or the headquarters of the party—in the first case, usually Moscow or Leningrad (Petrograd).

Central Committee—the executive committee of the party.

479

Central Executive Committee—the executive committee of the Soviet; the legislative body of the Soviet Government.

Cheka—political police organization of the Soviet Government, successor of the *Okhrana*. The name originated from the initial letters of *Chrezvychainaya Kommissiya* (Extraordinary Commission) for combating counter-revolutionary activities. Founded December 20, 1917, the Cheka limited its duties at first to "preliminary investigation," but on February 24, 1918 it extended its duties to executions, when it shot Prince Eboli on a charge of blackmail. Under its first leader, Felix Dzerzhinsky, it developed the system of hostages, of mass execution of individually innocent people in batches as "class enemies," and laid the groundwork for the notorious demonstration trials. Reorganized into the *G.P.U.* and later the *O.G.P.U.*, it continued its sanguinary career under Menzhinsky, when its operations were extended to mass arrests of dissident Communists and in rare instances their execution. Reorganized again into the *Nadzor*, its demonstration trials under Yagoda and Yezhov were extended to recalcitrant Communists and indeed to any Communists in disfavor with the regime. Its present head is Lavrentii Beriya, a rather belated convert to Communism and the leading concocter of flattering myths about Stalin. Notwithstanding its various names it is still popularly known as the *Cheka* and its operatives as *chekists*. Its range of activities is practically unlimited and its operations world-wide: its specialties include exploitation of forced labor, espionage, counterfeiting, assassination, and the like.

Compromisers—Professing socialists, principally Mensheviks and Essars, who in the opinion of the Bolsheviks were ever-ready to compromise their socialist principles for the sake of political collaboration with liberals, usually the Kadets.

Conciliators—Russian Social-Democrats who worked for the reconciliation of the warring factions, principally the Mensheviks and the Bolsheviks. Trotsky was for many years a conciliator.

Constituent Assembly—a body encompassing the purposes of both the Continental Congress and the Constitutional Convention of the American Revolution, which was supposed to determine the kind of government Russia was to have. Its deputies were elected by universal suffrage in the summer of 1917, when the Essars were the most popular party in the country. It met at the Tauride Palace in Petrograd and lasted less than 13 hours, from four o'clock in the afternoon of January 18, 1918, to forty minutes past four in the morning of January 19, when it was dispersed by Bolshevik troops, chiefly sailors and soldiers of Lettish regiments. Of its 815 deputies, 370 were Right Essars, 175 Bolsheviks, 40 Left Essars, 17 Kadets, 16 Mensheviks, and the remainder representatives of various national minorities' parties. Since even a bloc with the Left Essars could not overcome the majority of the Right Essars, the Bolsheviks, who had been among the loudest advocates of its convocation, regarded it as unrepresentative. After a futile effort to open it by an aged Essar, the Constituent Assembly was actually called to order by Sverdlov, President of the Central Executive Committee of the Soviets, which deprived it at once of its juridical basis, for it thus accepted its very existence only by the grace of the Soviets. The Essar Victor

Chernov was elected its President. After ten hours of turbulence, the Bolshevik deputation walked out demonstratively, followed an hour and a half later by its allies, the Left Essars. Then the Bolshevik troops finished the job. Later that day the Council of People's Commissars issued a decree of dispersal, the following day the Soviet Central Executive Committee issued a confirmatory decree, and a couple of days later the Third Congress of Soviets set its seal of approval on the dispersion and proclaimed itself the permanent government.

Council of People's Commissars—the cabinet of the Soviet Government; also known as the *Sovnarkom,* portmanteau word for *Soviet Narodnykh Kommissarov.*

December Insurrection—climax of the Revolution of 1905; see Chronological Guide.

Defeatists—international-minded socialists who favored the defeat of their own countries engaged in imperialist war.

Defensists—patriotic-minded socialists who favored suspension of anti-government activities in time of war and the support of their respective governments for the sake of defending their country against the common national enemy.

dukhan—a Caucasian or Near Eastern saloon or tavern.

duma—an ancient Russian word for *council,* of which *soviet* is a synonym; literally, *duma* means *meditation* or *thought;* specifically, the State Duma during the reign of Tsar Nicholas II was the Russian Parliament and the *dumas* of the various cities were analogous to municipal councils. See footnotes pp. 44, 70.

Economism—a movement among Russian Social-Democrats which laid the emphasis on trade-union activities rather than on purely political agitation; the economists' principal factional opponents were the *Iskrists,* who reversed the emphasis and denounced them as mere reformists and opportunists.

Essar—Social-Revolutionary; member of a peasant socialist party ideologically descended from the Populist movement (*narodnichestvo*); follow the Chronological Guide for stages of its development; also, the name of the party.

Essdek—Social-Democrat.

faction—a group within the party; cf. *fraction.*

February Revolution—the anti-monarchist revolution which began March 8, 1917.

Forwardists—a faction of Social-Democrats grouped around the publication *Vperyod* (Forward), a heterodox offshoot of the Bolsheviks, led by Bogdanov, Lunacharsky, Maxim Gorky.

fraction—a caucus of Communists outside the Communist Party operating jointly in the interests of the Communist Party—in trade unions, congresses, conferences, legislative assemblies, etc.—wherever there are three or more Communists; purpose: to establish Party control over the given non-Communist organization. The decisions of a fraction are final, beyond appeal and obligatory on all its members. Whenever the size of the fraction warrants it, a bureau is elected to guide its activities.

General Secretary—the senior secretary and chief executive officer of the party central committee.

G.P.U.—see: Cheka.

Green movement—see: footnote p. 282.

Jacobins—a general term applied to very radical revolutionists and specifically to the members of the Society of the Friends of the Constitution, who in the days of the Great French Revolution held their club meetings at first in the refectory, later in the library and after May, 1791, in the chapel of the Jacobin Monastery on the Rue St. Honoré in Paris. Notwithstanding popular misconceptions, the Jacobins were not bloodthirsty ruffians and horny-handed proletarians; they were for the most part writers, lawyers, physicians, merchants, artists and the like, the élite of the educated and the fairly prosperous. Among the presidents of their club in Paris were such gentlemen as Prince de Broglie, the Duke of Aiguillon, Vicomte de Noailles, Vicomte de Beauharnais. Indeed, proletarians were debarred from membership, if only because the annual fee was 24 livres and the entrance fee 12 livres. The Jacobins regarded themselves as "priests and missionaries of liberty" and their principal occupation was to prepare the raw material for the legislative activity of the National Assembly, the Legislative Assembly, and later the Convention. They were so influential in their day that they were generally regarded as the last court of appeal in practically all human affairs, especially by simple souls. In the Convention, where properly speaking there were no political parties but only deputies, the Jacobins were split into the Girondins, or Right Wingers, led by Brissot, who were for the most part deputies from the southern department of the Gironde and practically all other provinces except those of the north-east; the Mountain, or Left Wingers, led by Robespierre and Marat; and the Plain, or Centrists, led by Danton. Both the Gironde and the Mountain were democrats, republicans, supporters of the Revolution. But the Gironde, believing the Revolution essentially achieved, favored its canalization into constitutional routine, while the Mountain saw dangers ahead at home and abroad and therefore insisted on extraordinary measures in defense of the Revolution. The Gironde was supported by the prosperous and the respectable; the Mountain, by the masses. The guillotine became the final arbiter of their debates: the Mountain decapitated the Gironde and then the Plain—until the Mountain itself was overthrown on the 9th of Thermidor (July 27, 1794): Danton lost his head on April 5, Robespierre four months later, and a political reaction set in.

July Days—the turning point of 1917. On July 15 the Kadets announced their resignation from the Provisional Government on the pretext of disagreement with Kerensky and the other Socialist ministers on the question of granting autonomy to the Ukraine; they insisted on deferring the issue until the meeting of the Constituent Assembly. But their resignation was really a maneuver designed to browbeat the Essars and Mensheviks into greater submission to the Kadets and to throw the entire responsibility for the failures at the front on the Socialist ministers. The Petrograd masses, on the other hand, saw in the resignation of the Kadets an opportunity for the Soviet to terminate dual authority and take full power. They therefore went out into the streets on July 16—entire regiments of soldiers as well as factory workers —to demonstrate in favor of all power to the Soviet. By July 17 the number of demonstrants in Petrograd swelled to half a million. The Bolsheviks, considering the movement premature, advised against violence. The Central Executive Committee of the Soviet, controlled by the Mensheviks and the Essars, refused to assume the reins of government. The demonstrants were fired upon and replied with bullets. The demonstration proved fruitless and broke up. Then on July 18 charges were published by the former Bolshevik Duma deputy Alexinsky, who was a rabid patriot and defensist during the war, that Lenin was an agent of the German General Staff sent to Russia across Germany from his exile in Switzerland to foment disaffection in the Russian Army and disloyalty to the Provisional Government, in order to "soften" Russia for a crushing defeat by Germany. The same day mobs of patriots raided the offices of *Pravda,* and the following day the Provisional Government issued orders for the arrest of Lenin, Zinoviev, Trotsky, Kamenev and other Bolshevik and pro-Bolshevik leaders on similar charges. On July 20 the Provisional Government ordered the disarming of all Army units that had taken part in the demonstrations of July 16-18. With the Bolsheviks driven underground or into semi-legality, a reaction set in which developed into the next culminating point, the Kornilov Affair, after which the pendulum of 1917 swung again to the Left, the Bolsheviks rapidly gained influence, and 1917 reached its climax in the October Revolution.

Junkers—students of officers' schools.

Kadets—Constitutional Democrats—moderate liberals.

Keke—Georgian diminutive of Ekaterina (Catherine).

kinto—Georgian for street urchin, hooligan, clever schemer and cynic capable of exceedingly low cunning.

Liquidators—Social-Democrats who, after the defeat of the First Revolution became indisputable, advocated liquidation of underground tactics and participation instead in legal activities—such as, trade union, educational and similar innocuous work.

literaries—socialist writers.

makhorka—a cheap grade of tobacco.

Mauser—a repeating rifle widely used by the Russian army and police, invented by the German gunsmith Paul Mauser.

mauserist—gunman.

Mesamé-dasi—Georgian for *third group,* referring to Marxist intellectuals, as distinguished from those of the progressive nobility and the liberal bourgeoisie.

NEP—period of the New Economic Policy of the Soviet Government, instituted in the spring of 1921; it revived private trading to a limited extent.

nepman—a trader of the NEP period.

October—short for *October Revolution.*

October Revolution—the Revolution of the Bolsheviks, of November 7, 1917.

Okhrana—see footnote p. 89.

Old Bolshevik—a member of the Communist Party who joined the movement prior to 1917.

Old Guard—a variant of Old Bolshevik, sometimes used with specific reference to those who could trace their adherence to the Bolshevik faction as far back as 1903 or at least 1905.

Politburo—executive committee of the Central Committee of the Russian Communist Party. Formally its organization dates from the Eighth Congress (March 13-23, 1919), although it actually existed in one form or another prior to that. Originally it was the ruling body of the Party and of the Soviet state, in fact if not in name; its authority gradually shifted to Stalin. The number of its members and alternates changed from congress to congress. The first Politburo (elected in 1919) consisted of Lenin, Trotsky, Kamenev, Bukharin, Stalin. In 1920 its membership was expanded to seven, when the five above were supplemented by Preobrazhensky and Serebryakov. In 1922 its members were: Lenin, Trotsky, Zinoviev, Kamenev, Bukharin, Tomsky, Stalin. In 1923 (after the Twelfth Congress) its members were: Lenin, Trotsky, Stalin, Zinoviev, Kamenev, Tomsky and Rykov; its alternates: Bukharin, Kalinin, Molotov, Rudzutak. In 1924 (after the Thirteenth Congress) its members were: Stalin, Zinoviev, Kamenev, Bukharin, Rykov, Tomsky, united against Trotsky; its alternates: Dzerzhinsky, Molotov, Kalinin, Rudzutak, Sokolnikov, Frunze. In 1925 (after the Fourteenth Congress)—members: Stalin, Bukharin, Rykov, Tomsky, Voroshilov, Molotov, Kalinin, Zinoviev, Trotsky; alternates: Dzerzhinsky, Rudzutak, Petrovsky, Uglanov, Kamenev. After that removals and appointments were made between congresses. The members of the Politburo after the Fifteenth Congress (December, 1927) were: Stalin, Bukharin, Rykov, Tomsky, Molotov, Voroshilov, Kuibyshev, Rudzutak, Kalinin; alternates: Kirov, Kaganovich, Andreyev, Mikoyan, Petrovsky, Uglanov, S. Kossior, Chubar'. After the Sixteenth Congress (June-July, 1930), when Stalin became supreme boss and the Politburo was reduced practically to the status of the chorus in ancient Greek drama, its members were: Stalin, Kuibyshev, Molotov, Voroshilov, Kirov, Kaganovich, S. Kossior, Rudzutak, Kalinin, Rykov; alternates; Mikoyan, Andreyev, Chubar', Petrovsky, Syrtsov. After that, with few exceptions, very much the same names recur.

Populism—*Narodnichestvo*, from *narod* (the people), was a libertarian democratic movement, specifically Russian in its antecedents and hence agrarian in its ideology. It arose in the middle of the nineteenth century. Since its first protagonists were radical intellectuals, it was colored from its inception with the ideas of the utopian socialism then in vogue. Its first great protagonist, Nicholas Chernyshevsky, looked upon the peasantry (i.e., the people) as a revolutionary class, and the communal forms of peasant economy as the nucleus of a uniquely Russian kind of socialism. The movement grew (among intellectuals, of course) after the colossal fraud of the liberation of the serfs by Tsar Alexander II in 1861 became apparent, because it was hoped that the disappointed peasantry would be ripe for rebellion. But it wasn't. The industrialization of Russia progressed during the succeeding decades, more and more peasants moved to the industrial centers and became proletarians. But the Populists continued to hope that Russia could come to socialism without going through the purgatory of the capitalistic phase of historic development. In the seventies the Populists split into Bakuninists (the followers of the famous international Anarchist, Michael Bakunin) and Lavrists (the disciples of Peter Lavrov, friend and translator of Karl Marx). The Bakuninists argued that the first essential step was the destruction of the state, by means of a nation-wide insurrection of the peasantry, after which the free agrarian collectives (*obshchinas*) could band together into a non-statist federation: that was their idea of socialism. The Lavrists argued that the first prerequisite was educational—the cultural and intellectual level of the people (i.e., the peasantry) had to be raised; and that educational mission had to be performed through the dissemination of socialist ideas among the peasantry by "critically thinking individuals." Whereupon hundreds of young intellectuals abandoned their studies at various universities at home and abroad, forsook their comfortable homes, donned peasant garb or a worker's blouse, learned common trades, and went to live with the common people in order to teach them the way to freedom. This "going to the people" (*khozhdeniye v narod*) movement ended disastrously for the young idealists, who were not only persecuted by the tsarist government but not infrequently betrayed to the police by the very peasants they sought to help. After that (see: Chronological Guide) the Populists resorted to the terror as a political weapon, concentrating on the "central" terror—that is, against the central government and first of all, the tsar—hoping to dislodge the monarchy as well as the monarch and seize the reins of government. But the assassination of Alexander II (March, 1881) was not followed by an uprising of the people; instead, an even deeper reaction set in. Under the impact of that experience, the further growth of industry and the expansion of the class of city workers, many of the Populists turned to the Marxist movement. Others, disillusioned about the effectiveness of the terror, became liberal reformers. Still others, who regarded the growing army of proletarians as essentially peasants temporarily away from the plow and masquerading in city clothes, argued that artisan collectives (*artels*) could industrialize Russia far more effectively and painlessly than capitalistic industrialization, accused the Marxists of being defenders and apologists of capitalism and renegades to the ideals of their forefathers (the Populist heroes of yesterday who had fought for political liberty) because the Marxists acknowledged the progressive role of capitalism at a certain historic stage and, in the opinion of the Populists, laid too much emphasis on the economic phase of the struggle. Moribund Populism re-emerged early in the twentieth century as the Social-Revolutionary (Essar) Party, which during the first decade of the century revived the terror as a political weapon. Other stages of the movement are indicated in the Chronological Guide.

P.P.S.—Polish Socialist Party, led by Joseph Pilsudski, which was strongly nationalistic, as distinguished from the Social-Democracy of Poland and Lithuania, led by Rosa Luxemburg, which was internationalist.

practico—a socialist who specializes in organizational activities rather than in writing for the party.

Rabkrin—Russian portmanteau word for the People's Commissariat of Workers' and Peasants' inspection.

Recallists—a faction of Bolsheviks who advocated recall of the Social-Democratic deputies from the Duma.

social-chauvinist—a socialist turned chauvinist.

Soso—Georgian diminutive of Joseph.

soviet—Russian for *council*—and so translated into English, except when it is used to designate the specific institution which mobilized the masses, seized power and became (at first actually, later nominally) the government of Russia.

Soviet Army—same as Red Army.

Swamp—middle-of-the-roaders or centrists generally, and specifically those who took part in the Congress of the Social Democratic Labor Party of 1903 and during the split found themselves between the Bolsheviks and the Mensheviks.

Thermidor—generally a swing toward opportunism in a revolution, which leads toward reaction; specifically the reference is to the events that followed upon the 9th of Thermidor (July 27, 1794), when Robespierre and other Jacobin leaders of the Mountain in the Convention were overthrown by moderate Jacobins tired of the Terror and of revolutionary innovations.

Third Period—a policy rather than. an actual trend proclaimed by a Communist International plenum in 1929, predicated on the assumption that with the introduction of the first Five-Year Plan in the Soviet Union, Russia was marching toward unprecedented prosperity, while in the rest of the world the entire social structure was rapidly disintegrating and ripening for Communist revolution; hence the duty of Communists to mobilize the masses and train them for the impending insurrections in all countries except, of course, the Soviet Union. The policy had many stupid and ludicrous and some very tragic consequences—among the latter the splitting of the anti-Nazi forces in Germany, which helped to clear the road for the Hitler régime.

Third Section—see: *Okhrana*.

transporter—underground revolutionist specializing in smuggling of forbidden publications, people, arms, ammunition, etc.

Unification Congress—the Stockholm Congress of the Russian Social-Democratic Labor Party of 1906; see Chronological Guide.

verst—linear measure equivalent to about two-thirds of a mile.

Vienna *Pravda*—founded in Lwow, but after the first two issues moving to Vienna, *Pravda: Rabochaya Gazeta* (The Truth: Workers' Newspaper) was published between October 16, 1908 and May 6, 1912; in Vienna it was edited by Trotsky as the organ of a group of non-factional Social-Democratic writers.

Volunteer Army—synonymous with White Army.

War Department—synonymous with People's Commissariat of War.

zemstvò—county council; see: footnote p. 55.

INDEX

Abashidze (Georgian monk), 14, 17, 20, 90
Agrarian question, Lenin on, 73-75; Menshe-
 viks on, 73; Plekhanov on, 73, 75, 77;
 Rozhkov on, 76; Stalin on, 74-76, 78;
 Suvorov on, 76; at Stockholm Congress,
 73-78
Alexander II, Tsar, 10, 55n.
Alexander III, Tsar, 394
Alexinsky, Grigorii Alexeyevich, 152; on
 Bolshevik expropriators, 99; and Lenin,
 82
Alksnis (Red Army commander), 269
Alliluyev, Sergo (Stalin's father-in-law), 37,
 40, 143, 211, 243; on strike in Tiflis, 28;
 finds Stalin in Petersburg, 135; letters
 from Stalin, 121, 170, 174; helps Stalin
 hide, 122; on Stalin's struggle against
 Menshevism, 115; on hiding of Lenin, 212
Alliluyeva, Nadezhda (Stalin's second wife),
 213, 256, 379
Alsky, signs "Declaration of the Forty-Six,"
 370
Alyosha: See Dzhaparidze
Amilakhviri (Georgian Prince), 8
Anarchism, in Georgia, 57, 83; in Revolution
 of 1905, 83; "Anarchism and Socialism,"
 by Stalin, 83
Anarchists, 57, 83, 179; in Bolshevik Revo-
 lution, 337; Lenin and, 337; Trotsky and,
 337
Andreyev, Andrey, elected to Bolshevik Cen-
 tral Committee, 348
Anet, Claude (French journalist), 208
Angarsky, N. S. (Bolshevik memoirist),
 201; on Old Bolsheviks, 197, 198
Anglo-Russian Committee, 398
Anissimov (Menshevik) member, Central
 Executive Committee of Soviets, 211, 221
Antagulov (Soviet historian), on Bashkiria,
 263
Anthology for Five Years (pub. by Commis-
 sariat of Education), 271
Anti-Semitism, Stalin and, 152, 172, 399, 400
Antonov-Ovsyenko, Vladimir Alexeyevich
 (Bolshevik), 186, 247; recalled from Sar-
 atov, 312; Red Army commander, 272;
 Stalin on, 236
April theses, 196, 199, 205; Bukharin on, 198;
 Kamenev opposes, 201 (*see* Lenin, April
 Conference)

April, 1917, conference: *See* Conferences
Aralov, 312, 313
Arkomed, T., 30, 31; on Georgian justice, 36
Arshanov, 325
Artem, Fedor Andreyevich, 253; elected to
 Central Committee, 6th Bolshevik Con-
 gress, 221 (*see* Sergeyev)
Austria-Hungary, national question in, 152,
 153, 156
Austrian revolution of 1918, 259
Austrian school: *See* Austro-Marxists
Austrian social democracy, 152, 156
Austro-Marxists, 154-156, 158
Autonomous republics, Soviet conference of,
 261
Autonomy, of Daghestan, 260; of Gurian So-
 viet Republic, 260, 261
Axelrod, Pavel Borisovich, 59, on bourgeois
 revolution in Russia, 423, 424; Lenin
 breaks with, 157; letter from Potressov,
 110; Stalin on, 48

Badayev, Alexey Yegorovich (Bolshevik,
 Duma deputy), 143-145, 149, 170
Ba'ilov prison, Stalin in, 117; Vereshchak in,
 117
Bakinsky, Sergey (Ukrainian Bolshevik),
 confers with Stalin, 246
Baku, 24, 34, 40, 46, 64, 68, 114, 117, 118,
 122-125, 129, 130, 133, 138, 148, 178, 182,
 237, 248, 260, 262, 266; expropriations in,
 99, 102, 124; strikes in, 45, 47, 57; Men-
 sheviks in, 152; Party declines in, 124
Baku prison, 207, 209, 257, 414; Stalin in,
 172, 182
Balkan war, 155
Baransky, delegate to 1905 Bolshevik confer-
 ence in Tammerfors, 69
Barbusse, Henri (biographer of Stalin), 32;
 on Stalin's visit to Lenin, 108; and Beriya, 108
Barère, Bertrand, 401
Barmine, Alexandre, x
Barnaul, 325
Bashkir Soviet Republic, 263, 264; Stalin
 and, 263, 333
Basle, International Socialist Congress of
 1912 in, 146
Batum, 24, 29, 30, 32, 33, 35, 39, 40, 47, 57, 68,
 82, 118, 135, 237; strikes in, 31

488INDEX

Batum prison, Stalin in, 37
Baturin (Bolshevik literary), 141
Bauer, Otto (Austrian Social Democrat), on national question, 152, 158, 159
Bayliss, Mendel, ritual-murder trial victim, 154
"Bazarov" (Turgenev character), Lenin compared with, 59
Bazhanov, B., secretary of Stalin, 376; on mysterious death of Frunze, 418; on Stalin, 418, 419
B. C.: See Bolshevik Center
Beginning, The: See Nachalo
Beloborodov, A. A. G. (Urals Bolshevik), 414
Belosotsky: See Vladimir
Beltov: See Plekhanov
Berenda (Soviet military inspector), 317
Beriya, Lavrentii P., 17, 19, 29, 33, 46, 47, 55, 57, 58, 63, 82, 115, 122, 176; and Barbusse, 108; appointed head of O.G.P.U., 137; on London Party Congress, 60; on Stalin's fight against Menshevism, 44, 72
Berlin, 10, 105
Bern, 147, 178
Berzin, Jan Antonovich (Latvian Bolshevik), elected to Central Committee at July, 1917, Bolshevik Congress, 221; commander in Red Army, 272; on Southern front, 296, 297
Besoshvili (alias of Stalin): See Stalin
Bessodovsky, Grigorii (ex-Soviet Ambassador), on Stalin as expropriator, 106, 107; on execution of Tsarist family, 414
Bezo (alias of Stalin): See Stalin
Bibineishvili, B. (Bolshevik memoirist), on Kamo, 107, 108
Bible, the, 22
Biographies of Great Men, translation by Pavlenko, 35
"Black City": See Baku
Black hundreds (Tsarist pogromists), 95, 196
Bloody Sunday, 47, 56, 56n., 128, 427, 429, 430
Bluecher, Vasilli K., and Red Army, 271, 281; commander of Red Army, 269
Blumkin, Yakob, assassinates Count von Mirbach, 337; joins Bolsheviks, 337
Bobrov: See Natanson
Bodenstedt (author), on Georgian character, 2
Bogdanov (Alexander Alexandrovich Malinovsky), visits Lenin abroad, 49; elected to first Bolshevik Central Committee, 63; elected to Central Committee at 1907 London Congress, 91; elected to Bolshevik Center, 92; for boycott of Duma elections, 92; and Kamo, 105, 106; and Recallists, 111; and "Forward" group,

129; bloc with Trotsky and Martov, 129; Lenin breaks with, 157
Bogdanov (Menshevik), 210, 221
Bogolepov (Tsarist minister), 46n.
Bolshevik center, secretly elected at 1907 Party Congress in London, 91, 92, 114, 129, 184
Bolshevik, The (theoretical magazine), rejects Opposition articles, 398
Bolshevik party, xv: See Bolsheviks
Bolsheviks, at 1903 Party Congress in London, 59; split with Mensheviks, 43, 193; former adherents join Mensheviks, 43, 76, 77, 190; struggle against Mensheviks, 41, 43, 44, 55, 68, 91, 152, 162; collaborate with Mensheviks, 45, 69, 82, 144, 168, 181, 193, 203, 204, 225; party conciliators, 123, 144; called "Russian" faction, 152; members abandon party, 63, 93, 111; ultimatism of, 64, 65; Recallists among, 111; in Duma, 70n., 111, 122, 139, 141, 143, 145, 148-151, 159, 160, 168, 169; on boycott of Duma, 70-72, 92, 93, 292; in 1905 Petersburg Soviet, 83; at 1906 Congress in Stockholm, 72; at 1907 Congress in London, 89-92; Urals terrorism by, 96; and expropriations, 99; criticized as sect by Martov, 111; Okhrana reports on, 150, 160; at 1912 Conference in Prague, 150; dominant in Moscow, 163; conduct in World War, 168, 169, 175, 187; oppose Lenin's war stand, 168, 169, 175, 187; charged with treason, 169, 210; Duma deputies arrested, 169; deputies on trial, 169, 177, 178, 187; support Prince Lvov, 181, 192; revolutionary chauvinists among, 190; consider unity with Mensheviks, 193, 197, 203, 358; supporters of Provisional Government, 196, 197, 200; oppose Lenin on 1917 revolution, 198; accused as German agents, 210, 217, 222; driven underground again, 214; minority in Soviets, 89, 185; become dominant in Petrograd Soviet, 217, 226, 235; unite with Mezhrayontsi, 217, 242; discuss Pre-Parliament, 227, 242; offer compromise to Compromisers, 225; 1917 right wing of, 239, 240, 246; negotiations with Mensheviks and Essars by right wing of, 239; Lenin's ultimatum to right wing of, 240; 1917 growth of, 217, 225; coalition government with Left Essars, 241, 337, 340, 340n.; candidates to Constituent Assembly of, 242, 243; dissolve Constituent Assembly, 244; and peasantry, 219; program of, 223; Petersburg Committee of, 172, 186, 198, 207, 213, 215, 217; Moscow Committee of, 172, 200; and national question, 155, 156; in Georgia, 90, 266;